READINGS IN MANAGEMENT

SECOND EDITION

MAX D. RICHARDS

Professor of Management
Head, Division of Management
The Pennsylvania State University

WILLIAM A. NIELANDER

Professor of Marketing
Chairman, Department of Marketing
Arizona State College

Published by

SOUTH-WESTERN PUBLISHING COMPANY

Cincinnati   Burlingame, Calif.
Chicago   New Rochelle, N. Y.   Dallas

G56

Library of Congress Catalog Card Number: 63-15634

H163

Printed in the United States of America

PREFACE

The materials in this book represent typical management literature arranged in convenient and logical form. They provide a comprehensive explanation of the management process as it is viewed by management practitioners and scholars.

Experience with the first edition and advancements in the state of the management art dictate the changes in this edition; no changes were made for the mere sake of change. In general terms the second edition is somewhat more theoretical and somewhat more mathematical in content. It has, therefore, less orientation to technique.

The framework. The book is organized into six sections. In the first section, the elements of management that are basic to all management functions are examined. Each succeeding section is devoted to the study of one of the functions of management: planning, directing, controlling, organizing, and staffing. Where possible an overview article was included as an introduction to each subject, and the theoretical aspects of each subject tend to precede examination of applicable decision methods.

Although the framework of this book was selected to explain the administrative process through selected readings, it has proved helpful for other related purposes: (1) research in management; (2) evaluation of a particular manager's or group of managers' operations—a management audit; and (3) the development or training of managers.

Uses of the materials. These materials can be used in several ways. In the first instance they can be used to broaden and deepen one's understanding of the management process. For this purpose these articles can serve as a basic text in intermediate and advanced courses in management. In a similar way, a manager in business can employ these materials as a basic reading kit for the improvement of his understanding of management.

At the conclusion of each chapter, a bibliography of further materials has been prepared for advanced study within each area. Together with the text material, the bibliography provides a start on the framework for graduate study of management.

Since the outlines of several basic texts in management are similar to the outline of these readings, the use of these readings as supplementary text material is facilitated.

Coverage. Thousands of articles are available for inclusion in a book of management readings. In the field of operations research alone, hundreds of worthy articles exist. There are articles which present the results of comprehensive scientific research in particular areas. Other articles present the experiences of individuals or their companies on particular subjects. Still other articles present practical approaches to the solution of administrative problems. All three of these types of articles are included in these selections.

The point of view. An attempt has been made to present an objective point of view. Where important differences of opinion exist, articles presenting opposing viewpoints are included. No attempt has been made to present the opinions of one group of management thinkers to the exclusion of others. The book presents controversies in management thought rather than solutions to these controversies. Few would be so brash as to contend to have the answer for such controversies. It is important that these differences be kept in the forefront of management thinking so that research, study, and thought may be made toward their resolution.

Editorial comment. The purpose of the editorial comment, which has been kept to a minimum, is to explain the reason for an article being in a particular place and to set the stage for the reader's use of the article. Each manager and management student must place these materials within a framework which is meaningful to his own management experience and thought.

Acknowledgement. We are indebted first of all to the authors of the materials that are included in this volume. We also acknowledge the help and assistance of the editors and publishers of these materials in their original form. Without their help and permission, this collection could not have been brought to fruition.

Max D. Richards

William A. Nielander

CONTENTS

CHAPTER IV. THE SYSTEMS CONCEPT

CHAPTER V. COMMUNICATIONS AND INFORMATION

CHAPTER VI. DECISION MAKING

CHAPTER VII. OPERATIONS RESEARCH AND MANAGERIAL DECISIONS

SECTION B. PLANNING

CHAPTER VIII. SETTING OBJECTIVES

CHAPTER XII. LEADERSHIP METHODS

SECTION D. CONTROLLING

CHAPTER XIII. MANAGEMENT CONTROL

CHAPTER XIV. STANDARDS OF MEASUREMENT FOR CONTROL

CHAPTER XV. EXTERNAL CONTROL

SECTION E. ORGANIZING

CHAPTER XVI. ORGANIZATION THEORY

CHAPTER XXI. RECRUITING AND SELECTING MANAGERS

CHAPTER XXII. MANAGEMENT DEVELOPMENT

SECTION A. BASIC ELEMENTS IN MANAGEMENT

The purpose of this introductory section is to reveal the nature and scope of managerial activity in order to provide a background for the study of managerial functions, the subject matter of the other sections in this book. To this end, the philosophical implications of managerial power within and without the firm are first examined. In chapters devoted to systems, communications, decision-making, and operations research, consideration is then given to basic elements which are involved in the performance of each of the management functions.

Chapter 1

The Nature of Management

The purpose of this chapter is to set the stage for the study of management. In these selections the present scope and trends of managing theory and practice are examined.

In the first article Harold Koontz examines the several current theories as explanations or partial explanations of management behavior. Although one cannot help but feel that Koontz emphasizes the dissimilarities among these concepts rather than their similarities, his article provides the reader with a concept of the scope of management. In the second article Peter F. Drucker is less concerned with theory than with practice. Philosophically, however, Drucker may be considered close to Koontz's obvious preference—the process approach. While Harold J. Leavitt and Thomas L. Whisler leave the realm of present-day management practice to predict the nature of management activity in 1980, their article has many implications for present-day managers.

I. THE MANAGEMENT THEORY
JUNGLE [1]
Harold Koontz [2]

Although students of management would readily agree that there have been problems of management since the dawn of organized life, most would also agree that systematic examination of management, with few exceptions, is the product of the present century and more especially of the past two decades. Moreover, until recent years almost all of those who have attempted to analyze the management process and look for some theoretical underpinnings to help improve research, teaching, and practice were alert and perceptive practitioners of the art who reflected on many years of experience. Thus, at least in looking at *general* management as an intellectually based art, the earliest meaningful writing came from such experienced practitioners as Fayol, Mooney, Alvin Brown, Sheldon, Barnard, and Urwick. Certainly not even the most academic worshipper of empirical research can overlook the empiricism involved in distilling fundamentals from decades of experience by such discerning practitioners as these. Admittedly done without questionnaires, controlled interviews, or mathematics, observations by such men can hardly be accurately regarded as *a priori* or "armchair."

The noteworthy absence of academic writing and research in the formative years of modern management theory is now more than atoned for by a deluge of research and writing from the academic halls. What is interesting and perhaps nothing more than a sign of the unsophisticated adolescence of management theory is how the current flood has brought with it a wave of great differences and apparent confusion. From the orderly analysis of management at the shop-room level by Frederick Taylor and the reflective distillation of experience from the general management point of view by Henri

[1] From *Journal of the Academy of Management,* Vol. 4, No. 3 (December, 1961), pp. 174-188. Reprinted by permission of the *Journal of the Academy of Management.*
[2] Harold Koontz, Professor of Business Policy and Transportation, Graduate School of Business Administration, University of California at Los Angeles.

Fayol, we now see these and other early beginnings overgrown and entangled by a jungle of approaches and approachers to management theory.

There are the behavioralists, born of the Hawthorne experiments and the awakened interest in human relations during the 1930's and 1940's, who see management as a complex of interpersonal relationships and the basis of management theory the tentative tenets of the new and undeveloped science of psychology. There are also those who see management theory as simply a manifestation of the institutional and cultural aspects of sociology. Still others, observing that the central core of management is decision-making, branch in all directions from this core to encompass everything in organization life. Then, there are mathematicians who think of management primarily as an exercise in logical relationships expressed in symbols and the omnipresent and ever revered model. But the entanglement of growth reaches its ultimate when the study of management is regarded as a study of one of a number of systems and subsystems, with an understandable tendency for the researcher to be dissatisfied until he has encompassed the entire physical and cultural universe as a management system.

With the recent discovery of an ages-old problem area by social, physical, and biological scientists, and with the supersonic increase in interest by all types of enterprise managers, the apparent impenetrability of the present thicket which we call management theory is not difficult to comprehend. One can hardly be surprised that psychologists, sociologists, anthropologists, sociometricists, economists, mathematicians, physicists, biologists, political scientists, business administration scholars, and even practicing managers, should hop on this interesting, challenging, and profitable band wagon.

This welling of interest from every academic and practicing corner should not upset anyone concerned with seeing the frontiers of knowledge pushed back and the intellectual base of practice broadened. But what is rather upsetting to the practitioner and the observer, who sees great social potential from improved management, is that the variety of approaches to management theory has led to a kind of confused and destructive jungle warfare. Particularly among academic disciplines and their disciples, the primary interests of many would-be cult leaders seem to be to carve out a distinct (and hence "original") approach to management. And to defend this originality, and thereby gain a place in posterity (or at least to gain a publication which will justify academic status or promotion), it seems to have become too much the current style to downgrade, and sometimes misrepresent, what anyone else has said, or thought, or done.

In order to cut through this jungle and bring to light some of the issues and problems involved in the present management theory area so that the tremendous interest, intelligence, and research results may become more meaningful, it is my purpose here to classify the various "schools" of management theory, to identify briefly what I believe to be the major source of differences, and to offer some suggestions for disentangling the jungle. It is hoped that a movement for clarification can be started so at least we in the field will not be a group of blind men identifying the same elephant with our widely varying and sometimes viciously argumentative theses.

THE MAJOR "SCHOOLS" OF MANAGEMENT THEORY

In attempting to classify the major schools of management theory into six main groups, I am aware that I may overlook certain approaches and cannot deal with all the nuances of each approach. But it does seem that most of the approaches to management theory can be classified in one of these so-called "schools."

The management process school

This approach to management theory perceives management as a process of getting things done through and with people operating in organized groups. It aims to analyze the process, to establish a conceptual framework for it, to identify principles underlying it, and to build up a theory of management from them. It regards management as a universal process, regardless of the type of enterprise, or the level in a given enterprise, although recognizing, obviously, that the environment of management differs widely between enterprises and levels. It looks upon management theory as a way of organizing experience so that practice can be improved through research, empirical testing of principles, and teaching of fundamentals involved in the management process.[3]

---

[3] It is interesting that one of the scholars strongly oriented to human relations and behavioral approaches to management has recently noted that "theory can be viewed as a way of organizing experience" and that "once initial sense is made out of experienced environment, the way is cleared for an even more adequate organization of this experience." See Robert Dubin in "Psyche, Sensitivity, and Social Structure," critical comment in Robert Tannenbaum, I. R. Weschler, and Fred Massarik, *Leadership and Organization: A Behavioral Science Approach* (New York: McGraw-Hill Book Co., 1961), p. 401.

Often referred to, especially by its critics, as the "traditional" or "universalist" school, this school can be said to have been fathered by Henri Fayol, although many of his offspring did not know of their parent, since Fayol's work was eclipsed by the bright light of his contemporary, Frederick Taylor, and clouded by the lack of a widely available English translation until 1949. Other than Fayol, most of the early contributors to this school dealt only with the organization portion of the management process, largely because of their greater experience with this facet of management and the simple fact that planning and control, as well as the function of staffing, were given little attention by managers before 1940.

This school bases its approach to management theory on several fundamental beliefs:

1. That managing is a process and can best be dissected intellectually by analyzing the functions of the manager.
2. That long experience with management in a variety of enterprise situations can be grounds for distillation of certain fundamental truths or generalizations—usually referred to as principles—which have a clarifying and predictive value in the understanding and improvement of managing.
3. That these fundamental truths can become focal points for useful research both to ascertain their validity and to improve their meaning and applicability in practice.
4. That such truths can furnish elements, at least until disproved, and certainly until sharpened, of a useful theory of management.
5. That managing is an art, but one like medicine or engineering, which can be improved by reliance on the light and understanding of principles.
6. That principles in management, like principles in the biological and physical sciences, are nonetheless true even if a prescribed treatment or design by a practitioner in a given case situation chooses to ignore a principle and the costs involved, or attempts to do something else to offset the costs incurred (this is, of course, not new in medicine, engineering, or any other art, for art is the creative task of compromising fundamentals to attain a desired result).
7. That, while the totality of culture and of the physical and biological universe has varying effects on the manager's environment and subjects, as indeed they do in every other field of science and art, the theory of management does not need to encompass the field of all knowledge in order for it to serve as a scientific or theoretical foundation.

The basic approach of this school, then, is to look, first, to the functions of managers. As a second step in this approach, many of us have taken the functions of managers and further dissected them by distilling what we see as fundamental truths in the understandably complicated practice of management. I have found it useful to classify my analysis of these functions around the essentials involved in the following questions:

1. What is the nature of the function?
2. What is the purpose of the function?
3. What explains the structure of the function?
4. What explains the process of the function?

Perhaps there are other more useful approaches, but I have found that I can place everything pertaining to management (even some of the rather remote research and concepts) in this framework.

Also, purely to make the area of management theory intellectually manageable, those who subscribe to this school do not usually attempt to include in the theory the entire areas of sociology, economics, biology, psychology, physics, chemistry, or others. This is done not because these other areas of knowledge are unimportant and have no bearing on management, but merely because no real progress has ever been made in science or art without significant partitioning of knowledge. Yet, anyone would be foolish not to realize that a function which deals with people in their various activities of producing and marketing anything from money to religion and education is completely independent of the physical, biological, and cultural universe in which we live. And, are there not such relationships in other "compartments" of knowledge and theory?

The empirical school

A second approach to management I refer to as the "empirical" school. In this, I include those scholars who identify management as a study of experience, sometimes with intent to draw generalizations but usually merely as a means of teaching experience and transferring it to the practitioner or student. Typical of this school are those who see management or "policy" as the study and analysis of cases and those with such approaches as Ernest Dale's "comparative approach." [4]

This approach seems to be based upon the premise that, if we study the experience of successful managers, or the mistakes made in management, or if we attempt to solve management problems, we will somehow understand and learn to apply the most effective kinds of management techniques. This approach, as often applied, assumes

[4] *The Great Organizers* (New York: McGraw-Hill Book Co., 1960), pp. 11-28.

that, by finding out what worked or did not work in individual circumstances, the student or the practitioner will be able to do the same in comparable situations.

No one can deny the importance of studying experience through such study, or of analyzing the "how-it-was-done" of management. But management, unlike law, is not a science based on precedent, and situations in the future exactly comparable to the past are exceedingly unlikely to occur. Indeed, there is a positive danger of relying too much on past experience and on undistilled history of managerial problem-solving for the simple reason that a technique or approach found "right" in the past may not fit a situation of the future.

Those advocating the empirical approach are likely to say that what they really do in analyzing cases or history is to draw from certain generalizations which can be applied as useful guides to thought or action in future case situations. As a matter of fact, Ernest Dale, after claiming to find "so little practical value" from the principles enunciated by the "universalists," curiously drew certain "generalizations" or "criteria" from his valuable study of a number of great practitioners of management.[5] There is some question as to whether Dale's "comparative" approach is not really the same as the "universalist" approach he decries, except with a different distiller of basic truths.

By the emphasis of the empirical school on study of experience, it does appear that the research and thought so engendered may assist in hastening the day for verification of principles. It is also possible that the proponents of this school may come up with a more useful framework of principles than that of the management process school. But, to the extent that the empirical school draws generalizations from its research, and it would seem to be a necessity to do so unless its members are satisfied to exchange meaningless and structureless experience, this approach tends to be and do the same as the management process school.

The human behavior school

This approach to the analysis of management is based on the central thesis that, since managing involves getting things done with and through people, the study of management must be centered on interpersonal relations. Variously called the "human relations,"

[5] *Ibid.*, pp. 11, 26-28, 62-68.

"leadership," or "behavioral sciences" approach, this school brings to bear "existing and newly developed theories, methods, and techniques of the relevant social sciences upon the study of inter- and intrapersonal phenomena, ranging fully from the personality dynamics of individuals at one extreme to the relations of cultures at the other." [6] In other words, this school concentrates on the "people" part of management and rests on the principle that, where people work together as groups in order to accomplish objectives, "people should understand people."

The scholars in this school have a heavy orientation to psychology and social psychology. Their primary focus is the individual as a socio-psychological being and what motivates him. The members of this school vary from those who see it as a portion of the manager's job, a tool to help him understand and get the best from people by meeting their needs and responding to their motivations, to those who see the psychological behavior of individuals and groups as the total of management.

In this school are those who emphasize human relations as an art that the manager should advantageously understand and practice. There are those who focus attention on the manager as a leader and sometimes equate management to leadership, thus, in effect, tending to treat all group activities as "managed" situations. There are those who see the study of group dynamics and interpersonal relationships as simply a study of socio-psychological relationships and seem, therefore, merely to be attaching the term "management" to the field of social psychology.

That management must deal with human behavior can hardly be denied. That the study of human interactions, whether in the environment of management or in unmanaged situations, is important and useful one could not dispute. And it would be a serious mistake to regard good leadership as unimportant to good managership. But whether the field of human behavior is the equivalent of the field of management is quite another thing. Perhaps it is like calling the study of the human body the field of cardiology.

The social system school

Closely related to the human behavior school and often confused or intertwined with it is one which might be labeled the social system

<hr>

[6] R. Tannenbaum, I. R. Weschler, and F. Massarik, *Leadership and Organization* (New York: McGraw-Hill Book Co., 1961), p. 9.

school. This includes those researchers who look upon management as a social system, that is, a system of cultural interrelationships. Sometimes, as in the case of March and Simon,[7] the system is limited to formal organizations, using the term "organization" as equivalent to enterprise, rather than the authority-activity concept used most often in management. In other cases, the approach is not to distinguish the formal organization, but rather to encompass any kind of system of human relationships.

Heavily sociological in flavor, this approach to management does essentially what any study of sociology does. It identifies the nature of the cultural relationships of various social groups and attempts to show these as a related, and usually an integrated, system.

Perhaps the spiritual father of this ardent and vocal school of management theorists is Chester Barnard.[8] In searching for an answer to fundamental explanations underlying the managing process, this thoughtful business executive developed a theory of cooperation grounded in the needs of the individual to solve, through cooperation, the biological, physical, and social limitations of himself and his environment. Barnard then carved from the total of cooperative systems so engendered one set of interrelationships which he defines as "formal organization." His formal organization concept, quite unlike that usually held by management practitioners, is any cooperative system in which there are persons able to communicate with each other and who are willing to contribute action toward a conscious common purpose.

The Barnard concept of cooperative systems pervades the work of many contributors to the social system school of management. For example, Herbert Simon at one time defined the subject of organization theory and the nature of human organizations as "systems of interdependent activity, encompassing at least several primary groups and usually characterized, at the level of consciousness of participants, by a high degree of rational direction of behavior toward ends that are objects of common knowledge."[9] Simon and others have subsequently seemed to have expanded this concept of social systems to include any cooperative and purposeful group interrelationship or behavior.

This school has made many noteworthy contributions to manage-

---

[7] *Organizations* (New York: John Wiley & Sons, Inc., 1958).

[8] *The Functions of the Executive* (Cambridge, Massachusetts: Harvard University Press, 1938).

[9] "Comments on the Theory of Organizations," 46 *American Political Science Review*, No. 4 (December, 1952), p. 1130.

ment. The recognition of organized enterprise as a social organism, subject to all the pressures and conflicts of the cultural environment, has been helpful to the management theorist and the practitioner alike. Among some of the more helpful aspects are the awareness of the institutional foundations of organization authority, the influence of informal organization, and such social factors as those Wight Bakke has called the "bonds of organization." [10] Likewise, many of Barnard's helpful insights, such as his economy of incentives and his theory of opportunism, have brought the power of sociological understanding into the realm of management practice.

Basic sociology, analysis of concepts of social behavior, and the study of group behavior in the framework of social systems do have great value in the field of management. But one may well ask the question whether this *is* management. Is the field of management coterminous with the field of sociology? Or is sociology an important underpinning like language, psychology, physiology, mathematics, and other fields of knowledge? Must management be defined in terms of the universe of knowledge?

The decision theory school

Another approach to management theory, undertaken by a growing and scholarly group, might be referred to as the decision theory school. This group concentrates on rational approach to decision— the selection from among possible alternatives of a course of action or of an idea. The approach of this school may be to deal with the decision itself, or to the persons or organizational group making the decision, or to an analysis of the decision process. Some limit themselves fairly much to the economic rationale of the decision, while others regard anything which happens in an enterprise the subject of their analysis, and still others expand decision theory to cover the psychological and sociological aspect and environment of decisions and decision-makers.

The decision-making school is apparently an outgrowth of the theory of consumer's choice with which economists have been concerned since the days of Jeremy Bentham early in the nineteenth century. It has arisen out of such economic problems and analyses

[10] *Bonds of Organization* (New York: Harper & Brothers, 1950). These "bonds" or "devices" of organization are identified by Bakke as (1) the functional specifications system (a system of teamwork arising from job specifications and arrangements for association); (2) the status system (a vertical hierarchy of authority); (3) the communications system; (4) the reward and penalty system; and (5) the organization charter (ideas and means which give character and individuality to the organization, or enterprise).

as utility maximization, indifference curves, marginal utility, and economic behavior under risks and uncertainties. It is, therefore, no surprise that one finds most of the members of this school to be economic theorists. It is likewise no surprise to find the content of this school to be heavily oriented to model construction and mathematics.

The decision theory school has tended to expand its horizon considerably beyond the process of evaluating alternatives. That point has become for many only a springboard for examination of the entire sphere of human activity, including the nature of the organization structure, psychological and social reactions of individuals and groups, the development of basic information for decisions, an analysis of values and particularly value considerations with respect to goals, communications networks, and incentives. As one would expect, when the decision theorists study the small, but central, area of decision *making*, they are led by this keyhole look at management to consider the entire field of enterprise operation and its environment. The result is that decision theory becomes no longer a neat and narrow concentration on decision, but rather a broad view of the enterprise as a social system.

There are those who believe that, since management is characterized by its concentration on decisions, the future development of management theory will tend to use the decision as its central focus and the rest of management theory will be hung on this structural center. This may occur and certainly the study of the decision, the decision process, and the decision maker can be extended to cover the entire field of management as anyone might conceive it. Nevertheless, one wonders whether this focus cannot also be used to build around it the entire area of human knowledge. For, as most decision theorists recognize, the problem of choice is individual, as well as organizational, and most of what has been said that is pure decision theory can be applied to the existence and thinking of a Robinson Crusoe.

The mathematical school

Although mathematical methods can be used by any school of management theory, and have been, I have chosen to group under a school those theorists who see management as a system of mathematical models and processes. Perhaps the most widely known group I arbitrarily so lump are the operations researchers or operations analysts, who have sometimes anointed themselves with the rather pretentious name of "management scientists." The abiding belief of this group is that, if management, or organization, or planning, or decision making is a logical process, it can be expressed in terms of mathematical symbols and relationships. The central approach of this school is the model, for it is through these devices that the problem is expressed in its basic relationships and in terms of selected goals or objectives.

There can be no doubt of the great usefulness of mathematical approaches to any field of inquiry. It forces upon the researcher the definition of a problem or problem area, it conveniently allows the insertion of symbols for unknown data, and its logical methodology, developed by years of scientific application and abstraction, furnishes a powerful tool for solving or simplifying complex phenomena.

But it is hard to see mathematics as a truly separate school of management theory, any more than it is a separate "school" in physics, chemistry, engineering, or medicine. I only deal with it here as such because there has appeared to have developed a kind of cult around mathematical analysts who have subsumed to themselves the area of management.

In pointing out that mathematics is a tool, rather than a school, it is not my intention to underestimate the impact of mathematics on the science and practice of management. By bringing to this immensely important and complex field the tools and techniques of the physical sciences, the mathematicians have already made an immense contribution to orderly thinking. They have forced on people in management the means and desirability of seeing many problems more clearly, they have pressed on scholars and practitioners the need for establishing goals and measures of effectiveness, they have been extremely helpful in getting the management area seen as a logical system of relationships, and they have caused people in management to review and occasionally reorganize information sources and systems so that mathematics can be given sensible quantitative meaning. But with all this meaningful contribution and the greater sharpness and sophistication of planning which is resulting, I cannot see that mathematics is management theory any more than it is astronomy.

THE MAJOR SOURCES OF MENTAL ENTANGLEMENT IN THE JUNGLE

In outlining the various schools, or approaches, of management theory, it becomes clear that these intellectual cults are not drawing greatly different inferences from the physical and cultural environment surrounding us. Why, then, have there been so many differences between them and why such a struggle, particularly among our academic brethren to obtain a place in the sun by denying the approaches of others? Like the widely differing and often contentious denominations of the Christian religion, all have essentially the same goals and deal with essentially the same world.

While there are many sources of the mental entanglement in the management theory jungle, the major ones are the following:

The semantics jungle

As is so often true when intelligent men argue about basic problems, some of the trouble lies in the meaning of key words. The semantics problem is particularly severe in the field of management. There is even a difference in the meaning of the word "management." Most people would agree that it means getting things done through and with people, but is it people in formal organizations, or in all group activities? Is it governing, leading, or teaching?

Perhaps the greatest single semantics confusion lies in the word "organization." Most members of the management process school use it to define the activity-authority structure of an enterprise and certainly most practitioners believe that they are "organizing" when they establish a framework of activity groupings and authority relationships. In this case, organization represents the formal framework within an enterprise that furnishes the environment in which people perform. Yet a large number of "organization" theorists conceive of organization as the sum total of human relationships in any group activity; they thus seem to make it equivalent to *social* structure. And some use "organization" to mean "enterprise."

If the meaning of organization cannot be clarified and a standard use of the term adopted by management theorists, understanding and criticism should not be based on this difference. It hardly seems to me to be accurate for March and Simon, for example, to criticize the organization theories of the management process, or "universalist," school for not considering the management planning function as part of organizing, when they have chosen to treat it separately. Nor should those who choose to treat the training, selecting, guiding or leading of people under staffing and direction be criticised for a tendency to "view the employee as an inert instrument" or a "given rather than a variable." [11] Such accusations, proceeding from false premises, are clearly erroneous.

Other semantic entanglements might be mentioned. By some, decision-making is regarded as a process of choosing from among alternatives; by others, the total managerial task and environment. Leadership is often made synonymous with managership and is analytically separated by others. Communications may mean everything from a written or oral report to a vast network of formal and informal relationships. Human relations to some implies a psychiatric manipulation of people, but to others the study and art of understanding people and interpersonal relationships.

Differences in definition of management as a body of knowledge

As was indicated in the discussion of semantics, "management" has far from a standard meaning, although most agree that it at least involves getting things done through and with people. But, does it mean the dealing with all human relationships? Is a street peddler a manager? Is a parent a manager? Is a leader of a disorganized mob a manager? Does the field of management equal the fields of sociology and social psychology combined? Is it the equivalent of the entire system of social relationships?

While I recognize that sharp lines cannot be drawn in management any more than they are in medicine or engineering, there surely can be a sharper distinction drawn than at present. With the plethora of management writing and experts, calling almost everything under the sun "management," can one expect management theory to be regarded as very useful or scientific to the practitioner?

The *a priori* assumption

Confusion in management theory has also been heightened by the tendency for many newcomers in the field to cast aside significant observations and analyses of the past on the grounds that they are *a priori* in nature. This is an often-met accusation made by those who wish to cast aside the work of Fayol, Mooney, Brown, Urwick, Gulick, and others who are branded as "universalists." To make the assumption that the distilled experiences of men such as these represent *a priori* reasoning is to forget that experience in and with

[11] J. G. March, and H. A. Simon, *Organizations* (New York: John Wiley & Sons, Inc., 1958), pp. 29-33.

managing *is* empirical. While the conclusions that perceptive and experienced practitioners of the art of management are not infallible, they represent an experience which is certainly real and not "armchair." No one could deny, I feel sure, that the ultimate test of accuracy of management theory must be practice and management theory and science must be developed from reality.

The misunderstanding of principles

Those who feel that they gain caste or a clean slate for advancing a particular notion or approach often delight in casting away anything which smacks of management principles. Some have referred to them as platitudes, forgetting that a platitude is still a truism and a truth does not become worthless because it is familiar. (As Robert Frost has written, "Most of the changes we think we see in life are merely truths going in or out of favor.") Others cast away principles of Fayol and other practitioners, only to draw apparently different generalizations from their study of management; but many of the generalizations so discovered are often the same fundamental truths in different words that certain criticized "universalists" have discovered.

One of the favorite tricks of the managerial theory trade is to disprove a whole framework of principles by reference to one principle which the observer sees disregarded in practice. Thus, many critics of the universalists point to the well-known cases of dual subordination in organized enterprise, coming to the erroneous conclusion that there is no substance to the principle of unity of command. But this does not prove that there is no cost to the enterprise by designing around, or disregarding, the principle of unity of command; nor does it prove that there were not other advantages which offset the costs, as there often are in cases of establishing functional authorities in organization.

Perhaps the almost hackneyed stand-by for those who would disprove the validity of all principles by referring to a single one is the misunderstanding around the principle of span of management (or span of control). The usual source of authority quoted by those who criticize is Sir Ian Hamilton, who never intended to state a universal principle, but rather to make a personal observation in a book of reflections on his Army experience, and who did say, offhand, that he found it wise to limit his span to 3 to 6 subordinates. No modern universalist relies on this single observation, and, indeed, few can or will state an absolute or universal numerical ceiling. Since Sir Ian was not a management theorist and did not intend to be, let us hope that the ghost of his innocent remark may be laid to deserved rest!

What concerns those who feel that a recognition of fundamental truths, or generalizations, may help in the diagnosis and study of management, and who know from managerial experience that such truths or principles do serve an extremely valuable use, is the tendency for some researchers to prove the wrong things through either misstatement or misapplication of principles. A classic case of such misunderstanding and misapplication is in Chris Argyris' interesting book on *Personality and Organization*.[12] This author, who in this book and his other works has made many noteworthy contributions to management, concludes that "formal organization principles make demands on relatively healthy individuals that are incongruent with their needs," and that "frustration, conflict, failure, and short-time perspective are predicted as results of this basic incongruency."[13] This startling conclusion—the exact opposite of what "good" formal organization based on "sound" organization principles should cause, is explained when one notes that, of four "principles" Argyris quotes, one is not an organization principle at all but the economic principle of specialization and three other "principles" are quoted incorrectly.[14] With such a postulate, and with no attempt to recognize, correctly or incorrectly, any other organization and management principles, Argyris has simply proved that wrong principles badly applied will lead to frustration; and every management practitioner knows this to be true!

The inability or unwillingness of management theorists to understand each other

What has been said above leads one to the conclusion that much of the management theory jungle is caused by the unwillingness or inability of the management theorists to understand each other. Doubting that it is inability, because one must assume that a person interested in management theory is able to comprehend, at least in concept and framework, the approaches of the various "schools," I can only come to the conclusion that the roadblock to understanding is unwillingness.

[12] New York: Harper & Brothers, 1957.
[13] *Ibid.*, p. 74.
[14] *Ibid.*, pp. 58-66.

Perhaps this unwillingness comes from the professional "walls" developed by learned disciplines. Perhaps the unwillingness stems from a fear that someone or some new discovery will encroach on professional academic status. Perhaps it is fear of professional or intellectual obsolescence. But whatever the cause, it seems that these walls will not be torn down until it is realized that they exist, until all cultists are willing to look at the approach and content of other schools, and until, through exchange and understanding of ideas some order may be brought from the present chaos.

Disentangling the Management Theory Jungle

It is important that steps be taken to disentangle the management theory jungle. Perhaps, it is too soon and we must expect more years of wandering through a thicket of approaches, semantics, thrusts, and counter-thrusts. But in any field as important to society where the many blunders of an unscientifically based managerial art can be so costly, I hope that this will not be long.

There do appear to be some things that can be done. Clearly, meeting what I see to be the major sources of the entanglement should remove much of it. The following considerations are important:

1. *The need for definition of a body of knowledge.* Certainly, if a field of knowledge is not to get bogged down in a quagmire of misunderstandings, the first need is for definition of the field. Not that it need be defined in sharp, detailed, and inflexible lines, but rather along lines which will give it fairly specific content. Because management is reality, life, practice, my suggestion would be that it be defined in the light of the able and discerning practitioner's frame of reference. A science unrelated to the art for which it is to serve is not likely to be a very productive one.

Although the study of managements in various enterprises, in various countries, and at various levels made by many persons, including myself, may neither be representative nor adequate, I have come to the conclusion that management is the art of getting things done through and with people in *formally organized groups*, the art of creating an environment in such an organized group where people can perform as individuals and yet cooperate toward attainment of group goals, the art of removing blocks to such performance, the art of optimizing efficiency in effectively reaching goals. If this kind of definition of the field is unsatisfactory, I suggest at least an agreement that the area should be defined to reflect the field of the practitioner and that further research and study of practice be done to this end.

In defining the field, too, it seems to me imperative to draw some limits for purposes of analysis and research. If we are to call the entire cultural, biological, and physical universe the field of management, we can no more make progress than could have been done if chemistry or geology had not carved out a fairly specific area and had, instead, studied all knowledge.

In defining the body of knowledge, too, care must be taken to distinguish between tools and content. Thus mathematics, operations research, accounting, economic theory, sociometry, and psychology, to mention a few, are significant *tools* of management but are not, in themselves, a part of the *content* of the field. This is not to mean that they are unimportant or that the practicing manager should not have them available to him, nor does it mean that they may not be the means of pushing back the frontiers of knowledge of management. But they should not be confused with the basic content of the field.

This is not to say that fruitful study should not continue on the underlying disciplines affecting management. Certainly knowledge of sociology, social systems, psychology, economics, political science, mathematics, and other areas, pointed toward contributing to the field of management, should be continued and encouraged. And significant findings in these and other fields of knowledge might well cast important light on, or change concepts in, the field of management. This has certainly happened in other sciences and in every other art based upon significant science.

2. *Integration of management and other disciplines.* If recognition of the proper content of the field were made, I believe that the present crossfire of misunderstanding might tend to disappear. Management would be regarded as a specific discipline and other disciplines would be looked upon as important bases of the field. Under these circumstances, the allied and underlying disciplines would be welcomed by the business and public administration schools, as well as by practitioners, as loyal and helpful associates. Integration of management and other disciplines would then not be difficult.

3. *The clarification of management semantics.* While I would expect the need for clarification and uniformity of management

semantics would largely be satisfied by definition of the field as a body of knowledge, semantics problems might require more special attention. There are not too many places where semantics are important enough to cause difficulty. Here again, I would suggest the adoption of the semantics of the intelligent practitioners, unless words are used by them so inexactly as to require special clarification. At least, we should not complicate an already complex field by developing a scientific or academic jargon which would build a language barrier between the theorist and the practitioner.

Perhaps the most expeditious way out of this problem is to establish a commission representing academic societies immediately concerned and associations of practicing managers. This would not seem to be difficult to do. And even if it were, the results would be worth the efforts.

4. *Willingness to distill and test fundamentals.* Certainly, the test of maturity and usefulness of a science is the sharpness and validity of the principles underlying it. No science, now regarded as mature, started out with a complete statement of incontrovertibly valid principles. Even the oldest sciences, such as physics, keep revising their underlying laws and discovering new principles. Yet any science has proceeded, and more than that has been useful, for centuries on the basis of generalizations, some laws, some principles, and some hypotheses.

One of the understandable sources of inferiority of the social sciences is the recognition that they are inexact sciences. On the other hand, even the so-called exact sciences are subject to a great deal of inexactness, have principles which are not completely proved, and use art in the design of practical systems and components. The often-encountered defeatist attitude of the social sciences, of which management is one, overlooks the fact that management may be explained, practice may be improved, and the goals of research may be more meaningful if we encourage attempts at perceptive distillation of experience by stating principles (or generalizations) and placing them in a logical framework. As two scientists recently said on this subject:

> The reason for this defeatist point of view regarding the social sciences may be traceable to a basic misunderstanding of the nature of scientific endeavor. What matters is not whether or to what extent inexactitudes in procedures and predictive capability can eventually be removed . . . : rather it is *objectivity*, i.e., the intersubjectivity of findings independent of any one person's intuitive judgment, which

distinguishes science from intuitive guesswork however brilliant. . . . But once a new fact or a new idea has been conjectured, no matter how intuitive a foundation, it must be capable of objective test and confirmation by anyone. And it is this crucial standard of scientific objectivity rather than any purported criterion of exactitude to which the social sciences must conform.[15]

In approaching the clarification of management theory, then, we should not forget a few criteria:

1. The theory should deal with an area of knowledge and inquiry that is "manageable"; no great advances in knowledge were made so long as man contemplated the whole universe.
2. The theory should be *useful* in improving practice and the task and person of the practitioner should not be overlooked.
3. The theory should not be lost in semantics, especially useless jargon not understandable to the practitioner.
4. The theory should give direction and efficiency to research and teaching.
5. The theory must recognize that it is a part of a larger universe of knowledge and theory.

[15] O. Helmer, and N. Rescher, "On the Epistemology of the Inexact Sciences," (Santa Monica, California: The Rand Corporation, P-1513, 1958), pp. 4-5.

2. THE NATURE OF MANAGEMENT [1]

Peter F. Drucker [2]

THE ROLE OF MANAGEMENT

The manager is the dynamic, life-giving element in every business. Without his leadership the "resources of production" remain resources and never become production. In a competitive economy, above all, the quality and performance of the managers determine the success of a business, indeed they determine its survival. For the quality and performance of its managers is the only effective advantage an enterprise in a competitive economy can have.

Management is also a distinct and a leading group in industrial society. We no longer talk of "capital" and "labor"; we talk of "management" and "labor." The "responsibilities of capital" have disappeared from our vocabulary together with the "rights of capital"; instead, we hear of the "responsibilities of management," and (a singularly hapless phrase) of the "prerogatives of management." We are building up a comprehensive and distinct system of "education for management." And when the Eisenhower Administration was formed in 1952, it was formed consciously as a "Management Administration."

The emergence of management as an essential, a distinct and a leading institution is a pivotal event in social history. Rarely, if ever, has a new basic institution, a new leading group, emerged as fast as has management since the turn of this century. Rarely in human history has a new institution proven indispensable so quickly; and even less often has a new institution arrived with so little opposition, so little disturbance, so little controversy.

Management will remain a basic and dominant institution perhaps as long as Western civilization itself survives. For management is

[2] Peter F. Drucker, Author, Consultant, and Lecturer in the field of general management.

not only grounded in the nature of the modern industrial system and in the needs of the modern business enterprise to which an industrial system must entrust its productive resources—both human and material. Management also expresses basic beliefs of modern Western society. It expresses the belief in the possibility of controlling man's livelihood through systematic organization of economic resources. It expresses the belief that economic change can be made into the most powerful engine for human betterment and social justice— that, as Jonathan Swift first overstated it two hundred and fifty years ago, whoever makes two blades of grass grow where only one grew before deserves better of mankind than any speculative philosopher or metaphysical system builder.

This belief that the material can and should be used to advance the human spirit is not just the age-old human heresy "materialism." In fact, it is incompatible with materialism as the term has always been understood. It is something new, distinctly modern, distinctly Western. Prior to, and outside of, the modern West, resources have always been considered a limit to man's activities, a restriction on his control over his environment—rather than an opportunity and a tool of his control over nature. They have always been considered God-given and unchangeable. Indeed all societies, except the modern West, have looked upon economic change as a danger to society and individual alike, and have considered it the first responsibility of government to keep the economy unchangeable.

Management, which is the organ of society specifically, charged with making resources productive, that is, with the responsibility for organized economic advance, therefore reflects the basic spirit of the modern age. It is in fact indispensable—and this explains why, once begotten, it grew so fast and with so little opposition.

The importance of management

Management, its competence, its integrity and its performance will be decisive both to the United States and to the free world in the decades ahead. At the same time the demands on management will be rising steadily and steeply.

A "Cold War" of indefinite duration not only puts heavy economic burdens on the economy, which only continuous economic advance can make bearable; it demands ability to satisfy the country's military needs while building up, at the same time, an expanding peacetime economy. It demands, indeed, an unprecedented ability of the entire economy to shift back and forth between peacetime and defense production, practically at an instant's notice. This demand, on the satisfaction of which our survival may well depend, is above all a demand on the competence of the managements, especially of our big enterprises.

That the United States is the leader today, economically and socially, will make management performance decisive—and adequate management performance much harder. From the peak there is only one easy way to go: downwards. It always requires twice as much effort and skill to stay up as it did to climb up. In other words, there is real danger that in retrospect the United States of 1950 will come to look like the Great Britain of 1880—doomed to decline for lack of vision and lack of effort. There are evidences of a tendency in this country to defend what we have rather than advance further; capital equipment is getting old in many industries; productivity is improving fast only in the very new industries, and may be stagnant if not declining in many others. Only superior management competence and continuously improved management performance can keep us progressing, can prevent our becoming smug, self-satisfied and lazy.

Outside the United States management has an even more decisive function and an even tougher job. Whether Europe regains her economic prosperity depends, above all, on the performance of her managements. And whether the formerly colonial and raw-material producing countries will succeed in developing their economies as free nations or will go Communist, depends to a large extent on their ability to produce competent and responsible managers in a hurry. Truly, the entire free world has an immense stake in the competence, skill and responsibility of management.

THE JOBS OF MANAGEMENT

Despite its crucial importance, its high visibility and its spectacular rise, management is the least known and the least understood of our basic institutions. Even the people in a business often do not know what their management does and what it is supposed to be doing, how it acts and why, whether it does a good job or not. Indeed, the typical picture of what goes on in the "front office" or on "the fourteenth floor" in the minds of otherwise sane, well-informed and intelligent employees (including, often, people themselves in responsible managerial and specialist positions) bears striking resemblance to the medieval geographer's picture of Africa as the stamping ground of the one-eyed ogre, the two-headed pygmy, the immortal phoenix and the elusive unicorn. What then is management: What does it do?

There are two popular answers. One is that management is the people at the top—the term "management" being little more than euphemism for "the boss." The other one defines a manager as someone who directs the work of others and who, as a slogan puts it, "does his work by getting other people to do theirs."

But these are at best merely efforts to tell us who belongs in management (as we shall see, they don't even tell us that). They do not attempt to tell us what management is and what it does. These questions can only be answered by analyzing management's function. For management is an organ; and organs can be described and defined only through their function.

Management is the specific organ of the business enterprise. Whenever we talk of a business enterprise, say, the United States Steel Company or the British Coal Board, as deciding to build a new plant, laying off workers or treating its customers fairly, we actually talk of a management decision, a management action, a management behavior. The enterprise can decide, act and behave only as its managers do—by itself the enterprise has no effective existence. And conversely any business enterprise, no matter what its legal structure, must have a management to be alive and functioning. (In this respect there is no difference between private enterprise, the nationalized industries of Great Britain, such old-established government monopolies as a Post Office, and the "ministries" and "trusts" of Communist Russia.)

That management is the specific organ of the business enterprise is so obvious that it tends to be taken for granted. But it sets management apart from all other governing organs of all other institutions. The Government, the Army or the Church—in fact, any major institution—has to have an organ which, in some of its function, is not unlike the management of the business enterprise. But management as such is the management of a *business* enterprise. And the reason for the existence of a business enterprise is that it supplies economic goods and services. To be sure, the business enterprise must discharge its economic responsibility so as to strengthen society, and in accordance with society's political and ethical beliefs. But these are (to use the logician's term) accidental conditions limiting, modifying, encouraging or retarding the economic activities of the business enterprise. The essence of business enterprise, the vital principle that determines its nature, is economic performance.

The first function: economic performance

Management must always, in every decision and action, put economic performance first. It can only justify its existence and its authority by the economic results it produces. There may be great non-economic results: the happiness of the members of the enterprise, the contribution to the welfare or culture of the community, etc. Yet management has failed if it fails to produce economic results. It has failed if it does not supply goods and services desired by the consumer at a price the consumer is willing to pay. It has failed if it does not improve or at least maintain the wealth-producing capacity of the economic resources entrusted to it.

In this management is unique. A General Staff will ask itself quite legitimately whether its basic military decisions are compatible with the economic structure and welfare of the country. But it would be greatly remiss in its duty were it to start its military deliberations with the needs of the economy. The economic consequences of military decisions are a secondary, a limiting factor in these decisions, not their starting point or their rationale. A General Staff, being the specific organ of a military organization, must, by necessity, put military security first. To act differently would be a betrayal of its responsibility and dangerous malpractice. Similarly, management, while always taking into consideration the impact of its decisions on society, both within and without the enterprise, must always put economic performance first.

The first definition of management is therefore that it is an economic organ, indeed the specifically economic organ of an industrial society. Every act, every decision, every deliberation of management has as its first dimension an economic dimension.

Management's first job is managing a business

This apparently obvious statement leads to conclusions that are far from being obvious or generally accepted. It implies both severe limitations on the scope of management and manager, and a major responsibility for creative action.

It means in the first place that the skills, the competence, the experience of management cannot, as such, be transferred and applied to the organization and running of other institutions. In particular a man's success in management carries by itself no promise—let alone a guarantee—of his being successful in government. A career in management is, by itself, not a preparation for major political office—or for leadership in the Armed Forces, the Church, or a university. The skills, the competence and the experience that are common and therefore transferable are analytical and administrative —extremely important, but secondary to the attainment of the primary objectives of the various non-business institutions. Whether Franklin D. Roosevelt was a great President or a national disaster has been argued hotly in this country for twenty years. But the patent fact that he was an extremely poor administrator seldom enters the discussion; even his staunchest enemies would consider it irrelevant. What is at issue are his basic political decisions. And no one would claim that these should be determined by the supply of goods and services desired by the consumer at the price the consumer is willing to pay, or by the maintenance or improvement of wealth-producing resources. What to the manager must be the main focus is to the politician, of necessity, only one factor among many.

A second negative conclusion is that management can never be an exact science. True, the work of a manager can be systematically analyzed and classified; there are, in other words, distinct professional features and a scientific aspect to management. Nor is managing a business just a matter of hunch or native ability; its elements and requirements can be analyzed, can be organized systematically, can be learned by anyone with normal human endowment. Altogether, this entire book is based on the proposition that the days of the "intuitive" managers are numbered. This book assumes that the manager can improve his performance in all areas of management, including the managing of a business, through the systematic study of principles, the acquisition of organized knowledge and the systematic analysis of his own performance in all areas of his work and job and on all levels of management. Indeed, nothing else can contribute so much to his skill, his effectiveness and his performance. And underlying this theme is the conviction that the impact of the manager on modern society and its citizens is so great as to require of him the self-discipline and the higher standards of public service of a true professional.

And yet the ultimate test of management is business performance. Achievement rather than knowledge remains, of necessity, both proof and aim. Management, in other words, is a practice, rather than a science or a profession, though containing elements of both. No greater damage could be done to our economy or to our society than to attempt to "professionalize" management by "licensing" managers, for instance, or by limiting access to management to people with a special academic degree.

On the contrary, it is the test of good management that it enables the successful business performer to do his work—whether he be otherwise a good manager or a poor one. And any serious attempt to make management "scientific" or a "profession" is bound to lead to the attempt to eliminate those "disturbing nuisances," the unpredictabilities of business life—its risks, its ups and downs, its "wasteful competition," the "irrational choices" of the consumer—and, in the process, the economy's freedom and its ability to grow. It is not entirely accident that some of the early pioneers of "Scientific Management" ended up by demanding complete cartelization of the economy (Henry Gantt was the prime example); that the one direct outgrowth of American "Scientific Management" abroad, the German "Rationalization" movement of the twenties, attempted to make the world safe for professional management by cartelizing it; and that in our own country men who were steeped in "scientific management" played a big part in "Technocracy" and in the attempted nation-wide super-cartel of the National Recovery Act in the first year of Roosevelt's New Deal.

The scope and extent of management's authority and responsibility are severely limited. It is true that in order to discharge its business responsibility management must exercise substantial social and governing authority within the enterprise—authority over citizens in their capacity as members of the enterprise. It is also a fact that because of the importance of the business enterprise, management inevitably becomes one of the leading groups in industrial society. Since management's responsibility is always founded in economic performance, however, it has no authority except as is necessary to discharge its economic responsibility. To assert authority for management over the citizen and his affairs beyond that growing out of management's responsibility for business performance is usurpation of authority. Furthermore management can only be one leading group among several; in its own self-interest it can never and must never be *the* leading group. It has partial rather than comprehensive social responsibility—hence partial rather than comprehensive social authority. Should management claim to be *the* leading group—or even to be the most powerful of leading groups—it will either be rebuffed and, in the process, be shorn of most of the authority it can claim legitimately, or it will help into power a dictatorship that will deprive management as well as all other groups in a free society of their authority and standing.

But while the fact that management is an organ of the business enterprise limits its scope and potential, it also embodies a major responsibility for creative action. For management has to *manage*. And managing is not just passive, adaptive behavior; it means taking action to make the desired results come to pass.

The early economist conceived of the businessman and his behavior as purely passive: success in business meant rapid and intelligent adaptation to events occurring outside, in an economy shaped by impersonal, objective forces that were neither controlled by the businessman nor influenced by his reaction to them. We may call this the concept of the "trader." Even if he was not considered a parasite, his contributions were seen as purely mechanical: the shifting of resources to more productive use. Today's economist sees the businessman as choosing rationally between alternatives of action. This is no longer a mechanical concept; obviously what choice the businessman makes has a real impact on the economy. But still, the economist's "businessman"—the picture that underlies the prevailing economic "theory of the firm" and the theorem of the "maximization of profits"—reacts to economic developments. He is still passive, still adaptive—though with a choice between various ways to adapt. Basically this is a concept of the "investor" or the "financier" rather than of the manager.

Of course, it is always important to adapt to economic changes rapidly, intelligently and rationally. But managing goes way beyond passive reaction and adaptation. It implies responsibility for attempting to shape the economic environment, for planning, initiating and carrying through changes in that economic environment, for constantly pushing back the limitations of economic circumstances on the enterprise's freedom of action. What is possible—the economist's "economic conditions"—is therefore only one pole in managing a business. What is desirable in the interest of the enterprise is the other. And while man can never really "master" his environment, while he is always held within a tight vise of possibilities, it is management's specific job to make what is desirable first possible and then actual. Management is not just a creature of the economy; it is a creator as well. And only to the extent to which it masters the economic circumstances, and alters them by conscious, directed action, does it really manage. To manage a business means, therefore, to *manage by objectives*. Throughout this book this will be a keynote.

Managing managers

To obtain economic performance there must be an enterprise. Management's second function is therefore to make a productive enterprise out of human and material resources. Concretely this is the function of managing managers.

The enterprise, by definition, must be capable of producing more or better than all the resources that comprise it. It must be a genuine whole: greater than—or at least different from—the sum of its parts, with its output larger than the sum of all inputs.

The enterprise cannot therefore be a mechanical assemblage of resources. To make an enterprise out of resources it is not enough to put them together in logical order and then to throw the switch of capital as the nineteenth-century economists firmly believed (and as many of their successors among academic economists still believe). What is needed is a transmutation of the resources. And this cannot come from an inanimate resource such as capital. It requires management.

But it is also clear that the "resources" capable of enlargement can only be human resources. All other resources stand under the laws of mechanics. They can be better utilized or worse utilized, but they can never have an output greater than the sum of the inputs. On the contrary, the problem in putting non-human resources together is always to keep to a minimum the inevitable output-shrinkage through friction, etc. Man, alone of all the resources available to man, can grow and develop. Only what a great medieval political writer (Sir John Fortescue) called the "intencio populi," the directed, focused, united effort of free human beings, can produce a real whole. Indeed, to make the whole that is greater than the sum of its parts has since Plato's days been the definition of the "Good Society."

When we speak of growth and development we imply that the human being himself determines what he contributes. Yet, we habitually define the rank-and-file worker—as distinguished from the manager—as a man who does as he is directed, without responsibility or share in the decisions concerning his work or that of others. This indicates that we consider the rank-and-file worker in the same light as other material resources, and as far as his contribution to the enterprise is concerned as standing under the laws of mechanics. This is a serious misunderstanding. The misunderstanding, however, is not in the definition of rank-and-file *work*, but rather in the failure to see that many rank-and-file *jobs* are in effect managerial, or would be more productive if made so. It does not, in other words, affect the argument that it is managing managers that makes an enterprise.

That this is true is shown in the terms we use to describe the various activities needed to build a functioning and productive enterprise. We speak of "organization"—the formal structure of the enterprise. But what we mean is the organization of managers and of their functions; neither brick and mortar nor rank-and-file workers have any place in the organization structure. We speak of "leadership" and of the "spirit" of a company. But leadership is given by managers and effective primarily within management; and the spirit is made by the spirit within the management group. We talk of "objectives" for the company, and of its performance. But the objectives are goals for management people; the performance is management performance. And if an enterprise fails to perform, we rightly hire not different workers but a new president.

Managers are also the costliest resource of the enterprise. In the big companies one hears again and again that a good engineer or accountant with ten or twelve years of working experience represents a direct investment of $50,000 over and above the contribution he has made so far to the company's success. The figure is, of course, pure guess—though the margin of error may well be no greater than that in the accountant's meticulous and detailed calculation of the investment in, and profitability of, a piece of machinery or a plant. But even if the actual figure were only a fraction, it would be high enough to make certain that the investment in managers, though, of course, never shown on the books, outweighs the investment in every other resource in practically all businesses. To utilize this investment as fully as possible is therefore a major requirement of managing a business.

To manage managers is therefore to make resources productive by making an enterprise out of them. And management is so complex and multi-faceted a thing, even in a very small business, that managing managers is inevitably not only a vital but a complex job.

Managing worker and work

The final function of management is to manage workers and work. Work has to be performed; and the resource to perform it with is workers—ranging from totally unskilled to artists, from wheelbarrow pushers to executive vice-presidents. This implies organization of the work so as to make it most suitable for human beings, and organization of people so as to make them work most productively and effectively. It implies consideration of the human being as a resource —that is, as something having peculiar physiological properties, abilities and limitations that require the same amount of engineering attention as the properties of any other resource, e.g., copper. It implies also consideration of the human resource as human beings having, unlike any other resource, personality, citizenship, control over whether they work, how much and how well, and thus requiring motivation, participation, satisfactions, incentives and rewards, leadership, status and function. And it is management, and management alone, that can satisfy these requirements. For they must be satisfied through work and job and within the enterprise; and management is the activating organ of the enterprise.

There is one more major factor in every management problem, every decision, every action—not, properly speaking, a fourth function of management, but an additional dimension; time. Management always has to consider both the present and the long-range future. A management problem is not solved if immediate profits are purchased by endangering the long-range profitability, perhaps even the survival, of the company. A management decision is irresponsible if it risks disaster this year for the sake of a grandiose future. The all too common case of the management that produces great economic results as long as it runs the company but leaves behind nothing but a burned-out and rapidly sinking hulk is an example of irresponsible managerial action through failure to balance present and future. The immediate "economic results" are actually fictitious and are achieved by paying out capital. In every case where present and future are not both satisfied, where their requirements are not harmonized or at least balanced, capital, that is, wealth-producing resources, is endangered, damaged or destroyed.

The time dimension is inherent in management because management is concerned with decisions for action. And action is always aimed at results in the future. Anybody whose responsibility it is to act—rather than just to know—operates into the future. But there are two reasons why the time dimension is of particular importance in management's job, and of particular difficulty. In the first place, it is the essence of economic and technological progress that the time-span for the fruition and proving out of a decision is steadily lengthening. Edison, fifty years ago, needed two years or so between the start of laboratory work on an idea and the start of pilot-plant operations. Today it may well take Edison's successors fifteen years. A half century ago a new plant was expected to pay for itself in two or three years; today, with capital investment per worker ten times that of 1900, the pay-off period in the same industry is ten or twelve years. The human organization, such as a sales force or a management group, may take even longer to build and to pay for itself.

The second peculiar characteristic of the time dimension is that management—almost alone—has to live always in both present and future. A military leader, too, knows both times. But rarely does he have to live in both at the same time. During peace he knows no "present"; all the present is is a preparation for the future of war. During war he knows only the most short-lived "future"; he is concerned with winning the war at hand to the practical exclusion of everything else. But management must keep the enterprise successful and profitable in the present—or else there will be no enterprise left to enjoy the future. It must simultaneously make the enterprise capable of growing and prospering, or at least of surviving in the future—otherwise it has fallen down on its responsibility of keeping resources productive and unimpaired, has destroyed capital. (The only parallel to this time-squeeze is the dilemma of the politician between the responsibility for the common good and the need to be re-elected as a prerequisite to making his contribution to the common good. But the cynical politician can argue that promises to the voters and performance once in office need not resemble each other too closely. The manager's action on present results, however, directly determines future results, his action on future results—research expenditures, for instance, or plant investment—profoundly influences visible present results.)

The integrated nature of management

The three jobs of management: managing a business, managing managers and managing worker and work, can be analyzed separately, studied separately, appraised separately. In each a present and a future dimension can be distinguished. But in its daily work management cannot separate them. Nor can it separate decisions on present from decisions on future. Any management decision always affects all three jobs and must take all three into account. And the most vital decisions on the future are often made as decisions on the present—on present research budgets or on the handling of a grievance, on promoting this man and letting that one go, on maintenance standards or on customer service.

It cannot even be said that one job predominates or requires the greater skill or competence. True, business performance comes first —it is the aim of the enterprise and the reason for its existence. But if there is no functioning enterprise, there will be no business performance, no matter how good management may be in managing the business. The same holds true if worker and work are mismanaged. Economic performance that is being achieved by mismanaging managers is illusory and actually destructive of capital. Economic performance that is being achieved by mismanaging work and worker is equally an illusion. It will not only raise costs to the point where the enterprise ceases to be competitive; it will, by creating class hatred and class warfare, end by making it impossible for the enterprise to operate at all.

Managing a business has primacy because the enterprise is an economic institution; but managing managers and managing workers and work have primacy precisely because society is not an economic institution and is therefore vitally interested in these two areas of management in which basic social beliefs and aims are being realized.

In this book we shall always bring together both present and future. But we shall discuss separately each of the three major jobs of management: managing a business, managing managers, managing work and worker. We must, however, never allow ourselves to forget that in actual practice managers always discharge these three jobs in every one action. We must not allow ourselves to forget that it is actually the specific situation of the manager to have not one but three jobs at the same time, discharged by and through the same people, exercised in and through the same decision. Indeed, we can only answer our question: "What is management and what does it do?" by saying that it is a multi-purpose organ that manages a business and manages managers *and* manages worker and work. If one of these were omitted, we would not have management any more— and we also would not have a business enterprise or an industrial society.

3. MANAGEMENT IN THE 1980'S [1]

Harold J. Leavitt [2]
Thomas L. Whisler [3]

Over the last decade a new technology has begun to take hold in American business, one so new that its significance is still difficult to evaluate. While many aspects of this technology are uncertain, it seems clear that it will move into the managerial scene rapidly, with definite and far-reaching impact on managerial organization. In this article we would like to speculate about these effects, especially as they apply to medium-size and large business firms of the future.

The new technology does not yet have a single established name. We shall call it *information technology*. It is composed of several related parts. One includes techniques for processing large amounts of information rapidly, and it is epitomized by the high-speed computer. A second part centers around the application of statistical and mathematical methods to decision-making problems; it is represented by techniques like mathematical programing, and by methodologies like operations research. A third part is in the offing, though its applications have not yet emerged very clearly; it consists of the simulation of higher-order thinking through computer programs.

Information technology is likely to have its greatest impact on middle and top management. In many instances it will lead to opposite conclusions from those dictated by the currently popular philosophy of "participative" management. Broadly, our prognostications are along the following lines:

1. Information technology should move the boundary between planning and performance upward. Just as planning was taken from the hourly worker and given to the industrial engineer, we now expect it to be taken from a number of middle managers and given to as yet largely nonexistent specialists: "operations researchers," perhaps, or "organizational analysts." Jobs at today's middle-

[1] From *Harvard Business Review* (November-December, 1958), pp. 41-48. Reprinted by permission of the *Harvard Business Review*.
[2] Harold J. Leavitt, Professor of Industrial Administration and Psychology, Graduate School of Industrial Administration, Carnegie Institute of Technology.
[3] Thomas L. Whisler, Associate Professor of Industrial Relations, Graduate School of Business Administration, The University of Chicago.

management level will become highly structured. Much more of the work will be programed, i.e., covered by sets of operating rules governing the day-to-day decisions that are made.

2. Correlatively, we predict that large industrial organizations will recentralize, that top managers will take on an even larger proportion of the innovating, planning, and other "creative" functions than they have now.

3. A radical reorganization of middle-management levels should occur, with *certain classes* of middle-management jobs moving downward in status and compensation (because they will require less autonomy and skill), while other classes move upward into the top-management group.

4. We suggest, too, that the line separating the top from the middle of the organization will be drawn more clearly and impenetrably than ever, much like the line drawn in the last few decades between hourly workers and first-line supervisors.

The New Technology

Information technology has diverse roots—with contributions from such disparate groups as sociologists and electrical engineers. Working independently, people from many disciplines have been worrying about problems that have turned out to be closely related and cross-fertilizing. Cases in point are the engineers' development of servomechanisms and the related developments of general cybernetics and information theory. These ideas from the "hard" sciences all had a direct bearing on problems of processing information—in particular, the development of techniques for conceptualizing and measuring information.

Related ideas have also emerged from other disciplines. The mathematical economist came along with game theory, a means of ordering and permitting analysis of strategies and tactics in purely competitive "think-" type games. Operations research fits in here, too; OR people made use of evolving mathematical concepts, or devised their own, for solving multivariate problems without necessarily worrying about the particular context of the variables. And from social psychology ideas about communication structures in groups began to emerge, followed by ideas about thinking and general problem-solving processes.

All of these developments, and many others from even more diverse sources, have in common a concern about the systematic manipulation of information in individuals, groups, or machines. The relationships among the ideas are not yet clear, nor has the wheat been adequately separated from the chaff. It is hard to tell who started what, what preceded what, and which is method and which theory. But, characteristically, application has not, and probably will not in the future, wait on completion of basic research.

Distinctive features

We call information technology "new" because one did not see much use of it until World War II, and it did not become clearly visible in industry until a decade later. It is new, also, in that it can be differentiated from at least two earlier industrial technologies:

1. In the first two decades of this century, Frederick W. Taylor's *scientific management* constituted a new and influential technology—one that took a large part in shaping the design of industrial organizations.
2. Largely after World War II a second distinct technology, *participative management,* seriously overtook—and even partially displaced—scientific management. Notions about decentralization, morale, and human relations modified and sometimes reversed earlier applications of scientific management. Individual incentives, for example, were treated first as simple applications of Taylorism, but they have more recently been revised in the light of "participative" ideas.

The scientific and participative varieties both survived. One reason is that scientific management concentrated on the hourly worker, while participative management has generally aimed one level higher, at middle managers, so they have not conflicted. But what will happen now? The new information technology has direct implications for middle management as well as top management.

Current picture

The inroads made by this technology are already apparent, so that our predictions are more extrapolations than derivations.[4] But the significance of the new trends has been obscured by the wave of interest in participative management and decentralization. Information technology seems now to show itself mostly in the periphery of management. Its applications appear to be independent of central organizational issues like communication and creativity. We have tended until now to use little pieces of the new technology to generate information, or to lay down limits for subtasks that can then be used within the old structural framework.

---

[4] Two examples of current developments are discussed in "Putting Arma Back on Its Feet," *Business Week* (February 1, 1958), p. 84; and "Two-Way Overhaul Rebuilds Raytheon," *Business Week* (February 22, 1958), p. 91.

Some of this sparing use of information technology may be due to the fact that those of us with a large commitment to participative management have cause to resist the central implications of the new techniques. But the implications are becoming harder to deny. Many business decisions once made judgmentally now can be made better by following some simple routines devised by a staff man whose company experience is slight, whose position on the organization chart is still unclear, and whose skill (if any) in human relations was picked up on the playground. For example:

> We have heard recently of an electric utility which is considering a move to take away from generating-station managers virtually all responsibility for deciding when to use stand-by generating capacity. A typical decision facing such managers develops on hot summer afternoons. In anticipation of heavy home air-conditioning demand at the close of working hours, the manager may put on extra capacity in late afternoon. This results in additional costs, such as overtime premiums. In this particular geographical area, rapidly moving cold fronts are frequent. Should such a front arrive after the commitment to added capacity is made, losses are substantial. If the front fails to arrive and capacity has not been added, power must be purchased from an adjacent system at penalty rates—again resulting in losses.
>
> Such decisions may soon be made centrally by individuals whose technical skills are in mathematics and computer programing, with absolutely no experience in generating stations.

Rapid spread

We believe that information technology will spread rapidly. One important reason for expecting fast changes in current practices is that information technology will make centralization much easier. By permitting more information to be organized more simply and processed more rapidly it will, in effect, extend the thinking range of individuals. It will allow the top level of management intelligently to categorize, digest, and act on a wider range of problems. Moreover, by quantifying more information it will extend top management's control over the decision processes of subordinates.

If centralization becomes easier to implement, managers will probably revert to it. Decentralization has, after all, been largely negatively motivated. Top managers have backed into it because they have been unable to keep up with size and technology. They could not design and maintain the huge and complex communication systems that their large, centralized organizations needed. Information technology should make recentralization possible. It may also obviate other major reasons for decentralization. For example, speed and flexibility will be possible despite large size, and top executives will be less dependent on subordinates because there will be fewer "experience" and "judgment" areas in which the junior men have more working knowledge. In addition, more efficient information-processing techniques can be expected to shorten radically the feedback loop that tests the accuracy of original observations and decisions.

Some of the psychological reasons for decentralization may remain as compelling as ever. For instance, decentralized organizations probably provide a good training ground for the top manager. They make better use of the whole man; they encourage more active cooperation. But though interest in these advantages should be very great indeed, it will be counterbalanced by interest in the possibilities of effective top-management control over the work done by the middle echelons. Here an analogy to Taylorism seems appropriate:

> In perspective, and discounting the countertrends instigated by participative management, the upshot of Taylorism seems to have been the separating of the hourly worker from the rest of the organization, and the acceptance by both management and the worker of the idea that the worker need not plan and create. Whether it is psychologically or socially justifiable or not, his creativity and ingenuity are left largely to be acted out off the job in his home or his community. One reason, then, that we expect top acceptance of information technology is its implicit promise to allow the top to control the middle just as Taylorism allowed the middle to control the bottom.

There are other reasons for expecting fast changes. Information technology promises to allow fewer people to do more work. The more it can reduce the number of middle managers, the more top managers will be willing to try it.

We have not yet mentioned what may well be the most compelling reason of all: the pressure on management to cope with increasingly complicated engineering, logistics, and marketing problems. The temporal distance between the discovery of new knowledge and its practical application has been shrinking rapidly, perhaps at a geometric rate. The pressure to reorganize in order to deal with the complicating, speeding world should become very great in the next decade. Improvisations and "adjustments" within present organizational frameworks are likely to prove quite inadequate; radical rethinking of organizational ideas is to be expected.

Revolutionary effects

Speculating a little more, one can imagine some radical effects of an accelerating development of information technology—effects warranting the adjective "revolutionary."

Within the organization, for example, many middle-management jobs may change in a manner reminiscent of (but faster than) the transition from shoemaker to stitcher, from old-time craftsman to today's hourly worker. As we have drawn an organizational class line between the hourly worker and the foreman, we may expect a new line to be drawn heavily, though jaggedly, between "top management" and "middle management," with some vice presidents and many ambitious suburban junior executives falling on the lower side.

In one respect, the picture we might paint for the 1980's bears a strong resemblance to the organizations of certain other societies— e.g., to the family-dominated organizations of Italy and other parts of Europe, and even to a small number of such firms in our own country. There will be many fewer middle managers, and most of those who remain are likely to be routine technicians rather than thinkers. This similarity will be superficial, of course, for the changes we forecast here will be generated from quite different origins.

What organizational and social problems are likely to come up as by-products of such changes? One can imagine major psychological problems arising from the depersonalization of relationships within management and the greater distance between people at different levels. Major resistances should be expected in the process of converting relatively autonomous and unprogramed middle-management jobs to highly routinized programs.

These problems may be of the same order as some of those that were influential in the development of American unions and in focusing middle management's interest on techniques for overcoming the hourly workers' resistance to change. This time it will be the top executive who is directly concerned, and the problems of resistance to change will occur among those middle managers who are programed out of their autonomy, perhaps out of their current status in the company, and possibly even out of their jobs.

On a broader social scale one can conceive of large problems outside the firm, that affect many institutions ancillary to industry. Thus:

1. What about education for management? How do we educate people for routinized middle-management jobs, especially if the path from those jobs up to top management gets much rockier?
2. To what extent do business schools stop training specialists and start training generalists to move directly into top management?
3. To what extent do schools start training new kinds of specialists?

4. What happens to the traditional apprentice system of training within managerial ranks?
5. What will happen to American class structure? Do we end up with a new kind of managerial elite? Will technical knowledge be the major criterion for membership?
6. Will technical knowledge become obsolete so fast that managers themselves will become obsolete within the time span of their industrial careers?

MIDDLE-MANAGEMENT CHANGES

Some jobs in industrial organizations are more programed than others. The job that has been subjected to micromotion analysis, for instance, has been highly programed; rules about what is to be done, in what order, and by what processes, are all specified.

Characteristically, the jobs of today's hourly workers tend to be highly programed—an effect of Taylorism. Conversely, the jobs shown at the tops of organization charts are often largely unprogramed. They are "think" jobs—hard to define and describe operationally. Jobs that appear in the big middle area of the organization chart tend to be programed in part, with some specific rules to be followed, but with varying amounts of room for judgment and autonomy.[5] One major effect of information technology is likely to be intensive programing of many jobs now held by middle managers and the concomitant "deprograming" of others.

As organizations have proliferated in size and specialization, the problem of control and integration of supervisory and staff levels has become increasingly worrisome. The best answer until now has been participative management. But information technology promises better answers. It promises to eliminate the risk of less than adequate decisions arising from garbled communications, from misconceptions of goals, and from unsatisfactory measurement of partial contributions on the part of dozens of line and staff specialists.

Good illustrations of this programing process are not common in middle management, but they do exist, mostly on the production side of the business. For example, the programmers have had some successes in displacing the judgment and experience of production schedulers (although the scheduler is still likely to be there to act out the routines) and in displacing the weekly scheduling meetings of production, sales, and supply people. Programs are also being worked

[5] See Robert N. McMurry, "The Case for Benevolent Autocracy," *Harvard Business Review* (January-February, 1958), p. 82.

out in increasing numbers to yield decisions about product mixes, warehousing, capital budgeting, and so forth.[6]

Predicting the impact

We have noted that not all middle-management jobs will be affected alike by the new technology. What kinds of jobs will become more routinized, and what kinds less? What factors will make the difference?

The impact of change is likely to be determined by three criteria:

1. *Ease of measurement*—It is easier, at this stage, to apply the new techniques to jobs in and around production than in, say, labor relations, one reason being that quantitative measurement is easier in the former realms.
2. *Economic pressure*—Jobs that call for big money decisions will tend to get earlier investments in exploratory programing than others.
3. *The acceptability of programing by the present jobholder*—For some classes of jobs and of people, the advent of impersonal rules may offer protection or relief from frustration. We recently heard, for example, of efforts to program a maintenance foreman's decisions by providing rules for allocating priorities in maintenance and emergency repairs. The foreman supported this fully. He was a harried and much blamed man, and programing promised relief.

Such factors should accelerate the use of programing in certain areas. So should the great interest and activity in the new techniques now apparent in academic and research settings. New journals are appearing, and new societies are springing up, like the Operations Research Society of America (established in 1946), and the Institute of Management Sciences (established in 1954), both of which publish journals.

The number of mathematicians and economic analysts who are being taken into industry is impressive, as is the development within industry, often on the personal staffs of top management, of individuals or groups with new labels like "operations researchers," "organization analysts," or simply "special assistants for planning." These new people are a cue to the emergence of information technology. Just as programing the operations of hourly workers created the industrial engineer, so should information technology, as planning is withdrawn from middle levels, create new planners with new names at the top level.

[6] See the journals, *Operations Research* and *Management Science*.

So much for work becoming more routinized. At least two classes of middle jobs should move *upward* toward *de*programedness:

1. The programmers themselves, the new information engineers, should move up. They should appear increasingly in staff roles close to the top.
2. We would also expect jobs in research and development to go in that direction, for innovation and creativity will become increasingly important to top management as the rate of obsolescence of things and of information increases. Application of new techniques to scanning and analyzing the business environment is bound to increase the range and number of possibilities for profitable production. Competition between firms should center more and more around their capacities to innovate.

Thus, in effect, we think that the horizontal slice of the current organization chart that we call middle management will break in two, with the larger portion shrinking and sinking into a more highly programed state and the smaller portion proliferating and rising to a level where more creative thinking is needed. There seem to be signs that such a split is already occurring. The growth of literature on the organization of research activities in industry is one indication.[7] Many social scientists and industrial research managers, as well as some general managers, are worrying more and more about problems of creativity and authority in industrial research organizations. Even some highly conservative company presidents have been forced to break time-honored policies (such as the one relating salary and status to organizational rank) in dealing with their researchers.

Individual problems

As the programing idea grows, some old human relations problems may be redefined. Redefinition will not necessarily solve the problems, but it may obviate some and give new priorities to others.

Thus, the issue of morale versus productivity that now worries us may pale as programing moves in. The morale of programed personnel may be of less central concern because less (or at least a different sort of) productivity will be demanded of them. The execution of controllable routine acts does not require great enthusiasm by the actors.

[7] Much of the work in this area is still unpublished. However, for some examples, see Herbert A. Shepard, "Superiors and Subordinates in Research," *Journal of Business of the University of Chicago* (October, 1956), p. 261; and also Donald C. Pelz, "Some Social Factors Related to Performance in a Research Organization," *Administrative Science Quarterly* (December, 1956), p. 310.

Another current issue may also take a new form: the debate about the social advantages or disadvantages of "conformity." The stereotype of the conforming junior executive, more interested in being well liked than in working, should become far less significant in a highly depersonalized, highly programed, and more machine-like middle-management world. Of course, the pressures to conform will in one sense become more intense, for the individual will be required to stay within the limits of the routines that are set for him. But the constant behavioral pressure to be a "good guy," to get along, will have less reason for existence.

As for individualism, our suspicion is that the average middle manager will have to satisfy his personal needs and aspirations off the job, largely as we have forced the hourly worker to do. In this case, the Park Forest of the future may be an even more interesting phenomenon than it is now.

Changes at the Top

If the new technology tends to split middle management—thin it, simplify it, program it, and separate a large part of it more rigorously from the top—what compensatory changes might one expect within the top group?

This is a much harder question to answer. We can guess that the top will focus even more intensively on "horizon" problems, on problems of innovation and change. We can forecast, too, that in dealing with such problems the top will continue for a while to fly by the seat of its pants, that it will remain largely unprogramed.

But even this is quite uncertain. Current research on the machine simulation of higher mental processes suggests that we will be able to program much of the top job before too many decades have passed. There is good authority for the prediction that within ten years a digital computer will be the world's chess champion, and that another will discover and prove an important new mathematical theorem; and that in the somewhat more distant future "the way is open to deal scientifically with ill-structured problems—to make the computer coextensive with the human mind." [8]

Meanwhile, we expect top management to become more abstract, more search-and-research-oriented and correspondingly less directly

[8] See Herbert A. Simon and Allen Newell, "Heuristic Problem Solving: The Next Advance in Operations Research," *Operations Research* (January-February, 1958), p. 9.

involved in the making of routine decisions. Allen Newell recently suggested to one of the authors that the wave of top-management game playing may be one manifestation of such change. Top management of the 1980's may indeed spend a good deal of money and time playing games, trying to simulate its own behavior in hypothetical future environments.

Room for innovators

As the work of the middle manager is programed, the top manager should be freed more than ever from internal detail. But the top will not only be released to think; it will be *forced* to think. We doubt that many large companies in the 1980's will be able to survive for even a decade without major changes in products, methods, or internal organization. The rate of obsolescence and the atmosphere of continuous change which now characterize industries like chemicals and pharmaceuticals should spread rapidly to other industries, pressuring them toward rapid technical and organizational change.

These ideas lead one to expect that researchers, or people like researchers, will sit closer to the top floor of American companies in larger numbers; and that highly creative people will be more sought after and more highly valued than at present. But since researchers may be as interested in technical problems and professional affiliations as in progress up the organizational ladder, we might expect more impersonal, problem-oriented behavior at the top, with less emphasis on loyalty to the firm and more on relatively rational concern with solving difficult problems.

Again, top staff people may follow their problems from firm to firm much more closely than they do now, so that ideas about executive turnover and compensation may change along with ideas about tying people down with pension plans. Higher turnover at this level may prove advantageous to companies, for innovators can burn out fast. We may see more brain picking of the kind which is now supposedly characteristic of Madison Avenue. At this creating and innovating level, all the current work on organization and communication in research groups may find its payoff.

Besides innovators and creators, new top-management bodies will need programmers who will focus on the internal organization itself. These will be the operations researchers, mathematical programmers, computer experts, and the like. It is not clear where these kinds of people are being located on organization charts today, but our guess is that the programmer will find a place close to the top. He will probably remain relatively free to innovate and to carry out his own applied research on what and how to program (although he may eventually settle into using some stable repertory of techniques as has the industrial engineer).

Innovators and programmers will need to be supplemented by "committors." Committors are people who take on the role of approving or vetoing decisions. They will commit the organization's resources to a particular course of action—the course chosen from some alternatives provided by innovators and programmers. The current notion that managers ought to be "coordinators" should flower in the 1980's, but at the top rather than the middle; and the people to be coordinated will be top staff groups.

Tight little oligarchy

We surmise that the "groupthink" which is frightening some people today will be a commonplace in top management of the future. For while the innovators and the programmers may maintain or even increase their autonomy, and while the committor may be more independent than ever of lower-line levels, the interdependence of the top-staff oligarchy should increase with the increasing complexity of their tasks. The committor may be forced increasingly to have the top men operate as a committee, which would mean that the precise individual locus of decision may become even more obscure than it is today. The small-group psychologists, the researchers on creativity, the clinicians—all should find a surfeit of work at that level.

Our references to a small oligarchy at the top may be misleading. There is no reason to believe that the absolute numbers of creative research people or programmers will shrink; if anything, the reverse will be true. It is the *head men* in these areas who will probably operate as a little oligarchy, with subgroups and sub-subgroups of researchers and programmers reporting to them. But the optimal structural shape of these unprogramed groups will not necessarily be pyramidal. It is more likely to be shifting and somewhat amorphous, while the operating, programed portions of the structure ought to be more clearly pyramidal than ever.

The organization chart of the future may look something like a football balanced upon the point of a church bell. Within the football (the top staff organization), problems of coordination, individual autonomy, group decision making, and so on should arise more intensely than ever. We expect they will be dealt with quite independently of the bell portion of the company, with distinctly different methods of remuneration, control, and communication.

CHANGES IN PRACTICES

With the emergence of information of technology, radical changes in certain administrative practices may also be expected. Without attempting to present the logic for the statements, we list a few changes that we foresee:

1. With the organization of management into corps (supervisors, programmers, creators, committors), multiple entry points into the organization will become increasingly common.
2. Multiple sources of potential managers will develop, with training institutions outside the firm specializing along the lines of the new organizational structure.
3. Apprenticeship as a basis for training managers will be used less and less since movement up through the line will become increasingly unlikely.
4. Top-management training will be taken over increasingly by universities, with on-the-job training done through jobs like that of assistant to a senior executive.
5. Appraisal of higher management performance will be handled through some devices little used at present, such as evaluation by peers.
6. Appraisal of the new middle managers will become much more precise than present rating techniques make possible, with the development of new methods attaching specific values to input-output parameters.
7. Individual compensation for top staff groups will be more strongly influenced by market forces than ever before, given the increased mobility of all kinds of managers.
8. With the new organizational structure new kinds of compensation practices—such as team bonuses—will appear.

Immediate measures

If the probability seems high that some of our predictions are correct, what can businessmen do to prepare for them? A number of steps are inexpensive and relatively easy. Managers can, for example, explore these areas:

1. They can locate and work up closer liaison with appropriate research organizations, academic and otherwise, just as many companies have profited from similar relationships in connection with the physical sciences.

2. They can re-examine their own organizations for lost information technologists. Many companies undoubtedly have such people, but not all of the top executives seem to know it.

3. They can make an early study and reassessment of some of the organizationally fuzzy groups in their own companies. Operations research departments, departments of organization, statistical analysis sections, perhaps even personnel departments, and other "oddball" staff groups often contain people whose knowledge and ideas in this realm have not been recognized. Such people provide a potential nucleus for serious major efforts to plan for the inroads of information technology.

Perhaps the biggest step managers need to take is an internal, psychological one. In view of the fact that information technology will challenge many long-established practices and doctrines, we will need to rethink some of the attitudes and values which we have taken for granted. In particular, we may have to reappraise our traditional notions about the worth of the individual as opposed to the organization, and about the mobility rights of young men on the make. This kind of inquiry may be painfully difficult, but will be increasingly necessary.

BIBLIOGRAPHY, CHAPTER I

ANSHEN, MELVIN. "Management and Change." Melvin Anshen and George Leland Bach (eds.). *Management and Corporations, 1985.* New York: McGraw-Hill Book Company, Inc., 1960. 199-240.

APPLEY, LAWRENCE. *Management in Action.* New York: American Management Association, Inc. 1956.

BELLOWS, ROGER. "The Challenge to Tomorrow's Executive," *Advanced Management* (April, 1960), 6-10.

BURSK, EDWARD D. *The Management Team.* Cambridge: Harvard University Press, 1954.

DRUCKER, PETER F. *The Practice of Management.* New York: Harper & Brothers, 1954. Chapter 29.

FAYOL, H. *General and Industrial Management.* New York: Pitman Publishing Corporation, 1949. Chapter 5.

GREENEWALT, CRAWFORD H. "The Management Profession," *Advanced Management* (December, 1955), 5-7.

HARBISON, FREDERICK, and CHARLES A. MYERS. *Management in the Industrial World.* New York: McGraw-Hill Book Company, Inc., 1959.

HOUSE, ROBERT T., and JOHN McINTYRE. "Management Theory in Practice," *Advanced Management* (October, 1961), 16-18.

HURNI, MELVIN. "Characteristics of Management Science," *Management Technology* (December, 1960), 37-46.

KOONTZ, HAROLD. "Making Sense of Management Theory," *Harvard Business Review* (July-August, 1962), 24-46.

LIKERT, RENSIS. *New Patterns in Management.* New York: McGraw-Hill Book Company, Inc., 1961. Chapter 1.

SIMON, HERBERT A. *Administrative Behavior,* Second Edition. New York: The Macmillan Company, 1960. Chapters 1 and 2, Appendix.

TANNENBAUM, R. "The Manager Concept: A Rational Synthesis," *Journal of Business*, Vol. 22, No. 4 (October, 1949), 229-240.

URWICK, LYNDALL. "Management Can Be an Intelligent Occupation," *Advanced Management* (February, 1956), 6-9.

YODER, DALE. "Management Theories as Managers See Them," *Personnel* (July-August, 1962), 25-30.

Chapter II
Management's Responsibilities in Society

A business does not exist in isolation but in a society that includes hospitals, schools, churches, government agencies, and other organizations, groups, and individuals. It is advantageous for a business to operate within the general beliefs and accepted codes of conduct of the society, for wide deviations from the accepted codes may jeopardize the security of the firm in the society.

Society's social and ethical beliefs as well as its rules of conduct provide a business with the foundation for plans and actions. The purpose of this chapter is to examine how the business manager determines what these beliefs and codes are and to illustrate the impact of the beliefs and codes on the operation of the firm.

In the first article O. A. Ohmann discusses the manager's need for "a fine sensitivity to spiritual qualities," a need which he regards as an end in itself in addition to the value such qualities may have for the firm. Thus, Ohmann calls for a more selfless managerial behavior than that which is indicated by the articles written by Howard R. Bowen which summarize his study of the responsibilities businessmen believe they have toward society and the reasons why businessmen have these beliefs. In contrast to the article by Ohmann, Theodore Levitt's article presents views of the effects that overemphasis upon social responsibility can have upon the success of the firm.

4. "SKYHOOKS" WITH SPECIAL IMPLICATIONS FOR MONDAY THROUGH FRIDAY [1]

O. A. Ohmann [2]

During the last several years, while my principal job assignment has been management development, I have become increasingly impressed with the importance of intangibles in the art of administration. With the managerial revolution of the last generation and the transition from owner-manager to professional executive, there has appeared a growing literature on the science and art of administration. A shift in emphasis is noticeable in these writings over the past 30 years.

Following the early engineering approach typified by the work of Frederick Taylor and others, there next developed a search for the basic principles of organization, delegation, supervision, and control. More recently, as labor relations became more critical, the emphasis has shifted to ways of improving human relations. The approach to the problems of supervisory relationships was essentially a manipulative one. Textbooks on the techniques of personnel management mushroomed. Still later it became more and more apparent that the crux of the problem was the supervisor himself, and this resulted in a flood of "how to improve yourself" books. Meanwhile the complexities of the industrial community increased, and the discontents and tensions mounted.

It seems increasingly clear, at least to me, that while some administrative practices and personnel techniques may be better than others, their futility arises from the philosophical assumptions or value judgments on which this superstructure of manipulative procedure rests. We observe again and again that a manager with sound values and a stewardship conception of his role as boss can be a pretty effective leader even though his techniques are quite unorthodox. I am convinced that workers have a fine sensitivity to spiritual qualities and want to work for a boss who believes in something and in whom they can believe.

---

[1] From the *Harvard Business Review*, Vol. XXXIII, No. 3 (May-June, 1955), pp. 1-10. Reprinted by permission of the *Harvard Business Review*.
[2] O. A. Ohmann, Director of Organization Planning and Management Development for the Standard Oil Company of Ohio.

This observation leads me to suspect that we may have defined the basic purposes and objectives of our industrial enterprise too narrowly, too selfishly, too materialistically. Bread alone will not satisfy workers. There are some indications that our people have lost faith in the basic values of our economic society, and that we need a spiritual rebirth in industrial leadership.

Certainly no people have ever had so much, and enjoyed so little real satisfaction. Our economy has been abundantly productive, our standard of living is at an all-time peak, and yet we are a tense, frustrated, and insecure people full of hostilities and anxieties. Can it be that our *god of production* has feet of clay? Does industry need a new religion—or at least a better one than it has had?

I am convinced that the central problem is not the division of the spoils as organized labor would have us believe. Raising the price of prostitution does not make it the equivalent of love. Is our industrial discontent not in fact the expression of a hunger for a work life that has meaning in terms of higher and more enduring spiritual values? How can we preserve the wholeness of the personality if we are expected to worship God on Sundays and holidays and mammon on Mondays through Fridays?

I do not imply that this search for real meaning in life is or should be limited to the hours on the job, but I do hold that the central values of our industrial society permeate our entire culture. I am sure we do not require a bill of particulars of the spiritual sickness of our time. The evidences of modern man's search for his soul are all about us. Save for the communist countries there has been a world-wide revival of interest in religion. The National Council of Churches reports that 59% of our total population (or 92 million) now claim church affiliation. The November 22, 1954, issue of *Barron's* devoted the entire front page to a review of a book by Barbara Ward, *Faith and Freedom.*[8]

Perhaps even more significant is the renaissance in the quality of religious thought and experience. Quite evidently our religion of materialism, science, and humanism is not considered adequate. Man is searching for anchors outside himself. He runs wearily to the periphery of the spider web of his own reason and logic, and looks for new "skyhooks"—for an abiding faith around which life's experiences can be integrated and given meaning.

[8] Barbara Ward, *Faith and Freedom* (New York: W. W. Norton & Company, Inc., 1954).

Why "Skyhooks"?

Perhaps we should assume that this need for "skyhooks" is part of man's natural equipment—possibly a function of his intelligence—or if you prefer, God manifesting Himself in His creatures. It seems to me, however, that the recent intensification of this need (or perhaps the clearer recognition of it) stems in part from certain broad social, economic, political, and philosophical trends. I shall not attempt a comprehensive treatment of these, but shall allude to only a few.

Abundance without satisfaction

I have already indicated that on the economic front we have won the battle of production. We have moved from an economy of scarcity to one of abundance. We have become masters of the physical world and have learned how to convert its natural resources to the satisfaction of our material wants. We are no longer so dependent and so intimately bound to the world of nature. In a way we have lost our feeling of being part of nature and with it our humble reverence for God's creation.

While the industrialization of our economy resulted in ever-increasing production, it also made of individual man a production number—an impersonal, de-skilled, interchangeable production unit, measured in so many cents per hour. For most employees, work no longer promotes the growth of personal character by affording opportunities for personal decision, exercise of judgment, and individual responsibility. A recent issue of *Nation's Business* quotes the modern British philosopher, Alexander Lindsay, on this point as follows:

> Industrialism has introduced a new division into society. It is the division between those who manage and take responsibility and those who are managed and have responsibility taken from them. This is a division more important than the division between the rich and poor.[4]

Certainly the modern industrial worker has improved his material standard of living at the cost of becoming more and more dependent on larger and larger groups. Not only his dignity but also his security has suffered. And so he reaches out for new "skyhooks"—for something to believe in, for something that will give meaning to his job.

---

[4] John Kord Lagemann, "Job Enlargement Boosts Production," *Nation's Business*, December, 1954, p. 36.

Disillusionment with science

A second trend which seems to bear some relation to our urgent need for a faith grows out of our disillusionment with science. As a result of the rapid advance of science, the curtains of ignorance and superstition have been pulled wide on all fronts of human curiosity and knowledge. Many of the bonds of our intellectual enslavement have been broken. Reason and scientific method were called on to witness to the truth, the whole truth, and nothing but the truth. We were freed from the past—its traditions, beliefs, philosophies, its mores, moral and religion. Science became our religion and reason replaced emotion.

However, even before the atom bomb there was a growing realization that science did not represent the whole truth, that with all its pretensions it could be dead wrong, and, finally and particularly, that without proper moral safeguards the truth did not necessarily make men free. Atomic fission intensified the fear and insecurity of every one of us who contemplated the possibility of the concentration of power in the hands of men without morals. We want science to be in the hands of men who not only recognize their responsibility to man-made ethical standards (which are easily perverted) but have dedicated themselves to the eternal and absolute standards of God. Thus, while the evidence of material science has been welcomed, our own personal experiences will not permit us to believe that life is merely a whirl of atoms without meaning, purpose, beauty, or destiny.

Trend toward bigness

A third factor contributing to our insecurity is the trend toward bigness and the resulting loss of individuality. This is the day of bigger and bigger business—in every aspect of life. The small is being swallowed by the big, and the big by the bigger. This applies to business, to unions, to churches, to education, to research and invention, to newspapers, to our practice of the professions, to government, and to nations. Everything is getting bigger except the individual, and he is getting smaller and more insignificant and more dependent on larger social units. Whether we like it or not this is becoming an administrative society, a planned and controlled society, with ever-increasing concentration of power. This is the day of collectivism and public-opinion polls. It is the day when the individual must be *adjusted to the group*—when he must above all else be sensitive to the feelings and attitudes of others, must get an idea of how others expect him to act, and then react to this.

This is the insecure world which David Riesman has described so well in his book, *The Lonely Crowd*.[5] He pictures man as being no longer "tradition directed" as was primitive man, nor as in Colonial days is he "inner directed" as if by the gyroscope of his own ideals, but today he is "outer directed" as if by radar. He must constantly keep his antenna tuned to the attitudes and reactions of others to him. The shift has been from morals to morale and from self-reliance to dependence on one's peer group. However, the members of one's peer group are each responding to each other. Obviously these shifting sands of public opinion offer no stable values around which life can be consistently integrated and made meaningful. The high-water mark of adjustment in such a society is that the individual be socially accepted and above all else that he appear to be *sincere*.

This is certainly not a favorable environment for the development of steadfast character. It is essentially a neurotic and schizophrenic environment which breeds insecurity.

This socially dependent society also offers an ideal market for the wares of the "huckster," the propagandist, and the demagogue. Lacking a religious interpretation of the divine nature of man, these merchants in mass reaction have sought the least common denominator in human nature and have beamed the movies and newspapers at the ten-year mental level. One wonders if this approach to people does not make them feel that they have been sold short and that they are capable of much better than is expected of them. Has this demoralizing exposure of the cheapness of our values not intensified our search for something better to believe in?

On top of all these disturbing socioeconomic trends came the war. This certainly was materialism, science, and humanism carried to the logical conclusion. The war made us question our values and our direction. It left us less cocksure that we were right, and more fearful of ourselves as well as of others. It made us fearful of the power which we had gained, and led us to search our soul to determine whether we had the moral strength to assume the leadership role that had been given to us. We have been humbled in our efforts to play god and are about ready to give the job back. Note, however, that this is not a characteristic reaction to war. Typically wars have been followed by a noticeable deterioration of moral standards, traditional values, and social institutions.

Perhaps none of these rationalizations for our return to religion is entirely valid. I suspect that the search for some kind of over-

[5] David Riesman, *The Lonely Crowd* (New Haven, Yale University Press, 1950).

arching integrative principle or idea is the expression of a normal human need. Certainly history would indicate that man's need for a god is eternal even though it may be more keenly sensed in times of adversity. A religion gives a point of philosophical orientation around which life's experiences can be organized and digested. Without the equivalent, a personality cannot be whole and healthy. Short-term goals which need to be shifted with the changing tide do not serve the same integrative function as do the "skyhooks" which are fastened to eternal values. I do not personally regard the current religious revival as a cultural hangover, nor as a regression. Being a mystic I prefer instead to view the need for such a faith as the spark of the Creator in us to drive us on to achieve His will and our own divine destiny.

Why Monday Through Friday?

If we may grant for the moment that modern man *is* searching for deeper meanings in life, we may then ask, what has this to do with industry. If he needs "skyhooks," let him get them in church, or work out his own salvation. The business leaders of the past insisted that "business is business" and that it had little bearing on the individual's private life and philosophy.

There are several reasons why "skyhooks" must be a primary concern of the business administrator:

1. For the individual the job is the center of life, and its values must be in harmony with the rest of life if he is to be a whole and healthy personality.

2. This is an industrial society, and its values tend to become those of the entire culture.

3. The public is insisting that business leaders are in fact responsible for the general social welfare—that the manager's responsibilities go far beyond those of running the business. They have delegated this responsibility to the business executive whether he wishes to play this role or not.

4. Even if the administrator insists on a narrow definition of his function as merely the production of goods and services as efficiently as possible, it is nevertheless essential that he take these intangibles into account since they are the real secrets of motivating an organization.

5. Besides all this the administrator needs a better set of "skyhooks" himself if he is to carry his ever-increasing load of responsibility without cracking up. The fact that so many administrators are taking time to rationalize, defend, and justify the private enterprise system is an outward indication of this need for more significant meanings.

Anything Wrong with Capitalism?

We may ask, then, what specifically is wrong with our capitalistic system of private enterprise? What is wrong with production or with trying to improve our standard of living? What is wrong with a profit, or with private ownership of capital, or with competition? Is this not the true American way of life.[6]

Nothing is necessarily wrong with these values. There are certainly worse motives than the profit motive. A refugee from communism is reported to have observed: "What a delight to be in the United States where things are produced and sold with such a nice clean motive as making a profit."

I am not an economist, and it is beyond the scope of this article to attempt a revision of our economic theory. I am tempted, however, to make a couple of observations about these traditional economic concepts:

1. That while the values represented by them are not necessarily wrong, they are certainly pretty thin and do not challenge the best in people.
2. That many of the classical economic assumptions are outmoded and are no longer adequate descriptions of the actual operation of our present-day economy.

For example, the concept of economic man as being motivated by self-interest not only is outmoded by the best current facts of the social sciences, but also fails to appeal to the true nobility of spirit of which we are capable.

The concept of the free and competitive market is a far cry from the highly controlled and regulated economy in which business must operate today. General Motors does not appear to want to put Chrysler out of business, and apparently the union also decided to take the heat off Chrysler rather than to press its economic advantage to the logical conclusion. The assumption that everyone is out to destroy his competitors does not explain the sharing of technology through trade associations and journals. No, we also have tremendous capacity for cooperation when challenged by larger visions. We are daily denying the Darwinian notion of the "survival of the fittest" which, incidentally, William Graham Sumner, one of the nineteenth-century apologists for our economic system, used for justifying unbridled, self-interest and competition.

---

[6] For a comprehensive treatment of the criticisms of business see J. D. Glover, *The Attack on Big Business* (Boston, Division of Research, Harvard Business School, 1954).

Certainly the traditional concept of private ownership of capital does not quite correspond to the realities of today's control of large blocks of capital by insurance companies and trusteed funds.

The notion of individual security through the accumulation of savings has largely given way to the collectivist means of group insurance, company annuities, and Social Security.

The concept that all profits belong to the stockholders is no longer enthusiastically supported by either the government or the unions since both are claiming an increasing cut.

And so, while we may argue that the system of private enterprise is self-regulatory and therefore offers maximum individual freedom, the simple, cold fact is that it is in ever-increasing degree a managed or controlled economy—partly at the insistence of the voters, but largely as the result of the inevitable economic pressures and the trend toward bigness.[7]

Regardless of the rightness or wrongness of these changes in our system of enterprise, the changes have been considerable, and I doubt that classical economic theory can be used as an adequate rationale of its virtues. I am therefore not particularly optimistic about the efficacy of the current campaign to have businessmen "save the private enterprise system and the American way of life" by engaging in wholesale economic education, much of which is based on outmoded concepts.

Much as economic theory needs revision, I fear that this is not likely to cure our ills. Nor do I believe that profit-sharing or any other device for increasing the workers' cut (desirable as these efforts may be) will give us what we really want. It is rather another type of sharing that is needed, a sharing of more worthy objectives, a sharing of the management function, and a sharing of mutual respect and Christian working relationships.

Goals and purposes

What is wrong is more a matter of goals and purposes. . . . There is nothing wrong with production, but we should ask ourselves: *"Production for what?"* Do we use people for production or production for people? How can production be justified if it destroys personality and human values both in the process of its manufacture and by its end use? Clarence B. Randall of Inland Steel in his book, *A Creed for Free Enterprise*, says:

[7] See John Kenneth Galbraith, *American Capitalism* (Boston, Houghton Mifflin Company, 1952).

We have come to worship production as an end in itself, which of course it is not. It is precisely there that the honest critic of our way of life makes his attack and finds us vulnerable. Surely there must be for each person some ultimate value, some purpose, some mode of self-expression that makes the experience we call life richer and deeper.[8]

So far, so good, Mr. Randall. But now notice how he visualizes industry making its contribution to this worthy objective:

To produce more and more with less and less effort is merely treading water unless we *thereby release time and energy for the cultivation of the mind and the spirit* and for the achievement of those ends for which Providence placed us on this earth.[9]

Here is the same old dichotomy—work faster and more efficiently so that you can finish your day of drudgery and cultivate your soul on your own time. In fact he says: "A horse with a very evil disposition can nevertheless pull the farmer's plow." No, I am afraid the job *is* the life. *This* is what must be made meaningful. We cannot assume that the end of production justifies the means. What happens to people in the course of producing may be far more important than the end product. Materialism is not a satisfactory "skyhook." People are capable of better and want to do better. (Incidentally I have the impression that Mr. Randall's practices line up very well with my own point of view even if his words do not.)

Perhaps we should ask what is the really important difference between Russian communism and our system. Both worship production and are determined to produce more efficiently, and do. Both worship science. Both have tremendously improved the standard of living of their people. Both share the wealth. Both develop considerable loyalties for their system. (In a mere 40 years since Lenin started the communist revolution a third of the world's people have come to accept its allegiance.) True, in Russia capital is controlled by the state while here it is theoretically controlled by individuals, although in actual practice, through absentee ownership, it is controlled to a considerable extent by central planning agencies and bureaus, both public and private.

No, the real difference is in the philosophy about people and how they may be used as means to ends. It is a difference in the assumptions made about the origin of rights—whether the individual is endowed with rights by his Creator and yields these only voluntarily

[8] Clarence B. Randall, *A Creed for Free Enterprise* (Boston, Little, Brown and Company, 1952), p. 16.
[9] *Ibid.*

to civil authority designated by him, or whether rights originate in force and in the will of the government. Is God a myth, or is He the final and absolute judge to whom we are ultimately responsible? Are all standards of conduct merely man-made and relative, or absolute and eternal? Is man a meaningless happenstance of protoplasm, or is he a divine creation with a purpose, with potential for improvement, and with a special destiny in the over-all scheme of things?

These are some of the differences—or at least I hope that they still are. And what a difference these intangible, perhaps mythical, "skyhooks" make. They are nevertheless the most real and worthwhile and enduring things in the world. The absence of these values permitted the Nazis to "process" people through the gas chambers in order to recover the gold in their teeth.

THE ADMINISTRATOR CONTRIBUTES

This, then, is part of our general cultural heritage and is passed on to us in many ways. However, it really comes to life in people— in their attitudes, aspirations, and behaviors. And in a managerial society this brings us back to the quality of the individual administrator. He interprets or crystallizes the values and objectives for his group. He sets the climate within which these values either *do* or *do not* become working realities. He must define the goals and purposes of his group in larger and more meaningful perspective. He integrates the smaller, selfish goals of individuals into larger, more social and spiritual objectives for the group. He provides the vision without which the people perish. Conflicts are resolved by relating the immediate to the long-range and more enduring values. In fact, we might say this *integrative function* is the core of the administrator's contribution.

The good ones have the mental equipment to understand the business and set sound long-term objectives, but the best ones have in addition the philosophical and character values which help them to relate the over-all goals of the enterprise to eternal values. This is precisely the point at which deep-seated religious convictions can serve an integrative function since they represent the most long-range of all possible goals.[10] Most really great leaders in all fields of human endeavor have been peculiarly sensitive to their historic role in human destiny. Their responsibility and loyalty are to some distant vision which gives calm perspective to the hot issues of the day.

[10] For further elaboration see Gordon W. Allport, *The Individual and His Religion* (New York, The Macmillan Company, 1953).

This function of the administrator goes far beyond being a likable personality, or applying correct principles of organization, or being skillful in the so-called techniques of human relations. I am convinced that the difficulties which so many executives have with supervisory relationships cannot be remedied by cultivation of the so-called human relations skills. These difficulties spring rather from one's conception of his function or role as a boss, his notion about the origin and nature of his authority over others, the assumptions he makes about people and their worth, and his view of what he and his people are trying to accomplish together. To illustrate:

> If, for example, my personal goal is to get ahead in terms of money, position, and power; and if I assume that to achieve this I must best my competitors; that the way to do this is to establish a good production record; that my employees are means to this end; that they are replaceable production units which must be skillfully manipulated; that this can be done by appealing to the lowest form of immediate selfish interest; that the greatest threat to me is that my employees may not fully recognize my authority nor accept my leadership—if these are my values, then I am headed for trouble—all supervisory techniques notwithstanding.

I wish I could be quite so positive in painting the picture of the right values and approaches to management. I suspect there are many, many different right answers. No doubt each company or enterprise will have to define its own long-term purposes and develop its own philosophy in terms of its history, traditions, and its real function in our economy. I am also certain that no one philosophy would be equally useful to all managers. The character of an organization is, to a large extent, set by the top man or the top group, and it is inevitable that this be the reflection of the philosophy of these individuals. No one of us can operate with another's philosophy. I have also observed that in most enterprises the basic faith or spirit of the organization is a rather nebulous or undefined something, which nevertheless has very profound meaning to the employees.

A successful executive

Recognizing then the futility of advocating any one pattern of values, it occurs to me that it might, however, be suggestive or helpful if I told you something of the philosophy of one extremely successful executive whom I have pumped a good deal on this subject (for he is more inclined to live his values than to talk about them):

As near as I can piece it together, he believes that this world was not an accident but was created by God and that His laws regulate and control the universe and that we are ultimately *responsible to Him.* Man, as God's supreme creation, is in turn endowed with creative ability. Each individual represents a unique combination of talents and potentials. In addition, man is the only animal endowed with freedom of choice and with a high capacity for making value judgments. With these gifts (of heredity and cultural environment) goes an obligation to give the best possible accounting of one's stewardship in terms of maximum self-development and useful service to one's fellows in the hope that one may live a rich life and be a credit to his Creator.

This executive also assumes that each individual possesses certain God-given rights of self-direction which only *the individual* can voluntarily delegate to others in authority over him, and that this is usually done in the interest of achieving some mutual cooperative good. The executive therefore assumes that his *own* authority as boss over others must be exercised with due regard for the attendant obligations to his employees and to the stockholders who have temporarily and voluntarily yielded their rights in the interest of this common undertaking. (Notice that he does not view his authority as originating with or derived from his immediate superior.) This delegated authority must, of course, be used to advance the common good rather than primarily to achieve the selfish ambitions of the leader at the expense of the led.

He further assumes that the voluntary association of employees in industry is for the purpose of increasing the creativity and productivity of all members of the group and thus of bringing about increased benefits to all who may share in the ultimate use of these goods and services. What is equally important, however, is that in the course of this industrial operation each individual should have an opportunity to develop the maximum potential of his skills and that the working relationships should not destroy the individual's ability to achieve his greatest maturity and richness of experience. As supervisor he must set the working conditions and atmosphere which will make it possible for his employees to achieve this dual objective of increasing productivity and maximizing self-development.

These goals can best be achieved by giving employees maximum opportunity to exercise their capacity for decision making and judgment within their assigned area of responsibility. The supervisor is then primarily a coach who must instruct, discipline, and motivate all the members of the group, making it possible for each to exercise his special talent in order to maximize the total team contribution. Profits are regarded as a measure of the group's progress toward these goals, and a loss represents not only an improper but even an immoral use of the talents of the group.

There is nothing "soft" about his operation. He sets high quality standards and welcomes stiff competition as an additional challenge to his group. He therefore expects and gets complete cooperation and dedication on the part of everyone. Incidentally, he views the activity of working together in this manner with others as being one of life's most rewarding experiences. He holds that this way of life is something which we have not yet fully learned, but that its achievement is part of our divine destiny. He is firmly convinced that such conscientious efforts *will* be rewarded with success. He manages with a light touch that releases creativity, yet with complete confidence in the outcome.

This is probably a poor attempt at verbalizing the basic philosophy which this man lives so easily and naturally. I hope, however, that it has revealed something of his conception of his role or function as an executive, and his view of what he and his organization are trying to do together. With this account of his values I am sure that you would have no difficulty completing the description of his administrative practices and operating results. They flow naturally from his underlying faith, without benefit of intensive training in the principles and art of administration.

As you would suspect, people like to work for him—or with him. He attracts good talent (which is one of the real secrets of success). Those with shoddy values, selfish ambitions, or character defects do not survive—the organization is self-pruning. Those who remain develop rapidly because they learn to accept responsibility. He not only advocates but practices decentralization and delegation. His employees will admit that they have made mistakes, but usually add with a grin that they try not to make the same one twice. People respond to his leadership because he has faith in them and expects the best in them rather than the worst. He speaks well of the members of his organization, and they appear to be proud of each other and of their record of performance. He takes a keen interest in developing measurements of performance and in bettering previous records or competitive standards. He feels that no one has a right to "louse up a job"—a point on which he feels the stockholders and the Lord are in complete agreement.

While he does not talk much about "employee communications" nor stress formal programs of this type, his practice is to spend a large proportion of his time in the field with his operating people rather than in his office. He is "people oriented" and does a particularly good job of listening. The union committee members have confidence in his fairness, yet do a workmanlike job of bargaining. In administering salaries he seems to be concerned about helping the individual to improve his contribution so that a pay increase can be justified.

In his general behavior he moves without haste or hysteria. He is typically well organized, relaxed, and confident, even under trying circumstances. There is a high degree of consistency in his behavior and in the quality of his decisions because his basic values do not shift. Since he does not operate by expediency, others can depend on him; and this consistency makes for efficiency in the discharge of delegated responsibility. Those operating problems which do come to him for decision seem to move easily and quickly to a conclusion. His long-term values naturally express themselves in well-defined policies, and it is against this frame of reference that the decisions of the moment easily fall into proper perspective.

In policy-level discussions his contributions have a natural quality of objectivity because "self-concern" does not confuse. Others take him at face value because his motives are not suspect. When differences or conflicts do arise, his approach is not that of compromise; rather he attempts to integrate the partisan views around mutually acceptable longer-range goals. The issues of the moment then seem to dissolve in a discussion of the best means to the achievement of the objective. I have no doubt that he also has some serious problems, but I have tried to give a faithful account of the impression which he creates. There is a *sense of special significance* about his operation which is shared by his associates.

This Is the Key

It is precisely this "sense of special significance" which is the key to leadership. We all know that there are many different ways of running a successful operation. I am certainly not recommending any particular set of administrative practices—although admittedly some are better than others. Nor am I suggesting that his set of values should be adopted by others, or for that matter could be. What I am saying is that a man's real values have a subtle but inevitable way of being communicated, and they affect the significance of everything he does.

These are the vague intangibles—the "skyhooks"—which are difficult to verbalize but easy to sense and tremendously potent in their influence. They provide a different, invisible, fundamental structure into which the experiences of every day are absorbed and given meaning. They are frequently unverbalized, and in many organizations they defy definition. Yet they are the most real things in the world.

The late Jacob D. Cox, Jr., formerly president of Cleveland Twist Drill Company, told a story that illustrates my point:

Jimmy Green was a new union committee member who stopped in to see Mr. Cox after contract negotiations had been concluded. Jimmy said that every other place he had worked, he had always gone home grouchy; he never wanted to play with the children or take his wife to the movies. And then he said, "But since I have been working here, all that has changed. Now when I come home, the children run to meet me and we have a grand romp together. It is a wonderful difference and I don't know why, but I thought you would like to know." [11]

As Mr. Cox observed, there must be a lot of Jimmy Greens in the world who want an opportunity to take part freely in a cooperative effort that has a moral purpose.

[11] Jacob D. Cox, Jr., *Material Human Progress* (Cleveland, Cleveland Twist Drill Company, 1954), p. 104.

5. THE BUSINESSMAN'S VIEWS OF
HIS SPECIFIC RESPONSIBILITIES [1]   Howard R. Bowen [2]

CONCLUSIONS

Our survey of the opinions of leading businessmen regarding their social responsibilities leads to certain conclusions.

First, there is widespread and sincere interest in the subject.

Second, the pronouncements of businessmen regarding their general responsibilities (e.g., the concept of trusteeship for several interests) are frequent and eloquent. But businessmen are noticeably less articulate about the specific duties which flow from these general responsibilities. The new theories of the role of business in modern society are in a relatively primitive or formative state. Because of their newness and because of the intricacy of their implications, these theories have by no means developed into full-blown plans of action. This suggests that businessmen have much hard thinking and soul-searching ahead of them. It also suggests that they will need professional guidance in translating their general aims into concrete policies and actions. Such translation, since it would point up the practical implications of the general aims, might of course have the effect of modifying the aims themselves.

Third, the fact that businessmen are so unanimous in their belief in the need for public education implies that, in their opinions, the required adjustments are two-directional. On the one hand, businessmen must adjust their operations to the needs of society at large; on the other hand, society must develop attitudes and policies more favorable to business.

Fourth, the great concern of businessmen for better public relations, which they hope to achieve both by "education" of the public and by adoption of socially oriented policies, indicates the power of public opinion over business and suggests the efficacy of control or influence over business by means of moral sanctions exerted by an

[1] From *Social Responsibilities of the Businessman* (New York: Harper & Brothers, 1953), pp. 67-68. Reprinted by permission of Harper & Brothers.
[2] Howard R. Bowen, President, Grinnell College.

alert and articulate public. A change in the climate of opinion—without any change in formal controls—can doubtless exert great influence over businessmen.

Fifth, in spelling out their specific responsibilities, businessmen give noticeably more attention to those obligations which are clearly in their own long-run interest than to those which are not so clearly advantageous to them.[3] For example, they give great emphasis to developing better public relations, and to increasing productivity and efficiency. Doubtless, these are all desirable from the social point of view, but they are pre-eminently desirable from the point of view of business. When businessmen are concerned with general economic stability, they think of it in terms of the stability of their own operations—which has a strong flavor of self-interest. Those who advocate a low-price policy do so not only because it is good social policy but also because it is good business in the long run. The number who express concern about things which are not so clearly in the business interest are relatively few.

The fact that businessmen are interested in those responsibilities which are affected with the long-run private interest as well as the public interest should be cause for neither surprise nor regret. Rather, it should be a source of profound satisfaction that the private and the social interest are found to be coincident over significant areas, because action in the social interest is doubtless more reliable when it is reinforced by the private interest. The fact that businessmen consider certain actions which are in the social interest to be also in the long-run self-interest is due not to a sudden conversion of businessmen, but rather to a change in the climate of public opinion within which they are operating. It is self-interest in a new setting. The things that are expected of businessmen today—and which they, therefore, regard as their responsibilities—are based upon a shift in public attitudes regarding business and its role in our society. This implies that, under the pressure of public opinion, businessmen can be persuaded to accept new duties and obligations which today they do not accept simply because the public does not expect them to be accepted. The means of achieving higher morality in business behavior is to create public attitudes which enlarge the moral responsibilities of business. Once this is done, business, with its new and broadened concern for public approval, will respond.

---

[3] Cf. Alfred S. Cleveland, "N.A.M., Spokesman for Industry," *Harvard Business Review*, May, 1948, pp. 353-71.

6. WHY ARE BUSINESSMEN CONCERNED ABOUT THEIR SOCIAL RESPONSIBILITIES? [1]

Howard R. Bowen [2]

It is now time to draw together the threads of our argument in answer to the question: Why are today's businessmen concerned about their social responsibilities?

In asking the question, it was assumed that today's businessmen are, in fact, more concerned than were their predecessors; this assumption was supported by citing many illustrations of business policies and actions growing out of this concern, and by analyzing many statements of businessmen.

We can divide our answer to the question into three parts: (1) because they have been *forced* to be more concerned, (2) because they have been *persuaded* to be more concerned, and (3) because, owing largely to the separation of ownership and control in the large corporation, *conditions* have been *favorable* to the development of this concern. Let us consider each of these three parts of the answer separately.

First, businessmen have been forced to consider their responsibilities because they have been operating in a climate of opinion in which increased public regulation, or even public ownership, has been considered an ever-present threat. Moreover, they have been confronted with the relentless pressure of a determined labor movement. Businessmen as a group, therefore, well understood that a condition of business survival, or at least of continued relative business independence, would be the operation of their businesses in conformity with the new standards and new aspirations of the public. The shaping of business policies in accordance with publicly accepted standards had become imperative from the point of view of the businessmen's own long-run self-interest.[3]

---

[1] From *Social Responsibilities of the Businessman* (New York: Harper & Brothers, 1953), pp. 103-107. Reprinted by permission of Harper & Brothers.

[2] Howard R. Bowen, President, Grinnell College.

[3] An influential businessman, who has made helpful, though severe, criticisms of this book, feels that I have not given sufficient attention to the spiritual side of industry.

Second, businessmen have been persuaded to consider their social responsibilities. As members of the society they have acquired many of its attitudes and values; hence, they have come to share—in substantial degree but perhaps not completely—the standards of the society as to what a business ought to be like and how it ought to be operated. They have been influenced by business educators, by their direct contacts with the government and its problems, and by the necessity of grappling with new and different problems. Through the rise of a new scientific study of management, they have come to realize that many of the things expected of them (e.g., good working conditions and good human relations) are actually good business in that they promote efficiency and lower costs.

Third, as a result of the separation of ownership and control in the large corporation, the managerial function has been vested in professional salaried managers whose motivation and point of view tend to differ in important respects from that of owner-managers. These new managers are selected because of their qualifications as administrators and their acceptability to various groups affected by the corporation; they are on the whole highly educated and experienced; they are interested in professional achievement (which they define broadly) as well as in personal remuneration; they identify themselves closely with the corporation and view it as having indefinitely long life; they think in terms of the long-range welfare and interests of the corporation as such; they regard the corporation as something more than a mere creature of the stockholders. Also, as a result of the growth of the corporation in complexity and size, the management function has been subdivided so that decision-making has become a social process in which many persons participate and in which various points of view and diverse interests are expressed. In addition, many of our large corporations have attained a kind of maturity and stability which permits them to consider the long view and to take a philosophical approach to their role in society. The large size of these corporations makes obvious to their managers the relation between their decisions and the general welfare.

Adding these factors together, one can conclude that there are abundant explanations for the increasing concern of businessmen toward their social responsibilities—that this trend of business thought and action is firmly based upon fundamental features of the modern social environment and on fundamental motives of businessmen. In a sense, a kind of socialization or social responsiveness of business has been achieved spontaneously without resort to formal governmental apparatus—although the tacit threat of further control by government or labor has consistently been in the background.

One must not, of course, exaggerate the extent to which businessmen and their corporations have disavowed their selfish motives and turned their thoughts to the social welfare. One would have difficulty in sharing even today the enthusiasm of a leading businessman, who said, on the very eve of the Great Depression: "The tendency in the banking business toward cooperation for the protection of the public and the establishment of the highest ethical standards has come to its most perfect flowering in the last decade . . . ." Yet a reading of the literature about capitalism and its civilization covering the period of Dickens, of the Granger movement, of the "muckrakers," of the disenchanted 'twenties, of the Great Depression, and of the recent war and postwar years would provide heartening evidence that great progress has occurred both in thinking and in action.

This progress has been achieved primarily as a result of the changes in the social climate of opinion, attitudes, and values. It has been based, in the last analysis, on public opinion—and on what the public has expected of business. In general, business is sensitive to changes in the market for its goods and it is equally sensitive to changes in the market for the business system itself. In both markets, it will rise to what is expected of it—but it will not rise much higher than that. And if public opinion relaxes and expects less of business, some of the gains of a century could easily be lost.

It would be idle to debate whether, or to what extent, this growing social responsiveness of business rests on altruistic or selfish motives. There are elements of both. The fact that self-interest (interpreted broadly and for the long run) is so important gives one confidence in the persistence and further development of these trends.[4]

---

[4] Cf. C. E. Griffin, *Enterprise in a Free Society* (Homewood, Illinois: Richard D. Irwin, 1949), pp. 90-91.

The situation has been epitomized, with a touch of satire, by Senator Ralph E. Flanders:

"What is required is an evolution of our system, instead of its destruction. Our system is based on the faith announced by Adam Smith that, in the sum total, selfish interests work together for the general good. The time has come when that doctrine is no longer tenable in its historic form.

"If, however, we learn to distinguish between short-sighted selfish interests and long-range selfish interests, then the whole formula still applies and still will work with this simple readjustment of one of its elements. We may still be selfish, but let us be selfish in the long-range view. What harm will there be if the disinterested observer finds it difficult to distinguish our selfishness from old-fashioned virtue?"—H. F. Merrell, editor, "Businessmen's Responsibilities to Government," in *Responsibilities of Business Leadership* (Cambridge: Harvard University Press, 1948), pp. 38-39.

7. THE DANGERS OF SOCIAL RESPONSIBILITY [1]

Theodore Levitt [2]

Concern with management's social responsibility has become more than a Philistinic form of self-flattery practiced at an occasional community chest banquet or at a news conference celebrating a "selfless example of corporate giving" to some undeserving little college in Podunk. It has become more than merely intoning the pious declarations of Christian brotherhood which some hotshot public relations man has pressed into the outstretched hands of the company president who is rushing from an executive committee meeting to a League of Women Voters luncheon. It has become a deadly serious occupation—the self-conscious, soul-searching preoccupation with the social responsibilities of business, with business statesmanship, employee welfare, public trust, and with all the other lofty causes that get such prominent play in the public press.

Contrary to what some uncharitable critics may say, this preoccupation is not an attitudinizing pose. Self-conscious dedication to social responsibility may have started as a purely defensive maneuver against strident attacks on big corporations and on the moral efficacy of the profit system. But defense alone no longer explains the motive.

THE NONPROFIT MOTIVE

When outnumbered by its critics at the polls, business launched a counterattack via the communications front. Without really listening to what the critics alleged, business simply denied all that they were saying. But a few executives did listen and began to take a second look at themselves. Perhaps this criticism was not all captious. And so they began to preach to their brethren.

Before long something new was added to the ideological stockpile of capitalism. "Social responsibility" was what business needed, its

[1] From *Harvard Business Review* (September-October, 1958), pp. 41-50. Reprinted by permission of *Harvard Business Review*.

[2] Theodore Levitt, Lecturer, Graduate School of Business Administration, Harvard University.

own leaders announced. It needed to take society more seriously. It needed to participate in community affairs—and not just to take from the community but to give to it. Gradually business became more concerned about the needs of its employees, about schools, hospitals, welfare agencies, and even aesthetics. Moreover, it became increasingly clear that if business and the local governments failed to provide some of the routine social-economic amenities which people seemed clearly intent on getting, then that Brobdingnagian free-wheeling monster in far-off Washington would.

So what started out as the sincere personal viewpoints of a few selfless businessmen became the prevailing vogue for them all. Today pronouncements about social responsibility issue forth so abundantly from the corporations that it is hard for one to get a decent play in the press. Everybody is in on the act, and nearly all of them actually mean what they say! Dedication reverberates throughout the upper reaches of corporate officialdom.

Happy new orthodoxy

This, it is widely felt, is good. Business will raise itself in the public's esteem and thereby scuttle the political attacks against it. If the public likes big business, nobody can make capital by attacking it. Thus social responsibility will prolong the lifetime of free enterprise. Meanwhile, the profit motive is compromised in both word and deed. It now shares its royal throne with a multitude of noncommercial motives that aspire to loftier and more satisfying values. Today's profits must be merely adequate, not maximum. If they are big, it is cause for apologetic rationalization (for example, that they are needed to expand the company's ability to "serve" the public even better) rather than for boastful celebration. It is not fashionable for the corporation to take gleeful pride in making money. What *is* fashionable is for the corporation to show that it is a great innovator; more specifically, a great public benefactor; and, very particularly, that it exists "to serve the public."

The mythical visitor from Mars would be astonished that such a happy tableau of cooperative enterprise can create such vast material abundance. "People's Capitalism" is a resounding success. The primitive principle of aggrandizing selfishness which the Marxists mistakenly contend activates capitalism does not count at all. What we have instead is a voluntary association of selfless entrepreneurs singularly dedicated to creating munificence for one and all—an almost spiritually blissful state of cooperative and responsible enterprise. We are approaching a jet-propelled utopia. And, unlike some other periods in the short and turbulent history of capitalism, today has its practicing philosophers. These are the men busily engaged in the canonistic exposition of a new orthodoxy—the era of "socially responsible enterprise."

A lonely crowd

Occasionally some big business representative does speak less sanctimoniously and more forthrightly about what capitalism is really all about. Occasionally somebody exhumes the apparently antique notion that the business of business is profits; that virtue lies in the vigorous, undiluted assertion of the corporation's profit-making function. But these people get no embossed invitations to speak at the big, prestigeful, and splashy business conferences—where social responsibility echoes as a new tyranny of fad and fancy.

About a year ago, Frank O. Prior, then president and now board chairman of Standard Oil Company (Indiana), made a speech that was in part reminiscent of the late but apparently unlamented tycoon:

> Without terminological pretensions, pseudodialectical profundity, or rhetorical subtlety, he called on his big business colleagues to run their businesses as they are intended to be run—for profit. Regarding people who publicly consider profit making a doubtful morality, he called on his colleagues to "move over to the offensive," "to stand up and fight," to talk about profits in terms of their central function, and to throw all sentiment to the wolves.
>
> His remarks must have sounded strange and harsh to people accustomed to a decade of viewing the corporation as a sort of miniature welfare state. Good human relations, he said, makes sense only when it "rests on a foundation of economic good sense and not just on sentiment. Sentiment has a tendency to evaporate whenever the heat is on. Economic good sense is durable."
>
> Then he said: "You aren't supposed to use language like that these times. You're supposed to talk about high ideals using high-flown words. You're expected to be mainly aware of what they call social responsibility. . . . This is fine, but I still say management's No. 1 problem is profits."

And where was this vigorous affirmation of no-nonsense capitalism made? Was it Chicago, the seat of Standard's home office and one of the few places where some think the old orthodoxy retains some semblance of primeval integrity? No. This was too unreconstructed a view even for Chicago, the city of broad shoulders. So the Chamber of Commerce of distant and isolated Casper, Wyoming, provided the platform. And even there Prior could not afford to let his forthright remarks stand as boldly as he started out. The corporation, he allowed, must develop "a fuller sense of responsibility and a much broader outlook on the facts of life"—and prices should be "fair." [3]

The fact is, the profit motive is simply not fashionable today among emancipated conferees of the Committee for Economic Development or even in the National Association of Manufacturers. It has been dying a lingering, unmourned death for ten years. Rarely can a big business leader eulogize it today without being snubbed by his self-consciously frowning peers.

Things have come to a remarkable pass. And if anyone doubts it, let him contemplate the spectacle of a recent NAM convention interrupting its urgent deliberations to hear Siobhan McKenna reading Yeats's poetry, presumably to set an appropriate tone of cultural emancipation and dedication. Can anybody picture this happening 25 years ago? Or the board chairman of Sears, Roebuck & Co., stating, as he did last year, that not only is business's first responsibility social but business executives, like Secretary Benson's farmers, should look less to their pocketbooks and more to their spirits? Not even his suggestion that the top brass are overpaid ruffled any managerial feathers. [4]

The self-persuaders

There is nothing mysterious about the social responsibility syndrome. It does not reflect a change in businessmen's nature or the decay of self-interest. Quite to the contrary, often it is viewed as a way of maximizing the lifetime of capitalism by taking the wind out of its critics' sails. Under direct questioning it will be confessed that actvities such as supporting company intramural athletic programs, hiring a paid director for a company choral society, or underwriting employee dramatic performances (even on company time) are not charity. They are hardheaded tactics of survival against the onslaught of politicians and professional detractors. Moreover, they build morale, improve efficiency, and yield returns in hard cash.

In other words, it pays to play. If it does not pay, there is no game. For instance, when it comes to choosing between the small Arkansas supplier whose town would be ruined if orders stopped

[3] Speech delivered May 6, 1957.
[4] Theodore V. Houser, 1957 McKinsey Foundation Lectures, reprinted as *Big Business and Human Values* (New York: McGraw-Hill Book Company, Inc., 1957).

and the Minneapolis supplier who can make it cheaper, there is no doubt that even the most socially responsible corporation will take the latter. It can always fall back on responsibility to its employees, stockholders, or customers, and still pretend it is being fashionable.

In some respects, therefore, all this talk *is* merely talk. It stops at the pocketbook. How, then, can it be dangerous? I think the answer is very simple: what people say, they ultimately come to believe if they say it enough, and what they believe affects what they do. To illustrate how innocent talk, intended in some respects simply for show, can haunt and change the very people who make it, look at what has happened to the Republican Party in the last few years. The example is only too painfully obvious to many executives:

> For years the party fought the New Deal tooth and claw. Ulti-mately, in order to turn the Democrats out, it began matching the New Deal promise for promise. Republicans, it said, were not opposed to these measures; they simply wanted to do everything better and cheaper. The welfare state, it was emphasized, was lacking in sound business management.
>
> Having finally ascended to office and proposing to stay in, a good many Republicans are now surprised to find themselves actually *doing* what they had promised during the election campaign. Some of the stalwarts who had lowered themselves to making expedient panegyric speeches about Modern Republicanism are now fighting a losing battle against its implementation.

The talk about social responsibility is already more than talk. It is leading into the believing stage; it has become a design for change. I hope to show why this change is likely to be for the worse, and why no man or institution can escape its debilitating consequences.

A New Feudalism

The function of business is to produce sustained high-level profits. The essence of free enterprise is to go after profit in any way that is consistent with its own survival as an economic system. The catch, someone will quickly say, is "consistent with." This is true. In addition, lack of profits is not the only thing that can destroy busi-ness. Bureaucratic ossification, hostile legislation, and revolution can do it much better. Let me examine the matter further. Capitalism as we like it can thrive only in an environment of political democ-racy and personal freedom. These require a pluralistic society— where there is division, not centralization, of power; variety, not unanimity, of opinion; and separation, not unification, of workaday economic, political, social, and spiritual functions.

We all fear an omnipotent state because it creates a dull and frightening conformity—a monolithic society. We do not want a society with one locus of power, one authority, one arbiter of propriety. We want and need variety, diversity, spontaneity, competition—in short, pluralism. We do not want our lives shaped by a single viewpoint or by a single way of doing things, even if the material consequences are bountiful and the intentions are honorable. Mussolini, Stalin, Hitler, Franco, Trujillo, Peron, all show what happens when power is consolidated into a single, unopposed, and unopposable force.

We are against the all-embracing welfare state not because we are against welfare but because we are against centralized power and the harsh social discipline it so ineluctably produces. We do not want a pervasive welfare state in government, and we do not want it in unions. And for the same reasons we should not want it in corporations.

Dangerous power

But at the rate we are going there is more than a contingent probability that, with all its resounding good intentions, business statesmanship may create the corporate equivalent of the unitary state. Its proliferating employee welfare programs, its serpentine involvement in community, government, charitable, and educational affairs, its prodigious currying of political and public favor through hundreds of peripheral preoccupations, all these well-intended but insidious contrivances are greasing the rails for our collective descent into a social order that would be as repugnant to the corporations themselves as to their critics. The danger is that all these things will turn the corporation into a twentieth-century equivalent of the medieval Church. The corporation would eventually invest itself with all-embracing duties, obligations, and finally powers—ministering to the whole man and molding him and society in the image of the corporation's narrow ambitions and its essentially unsocial needs.

Now there is nothing wrong as such with the corporation's narrow ambitions or needs. Indeed, if there is anything wrong today, it is that the corporation conceives its ambitions and needs much too broadly. The trouble is not that it is too narrowly profit-oriented, but that it is not narrowly profit-oriented *enough*. In its guilt-driven urge to transcend the narrow limits of derived standards, the modern corporation is reshaping not simply the economic but also the institutional, social, cultural, and political topography of society.

And there's the rub. For while the corporation also transforms itself in the process, at bottom its outlook will always remain narrowly materialistic. What we have, then, is the frightening spectacle of a powerful economic functional group whose future and perception are shaped in a tight materialistic context of money and things but which imposes its narrow ideas about a broad spectrum of unrelated noneconomic subjects on the mass of man and society.

Even if its outlook were the purest kind of good will, that would not recommend the corporation as an arbiter of our lives. What is bad for this or any other country is for society to be consciously and aggressively shaped by a single functional group or a single ideology, whatever it may be.

If the corporation believes its long-run profitability to be strengthened by these peripheral involvements—if it believes that they are not charity but self-interest—then that much the worse. For, if this is so, it puts much more apparent justification and impulse behind activities which are essentially bad for man, bad for society, and ultimately bad for the corporation itself.

Example of labor

The belief that one institution should encompass the complete lives of its members is by no means new to American society. One example can be taken from the history of unionism:

> In the latter part of the nineteenth century America's budding labor unions were shaken by a monumental internal struggle for power. On the one side were the unctuous advocates of the "whole man" idea of the union's function. For them the union was to be an encompassing social institution, operating on all conceivable fronts as the protector and spokesman of the workingman at large. In the process they acknowledged that the union would have to help shape and direct the aspirations, ideas, recreations, and even tastes—in short, the lives— of the members and the society in which they functioned.
>
> Opposing this view were the more pragmatic "horny-handed sons of toil," the "bread and butter" unionists. All they wanted, in the words of Samuel Gompers, was "more, more, more." At the time it was widely believed that this made Gompers a dangerous man. Lots of pious heads shook on the sidelines as they viewed the stark contrast between the dedicated "uplifters" and Gompers' materialistic opportunism. Who would not side with the "uplifters"? Yet Gompers won, and happily so, for he put American unionism on the path of pure-and-

simple on-the-job demands, free of the fanciful ideological projects and petty intellectualism that drain the vitality of European unions.

As late as the early 1930's the American Federation of Labor remained true to Gompers' narrow rules by opposing proposed Social Security legislation. And when, in the 1930's, the communists and the pseudo humanitarians pushed the "whole man" concept of unionism, they also lost. Today, however, without ideologically sustained or conscious direction, the more "progressive" unions have won the battle for what the nineteenth century ideologists lost. With all their vast might and organizational skill, these unions are now indeed ministering to the whole man:

1. Walter Reuther's United Auto Workers runs night schools, "drop-in" centers for retired members, recreation halls; supports grocery cooperatives; publishes and broadcasts household hints, recipes, and fashion news; and runs dozens of social, recreational, political, and action programs that provide something for every member of the family every hour of the day.
2. David Dubinsky's International Ladies' Garment Workers' Union has health centers, citizenship and hobby classes, low-cost apartment buildings, and a palatial summer resort in the Poconos.
3. A Toledo union promotes "respectability" in clothes and hair styles among teenagers as a way of counteracting leather-jacketed, duck-tail, rock-'n-roll delinquency.

Thus, the union is transformed in such cases from an important and desirable economic functional group into an all-knowing, all-doing, all-wise father on whom millions become directly dependent for womb-to-tomb ministration.

Toward a monolithic society

This is the kind of monolithic influence the corporation will eventually have if it becomes so preoccupied with its social burden, with employee welfare, and with the body politic. Only, when the corporation does this, it will do a much more thorough job than the union. For it is more protean and potentially more powerful than any democratic union ever dreamed of being. It is a self-made incubator and instrument of strength, more stable and better able to draw and hold a following than is the union. It creates its own capital and its own power by the sheer accident of doing what it is expected to do. (By contrast, the union can do nothing unless the corporation has done its job first. The union is essentially a luxury institution, not a necessity.)

I think it is significant that the right kinds of appeals to workers based on the corporation's materialistic self-interest are generally more successful than vague abstractions like "People's Capitalism."

This is a truth the Soviet adherents to the materialistic philosophy stubbornly refused to learn as they tried with repeated failure to intrude ideological clack where only materialistic motives could work. Their denial of their own materialistic ideology finally surrendered to hard cash, first in the form of the "new economic policy," later through the system of "socialist competition," and now as industrial and agricultural decentralization.

If the corporate ministry of man turns out to be only half as pervasive as it seems destined to be, it will turn into a simonist enterprise of Byzantine proportions. There is a name for this kind of encircling business ministry, and it pains me to use it. The name is fascism. It may not be the insidious, amoral, surrealistic fascism over which we fought World War II, or the corrupt and aggrandizing Latin American version, but the consequence will be a monolithic society in which the essentially narrow ethos of the business corporation is malignantly extended over everyone and everything.

This feudalistic phantasmagoria may sound alarmist, farfetched, or even patently ridiculous. For one thing, it will be said, not all corporations see alike on all things. At the very least there will be the pluralism of differences arising out of corporate differences in productive functions and their differences as competitors. But look at it this way: When it comes to present-day corporate educational, recreational, welfare, political, social, and public relations programs, attitudes, ideas, promotions, and preferences, how much difference is there? Are they more alike or more unlike? Are they growing more similar or more dissimilar?

It may also be protested, "What is wrong with the corporate ideology, anyway? Who will deny the material abundance, the leisure, and even the aesthetic values it has created and fostered in the United States? Nobody!" But that is irrelevant. The point is: we do not want a monolithic society, even if its intentions are the best. Moreover, a group's behavior in the pluralistic, competitive past is no guarantee of its behavior once it reaches complete ascendance.

End of capitalism

The power which the corporation gains as a sort of commercial demichurch it will lose as an agency of profit-motive capitalism. Indeed, as the profit motive becomes increasingly sublimated, capitalism will become only a shadow—the torpid remains of the creative dynamism which was and might have been. It will thrive in name

only, at the convention rostrums and the chambers of commerce—
a sort of verbal remains of the real thing, shakily sustained by
pomp and ceremony. Like Rome, it will never know that when it
believed itself at the height of its glory, it was undergoing its denoue-
ment. The incubus of the corporate ministry of man will be completely enthroned while capitalism withers away, a victim of its own
haloed good intentions.

Power Incorporated

The trouble with our society today is not that government is
becoming a player rather than an umpire, or that it is a huge welfare
colossus dipping into every nook and cranny of our lives. The trouble
is, all major functional groups—business, labor, agriculture, *and* government—are each trying so piously to outdo the other in intruding
themselves into what should be our private lives. Each is trying to
mold the whole man into its own image according to its own needs
and tastes. Each is seeking to extend its own narrow tyranny over
the widest possible range of our institutions, people, ideas, values,
and beliefs, and all for the purest motive—to do what it honestly
believes is best for society.

And that is precisely what is wrong. It is this aspect of purity
and service that is so nightmarish. It is perfectly legitimate for each
group to fight for its survival by seeking to influence others. But
somehow the past decade has produced a new twist: self-serious
self-righteousness. And there is nothing more dangerous than the
sincere, self-righteous, dedicated proselyte sustained by the mighty
machinery of a powerful institution—particularly an economic institution. The reformer whose only aim is personal aggrandizement and
whose tactics are a vulgar combination of compulsive demagoguery
and opportunistic cynicism is much less dangerous than the social
evangelist who, to borrow from Nitzsche, thinks of himself as "God's
ventriloquist." As Greek tragedies show, there is nothing more corrupting than self-righteousness and nothing more intolerant than an
ardent man who is convinced he is on the side of the angels.

When the spokesmen for such causes begin to make speeches and
write books about their holy mission, to canonize their beliefs into
faith, conviction, and doctrine, and to develop ways of thinking by
which their particular institutional ambitions are ideologically sustained—that is the time for us to begin trembling. They will then

have baptized their mission with a book—still the most powerful instrument of change devised by man.

American capitalism does not yet possess a dramatic ideological statement of the kind just described. But it is getting there. During the past decade business executives' bylines have appeared under an increasing number of book and article titles connoting a sense of mission, of reaching out—for example, *A Creed for Free Enterprise*,[5] "'Skyhooks' (With Special Implications for Monday Through Friday),"[6] *New Frontiers for Professional Managers*,[7] and "Business Leadership and a Creative Society."[8] That such titles should be chosen and that they should appeal to the management community are, I believe, significant signs of the times. There is no doubt that the sense of zeal and social responsibility is increasing.

So far the movement is a young and rather unassuming one. But when it really gathers momentum, when its forms become crystallized and its primal innocence becomes more professionalized, its success should amaze us. The corporation is not handicapped by the cumbersome authority that has always characterized the church and the state. It can make its authority sweet as honey by making itself the embodiment of material welfare, of unbounded security, of decorous comfort, amusing diversion, healthful recreation, and palatable ideology. It can far surpass even the medieval Church in efficiency and power.

It may have no intention of doing this (and I firmly believe that this is the last thing that the apostles of corporate humanity want), but what we get is seldom what we want. History is fortuitous. It does not move on tracks made by rational social engineers.

Separate functions

Business wants to survive. It wants security from attack and restriction; it wants to minimize what it believes is its greatest potential enemy—the state. So it takes the steam out of the state's lumbering engines by employing numerous schemes to win its employees and the general public to its side. It is felt that these are the best possible investments it can make for its own survival. And that is

---

[5] Clarence B. Randall (Boston: Little, Brown and Company, 1952).
[6] O. A. Ohmann, *Harvard Business Review* (May-June, 1955), p. 41.
[7] Ralph J. Cordiner (New York: McGraw-Hill Book Company, Inc., 1956).
[8] Abram T. Collier, *Harvard Business Review* (January-February, 1953), p. 29.

precisely where the reasoning has gone wrong. These investments are only superficially *easy* solutions, not the best.

Welfare and society are not the corporation's business. Its business is making money, not sweet music. The same goes for unions. Their business is "bread and butter" and job rights. In a free enterprise system, welfare is supposed to be automatic; and where it is not, it becomes government's job. This is the concept of pluralism. Government's job is not business, and business's job is not government. And unless these functions are resolutely separated in all respects, they are eventually combined in every respect. In the end the danger is not that government will run business, or that business will run government, but rather that the two of them will coalesce, as we saw, into a single power, unopposed and unopposable.

The only political function of business, labor, and agriculture is to fight each other so that none becomes or remains dominant for long. When one does reach overwhelming power and control, at the very best the state will eventually take over on the pretense of protecting everybody else. At that point the big business executives, claiming possession of the tools of large-scale management, will come in, as they do in war, to become the bureaucrats who run the state.

The final victor then is neither government, as the representative of the people, nor the people, as represented by government. The new leviathan will be the professional corporate bureaucrat operating at a more engrossing and exalted level than the architects of capitalism ever dreamed possible.

The functions of the four main groups in our economy—government, business, labor, agriculture—must be kept separate and separable. As soon as they become amalgamated and indistinguishable, they likewise become monstrous and restrictive.

TENDING TO BUSINESS

If businessmen do not preach and practice social responsibility, welfare, and self-restraint, how can management effectively deal with its critics, the political attacks, the confining legislation—that is, the things which have induced it to create its own private welfare state? The answer is fairly simple: to perform its main task so well that critics cannot make their charges stick, and then to assert forthrightly its function and accomplishments with the same aroused spirit that made nineteenth-century capitalism as great as it was extreme.

Present failures

It seems clear that today's practices fall far short of this prescription. When it comes to material things, the accomplishments of American capitalism are spectacular. But the slate is not clean. American capitalism also creates, fosters, and acquiesces in enormous social and economic cancers. Indeed, it fights against the achievement of certain forms of economic and social progress, pouring millions into campaigns against things which people have a right to expect from their government and which they seem to want their government to provide. For example:

1. Business motives helped to create slums, and now business seems all too frequently to fight their abolition. The free operation of the profit motive has not abolished them. Indeed, it sustains them. But if abolishing slums is not a sound business proposition, business should cease its campaign against government doing a job which nobody in his right mind can deny should be done. If supporting state and federal efforts at urban renewal does not raise the public's esteem of business's good intentions, few things will. Certainly self-righteous claims of good intentions are not enough.

2. The same is true of health insurance, pensions, school construction, and other proposals for activities which are best handled by government (for reasons of administration as well as of ability to meet the commitments) and are therefore logical government functions. Businessmen will simply have to accept the fact that the state can be a powerful auxiliary to the attainment of the good life. This is particularly so in a free enterprise economy where there is a natural division of social and economic functions, and where this division is fortified by countervailing institutional checks and balances.

Yet in both word and deed business constantly denies the potentially beneficial role of the state. Where it does not fight the public interest, it often adopts a placid air of indifference or a vapid neutrality. Its most shameful indifference is in matters of civil rights. Although business operates in a system where the guarantee of civil rights is the bedrock of its own effective existence, management seldom raises a voice in support of civil rights—whether the issue is legislation or protecting some anonymous Joe Doakes against a Congressional kangaroo-court committee supposedly developing information for legislation.

Business must learn to speak for Joe Doakes when civil rights are involved. In doing this it would actually be speaking for itself. Civil rights are a single cloth; they cannot be curtailed for some without being curtailed for everybody. Hence to speak for Joe Doakes is to act in one's self-interest—especially in management's case, for when civil rights are gone, business loses not only freedom but also money.

Sensible welfare

I am not arguing that management should ignore its critics. Some of them have made a good case from time to time against business's social delinquencies and against its shortsightedness in fighting practically all of Washington's efforts to provide security. (Indeed, if business had not always fought federal welfare measures, perhaps the unions would not have demanded them from business itself.)

Nor am I arguing that management has no welfare obligations at all to society. Quite to the contrary. Corporate welfare makes good sense *if* it makes good economic sense—and not infrequently it does. But if something does not make economic sense, sentiment or idealism ought not let it in the door. Sentiment is a corrupting and debilitating influence in business. It fosters leniency, inefficiency, sluggishness, extravagance, and hardens the innovationary arteries. It can confuse the role of the businessman just as much as the profit motive could confuse the role of the government official. The governing rule in industry should be that *something is good only if it pays.* Otherwise it is alien and impermissible. This is the rule of capitalism.

No matter how much business protests that saying this is redundant because it is exactly the rule being practiced, the fact is that it is *seldom* followed. Businessmen only say they practice it because it is another one of those sacred articles of the capitalist faith that must be regularly reaffirmed in speech and print. Their words are belied by some of their most common policies, such as:

1. *The growing constellation of employee welfare programs.* Do they really make good economic sense for the individual firm? I say they do not. Most company welfare measures—such as retirement, unemployment, and health benefits—are forms of mass insurance. They make economic sense only when operated on a compulsory national basis. The only conceivable basis on which it can be argued that they make economic sense when operated by individual companies is that they help attract and hold manpower. And that is seldom the primary motive. If there were adequate national mass insurance, the company that wants to attract and hold more and better manpower needs only to pay more. The whole thing would be cheaper and more efficient.
2. *Stock purchase plans.* These plans, which are one of the sacred appurtenances of "People's Capitalism," are justifiable only if they

provide direct incentives to differentially superior performance. They are a menace and a drag on the economy when (as is often the case) their real object is to let the corporate insiders in on some easy capital gains gravy, or to immobilize the labor market by tying people to a particular company.

If the public wants protection against the uneven consequences of all-out capitalism, let it run to its unions and to government. If business wants protection against unions and government, let it fight for its cause on the open battlefield of manful contention—on the front of economic and political pressures. We are not back in the age of the robber barons, with its uneven matching of economic and political functional groups. Business, government, and unions are now each big and powerful enough to take care of themselves. As Mao Tse-Tung once prescribed for China, "Let all flowers bloom together; let rival schools of thought contend."

CONCLUSION

Business will have a much better chance of surviving if there is no nonsense about its goals—that is, if long-run profit maximization is the one dominant objective in practice as well as in theory. Business should recognize what government's functions are and let it go at that, stopping only to fight government where government directly intrudes itself into business. It should let government take care of the general welfare so that business can take care of the more material aspects of welfare.

The results of any such single-minded devotion to profit should be invigorating. With none of the corrosive distractions and costly bureaucracies that now serve the pious cause of welfare, politics, society, and putting up a pleasant front, with none of these draining its vitality, management can shoot for the economic moon. It will be able to thrust ahead in whatever way seems consistent with its money-making goals. If laws and threats stand in its way, it should test and fight them, relenting only if the courts have ruled against it, and then probing again to test the limits of the rules. And when business fights, it should fight with uncompromising relish and self-assertiveness, instead of using all the rhetorical dodges and pious embellishments that are now so often its stock in trade.

Practicing self-restraint behind the cloak of the insipid dictum that "an ounce of prevention is worth a pound of cure" has only limited justification. Certainly it often pays not to squeeze the last dollar out of a market—especially when good will is a factor in the long-term outlook. But too often self-restraint masquerades for capitulation. Businessmen complain about legislative and other attacks on aggressive profit seeking but then lamely go forth to slay the dragon with speeches that simply concede business's function to be service. The critic quickly pounces on this admission with unconcealed relish—"Then why *don't* you serve?" But the fact is, no matter how much business "serves," it will never be enough for its critics.

The strenuous life

If the all-out competitive prescription sounds austere or harsh, that is only because we persist in judging things in terms of utopian standards. Altruism, self-denial, charity, and similar values are vital in certain walks of our life—areas which, because of that fact, are more important to the long-run future than business. But for the most part those virtues are alien to competitive economics.

If it sounds callous to hold such a view, and suicidal to publicize it, that is only because business has done nothing to prepare the community to agree with it. There is only one way to do that: to perform at top ability and to speak vigorously *for* (not in defense of) what business does. Prior's stand on human relations, quoted earlier, is a good point of departure. But it is only a beginning.

In the end business has only two responsibilities—to obey the elementary canons of everyday face-to-face civility (honesty, good faith, and so on) and to seek material gain. The fact that it is the butt of demagogical critics is no reason for management to lose its nerve—to buckle under to reformers—lest more severe restrictions emerge to throttle business completely. Few people will man the barricades against capitalism if it is a good provider, minds its own business, and supports government in the things which are properly government's. Even today, most American critics want only to curb capitalism, not to destroy it. And curbing efforts will not destroy it if there is free and open discussion about its singular function.

To the extent that there is conflict, can it not be a good thing? Every book, every piece of history, even every religion testifies to the fact that conflict is and always has been the subject, origin, and life blood of society. Struggle helps to keep us alive, to give élan to life. We should try to make the most of it, not avoid it.

Lord Acton has said of the past that people sacrificed freedom by grasping at impossible justice. The contemporary school of business morality seems intent on adding its own caveat to that unhappy consequence. The gospel of tranquility is a soporific. Instead of fighting for its survival by means of a series of strategic retreats masquerading as industrial statesmanship, business must fight as if it were at war. And, like a good war, it should be fought gallantly, daringly, and, above all, *not* morally.

BIBLIOGRAPHY, CHAPTER II

ANDLINGER, GERHARD R. "The Crucible of Our Business Creeds," *Business Horizons* (Summer, 1959), 34-44.

AUSTIN, ROBERT W. "Code of Conduct for Executives," *Harvard Business Review* (September-October, 1961), 53-61.

BOULDING, KENNETH E. "Religious Foundations of Economic Progress," *Harvard Business Review* (May-June, 1952), 33-40.

DONHAM, WALLACE B. *Administration and Blind Spots*. Boston: Division of Research, Harvard Graduate School of Business Administration, 1954.

DUDDY, E. A. "The Moral Implications of Business as a Profession," *Journal of Business*, Vol. XVII (April, 1945), 63-72.

HAWLEY, CAMERON. *Cash McCall*. Boston: Houghton Mifflin Company, 1955.

JOHNSON, HAROLD L. "Can the Businessman Apply Christianity?" *Harvard Business Review* (September-October, 1957), 68-76.

KAUFMANN, WALTER A. "A Philosopher's View," *Ethics and Business*. The Bureau of Business Research, The Pennsylvania State University (1962), 35-54.

MURROW, EDWARD R. "How TV Can Help Us Survive," *TV Guide* (December 13-19), 1958, 22-27.

PETIT, THOMAS A. "The Legitimacy of Management Power," *Business Horizons* (Spring, 1962), 91-96.

SILVERSTEIN, SAUL. "Five Areas of Management Reappraisal," *Dun's Review and Modern Industry* (March, 1956), 41-42, 82-85.

SMITH, GEORGE A., JR. *Business, Society, and the Individual*. Homewood, Illinois: Richard D. Irwin, Inc., 1962.

Chapter III
Human Relations and Behavior

As one of the fundamental considerations or variables in making business decisions, managers must consider the human element. The purpose of this chapter is to introduce behavioral concepts with respect to the nature of human activity in organizations. These concepts have had a variety of labels and have, at times, been the subject of high-pressure promotion by their proponents. It is the belief of the authors, however, that elements of human behavior are important factors in some decisions and unimportant in others.

Knowledge of the importance of human behavior is the first step in assigning human relations activities a proper role in managerial decisions. In the articles selected for this chapter, David G. Moore explains the present state of behavioral theory; Raymond A. Bauer indicates that so-called human irrationality has logical bases if time and trouble is taken to identify individual motives; Douglas M. McGregor explains the behavior of the individual in the organization within the larger framework of the Maslovian hierarchy of needs concept; and F. F. Bradshaw challenges the concept that the "natural science" label applies only to physical and biological phenomena.

The materials in this chapter are closely related to the concepts presented in Chapter XI and, to some extent, in Chapter XII. These materials are also applicable to the wider ranges of decision making considered throughout the book.

8. THE PRESENT STATE OF THE
BEHAVIORAL SCIENCES [1]

David G. Moore [2]

*   *   *

The student of business administration can take away from the behavioral sciences, pure or applied, only what the behavioral sciences can offer. Much depends, therefore, on the current state of development of these sciences. It goes without saying that the behavioral sciences are not exact sciences like physics or chemistry. Human behavior cannot be readily predicted from a relatively few general laws or principles. In teaching the behavioral science, you cannot begin with elementary propositions and gradually build up a complex system of interdependent propositions which can be manipulated at abstract, mathematical levels. The behavioral sciences are still in an empirical, observational phase. James B. Conant defines science as "an attempt either to lower the degree of empiricism or to extend the range of theory." The practical arts in this view are almost one hundred percent empirical; physics, on the other hand, is almost one hundred percent theoretical—theoretical in the sense that predictions can be made by deduction from general laws and theories. It is apparent that the behavioral sciences have many years of development before they reach a theoretical phase. They are still wrestling with problems of observation and the classification of patterns of human behavior; in other words, they are hardly at the point of the beginning of a science. Only recently can it be said that the observations of the behavioral scientist are better than those of the practical man in the field.

There are a number of reasons why the behavioral sciences have developed so slowly. In the first place, it is difficult to deal experimentally with human beings or with human interaction. Laboratory

[1] From "Contributions to Management Philosophy from the Behavioral Sciences," *Proceedings of Annual Meeting of the Academy of Management* (December 28, 1960), pp. 10-16. Reprinted by permission of the *Journal of the Academy of Management*.
[2] David G. Moore, Professor, Department of Personnel and Production Administration, Michigan State University.

experimentation involves a deliberate control over variables; but, with human beings, the laboratory introduces a new and important variable as the Western Electric researchers found out. Furthermore, it is often unethical, even immoral, to experiment with the personal lives of other human beings. More than this, it is difficult to control subjectivity in the observation of the behavior of others. The observer is always part of the situation which he is attempting to observe. His mere presense alters behavior. But, even more important, he himself becomes inextricably involved with the situation, oftentimes perceiving what he unconsciously wants to perceive and projecting many of his own needs and emotions into his research. It takes a high degree of discipline and self-awareness to become a good observer of the behavior of others.

In the second place, human behavior is complex. It is always the product of an evolving, dynamic, current reality and an equally dynamic, changing interpretation of this reality. It involves the past plus the present plus a perceived future. When you observe a man's behavior, you cannot tell at first blush whether he is reacting to past events, present circumstances, future possibilities, or all three. He has a sense of time; he has memories and anticipations. He is capable of integrating a myriad of experiences from within, from without, from close-by, from far-away.

In the third place, a human being is not totally a creature of his environment. He integrates his past and present experiences and his anticipation of the future; he perceives and interprets events in terms of his needs and sentiments. In other words, behind his actions and reactions are underlying motives which must be understood if his behavior is to be understood. With people, we must always ask the question, why? This is not true, of course, of physical phenomena. We don't have to ask why the sun rises; it does and that is enough. Nowhere is the problem of underlying motives better illustrated than in marketing research. One example of early motivation research involved a study of the reactions of housewives in a particular neighborhood to venetian blinds versus lace curtains. One group of housewives clearly liked venetian blinds; another group was partial to lace curtains. When asked their reasons for choosing one or the other, both groups maintained that curtains or blinds, whatever their particular preference, were "easier to keep clean." Logic tells us that venetian blinds and lace curtains cannot both be easier to keep clean. Obviously, the housewives in this case were not revealing their true underlying motives; they were simply saying what housewives were supposed to say about their behavior. Careful study revealed that the two groups of housewives enjoyed quite different ways of life. One group was older, more conservative, somewhat hidebound; the other group was younger, modern, more liberal. The two styles of window covering symbolized their different ways of life. The venetian blinds announced to the whole neighborhood, "Here lives a modern family." The lace curtains declared, "Here is a conservative family."

Because of the difficulties involved in studying human behavior, the problems of interpretation, the dynamic, changing, evolving panorama of human affairs, and the problems of underlying motivation, the behavioral sciences have progressed slowly. However, over the past twenty years, with the great increase in social research, techniques of observation and analysis have been considerably improved in the human sciences. While there is as yet no generally accepted theoretical science of man, there are useful models of behavior, both psychological and social; there are insightful concepts which focus light on various aspects of human behavior; there are well-developed methods of investigation; there are improved analytic techniques which provide greater objectivity in the analysis of human affairs; and there is finally a wealth of material describing various patterns of human behavior in diverse settings. In short, the behavioral sciences have progressed far beyond the commonsensical observations and judgments of the layman. The administrator or student who feels that he has acquired through some natural process all of the insights and skills that he needs to understand human behavior and make judgments about others is fooling himself. Indeed, most people are completely unaware of the limitations of their personal experiences and the highly subjective, class-bound nature of their observations and judgments. Yet, because they have had to come to grips with human relations throughout their lives, they somehow develop a certainty of judgment which they would never feel in the considerably less complex physical sciences. . . .

9. WHO SAYS PEOPLE ACT
IRRATIONALLY? [1]

Raymond A. Bauer [2]

What place does a psychologist—or a behavioral scientist—have in a business enterprise? If you ask a modern manager, he will probably reply along these lines:

> Well, we've discovered that people in our company act very irrationally from time to time. We need help in dealing with and working along with their illogical behavior.

Many businessmen, as a matter of fact, take great pride in their appreciation of what they call "human irrationality." Accepting the idea that people often behave "illogically" is supposed to be a major step forward in business administration.

Board up that pigeonhole!

Actually, this tendency to file human behavior into neat pigeonholes marked "rational" and "irrational" is doing more harm than good. As ordinarily done, it is an unsound practice, and, in addition, may well be weakening the manager's effectiveness within his organization.

To show what I mean, let us first look at this idea that many people occasionally behave "irrationally" in a business operation.

What does the businessman usually have in mind when he says a worker is acting in an illogical manner? He commonly is thinking of some recent incident in his own company which involved an employee who, let us say, consistently refused to clear design changes on a production item with the engineering department, although company policy demanded that he do so.

This kind of behavior seems irrational to the manager because it conflicts with the goals of the company, or the smooth operation of

[1] From *Harvard Business School Bulletin* (December, 1958), pp. 13-19. Reprinted by permission of Raymond A. Bauer and *Harvard Business Review*.
[2] Raymond A. Bauer, Ford Foundation Visiting Professor, Harvard Business School, 1958.

the shop, or the worker's chance for promotion or a wage increase. But the trouble is that the employee may have a wholly different set of goals. Maybe he is more interested in working out his own ideas, or building up his prestige with his fellow employees, or being a non-conformist, or forcing a change in the system than he is in fattening his pay envelope or being a cooperative cog in the corporate wheel or contributing to the efficiency of the company. If these are his goals, his refusal to abide by company policy is perfectly logical and rational.

It seems to me that the economists have tricked us with a sort of academic shell game. They have usurped the labels "logical" and "rational" for the things that human beings do which fit in with the traditional goals which the economists have set for people—primarily the advancement of their own material standard of living—and have relegated other purposes that men and women have to the limbo of the irrational. They assume that anything a man does which will make him more money is "rational" while those actions he takes which interfere with the increase of his earnings are "irrational." I submit that this is a narrow way of looking at people; and, in some ways, pretty illogical itself.

What, after all, is so "rational" or "logical" about pursuing a dollar so hard that you injure your health, alienate your friends, break up your family, and disrupt your self-esteem?

Different team—different goal

We are likely, then, to hang the label of "irrational" on a man when we disagree with the goals he has selected for himself. But there is no inherent reason why, at any given moment, a man should prefer earning additional money over resting or gaining the approval of his fellow workers. There is no one set of human objectives which, in themselves, can be called more rational than another set.

This is true even for the famous farmer who kissed the cow. When we say he acted illogically, we are making an assumption that, like us, he preferred girls to cattle. But suppose he just happens to like cows better than girls—then his display of affection makes perfectly good sense.

I will agree that you can think through this bizarre action and come up with a perfectly sound conclusion that it is irrational. You can, for instance, surmise that the farmer is looking for a relationship of companionship and affection. If this is so, kissing a cow is illogical, because he is never going to be able to establish the kind of fellowship for which he is seeking with an animal. His behavior, therefore, is indeed illogical because it is not going to take him to his goal.

But here you are putting the whole weird business in a different context; you are not judging his goals and calling them sane or insane; you are passing judgment on the way he has chosen to reach them. The use of the word "irrational" when applied to *means* makes perfectly good sense. Unfortunately, however, we don't usually make this fine distinction in our day-to-day use of the term.

Management falls into a trap

To leave the barnyard and return to industry, you can say: Worker A is not acting logically when he does not do everything within his power to maximize his earnings because in the long run he will gain more esteem, be more comfortable, and so on if he makes more money. Here, similarly, you are saying that you do not disagree with his purposes, but think that he has done a lousy job of figuring out how to reach them. The rest of us don't necessarily have to agree with you when you make a statement of this kind, but at least we will agree that it is a correct use of the terms "logical" and "illogical."

Why do managers so often trap themselves in this confusion between a man's target and the way he has chosen to hit it? There are, perhaps, four reasons:

1. The goals of the manager are much more likely to be tied up with the goals of the organization than are those of the employee. It is to the businessman's direct self-interest that the company be efficient and successful, whereas this may not be anywhere near as important to the worker; *he* can always go elsewhere, with no black marks on *his* record, if the firm stumbles.
2. An executive's self-esteem and the respect of his fellows depends to a considerable degree on how well he does his job, while the worker in the shop may find that his great renown and satisfaction comes from his success in the bowling alley.
3. The behavior of managers is more often accepted as "good for the company" than similar activity on the part of the employee. For example, when the boys from the line step across the street for a beer at lunch time and come back logy and late, the foreman assumes that the long-range efficiency of his shift has been cut. But when a few of the executives stay equally long at lunch over a martini, their behavior is regarded as "good" because it "welds the team together" even if they haven't talked shop. Actually, industrial sociologists are beginning to argue that the occasional lunch-time beer for the man on the line tends to serve the same purpose as the manager's martini.
4. Managers too often unconsciously accept the textbook maxim that making more dough is the best—or the only—way to gain happiness, psychic satisfaction, and respect. Actually, of course, they know

better, for they rarely run their own lives that way. Dean Teele
has pointed out that few professional managers have set bigger
salaries as their sole purpose in life: only the miser pursues money
for its own sake, and even in his case it stands for something else.
We use money to gain comfort, prestige, recreation, affection—and,
as individuals, we readily recognize that bank checks can't buy many
of the things we want out of life. Thus, the manager himself quickly
agrees that money isn't everything for him—in fact, that it is useful
only as an aid to help him secure other valuables—but still he labels
"illogical" the worker who pursues some of these other objectives
directly in the plant at the possible sacrifice of his earnings.

All this adds up to one idea: that the reason why businessmen
fall into the ready assumption that "Joe is sure acting nuts today"
is because they are looking at Joe with a set of blinders on. They are
considering him solely in terms of the objectives of the company and
measuring him against the shape of the so-called "economic man,"
that convenient fiction created to serve the perfectly legitimate needs
of the economist. Unfortunately, the economic man is usually not
the whole man—though he surely is a part—and the company's goals
are not always the workers' goals. To put it baldly, too many executives apply the word "irrational" to Joe simply because he is lousing
up their operation, without really thinking through the situation in
the terms that Joe sees it.

Sometimes, managers will consider a man "irrational" when the
fact is that he couldn't behave in a way they would accept even if he
wanted to. Suppose that you and I were watching a football game.
Our team has the ball; a back breaks through the line and into the
secondary, and heads for the goal line. Suddenly, from nowhere, an
opposing player streaks out of the melee, chases our man, and pulls
him down from behind. If I were to turn to you and say: "How
irrational of our ball carrier! He should have run faster," I could
perfectly well expect you to reply: "And what the hell makes you
think he *could* run faster?"

If this example sounds ridiculous and far removed from a business situation, how about this one:

> A salesman is called in by his supervisor and given a full-fledged
> laying out. If the salesman listened carefully he would discover that
> he was a bum, a scoundrel, stupid, incompetent, repulsive, and dis-
> honest. If he is to keep his job, he has to accept this image of himself
> and then do something about mending his ways. Two weeks later,
> nothing has changed; despite this classic lacing, he is still the same old
> guy. Naturally enough, the supervisor shakes his head and says, "Boy,
> is that guy nuts. I warned him; I told him what was the matter with
> him as clearly as I could; and still he keeps on acting the same way and
> pulling the same dumb stunts."

Self-defense *is* logical

The problem, of course, is that we are asking the salesman to accept a pretty horrible image of himself as a preface to improving his performance. He has to admit that he is a real deadbeat and start from there because that is the way the manager set up the situation for him. We shouldn't be surprised that he cannot do this; the full impact of the message will not get across, he may not hear some things correctly, he will forget others, and he will rationalize both his behavior and that of the boss. As he takes this terrific pounding, self-defense is the most logical response in the world. He needs to protect himself, and he will do it by any means possible. This self-defense may well prevent him from looking at himself objectively and doing something effective about the changes the boss requires. He may, under these circumstances, be literally unable to do anything about his poor sales record.

Hard to change our pattern

Yet the sales manager will call this sturdy self-defense "irrational." Actually, the only "rational" step for the poor man to take, other than covering himself psychologically, would be to go home and blow his brains out or head for the mental hospital—and the top man would certainly call *that* "illogical!"

This human need to guard one's self-respect is natural and universal. It is a perfectly rational goal, though the means we take to reach it may not always be so rational, and the overpowering necessity to protect one's inner self may make it literally impossible for a man "to run any faster." Furthermore, I should remind you, it is pretty difficult for any of us to change our basic patterns of behavior under the best of circumstances. As John P. Marquand wrote in *Sincerely, Willis Wayde*, "You could read these works, you could attend lectures, but in the end it always seemed to Willis that you were still alone. In the watches of the night at least, you were always you." [3]

Let me, finally, underline the point that men will behave in ways which will seem extremely irrational to managers in order to win and hold the self-esteem of their fellows. No one who has driven by the Harvard Business School, let alone attended it, could have failed to hear about the Hawthorne experiment—and the clique behavior of

[3] Little Brown & Company, 1955, p. 218.

the bank-wiring crew which refused to raise production because of group pressure even though they could make more money individually by doing so.

We need their good will

Actually, I would go further than simply reminding you that this is perfectly logical behavior, and hazard a guess that some of this sort of business, though it may seem harmful to the organization at first glance, may, in fact, be beneficial. Any man in any organization—at any level, I hasten to add—is at least partially dependent on the good will of his associates; the man who gets along well with others can expect to be helped out, while his opposite number may be actively blocked. That much is clear. From the viewpoint of the company, good group morale, built up partly by joking, horseplay, and mutual concessions, is essential.

Take a tip from Mr. Roberts

In this connection, I can't help remembering the crew in *Mister Roberts*. Though the wild night ashore at Elysium got the skipper and the sailors into plenty of trouble, and could hardly have been called constructive organizational behavior, the raid on the Colonel's party and the visit to the home of the French consul did more for the morale of that group of discontented men than any approved recreational program could ever have achieved.

Throughout this article, I have spoken rather glibly of "the economist" and "the businessman." Actually, this simple labeling is quite illogical. In the first place, my criticisms do not apply to all economists or all businessmen by any manner of means; in the second place, they *do* apply to plenty of people in other lines of endeavor who try to squeeze free human spirits into square boxes marked "This is how people ought to behave."

Perhaps in all this I have been beating a dead horse. Maybe not very many managers look on the behavioral sciences as being concerned with the "irrational" ways in which people conduct themselves. But I am afraid that I am not convinced this is so; this is a horse which had better be dead, and I have been disturbed by what I took to be some signs of life stirring in it.

I am disturbed for two reasons: first, I naturally resent the notion that my colleagues and I are dealing with the off-beat and way-out aspects of people. It makes me feel a little like an odd ball myself. Secondly, I suspect that this easy notion of "rational" versus "nonrational" behavior when it creeps into an executive's thinking results in a pose of condescension which does the administrator himself little good and stands in the way of his efforts to do an effective job. More than once I have read and heard—in the words of quite "advanced" men—the statement that management acts rationally, but they must not expect the workers to do so. Management is thus taught to look for and tolerate illogical behavior among its employees.

Any inner assumptions of others' irrationality will communicate itself quickly, and the manager will find himself out of tune with the people who are working for and with him. Furthermore, sound administration rests on a good understanding of the facts in a given situation, and the emotions and feelings of people are facts. An executive limits the accuracy of his analysis if he assumes that anything his associates are doing which does not make immediate sense to him is a little screwy. He would do well to go back and take another broader, more businesslike look and then use the terms "irrational" and "illogical" far more sparingly, and in the context of the means a man takes to reach his ends, rather than the ends he chooses.

Just what is your logic?

Perhaps it would be best in closing to make clear that there are two things I am *not* saying. I am not saying that there is no such thing as being illogical or irrational, but rather that the terms are misapplied all too frequently. "Illogical" and "irrational" are entirely proper terms to apply when they refer to the fact that someone has slipped a cog in figuring how to get from A to B to C.

I am also not saying that because much behavior is logical from the point of view of the individual it is any more desirable from the point of view of the organization. What I hope, however, is that the search for *his* logic may make the manager more effective in dealing with his behavior.

10. THE HUMAN SIDE OF ENTERPRISE [1]

Douglas Murray McGregor [2]

It has become trite to say that industry has the fundamental know-how to utilize physical science and technology for the material benefit of mankind, and that we must now learn how to utilize the social sciences to make our human organizations truly effective.

To a degree, the social sciences today are in a position like that of the physical sciences with respect to atomic energy in the thirties. We know that past conceptions of the nature of man are inadequate and, in many ways, incorrect. We are becoming quite certain that, under proper conditions, unimagined resources of creative human energy could become available within the organizational setting.

We cannot tell industrial management how to apply this new knowledge in simple, economic ways. We know it will require years of exploration, much costly development, research, and a substantial amount of creative imagination on the part of management to discover how to apply this growing knowledge to the organization of human effort in industry.

MANAGEMENT'S TASK: THE CONVENTIONAL VIEW

The conventional conception of management's task in harnessing human energy to organizational requirements can be stated broadly in terms of three propositions. In order to avoid the complications introduced by a label, let us call this set of propositions "Theory X":

1. Management is responsible for organizing the elements of productive enterprise—money, materials, equipment, people—in the interest of economic ends.
2. With respect to people, this is a process of directing their efforts, motivating them, controlling their actions, modifying their behavior to fit the needs of the organization.
3. Without this active intervention by management, people would be passive—even resistant—to organizational needs. They must there-

[1] From *The Management Review* (November, 1957), pp. 22-28, 88-92. Reprinted by permission Douglas Murray McGregor and *The Management Review*.
[2] Douglas Murray McGregor, School of Industrial Management, Massachusetts Institute of Technology.

tion" 98 •

fore be persuaded, rewarded, punished, controlled—their activities must be directed. This is management's task. We often sum it up by saying that management consists of getting things done through other people.

4. The average man is by nature indolent—he works as little as possible.
5. He lacks ambition, dislikes responsibility, prefers to be led.
6. He is inherently self-centered, indifferent to organizational needs.
7. He is by nature resistant to change.
8. He is gullible, not very bright, the ready dupe of the charlatan and the demagogue.

The human side of economic enterprise today is fashioned from propositions and beliefs such as these. Conventional organization structures and managerial policies, practices, and programs reflect these assumptions.

In accomplishing its task—with these assumptions as guides— management has conceived of a range of possibilities.

At one extreme, management can be "hard" or "strong." The methods for directing behavior involve coercion and threat (usually disguised), close supervision, tight controls over behavior. At the other extreme, management can be "soft" or "weak." The methods for directing behavior involve being permissive, satisfying people's demands, achieving harmony. Then they will be tractable, accept direction.

This range has been fairly completely explored during the past half century, and management has learned some things from the exploration. There are difficulties in the "hard" approach. Force breeds counter-forces: restriction of output, antagonism, militant unionism, subtle but effective sabotage of management objectives. This "hard" approach is especially difficult during times of full employment.

There are also difficulties in the "soft" approach. It leads frequently to the abdication of management—to harmony, perhaps, but to indifferent performance. People take advantage of the soft approach. They continually expect more, but they give less and less.

Currently, the popular theme is "firm but fair." This is an attempt to gain the advantages of both the hard and the soft approaches. It is reminiscent of Teddy Roosevelt's "speak softly and carry a big stick."

Is the Conventional View Correct?

The findings which are beginning to emerge from the social sciences challenge this whole set of beliefs about man and human nature and about the task of management. The evidence is far from conclusive, certainly, but it is suggestive. It comes from the laboratory, the clinic, the schoolroom, the home, and even to a limited extent from industry itself.

The social scientist does not deny that human behavior in industrial organization today is approximately what management perceives it to be. He has, in fact, observed it and studied it fairly extensively. But he is pretty sure that this behavior is *not* a consequence of man's inherent nature. It is a consequence rather of the nature of industrial organizations, of management philosophy, policy, and practice. The conventional approach of Theory X is based on mistaken notions of what is cause and what is effect.

Perhaps the best way to indicate why the conventional approach of management is inadequate is to consider the subject of motivation.

PHYSIOLOGICAL NEEDS

Man is a wanting animal—as soon as one of his needs is satisfied, another appears in its place. This process is unending. It continues from birth to death.

Man's needs are organized in a series of levels—a hierarchy of importance. At the lowest level, but pre-eminent in importance when they are thwarted, are his *physiological needs*. Man lives for bread alone, when there is no bread. Unless the circumstances are unusual, his needs for love, for status, for recognition are inoperative when his stomach has been empty for a while. But when he eats regularly and adequately, hunger ceases to be an important motivation. The same is true of the other physiological needs of man—for rest, exercise, shelter, protection from the elements.

A satisfied need is not a motivator of behavior! This is a fact of profound significance that is regularly ignored in the conventional approach to the management of people. Consider your own need for air: Except as you are deprived of it, it has no appreciable motivating effect upon your behavior.

SAFETY NEEDS

When the physiological needs are reasonably satisfied, needs at the next higher level begin to dominate man's behavior—to motivate him. These are called *safety needs*. They are needs for protection against danger, threat, deprivation. Some people mistakenly refer to these as needs for security. However, unless man is in a dependent relationship where he fears arbitrary deprivation, he does not demand security. The need is for the "fairest possible break." When he is confident of this, he is more than willing to take risks. But when he feels threatened or dependent, his greatest need is for guarantees, for protection, for security.

The fact needs little emphasis that, since every industrial employee is in a dependent relationship, safety needs may assume considerable importance. Arbitrary management actions, behavior which arouses uncertainty with respect to continued employment or which reflects favoritism or discrimination, unpredictable administration of policy —these can be powerful motivators of the safety needs in the employment relationship *at every level*, from worker to vice president.

SOCIAL NEEDS

When man's physiological needs are satisfied and he is no longer fearful about his physical welfare, his *social needs* become important motivators of his behavior—needs for belonging, for association, for acceptance by his fellows, for giving and receiving friendship and love.

Management knows today of the existence of these needs, but it often assumes quite wrongly that they represent a threat to the organization. Many studies have demonstrated that the tightly knit, cohesive work group may, under proper conditions, be far more effective than an equal number of separate individuals in achieving organizational goals.

Yet management, fearing group hostility to its own objectives, often goes to considerable lengths to control and direct human efforts in ways that are inimical to the natural "groupiness" of human beings. When man's social needs—and perhaps his safety needs, too—are thus thwarted, he behaves in ways which tend to defeat organizational objectives. He becomes resistant, antagonistic, uncooperative. But this behavior is a consequence, not a cause.

EGO NEEDS

Above the social needs—in the sense that they do not become motivators until lower needs are reasonably satisfied—are the needs of greatest significance to management and to man himself. They are the *egoistic needs*, and they are two kinds:

1. Those needs that relate to one's self-esteem—needs for self-confidence, for independence, for achievement, for competence, for knowledge.
2. Those needs that relate to one's reputation—needs for status, for recognition, for appreciation, for the deserved respect of one's fellows.

Unlike the lower needs, these are rarely satisfied; man seeks indefinitely for more satisfaction of these needs once they have become important to him. But they do not appear in any significant way until physiological, safety, and social needs are all reasonably satisfied.

The typical industrial organization offers few opportunities for the satisfaction of these egoistic needs to people at lower levels in the hierarchy. The conventional methods of organizing work, particularly in mass-production industries, give little heed to these aspects of human motivation. If the practices of scientific management were deliberately calculated to thwart these needs, they could hardly accomplish this purpose better than they do.

SELF-FULFILLMENT NEEDS

Finally—a capstone, as it were, on the hierarchy of man's needs—there are what we may call the *needs for self-fulfillment*. These are the needs for realizing one's own potentialities, for continued self-development, for being creative in the broadest sense of that term.

It is clear that the conditions of modern life give only limited opportunity for these relatively weak needs to obtain expression. The deprivation most people experience with respect to other lower-level needs diverts their energies into the struggle to satisfy *those* needs, and the needs for self-fulfillment remain dormant.

MANAGEMENT AND MOTIVATION

We recognize readily enough that a man suffering from a severe dietary deficiency is sick. The deprivation of physiological needs has behavioral consequences. The same is true—although less well recognized—of deprivation of higher-level needs. The man whose needs for safety, association, independence, or status are thwarted is sick just as surely as the man who has rickets. And his sickness will have behavioral consequences. We will be mistaken if we attribute his resultant passivity, his hostility, his refusal to accept responsibility to his inherent "human nature." These forms of behavior are *symptoms* of illness—of deprivation of his social and egoistic needs.

The man whose lower-level needs are satisfied is not motivated to satisfy those needs any longer. For practical purposes they exist no longer. Management often asks, "Why aren't people more productive? We pay good wages, provide good working conditions, have excellent fringe benefits and steady employment. Yet people do not seem to be willing to put forth more than minimum effort."

The fact that management has provided for these physiological and safety needs has shifted the motivational emphasis to the social and perhaps to the egoistic needs. Unless there are opportunities *at work* to satisfy these higher-level needs, people will be deprived; and their behavior will reflect this deprivation. Under such conditions, if management continues to focus its attention on physiological needs, its efforts are bound to be ineffective.

People *will* make insistent demands for more money under these conditions. It becomes more important than ever to buy the material goods and services which can provide limited satisfaction of the thwarted needs. Although money has only limited value in satisfying many higher-level needs, it can become the focus of interest if it is the *only* means available.

THE CARROT-AND-STICK APPROACH

The carrot-and-stick theory of motivation (like Newtonian physical theory) works reasonably well under certain circumstances. The *means* for satisfying man's physiological and (within limits) his safety needs can be provided or withheld by management. Employment itself is such a means, and so are wages, working conditions, and benefits. By these means the individual can be controlled so long as he is struggling for subsistence.

But the carrot-and-stick theory does not work at all once man has reached an adequate subsistence level and is motivated primarily by higher needs. Management cannot provide a man with self-respect, or with the respect of his fellows, or with the satisfaction of needs for self-fulfillment. It can create such conditions that he is encouraged and enabled to seek such satisfactions for *himself,* or it can thwart him by failing to create those conditions.

But this creation of conditions is not "control." It is not a good device for directing behavior. And so management finds itself in an odd position. The high standard of living created by our modern technological know-how provides quite adequately for the satisfaction of physiological and safety needs. The only significant exception is where management practices have not created confidence in a "fair break"—and thus where safety needs are thwarted. But by making possible the satisfaction of low-level needs, management has deprived itself of the ability to use as motivators the devices on which conventional theory has taught it to rely—rewards, promises, incentives, or threats and other coercive devices.

The philosophy of management by direction and control—*regardless of whether it is hard or soft*—is inadequate to motivate because the human needs on which this approach relies are today unimportant motivators of behavior. Direction and control are essentially useless in motivating people whose important needs are social and egoistic. Both the hard and the soft approach fail today because they are simply irrelevant to the situation.

People, deprived of opportunities to satisfy at work the needs which are now important to them, behave exactly as we might predict—with indolence, passivity, resistance to change, lack of responsibility, willingness to follow the demagogue, unreasonable demands for economic benefits. It would seem that we are caught in a web of our own weaving.

A New Theory of Management

For these and many other reasons, we require a different theory of the task of managing people based on more adequate assumptions about human nature and human motivation. I am going to be so bold as to suggest the broad dimensions of such a theory. Call it "Theory Y," if you will.

1. Management is responsible for organizing the elements of productive enterprise—money, materials, equipment, people—in the interest of economic ends.
2. People are *not* by nature passive or resistant to organizational needs. They have become so as a result of experience in organizations.
3. The motivation, the potential for development, the capacity for assuming responsibility, the readiness to direct behavior toward organizational goals are all present in people. Management does not put them there. It is a responsibility of management to make it possible for people to recognize and develop these human characteristics for themselves.
4. The essential task of management is to arrange organizational conditions and methods of operation so that people can achieve their own goals *best* by directing *their own* efforts toward organizational objectives.

This is a process primarily of creating opportunities, releasing

potential, removing obstacles, encouraging growth, providing guidance. It is what Peter Drucker has called "management by objectives" in contrast to "management by control." It does *not* involve
the abdication of management, the absence of leadership, the lowering
of standards, or the other characteristics usually associated with the
"soft" approach under Theory X.

Some Difficulties

It is no more possible to create an organization today which will
be a full, effective application of this theory than it was to build an
atomic power plant in 1945. There are many formidable obstacles to
overcome.

The conditions imposed by conventional organization theory and
by the approach of scientific management for the past half century
have tied men to limited jobs which do not utilize their capabilities,
have discouraged the acceptance of responsibility, have encouraged
passivity, have eliminated meaning from work. Man's habits, attitudes, expectations—his whole conception of membership in an industrial organization—have been conditioned by his experience under
these circumstances.

People today are accustomed to being directed, manipulated, controlled in industrial organizations and to finding satisfaction for
their social, egoistic, and self-fulfillment needs away from the job.
This is true of much of management as well as of workers. Genuine
"industrial citizenship"—to borrow again a term from Drucker—is
a remote and unrealistic idea, the meaning of which has not even
been considered by most members of industrial organizations.

Another way of saying this is that Theory X places exclusive
reliance upon external control of human behavior, while Theory Y
relies heavily on self-control and self-direction. It is worth noting
that this difference is the difference between treating people as children and treating them as mature adults. After generations of the
former, we cannot expect to shift to the latter overnight.

Steps in the Right Direction

Before we are overwhelmed by the obstacles, let us remember that
the application of theory is always slow. Progress is usually achieved
in small steps. Some innovative ideas which are entirely consistent
with Theory Y are today being applied with some success.

Decentralization and delegation

These are ways of freeing people from the too-close control of conventional organization, giving them a degree of freedom to direct their own activities, to assume responsibility, and, importantly, to satisfy their egoistic needs. In this connection, the flat organization of Sears, Roebuck and Company provides an interesting example. It forces "management by objectives," since it enlarges the number of people reporting to a manager until he cannot direct and control them in the conventional manner.

Job enlargement

This concept, pioneered by I.B.M. and Detroit Edison, is quite consistent with Theory Y. It encourages the acceptance of responsibility at the bottom of the organization; it provides opportunities for satisfying social and egoistic needs. In fact, the reorganization of work at the factory level offers one of the more challenging opportunities for innovation consistent with Theory Y.

Participation and consultative management

Under proper conditions, participation and consultative management provide encouragement to people to direct their creative energies toward organizational objectives, give them some voice in decisions that affect them, provide significant opportunities for the satisfaction of social and egoistic needs. The Scanlon Plan is the outstanding embodiment of these ideas in practice.

Performance appraisal

Even a cursory examination of conventional programs of performance appraisal within the ranks of management will reveal how completely consistent they are with Theory X. In fact, most such programs tend to treat the individual as though he were a product under inspection on the assembly line.

A few companies—among them General Mills, Ansul Chemical, and General Electric—have been experimenting with approaches which involve the individual in setting "targets" or objectives *for himself* and in a *self*-evaluation of performance semiannually or annually. Of course, the superior plays an important leadership role in this process—one, in fact, which demands substantially more competence than the conventional approach. The role is, however, considerably more congenial to many managers than the role of "judge" or "inspector" which is usually forced upon them. Above all, the individual is encouraged to take a greater responsibility for planning and appraising his own contribution to organizational objectives; and the accompanying effects on egoistic and self-fulfillment needs are substantial.

Applying the Ideas

The not infrequent failure of such ideas as these to work as well as expected is often attributable to the fact that a management has "bought the idea" but applied it within the framework of Theory X and its assumptions.

Delegation is not an effective way of exercising management by control. Participation becomes a farce when it is applied as a sales gimmick or a device for kidding people into thinking they are important. Only the management that has confidence in human capacities and is itself directed toward organizational objectives rather than toward the preservation of personal power can grasp the implications of this emerging theory. Such management will find and apply successfully other innovative ideas as we move slowly toward the full implementation of a theory like Y.

The Human Side of Enterprise

It is quite possible for us to realize substantial improvements in the effectiveness of industrial organizations during the next decade or two. The social sciences can contribute much to such developments; we are only beginning to grasp the implications of the growing body of knowledge in these fields. But if this conviction is to become a reality instead of a pious hope, we will need to view the process much as we view the process of releasing the energy of the atom for constructive human ends—as a slow, costly, sometimes discouraging approach toward a goal which would seem to many to be quite unrealistic.

The ingenuity and the perseverance of industrial management in the pursuit of economic ends have changed many scientific and technological dreams into common place realities. It is now becoming clear that the application of these same talents to the human side of enterprise will not only enhance substantially these materialistic achievements, but will bring us one step closer to "the good society."

BIBLIOGRAPHY, CHAPTER III

APPLEY, LAWRENCE. "Peer Pressure," *Management News* (November, 1956), 1, 2.

BERNTHAL, WILMAR F. "Integrating the Behavioral Sciences and Management," *Journal of the Academy of Management* (December, 1960), 161-166.

BLACK, JAMES M. "Farewell to the Happiness Boys," *Management Review* (May, 1961), 38-47.

DRUCKER, PETER F. "Big Business and the National Purpose," *Harvard Business Review* (March-April, 1962), 49-59.

DAVIS, KEITH. *Human Relations at Work*. New York: McGraw-Hill Book Company, Inc., 1962.

KAHN, ROBERT L. "The Importance of Human Relations Research for Industrial Productivity," *New Solutions to Production Problems*, Manufacturing Series No. 200. New York: American Management Association, Inc., 1952, 15-28.

KATZ, ROBERT L. "Human Relations Skills Can Be Sharpened," *Harvard Business Review*, Vol. 34, No. 4 (January-February, 1955), 33-42.

—————. "Toward a More Effective Enterprise," *Harvard Business Review* (September-October, 1960), 80-102.

LARKE, ALFRED G. "Human Relations Research," *Dun's Review and Modern Industry* (July, 1956), 42-44.

McGREGOR, DOUGLAS. "Line Management's Responsibility for Human Relations," *Building Up the Supervisor's Job*, Manufacturing Series No. 213. New York: American Management Association, Inc. (1953), 27-35.

McNAIR, MALCOLM. "What Price Human Relations," *Harvard Business School Bulletin* (Winter, 1956).

MILLER, DELBERT C. "How Behavioral Scientists Can Help Business," *Business Horizons* (Summer, 1960), 32-37.

MOORE, DAVID G. "Behavioral Science and Business Education," *Journal of the Academy of Management* (December, 1960), 187-191.

—————. "Human Behavior and Industry," *Journal of Business*, Vol. XXVIII (1958), 38-40.

SCHOEN, DONALD R. "Human Relations: Boon or Bogle?" *Harvard Business Review*, Vol. 35, No. 6 (1957), 41-47.

WHYTE, WILLIAM F., et al., *Money and Motivation*. New York: Harper & Brothers, 1955.

Chapter IV
The Systems Concept

The concept of a system not only means many different things in different contexts but also means many different things to different people in the same context. One of the appeals of a systems concept is its generality or universality of application when explaining behavior in widely different contexts, and the attempts to develop a general systems theory are directed toward universality. In managing business organizations, however, a somewhat narrower view of systems is helpful in explaining and integrating into meaningful relationships such elements as decision-making, information, data processing, and mathematical models.

Toward the end of an explanation of systems in the first article of this chapter, Robert Chin develops the parts making up a system and carries these ideas forward into the area of developmental models. In the next article Elias H. Porter contends that organizational behavior, which is explainable by means of several different behavioral theories, is perhaps explained more meaningfully through the concept of a system of information flows. Murray A. Geisler and Wilbur A. Steger, in the final article, suggest the simulation of system elements and communication flows in designing new management systems.

11. THE UTILITY OF SYSTEM MODELS AND DEVELOPMENTAL MODELS FOR PRACTITIONERS[1]

Robert Chin[2]

All practitioners have ways of thinking about and figuring out situations of change. These ways are embodied in the concepts with which they apprehend the dynamics of the client-system they are working with, their relationship to it, and their processes of helping with its change. For example, the change-agent encounters resistance, defense mechanisms, readiness to change, adaptation, adjustment, maladjustment, integration, disintegration, growth, development, and maturation as well as deterioration. He uses concepts such as these to sort out the processes and mechanisms at work. And necessarily so. No practitioner can carry on thought processes without such concepts; indeed, no observations or diagnoses are ever made on "raw facts," because facts are really observations made within a set of concepts. But lurking behind concepts such as the ones stated above are assumptions about how the parts of the client-system fit together and how they change. For instance, "Let things alone, and natural laws (of economics, politics, personality, etc.) will work things out in the long run." "It is only human nature to resist change." "Every organization is always trying to improve its ways of working." Or, in more technical forms, we have assumptions such as: "The adjustment of the personality to its inner forces as well as adaptation to its environment is the sign of a healthy personality." "The coordination and integration of the departments of an organization is the task of the executive." "Conflict is an index of malintegration, or of change." "Inhibiting forces against growth must be removed."

It is clear that each of the above concepts conceals a different assumption about how events achieve stability and change, and how anyone can or cannot help change along. Can we make these assump-

---

[1] From *The Planning of Change*, by Warren G. Bennis, Kenneth D. Benne, and Robert Chin, © 1961, Holt, Rinehart and Winston, Inc., New York. Reprinted by permission.

[2] Robert Chin, Director of Research, Human Relations Center, Boston University.

tions explicit? Yes, we can and we must. The behavioral scientist does exactly this by constructing a simplified *model* of human events and of his tool concepts. By simplifying he can analyze his thoughts and concepts, and see in turn where the congruities and discrepancies occur between these and actual events. He becomes at once the observer, analyzer and modifier of the system [3] of concepts he is using.

The purpose of this paper is to present concepts relevant to, and the benefits to be gained from using, a "system" model and a "developmental" model in thinking about human events. These models provide "mind-holds" to the practitioner in his diagnosis. They are, therefore, of practical significance to him. This suggests one essential meaning of the oft-quoted and rarely explained phrase that "nothing is so practical as a good theory." We will try to show how the "systems" and "developmental" approaches provide key tools for a diagnosis of persons, groups, organizations, and communities for purposes of change. In doing so, we shall state succinctly the central notions of each model, probably sacrificing some technical elegance and exactness in the process. We shall not overburden the reader with citations of the voluminous set of articles from which this paper is drawn.

We postulate that the same models can be used in diagnosing different sizes of the units of human interactions—the person, the group, the organization, and the community.

One further prefatory word. We need to keep in mind the difference between an "analytic" model and a model of concrete events or cases. For our purposes, *an analytic model* is a constructed simplification of some part of reality that retains only those features regarded as essential for relating similar processes whenever and wherever they occur. *A concrete model* is based on an analytic model, but uses more of the content of actual cases, though it is still a simplification designed to reveal the essential features of some range of cases. As Hagen [4] puts it: "An explicitly defined analytic model helps the theorist to recognize what factors are being taken into account and *what relationships among them are assumed* and hence to know the basis of his conclusions. The advantages are ones of both exclusion and inclusion. A model lessens the danger of overlooking the indirect effects of a change of a relationship" (our italics). We mention this distinction since we find a dual usage that has plagued

---

[3] "System" is used here as any organized and coherent body of knowledge. Later we shall use the term in a more specific meaning.

[4] E. Hagen, chapter on "Theory of Social Change," unpublished manuscript.

behavioral scientists, for they themselves keep getting their feet entangled. We get mixed up in analyzing "the small group as a system" (analytic) and a school committee as a small group (concrete) or a national social system (analytic) and the American social system (concrete) or an organizational system (analytic) and the organization of a glue factory (concrete). In this paper, we will move back and forth between the analytic usage of "model" and the "model" of the concrete case, hopefully with awareness of when we are involved in a semantic shift.

THE "SYSTEM" MODEL

Psychologists, sociologists, anthropologists, economists, and political scientists have been "discovering" and using the system model. In so doing, they find intimations of an exhilarating "unity" of science, because the system models used by biological and physical scientists seem to be exactly similar. Thus, the system model is regarded by some system theorists as universally applicable to physical and social events, and to human relationships in small or large units.

The terms or concepts that are a part of the system model are "boundary," "stress or tension," "equilibrium," and "feedback." All these terms are related to "open system," "closed system," and "intersystem" models. We shall first define these concepts, illustrate their meaning, and then point out how they can be used by the change-agent as aids in observing, analyzing, or diagnosing—and perhaps intervening in—concrete situations.

The major terms

System. Laymen sometimes say, "you can't beat the system" (economic or political), or "he is a product of the system" (juvenile delinquent or Soviet citizen). But readers of social science writings will find the term used in a rather more specific way. It is used as an abbreviated term for a longer phrase that the reader is asked to supply. The "economic system" might be read as: "we treat price indices, employment figures, etc., as if they were closely interdependent with each other and we temporarily leave out unusual or external events, such as the discovery of a new gold mine." Or in talking about juvenile delinquency in "system" terms, the sociologists choose to treat the lower-class values, lack of job opportunities, ragged parental images, as interrelated with each other, in back-and-forth cause-and-effect fashion, as determinants of delinquent behavior. Or the industrial sociologist may regard the factory as a "social system," as people working together in relative isolation from the outside, in order to examine what goes on in interactions and interdependencies of the people, their positions, and other variables. In our descriptions and analyses of a particular concrete system, we can recognize the shadowy figure of some such analytic model of "system."

The analytic model of system demands that we treat the phenomena and the concepts for organizing the phenomena as if there existed organization, interaction, interdependency, and integration of parts and elements. System analysis assumes structure and stability within some arbitrarily sliced and frozen time period.

It is helpful to visualize a system [5] by drawing a large circle. We place elements, parts, variables, inside the circle as the components, and draw lines among the components. The lines may be thought of as rubber bands or springs, which stretch or contract as the forces increase or decrease. Outside the circle is the environment, where we place all other factors which impinge upon the system.

Boundary. In order to specify what is inside or outside the system, we need to define its "boundary" line. The boundary of a system may exist physically: a tightly corked vacuum bottle, the skin of a person, the number of people in a group, etc. But, in addition, we may delimit the system in a less tangible way, by placing our boundary according to what variables are being focused upon. We can construct a system consisting of the multiple roles of a person, or a system composed of varied roles among members in a small work group, or a system interrelating roles in a family. The components or variables used are roles, acts, expectations, communications, influence and power relationships, and so forth, and not necessarily persons.

The operational definition of *boundary* is: the line forming a closed circle around selected variables, where there is less interchange of energy (or communication, etc.) *across* the line of the circle than *within* the delimiting circle. The multiple systems of a community may have boundaries that do or do not coincide. For example, treating the power relationships may require a boundary line different from that for the system of interpersonal likes or dislikes in a com-

---

[5] A useful visual aid for "system" can be constructed by using paper clips (elements) and rubber bands (tensions) mounted on a peg board. Shifting of the position of a clip demonstrates the interdependency of all the clips' positions, and their shifting relationships.

munity. In small groups we tend to draw the same boundary line for the multiple systems of power, communications, leadership, and so on, a major advantage for purposes of study.

In diagnosing we tentatively assign a boundary, examine what is happening inside the system and then readjust the boundary, if necessary. We examine explicitly whether or not the "relevant" factors are accounted for within the system, an immensely practical way of deciding upon relevance. Also, we are free to limit ruthlessly, and neglect some factors temporarily, thus reducing the number of considerations necessary to be kept in mind at one time. The variables left outside the system, in the "environment" of the system, can be introduced one or more at a time to see the effects, if any, on the interrelationship of the variables within the system.

Tension, stress, strain, and conflict. Because the components within a system are different from each other, are not perfectly integrated, or are changing and reacting to change, or because outside disturbances occur, we need ways of dealing with these differences. The differences lead to varying degrees of tension within the system. *Examples:* males are not like females, foremen see things differently from workers and from executives, children in a family grow, a committee has to work with a new chairman, a change in the market condition requires a new sales response from a factory. To restate the above examples in conceptual terms: we find built-in differences, gaps of ignorance, misperceptions, or differential perceptions, internal changes in a component, reactive adjustments and defenses, and the requirements of system survival generating tensions. Tensions that are internal and arise out of the structural arrangements of the system may be called *stresses and strains* of the system. When tensions gang up and become more or less sharply opposed along the lines of two or more components, we have *conflict*.

A word of warning. The presence of tensions, stresses or strains, and conflict within the system often are reacted to by people in the system as if they were shameful and must be done away with. Tension reduction, relief of stress and strain, and conflict resolution become the working goals of practitioners but sometimes at the price of overlooking the possibility of increasing tensions and conflict in order to facilitate creativity, innovation, and social change. System analysts have been accused of being conservative and even reactionary in assuming that a social system always tends to reduce tension, resist innovation, abhor deviancy and change. It is obvious, however, that tension and conflict are "in" any system, and that no living system exists without tension. Whether these facts of life in a system are to be abhorred or welcomed is determined by attitudes or value judgments not derivable from system theory as such.

The identification of and analysis of how tensions operate in a system are by all odds *the* major utility of system analysis for practitioners of change. The dynamics of a living system are exposed for observation through utilizing the concepts of tension, stress and strain, and conflict. These tensions lead to activities of two kinds: those which do not affect the structure of the system (dynamics), and those which directly alter the structure itself (system change).

Equilibrium and "steady state." A system is assumed to have a tendency to achieve a balance among the various forces operating within and upon it. Two terms have been used to denote two different ideas about balance. When the balance is thought of as a fixed point or level, it is called "equilibrium." "Steady state," on the other hand, is the term recently used to describe the balanced relationship of parts that is not dependent upon any fixed equilibrium point or level.

Our body temperature is the classic illustration of a fixed level (98.6° F.), while the functional relationship between work units in a factory, regardless of the level of production, represents a steady state. For the sake of simplicity, we shall henceforth stretch the term "equilibrium" to cover both types of balance, to include also the idea of "steady state."

There are many kinds of equilibria. A *stationary equilibrium* exists when there is a fixed point or level of balance to which the system returns after a disturbance. We rarely find such instances in human relationships. A *dynamic equilibrium* exists when the equilibrium shifts to a new position of balance after disturbance. Among examples of the latter, we can observe a *neutral* type of situation. *Example:* a ball on a flat plane. A small push moves it to a new position, and it again comes to rest. *Example:* a farming community. A new plow is introduced and is easily incorporated into its agricultural methods. A new level of agricultural production is placidly achieved. A *stable type of situation* exists where the forces that produced the initial equilibrium are so powerful that any new force must be extremely strong before any movement to a new position can be achieved. *Example:* a ball in the bottom of a goblet. *Example:* an organization encrusted with tradition or with clearly articulated and entrenched roles is not easily upset by minor events. An *unstable type of situation* is tense and precarious. A small disturbance produces large and rapid movements to a new position. *Example:* a ball balanced on the rims of two goblets placed side by side. *Example:* an organization with a precarious and tense balance between two modes of leadership style. A small disturbance can cause a large swing to one direction and a new position of equilibrium. *Example:* a community's balance of power between ethnic groups may be such that a "minor" disturbance can produce an upheaval and movement to a different balance of power.

A system in equilibrium reacts to outside impingements by: (*1*) resisting the influence of the disturbance, refusing to acknowledge its existence, or by building a protective wall against the intrusion, and by other defensive maneuvers. *Example:* A small group refuses to talk about a troublesome problem of unequal power distribution raised by a member. (*2*) By resisting the disturbance through bringing into operation the homeostatic forces that restore or re-create a balance. The small group talks about the troublesome problem of a member and convinces him that it is not "really" a problem. (*3*) By accommodating the disturbances through achieving a new equilibrium. Talking about the problem may result in a shift in power relationships among members of the group.

The concepts of equilibrium (and steady state) lead to some questions to guide a practitioner's diagnosis.

1. What are the conditions conducive to the achievement of an equilibrium in this case? Are there internal or external factors producing these forces? What is their quality and tempo?
2. Does the case of the client-system represent one of the typical situations of equilibrium? How does judgment on this point affect intervention strategy? If the practitioner feels the situation is tense and precarious, he should be more cautious in intervention than in a situation of stable type.
3. Can the practitioner identify the parts of the system that represent greatest readiness to change, and the greatest resistance to and defense against change? Can he understand the functions of any variable in relation to all other variables? Can he derive some sense of the direction in which the client system is moving, and separate those forces attempting to restore an old equilibrium and those pushing toward a new equilibrium state?

Feedback. Concrete systems are never closed off completely. They have inputs and outputs across the boundary; they are affected by and in turn affect the environment. While affecting the environment, a process we call output, systems gather information about how they are doing. Such information is then fed back into the system as input to guide and steer its operations. This process is called feedback. The "discovery" of feedback has led to radical inventions in the physical world in designing self-guiding and self-correcting instruments. It has also become a major concept in the behavioral sciences, and a central tool in the practitioner's social technology. *Example:* In reaching for a cigarette we pick up tactile and visual cues that are used to guide our arm and finger movements. *Example:* Our interpersonal communications are guided and corrected by our picking up of effect cues from the communicatees. *Example:* Improving the feedback process of a client system will allow for self-steering or corrective action to be taken by him or it. In fact, the single most important improvement the change-agent can help a client system to achieve is to increase its diagnostic sensitivity to the effects of its own actions upon others. Programs in sensitivity training attempt to increase or unblock the feedback processes of persons; a methodological skill with wider applicability and longer-lasting significance than solving the immediate problem at hand. In diagnosing a client system, the practitioner asks: What are its feedback procedures? How adequate are they? What blocks their effective use? Is it lack of skill in gathering data, or in coding and utilizing the information?

Open and closed systems

All living systems are open systems—systems in contact with their environment, with input and output across system boundaries. What then is the use of talking about a closed system? What *is* a closed system? It means that the system is temporarily assumed to have a leak-tight boundary—there is relatively little, if any, commerce across the boundary. We know that no such system can be found in reality, but it is sometimes essential to analyze a system as if it were closed so as to examine the operations of the system as affected "only by the conditions previously established by the environment and not changing at the time of analysis, plus the relationships among the internal elements of the system." The analyst then opens the system to a new impact from the environment, again closes the system, and observes and thinks out what would happen. It is, therefore, fruitless to debate the point; both open and closed system models are useful in diagnosis. Diagnosing the client as a system of variables, we have a way then of managing the complexity of "everything depends upon everything else" in an orderly way. Use of system analysis has these possibilities: (a) diagnosticians can avoid the error of simple cause-and-effect thinking; (b) they can justify what is included in observation and interpretation and what is temporarily excluded; (c) they can predict what will happen if no new or outside force is applied; (d) they are guided in categorizing what is relatively enduring and stable, or changing, in the situation; (e) they can distinguish between what is basic and what is merely symptomatic; (f) they can predict what will happen if they leave the events undisturbed and if they intervene; and (g) they are guided in selecting points of intervention.

Intersystem model

We propose an extension of system analysis that looks to us to be useful for the problems confronting the change-agent. We urge the adoption of an intersystem model.

An intersystem model involves two open systems connected to each other.[6] The term we need to add here is *connectives*. Connectives represent the lines of relationships of the two systems. Connectives tie together parts (mechanics) or imbed in a web of tissue the separate organs (biology); connectives in an industrial establishment are the defined lines of communication, or the leadership hierarchy and authority for the branch plants; or they represent the social contract entered into by a therapist and patient; or mutual role expectations of consultant and client; or the affective ties between family members. These are conjunctive connectives. But we also have conflicts between labor and management, teenage gang wars, race conflicts, and negative emotional responses to strangers. These are disjunctive connectives.

Why elaborate the system model into an intersystem model? Cannot we get the same effect by talking about "sub-systems" of a larger system? In part we can. Labor-management conflicts, or interpersonal relations, or change-agent and client relationships can each be treated as a new system with sub-systems. But we may lose the critical fact of the autonomy of the components, or the direct interactional or transactual consequences for the separate components when we treat the sub-systems as merely parts of a larger system.

[6] A visualization of an intersystem model would be two systems side by side, with separately identified links. Two rubber band-paper clip representatives can be connected with rubber bands of a different color, representing the connectives.

The intersystem model exaggerates the virtues of autonomy and the limited nature of interdependence of the interactions between the two connected systems.

What are some of the positive advantages of using intersystem analysis? First, the external change-agent, or the change-agent built into an organization, as a helper with planned change does not completely become a part of the client-system. He must remain separate to some extent; he must create and maintain some distance between himself and the client, thus standing apart "in another system" from which he re-relates. This new system might be a referent group of fellow professionals, or a body of rational knowledge. But create one he does and must. Intersystem analysis of the change-agent's role leads to fruitful analysis of the connectives—their nature in the beginning, how they shift, and how they are cut off. Intersystem analysis also poses squarely an unexplored issue, namely the internal system of the change-agent, whether a single person, consultant group, or a nation. Helpers of change are prone at times not to see that their own systems as change-agents have boundaries, tensions, stresses and strains, equilibria, and feedback mechanisms which may be just as much parts of the problem as are similar aspects of the client-systems. Thus, relational issues are more available for diagnosis when we use an intersystem model.

More importantly, the intersystem model is applicable to problems of leadership, power, communication, and conflict in organizations, intergroup relations, and international relations. *Example:* Leadership in a work group with its liaison, negotiation, and representation functions is dependent upon connectives to another group and not solely upon the internal relationships within the work group. Negotiators, representatives, and leaders are parts of separate systems each with its own interdependence, tensions, stresses, and feedback, whether we are thinking of foreign ministers, Negro-white leaders, or student-faculty councils.

In brief, the intersystem model leads us to examine the interdependent dynamics of interaction both within and between the units. We object to the premature and unnecessary assumption that the units always form a single system. We can be misled into an utopian analysis of conflict, change-agent relations to client, and family relations if we neglect system differences. But an intersystem model provides a tool for diagnosis that retains the virtues of system analysis, adds the advantage of clarity, and furthers our diagnosis of the influence of various connectives, conjunctive and disjunctive, on the two systems. For change-agents, the essence of collaborative planning is contained in an intersystem model.

DEVELOPMENTAL MODELS

Practitioners have in general implicitly favored developmental models in thinking about human affairs, while social scientists have not paid as much attention to these as they have to system models. The "life sciences" of biology and psychology have not crystallized nor refined their common analytic model of the development of the organism, despite the heroic break-throughs of Darwin. Thus, we are forced to present only broad and rough categories of alternative positions in this paper.

Since there is no standard vocabulary for a developmental model, we shall present five categories of terms that we deem essential to such models: direction, states, forces, form of progression, and potentiality.

The major terms

Developmental models. By developmental models, we mean those bodies of thought that center around growth and directional change. Developmental models assume change; they assume that there are noticeable differences between the states of a system at different times; that the succession of these states implies the system is heading somewhere; and that there are orderly processes which explain how the system gets from its present state to wherever it is going. In order to delimit the nature of change in developmental models we should perhaps add the idea of an increase in value accompanying the achievement of a new state. With this addition, developmental models focus on processes of growth and maturation. This addition might seem to rule out processes of decay, deterioration, and death from consideration. Logically, the developmental model should apply to either.

There are two kinds of "death" of concern to the practitioner. First, "death" or loss of some part or subvalue, as a constant concomitant of growth and development. Theories of life processes have used concepts such as katabolic (destructive) processes in biology, death instincts in Freud's psychology, or role loss upon promotion. On balance, the "loss" is made up by the "gains," and thus there is an increase in value. Second, "death" as planned change for a group or organization—the dissolution of a committee or community organization that has "outlived its purpose and function," and the termination of a helping relationship with deliberateness and collaboration of participants is properly included as part of a developmental model.

Direction. Developmental models postulate that the system under scrutiny—a person, a small group, interpersonal interactions, an organization, a community or a society—is going "somewhere"; that the changes have some direction. The direction may be defined by (*a*) some *goal* or end state (developed, mature); (*b*) the *process* of becoming (developing, maturing) or (*c*) the degree of achievement *toward* some goal or end state (increased development, increase in maturity).

Change-agents find it necessary to believe that there is direction in change. *Example:* self-actualization or fulfillment is a need of the client-system. When strong directional tendencies are present, we modify our diagnosis and intervention accordingly. A rough analogy may be helpful here. A change-agent using a developmental model may be thought of as a husbandman tending a plant, watching and helping it to grow in its own natural direction of producing flowers. He feeds, waters, and weeds. Though at times he may be ruthless in pinching off excess buds, or even in using "grafts," in general he encourages the plant to reach its "goal" of producing beautiful flowers.

Identifiable state. As the system develops over time, the different states may be identified and differentiated from one another. Terms such as "stages," "levels," "phases," or "periods" are applied to these states. *Example:* psychosexual definition of oral, and anal stages, levels of evolution of species, or phases of group development.

No uniformity exists in the definition and operational identification of such successive states. But since change-agents do have to label the past, present, and future, they need some terms to describe successive states and to identify the turning points, transition areas, or critical events that characterize change. Here, system analysis is helpful in defining how parts are put together, along with the tensions and directions of the equilibrating processes. We have two polar types of the shifts of states: (*a*) small, nondiscernible steps or increments leading to a qualitative jump. (*Example:* black hair gradually turning gray, or a student evolving into a scholar); (*b*) a cataclysmic or critical event leading to a sudden change. (*Example:* a sickness resulting in gray hair overnight, or an inspirational lecture by a professor.) While the latter type seems more frequently to be externally induced, internal factors of the system can have the same consequence. In other words, the internal disequilibration of a balance may lead to a step-jump of the system to a new level. Personality stages, group stages, and societal phases are evolved and precipitated from internal and from external relations.

Form of progression. Change-agents see in their models of development some form of progression or movement. Four such forms are typically assumed. First, it is often stated that once a stage is worked through, the client-system shows continued progression and normally never turns back. (Any recurrence of a previous state is viewed as an abnormality. Freudian stages are a good example: recurrence of a stage is viewed as regression, an abnormal event to be explained.) Teachers expect a steady growth of knowledge in students, either in a straight line (linear) or in an increasingly accelerating (curvilinear) form.

Second, it is assumed that change, growth, and development occur in a *spiral* form. *Example:* A small group might return to some previous "problem," such as its authority relations to the leader, but now might discuss the question at a "higher" level where irrational components are less dominant.

Third, another assumption more typically made is that the stages are really phases which occur and recur. There is an oscillation between various states, where no chronological priority is assigned to each state; there are cycles. *Example:* Phases of problem-solving or decision-making recur in different time periods as essential to progression. Cultures and societies go through phases of development in recurrent forms.

Fourth, still another assumption is that the form of progression is characterized by a branching out into *differentiated* forms and processes, each part increasing in its specialization, and at the same time acquiring its own autonomy and significance. *Example:* biological forms are differentiated into separate species. Organizations become more and more differentiated into special task and control structures.

Forces. First, forces or casual factors producing development and growth are most frequently seen by practitioners as "natural," as part of human nature, suggesting the role of genetics and other in-born characteristics. At best, environmental factors act as "triggers" or "releases," where the presence of some stimulus sets off the system's inherent growth forces. For example, it is sometimes thought that the teacher's job is to trigger off the natural curiosity of the child, and that growth of knowledge will ensue. Or the leadership of an organization should act to release the self-actualizing and creative forces present in its members.

Second, a smaller number of practitioners and social scientists think that the response to new situations and environmental forces is a coping response which gives rise to growth and development. Third, at this point, it may be useful to remind ourselves of the earlier discussion of the internal tensions of the system, still another cause of change. When stresses and strains of a system become too great, a disruption occurs and a set of forces is released to create new structures and achieve a new equilibrium.

Potentiality. Developmental models vary in their assumptions about potentialities of the system for development, growth, and change. That is, they vary in assumptions about the capabilities, overt or latent, that are built into the original or present state so that the necessary conditions for development may be typically present. Does the "seed"—and its genetic characteristics—represent potentialities? And are the supporting conditions of its environment available? Is the intelligence or emotional capability or skill-potential sufficient for development and change in a social and human process?

Change-agents typically assume a high degree of potentiality in the impetus toward development, and in the surrounding conditions that effectuate the potential.

Utility to practitioners

The developmental model has tremendous advantages for the practitioner. It provides a set of expectations about the future of the client-system. By clarifying his thoughts and refining his observations about direction, states in the developmental process, forms of progression, and forces causing these events to occur over a period of time, the practitioner develops a time perspective which goes far beyond that of the more here-and-now analysis of a system-model, which is bounded by time. By using a developmental model, he has a directional focus for his analysis and action and a temporal frame of reference. In addition, he is confronted with a number of questions to ask of himself and of his observations of the case: Do I assume an inherent end of the development? Do I impose a desired (by me) direction? How did I establish a collaboratively planned direction? What states in the development process may be expected? What form of progression do I foresee? What causes the development? His diagnoses and his interventions can become strategic rather than merely tactical.

The Change-Agent and Models

The primary concern of this paper has been to illustrate some of the major kinds of analytic models and conceptual schemes that have been devised by social scientists for the analysis of change and of changing human processes. But we need to keep in mind that the concern with diagnosis on the part of the social scientist is to achieve understanding, and to educe empirically researchable hypotheses amenable to his methods of study. The social scientist generally prefers not to change the system, but to study how it works and to predict what would happen if some new factor were introduced. So we find his attention focused on a "theory of change," of how the system achieves change. In contrast, the practitioner is concerned with diagnosis: how to achieve understanding in order to engage in change. The practitioner, therefore, has some additional interests, he wants to know how to change the system, he needs a "theory of changing" the system.

A theory of changing requires the selection, or the construction, by theoretically minded practitioners, of thought-models appropriate to their intended purpose. This has to be done according to explicit criteria. A change-agent may demand of any model answers to certain questions. The responses he receives may not be complete nor satisfactory since only piece-meal answers exist. At this period in the development of a theory of changing, we ask four questions as our guide lines for examining a conceptual model intended for the use of change-agents.

The first question is simply this: does the model account for the stability and continuity in the events studied at the same time that it accounts for changes in them? How do processes of change develop, given the interlocking factors in the situation that make for stability? Second, where does the model locate the "source" of change? What place among these sources do the deliberate and conscious efforts of the client-system and change-agent occupy? Third, what does the model assume about how goals and directions are determined? What or who sets the direction for movement of the processes of change? Fourth, does the model provide the change agent with levers or handles for affecting the direction, tempo, and quality of these processes of change?

A fifth question running through the other four is this: How does the model "place" the change-agent in the scheme of things? What is the shifting character of his relationship to the client-system, initially and at the termination of relationship, that affects his perceptions and actions? The questions of relationship of change-agent to others needs to be part and parcel of the model since the existential relationships of the change-agent engaged in processes of planned change become "part of the problem" to be investigated.

The application of these five questions to the models of systems and models of development crystallizes some of the formation of ingredients for a change-agent model for changing. We can now summarize each model as follows:

A "system" model emphasizes primarily the details of how stability is achieved, and only derivatively how change evolves out of the incompatibilities and conflicts in the system. A system model assumes that organization, interdependency, and integration exist among its parts and that change is a derived consequence of how well the parts of the system fit together, or how well the system fits in with other surrounding and interacting systems. The source of change lies primarily in the structural stress and strain externally induced or internally created. The process of change is a process of tension reduction. The goals and direction are emergent from the structures or from imposed sources. Goals are often analyzed as set by "vested interests" of one part of the system. The confronting symptom of some trouble is a reflection of difficulties of adaptability (reaction to environment) or of the ability for adjustment (internal equilibration). The levers or handles available for manipulation are in the "inputs" to the system, especially the feedback mechanisms, and in the forces tending to restore a balance in the system. The change-agent is treated as separate from the client-system, the "target system."

The developmental model assumes constant change and development, and growth and decay of a system over time. Any existing stability is a snapshot of a living process—a stage that will give way to another stage. The supposition seems to be that it is "natural" that change should occur because change is rooted in the very nature of living organisms. The laws of the developmental process are not necessarily fixed, but some effects of the environment are presumably necessary to the developmental process. The direction of change is toward some goal, the fulfillment of its destiny, granting that no major blockage gets in the way. "Trouble" occurs when there is a gap between the system and its goal. Intervention is viewed as the removal of blockage by the change-agent, who then gets out of the way of the growth forces. Developmental models are not very sharply

ASSUMPTIONS AND APPROACHES OF THREE ANALYTIC MODELS

	Models of change		
ASSUMPTIONS AND APPROACHES TO:	SYSTEM MODEL	DEVELOPMENTAL MODEL	MODEL FOR CHANGING
1. *Content*			
Stability	Structural integration	Phases, stages	Unfreezing parts
Change	Derived from structure	Constant and unique	Induced, controlled
2. *Causation*			
Source of change	Structural stress	Nature of organisms	Self and change-agent
Causal force	Tension reduction		Rational choice
3. *Goals*			
Direction	Emergent	Ontological	Deliberate selection
Set by	"Vested interests"		Collaborative process
4. *Intervention*			
Confronting symptoms	Stresses, strains, and tensions	Discrepancy between actuality and potentiality	Perceived need
Goal of intervening	Adjustment, adaptation	Removal of blockages	Improvement
5. *Change-Agent*			
Place	Outside the "target" system	Outside	Part of situation
Role	External diagnoser and actor	External diagnoser and actor	Participant in here and now

analyzed by the pure theorist nor formally stated, usually, as an analytic model. In fact, very frequently the model is used for studying the unique case rather than for deriving "laws of growth"; it is for descriptive purposes.

The third model—a model for "changing," is a more recent creation. It incorporates some elements of analyses from system models, along with some ideas from the developmental model, in a framework, where direct attention is paid to the induced forces producing change. It studies stability in order to unfreeze and move some parts of the system. The direction to be taken is not fixed or "determined," but remains in large measure a matter of "choice" for the client-system. The change-agent is a specialist in the technical processes of facilitating change, a helper to the client-system. The models for changing are as yet incompletely conceptualized. The intersystem model may provide a way of examining how the change-agent's relationships, as part of the model, affect the processes of change.

We can summarize and contrast the three models with a chart [page 126]. We have varying degrees of confidence in our categories, but, as the quip says, we construct these in order to achieve the laudable state of "paradigm lost." It is the readers' responsibility to help achieve this goal!

The Limitations

It is obvious that we are proposing the use of systematically constructed and examined models of thought for the change-agent. The advantages are manifold and—we hope—apparent in our preceding discussion. Yet we must now point out some limitations and disutility of models.

Models are abstractions from the concreteness of events. Because of the high degree of selectivity of observations and focus, the "fit" between the model and the actual thought and diagnostic processes of the change-agent is not close. Furthermore, the thought and diagnostic processes of the change-agent are not fixed and rigid. And even worse, the "fit" between the diagnostic processes of the change-agent and the changing processes of the "actual" case, is not close. Abstract as the nature of a model is, as applied to the change-agent, students of the change-agent role may find the concepts of use. But change-agents' practices in diagnosing are not immediately affected by models' analyses.

Furthermore, there are modes of diagnosing by intervening, which do not fall neatly into models. The change agent frequently tries out an activity in order to see what happens and to see what is involved in the change. If successful, he does not need to diagnose any further, but proceeds to engage in further actions with the client. If unsuccessful, however, he may need to examine what is going on in more detail.

The patch work required for a theory and model of changing requires the suspension of acceptance of such available models. For this paper has argued for some elements from both the system models and the developmental models to be included in the model for practitioners, with the use of a format of the intersystem model so as to include the change-agent and his relationships as part of the problem. But can the change-agent wait for such a synthesis and emerging construction? Our personal feeling is that the planning of change cannot wait, but must proceed with the available diagnostic tools. Here is an intellectual challenge to the scientist-scholar of planned change that could affect the professions of practice.

12. THE PARABLE OF THE SPINDLE [1]

Elias H. Porter [2]

More and more we hear the word "systems" used in discussions of business problems. Research people are studying systems, experts are looking at organizations as systems, and a growing number of departments and companies have the word "systems" in their names.

Just what *is* a system in the business sense? What does it do? What good is it to management? To answer these questions I shall first use a parable from the restaurant industry. What, you may ask, can executives in manufacturing, retailing, or service systems learn from restaurant systems? I readily admit that if you envisage only menus, customers, waitresses, and cooks in a restaurant, you will find no transferable knowledge. But if you see (as I hope you will) inputs, rate variations, displays, feedback loops, memory devices, queuing, omissions, errors, chunking, approximating, channeling, and filtering in a restaurant system—then you should indeed find some practical value in my parable.

The implications of the parable will be discussed specifically in the second part of the article, after we have reduced it to a paradigm.

THE PARABLE

Once upon a time the president of a large chain of short-order restaurants attended a lecture on "Human Relations in Business and Industry." He attended the lecture in the hope he would learn something useful. His years of experience had led him to believe that if human relations problems ever plagued any business, then they certainly plagued the restaurant business.

The speaker discussed the many pressures which create human relations problems. He spoke of psychological pressures, sociological pressures, conflicts in values, conflicts in power structure, and so on.

[1] From *Harvard Business Review* (May-June, 1962), pp. 58-66. Reprinted by permission of the *Harvard Business Review*.
[2] Elias H. Porter, Research Director of Plans and Operations, System Development Corporation, Santa Monica, California.

The president did not understand all that was said, but he did go home with one idea. If there were so many different sources of pressure, maybe it was expecting too much of his managers to think they would see them all, let alone cope with them all. The thought occurred to him that maybe he should bring in a team of consultants from several different academic disciplines and have each contribute his part to the solution of the human relations problems.

And so it came to pass that the president of the restaurant chain and his top-management staff met one morning with a sociologist, a psychologist, and an anthropologist. The president outlined the problem to the men of science and spoke of his hope that they might come up with an interdisciplinary answer to the human relations problems. The personnel manager presented exit-interview findings which he interpreted as indicating that most people quit their restaurant jobs because of too much sense of pressure caused by the inefficiencies and ill tempers of co-workers.

This was the mission which the scientists were assigned: find out why the waitresses break down in tears; find out why the cooks walk off the job; find out why the managers get so upset that they summarily fire employees on the spot. Find out the cause of the problems, and find out what to do about them.

Later, in one of the plush conference rooms, the scientists sat down to plan their attack. It soon became clear that they might just as well be three blind men, and the problem might just as well be the proverbial elephant. Their training and experience had taught them to look at events in different ways. And so they decided that inasmuch as they couldn't speak each others' languages, they might as well pursue their tasks separately. Each went to a different city and began his observations in his own way.

The sociologist

First to return was the sociologist. In his report to top management he said:

> I think I have discovered something that is pretty fundamental. In one sense it is so obvious that it has probably been completely overlooked before. It is during the *rush hours* that your human relations problems arise. That is when the waitresses break out in tears. That is when the cooks grow temperamental and walk off the job. That is when your managers lose their tempers and dismiss employees summarily.

After elaborating on this theme and showing several charts with sloping lines and bar graphs to back up his assertions, he came to his diagnosis of the situation. "In brief, gentlemen," he stated, "you have a sociological problem on your hands." He walked to the blackboard and began to write. As he wrote, he spoke:

> You have a stress pattern during the rush hours. There is stress between the customer and the waitress. . . .
> There is stress between the waitress and the cook. . . .
> And up here is the manager. There is stress between the waitress and the manager. . . .
> And between the manager and the cook. . . .
> And the manager is buffeted by complaints from the customer.
> We can see one thing which, sociologically speaking, doesn't seem right. The manager has the highest status in the restaurant. The cook has the next highest status. The waitresses, however, are always "local hire" and have the lowest status. Of course, they have higher status than bus boys and dish washers but certainly lower status than the cook, and yet they give orders to the cook.
> It doesn't seem right for a lower status person to give orders to a higher status person. We've got to find a way to break up the face-to-face relationship between the waitresses and the cook. We've got to fix it so that they don't have to talk with one another. Now my idea is to put a "spindle" on the order counter. The "spindle," as I choose to call it, is a wheel on a shaft. The wheel has clips on it so the girls can simply put their orders on the wheel rather than calling out orders to the cook.

When the sociologist left the meeting, the president and his staff talked of what had been said. It made some sense. However, they decided to wait to hear from the other scientists before taking any action.

The psychologist

Next to return from his studies was the psychologist. He reported to top management:

> I think I have discovered something that is pretty fundamental. In one sense it is so obvious that it has probably been completely overlooked before. It is during the *rush hours* that your human relations problems arise. That is when the waitresses break out in tears. That is when the cooks grow temperamental and walk off the job. That is when your managers lose their tempers and dismiss employees summarily.

Then the psychologist sketched on the blackboard the identical pattern of stress between customer, waitress, cook, and management. But his interpretation was somewhat different:

Psychologically speaking we can see that the manager is the father figure, the cook is the son, and the waitress is the daughter. Now we know that in our culture you can't have daughters giving orders to the sons. It louses up their ego structure.

What we've got to do is to find a way to break up the face-to-face relationship between them. Now one idea I've thought up is to put what I call a "spindle" on the order counter. It's kind of a wheel on a shaft with little clips on it so that the waitresses can put their orders on it rather than calling out orders to the cook.

What the psychologist said made sense, too, in a way. Some of the staff favored the status-conflict interpretation while others thought the sex-conflict interpretation to be the right one; the president kept his own counsel.

The anthropologist

The next scientist to report was the anthropologist. He reported to top management:

I think I have discovered something that is pretty fundamental. In one sense it is so obvious that it has probably been completely overlooked before. It is during the *rush hours* that your human relations problems arise. That is when the waitresses break out in tears. That is when the cooks grow temperamental and walk off the job. That is when your managers lose their tempers and dismiss employees summarily.

After elaborating for a few moments he came to his diagnosis of the situation. "In brief, gentlemen," he stated, "you have an anthropological problem on your hands." He walked to the blackboard and began to sketch. Once again there appeared the stress pattern between customer, waitress, cook, and management:

We anthropologists know that man behaves according to his value systems. Now, the manager holds as a central value the continued growth and development of the restaurant organization. The cooks tend to share this central value system, for as the organization prospers, so do they. But the waitresses are a different story. The only reason most of them are working is to help supplement the family income. They couldn't care less whether the organization thrives or not as long as it's a decent place to work. Now, you can't have a noncentral value system giving orders to a central value system.

What we've got to do is to find some way of breaking up the face-to-face contact between the waitresses and the cook. One way that has occurred to me is to place on the order counter an adaptation of the old-fashioned spindle. By having a wheel at the top of the shaft and putting clips every few inches apart, the waitresses can put their orders on the wheel and not have to call out orders to the cook. Here is a model of what I mean.

Triumph of the spindle

When the anthropologist had left, there was much discussion of which scientist was right. The president finally spoke. "Gentlemen, it's clear that these men don't agree on the reason for conflict, but all have come up with the same basic idea about the spindle. Let's take a chance and try it out."

And it came to pass that the spindle was introduced throughout the chain of restaurants. It did more to reduce the human relations problems in the restaurant industry than any other innovation of which the restaurant people knew. Soon it was copied. Like wild fire the spindle spread from coast to coast and from border to border.

So much for the parable. Let us now proceed to the paradigm.

THE PARADIGM

Each of the three scientists had seen a different problem: status conflict, sex rivalry, and value conflict. Maybe it was none of these but simply a problem in the division of work between men and machines and how they are related one to the other: a problem of system design. Let us explore this possibility by observing the functions which the spindle fulfills.

Functions served

First of all, the spindle acts as a memory device for the cook. He no longer needs to remember all the orders given him by the waitresses. This makes his job easier and less "stressful"—especially during the rush hours.

Secondly, the spindle acts as a buffering device. It buffers the cook against a sudden, overwhelming load of orders. Ten waitresses can place their orders on the spindle almost simultaneously. The cook takes them off the spindle according to his work rate—not the input rate. This makes his job easier, more within reach of human capacity—especially during the rush hours.

Thirdly, the spindle acts as a queuing device—in two ways. It holds the order in a proper waiting line until the cook can get to them. When dependent on his memory only, the cook can get orders mixed up. It also does all the "standing in line" for the waitresses. They need never again stand in line to pass an order to the cook. This makes their jobs easier—especially during the rush hours.

Fourthly, the spindle permits a visual display of all the orders waiting to be filled. The cook can often see that several of the orders call for the same item. He can prepare four hamburgers in about the same time as he can prepare one. By reason of having "random access" to all the orders in the system at that point he is able to organize his work around several orders simultaneously with greater efficiency. This makes his job easier—especially during the rush hours.

To appreciate the fifth function which the spindle serves, we must go back to the procedures used before the advent of the spindle. In looking at these procedures we are going to examine them in "general system behavior theory" terms:

On the menu certain "information" exists in the physical form of printed words. The customer "transforms" this information into the physical form of spoken words. The information is once again transformed by the waitress. Now it exists in the physical form of written notes made by the waitress. Once again the information is transformed as the waitress converts her notes into spoken words directed to the cook. The cook transforms the information from the physical form of spoken words to the physical form of prepared food. We have an "information flow" which looks like this:

$$\text{Menu} \xrightarrow{\substack{\text{Printed} \\ \text{Words}}} \text{Customer} \xrightarrow{\substack{\text{Spoken} \\ \text{Words}}} \text{Waitress} \xrightarrow{\substack{\text{Written} \\ \text{Notes}}} \xrightarrow{\substack{\text{Spoken} \\ \text{Words}}} \text{Cook} \xrightarrow{\substack{\text{Prepared} \\ \text{Food}}}$$

Now every so often it happened that an error was made, and the customer didn't get what he ordered. Of course you and I would have been the first to admit that we had made an error, but not all cooks and waitresses have this admirable character trait. This is rather understandable since the waitress was trying to do things correctly and rapidly (she wanted all the tips she could get!), and when she was suddenly confronted with the fact that an error had been made, her first reaction was that the cook had goofed. The cook, on the other hand, was trying to do his best. He knew in his own heart that he had prepared just what she had told him to prepare. "It's the waitress' fault," was his thought.

So what did the cook and waitress learn? Did they learn to prevent a recurrence of the error? Indeed not! The waitress learned that the cook was a stupid so-and-so, and the cook learned that the waitress was a scatterbrained so-and-so. This kind of emotionalized learning situation and strainer-of-interpersonal-relations any organization can do without—especially during the rush hours.

Changes effected

Consider now how the spindle changes all this. The waitress prepares the order slip and the cook works directly from it. If the waitress records the order incorrectly, it is obvious to her upon examining the order slip. Similarly, if the cook misreads the slip, an examination of the order slip makes it obvious to him. The fifth function of the spindle, then, is to provide "feedback" to both waitress and cook regarding errors. The spindle markedly alters the emotional relationship and redirects the learning process.

As errors are examined under conditions of feedback, new responses are engendered. The cook and waitress may find the present order slip to be hard to read, and they may request the manager to try out a different style of order slip. Now they are working together to solve the system's problems rather than working against each other and disregarding the system's problems. Maybe they find that abbreviations cause some random errors. For example, it might be that HB (Hamburger) and BB (Beefburger) get mixed up just a little too often, so the cook and waitress get together with the manager and change the name of Beefburger to Caravan Special on the menu because the new symbol (CS) will transmit itself through the system with much less ambiguity—especially during the rush hours.

HANDLING OVERLOAD

Had I been asked a few years ago to advise on human relations problems in the restaurant industry as a professional psychologist, my approach would have been limited to what I now call a "component" approach. My thinking would have been directed at the components in the system—in this case, the people involved. I would have explored such answers as incentive schemes, human relations training, selection procedures, and possibly some time-and-motion studies. My efforts would have been limited to attempts to *change the components to fit in with the system as designed no matter how poor the design might be.*

But now I would first concern myself with the "information" which must be "processed" by the system. My concern would be centered on the functions which would have to be performed by the system and how they might best be performed. I would concern myself especially with how the system is designed to handle conditions of information overload.

It is significant that in our parable the three scientists each discovered that the human relations problems arose mostly during the rush hours, in the period of "information overload." How a system responds to conditions of overload depends on how the system is designed. Let us look at how various design features permit the handling of conditions of overload in a number of different kinds of systems.

Increase in channels

One of the most common adjustments that a system makes to an excess input load is to increase the number of "channels" for handling the information. Restaurants put more waitresses and cooks on the job to handle rush-hour loads. The Post Office hires extra help before Christmas. The telephone system has recently introduced automatic-switching equipment to handle heavy communication loads; when the load gets to a certain point, additional lines are automatically "cut in" to handle the additional calls. Even our fire departments increase "channels." If there is not enough equipment at the scene, more is called in. Department stores put on additional clerks to handle holiday crowds. Military commanders augment crews in anticipation of overload conditions. Extra communication lines may be called up. More troops are deployed.

Almost everywhere we look we see that systems are very commonly designed to increase or decrease the number of channels according to the load.

Waiting lines

But there comes a time when just increasing the number of channels is not enough. Then we see another common adjustment process, that of "queuing" or forming a waiting line. There are few readers who have not had the experience of waiting in a restaurant to be seated. Other examples are common. Raw materials are stored awaiting production processes. Orders wait in queue until filled.

Manufactured goods are stored on docks awaiting shipment. The stock market ticker tape falls behind.

We have already seen how the spindle makes it unnecessary for the waitresses to queue to give orders. And we are all familiar with the modern custom in most restaurants of having a hostess take our names and the size of our party. What happens when the hostess takes our names down on paper? For one, we do not have to go through the exasperating business of jostling to hold our position in line. Also, the "holding of proper position" is done by machine; that is, it is done by the list rather than by our elbows.

Use of filtering

The hostess' list also illustrates the way in which a system can make still a third type of adjustment, that of "filtering." Because she jots down the size of the group, she can now selectively pull groups out of the queue according to the size of the table last vacated. Some readers will recall that many restaurants used to have all tables or booths of the same size and that everyone was seated in turn according to how long he had waited. It used to be infuriating for a party of four to see a single person being seated at a table for four while they continued to wait. The modern notion of accommodations of varying sizes, combined with the means for filtering, makes the use of floor space much more efficient and the waiting less lengthy. We can see filtering in other systems as well:

1. The Post Office handles registered mail before it handles other mail, delivers special delivery letters before other letters.
2. In the case of our other most important communication system, the telephone system, there is no way for dial equipment to recognize an important call from an unimportant call; it cannot tell whether a doctor is dialing or the baby is playing. However, where long-distance calls must go through operators, there is a chance for filtering. For instance, in trying to place a call to a disaster area the operator may accept only those calls which are of an emergency nature.
3. Military systems assign priorities to messages so as to assure differential handling.
4. Orders may be sent to production facilities in bunches that make up a full workday rather than in a first-in-first-out pattern. Special orders may be marked for priority attention.

Variations of omission

A system can be so designed as to permit "omissions," a simple rejection or nonacceptance of an input. The long-distance operator may refuse to accept a call as a means of preventing the lines from becoming overloaded. The dial system gives a busy signal and rejects the call. A manufacturing organization may reject an order it cannot fill within a certain time. A company may discontinue manufacture of one line temporarily in order to catch up on a more profitable line that is back-ordered.

As another example of how the design determines what adjustments the system can make, consider the way the short-order restaurant system design utilizes the omission process.

If waiting lines get too long, customers will turn away. That is not good for business, so restaurants often practice another kind of omission. On the menu you may find the words, "No substitutions." Instead of rejecting customers, the restaurants restrict the range of inputs they will accept in the way of orders. Thus time is saved in preparing the food, which in turn cuts down the waiting time in the queue.

The goal of most restaurants is to process as many customers per unit time as is possible. With a fixed profit margin per meal served, the more meals served, the more profit. But when people are in the queue, they are not spending money. One solution to this is the installation of a bar. This permits the customers to spend while waiting. It is a solution enjoyed by many customers as well as by management.

Chunking & approximating

Another big timesaver in the restaurant system is the use of a fifth adjustment process, that of "chunking." Big chunks of information can be passed by predetermined arrangements. You may find a menu so printed that it asks you to order by number. The order may be presented to the cook as "4D" (No. 4 Dinner), for example. The cook already knows what makes up the dinner and does not need to be told each item with each order. Preplanning permits chunking, and chunking frees communication channels.

Somewhat akin to the chunking process is a sixth adjustment process, "approximating." To illustrate:

1. A business forecaster may not be able to make an exact count of future sales, but he may predict confidently that the sales will be small, moderate, or large.
2. An overburdened Post Office crew may do an initial sorting of mail as "local" or "out of town."

3. An airborne radar crew may report a "large formation" headed toward the coast.
4. An intelligence agency may get a report of "heightened" air activity in a given area.
5. An investment house may predict "increased" activity in a certain line of stocks.
6. Stock market reports state that industrials are "up" and utilities are "down."

Approximating thus means making a gross discrimination of the input rather than making a fine discrimination.

Trading errors

A rather unusual adjustment process that a system can adopt to cope with overload is to accept an increase in the number of errors made. It is almost as if systems said to themselves, "It's better to make mistakes than not to deal with the input." For example, the sorting of mail is not checked during rush periods. Mail which is missent must be returned, but in a rush that risk is worth the cost; more mail gets sent where it is supposed to go even though there are more errors. Thus, quality control is given up for the sake of speed. On the other hand, some systems are so designed as to be insensitive to errors. The telephone system will permit you to dial as many wrong numbers as you are capable of dialing.

It is interesting to see in the restaurant system design a deliberate making of errors of one sort in order to prevent the making of errors of another sort during rush hours.

Picture yourself and a couple of friends dropping into a restaurant during the middle of an afternoon. You are the only customers there. The waitress takes your order. You ask for a hamburger with "everything on it." The next person asks for a hamburger but wants only lettuce and a slice of tomato on it. The third person asks for a hamburger but specifies relish and mayonnaise. The work load is low. There is time to individualize orders.

But during rush hours it would be too easy to make errors. Then the cook prepares only the meat and bun. The waitress goes to a table where there are bowls with lettuce leaves and tomato slices and little paper cups of relish and mayonnaise. On each plate she places a lettuce leaf, a tomato slice, a cup of relish, and a cup of mayonnaise. In most instances she will have brought something that the customer did not order, and in this sense she would have made an "error"; but she would have avoided the error of not bringing the customer something he *did* want.

Other examples of the same type are common. For instance, a sales department sends out brochures to everyone who inquires about a product so as not to miss someone who is really interested. Again, the Strategic Air Command, as a central policy, uses this deliberate making of one type of "error" to avoid a possible error of more severe consequences. The commander may order the force launched under "positive control." It is better to have launched in error than to be caught on the ground and destroyed.

CONCLUSION

And so we see that there is a new frame of reference, a new point of view coming into use in approaching the problems of organizations. This new frame of reference looks at organizations as systems which (1) process information, transforming the information from one form into another, and (2) are or are not designed to cope with the conditions of overload that may be imposed on them. This new frame of reference is expressed as an interest in how the structure or design of an organization dynamically influences the operating characteristics and the capacities of the system to handle various conditions of information overload.

At the University of Michigan there are some 50 scientists whose primary interests lie in looking for similarities and differences in system behavior at all levels. They examine single cells, whole organs, individuals, groups, and societies for the manners in which these systems cope with their environments in common and in unique ways. They search the work of other scientists for clues to system behavior at one level that is followed at higher or lower orders of organization. As for the application of this "system frame of reference," one finds such organizations as System Development Corporation, the RAND Corporation, and the MITRE Corporation using it in approaching the complex problems of advanced military systems. Here is just a sampling of specific developments that bear close watching:

1. Because it is possible to view organizations as systems which process data in a continuous sequence of "information transformations" and which may make numerous types of adjustments at the points of transformation, a wholly new concept of training has arisen. In the past, training in business and industry as well as in the military was largely limited to training a man or men to do a given task in a certain way. Now training can be provided that teaches a man or men to adopt adjustment processes suited to the design of the system and the condition of overload. In other words, training for

flexibility rather than rigidity is now possible. It should not be long before internal competition is replaced by internal cooperation as the main means of enhancing production.

2. Because it is possible to view a business or industry as an information processing system, it is possible to simulate the information flow on digital computers and, by controlling the adjustment processes at each point where the data are transformed, to learn what effects and costs would be involved in change. The manager will then be able to test his policies realistically on the computer before committing himself in action. A computer program called SIMPAC (Simulation Package) has already been developed at System Development Corporation for this purpose.

3. A digital computer program capable of "learning" has been developed. By analyzing how data can be sensed, compared with other data, and stored in the computer's "memory," scientists have been able to "teach" a prototype computer program to recognize letters of the alphabet, cartoon characters, and spoken words. One can look forward to the day when, opening a bank account, he will be asked to sign his name in a variety of situations—e.g., standing, sitting, bending over, and maybe even after a couple of martinis. The computer will learn to recognize his signature from these samples, and at the clearinghouse, after that, his account will be automatically debited and the payee's account automatically credited.

Ludwig von Bertalanffy, the father of general system theory, predicted that general system theory would unify the sciences, thus making it possible for a scientist trained in one area to talk in common terms with another scientist trained in another area.[3] It also seems certain that business and industry will soon profit from the application of the theory of how systems behave.

[3] "General System Theory," *General Systems*, Volume I (Ann Arbor: Society for General Systems Research, 1956), pp. 1-10.

13. HOW TO PLAN FOR MANAGE-
MENT IN NEW SYSTEMS [1]

Murray A. Geisler [2]
Wilbur A. Steger [3]

Businessmen have long known that they can, if they wish, find out a great deal in advance about how a new machine or inventory system will work by using methods of simulation. These methods range all the way from wind tunnels to elaborate sets of formulas and computers. But until recently there has been no way of learning much about how a *management team* will work in a radically new system. How will executives as a group affect the operation of, say, a completely reorganized plant, or a brand new division set up to produce and handle a revolutionary new product?

The absence of such information has been crucial to planners. Who can doubt that the management factor is sometimes more important than all the mechanical, nonhuman aspects of the new system combined? And so, despite the most careful work of operations research experts, systems engineers, and others, the expected efficiency of a proposed new system has again and again become the subject of a free-wheeling guessing game among the top executives concerned.

Now, thanks to the recently developed approach we shall describe presently, this situation is no longer so uncertain. Managerial operations *can* be simulated; much of their probable impact *can* be understood in advance. Actual tests demonstrate, for instance, that even in a radically new system much can be foretold about such questions as:

1. Will executives function more or less effectively (in terms of conventional organizational goals) than some person or group predicts?
2. What policies and rules will work best in the handling of specific problems like maintenance?

[1] From *Harvard Business Review* (September-October, 1962), pp. 103-110. Reprinted by permission of the *Harvard Business Review*.
[2] Murray A. Geisler, Assistant for Research, Logistics Department, The Rand Corporation.
[3] Wilbur A. Steger, Vice President, ConSad Corporation, and a consultant to Rand and Aerospace Corporation.

3. How should responsibility for decisions be divided between head-quarters groups and managers in the field?

In this article we shall describe the new approach, show how it works, and consider its limitations. In parts of our discussion we shall purposely err on the technical rather than the popular side, for some of the issues involved are of deep concern to men in operations research and other staff specialties who have wrestled with simulation problems before.

Main Features

The approach to be described was specifically developed by The RAND Corporation to help the U. S. Air Force contend with certain management planning problems. But it might just as well have been developed for any number of private corporations since many of the Air Force's questions were the same as those asked by industrial executives. For instance, what will be the impact on management of a changed organization, new types and flows of information, or changes in the types of decisions called "routine"? What unexpected problems will managers have to solve when the new business, product, or system is set up? Such questions are harder than usual to answer because the new system cannot be seen; in fact, it may not become operational for several years.

The new approach is called "game simulation." It is called this because it has both the relatively unstructured characteristics of business games (and war games) and the rigid, controlled qualities of traditional computer simulations.[4] To mention just the main features of the approach:

1. Executives, staff specialists, and/or others participate and make the decisions.
2. The situations they work in are simulated with the help, where necessary, of computers.
3. The participants confront many variations of detailed situations relevant to the specific problem under investigation.
4. The floor-run efforts of these studies are usually large-scale (as research studies go), involving as many as 25 to 50 participants and staff personnel.
5. Background research for the exercises *may* require as much time as

[4] See, for example, Harvey N. Shycon and Richard B. Maffei, "Simulation—Tool for Better Distribution," *Harvard Business Review* (November-December, 1960), p. 65.

12 months of hypothesis formulation, computer modeling, practice mockups, and data gathering.
6. Following the runs of the floor research, it may take six months to analyze and report the results.

Better predictions

We come now to a very significant point about the game-simulation approach. It is a point that can be appreciated most keenly by experienced executives.

Most attempts to simulate systems and situations with computers have abstracted the human element, so to speak; that is, they have set it apart as a separate factor making it only a link in the system. Ordinarily, the result has been to degrade or reduce the performance of the system. This is not so with the game-simulation approach. It is just as useful in situations where managers team together to make the system *more* effective as it is in situations where they tend to reduce performance.

We are all familiar with ways in which people affect systems in this manner. We have seen them:

1. Learning better how to plan and control funds, supplies, and other resources to achieve management goals.
2. Improvising on and improving the operation of the system itself.
3. Improving their understanding of—or perhaps even seeking—higher system goals.
4. Making complex decisions where the "rationality" of the decisions is difficult to define in precise, mathematical ways. All these effects are important in business operations.

But we cannot represent them in numbers and equations for computers, nor can we predict them accurately from previous experience for a new and untested system.

In view of the great bearing management insights and decisions will have on the choice of resources for supporting a not-yet-existing and radically different system, their importance in the planning stage, *as in the management system eventually evolved*, cannot be overemphasized. If, during the operational phases of a system's life, an efficient management system will permit the freeing of resources over time (while still getting the job done), planners must know this in advance if they are to make decisions efficiently. Perhaps even more important, no resources *will* become free if the management portion of the system is not developed *before* the rest of the system becomes operational.

These statements are not mere supposition. Experience backs them up. Many systems in the past, both military and commercial, have failed to attain their full effectiveness until several years after their initial operation—sometimes too late to satisfy the needs they were designed to meet. One military aircraft weapon system, for example, took more than ten years to reach its full potential. The fact is, only negligible changes were made in the "hardware" portion of the system itself, complex as it was; the more-than-*tenfold* increase in system performance during the period was almost entirely attributable to that intangible known as "management"! Thus the aim of game simulation is to speed up development in cases like the preceding one—and help get it started, at the outset of operations, at a higher level.

At least two lessons become clear when experiences like the foregoing are subjected to analysis:

1. A management system is so complex—involving as it does so many manifestations of man's sometimes unpredictable behavior in large organizations—that it takes a great deal of thought and time to embody slight changes from an older management system in a newer organization. Particularly when these changes require formal alterations in the organization's information systems, or in the organizational structure itself, it may take years to introduce them. In the military, for example, such changes have been known to take as long to become operational as have the development, testing, and production of a modern hardware system itself.

2. Many management improvements are related directly to a particular system's "hardware" (e.g., a certain kind of warehouse or transportation) and are the result of some form of "inductive learning" about that hardware. But it takes time to develop and incorporate such improvements consistently throughout an organization. Furthermore, potentially desirable combinations may never be realized in most companies because radical changes are not likely to be tried except under the experimental and research conditions visualized for our game-simulation approach. Once the fat is in the fire, with machines to run, schedules to meet, and jobs to keep, men are naturally less likely to do a lot of experimenting.

FASTER LEARNING

To appreciate more fully why game-simulation techniques can be an invaluable aid to designers of complex management systems, let us examine the learning process closely. Learning might be broken down into these four working categories:

1. How to perform the *routine* tasks in a new system more efficiently.

2. How to define the system's goals (main objectives as well as more limited ones, viz., "sub-goals").
3. How to deal with the uncertainty and the unanticipated problems that arise in the system.
4. How to make the system more effective, using inductive learning (e.g., observation, reflection, imagination, and so forth).

Let us proceed to examine each of these four categories in turn.

Routine tasks

When top management thinks ahead about a new organization, it is not easy to judge what the routine jobs will be and how they could be done better. For example, one man's work will be affected by another's, and in many systems there will be a whole series of inter-related administrative activities to keep track of. Many of them might be classified as follows:

1. *Filtering*—separating, assigning priorities to, and screening data for routine handling.
2. *Load sharing*—relieving overloaded situations.
3. *Load balancing*—taking supervisory action to adjust the work load of subordinates.
4. *Adapting*—employing forces appropriately in changing situations.
5. *Adjusting*—dealing flexibly with new situations or problems.
6. *Communicating*—receiving and imparting information.
7. *Interacting*—handling the interrelationships of managers and employees.
8. *Coordinating*—acting in common with others.
9. *Checking*—preventing, detecting, and correcting errors.
10. *Expediting*—speeding up progress and dispatching work promptly.[5]

Combinations of these elements are undoubtedly what cause humans to have a "routine" impact on a system's cost or effectiveness. The problem facing a member of a complex system—or an evaluator of his performance—is that it is difficult to know which behavior (except for certain extreme activities) increases system effectiveness per budget dollar and which decreases it. Where it is possible to model a complex system *abstractly*, but with sufficient realism to study the effect of certain aspects of human behavior on organizational effectiveness, substantial gains can be expected. This is particularly true when the environment does not yet actually exist, as

---

[5] See Alvin M. Freed, *Measuring Human System Behavior in the Operational Man-Machine System*, System Development Corporation, Document SD-3325 (January 8, 1960), pp. 21-22.

would be so in the case of a not-yet-operational weapon or an "improved" management policy (on paper).

Defining goals

As anyone knows who has worked with complex systems, the functions of groups in a large organization often cannot be described simply in terms of independent subproblems each with its own subcriteria, one tied to the next in an ascending order; there are too many interactions between *apparently* independent elements. A great deal of cooperation and coordination is necessary under the most ordinary of conditions. Where the output of one group depends on the operations (or the combinations of inputs) used in another group, or where both groups draw on the same inputs, decentralization of responsibility for achieving goals is not compatible with over-all "maximization" of performance. This makes the problem of assigning jobs and tasks to accomplish—a tough one under the best of circumstances—very difficult.

To compound the difficulty, over-all standards and criteria for evaluating organizational performance often can be developed only by working with the problems over a period of time.

Game simulation is one important aid in solving this problem, particularly when no analogous organizations exist or when one exists but cannot be experimented with. To mention just a few of the advantages:

1. Coordination and cooperation between groups participating is a bargaining process with game overtones. There is both the reality of people at work and an atmosphere of freedom to experiment.
2. If participants set too conservative a goal for themselves at first (which is likely in a new and uncertain situation), they can raise their sights gradually as they gain experience.
3. When experimenting with simulated organizations, it is feasible to reshuffle functions and subgoals among portions of the organizations.
4. It is not necessary to equate the individual's goals and those of the organization he works in. In industry, the sacrificing of the individual's goals to the organization's—or the devising of organizations that can "maximize the sum" of organization and individual goals— now poses significant problems in distinguishing what is done from what could be done.[6]

[6] Mason Haire, "Psychology and the Study of Business," in *Social Science Research on Business: Product and Potential,* by Robert A. Dahl, Mason Haire, and Paul F. Lazarsfeld (New York: Columbia University Press, 1959), p. 71.

Dealing with uncertainty

Discussions of uncertainty, expectation formation, and decision making have revealed many unresolved differences of opinion. One school of thought, the Simon-Newell school, characterizes "rational" decision making in the face of uncertainty as consisting of "unprogramed" (and therefore "unprogramable in advance") decisions. According to this view, before the choices can be brought within the limits of human computation, simplified constructs of reality first have to be approximated by the decision-maker.[7] Here the advantages of game simulation are clear, for the conditions to be experienced can be simulated.

However, others emphasize the relatively *nonprobabilistic* aspects of uncertainty; what they have in mind is the fact that decision-makers (a) do not know all the consequences attached to a given alternative and (b) do not possess a complete ordering of alternatives for all possible sets of circumstances. Search actions and innovation are the first choices in such situations; activities designed to reduce uncertainty are favored by managers. Such processes depart (except in the broadest sense) from the rational assessment of probabilities on which so much of statistical decision theory is based.

Is game simulation impractical if this view of decision making is held, or where decisions seem to have more of this character than of rationality and probability? We do not think so. Nor do we feel that such decisions must be regarded as "unanalyzable." After all, human decision making of this sort has been analyzed by empirical scientists—economists, psychologists, and historians—for many years. If the best estimate of the real-life problems of a not-yet-existing complex system is that it will involve nonprobabilistic uncertainties, manned simulation can be very helpful, indeed, in predicting the outcome of that system—or of an alternative system—provided that the modeled environment can simulate, in a rich enough manner, the *kinds* of uncertainties that will arise and exist.

Inductive learning

In almost every new organization or project there is a good possibility that performance will fall below the expected or desirable level and cause people to search for better solutions. Manned simulations seem to offer today's most practicable way of putting our

---

[7] Geoffrey P. E. Clarkson and Herbert A. Simon, "Simulation of Individual and Group Behavior," *American Economic Review* (December, 1960), pp. 920-932.

cheapest "thinking machines"—people—into the largest possible variety of learning-producing situations.

But some will ask, why not work out the possibilities for improvement concisely, speedily, and comprehensively with "computerized" simulations? One reason is that humans do not think the way computers do—and remember, it is *managerial* performance that we are concerned with. For situations of even moderate complexity, the human organism does not possess the input speed, memory, computing capacity, and *systematically* reached preference scales required by computer programs. This being true, many choices facing a decision-maker in a complex system will involve—at least at first glance—uncertain and (on the surface) incomparable alternatives.

It is at this point that heuristic reasoning—"reasoning not regarded as final and strict, but as provisional and plausible only, whose purpose is to discover the solution of the present problem" [8]— becomes good reasoning, which should unashamedly be put in the place of processes demanding rigorous proofs. Many of the good solutions to problems in both the real world and in a laboratory simulation of a complex system must be of this variety. This does not mean that no further research into the "goodness" of a solution should be performed, following an apparent improvement that a participant has made on the basis of insight. *Where practical* (it may prove to be so in a distressingly small number of cases), analysis of the "goodness" of heuristic solutions can indeed be attempted by all-computer methods.

Another reason for using the game-simulation approach has to do with human errors. The neglect of the level of human-introduced error often leads planners to a very poor prediction of system performance. Such errors can be due to the mismatching of machines to the physiology of man, but often they are due to a poor display of information, excessive demands on human problem-solving ability, and the like. For this reason the efficiency of a system design which takes account of such errors in man-machine systems may not compare very well with one that disregards this possibility!

Case Study

Now let us examine an actual case in the use of game simulation. The case involved a new, highly complex weapon system that was

---

[8] György Polya, *How To Solve It* (New York: Doubleday Anchor Books, 1957), p. 113.

about to be phased into the operations of the U. S. Air Force. The need was to assess alternative systems of management for the project. Despite the military setting, the situation involved various problems similar to those that large, private corporations face in long-range planning—for example, efforts to anticipate how proposed investment policies or organizational changes will fare in the future.

While the particular situation represented by this case was very complex, with long lead times, it should be borne in mind that problems do not *have* to be so enormous to justify the use of game simulation. This approach can of course be scaled down so that it will be appropriate in simpler situations.

The problem

Here, in brief, are a few elements of the problem that RAND studied (the project was called Laboratory Problem II):

> The Air Force wanted to adapt the typical information and feedback processes of a control system to the military environment posed by ballistic missiles in the 1963-1965 time period. These missiles, dispersed over a wide geographic area, had to be maintained on a high level of alert, responsive to sudden emergencies. Since the cost of the missile systems was very great, efforts were continually being made to hold to a minimum the resources needed to do an acceptable job. One way to do this was to be able to shift resources (within the constraints of possible sudden war) from one place to another responsively, since the demands for resources at any one place were typically sporadic and low. Further, the support costs in equipment and facilities comprised so large a fraction of the total system cost that minimum missile-system downtime was desirable not only for military but for economic reasons.
>
> The scheduling rules assigning missiles to various degrees of alert and assigning the resources to repair missiles requiring preventive or other prescribed maintenance were found to be the critical decisions in the squadron. The formulation of precise scheduling rules by mathematical analysis was found to be very difficult because of the many combinations of conditions and constraints that had to be considered. In effect, the implications of the schedule had to be determined by support units (or missile "black boxes"), and there were over 50,000 such support units on the operational missile system in a tactical unit. Finally, the schedule was affected, to some extent, in each simulated 15-minute period, as one or more missiles or supporting resources changed status.

Gains achieved

What were the results of the game-simulation study? Some of the most significant ones follow:

1. Useful scheduling rules were developed by trying many rules of thumb during the experiment. The rules that seemed to work best were called "opportunistic scheduling." Under these rules, all prescribed maintenance was deferred as long as the policies permitted. Then, when a missile malfunctioned, all possible prescribed maintenance that could be done concurrently was accomplished at that time. In this way, missiles were taken off alert for as little time as possible for prescribed maintenance. It is interesting to note that the preferred rules of thumb were not conceived before the experiment was begun but were instead evolved, to a significant degree, by the participants from the Air Force.

2. Under the stress of a very difficult set of problems and a relatively new environment, the "predicted" effectiveness of the management team did not materialize. When simpler models had been used, or non-Air Force personnel had been used in practice mock-ups, the over-all results were not the same. Under relatively conventional decision rules, *over-all effectiveness from 10% to 20% less than was eventually produced (during the actual floor flow-runs) was the best rough estimate.*

3. The squadron headquarters found that it could not centrally handle all the decisions in the system, many of which were tied closely to local situations. It therefore worked out conditions under which officers at the place of launch could act without prior approval of the squadron headquarters and also conditions under which prior approval would be necessary. These conditions were further developed in the study into rules of thumb or "heuristic rules," since the relationships appeared to be too complicated for analytic solution.

4. The data produced by the squadron managers in the course of their minute-to-minute operational decision making were also used by them and higher headquarters for longer run or planning decisions. These data were used to estimate resource demands and utilization, which provided the basis for determining required manning, equipping, and stockage of the launch installations and squadron echelons. These data reflected the particular decision rules used to schedule the employment of the resources, and so there was a direct relationship between the short-run operational decision rules (like minute-to-minute scheduling) and the longer run planning decisions (like determination of the resource requirements of the squadron).

Requirements

Clearly, the "opportunistic" rules that evolved during the experiment required a highly responsive organization and information system; managers had to be ready to react instantaneously to any missile malfunction, change in resource status, or other development under conditions of wide dispersion. As a missile or resource changed status, the information in the system was therefore updated through appropriate inputs. As a new situation occurred, each of the managers interrogated the information system for the implications it had for his function (such as operations, supply, or maintenance), revised his schedule accordingly, and assigned available resources to the urgent activities.

During the experiment, the information system was able to respond instantaneously to such interrogations, because all the necessary information had been placed in a very large random-access memory which could be interrogated quickly. Since the system status changed very rapidly, an input system had to be devised which would quickly update the status. This meant that input data had to be minimized, which in turn was done by requiring only a single input of each necessary data element that served all managers.

Since the organization had to respond very quickly to emergencies, a good deal of functional integration was required. Operations, maintenance, and supply in the squadron headquarters had to work closely as a team since each was affected by emergencies. In addition, close communication between the launch installations and the squadron headquarters had to be maintained. To do this, report formats were evolved which helped to present to each manager the consequences of another function's decisions for him, and the consequences of his decisions for them. In this way, each manager was able to react rapidly to decisions that might affect his plans.

Conclusion

The idea of using executives in simulations of future organizations, projects, and problems to improve the operation of the management system is a new one. The study just described is only one of a few that have been undertaken. Hence it is important to keep game simulation in perspective—its broad values and limitations—so that companies will adopt and invest in it wisely.

Distinguishing features

The high costs of the new approach, both in dollars and design effort, require that the problems attacked be complex and important, and the research budgets large. In some respects, this approach is similar to techniques more widely used in systems research: gaming and computer simulation analyses. This is because the attempt has been made to borrow and combine some of the better features of both—the flexibility and inventiveness of the former and the quickly generated "realism" of the latter for more routine aspects—so as to achieve a comparatively rigorous *prediction* of the decision-making behavior of managers in realistic situations. How will they operate? How will their work affect the efficiency of the new system?

In effect, the peculiar advantage being claimed for the type of simulation under discussion here is that the knowledge gained about the future management system is frequently *new*, that is, never discovered before. Note the contrast with business games. In business games ideas are often uncovered that are new to the participant but *not* new to the businessmen who have been playing the games for many years. In addition, the game-simulation technique has enough realism in detail and inputs to enable a thorough evaluation of the "goodness" of the learning experienced during the exercise.

The distinguishing features of the game-simulation technique can be summarized as follows:

1. The focus, during the planning stages of a system, is on what the *management* portion of it should look like when it goes into operation.
2. It fosters the development of creative insights into the proposed management system. These insights can be valuable in training and preparing men for operating responsibilities.
3. Decision-making, organizational, and informational questions are set up and analyzed in a nonmathematical way (although statistics may enter into the decisions, as in real life).
4. As for the men participating in the game-simulation exercises, their ability to learn quickly and accurately is enhanced by several important factors:
   a. Time compression permits a rapid "feedback" to decision makers.
   b. They can see the entire "system," albeit in an abstract way; their view is not limited to special functions.
   c. The decision-makers see the measurable impact of their choices more clearly.
   d. Considerably less "punishment" is in store for the men making mistakes in a game simulation than in the real world.

Limitations

The millennium has not yet arrived. Many obstacles must still be surmounted before game simulation can become a *widely* used research tool. For example:

1. *The high costs of a simulation like that described for the Air Force.* The costs of the wide scope, great detail, and the use of humans in simulations make this sort of experiment usable primarily for designing larger, complex "man-machine" systems. Of course, some of these costs would have to be borne by any sizable study of a control system, but others can be reduced by turning to suitable compiler programs and by using only the degree of detail necessary to obtain

the desired results. The costs should not, therefore, always be as high as at present.

2. *Experimental design problems.* Manned simulation experiments cannot produce, for an equal research budget, the same number and length of runs that their all-computer brethren can. This makes it difficult to perform the desired amount of sensitivity testing or to run studies long enough to wipe out, fully, the effects of initial conditions. However, work is proceeding at RAND and elsewhere on experimental design techniques to mitigate these effects.

3. *Inability to produce optimal designs.* Simulations, by their very nature, produce at best highly preferred—but not optimal—policies. Bear in mind, though, that the development of all-computer simulation and analytic models based on manned simulation as a breadboard model should help considerably to improve and refine results.

4. *Defining a suitable level of scope and detail.* The system-designer might wish the simulation activity to produce answers to highly specific questions, but this requires the simulation activity to represent great amounts of detail and many functions and organizations. This is costly and makes analysis more difficult. Therefore, we must better understand how to deal with management control problems in an abstract way for simulation purposes, yet realistically enough to produce valid design factors for real-world application.

In addition to these, an important limitation cannot have escaped the attention of those trained in more analytical methods: no one can claim to predict system performance with a high degree of confidence while using this method. Otherwise, one would have to assert that all of man's managerial inventiveness had been exhausted *prior* to the system's initial operation! Nevertheless, to the extent that the game-simulation approach succeeds in rapidly producing managerial insights that can later be incorporated in the operating system, performance prediction is enhanced. No simulation, however perfect, can exhaust the possibility that men will later improve the system's performance in operation even more than they did in the study. Nevertheless, such a simulated environment will aid planners in determining which human actions will not *degrade* a complex system's performance but, rather, will work toward its betterment.

On balance, therefore, game simulation seems to have proved itself well. Without such an approach man's role in new management systems cannot be adequately evaluated; and, without an evaluation of their role, the whole structure of plant, equipment, and people is hard to appraise. It is especially significant that the new approach can help planning executives determine what kinds of managerial action will not degrade a complex system's performance but will help to make it work better.

BIBLIOGRAPHY, CHAPTER IV

BEER, STAFFORD. *Cybernetics and Management.* New York: John Wiley & Sons, Inc., 1959.

BOULDING, KENNETH E. "General Systems Theory—The Skeleton of Science," *Management Science* (April, 1956), 197-208.

CHAPIN, NED. *An Introduction to Automatic Computers.* New York: D. Van Nostrand Company, Inc., 1957. Chapter 4.

CHAPMAN, R., and J. L. KENNEDY. "The Background and Implication of the Rand Corporation Systems Research Laboratory Studies," Rubenstein and Haberstroh, *Some Theories of Organization.* Homewood, Illinois: The Dorsey Press Inc., 1960. 139.

ECKMAN, DONALD P. *Systems: Research and Design.* New York: John Wiley & Sons, Inc., 1961.

EDWARDS, WARD. "The Theory of Decision Making," *Some Theories of Organization,* Rubenstein and Haberstroh. Homewood, Illinois: The Dorsey Press, Inc., 1960.

GALLAGHER, JAMES D. *Management Information Systems and the Computer.* New York: American Management Association, Inc., 1961.

GOODE, HARRY H., and ROBERT E. MACHOL. *System Engineering.* New York: McGraw-Hill Book Company, Inc., 1957.

JOHNSON, RICHARD A., et al., *The Theory and Management of Systems.* New York: McGraw-Hill Book Company, Inc., 1962.

JONAS, H. "Critique of Cybernetics," *Social Research* (July, 1953), 172-192.

KAPPLER, M. O. *Automated Information Processing in Command Control Systems,* System Development Corporation, SP159 (April 11, 1960).

MILLER, D. W., and M. K. STARR. *Executive Decisions and Operations Research.* Englewood Cliffs, New Jersey: Prentice-Hall, Inc., 1960. Chapter 2.

OPTNER, STANFORD L. *Systems Analysis for Business Management.* Englewood Cliffs, New Jersey: Prentice-Hall, Inc., 1960. 3-30.

TAYLOR, SIDNEY W. "Systems . . . Panoramic Approach to Management," *Armed Forces Management* (May, 1958), 30-32.

WEINWURM, G. F. "Computer Management Control Systems Through the Looking Glass," *Management Science* (July, 1961), 411.

Chapter V

Communications and Information

Communication of information in organizations provides data for managers to plan and control operations. Throughout organizations there are information processing groups whose responsibility it is to transform raw and semiprocessed data into forms for managerial decisions. In spite of these needs and activities, providing information in proper form, content, and at appropriate intervals remains a major problem in business organizations.

In Article 14 D. Ronald Daniel discusses the needs for information and the methods to be used in designing systems of information flows. Schuyler Dean Hoslett in Article 15 probes the basic reasons that misunderstanding and communication failures occur in groups. In the next article Keith Davis substantiates these failures to establish better communications as he shows that patterns of communication within the management structure do not necessarily take the forms envisaged by the planners of the formal communication systems. Since failures in communication often are attributable to misunderstanding by the receiver of data, the final selection in the chapter is devoted to the subject of listening.

It should be noted that communication has both its formal aspects as required by the decision centers in the organization structure and its informal aspects as required by informal groupings.

14. MANAGEMENT INFORMATION CRISIS [1]

D. Ronald Daniel [2]

In late 1960 a large defense contractor became concerned over a major project that was slipping badly. After 15 months costs were running far above the estimate and the job was behind schedule. A top-level executive, assigned as program manager to salvage the project, found he had no way of pinpointing what parts of the system were causing the trouble, why costs were so high, and which subcontractors were not performing.

Recently an American electronics company revamped its organization structure. To compete more aggressively in international markets, management appointed "area managers" with operating responsibility—e.g., in Latin America, Western Europe, and the Far East. After nine months it was apparent that the new plan was not coming up to expectations. On checking with three newly created area managers, the company president heard each say, in effect:

1. *In half of the countries in my area the political situation is in flux, and I can't anticipate what's going to happen next.*
2. *I'm still trying to find out whether our operating costs in Austria are reasonable.*
3. *I don't know where in South America we're making a profit.*

A small but highly successful consumer products company recently followed the lead of its larger competitors by establishing product-manager positions. Although outstanding men were placed in the new jobs, an air of general confusion soon developed, and the product managers began to show signs of frustration. After much study it became apparent that an important cause of the trouble was that no one had determined what kind of information the product managers would need in order to perform their new functions.

[1] From *Harvard Business Review*, Vol. 39, No. 5 (September-October, 1961), pp. 111-121. Reprinted by permission of the *Harvard Business Review*.

[2] D. Ronald Daniel, McKinsey & Company, Inc.

In retrospect it is obvious that these three companies were plagued by a common problem: inadequate management information. The data were inadequate, not in the sense of there not being enough, but in terms of relevancy for setting objectives, for shaping alternative strategies, for making decisions, and for measuring results against planned goals.

Assessing the Gap

In each company the origin of the problem lay in the gap between a static information system and a changing organization structure. This difficulty is not new or uncommon. There is hardly a major company in the United States whose plan of organization has not been changed and rechanged since World War II. And with revised structures have come new jobs, new responsibilities, new decision-making authorities, and reshaped reporting relationships. All of these factors combine to create new demands for information —information that is usually missing in existing systems. As a result, many leading companies are suffering a major information crisis—often without fully realizing it.

Far-reaching trends

Some idea of the scope of this problem can be gained by reviewing the intensity of the three major causes of recent organization changes in American business.

Growth. Since 1945 the Gross National Product has risen 135%. In specific industries the growth rate has been even greater. Plastic production, for example, tripled between 1948 and 1958; electronics sales nearly quadrupled in the decade from 1950 to 1960. Many individual companies have shown even more startling growth. This growth, in turn, has fostered organizational change:

1. Divisions have been created and decentralization has been encouraged.
2. Greater precision in defining line-staff relationships has been necessitated.
3. Organization structures that were once adequate for $50-millon businesses have proved unworkable for $500-million enterprises.

Diversification. Merger and acquisition have accounted for the growth of many large organizations. For these companies, the task of finding, evaluating, and consummating diversification deals—and assimilating newly acquired products and businesses—has required continuous organizational adjustment. Some corporations have diversified by developing new product lines to satisfy shifting market requirements; some have used other means. But always the effect has been the same: different organization structures for parts of or perhaps for the entire enterprise.

International operations. There has been a threefold increase in the value of United States investments abroad since World War II. Major companies that once regarded foreign markets as minor sources of incremental profits, or as markets for surplus production, now look overseas for the bulk of their future profits and growth. They are setting up manufacturing and research as well as marketing organizations in foreign countries. Consequently, we are growing used to seeing a company's "export department" evolve into the "international division," and national companies grow into world-wide enterprises.[3] All this calls for extensive modifications of organization structure.

The impact of any one of the above factors alone would be sufficient to create great change in an enterprise, but consider that in many cases at least two, and sometimes all three, have been at work. It is easy to see why so many company organization structures do become unstable and how this creates a management information problem large enough to hamper some firms and nearly paralyze others.

Linking systems and needs

Organization structure and information requirements are inextricably linked. In order to translate a statement of his duties into action, an executive must receive and use information. Information in this case is not just the accounting system and the forms and reports it produces. It includes *all* the data and intelligence—financial and nonfinancial—that are really needed to plan, operate, and control a particular enterprise. This embraces external information such as economic and political factors and data on competitive activity.

When viewed in this light, the impact of organization structure on needs for management information becomes apparent. The trouble

---

[3] See Gilbert H. Clee and Alfred di Scipio, "Creating a *World* Enterprise," *Harvard Business Review* (November-December, 1959), p. 77.

is that in most companies it is virtually taken for granted that the information necessary for performance of a manager's duties flows naturally to the job. To a certain extent this is so. For example, internally generated information—especially accounting information —does tend to flow easily to the job or can be made to do so. Also, in companies doing business in only one industry and having a small, closely knit management group much vital interdepartmental and general information is conveyed by frequent face-to-face contact and coordination among executives. Economic and competitive information from outside is similarly transmitted, the bulk of it coming into the concern informally. Further, through trade contacts, general reading, and occasional special studies, executives toss bits of information into the common pool and draw from it as well.

The point is, however, that while such an informal system can work well for small and medium-size companies in simple and relatively static industries, it becomes inadequate when companies grow larger and especially when they spread over several industries, areas, and countries. At this point, most large companies have found that information has to be conveyed in a formal manner and less and less through direct observation.

Unfortunately, management often loses sight of the seemingly obvious and simple relationship between organization structure and information needs. Companies very seldom follow upon reorganizations with penetrating reappraisals of their information systems, and managers given new responsibilities and decision-making authority often do not receive all the information they require.

Causes of confusion

The cornerstone for building a compact, useful management information system is the determination of each executive's information needs. This requires a clear grasp of the individual's role in the organization—his responsibilities, his authorities, and his relationships with other executives. The task is then to:

1. Design a network of procedures that will process raw data in such a way as to generate the information required for management use.
2. Implement such procedures in actual practice.

Such action steps, while demanding and time-consuming, have proved to be far less difficult than the creative and conceptual first step of defining information requirements. Seldom is the open approach of asking an executive what information he requires successful. For one thing, he may find it difficult to be articulate because the organization structure of his company is not clearly defined.

Further, and more important, there is a widespread tendency among operating executives to think of information exclusively in terms of their companies' accounting systems and the reports thus generated. This way of thinking can be a serious deterrent because:

1. Many conventional accounting reports cause confusion in the minds of nonfinancially trained executives. Take, for example, the profit-and-loss statement, with its arbitrary treatment of inventories, depreciation, allocated overhead expenses, and the like, or the statistical sales report, which is often a 40-page, untitled, machine-prepared tabulation of sales to individual customers. Such reports have made an indelible impression on managers' thinking, coloring their understanding and expectations of reports in general.
2. By its very nature traditional accounting fails to highlight many important aspects of business operations. Accounting systems often are designed primarily to meet SEC, Internal Revenue, and other statutory requirements—requirements that, more often than not, fail to correspond to management's information needs. Accounting describes the past in dollars, usually without discriminating between the critical and noncritical elements of a business—the elements that control competitive success in a particular industry and the elements that do not.
3. Accounting reports generally describe what has happened inside a company. Just consider what this approach omits:
   a. Information about the future.
   b. Data expressed in nonfinancial terms—e.g., share of market, productivity, quality levels, adequacy of customer service, and so on.
   c. Information dealing with external conditions as they might bear on a particular company's operations.

   Yet all of these items are essential to the intelligent managing of a business.

PLANNING NEEDS DEFINED

The key to the development of a dynamic and usable system of management information is to move beyond the limits of classical accounting reports and to conceive of information as it relates to two vital elements of the management process—planning and control. In the pages to follow I shall focus largely on the planning aspect.

We hear more and more these days about new techniques for inventory, cost, and other types of control, but information systems for business planning still represent a relatively unexplored horizon.

Planning, as used in this article, means: setting objectives, formulating strategy, and deciding among alternative investments or courses of action. This definition can be applied to an entire company, an integrated division, or a single operating department.

As Exhibit I shows, the information required to do planning of this kind is of three basic types:

1. *Environmental information.* Describes the social, political, and economic aspects of the climate in which a business operates or may operate in the future.
2. *Competitive information.* Explains the past performance, programs, and plans of competing companies.
3. *Internal information.* Indicates a company's own strengths and weaknesses.

Now let us consider each of these categories in some detail.

Environmental information

The environmental data category is one of the least formalized and hence least used parts of a management information system in most companies. Specific examples of the data included in this category are:

1. Population—current levels, growth trends, age distribution, geographical distribution, effect on unemployment.
2. Price levels—retail, wholesale, commodities, government regulation.
3. Transportation—availability, costs, competition, regulation.
4. Foreign trade—balance of payments, exchange rates, convertibility.
5. Labor force—skills, availability, wages, turnover, unions.

To this list a company operating internationally would add another item—systematic collection and interpretation, on a country-by-country basis, of information on political and economic conditions in the foreign areas where business is being done. Here is an example of what can be accomplished:

A well-established internationl corporation with a highly sophisticated management makes a three-pronged effort to get data on local political and economic conditions. (a) There is a small but highly competent and well-paid four-man staff at corporate headquarters which travels extensively and publishes, using its own observations plus a variety of other sources, a weekly commentary on world events as they relate to the company. (b) This corporation has trained all its country managers to be keen observers of their local scene and to report their interpretive comments to headquarters regularly. (c) There is a little-talked-about group of "intelligence agents" who are not on the company's official payroll but are nevertheless paid for the information they pass along.

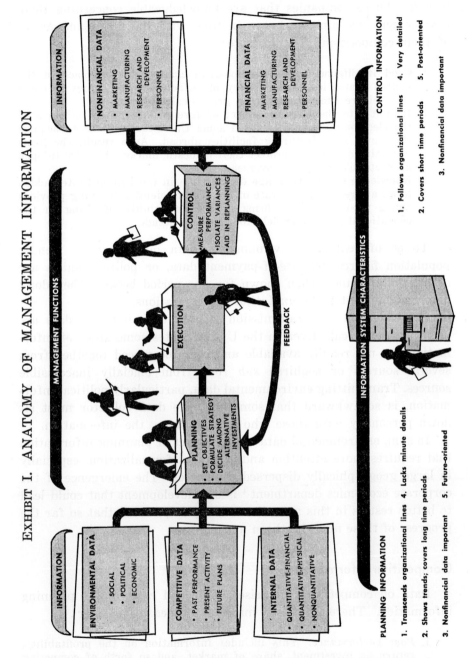

EXHIBIT I. ANATOMY OF MANAGEMENT INFORMATION

Certainly, not every organization has to go to these ends to keep itself informed of the situation in which it operates. However, those organizations that ignore environmental data or that leave its collection to the informal devices of individual executives are inviting trouble. Those companies that are knowledgeable concerning their environment are almost always in tune with the times and ahead of their competition. To illustrate:

1. Good intelligence on the sociological changes taking place in the United States led several heavy manufacturing companies to enter the "leisure time" field with a great deal of success.
2. Insight into the possible impact of foreign labor costs on parts of the electronics industry caused some U. S. corporations to acquire their own manufacturing facilities abroad. As a result, the firms were able not only to protect their domestic markets but also to open up profitable operations overseas.
3. Knowledge of trends in age distribution in the United States added to an awareness of the rate of change of scientific learning provides ample proof for some firms of the desirability of being in the educational publishing field for the next decade.

To be of real use, environmental data must indicate trends; population figures, balance-of-payment data, or political shifts are of little significance when shown for one period because they don't help management make *analytical* interpretations.

The collection and transmission of good environmental data are often problematical. Even in the United States some kinds of information are not readily available and must be pieced together from several sources or acquired *sub rosa* from officially inaccessible sources. Transmitting environmental data, particularly political information, is so awkward that sometimes the data collector must sit down personally with those who need to know the information.

In sum, environmental data are an aspect of planning information that requires more attention and warrants formalization, especially in large geographically dispersed companies. The emergence of the corporate economics department [4] is one development that could lead to better results in this area, but it is my impression that so far the progress of these units has been uneven.

Competitive information

Data on competition comprise the second category of planning information. There are three important types to consider:

1. *Past performance.* This includes information on the profitability, return on investment, share of market, and so forth of competing

[4] Clark S. Teitsworth, "Growing Role of the Company Economist," *Harvard Business Review* (January-February, 1959), p. 97; and the article by Henry B. Arthur in this issue, p. 80.

companies. Such information is primarily useful in identifying one's competitors. It also is one benchmark when setting company objectives.

2. *Present activity.* This category covers new product introductions, management changes, price strategy, and so on—all current developments. Good intelligence on such matters can materially influence a company's planning; for example, it may lead to accelerating research programs, modifying advertising strategy, or switching distribution channels. The implication here is not that a company's plans should always be defensive and prompted by a competitor's moves but simply that anything important a competitor does should be recognized and factored into the planning process.

3. *Future plans.* This includes information on acquisition intentions, facility plans, and research and development efforts.

Competitive information, like environmental data, is an infrequently formalized part of a company's total information system. And so there seldom is a concerted effort to collect this kind of material, to process it, and to report it to management regularly. But some interesting exceptions to this general lack of concern exist:

1. Oil companies have long employed "scouts" in their land departments. These men report on acreage purchases, drilling results, and other competitive activity that may be pertinent to the future actions of their own company.

2. Business machine companies have "competitive equipment evaluation personnel" who continually assess the technical features of competitors' hardware.

3. Retail organizations employ "comparison shoppers" who appraise the prices and quality of merchandise in competitive stores.

Commercial intelligence departments are appearing more and more on corporate organization charts. An excerpt from the charter of one such group states its basic responsibility thus:

> To seek out, collect, evaluate, and report information covering the past performance and future plans of competitors in such a manner that the information will have potential utility in strategic and operational planning of the corporation. This means that in addition to reporting factual information, emphasis should be on determining the implications of such information for the corporation.

Internal information

The third and final basic category of planning information is made up of internal data. As it relates to the total planning process, internal data are aimed at identifying a company's strengths and weaknesses—the characteristics that, when viewed in the perspective of the general business environment and in the light of competitive activity, should help management to shape its future plans. It is useful to think of internal data as being of three types:

1. *Quantitative-financial*—e.g., sales, costs, and cost behavior relative to volume changes.
2. *Quantitative-physical*—e.g., share of market, productivity, delivery performance, and manpower resources.
3. *Nonquantitative*—e.g., community standing and labor relations.

In reporting internal data, a company's information system must be discriminating and selective. It should focus on "successive factors." In most industries there are usually three to six factors that determine success; these key jobs must be done exceedingly well for a company to be successful. Here are some examples from several major industries:

1. In the automobile industry, styling, an efficient dealer organization, and tight control of manufacturing costs are paramount.
2. In food processing, new product development, good distribution, and effective advertising are the major success factors.
3. In life insurance, the development of agency management personnel, effective control of clerical personnel, and innovation in creating new types of policies spell the difference.

The companies which have achieved the greatest advances in information analysis have consistently been those which have developed systems that have (a) been selective and (b) focused on the company's strengths and weaknesses with respect to its acknowledged success factors. By doing this, the managements have generated the kind of information that is most useful in capitalizing on strengths and correcting weaknesses. To illustrate:

> An oil company devised a system of regularly reporting its "finding" costs—those costs incurred in exploring for new reserves of oil divided by the number of barrels of oil found. When this ratio trended upward beyond an established point, it was a signal to the company's management to consider the acquisition of other oil companies (together with their proved reserves) as a less expensive alternative to finding oil through its own exploratory efforts.

In the minds of most executives the accounting system exists primarily to meet the company's internal data needs; yet this is often an unreasonable and unfulfilled expectation. Accounting reports rarely focus on success factors that are nonfinancial in nature. Moreover, accounting practices with respect to allocation of expenses, transfer prices, and the like, often tend to obscure rather than clarify the underlying strengths and weaknesses of a company. This inadequacy should not be surprising since the *raison d'être* of many accounting systems is not to facilitate planning but rather to ensure the fulfillment of management's responsibility to the stockholders, the government, and other groups.

Tailoring the Requirements

If a company is to have a comprehensive, integrated system of information to support its planning process, it will need a set of management reports that regularly covers the three basic categories of planning data—i.e., environmental, competitive, and internal. The amount of data required in each area will naturally vary from company to company and will depend on such factors as the nature of the industry, the size and operating territory of the company, and the acceptance by management of planning as an essential function. However, it is important in every case for management to *formalize* and *regularize* the collection, transmission, processing, and presentation of planning information; the data are too vital to be ignored or taken care of by occasional "special studies." It is no accident that many of the most successful companies in this country are characterized by well-developed planning information systems.

What is gained if such an approach is taken? What difference does it make in operations? We do not need to conjecture to answer these questions; we can turn to concrete company experience. For instance, Exhibit II illustrates how the information used by the marketing department of an oil company changed as a result of a thorough study of the information needed to formulate effective plans. In this instance, the study indicated an increase in the data required by the vice president and his staff. (However, this result is not inevitable; it holds only for this particular situation. In other circumstances reviews of this kind have led to significant *cutbacks* in information.)

Several points should be noted in examining Exhibit II:

1. The information shown is not all for the *personal* use of the vice president, although much of it is generated and used in his field.
2. For simplicity, most of the information listed in the exhibit was presented to company executives in graphic form.
3. The exhibit highlights only the reports used for retail gasoline marketing; omitted are fuel oil marketing, commercial and industrial marketing, and other topics which the new reporting system also covered.

EXHIBIT II. COMPARATIVE ANALYSIS OF MARKETING PLANNING INFORMATION

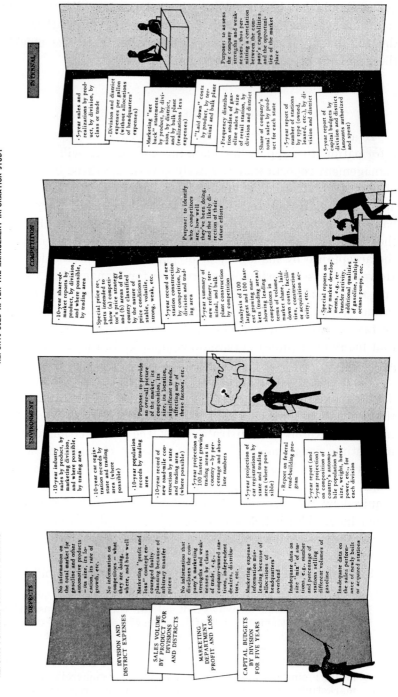

Many companies have found that the most effective approach to determining requirements for planning information, whether it be for one executive or an entire company, is to relate the three types of planning data described earlier to the steps in the planning process —i.e., setting objectives, developing strategy, and deciding among alternative investments. Thus, one asks himself questions like these:

1. What political data are needed to set reasonable objectives for this company?
2. What sociological and economic data about the areas in which this company operates are needed to formulate new product strategy?
3. What competitive intelligence is necessary to develop share-of-market objectives?
4. What internal cost information is needed to choose between alternative facility locations?

Contrast with control

In Exhibit I, I have listed the five principal characteristics of planning data compared with the characteristics of control data. Note that in all but one case (nonfinancial information) they are different. It is most important to keep these differences in mind, lest the "fuel" for the planning system be confused with the "fuel" for the control system, and vice versa. Hence, I should like to emphasize the contrasts here:

1. *Coverage.* Good planning information is not compartmentalized by functions. Indeed, it seeks to transcend the divisions that exist in a company and to provide the basis on which *integrated* plans can be made. In contrast, control information hews closely to organizational lines so that it can be used to measure performance and help in holding specific managers more accountable.
2. *Length of time.* Planning information covers fairly long periods of time—months and years rather than days and weeks—and deals with trends. Thus, although it should be regularly prepared, it is not developed as frequently as control information.
3. *Degree of detail.* Excessive detail is the quicksand of intelligent planning. Unlike control, where precision and minute care do have a place, planning (and particularly long-range planning) focuses on the major outlines of the situation ahead. In the words of two authorities, L. Eugene Root and George A. Steiner, "The further out in time the planning, the less certain one can be about the precision of numbers. As a basic principle in planning it is understood that, in the longer range, details merge into trends and patterns." [5]

[5] "The Lockheed Aircraft Corporation Master Plan," in *Long-Range Planning for Management,* edited by David W. Ewing (New York: Harper & Brothers, 1958), p. 151.

4. *Orientation.* Planning information should provide insights into the future. Control information shows past results and the reasons for them.

FUTURE DEVELOPMENTS

The heightened interest of management in its information crisis is already unmistakable. Dean Stanley F. Teele of the Harvard Business School, writing on the process of change in the years ahead, states, "I think the capacity to manage knowledge will be still more important to the manager. . . . The manager will need to increase his skill in deciding what knowledge he needs." [6]

Ralph Cordiner of General Electric Company in his book, *New Frontiers for Professional Managers,* writes:

> It is an immense problem to organize and communicate the information required to operate a large, decentralized organization. . . .
> What is required . . . is a . . . penetrating and orderly study of the business in its entirety to discover what specific information is needed at each particular position in view of the decisions to be made there. . . .[7]

Invariably, increasing attention of leaders in education and industry precedes and prepares the way for frontal attacks on business problems. In many organizations the initial reaction to the management information problem is first evidenced by a concern over "the flood of paper work." Eventually, the problem itself is recognized—i.e., the need to define concisely the information required for intelligent planning and control of a business.

Following this awakening interest in business information problems, we are likely to see the acceleration of two developments already in view: (a) improved techniques relating to the creation and operation of total information systems, and (b) new organizational approaches to resolving information problems.

Improved techniques

While the crisis in management information has been growing, tools that may be useful in its solution have been under development. For example, the evolution of electronic data-processing systems, the

[6] "Your Job and Mine," *The Harvard Business School Bulletin* (August, 1960), p. 8.
[7] New York: McGraw-Hill Book Company, Inc., 1956, p. 102.

development of supporting communications networks, and the formulation of rigorous mathematical solutions to business problems have provided potentially valuable tools to help management attack its information problems. Specifically, progress on three fronts is an encouraging indication that this kind of approach will prove increasingly fruitful:

1. Managements of most companies are far more conversant with both the capabilities and the limitations of computer systems than they were five years ago. This growing understanding has done much to separate fact from fancy. One key result should be the increasing application of electronic data-processing concepts to the more critical, less routine problems of business.
2. Computer manufacturers and communications companies are learning the worth of their products. They show signs of recognizing that it is not hardware but an information system which is extremely valuable in helping to solve management's problems.
3. Significant improvements have been made in the techniques of harnessing computers. Advances in automatic programing and developments in creating a common business language are gratifying evidence that the gap is being narrowed between the technical potential of the hardware and management's ability to exploit it.

Organizational moves

The development of new organizational approaches is less obvious. Earlier in this article I noted that: (a) progress in the systematic collection and reporting of information dealing with a company's environment or with its competitive situation has been slow, and (b) traditional accounting reports are often inadequate in providing the data needed for business planning. These conditions may result from a very basic cause; namely, that most organization structures do not pin down the responsibility for management information systems and tie it to specific executive positions. Controllers and other financial officers usually have been assigned responsibility for *accounting* information—but this, of course, does not meet the total need.

Nowhere has the absence of one person having specific and *total* responsibility for management information systems had a more telling effect than in defense contractor companies. In such organizations the usual information problems have been compounded by the rapid rate of technological advance and its attendant effect upon product obsolescence, and also by the requirement for "concurrency," which means that a single product or product complex is developed, tested, produced, and installed simultaneously. Under these conditions, some companies have been nearly paralyzed by too much of the wrong information.

Having recognized this problem, several corporations have attacked it by creating full-time management information departments. These groups are responsible for:

1. Identifying the information needs for all levels of management for both planning and control purposes. As prerequisites to this responsibility it is necessary to (a) define the authority and duties of each manager and (b) determine the factors that really contribute to competitive success in the particular business in question.
2. Developing the necessary systems to fulfill these information needs.
3. Operating the data-processing equipment necessary to generate the information which is required.

To some extent these departments, reporting high in the corporate structure, have impinged on responsibilities traditionally assigned to the accounting organization since they are concerned with financial as well as nonfinancial information. But to me this overlapping is inevitable, particularly in companies where the financial function operates under a narrow perspective and a preoccupation with accountancy. The age of the information specialist is nearing, and its arrival is inextricably tied in with the emergence of some of the newer tools of our management sciences. This notion is not far removed from the concept of Harold J. Leavitt and Thomas L. Whisler, who foresee the evolution of information technology and the creation of a "programing elite." [8]

Conclusion

The day when management information departments are as common as controller's departments is still years away. But this should not rule out concerted efforts to improve a company's information system. In fact, I would expect many broad-gauged controller's organizations to assume the initiative in their companies for such programs.

To this end, the nine questions listed in Exhibit III are for the executive to ask himself as a guide to assessing the improvement potential in his organization's planning information. If the answers to these questions tend to be negative, the chances are strong that changes are in order.

---

[8] "Management in the 1980's," *Harvard Business Review* (November-December, 1958), p. 41. (See Article 3.)

Exhibit III
HOW GOOD IS YOUR PLANNING INFORMATION?

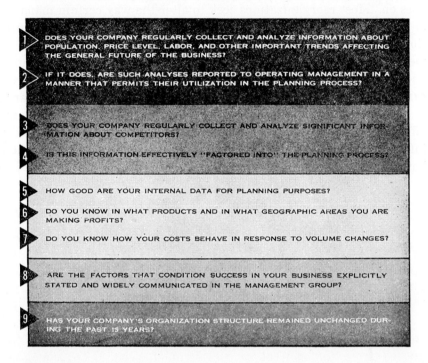

1 DOES YOUR COMPANY REGULARLY COLLECT AND ANALYZE INFORMATION ABOUT POPULATION, PRICE LEVEL, LABOR, AND OTHER IMPORTANT TRENDS AFFECTING THE GENERAL FUTURE OF THE BUSINESS?

2 IF IT DOES, ARE SUCH ANALYSES REPORTED TO OPERATING MANAGEMENT IN A MANNER THAT PERMITS THEIR UTILIZATION IN THE PLANNING PROCESS?

3 DOES YOUR COMPANY REGULARLY COLLECT AND ANALYZE SIGNIFICANT INFORMATION ABOUT COMPETITORS?

4 IS THIS INFORMATION EFFECTIVELY "FACTORED INTO" THE PLANNING PROCESS?

5 HOW GOOD ARE YOUR INTERNAL DATA FOR PLANNING PURPOSES?

6 DO YOU KNOW IN WHAT PRODUCTS AND IN WHAT GEOGRAPHIC AREAS YOU ARE MAKING PROFITS?

7 DO YOU KNOW HOW YOUR COSTS BEHAVE IN RESPONSE TO VOLUME CHANGES?

8 ARE THE FACTORS THAT CONDITION SUCCESS IN YOUR BUSINESS EXPLICITLY STATED AND WIDELY COMMUNICATED IN THE MANAGEMENT GROUP?

9 HAS YOUR COMPANY'S ORGANIZATION STRUCTURE REMAINED UNCHANGED DURING THE PAST 15 YEARS?

The impact of the information crisis on the executive will be significant. To an increasing extent, a manager's effectiveness will hinge on the quality and completeness of the facts that flow to him and on his skill in using them. With technology changing at a rapid rate, with the time dimension becoming increasingly critical, and with organizations becoming larger, more diversified in product lines, and more dispersed geographically, it is inevitable that executives will rely more and more on formally presented information in managing their businesses.

What is more, some organizations are concluding that the easiest and most effective way to influence executive action is to control the flow of information into managerial positions. This notion holds that the discipline of information can be a potent factor in determining just what an executive can and cannot do—what decisions he can make, what plans he can draw up, what corrective steps he can take.

To the extent that this is true, information systems may be increasingly used to mold and shape executive behavior. Better data handling might well become a substitute for much of the laborious shuffling and reshuffling of positions and lines of authority that now goes on. Most reorganizations seek to alter the way certain managers or groups of managers operate. But simply drawing new organization charts and rewriting job descriptions seldom ensure the implementation of new concepts and relationships. The timing, content, and format of the information provided to management, however, *can* be a strong influence in bringing about such purposeful change.

Thus, developments in management information systems will affect the executive in two ways. Not only will the new concepts influence what he is able to do, but they will to a great extent control how well he is able to do it.

15. BARRIERS TO COMMUNICATION [1]

Schuyler Dean Hoslett [2]

Much remains to be desired in the field of industrial communication, and management is well aware of it. But what, specifically, are the obstacles that must be overcome and the conditions that must be met before the communications problems will find a more general solution? This article examines the areas in which shortcomings seem most pronounced and recommends several courses of action which management can undertake to advantage.

An Initial Barrier to effective communication in organizations is the plain fact that many organizations really do not expect substantial two-way communication. While the phrase "two-way communication" is on the lips of many, too often it is conceived of in terms of sending orders and questions down from the top; in receiving reports and explanations up from the bottom. If the phrase is to have full meaning, there must be a complete cycle, including reports and explanations down (as well as up) and requests, criticisms, and questions up (as well as down).

Why this view is not more generally accepted is explained in part by historical considerations. That is to say, management thinking today still has strong overtones of an earlier authoritarianism and paternalism. When these philosophies were in full flower, it was commonly accepted that there were two types of persons: the order-givers and the order-receivers. Orders were not to be questioned, but obeyed; suggestions from order-receivers were out of place. Today one school of management philosophy emphasizes participant-centered administration—a philosophy which, in one of its aspects, pays some genuine service to the kind of substantial two-way communication mentioned above. But there is a strong time or administrative-practice lag. Thus, many organizations still think of two-way communication in the limited terms suggested at the outset of this article. Perhaps in time, and with further experience with the method, participant-centered administration will be the rule and semblances of authoritarianism and paternalism the exception. But

[1] From *Personnel*, Vol. 28, No. 2 (September, 1951), pp. 108-114. Reprinted by permission of the American Management Association.
[2] Schuyler D. Hoslett, Executive Assistant to the Chairman of the Board, Reuben H. Donnelly Corporation.

even if this goal is widely desired, and there is a full measure of acceptance of the concept of two-way communication, there remains substantial obstacles to its achievement.

The status relationship

One of these is a fundamental barrier raised by the *status relationships* existent in every organization. The placing of persons in superior and subordinate relationships in the formal structure necessarily inhibits the free flow of information, ideas, suggestions, questions. It is well known that the subordinate tends to tell his superior what the latter is interested in, not to disclose what he doesn't want to hear, and to cover up problems and mistakes which may reflect on the subordinate. He tends to tell the boss those things which will enhance his position and indicate his success in meeting the problems of the day. This creates distortion in the upward flow of communication matched by distortion in the downward flow. The latter results in part from the seeming necessity to maintain status differences: The superior feels he cannot fully admit to his subordinate those problems, conditions, or results which may reflect adversely on his ability and judgment. To do so would undermine his position as a superior being in the formal organization. Further distortion occurs because the subordinate is continuously engaged in interpreting and misinterpreting the words, attitudes, and actions of his superior.

*   *   *

This seems clear: The fact of the superior-subordinate relationship is a constant in any organization. The relationship itself cannot be legislated out of existence. It follows, then, that any basic attack on barriers to communication must deal with the task of mitigating the inhibiting effects of this relationship. This means that in every possible way, including formal training, status differences must be de-emphasized. Somehow an "atmosphere of approval" for communication must be created to such a degree that the parties will *mutually* accept criticism, welcome suggestions, and admit of problems, meeting these situations without trading on their formal positions of authority and responsibility. For unless this kind of relationship can be developed, effective communication cannot take place.

Individual face-to-face contacts

This brings us to a specific barrier to communication related to the status problem—the lack of productive face-to-face contacts in organizations. These contacts are in two classes: (1) the individual face-to-face contacts of superior and subordinate, and (2) the group face-to-face contacts in informal and formal meetings. Regarding the former, it is obviously essential to have known channels of communications within the hierarchy. This is a common management precept. What appears to be one of the unrecognized barriers at this level is in a failure to utilize the channels most productively—specifically the failure of the superior to listen to what the subordinate has to say before he offers information, comment, or advice on the subject under discussion. Thus, advice or information is given without a full understanding of the issue or problem being presented. (This is a part of the accepted status relationship also: the supervisor talks; the subordinate listens.) Moreover, there seems to be a marked tendency not to listen to the emotional content of what the subordinate is saying, resulting in a failure to understand his *feelings* on the subject. When a response indicating no recognition of emotional or "feeling" content is given, and the issue is of real concern to the subordinate, the latter will obviously feel that he had not been fully understood. Without this understanding further communication in mutually acceptable and useful terms is curtailed. An example will illustrate the point. A worker says:

> The big shots in this place certainly don't pay much attention to the people who do the work. When they want someone for a supervisor, I think they pick out their friends and "yes men"—they don't look at your record on the job. I stay on the job and get my work done on time with no complaints, and often do things that I don't really have to, but nobody notices you if you aren't out making friends with the boss.

How should the superior respond? In all likelihood he will respond to an aspect of the logic of the stated complaint—will say, "What superiors do you know who are 'yes men'?" or "What things do you do that you don't have to?" "How do you know nobody has noticed you?" or, even more likely, "What you say just isn't so—forget about it." Such replies very well stifle the development of any real understanding of the problem. But if the superior understands the emotional content of what the worker is saying, and initially responds to it, he may reply something as follows: "You feel that your work hasn't been appreciated or recognized." The latter reply facilitates further communication leading to an understanding of the problem as the worker sees it. This in turn may pave the way to a possible solution by the worker himself. In any event it releases the feelings of the worker so that he is psychologically prepared to accept information from the superior—and if needed, advice. At the same time the superior has placed himself in a position to give more useful information or advice since he understands the problem, including its emotional aspect, more fully.

Thus, it appears that the non-directive interviewing technique, which is a listening technique of demonstrated value in dealing with personal problems, has in a modified form a useful function to perform in the subordinate-superior relationship. We can make use of its basic components—listening and responding to emotional content—in our everyday work relationships.

Group face-to-face contacts

Formal and informal meetings have long been thought of as a tool of communication—in the past with an emphasis on downward communication; at the present with an increasing emphasis on upward communication of the real "facts of life" at the lower levels. Going beyond this, there have been experiments in group decision-making. In certain situations it has been found that a group decision is better than the decision of any individual member of the group. It has also been shown that when members of a group participate in the making of a decision at their own level of competence, it is better accepted and executed than a decision merely handed down from above.

These newer emphases on group meetings for upward communication and/or for group decision have served to focus attention on one prerequisite of group success—a flow of uninhibited communication within the group structure. To stimulate this flow we need the same fundamental condition prescribed for effective individual face-to-face contacts—that is, the same permissiveness, the same atmosphere of approval for expression, is a *sine qua non* in both instances. This seems true whether or not the group is gathered for purposes of decision-making or for the interchange of facts and ideas for the consideration of a formal leader in making a decision.

If this atmosphere is essential, on what is it based? Clearly it is based primarily upon the attitudes and behavior of the superiors—for it is these factors which promote a given atmosphere. But unfortunately, we do not always find persons in positions of authority whose attitudes and conduct are conducive to free communication. If such persons cannot be replaced, this question is raised: Can one change attitudes and behavior? Broadly speaking, our attempts to do this through training have been disappointing. Lecture and discussion courses on human relations probably have had some effect on attitudes, but the translation of this change in attitude to a behavior change in the workplace has occurred to only a very limited extent. Assuredly this is the hardest of training problems, but it is also a basic problem. Until some fruitful means are devised for meeting it, improvement in communication must necessarily remain retarded.

One hope for success lies in the role-playing method of training.

*   *   *

One important advantage of this method is the promotion of *active* participation to a much higher degree than is possible in lecture sessions or is likely to take place in group discussion. Consequently there is a greater freedom and range of expression regarding both problems and solutions. The sessions tend to "bring out basic problems of concern to supervisors, develop insight among them into these problems, give opportunity for constructive practice in situations confronting them, and give insight both to the leader and the group into the motives, problems and attitudes of employees." Ordinary training sessions must necessarily center on talk about the problems of attitude and behavior, while in the role-playing session, people not only talk about the problems but do something about them —through the taking of roles—in the same practice-sessions. This practice occurs in the relative security of the training room so that the transposition of improved practice from the training room to the workplace is made easier.

While we have no quantitative proof of the efficiency of this method (as a matter of fact, we have very little quantitative proof of the value of other supervisory training techniques), and one should not over-emphasize the value of a single technique, the limited use of role-playing observed to date gives promise of its potential usefulness in improving behavior *skills*. But influence must be brought to bear also on supervisors' *attitudes* because in the long-run behavior is the expression of those attitudes. Role-playing no doubt produces some effect on attitudes, but we should not yet throw lecture and discussion methods overboard as valueless for this purpose. Some experiments point to good results through a combination of the three methods: lecture, discussion, and role-playing. Clearly, further experimentation and evaluation of results are indicated.

The written word in communication

This leads me to comment on one other barrier to communication —undue reliance on the written word in the form of bulletins, magazines, newspapers, booklets, and the like. This is not to say, obviously, that one cannot communicate through the written or printed word. The point is rather that a good many administrators seem to be making a fundamental mistake in considering the mimeograph or printing press as a substitute for sound face-to-face relationships. This is especially highlighted in some business establishments where employees are bombarded with "slick," easy-to-read, well-illustrated publications which attempt to persuade them to an acceptance of the company's point of view regarding policies, distribution of profits, pensions, free enterprise, etc. It bears repeating that there cannot be any real communication through these media unless there is a relationship characterized by a fair degree of mutual trust and confidence in the first place—a relationship which is based, as we have noted, on attitude and behavior (the latter both in an individual and in an organization-wide sense) rather than words. If there is a background of antagonism or distrust or insecurity between management and workers, such printed material, however "slick" it may be, will not be accepted. This simple but fundamental fact governing communication is too much overlooked.

Three problem areas

Other barriers are raised, of course, in the way in which written media are used. It is not my intention here to provide a list of rules for the use of written media, but rather to suggest three areas in which shortcomings seem especially pronounced. The first of these is the failure to explain the purpose of the "directional" type of management communication such as the order, or procedure, or "directive." Chester Barnard has laid down the useful rule that a communication must appeal to the receiver as consonant with the organization's purpose and with his own personal interest. These conditions are more likely to be met if at the outset the receiver is told not only *what* he should do, but is told *why* he should do it. The communication must have a high explanatory, and to some degree persuasive, quality. The absence rather than the presence of this quality seems to be a common characteristic of management's "directional" communications.

A second barrier to understanding through the written word is in writing above the level of the readership. Here Barnard's rule that a communication will not be accepted unless the receiver can and does understand it is to the point. Henry C. Link reports that a recent analysis of 69 articles selected at random from 13 representative employee papers, 37—or over half—were on a readability level of difficult to very difficult, that is, above the educational level of 67 to 95 per cent of the adult population. Another survey of 25 management and 25 union publications for employees showed that, on the average, they were pitched at a level of *understanding* (readability) of employees with a high school or college education. In terms of *human interest*, the majority of both house organs and union newspapers were only "mildly interesting" or "dull." The authors conclude that "management editors and union editors alike need to work strenuously toward language simplification and enhanced human interest values. If they do this, their publications will be readily understood by rank-and-file employees with a limited educational background." This subject requires nothing more than an emphasis here since the techniques for making copy understandable and interesting have been elaborated in a number of places.

A third shortcoming which bears attention is the failure to ascertain the response to communications. For the most part we do not know the effectiveness of the written—or for that matter, the oral—word. In view of the high cost of communication, it seems fairly elementary that we should occasionally spend something additional to ascertain the results we obtain in terms of understanding and/or acceptance. One of the few examples of an explicit test of the response to communication has been furnished by John Corson. A questionnaire survey of the field staff of the Bureau of Old Age and Survivors Insurance indicated that 20 per cent of the field workers displayed varying degrees of misunderstanding of the instructional materials issued from headquarters during the previous month. Significantly, this misunderstanding occurred among employees who needed a precise understanding of the operating instructions in order to perform their work accurately. This kind of test undertaken periodically provides specific means for the evaluation and improvement of written communication; it is suggestive of action other organizations can undertake to advantage.

Conclusion

In conclusion, any basic attack on the problem of communication must be made primarily in terms of improving the face-to-face relationships of individuals and of groups at the several levels of the organization. This in turn requires more attention to attitudes and behavior—and to their modification when they are not productive of an atmosphere of approval in which communication of a realistic, stimulating, critical but helpful kind can take place. Written media must be considered as supplementary to—not substitutes for—productive face-to-face relationships. Without satisfactory relationships, written media may, in fact, produce less rather than more understanding and acceptance.

16. COMMUNICATION WITHIN MANAGEMENT [1]

Keith Davis [2]

Communication has become a very popular subject these days. There are many, in fact, who would say it is being over emphasized. Yet there is one aspect of communication which, amidst all the tumult and shouting, has been somewhat neglected. That phase is communication within the management group itself. This subject is usually called management communication or intra-management communication; regardless of its name, it represents a major area of the communication problem in business.

The general tendency, apparently, has been to say, "Let's improve employee communication; management can take care of itself." To be sure, employees far outnumber managers and communication programs are understandably focused primarily toward this group, but these conditions do not justify the neglect of management communication.

In ancient history the Tower of Babel exemplified the significance of communication in the accomplishment of a group work. Today we recognize even more clearly that communication, in management or out of it, is organic or basic to organized group activity. No group can long endure without it, because it is the nerve system which permits a group to function as a whole.

Picture for a moment a situation in which a superintendent and his foremen are working under conditions which prohibit communication. Some of the most obvious results of the "wall of silence" that surrounds them are:

1. The foremen do not know clearly what the superintendent wants them to do.
2. The foremen do not know what other foremen are doing. They cannot coordinate.
3. The superintendent cannot effectively give orders and instructions to his personnel, which means he is unable to direct their efforts toward the organization's objectives.

[1] From *Personnel*, Vol. XXXI, No. 3 (November, 1954), pp. 212-217. Reprinted by permission of the American Management Association.
[2] Keith Davis, Author, consultant and Professor of Management, Arizona State University.

4. The superintendent does not know clearly what his foremen are doing. Thus, for example, he is unable to motivate because he does not know their needs and reactions, and he cannot control because he is ignorant of their progress.

Truly communication is essential to perform any organized group activity. A group cannot coordinate and function as a whole without it.

Why emphasize management communication?

There are good reasons why management communication deserves emphasis at this stage in the development of the communication art.

First, management communication is *prerequisite* to worker communication. Obviously, management cannot communicate to workers unless management itself is informed. Not only must management *know* (that is, be informed) but it also must *understand* the information well enough to interpret it to others. Top management often fails to recognize this simple fact. For example, top management in one company expected its foremen to interpret the incentive plan to workers but failed to explain the plan adequately to the foremen. Even though the foremen had stacks of papers describing the plan, they did not understand it and, therefore, were unable to interpret it to the workers. Just as a photograph can be no clearer than the negative from which it is printed, the manager cannot transmit more clearly than he understands.

Management communication also is essential if a manager is to make proper judgments and decisions. The manager is often completely isolated from the point of performance, and he can serve as a "decision center" only to the extent that reports and other information reach him. This requires two-way communication. The specialization of decision-making functions is largely dependent upon the ability to develop adequate channels of communication to and from decision centers. This reason alone should be enough to convince management that its own communication patterns need continuous analysis and appraisal.

Another reason for emphasizing management communication is that the scope of a manager's influence is typically greater than a worker's. Inadequate communication to any single manager can have a direct effect on profit, productivity, or morale, because his wide span of control and coordination affects many people and different activities. Inadequate information to a worker usually affects only his job and a few others, but poor information to a manager may affect the work of hundreds of persons.

Management communication deserves emphasis also because most of the links in the chain of communication, from top to bottom and bottom to top, are in the management group. A communication from a worker to top management, for example, may go through five persons—all managers. Each link in that chain, except the first, is within the management group. Each link affords a new opportunity for distortion, fading, and delay. Each executive in the chain has an opportunity to filter information, passing on only what he thinks is important or what he thinks his receiver wants to hear. Thus the problems of upward and downward communication in business, measured in terms of links in the communication chain, fall mostly within the management strata.

Finally, management communication is important because, even though members of management are not defined as "employees" in labor relations laws, they are in fact *employees*, which means that they have needs for communication and understanding just like any other employees. A manager who is not "in the know" lacks both the incentive to improve and the ability to make decisions. His attitude is, "If I don't know what's going on around here, why should I worry about what happens? If other executives don't cooperate with me, why should I cooperate with them?"

The five conditions just discussed indicate that management communication deserves at least equal emphasis with employee communication. The two are merely different sides of the same coin, and one cannot improve very far beyond the other, because one is dependent upon the other for the good of the company as a whole.

Communication analysis

The first step in developing good management communication is to find what problems exist in the individual business and then proceed to remedy them. Problems can be determined by judgment on the basis of general observation and knowledge, but the more scientific approach is actually to make first-hand analysis within the company involved. In this way the specific problems that require action can be isolated and identified.   .

There are now available several methods of making such an analysis. They range all the way from a simple questionnaire asking "Do you know this?" to an elaborate study of the overall communication *process* itself. Obviously, the latter is more effective because it takes into account causes as well as results, whereas the former appraises only results.

One promising method of communication process study is called "ecco analysis." [8] It uses a simple questionnaire or interview to determine communication chains about particular units of information. Each unit is traced from its origin as it spreads throughout the organization. In this manner one can determine the people who communicate actively, the degree to which certain managers or departments are isolated from communication chains, the extent to which different media are used, the activity of the grapevine, and many other related factors.

The communication network in one company

The use of "ecco" analysis can be illustrated by examples of results achieved with this method in one company. This manufacturing firm employed about 700 persons, but the research covered only the management group. The communication pattern consistently was a "cluster chain," in which only a few of the informed persons communicated, and they usually informed several persons instead of only one. (The accompanying illustration shows the difference between the "cluster chain" and an ordinary single-strand chain in which A tells B, who tells C, who tells D, and so on.)

The cluster chain means that most people in management acted as passive receivers, and only a few (10 to 30 per cent in most cases) re-communicated the information originally to another person. These "communicators" are often called liaison individuals. Membership in the liaison group was different for each unit of information, depending on factors such as requirements of the formal organization and personal interest in the subject. There was no established, consistent group of communicators, but some persons tended more than others to be active in communication.

The predominant flow of communication in this company was downward (measured in terms of the formal organizational levels), regardless of the persons involved or the type of information. The grapevine was very active, but even there, communication predominantly flowed downward. The evidence clearly showed that upward communication was inadequately developed. There was, in fact, negligible communication between foremen and other members of management, except for formal contacts between a foreman and his direct supervisor. Here was an area requiring management's conscious effort for improvement.

[8] This and other methods of analysis are described in Keith Davis, "A Method of Studying Communication Patterns in Organizations," *Personnel Psychology*, Autumn, 1953, pp. 301-312.

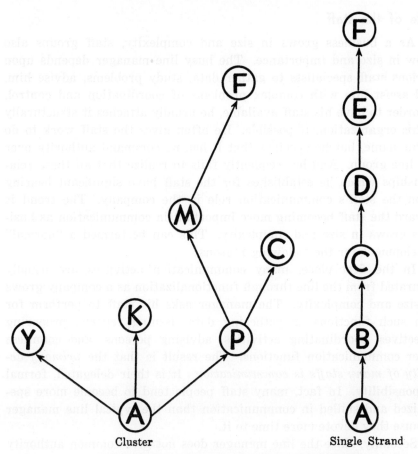

Cluster   Single Strand

TWO BASIC COMMUNICATION PATTERNS

Certain departmental groups of foremen were also well isolated from most downward communication, especially the grapevine. This problem required attention, too, because it was usually tied in with social isolation or geographical separation.

Staff persons were somewhat more active communicators in this company than line persons. The staff both received and transmitted proportionately more information than the line.

The foregoing examples should illustrate that communication analysis is beyond the stage of "by guess and by golly." Important basic data about a firm's individual situation can now be determined accurately and scientifically, as in other areas of management analysis.

In this field study both the grapevine and the staff group were shown to be especially active. Because of their importance these two subjects warrant further discussion on a general basis.

Role of the staff

As a business grows in size and complexity, staff groups also grow in size and importance. The busy line manager depends upon various staff specialists to gather data, study problems, advise him, and assist him with complex problems of coordination and control. In order to have his staff available, he usually attaches it structurally to his organization, if possible. He often gives the staff work to do in his name, but he specifies that it has no command authority over the line group. And he frequently fails to realize that all these relationships which he establishes for the staff have significant bearing upon the staff's communication role in the company. The trend is toward the staff becoming more important in communication as business grows in size and complexity. This can be termed a "normal" development for the following reasons:

In the first place, many communication activities are usually separated from the line through functionalization as a company grows in size and complexity. The manager asks his staff to perform for him such functions as gathering data, issuing reports, preparing directives, coordinating activities, advising persons, and countless other communication functions. The result is that the *primary activity of many staffs is communication*. It is their delegated, formal responsibility. In fact, many staff people tend to become more specialized and skilled in communication than the typical line manager because they devote more time to it.

Secondly, since the line manager does not give common authority to staff people, they have greater motivation to communicate, because they realize that their success is more dependent upon "selling" their ideas to others. Line managers, on the other hand, are often lulled into poor communication by the fact that they have authority to order an action even when they cannot sell it.

A third reason for the communication importance of the staff is that it is usually set in the organization structure so that it has shorter communication chains to higher management. For example, a foreman in a large factory might have to go through five levels to reach the executive vice president, but a personnel specialist might reach him through three levels. This permits staff members to have the "ear" of top management and to short-circuit the line. The result is both good and bad. Communication upward and downward tends to be improved, but lower management often waits in insecurity with the fear that it is being by-passed, or criticized without an opportunity to answer.

A fourth reason for the staff's communication activity is that it is more mobile than the line, certainly at the lower levels of the organization. Staff specialists and executives in such areas as personnel and control find that their duties both require and allow them to get out of their offices and visit other areas without someone wondering if they are "not working." They also find it easier to get away for coffee or just to visit. All of this means that staff people have the chance to receive and spread information widely and regularly.

Finally, the staff is often more involved in the chain of procedure than is the line. For example, a production control problem may clear through five staff persons but only three line persons, which means that more staff people than line people often know about many line actions.

Since staff people have so many reasons, both formal and informal, for communicating, the over-all result is that they do transmit and receive information actively. They have the information, the skill, the motivation, the contacts, and the organizational position. Management must recognize this active communication role of staff and make full use of it in management communication.

The grapevine in management

Informal communication is often called "the grapevine." It arises from the social and personal interests of people, rather than the formal requirements of an organization. The term "grapevine" probably arose because it was thought to be a long, winding means of communication from one point to another—like a real grapevine. But it is now recognized that the grapevine is often faster and more direct than so-called direct, formal channels of information.

The grapevine is typically considered to apply to workers. Observation, confirmed by research, indicates that it is just as active among management. Wherever there are people, there are grapevines. This means that the grapevine is a significant influence among management, either for or against organization objectives. It can make or break individual managers or general morale in management.

The grapevine is especially fast and active when news is significant, which means that it will undermine a formal system for significant news unless the formal system is kept flexible and fast. The grapevine quickens its pace when people are insecure, as when a reorganization is "in the wind" or a reduction in force is probable. Since the grapevine has no reliable source to which participants can refer to confirm facts, the grapevine carries rumor or distorted information rather easily. Since participants in a grapevine cannot easily be held responsible for distortion, as they could be in formal communication, each participant is freer to treat facts lightly.

In the management group the grapevine is more spontaneous and flexible than formal communication. For example, it can easily bypass managers in the chain of command because it is not confined by formal procedure. Under certain conditions, this can be beneficial, but often it short-circuits other managers and undermines executive relationships.

Since the grapevine is active and significant within the management group, it deserves more attention by members of management. They need to study it, learn how it works and who its key connections are, and develop ways to keep it positive rather than negative. It is a regular part of the management environment.

Studies show that the management grapevine can be influenced because its patterns are partly predictable. For example:

1. People talk most when the news is recent.
2. People talk about things that effect their work.
3. People talk about people they know.
4. People working near each other are likely to be on the same grapevine.
5. People who contact each other in the chain of procedure, tend to be on the same grapevine.

No matter what the causes of grapevines, they will continue. *Grapevines represent a normal management activity.*

The job ahead

Management communication is not to be overlooked with the comment that, "It will take care of itself." In many respects, it is prerequisite to good employee communication, and both are essential to coordinated, effective operations. Because management and employee communication are interdependent, one cannot rise far above the other in over-all quality.

Management communication will be improved, not by airy speculation in the front office, but by actual study of each company's management communication system to determine needs and problems. Present-day research indicates that the grapevine and the staff are quite significant components of a firm's management communication network. They should be given early attention in a company's communication program.

17. LISTENING IS GOOD
BUSINESS [1]

Ralph G. Nichols [2]

In the year 1940, Dr. Harry Goldstein completed an important educational research project at Columbia University. Two very significant observations emerged from it. *One:* he discovered that it is perfectly possible for us to listen to speech—without any significant loss of comprehension—at three times the normal speaking rate. *Two:* he suggested that America may have overlooked a very important element in her educational system, that of refining our ability to listen.

Quite a few people read this study, and wondered about it; but not very many did anything about it. Shortly after that, however, Richard Hubbell, an important figure in the television industry, produced a new book. In it he declared without equivocation that 98 per cent of all that a man learns in his lifetime he learns through his eyes or through his ears.

Hubbell's book threw a spotlight upon a long-neglected organ we own—our ears; and it threw into focus one of the most important educational researches of our time. Dr. Paul Rankin of Ohio State University was determined to find out what proportion of our waking day we spend in verbal communication. He kept a careful log on 65 white-collar workers at 15-minute intervals for two months on end. Here is what he found:

> Seven out of every ten minutes that you and I are conscious, alive and awake we are communicating verbally in one of its forms; and that communication time is devoted nine per cent to writing, 16 per cent to reading, 30 per cent to speaking, and 45 per cent to listening.

OUR UPSIDE-DOWN SCHOOLS

With respect to training in these communication skills, America has built her school system upside-down. Primary and secondary

[1] From *Management of Personnel Quarterly*, Vol. 1, No. 2 (Winter, 1962), pp. 2-9. Reprinted by permission of Ralph G. Nichols and The University of Michigan, Bureau of Industrial Relations.
[2] Ralph G. Nichols, Department of Rhetoric, University of Minnesota.

schools devote some 12 years to teaching a youngster how to write a sentence, in the hope that sometime he will be able to write a full paragraph, and then a complete report. Countless tax dollars and teacher hours of energy are spent in improving the least-used channel of communication.

For some inexplicable reason we chop off all reading improvement training at the end of the eighth grade. From that time on the reading we do is of an extensive, voluntary and general character. Then we moan because America averages out as a nation of eighth grade readers. In view of the eight years of training we receive at best, we shouldn't be shocked at that fact. However, a lot of tax dollars are devoted to improving this second least-used channel of communication.

Then we come to something important quantitatively—speech itself. Thirty per cent of our communication time is spent in it; yet speech training in America is largely an extra-curricular activity. In a typical school you will find an all-school play once or twice a year. There may be a debating team with a couple of lawyers' sons on it. There will be an orator, an extemporary speaker, and that is about the size of it. You will find it very difficult to discover a high school where even one semester of speech training is required of the students.

Then we come to listening. Forty-five per cent of our communication time is spent in it. In 1948, when I first became concerned about this field, hardly anyone had considered refining his listening ability.

I asked my University for a sabbatical leave that year, and spent 12 months doing research, trying to identify the characteristics of a good and bad listener. First, I learned that nobody knew much about effective listening. Only one small girls' college in Missouri, Stephens College, was teaching listening. Only three experimental and scientific research reports in the field of listening comprehension had been published in 1948. By comparison, over 3,000 scientific studies had been published in the field of reading comprehension.

TEN YEARS MAKE A DIFFERENCE

By 1958 a very dramatic change had occurred. Most of our leading universities were teaching listening under that label. Today these schools are not only teaching listening—they are conducting graduate-level research in the field. Today scores of businesses and industries have instituted listening training programs for selected management personnel. Several departments of the Federal Government have followed suit.

A number of units of our military service have started listening training programs. Effective listening has practical application to current business practices. For example, there is a growing conviction that most salesmen talk too much and listen too little. There is a good deal of evidence accumulating to support this conviction.

Two Central Questions

In view of this tremendous surge of interest in listening in just ten years' time, I should like to raise two questions and very closely pursue answers to them.

Question No. 1: Is efficient listening a problem in business and industrial management?

For our first bit of insight on this, I should like to revert to the classroom for just a moment, for the first person to produce important evidence on it was H. E. Jones, a professor at Columbia University. He was in charge of all the beginning psychology classes there, and he frequently lectured to a population of some 476 freshmen.

It seemed to him, when he gave comprehension tests on his lecture content, that the students weren't getting very much of what he was trying to say. He hit upon a novel idea for an experiment and, with the cooperation of 50 of his colleagues on the Columbia faculty, he proceeded with the study. Each professor agreed to prepare and deliver a ten-minute lecture on his own subject to Jones' students. Each one submitted his lecture excerpt to Jones ahead of time, and Jones painstakingly built an objective test over the contents. Half of the questions in each quiz demanded a recalling of facts, and the other half required the understanding of a principle or two imbedded in the lecture excerpt.

Efficiency Level—25 Per Cent

Professor No. 1 came in, gave his ten-minute lecture, disappeared, and the group was questioned on its content. No. 2 followed. At the end of the 50th presentation and the 50th quiz, Jones scored the papers and found that freshmen were able to respond correctly to only about 50 per cent of the items in the test. Then came the shock. Two months later he reassembled the 476 freshmen and gave them the whole battery of tests a second time. This time they were able to respond correctly to only 25 per cent of the items in the quizzes. Jones was forced to conclude, reluctantly, that without training, Columbia University freshmen operate at a 25 per cent level of efficiency when they listen.

I couldn't believe it could be that bad. I decided to repeat the experiment at the University of Minnesota, and did so. I didn't let two months go by, for I was pretty certain that the curve of forgetting takes the downward swoop long before two months pass. I let two weeks pass, and got exactly the same statistics: 50 per cent response in the immediate test situation; 25 per cent after two weeks had passed. Several other universities have conducted the same experiment, and all have come up with similar statistics.

I think it is accurate and conservative to say that we operate at precisely a 25 per cent level of efficiency when listening to a ten-minute talk. How do you like that? I know you are interested in efficiency. Some of us like to talk in terms of 90, 93, 95 or even 98 per cent efficiency in the things we do—yet in the thing we do most frequently in all our lives (save possibly for breathing), we probably operate at about a 25 per cent level of efficiency.

Is this important in business and industrial management? Let us consider some evidence that will be nearer to your heart.

Evidence from Industry

A few years ago a young man went to a speech professor at a large state university and said that he would like to acquire a Ph.D. degree in the field of speech. My professorial friend said, "Well, your credentials look good enough; but instead of doing a Ph.D. in the speech field, I would like you to do it in the field of listening. I have a project in mind. Take a notebook; go to this firm in New Orleans; and interview all the management people you can get in to see during one week. Ask them these questions." Then he gave the student a list of questions he was to ask of each manager.

The young man disappeared, and came back a week later. He had a little notebook full of testimony that he had acquired from these management people. The gist of it was that they worked for a tremendous organization, that they had a great future, that they felt they had one of the finest communication systems ever devised in any business or industry.

They said, "Our workers know what they are trying to do. They understand our program. We have the most loyal group of employees to be found anywhere. The morale in our outfit is tremendous. The future looks good."

"Okay," said my friend the speech professor. "Put on a pair of coveralls. Go down to that same firm and see Joe Walker, head of the company's trucking department. You are to work for him for one year. Every day, carry a notebook in your inside pocket, and whenever you hear the employees say anything about their management—write it down in your notebook."

Twelve months later the student came back with a great stack of notebooks. My friend spent several weeks pouring over the testimony in them, and when he got through announced that it was the most vicious, malicious, denunciatory attack of one group upon another he ever had seen.

Trying to find out what the employees really knew of their firm's policies, procedures, and philosophy, he concluded that the workers understood *less* than 25 per cent of what their managers thought they understood.

I doubted this generalization and discussed my skepticism with Erle Savage, a senior partner of the Pidgeon Savage Lewis Cor-

Dilution of information occurs as a result of improper Communications flow ..

| 100% BOARD | 63% VICE PRESIDENT | 56% GENERAL SUPERVISOR | 40% PLANT MANAGER | 30% GENERAL FOREMAN | 20% WORKER |

Reproduced By Special Permission of Pidgeon Savage Lewis, Inc.

poration of Minneapolis, an advertising and communications firm. He looked at me when I told him about the study, and said, "Professor, don't be so skeptical. As a matter of fact, the picture is even worse than your friend reports it to you. My company has just made a very careful study of the communicative efficiency of 100 representative business and industrial managements. This chart shows the composite picture of what we discovered."

As you can see, there is a tremendous loss of information—37 per cent—between the Board of Directors and the Vice-Presidential level. General supervisors got 56 per cent of the information; plant managers 40 per cent; and general foremen received only 30 per cent of what had been transmitted downward to them. An average of only 20 per cent of the communication sent downward through the five levels of management finally gets to the worker level in the 100 representative American companies.

Studies have dug deeper. What kind of person is the employee who understands only 20 per cent of what his management thinks (and hopes) he understands? The 20 per cent-informed individual is usually a negative-minded fellow. He believes that there are big fat managers up there at the top, exploiting him, hogging most of the profits and not giving a proper share to him. His first inclination may be to steal something in order to get even—and the easiest thing to steal in our economy is time. One can check in late and pretend he got there early. Or he can leave early and report he left late. It is always easy to slow down at the desk or on the assembly line or wherever one is working. All this is costly business. If this doesn't satisfy him, a person can start stealing tools or equipment. People have been found carrying out a hammer or saw beneath overcoats as they walk out at night. One person was even caught with a nickel roll of toilet tissue under his jacket—trying to get even.

Upward Communication

Communicative efficiency down through the levels of management is terribly poor, and we are only beginning to appreciate the enormity of the problem. But I am much more concerned about another kind of communication. I am much more excited about the efficiency or inefficiency of upward communication than of that which passes downward through the channels. Why? Because I hold the deep conviction that the efficiency of downward communication is going to be improved significantly only when top management better understands the attitudes, the opinions, the ideas and the suggestions of the people at the bottom of the whole structure.

What kind of efficiency do we have when the levels of management report upward? We have begun to collect a lot of evidence on that. A recent study made of 24 industrial plants reveals a very peculiar thing. In the early stages of their study the researchers recognized that ten distinct factors are probably the most important in the morale of any employee group. They asked managers to rate these ten morale factors in the order of their importance as they thought they were influencing the employee group.

The managers put these three factors in the bottom three ranks. Eight: full appreciation of work done. Nine: feeling "in" on things. Ten: sympathetic help on personal problems.

Then the researchers went to the employee group and asked them to rate the ten morale factors in the rank-order of their actual influence. They rated these factors as follows: First: full appreciation of work done. Two: feeling "in" on things. Three: sympathetic help on personal problems.

It is almost incredible that management could guess exactly wrong, putting the three most important factors in the three least important spots; but this kind of evidence emerges again and again when objective studies are made of how well management really understands the attitudes and opinions of the employee group.

Attempts to Improve

Knowing this, a number of forward-looking firms and businesses in America are making very serious attempts to do something about it. A lot of different techniques have been tried. The old one, of course, was to have the boss know everybody. Many a president took great pride in the fact that he knew everybody on his payroll. Many of them liked to spend half a day walking through the shop or plant, shaking hands with all the workers.

This didn't work badly as long as the number was small enough to make it possible. But soon our companies got too big; so then we tried different systems.

We have had labor-management meetings in which labor was supposed to "speak out." We have had elected representatives of labor meet with selected management people. Neither of these things worked very well. We have tried hiring a chaplain as a special counselor, with the open invitation to everyone in the whole organization to go and talk to the chaplain at any time. This method might have succeeded had not some malcontented employee started a rumor that the chaplain was a stool pigeon "planted" by the board of directors. Of course, the potential value of this technique was soon lost.

Labor reporters for the house publications have been tried. We have tried suggestion and complaint boxes, father confessors, opinion and attitude surveys; and even though each device probably has some merit to it, in every case it has a built-in weakness.

THE CENTRAL REMEDY

Their failing is that they *are* merely devices or techniques, and as such it seems to me they do not get at the head of the problem, which is sympathetic listening by one man to another. My feelings were pretty well restated in a study made by Loyola University researchers. They spent 18 months making this study. They were trying to find out what the attributes of a good manager really are. They finally came up with this generalization:

> Of all the sources of information a manager has by which he can come to know and accurately size up the personalities of the people in his department, listening to the individual employee is the most important.

The most stereotyped report they got from worker after worker who like their superiors was this one: "I like my boss. He listens to me. I can talk to him."

Frank E. Fischer, managing director of the American Management Association's School of Management, summarizes the situation in one sentence. He says, "Efficient listening is of such critical importance to industry, that as research and methodology improve, I feel that training departments will have to offer courses in this field."

Granted that such a course is needed, how do you keep a listening training program alive in an industry? There is only one possible justification for keeping it alive, and that is if it is paying you money. If it is not paying off, get rid of it.

A few years ago a large firm located near Chicago was having a lot of trouble. They had been losing money in one particular plant for several months, and they tried a number of devices to get the plant operating productively again. Finally, hunting around for some new idea, they hired an outside psychologist to come in to teach all of their foremen how to listen. The psychologist got all the foremen into a room and essentially taught them how to grunt. He said, "When your men come in and complain to you about not having enough baths or not enough rest rooms or all of the other grievances they have, I want you to look sympathetic and say 'hmmm' and nod affirmatively to them. Don't argue or talk back. Ask questions if you want to, such as 'Well, what did your wife say?' or 'Do all the boys think this way?' Throw out little questions like these, but you are never to debate with one of these fellows. And you must all practice until you can say 'hmmm,' looking sympathetic while you're saying it." He coached these fellows for a couple of weeks and sent them back to their jobs.

As usual, streams of complainers made their way to the foremen's offices. To their surprise, instead of getting rude treatment, they found a man saying, "Hmmm, is that so? Well, what did you do then, Joe?" Several of them acted as though they were bulls in a china shop, muttered a half-baked apology of some kind, and backed out. The result was that after three months had gone by some 90 per cent of the grievances had disappeared, and the plant was making money again. The management of the plant was so sold on listening training that they decided if it was good for foremen, it would be just as well to have the plant managers learn how to listen too. They soon spread it through all of their levels of management.

I have pursued my first question long enough, is inefficient listening a problem in business and industrial management? I trust that perhaps you will concede it is.

Question No. 2: What can be done about it?

A few years ago I screened out the 100 worst listeners and the 100 best listeners I could identify in my University's freshman population. Standardized listening tests and lecture-comprehension tests were used, and we had two widely contrasting groups. These poor suffering 200 freshmen were then subjected to about 20 different kinds of objective tests and measures. I got scores on their reading, writing, speaking, mathematical and scientific aptitudes; six different types of personality inventories and each one filled out a lengthy questionnaire. In addition, I had a personal interview with each of the 200.

Ten Bad Habits

When I got all done it seemed to me that ten things clearly differentiated a good listener from a bad one. I published an article about "The Ten Worst Listening Habits of the American People." Other universities read the article and repeated the study. Essentially, they came to the same conclusions. Thus, for whatever it is worth, I should like to enumerate and comment briefly on what seems to be the ten worst listening habits that afflict us. Why? Because listening training is largely the business of eliminating these bad listening habits, and replacing them with their counterpart skills.

I. Calling the subject uninteresting

Bad listening habit number one is to declare the subject uninteresting. The chairman announces a topic, or perhaps the bad listener reads it on the program and says to himself, "Gee, how dull can they get, anyhow? You'd think for the money they shell out they could get a decent speaker on a decent subject. This is such a dull topic that I think I'll worry about that secretary of mine. Am I going to keep her on another year, or am I going to sack her right now?" A lot of us store up these mental tangents to use in moments of boredom, and this is what the bad listener *always* does.

The good listener starts at the same point, but goes to a different conclusion. He says, "Gee, that sounds like a dull subject. I don't know what it has to do with me in my business. However, I'm trapped here, I can't get up and walk out. It would be terribly embarrassing and very conspicuous. Inasmuch as I am trapped, I guess I'll tune in on this guy to see if he has anything to say that I can use."

And the key to good listening in the first instance is that three-letter word—"use." The good listener is a sifter, a screener, a winnower, always hunting for something worthwhile or practical that he can store away in the back of his mind and put to work for him in the days or months ahead.

This is a selfish activity, but a very profitable one. We openly acknowledge the selfish character of it, and urge our trainees to become better listeners by hunting for the useful and practical. G. K. Chesterton put it beautifully many years ago in these words: "In all this world there is no such thing as an uninteresting subject. There are only uninterested people."

2. Criticizing the delivery

Bad listening habit number two is criticizing the speaker's delivery. A bad listener does it almost every time. The speaker starts to talk, and the man thinks, "Gee, is that the best they can get? This man can't even talk. All he does is try to read from his notes. Hasn't anyone ever told him to look his listeners in the eye when he talks to them? I have never heard a voice as unpleasant as this fellow's. All he does is fidget, snort and cough. Nobody could get anything from such a character. I'll tune him out and worry about that sales pitch I have to make next week." And off he goes on a mental tangent.

The good listener moves in a different direction. He says, "I don't know when I have heard such an inept speaker. You'd think they would get a better man than that for what they pay him. But wait a minute! This guy knows something I don't know, or he wouldn't be up there. Inasmuch as I have paid tuition or a registration fee, I'll dig his message out of him if it kills me. I'll concentrate on his content and forget about the lack of smoothness in this character's delivery."

After an hour or two of concentrating on content, he doesn't even remember the eccentricities and the oddities of the speaker. He begins to get interested in the subject. Actually, the speaker does very little of the learning. If learning takes place, it is because of action inside the brain of the listener—the man out front.

Suppose that right now a janitor interrupted you, yelling in broken, profane English, "Get the hell out of here! The building is on fire!" You wouldn't lean backward and say, "Please, sir, will you not couch that admonition in better rhetoric?" You would rush pell-mell out of the room, as you know. That is my point. The message is ten times as important as the clothing in which it comes. Form has little to do with the significance of the communication taking place.

3. Getting overstimulated

I feel like an authority on this one, for I have been overstimulated as long as I can remember. I get so excited about people and things that I just can't control myself. How does it work? A speaker starts to develop his topic. I am out in the audience, and before he talks three or four minutes he walks rough-shod on one of my pet biases or convictions. Immediately I want to throw up my hand and challenge him on the spot. If it is too formal a spot, I will sit there and gnash my teeth and figure out the meanest, dirtiest, most embarrassing question I can hurl at him. I have often sat for 30 minutes composing the most embarrassing question that could possibly be phrased for the speaker to answer. If that doesn't fit, I will sit and build a great rebuttal speech. Maybe I know of a little evidence that contradicts something he has presented, and I will plan my rebuttal effort.

All too often I have hurled my nasty question or great rebuttal at the speaker, only to find him looking at me in complete wonderment and saying "Nichols, didn't you hear when I went on to say that so-and-so was also true?" I hadn't. My listening efficiency had dropped to a zero per cent level because I had been overstimulated and excited about my contribution to come.

It happens all the time. And it is important! We now think it is so important that we put at the top of each blackboard in every classroom where we teach listening—and, by the way, we teach 25 per cent of the incoming freshmen on my campus to be better listeners because we don't think many will get through college if we don't—this slogan: "Withhold Evaluation until Comprehension is Complete." It sounds kind of abstract and meaningless, but it isn't. In smaller words we might say, "Hear the man out before you judge him." Unless you fully comprehend his point, you are going to make a snap judgment of it, and at least half the time you are going to guess wrong.

4. Listening only for facts

Bad listening habit number four is listening only for facts. I know that you have great respect for facts. I have, too; but a curious thing exists about those facts. I personally asked the 100 worst listeners I could locate what they concentrated on in a listening situation. Ninety-seven of the 100 testified proudly that they "listened for the facts." The truth was that they got a few facts, garbled a shocking number, and completely lost the bulk of them.

I asked the 100 best listeners what they concentrated on in a listening situation, and a bit timidly and apologetically they testified in equal proportion, "When we listen we try to get the gist of it—the main idea."

The truth was that these idea listeners *had* recognized generalizations or principles, and had used them as connecting threads to give sense and system to the whole talk. Two days later they somehow appended more facts to these connecting threads than the bad listeners were able to catalogue and report.

We had to conclude that if one wants to be a good listener he should try to get the gist of the discourse—the main thread, the idea, the principle, the concept, the generalization. We should quit worrying about the facts. Facts can be retained only when they make sense, and they may make sense only when they support a generalization of some kind.

5. Outlining everything

Bad listening habit number five is trying to make an outline of everything. This is a curious business. We found that the 100 worst listeners thought that notetaking and outlining were synonymous. They knew only one way to take notes—to make an outline of the speech. There is nothing wrong with outlining if the speaker is following an outline pattern of organization. He should be, I would concede. However, between today and the day you and I die, probably not one-third of the speakers we hear are going to have organized their discourses carefully on an outline pattern or scheme—and one of the most frustrating things in this world is to try to outline the un-outlinable.

The student who does it always comes out with a sheet of notebook paper that is a perfect and beautiful thing in terms of symmetry— all the margins and indentations perfectly ordered, the symbols all nicely subordinated; and there is meaningless jargon after each symbol. Two months later, when he tries to review his notes, they have no meaning whatsoever.

We asked the 100 best listeners what they did for notetaking and they said, "It all depends on the speaker. We listen for a while and do nothing. When we figure out if he is organized or not, we sometimes write little abstracts. We listen three or four minutes and write a one-sentence summary of what has been said. Sometimes we annotate the workbook or textbook as we listen. Sometimes we use the 'fact versus principle' technique."

I am fascinated about this last technique for I feel it is highly effective. They have two sheets of notebook paper side by side when they go in to hear a lecture. At the top of one sheet they write the word "facts," and at the top of the opposite sheet they write the word "principles." Then they sort of lean back thinking. "Produce, Mister, produce!" They merely list in vertical columns the facts or principles produced. The system calls for a minimum of writing. If the man is a phony and has no ideas, they have two blank sheets of paper. If he happens to be a producer (and some of them are), you will find him grinding out from 20 to 40 facts every time he gives a talk, with two or three very important principles on the other side. These are the best possible notes to have when we come to a period for review.

Our conclusion had to be that the good listener is a flexible character who has many systems of taking notes, and that he carefully picks out the best one for the type of speaker he hears.

6. Faking attention

Bad listening habit number six is faking attention to the speaker. As a schoolteacher, for many years I felt I was going over big if I looked over the classroom and saw the bulk of my students with their chins in their hands looking up at me in this fashion. I was always pleased to see the girls in the first rows in this posture. I thought they were tuning me in.

We now know that the surest index to inattention in all this world is this posture on the part of the listener. Having paid the speaker the overt courtesy of appearing to tune him in, the listener feels conscience-free to take off on one of a thousand mental tangents, and that is precisely where he has gone. If you ever face an audience and, looking out across the room, see the bulk of your listeners in this pose, stop short in your talk and tell them to stand up and do calisthenics with you to get their blood circulating again.

Efficient listening is characterized by a quicker action of the heart, a faster circulation of blood, a small rise in body temperature. It is energy-burning and energy-consuming. It is dynamic and constructive.

7. Tolerating or creating distractions

Bad listening habit number seven is . . . so obviously clear that I will not elaborate on it.

8. Evading the difficult

Bad listening habit number eight is much more important. This is avoiding difficult and technical presentations.

We asked our 100 worst listeners what they did in terms of listening to radio and television. We found that these 100 worst listeners were authorities on Bob Hope, Red Skelton and the Lone Ranger. Apparently they had spent their lives listening to these programs. Not one of those bad listeners had ever sat clear through the "Chicago Round Table," "Town Meeting of the Air," "Meet the Press," "Invitation to Learning," "See It Now," or "You Are There."

We asked the 100 best listeners, and they knew all about Bob Hope and Red Skelton, to be sure; but, voluntarily or otherwise, they had many times sat through some of these more difficult, technical and educational programs on radio and television.

Pursuing this aspect of good listening, we finally concluded that the one word in the dictionary that best describes the bad listener is the word "inexperienced." It is true he spends 45 per cent of his communication day listening to something, but that something is always easy, recreational or narrative in character. He avoids, as though it were poison, anything tough, technical or expository in character.

Take a youngster who has never heard anything more difficult than Bob Hope and put him in an auditorium with 300 other freshmen; trot out the best professor of biochemistry on the faculty and let him start a lecture. The boy says, "Gee, what am I doin' here? What's he talkin' about?" He cancels that course and maybe heads into an economics class. It is just as rough over there. Inside of three months he washes out of school and is gone. He is inundated. For every two freshmen who come to our university and college campuses in America today, one washes out before the end of his sophomore year—and often before the end of his freshman year.

At the other end of the curriculum, in most instances, for every one graduate to whom we can award a four-year degree there are two employers waiting to bid for his services. Fifty per cent mortality on the intake! And we meet half of the demand on the outgo! I claim this is critical.

I am not sure how long we can stay in the world competition we are engaged in with this horrible loss of trained manpower. I get excited about it, perhaps overexcited. I actually feel that if we could get a little training grade by grade, ten minutes a week, in tough technical material, we would have a tremendous decrease of that 50 per cent mortality at the college level. America needs more educated men and women to improve her economy and her culture.

9. Submitting to emotional words

Bad listening habit number nine is letting emotion-laden words throw us out of tune with the speaker.

This is a curious business; but it is a fact that a single word may have such an emotional load in it that it throws some listener or group of listeners right out of perspective.

When I was in college I was on the debate team, and my colleague was a Negro boy whose first name was Lionel. He was intelligent and an excellent speaker; and we did all right until we met a certain college away from home. Inadvertently in that debate one of the opposition said, "The niggers will be coming over." I happened to be looking at Lionel's black throat, saw the blood rush upward into his black face, and realized he was the next speaker in the debate, and he went out and made a tremendous ten-minute speech on the race problem in America. It was a great talk—but we were supposed to be debating the Philippine Island question. We lost that debate.

Word got around, and every debate tournament we entered we lost because the opposition soon learned that all they had to do to lick us was to drop the word "nigger" into the conversation and we would go berserk. To this day if anybody says that word in my hearing, I begin to erupt emotionally and am unable to think for three or four minutes.

I don't know what words throw you out of tune with a speaker, but I will warrant that a few of these may affect you. We have pinned down a number of them. We know that the word "mother-in-law" sometimes does it. The word "evolution" does it sometimes. "Automation" and "big business" are troublemakers. "Income tax," "landlord," "landlady," "Harry Truman," and "Sherman Adams" are all fighting words that have tended to disrupt listening efficiency for some people at some time or other. Last year I learned that department store personnel do not want to be called "clerks." Unfortunately I had used the word "clerks" in a talk, and I had five women reproach me afterwards. They wished to be called "retail sales personnel."

One of the most important studies that could be made would be for some researcher to identify the 100 greatest word barriers to learning. I wish I knew what they were. If we knew what 100 words cause most of our difficulty as barriers to communication, we could consider them grade by grade; we could lay them out in the open, discuss them, rationalize them and get them behind us. How silly it is to let a simple word—merely a symbol of something—get us so excited as to disrupt our listening efficiency; yet this goes on all the time.

10. Wasting through power

I have left bad listening habit No. 10 until the last because I think it is by far the most important of all. It is wasting the differential between thought speed and speech speed.

On the average in America we talk 125 words per minute; but if you put a man up in front of an audience and get that degree of formality in the situation that always ensues when he starts speaking informatively or instructionally to a group seated before him, he slows down. In America we average 100 words per minute when we speak informatively to an audience. How fast do people out front listen? Or, to put it more accurately, how fast do listeners think in words per minute when they listen? We know from three different studies that you will never face an audience of any size at all that does not think at an easy cruising speed of 400 to 500 words per minute. The difference between speech speed and thought speed operates as a tremendous pitfall. It is a snare and a delusion. It is a breeder of false security, and a breeder of mental tangents.

MENTAL TANGENTS AT WORK

I believe I can give you fairly good insight as to what a male engineer thinks about when he is listening to a professor of engineering. Travel with me mentally, and imagine you are a group of senior engineering students about ready to graduate.

I am an old professor of engineering, and I walk in and glower at you at the beginning of your last class in your senior year, and I say, "Well, you think you're going to make it, eh? Some of you are going to get your sheepskins—but I'll tell you now that there are a few of you who aren't going to make it. We're going to flunk a couple of you. If you *do* make it, there is something you must remember as long as you live. The successful engineer is the man who appreciates the value and the worth of a slide rule! He is the man who never goes anywhere without one in his pocket or at his belt.

"Because a slide rule is the most important requirement for a successful career in engineering, I am going to spend this last class hour with you reviewing the mathematic computations possible when using it."

What do the students think about? One is thinking: "This old goat going over that again? I got that in physics when I was a junior in high school. They told me all about it again in my senior year, and again as a freshman and sophomore in college. How can a man stall that way and take taxpayers' money for a salary? Guess I'll worry about that soft tire on my Ford. I noticed the right rear was a little soft this morning. If that darned thing is flat when I get out of here, am I going to change it or let 'er sit until tomorrow, and get some help on it?"

He worries 50 seconds about the tire and then he checks in on the professor. The professor is now adding two digit figures on the slide rule. It is old stuff. Out goes the student worrying now about an approaching chemistry quiz. He spends 50 seconds on the chemistry quiz and ten seconds on the professor. In again, and out again. It wouldn't be so bad, if he always checked in for the ten!

Sooner or later this male engineering student gets to that inevitable tangent that occurs to every male at the college level. He begins to wonder which woman to call for a date Saturday night. "I wonder if I should call Susie. She's plump and jolly and I've had her out a lot of times and she's a lot of fun. She always makes candy that's so darned good!" He figures he could easily get a date with Susie—and then a thought strikes him. "I wonder if I could rate a date with Martha who came in from out of town. I don't know her last name, but gee, what a woman! That gal is tall, sinuous and glamorous. When she walks it's like watching a snake crawl. If I could rate a date with that creature, brother!" And this lad is off on a mental tangent from which there is no return!

The next thing he hears is the bell at the end of the hour.

As the bell rings he hears the old professor say, "Remember, when you take the cube root do it step by step, as a. . . ."

"Cube root? I never heard of it!" In absolute panic he grabs a friend going out the back door and he says, "How do you do cube root?" And the friend doesn't know either, for he has been out on a mental tangent too.

This is why we listen at an average efficiency level of 25 per cent. It is because of the constant allurement of mental tangents. It seems to be almost impossible to keep our minds free from them.

What is the answer? It is obvious. If you can think four times faster than any man can talk to you, this should be a source of power;

it should not be a weakness. As it operates without training it is a liability, but with training it can be converted into a tremendous asset.

MENTAL MANIPULATIONS

These activities, these mental manipulations, are three in number. Wherever you find listening training succeeding today, you will find them in the training program.

I. Anticipate speaker's next point

Number one is to anticipate what the speaker is going to say next. One of the best things we can possibly do is to dash ahead of him mentally and try to guess what his next main point is likely to be. If we guess it is going to be point A and it turns out to be point A, learning is reinforced, nearly doubled; for that point comes twice into our brain centers instead of once.

If we guess wrong, what then? If we guess it is going to be point A and it turns out to be point Z, we can't help ourselves. We begin to compare Z with A, and wonder why he didn't make A his next point.

When we compare the thought we felt he was going to make with the one he actually produced, we begin to apply the oldest law of learning in the books—which is that we learn best by comparison and contrast. To anticipate—to "guess ahead," is the one wager in life we cannot lose. Whether we guess right or wrong, we win.

2. Identify elements

Mental exercise number two is to identify the supporting elements the speaker uses in building his points. By and large, we use only three ways to build points. We explain the point, we get emotional and harangue the point, or we illustrate the point with a factual generalization following the illustration.

The sophisticated listener knows this. He spends a little of the differential between thought speed and speaking speed to identify what is being used as point-support material. This becomes very profitable in terms of listening efficiency.

3. Make mental summaries

Finally and most important, the good listener throws in periodic mental summaries as he listens. At the end of about three or four minutes, if the speaker draws a long breath or walks around the lectern, or takes a swallow of water, or if there is any pause at all, the sharp listener dashes clear back to the beginning of the discourse and makes a quick mental summary of what has been said up to the point of the break. We call these "dashes" mental recapitulations. There ought to be half a dozen or more in every lengthy talk we hear. They are the greatest dividend-payer in listening efficiency that we can possibly master and practice.

These periodic listening summaries are tremendous reinforcements of learning; and the beautiful thing about it is that we use to our own profit the ever-present differential between thought speed and speech speed.

A LOOK AHEAD

I would predict that within another five years or so no employer of white-collar personnel in America is going to sign up a young college or high school graduate without first inquiring about his listening index. If the young man asking you for a job says, "Well, my index is 17," I would advise you not to sign him up. We can no longer afford the luxury of a bad listener on our payrolls. One bad listener can cause more damage in the complex economy in which we operate than all your good listeners can compensate for. But if he says, "My listening index is 91," sign him up; for he is going to be a producer for you.

BIBLIOGRAPHY, CHAPTER V

BELLO, FRANCIS. "The Information Theory," *Fortune* (December, 1953), 136-158.

CHRISTIAN, ROGER W. "Controlled Plant Information," *Factory Management and Maintenance* (August, 1960), 61-81.

DAVIS, KEITH. "Management Communication and the Grapevine," *Harvard Business Review* (September-October, 1953), 43-49.

EVANS, MARSHALL K., and LOU R. HAGUE. "Master Plan for Information Systems," *Harvard Business Review* (January-February, 1962), 92-103.

EARL, ELMER W., JR. "Fundamentals of Communications," *Management Record* (September, 1954), 330-333.

JACKSON, JAY M. "The Organization and Its Communication Problem," *Advanced Management* (February, 1959), 17-20.

MASSIE, JOSEPH L. "Automatic Horizontal Communication in Management," *Journal of the Academy of Management* (August, 1960), 87-91.

PIERSOL, D. T. "Communication Practices of Supervisors in a Mid-Western Corporation," *Advanced Management* (February, 1958), 20-21.

ROBERTSON, R. R., JR., and F. J. ROETHLISBERGER. "The Growing Need for Good Communications in Industry," Bursk and Fenn (Eds.). *Planning the Future Strategy of Your Business.* New York: McGraw-Hill Book Company, Inc., 1956, 129-141.

SCHOLZ, WILLIAM. "Communications for Control," *Advanced Management* (November, 1959), 13-15.

SMITH, CHARLES B. "What Do You Mean?" *Personnel Journal* (June, 1961), 79-83.

STANTON, TED. " 'Information Scientists,' Industry's Link with Outside Research," *Management Review* (March, 1961), 33-35.

TRIPICIAN, JOSEPH F. "Face to Face—Appraisal as a Communications Tool," *Personnel* (July-August, 1961), 67-75.

VAUGHAN, J. L. "Communications for the Layman," *Business Topics* (Winter, 1961), 63-75.

ZELKO, HAROLD P. "How Effective Are Your Company Communications?" *Advanced Management* (February, 1956), 10.

Chapter VI
Decision Making

The decision process is often considered the focus of managerial activity. Planning, controlling, organizing, and other managerial functions or processes can be considered as different areas for decisions. Statistical methods and mathematical models, as aids in analysis or judgment, are tools for making these decisions. Human relations and behavioral elements in management are variables to consider in making decisions. In addition, a system can be considered as a model of the decision process with its accompanying information patterns. Thus, the whole range of subjects in management literature is directly linked to decision making.

The article by Charles Z. Wilson and Marcus Alexis explains different types of decision systems and shows the implicit assumptions we invoke in closed system approaches. Peter F. Drucker approaches decision making in the more specific context of the stages within the process of choice. In Article 20 M. C. Branch provides a perspective for the intuitive and the "more logical" decision approaches.

In spite of the analysis or judgment we are able to bring to bear upon a problem, its solution may remain elusive. To break out of patterns of routine or tried and true methods, innovation in decision making is necessary. Methods conducive to higher creativity are suggested by Charles S. Whiting in Article 21, and the organizational conditions which encourage creative decisions are discussed in Article 22 by Frederic D. Randall.

18. BASIC FRAMEWORKS FOR
DECISIONS [1]

Charles Z. Wilson [2]
Marcus Alexis [3]

Introduction

Decision making has been an integral part of the management literature for more than half a century. But because of an immoderate emphasis on decision making as an hierarchial "right," explorations of the behavioral aspects of the decision process(es) were at a minimum for much of this time. It was not until the early 50's that developments in decision theory gained a noticeable momentum. During this period we witnessed, on the one hand, the emergence of more powerful and sophisticated tools of mathematics and statistics; and, on the other hand, a revitalization of the social sciences. Together these developments forged the intellectual setting from which much of the current contributions to decision theory evolves.[4]

Unfortunately, however, the bulk of the literature on decision theory is developed along rigorous lines and spanned across several disciplines requiring more than a modest amount of mathematics, statistics, psychology, sociology and economics. Much of these materials are incomprehensible to the non-specialist and in many cases pose a formidable challenge for the specialist. The purpose of this paper is to present a panoramic view of frameworks and related decision concepts underlying the wide range of decision models now in use. For the purposes of this paper, the discussion is anchored

[1] From *Journal of the Academy of Management* (August, 1962), pp. 150-164. Reprinted by permission of the *Journal of the Academy of Management*.
[2] Charles Z. Wilson, Ford Faculty Fellow, Carnegie Institute of Technology and Associate Professor of Management, DePaul University.
[3] Marcus Alexis, Ford Faculty Fellow, Harvard University and Associate Professor of Business Administration, University of Rochester.
[4] There are several interesting summaries of developments in social science fields. See Ward Edwards, "The Theory of Decision Making," *Psychological Review*, 51 (September, 1954), pp. 380-471; William J. Gore and Fred S. Silander, "A Bibliographical Essay on Decision Making," *Administrative Science Quarterly*, 4 (June, 1959), pp. 97-121.

For a survey of quantitative developments, see Robert Schlaifer, *Probability and Statistics for Business Decisions* (New York: McGraw-Hill Book Company, Inc., 1959); Herman Chernoff and Lincoln E. Moses, *Elementary Decision Theory* (New York: John Wiley & Sons, 1959) and R. M. Thrall, C. H. Coombs, and R. L. Davis, *Decision Processes* (New York: John Wiley & Sons, 1954).

to two general types of frameworks. We have designated one type of framework as "closed." This is the classical decision situation where a decision maker faces a known set of alternatives and selects one or several of such courses of action by a "rational selection" process.[5] The second general type of framework is designated as "open." It parallels the "adaptive" or "learning" model.[6] This particular kind of framework is designed to facilitate a more complex view of the decision process. The act of choice spans many dimensions of behavior; rational as well as nonrational aspects.

"Open" and "closed" decision models, of course, are not mutually exclusive. One of the contentions of this paper is that both general types of decision models result from the same set of basic decision elements. Differences between the types stem mainly from the recognition and degree of emphasis accorded certain of the elements.

Decision elements

Of major interest to students of decision theory is the "complete" decision model. For a decision model to be "complete," that is, universally applicable, it must be able to prescribe behavior in the most complex as well as simplest cases. It must be capable of reflecting all dimensions of choice situations. Needless to say, the search for the "complete" model is a shifting goal and perhaps will continue to elude dynamic, aspiring researchers. The persistent research nevertheless has been rewarding. As a by-product of attempts to define and outline the "complete" model, we have come to recognize at least six elements common to all decisions: (1) the state of nature; (2) the decision maker; (3) the goals or ends to be served; (4) the relevant alternatives and the set of actions from which a choice will be made; (5) a relation which produces an ordering of alternatives in some arrangement; and (6) the choice itself, the selection of one or some combination of alternatives.

The state of nature refers to those aspects of the decision maker's environment which affect his choice. Included herein are the relationships between choices and outcomes. These relationships may be

[5] Herbert A. Simon, "Some Strategic Considerations in the Construction of Social Science Models," *Mathematical Thinking in the Social Sciences*, Paul F. Lazarsfeld (Ed.) (Glencoe: The Free Press, 1954).

[6] Kenneth J. Arrow, "Utilities, Attitudes, Choice: A Review Article," *Econometrica*, 26 (January, 1958), pp. 1-23.

random, that is, probabilistic. It is also possible for the relationships not to be known by the decision maker.

The individual or group making a choice is referred to as the decision maker. The decision maker is influenced not only by facts of the choice situation; he is also a product of his environment—the total set of social, political and economic forces around him.

By goals or ends are meant those objectives which the decision maker seeks to attain. In some choice situations the goals are clearly defined and operative. In others, such as the sequential choice situation, where choices are influenced by past choice(s) and outcome(s), goals are not always identifiable, operational or stable.

Alternatives, ordering of relations, and choice will not be discussed here because of the depth of coverage given in the sections immediately following.

By specifying the nature of these elements or in some cases according them mere recognition, it is possible to define a range of frameworks.

"Closed" Decision Models

Organizations are goal-oriented systems. That is, they are designed to improve the planning, problem-solving and decision-making abilities of individuals in pursuit of common goals. Therefore, it is not surprising that the most commonly used and accepted analytical framework for choice behavior or decision making in organizations is the "closed" decision model.

At the center of this framework is a concept of rationality rooted in the consciousness of individual choice behavior. Usually an individual is faced in a given situation with a number of choices or several possible courses of action. Each course of action is likely to lead to a unique consequence or to one of several possible consequences. We call an individual rational if he takes into account the possible consequences of actions open to him, if he is aware of a certain preference ordering and considers it, and if, in the light of such knowledge, he chooses that course of action which, in his estimation, leads to the best or most preferred consequence. In terms of the six elements common to all decision models, the ideal rational man makes a choice(s) on the basis of:

1. A known set of relevant alternatives with corresponding outcomes.
2. An established rule or relation which produces an ordering of the alternatives.

3. Maximizing something such as money rewards, income, physical goods or some form of utility.

Many of the widely accepted decision models in management science assume a kind of administrative rationality similar to that prescribed for the ideal rational man.[7] Such models are structured in "closed" frameworks. They are "closed" because of the minimal weight given to the environment of the decision maker, and the complexity of the act of choice as such.

Linear programming problems are particularly interesting examples of rational choice or "closed" decision making. Consider this simple production decision. Company T has two products, A and B, which can be produced in two different departments, I and II. The departments have different production capacities and unit profit per item of production. The decision is to select that combination of products A and B which best utilizes the total available capacity. Let's suppose that the following is given:

X_a, X_b—are possible quantities of product A and B

2.00, 2.50—are unit profits (dollars) for product A and B

.50, 1.0 —are percentages of capacity required to produce a unit of product A and B in department I

.80, .50—are percentages of capacity required to produce a unit of product A and B in department II

Then the model for our decision consists of an objective function

1. profit $= 2.00X_a + 2.50X_b$

to be maximized subject to

2. Dept. I: $.50X_a + 1.00X_b \leq 100\%$
   Dept. II: $.80X_a + .50X_b \leq 100\%$

and

3. $X_a > 0$ and $X_b > 0$.

That is, the production of any one of the departments must not exceed its full capacity but always be positive.

The goals or ends to be served are represented by profits. In other

[7] David W. Miller and Martin K. Starr, *Executive Decisions and Operations Research* (Englewood Cliffs, New Jersey: Prentice-Hall, 1960); also C. West Churchman, Russell L. Ackoff, and E. Leonard Arnoff, *Operations Research* (New York: John H. Wiley & Sons, 1957).

words, profits are a substitute for the whole structure of organization goals.

The decision maker can identify all feasible alternatives. The objective function combined with the constrained set of production possibilities makes possible the generation of a complete set of feasible solutions. The growth of computer operations and effective information systems has greatly enhanced this particular aspect of "closed" models.

Finally, problem solving algorithms such as the simplex method not only generate but also order feasible solutions and hence assure the selection of an "optimal" course of action.[8] Linear programming applications, in general, use restricted but very powerful "closed" models.

Games of strategy (Game Theory) are also structured in "closed" frameworks.[9] There are (1) clearly defined goals; (2) a number of alternatives open at each phase of the situation and; (3) players or participants who can estimate the consequences of their choices. The latter implies taking into consideration that outcomes are determined not only by one's own choice but also by choices of others. Thus, we have a "rational routine": identify alternatives, order, and select "best" course of action in light of predetermined goals.

There are countless other examples of "closed" models. Organizational decision making in general is concerned with sets of problems that can be framed in the typical "closed" choice situation. Limited resources, if not other factors, will act as ultimate restraints. "Closed" models, therefore, have enjoyed an increasing popularity. Recent developments have served to broaden the applicability of "closed" decision models by giving extensive attention to several states of nature often ignored. The remainder of this section will be devoted to a discussion of the impact of these developments on those decision elements emphasized in "closed" frameworks.

Alternatives: action-outcome relations

One way that different states of nature affect decision models is through the correspondence between alternatives (choices) and the

---

[8] There are other algorithms but the simplex approach is most widely used. See George B. Dantzig, "Maximization of a Linear Function of Variables Subject to Linear Inequalities," *Activity Analysis of Production and Allocation*, T. C. Koopmans (Ed.) (New York: John Wiley & Sons, 1951).

[9] Anatol Rapoport, *Fights, Games and Debates* (Ann Arbor: University of Michigan Press, 1960), Chapter 6.

possible outcome (consequences). There exist three knowledge states of choice-outcome relations.[10]

1. *Certainty*. It is assumed that there is complete and accurate knowledge of the consequence of each choice.
2. *Uncertainty*. The consequences of each choice cannot be defined by a correspondence relationship even within a probabilistic framework.
3. *Risk*. It is assumed that accurate knowledge about the probability distribution of the consequence of each alternative exists.

Certainty implies a state of awareness on the part of decision makers that seldom exists. The emphasis on certainty or deterministic foundations in decision making is a holdover from the early associations of social and physical sciences. Some contended that the laws of the physical sciences and the related deterministic quantitative methodology might be extended to social behavior.[11] But the contemporary revolution in both social and physical sciences has done much to minimize this view.

Genuine uncertainty is untenable in "closed" decision models. A basic premise in all "closed" decision models is that alternatives and consequences as well as goals are given. Thus, at least equal probabilistic measures can be assigned to possible outcomes of a given course of action. The current developments in subjective probability have done much to eliminate states of genuine uncertainty.

It is fair to say that models of risk dominate the kinds of foundations assumed in decision theory. The likelihood of each of the possible outcomes resulting from a particular course of action can generally be stated in either an objective or subjective probabilistic frame of reference. This is true if *all* outcomes for a given course of action cannot be specified independently. The U. S. Department of Commerce cannot, for example, list all of the consequences of a $5 billion decline in new plant expenditure. But it is nevertheless feasible for government economists to determine within a probabilistic framework the likelihood of certain major consequences.

Certainty and uncertainty may be thought of as limiting cases of risk.

Objective probability. Objective probability is fashioned from the regularity of *en masse* behavior. Its operational meaning flows from

[10] James G. March and Herbert A. Simon, *Organizations* (New York: John Wiley & Sons, 1959), p. 137.
[11] Rashevsky, for example, illustrates how much of the methodology of physical sciences is applicable to social behavior. See James S. Coleman, "An Expository Analysis of Rashevsky's Social Behavior Models," Lazarsfeld, *op. cit.*, pp. 105-165.

the Law of Large Numbers which asserts: the probability of any specified departure from the expected relative frequency of an event becomes smaller and smaller as the number of events considered becomes larger and larger. Stating this differently, given a large number of events and the relative frequency with which each event takes place, a stated probability of a particular event becomes more reliable as the number of events considered are increased.

We may define the objective or *a priori* probability of an event as the relative frequency with which an event would take place, given a large but finite number of observations. More generally, the probability of an event E, denoted by $P(E)$, can be represented by the ratio:

$$\frac{\text{number of possible outcomes of E}}{\text{total number of possible experiment outcomes}}$$

Experiment is assumed to be any set of observed phenomena. The total number of outcomes in this case is finite and countable and the number of outcomes of E are less than or equal to the total number of outcomes. In all cases where E is not the only possible outcome, a sufficiently large number of outcome observations will show E to be less than the total and hence $P(E)$ to be less than 1.

$P(E)$ is the probability measure of a simple event, one which is not related to the occurrence of any other event. If A denotes a choice and a_1, a_2, a_3 . . . a_n denote a set of outcomes, $P(a_1|A)$, $P(a_2|A)$, $P(a_3|A)$ . . . $P(a_n|A)$ are compound events; more specifically, they are *conditional probability* measures of a_1, a_2, a_3 . . . a_n when A is chosen. The values of $P(a_1|A)$, $P(a_2|A)$, $P(a_3|A)$ . . . $P(a_n|A)$ may be determined experimentally as in coin tossing or by empirically derived frequency distributions. *Extensive* experience is a basic requirement for "good" objective probability measures. One, for example, could toss a die six times to determine the probability or likelihood of the number two occurring. Suppose one observes that two (2) occurs $\frac{1}{3}$ of the time; i.e., $P(X{=}2) = \frac{1}{3}$ where X is a number on the die. This is an objective measure of the relative frequency of the number two occurring in a toss of the die but it is *not* the probability of two (2). We identify the probability of an event with the relative frequency over a *large number* of tosses. If an unbiased die is tossed a sufficiently large number of times, the relative frequency and, hence, the probability of a two (2) is $\frac{1}{6}$; $P(X{=}2) = \frac{1}{6}$.

Also, care must be exercised to insure the selection of the "right" statistical model. Contrary to popular beliefs, the normal distribution does not always work well as a generalized theoretical framework for estimating probability measures.[12] In many cases, getting the "right" theoretical framework poses an extremely difficult problem. Selecting the statistical model may be as important an operation in obtaining objective probabilistic measures as acquiring sufficient experience.

Reasonably accurate frequency distributions are available for many types of "closed" decision models. Electric power companies, for example, have years of experience to serve as a basis for estimating the probabilities of generating outages. Likewise, commercial airlines would have little difficulty in estimating the probability of "no-show" reservations.

In recent years, there has been a growing concern about non-recurring decisions. How does one construct a probabilistic foundation when decisions are unique? To the extent that there are unique elements in United States-Cuba relations, it is impossible to assign objective probability measures to the success or failure of particular actions. To date no uniformly acceptable solution method has been devised.

Equally as important, but more hopeful of solution, is the problem of convincing decision makers to use available data. The availability of objective probability measures is no assurance that they will be used in the decision process. The decision maker and experimenter are often different persons and the decision maker may not base his action on objective probabilities developed by the experimenter. If the "staff man" informs the line manager that an alternative T will result in outcome t_1 20% of the time or $P(t_1/T) = .20$, does the superior accept this estimate or adjust it upward (downward)?

Subjective probability. Subjective probability has a long history, dating back to Jacob Bernoulli in the 17th Century. Renewed interest in the subject has been generated because of the probabilistic base of many decision models and the recognition that decision makers are not always completely informed. Unlike its objective relation, subjective probability is heavily behavioral in its approach.[13] The

---

[12] The central-limit theorem tells us that a population with finite variance and mean has the property that the distribution of sample means drawn from it approaches the normal distribution. But this is only true if the variance is finite!

[13] Leonard J. Savage, *The Foundation of Statistics* (New York: John Wiley & Sons, 1954).

decision maker is not assumed to maximize on the basis of objective probabilities. He interprets action-outcome likelihoods in terms of personal perceptions. Unless very well informed, his estimates are likely to be different than the objective probabilities. Some experimental evidence strongly suggests a linear correspondence between subjective and objective probability but this does not necessarily mean that decision makers using subjective probability estimates behave *as if* they were acting on the basis of objective probability data. For one thing, behavior is related not only to the estimate of probability but to the subjective value of the expected outcome.

Evidence suggests that the decision maker acts on the basis of some combination of the following:

1. Degrees of belief in relative frequency basis of objective probability.
2. Perceptions of objective probability.
3. Evaluation of the importance of the situation.
4. Revocability of the decision.

Subjective probabilities may depart from objective measures because of any one of the factors.

The objective probability that an unbiased coin will fall heads on any toss is equal to the probability that it will fall tails. Thus they are both equal to one-half. An observer who is not familiar with the laws of probability might conclude that after a series of heads the coin is more likely to fall heads than tails on succeeding trials. In other words, the observer's limited experience of coin tossing leads him to "believe" that the probability of heads is greater than that of tails. The future actions of the individual may be affected by this perceptive estimate regardless how objective or reliable given probability measures may be.

Any model which seeks to predict decision behavior must recognize the likely discrepancy between personalistic (subjective) and objective probabilities.

Utility: ordering of alternatives

Another way of broadening the "closed" decision model to reflect a more "complete" set of elements is through the preference ordering of alternatives by the decision maker. The ordering of alternatives is an operation defined in the domain of the individual's value system. Early writers on utility discussed the ordering of alternatives as an ordinal ranking process (first, second, etc.). To this extent, a range of social or environmental forces shaping the individual's values are brought to bear indirectly in "closed" decision models.

Decision models today require that utility theory be developed beyond the ordinal stage. Each outcome must have an assigned, interval-scaled value. Structuring utility functions with such properties is not always feasible. Except where money or some easily measurable commodity can be taken as equivalent to measures of utility or at least related in an ascertainable manner, the determination of utilities, or even proof of their existence, is a most difficult matter.[14]

Contemporary utility theory starts with a set of human behavior axioms consistent with the generally prescribed concept of rationality in decision choice models. Each axiom is assumed to be testable.[15] That is, the axioms are stated such that the experimenter can assign operational meanings and relations to terms using the disciplines of logic and measure theory.

To date, several axiomatic systems for a theory of utility have been developed. Some are more "complete" than others. A "complete" axiomatic system must include what is known as the closure axiom. This axiom asserts that a person always prefers one of two outcomes or else is indifferent.

The one axiom common to all systems of rational behavior and subject to the most attention is the transitivity axiom. This axiom reads: If A is preferred to B, and B is preferred to C, then A is preferred to C. Without transitivity, we could not "link" the many sub-preference systems of an individual.

Developing the utility index. The discussions on utility theory seem to indicate the following are necessary for the construction of a utility index:

1. A set of mutually exclusive independent events.
2. An axiomatic system permitting the assignment of numerical values to each outcome.
3. A probability measure of each outcome possibility.
4. The assumption that the decision maker is a maximizer.
5. A willingness to gamble on the part of the decision maker.

To construct a utility index, we must be able to derive an interval scale which satisfies the requirement that none of the empirically

    [14] C. West Churchman, *Prediction and Optimal Decisions* (Englewood Cliffs, New Jersey: Prentice-Hall, Inc., 1961), Chapter 8.
    [15] Churchman, *Ibid.*

determined relations are disturbed. This is accomplished if the ratio of two pairs of measures taken on different scales will always be the same. A linear transformation satisfies this requirement.[16] Consider the following example.

A university research team is interested in measuring the subjective value of money to each of a group of students. To measure these subjective values (utilities), the researchers construct an experiment (a choice situation) in which the student is given the alternative of a specified but uncertain (risky) cash prize and of a certain (non-risky) cash prize. To distinguish between the risky and non-risky prizes, the former is referred to as an expected prize and the other as cash reward.

The expected prize is always some probability combination of zero and $1,000. The cash reward varies. A utility value of 100 is arbitrarily assigned to $1,000 and a utility value of zero to zero dollars. The utility of any cash reward is found by multiplying the probability of $1,000 by 100.

By now it is clear that the expected prize is nothing more than a gamble with a payoff of either zero or $1,000. Each gamble is independent of all other gambles and income is stated in numerical terms. Thus we have all the necessary requirements for the construction of an interval scale.

The scale is constructed by finding gambles and cash prizes to which students are indifferent. If a student is indifferent between a gamble involving a 50-50 chance of zero or $1,000 and a cash income of $400, we say *that the utility of $400 is equal* to $\frac{1}{2}(0) + \frac{1}{2}(100)$ or 50. The student may then be found to be indifferent between a cash income of $600 and a gamble in which the probability of zero is .25 and of $1,000 is .75. The interval scale value of $600 is then equal to $\frac{1}{2}(0) + \frac{3}{4}(100)$ or 75.

This procedure is continued for a large number of cash rewards and expected prizes involving $1,000 and zero. From the data collected, it is possible to express the preference of each student as a mathematical function of money and utility. Utility functions so constructed are not interpersonally comparable. In general it is not possible to construct a function for the students as a group. An exception, of course, would be possible only if all the students had the same subjective valuation of money; that is, they had the same interval scale. This is highly unlikely.

[16] Anatol Rapoport, *op. cit.*, pp. 124-128.

It is easy to generalize from the gamble about the students to ones involving different sums. All that is required for an interval scale is a method by which utility can be expressed as a linear transformation.

Stochastic choice. Ordinarily if individuals do order all alternatives, they will not be able to assign consistent utility to the same alternatives in repetitive situations without some error. This is particularly true if A is only slightly preferred to B. Instead of asserting absolutely that A is preferred to B, it would be more realistic to say, for example, that A is preferred to B "95% of the time." Or B may be preferred to A "5% of the time." In general such probabilistic preferences would give a more plausible interpretation of "indifferent" or "preferred." By weakening the "consistency requirement" in the axiomatic framework of preference orderings, extensive empirical testing would be more meaningful.[17]

With either one of the above approaches to preference ordering, there are serious obstacles to empirically deriving utility indexes.

Experiments that have been conducted to date indicate the need for an unusually high degree of sophistication in research methods.[18] This complicates the task of enlarging the collection of empirically derived utility functions. Thus it appears that for times to come, the underlying assumptions and valuations of the decision maker in choice situations will remain beyond our reach.

Optimization or suboptimization?

The decision maker may act as if he is maximizing in "closed" decision models. But his decisions may not *in fact* be "optimal" for the organization. In organizational decision making, the decision maker may be restricted by the hierarchical arrangement of the organizations and the flows of information through channels. The "closed" decision model for most organizational decision-making postures may therefore depart from the popularized concept of "maximizing" behavior.

---

[17] Herbert A. Simon, "Theories of Decision-Making in Economics and Behavioral Science," *American Economic Review*, 49, No. 3 (June, 1959), p. 262.

[18] See, for example, Donald Davidson, Patrick Suppes and Sidney Siegel, *Decision Making: An Experimental Approach* (Stanford: Stanford University Press, 1957).

Suboptimization is more typical of organizational decision making. The decision maker acts on the basis of the decision framework and information available to his particular unit or department in the hierarchy. He makes decisions from a "local" point of view.

Such decisions may be optimal for any given department, but less than optimal for the organization as a whole. The organization is affected by the total set of effects; a department may not be. Decisions beneficial to one department may create difficulties elsewhere in the organization which are much greater than the benefits received by the decision maker's department.

A company may decide to charge divisions for the use made of warehousing to assure economic utilization of facilities. The division managers have the alternative of using outside space if it is less costly. If the divisions are charged on the basis of the number of square feet occupied, it is easy for the decision maker to compare the cost of using company facilities versus independent warehouses. If company warehouses are partially empty and a division uses outside warehousing because it is less costly, the decision may well be "best" from the point of view of the division's income statement, but this is not the case for the company as a whole. The additional cost of storing in company facilities would have been zero and company profits would have been higher.

Summarizing the discussion on "closed" decision models, we find that the applicability of such models can be increased by modifying certain of the basic assumptions and relations such as action-outcome sequences and preferences orderings under different states of nature. Undoubtedly these modifications tend to broaden and add some realism to "closed" decision models, but even after such revisions, the theoretical foundations of "closed" models are inadequate to serve as points of departure for a general understanding of the human decision processes. The decision processes are far more dynamic than those depicted by the scheme of a "closed" model.

Goals are not defined in as clear-cut a manner as choice-decision models hypothesize. Goal-striving behavior occurs within a range of structure of goals. The selection of a particular goal or goal structure is itself a decision. Moreover, information is generally inadequate to identify all alternatives, and relevant alternatives are not necessarily stable; they may change with successive decisions.

There is serious doubt as to the ability of the "closed" decision model to simulate complex choice behavior, although it may do very well for simple choices.

"Open" Decision Models

In "closed" models a few dimensions of the decision environment are selected and admitted into the decision process; action-outcome relations, utility and so on. The decision maker is assumed to be a logical, methodical maximizer. In contrast, the "open" decision model parallels an "open system." Like the open system, it is continually influenced by its total environment. And, of course, it also influences the environment. Decisions shape as well as mirror environment. Contrary to main elements of "closed" decision models, it does not assume that the decision maker can recognize all goals and feasible alternatives. A more realistic view of the decision maker is emphasized. He is a complex mixture of many elements—his culture, his personality, and his aspirations.

Behavioral foundations of "open" decision model

The "open" decision model accents the individual's ability to control his behavior. For the most part, human behavior is learned and not controlled by biological forces shaped by "inborn" dimensions. This means that behavior is the outcome of conscious and unconscious "selective processes" and therefore must reflect the limitations of human cognition and the complexity of man's total environment.

Human cognition. Between the stimulus or "cue" and the ultimate action which follows, lies a filtering system or image.[19] The image is a construct of relationships, experiences, values and emotions. It is characterized by an internal capacity to grow from within as well as from the retention of external experiences. This point is illustrated by man's capacity to create, from series of unrelated events, ideas that become the sources of monumental essays, names, symphonies or organizations.[20]

The image is the key element in cognitive behavior. It contains not only what is, but what might be. Man not only knows, but knows that he knows.[21] The decision maker's decision reflects his perceptions of people, roles, and organizations in addition to his own values and emotions. Even the most intelligent of us act on the basis of images including more than the objective facts of the decision situation.

---

[19] Kenneth E. Boulding, *The Image* (Ann Arbor: University of Michigan Press, 1956).
[20] Boulding, *op. cit.,* pp. 25-27.
[21] Boulding, *Ibid.*

But despite man's power to behave "rationally," that is to say, his ability to select and order his responses to stimuli, he is bounded by a limited perspective. He possesses limited computational skills and, therefore, does not always make the best use of available information. Often he is inclined to deal with simplified models of real situations.[22]

Thus, the assumptions of "closed" decision models loses meaning in the context of an "open" system. An individual cannot weigh *all* alternatives. And still further, if the decision maker does not possess the ability to recognize and weigh the many choices that may be available, how does he "maximize" in the sense prescribed by "closed" decision models?

Role behavior. If each individual's decision is the result of a personalized selection process, how then does an organization, or for that matter society, channel such personal-centered behavior toward group defined ends? The answer lies in the make-up of the image. It is true that the image is a nondescript framework of experiences, values and expectations. But it is also characterized by order. Some experiences and expectations are collected and "stored" as single entities. Such programs of experiences and expectations become the basis for standardized responses to recurring stimuli. The whole collection of experiences and expectations, some developed from recurring and others from nonrecurring situations, are said to form premises for individual decisions.

Thus, to the extent that the organization is able to plant dominating premises, it is able to control and unify the behavior of participants. Organization structures provide status systems with roles defined. These become premises for individual decisions and hence behavior. The organization likewise provides experiences and information through training and communication. These, too, are premises for decisions and can become powerful means of influencing individuals toward organizational goals.[23] The role system, however, is perhaps the most discussed method of standardizing individual behavior.

For society as a whole, we also get individual behavior that is generally structured by premises reflecting experiences and expecta-

---

[22] Simon, Herbert A., *Models of Man* (New York: John Wiley & Sons, Inc., 1957), p. 197.
[23] Simon, Herbert A., *Administrative Behavior* (2nd ed.; New York: The Macmillan Company, 1957), pp. 123-125.

tions associated with roles. Public approval is often dependent on the way one acts and his role. For some roles—motherhood, fatherhood, doctor, etc., there are well-defined sets of standardized behaviors or norms that must be adhered to by the "acting" individuals. Fathers are expected to be the breadwinners in the American family; they are expected to assume financial responsibility. The laws of society frequently reflect the expectations as to how one is to act in a role. Fathers may be jailed for nonsupport. Creditors may sue husbands for debts incurred by their wives. Every person acts out at least one role for which there is an expected pattern. It may be his role as a citizen, soldier, teacher, student, corporate officer or public official.

Decisions in "open" models

The single-choice "open" decision model in some ways resembles a dynamic means-end or "closed" scheme. That is, the decision is made within the framework of a predetermined goal and established alternative. But the comparison ends there. Consider the model in Figure 1.

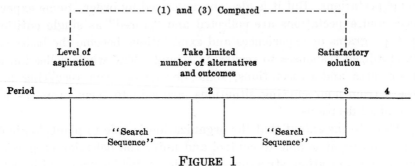

FIGURE 1

A SINGLE CHOICE "OPEN" MODEL

The decision maker passes through three time periods:

Period 1. The individual starts out with an idealized goal structure. He defines one or more action goals as a "first approximation" of the "ideal goal" in the structure. The action goal(s) may be considered as representative of the decision maker's *Aspiration Level.*[24]

Period 2. The individual engages in search activity and defines a limited number of outcomes and alternatives. He does not attempt

---

[24] Kurt Lewin, *et al.*, "Level of Aspiration," *Personality and the Behavior Disorders,* Vol, 1, J. Mcv. Hunt (Ed.) (New York: Ronald Press, 1944),

to establish the relations rigorously. His analysis proceeds from loosely defined rules of approximation. The limited alternatives defined establish a starting point for further search toward a solution.

Period 3. Search among the limited alternatives is undertaken to find a "satisfactory" as contrasted with an "optimal" solution. "Satisfactory" is defined in terms of the aspiration level or action goals.

A number of differences between "closed" and "open" decision models which are not always apparent are highlighted:

1. Predetermined goals are replaced by some unidentified structure which is approximated by an aspiration level.
2. All alternatives and outcomes are not predetermined; neither are the relationships between specific alternatives and outcomes always defined.
3. The ordering of all alternatives is replaced by a search routine which considers fewer than all alternatives.
4. The individual does not maximize but seeks to find a solution to "satisfy" an aspiration level.

Even in a single choice situation, the "open" model offers a "deeper" description of the choice process than "closed" decision models. If choices are defined in a stochastic context, this model can be predictive.

The multiple choice "open" model

The multiple choice "open" model is a more ambitious attempt to emphasize cognition processes in decision making. The model is a hierarchy of "single" decisions"; each successive decision is an attempt to improve the outcome in light of new information gained in the previous decisions. It provides a highly realistic simulation of human problem-solving.

The key element in the multiple-choice "open" model is the attainment discrepancy or the difference between the levels of aspiration and achievement. In most cases, some attainment discrepancy is almost certain because of the decision maker's inability to equate with any degree of precision a given outcome with his aspiration level. Generally an outcome can only be identified with a region about the aspiration level. A given outcome is satisfactory (unsatisfactory) or successful (unsuccessful) according to the magnitude of the attainment discrepancy. In our model, only significant discrepancies (plus or minus) are considered.

The attainment discrepancy controls the *modus operandi* for reaching a stable solution in "open" models. The size and direction of the discrepancy induce adjustments in both the level of aspiration and search activity.[25]

In Figure 2, it is explicitly assumed that a "plus" discrepancy increases the level of aspiration and decreases the range of search for solutions. A "negative" discrepancy decreases the level of aspirations and broadens the range of search. These behavioral attributes are specifically defined to assure "bound" properties in the model. This means that the range of fluctuations is restricted. The decision and aspiration level fluctuates between positions of minimum and maximum potential. Lewin *et al.* introduce "bound" properties in a

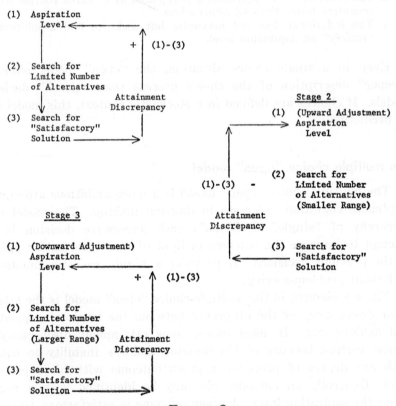

FIGURE 2

THE MULTIPLE CHOICE "OPEN" DECISION MODEL

[25] Simon, *Model of Man, op. cit.*, p. 253.

similar model by making the attainment of "highly satisfactory solutions" highly improbable, and "highly unsatisfactory solutions" highly probable. The effect of this approach is to make search desirable and probable given an unsatisfactory solution. But as reasonably satisfactory solutions are reached, search becomes undesirable and improbable. There must exist a solution where search activity will cease altogether.

The model in Figure 2 is an adaptive one. The decision maker reacts to the outcome by adjusting his goals (aspiration level) and hence his definition of an acceptable outcome.

The "open" decision model promises a number of fruitful paths toward a "complete" decision model. But it, too, has limitations. The main limitation (rather serious at this point) is the difficulty of discovering and measuring attributes of complex choice situations. Beyond this such models are a source of encouragement for students of decision-making. "Open" decision models add realism to the decision-making framework. The human capacities of the decision maker are given some measure of recognition. "Open" decision models offer a richer explanation of the human decision-making framework; the dynamics of choice are introduced. Finally, "open" decision models bring to bear the totality of forces—external and internal to the decision maker—influencing a decision.

Conclusions

There is a growing disenchantment with "closed" decision models in economic and management science circles.[26] A serious reconsideration of decisions that confront the organization decision maker and the required decision foundations appears to be in order. At this point there is evidence that the most vital decisions are non-recurring. "Search" is required to find feasible alternatives. And often this "search" must not be constrained by the bounds of some preferred solution. Problems solving requires a flexible and dynamic framework. Organizations grow and thus have growing aspirations; so must their problems and what constitute acceptable solutions. The future of "open" decision models, in light of these straws in the wind, seems highly promising.

[26] See, for example, Charles Hitch, "Uncertainties in Operations Research," *Journal of Operations Research*, Vol. 8, No. 4 (July-August, 1960), pp. 437-45, and Kenneth J. Arrow, "Decision Theory and Operations Research," *Journal of Operations Research*, Vol. 5, No. 6 (December, 1957), pp. 765-774.

19. MAKING DECISIONS [1]

Peter F. Drucker [2]

Whatever a manager does he does through making decisions. Those decisions may be made as a matter of routine. Indeed, he may not even realize that he is making them. Or they may affect the future existence of the enterprise and require years of systematic analysis. But management is always a decision-making process.

The importance of decision-making in management is generally recognized. But a good deal of the discussion tends to center on problem-solving, that is, on giving answers. And that is the wrong focus. Indeed, the most common source of mistakes in management decisions is the emphasis on finding the right answer rather than the right question.

The only kind of decision that really centers in problem-solving is the unimportant, the routine, the tactical decision. If both the conditions of the situation and the requirements that the answer has to satisfy, are known and simple, problem-solving is indeed the only thing necessary. In this case the job is merely to choose between a few obvious alternatives. And the criterion is usually one of economy: the decision shall accomplish the desired end with the minimum of effort and disturbance.

In deciding which of two secretaries should go downstairs every morning to get coffee for the office—to take the simplest example—the one question would be: What is the prevailing social or cultural etiquette? In deciding the considerably more complex question: Shall there be a "coffee break" in the morning, there would be two questions: Does the "break" result in a gain or in a loss in work accomplished, that is, does the gain in working energy outweigh the lost time? And (if the loss outweighs the gain): Is it worth while to upset an established custom for the sake of the few minutes? Of course, most tactical decisions are both more complicated and more important. But they are always one-dimensional, so to speak:

[1] From *The Practice of Management* (New York: Harper & Brothers). Copyright, 1954, by Peter F. Drucker; English copyright by William Heinemann Ltd. Reprinted by permission of Peter F. Drucker, Harper & Brothers, and William Heinemann Ltd.

[2] Peter F. Drucker, Author, Consultant, and Lecturer in the field of general management.

The situation is given and the requirements are evident. The only problem is to find the most economical adaptation of known resources.

But the important decisions, the decisions that really matter, are strategic. They involve either finding out what the situation is, or changing it, either finding out what the resources are or what they should be. These are the specifically managerial decisions. Anyone who is a manager has to make such strategic decisions, and the higher his level in the management hierarchy, the more of them he must make.

Among these are all decisions on business objectives and on the means to reach them. All decisions affecting productivity belong here: they always aim at changing the total situation. Here also belong all organization decisions and all major capital-expenditures decisions. But most of the decisions that are considered operating decisions are also strategic in character: arrangement of sales districts or training of salesmen; plant layout or raw-materials inventory; preventive maintenance or the flow of payroll vouchers through an office.

Strategic decisions—whatever their magnitude, complexity or importance—should never be taken through problem-solving. Indeed, in these specifically managerial decisions, the important and difficult job is never to find the right answer, it is to find the right question. For there are few things as useless—if not as dangerous—as the right answer to the wrong question.

Nor is it enough to *find* the right answer. More important and more difficult is to make effective the course of action decided upon. Management is not concerned with knowledge for its own sake; it is concerned with performance. Nothing is as useless therefore as the right answer that disappears in the filing cabinet or the right solution that is quietly sabotaged by the people who have to make it effective. And one of the most crucial jobs in the entire decision-making process is to assure that decisions reached in various parts of the business and on various levels of management are compatible with each other, and consonant with the goals of the whole business.

Decision-making has five distinct phases: Defining the problem; analyzing the problem; developing alternate solutions; deciding upon the best solution; converting the decision into effective action. Each phase has several steps.

Making decisions can either be time-wasting or it can be the manager's best means for solving the problem of time utilization. Time should be spent on defining the problem. Time is well spent on analyzing the problem and developing alternate solutions. **Time is necessary to make the solution effective. But much less time should be spent on finding the right solution.** And any time spent on selling a solution after it has been reached is sheer waste and evidence of poor time utilization in the earlier phases.

Defining the problem

Practically no problem in life—whether in business or elsewhere —ever presents itself as a case on which a decision can be taken. What appear at first sight to be the elements of the problem rarely are the really important or relevant things. **They are at best symptoms.**

Management may see a clash of personalities; the real problem may well be poor organization structure. Management may see a problem of manufacturing costs and start a cost-reduction drive; the real problem may well be poor engineering design or poor sales planning. Management may see an organization problem; the real problem may well be lack of clear objectives.

The first job in decision-making is therefore to find the real problem and to define it. And too much time cannot be spent on this phase. The books and articles on leadership are full of advice on how to make fast, forceful and incisive decisions. But there is no more foolish—and no more time-wasting—advice than to decide quickly what a problem really is.

Symptomatic diagnosis—the method used by most managers— is no solution. It is based upon experience rather than upon analysis, which alone rules it out for the business manager who cannot systematically acquire this experience. We cannot put sick businesses into a clinic and exhibit them to students as we do with sick people. We cannot test whether the manager has acquired enough experience to diagnose correctly before letting him loose on actual problems. We can—and do—use cases to prepare men to make business decisions. But the best of cases is still a dead specimen preserved, so to speak, in alcohol. It is no more a substitute for the real business problem than the specimens in the anatomical museum are a substitute for the live patient in the clinical ward.

Moreover, symptomatic diagnosis is only permissible where the symptoms are dependable so that it can be assumed that certain visible surface phenomena pertain to certain definite diseases. The doctor using symptomatic diagnosis can assume that certain symptoms do not, on the whole, lie (though even the physician today tries to substitute strict, analytical methods for symptomatic diagnosis). The manager, however, must assume that symptoms do lie. Knowing that very different business problems produce the same set of symptoms, and that the same problem manifests itself in an infinite variety of ways, the manager must analyze the problem rather than diagnose it.

To arrive at the definition of the problem he must begin by finding the "critical factor." This is the element (or elements) in the situation that has to be changed before anything else can be changed, moved, acted upon.

A fairly large kitchenware manufacturer bent all management energies for ten years toward cutting production costs. Costs actually did go down; but profitability did not improve. Critical-factor analysis showed that the real problem was the product mix sold. The company's sales force pushed the products that could be sold the easiest. And it put all its emphasis on the most obvious sales appeal: lower price. As a result the company sold more and more of the less profitable lines where its competitors made the least efforts. And as fast as it reduced manufacturing costs it cut its price. It gained greater sales volume—but the gain was pure fat rather than growth. In fact, the company became progressively more vulnerable to market fluctuations. Only by defining the problem as one of product mix could it be solved at all. And only when the question was asked: What is the critical factor in this situation? could the right definition of the problem be given.

To find the critical factor by straight analysis of the problem is not always easy. Often two subsidiary approaches have to be used. Both are applications of a principle developed by the classical physicists of the eighteenth century to isolate the critical factor: the principle of "virtual motion." One approach assumes that nothing whatever will change or move, and asks: What will then happen in time? The other approach projects backward and asks: What that could have been done or left undone at the time this problem first appeared, would have materially affected the present situation?

One example of the use of these two approaches is the case of a chemical company that faced the need to replace the executive vice-president who had died suddenly. Everybody agreed that the dead man had made the company; but everybody agreed also that he had been a bully and a tyrant and had driven out of the company all independent people. Consequently the problem, as management saw it, seemed to be that of deciding between not filling the job at all or filling it with another strong man. But if the first were done who would run the company? If the second, would there not be another tyrant?

The question of what would happen if nothing were done revealed both that the problem was to give the company a top management, and that action had to be taken. Without action the company would be left without top management. And sooner or later—probably sooner—it would decline and disintegrate.

The question of what could have been done ten years ago then brought out that the executive vice-president, his function and his personality were not the problem at all. The problem was that the company had a president in name but not in fact. While the executive vice-president had had to make all the decisions and take full responsibility, final authority and its symbols were still vested in a president who guarded his rights jealously, though he had abdicated in effect. Everything that could have been done ten years earlier to secure to the company the benefit of the dead man's strength and safeguard it against his weaknesses would have required clear establishment of the man's authority and responsibility as the top man. Then constitutional safeguards—team organization of the top job; assignment of the objective-formulating part of the job to the vice-presidents operating as a planning committee, or federal decentralization of product businesses—could have been provided. This analysis thus revealed that removal of the president was the first thing that had to be done.

The second step in the definition of the problem is to determine the conditions for its solution.

The objectives for the solution must be thought through.

In replacing the deceased executive vice-president the objectives for the solution of the problem were fairly obvious. It had to give the company an effective top management. It had to prevent a recurrence of one-man tyranny. And it had to prevent the recurrence of a leaderless interregnum; it had to provide tomorrow's top managers.

The first objective ruled out the solution most favored by some of the vice-presidents: an informal committee of functional vice-presidents working loosely with the nominal president. The second ruled out the solution favored by the Board chairman: recruitment of a successor to the executive vice-president. The third objective demanded that, whatever the organization of top management, federally decentralized product businesses had to be created to train and test future top managers.

The objectives should always reflect the objectives of the business, should always be focused ultimately on business performance and business results. They should always balance and harmonize the immediate and the long-range future. They should always take into account both the business as a whole and the activities needed to run it.

At the same time the rules that limit the solution must be thought through. What are the principles, policies and rules of conduct that have to be followed? It may be a rule of the company never to borrow more than half its capital needs. It may be a principle never to hire a man from the outside without first considering all inside managers carefully. It may be considered a requirement of good manager development not to create crown princes in the organization. It may be established policy that design changes must be submitted to manufacturing and marketing before being put into effect by the engineering department.

To spell out the rules is necessary because in many cases the right decision will require changing accepted policies or practices. Unless the manager thinks through clearly what he wants to change and why, he is in danger of trying at one and the same time both to alter and to preserve established practice.

The rule is actually the value-system within which the decision has to be made. These values may be moral; they may be cultural; they may be company goals or accepted principles of company structure. In their entirety they constitute an ethical system. Such a system does not decide what the course of action should be; it only decides what it should not be. Management people often imagine that the Golden Rule of doing unto others as you would have them do unto you, is a rule of action. They are wrong; the Golden Rule only decides what action should not be taken. Elimination of the unacceptable courses of action is in itself an essential prerequisite to decision. Without it there will be so many courses to choose from as to paralyze the capacity to act.

Analyzing the problem

Finding the right question, setting the objectives and determining the rules together constitute the first phase in decision-making. They define the problem. The next phase is analyzing the problem: classifying it and finding the facts.

It is necessary to classify the problem in order to know who must make the decision, who must be consulted in making it and who must be informed. Without prior classification, the effectiveness of the ultimate decision is seriously endangered; for classification alone can show who has to do what in order to convert the decision into effective action.

The principles of classification have been discussed earlier. There are four: the futurity of the decision (the time-span for which it commits the business to a course of action and the speed with which the decision can be reversed) ; the impact of the decision on other areas and functions; the number of qualitative considerations that enter into it; and the uniqueness or periodicity of the decision. This classification alone can insure that a decision really contributes to the whole business rather than solves an immediate or local problem at the expense of the whole. For the classification proposed sorts out problems according to their correlation both with over-all business goals and with the goals of the component that the individual manager runs. It forces the manager to see his own problem from the point of view of the enterprise.

"Get the facts" is the first commandment in most texts on decision-making. But this cannot be done until the problem has first been defined and classified. Until then, no one can know the facts; one can only know data. Definition and classification determine which data are relevant, that is, the facts. They enable the manager to dismiss the merely interesting but irrelevant. They enable him to say what of the information is valid and what is misleading.

In getting the facts the manager has to ask: What information do I need for this particular decision? He has to decide how relevant and how valid are the data in his possession. He has to determine what additional information he needs and do whatever is necessary to get it.

These are not mechanical jobs. The information itself needs skillful and imaginative analysis. It must be scrutinized for underlying patterns which might indicate that the problem has been wrongly defined or wrongly classified. In other words, "getting the facts" is only part of the job. Using the information as a means to test the validity of the whole approach is at least as important.

A monthly trade magazine found itself in financial difficulties. The problem was defined as one of advertising rates. But analysis of the facts and figures showed something no one at the magazine had ever suspected: whatever success the magazine had had was as a source of news for its subscribers. The subscribers were oversupplied with weighty monthlies; they lacked a smaller news publication and valued the particular magazine the more the closer it came to a news magazine in format and editorial content. As a result of this analysis of readership figures the whole problem was redefined: How can we become a news magazine? And the solution was: by becoming a weekly. It was the right solution, too, as the magazine's subsequent success showed.

The manager will never be able to get all the facts he should have. Most decisions have to be based on incomplete knowledge—either because the information is not available or because it would cost too much in time and money to get it. To make a sound decision, it is not necessary to have all the facts; but it is necessary to know what information is lacking in order to judge how much of a risk the decision involves, as well as the degree of precision and rigidity that the proposed course of action can afford. For there is nothing more treacherous—or, alas, more common—than the attempt to make precise decisions on the basis of coarse and incomplete information. When information is unobtainable, guesses have to be made. And only subsequent events can show whether these guesses were justified or not. To the decision-making manager applies the old saying of doctors: "The best diagnostician is not the man who makes the largest number of correct diagnoses, but the man who can spot early, and correct right away, his own mistaken diagnosis." To do this, however, the manager must know where lack of information has forced him to guess. He must define the unknown.

Developing alternative solutions

It should be an invariable rule to develop several alternative solutions for every problem. Otherwise there is the danger of falling into the trap of the false "either-or." Most people would protest were one to say to them: "All things in the world are either green or red." But most of us every day accept statements—and act on them—that are no whit less preposterous. Nothing is more common than the confusion between a true contradiction—green and non-green, for instance—which embraces all possibilities, and a contrast—green and red, for instance—which lists only two out of numerous possibilities. The danger is heightened by the common human tendency to focus on the extremes. All color possibilities are indeed expressed in "black or white," but they are not contained in it. Yet, when we say "black or white," we tend to believe that we have stated the full range simply because we have stated its extremes.

The old plant of a small, plumbing equipment manufacturer had become obsolete and threatened the company with the total loss of market position in a highly competitive and price conscious industry.

Management rightly concluded that it had to move out of the plant. But because it did not force itself to develop alternate solutions, it decided that it had to build a new plant. And this decision bankrupted the company. Actually nothing followed from the finding that the old plant had become obsolete but the decision to stop manufacturing there. There were plenty of alternative courses of action: to subcontract production, for instance, or to become a distributor for another manufacturer not yet represented in the territory. Either one would have been preferable, would indeed have been welcomed by a management that recognized the dangers involved in building a new plant. Yet, management did not think of these alternates until it was too late.

Another example is that of a big railroad which, in the postwar years, experienced a sharp increase in traffic volume. It was clear that facilities had to be expanded. The bottleneck seemed to be the company's biggest classification yard. Situated halfway between the main terminal points the yard handled all freight trains, breaking them up and rearranging them. And the jam in the yard had become so bad that trains were sometimes backed up for miles outside either end and had to wait twenty-four hours before they could even get in. The obvious remedy was to enlarge the yard. And this was accordingly done at a cost running into many millions. But the company has never been able to use the enlarged facilities. For the two subsidiary yards that lie between the main yard and the two terminals, north and south respectively, simply could not handle such additional loads as would be imposed on them were the new facilities put to use. Indeed it speedily became clear that the real problem all along had been the limited capacity of the subsidiary yards. The original main yard would have been able to handle a good deal more traffic if only the subsidiary yards had been larger and faster. And the enlargement of these two yards would have cost less than a fifth of the sum that was wastefully invested in enlarging the main yard.

These cases reveal how limited most of us are in our imagination. We tend to see one pattern and to consider it the right if not the only pattern. Because the company has always manufactured its own goods, it must keep on manufacturing. Because profit has always been considered the margin between sales price and manufacturing costs, the only way to raise profitability is cutting production costs. We do not even think of subcontracting the manufacturing job or of changing the product mix.

Alternative solutions are the only means of bringing our basic assumptions up to the conscious level, forcing ourselves to examine them and testing their validity. Alternative solutions are no guarantee of wisdom or of the right decision. But at least they prevent our making what we would have known to be the wrong decision had we but thought the problem through.

Alternative solutions are in effect our only tool to mobilize and to train the imagination. They are the heart of what is meant by the "scientific method." It is the characteristic of the really first-class scientist that he always considers alternative explanations, no matter how familiar and commonplace the observed phenomena.

Of course, searching for and considering alternatives does not provide a man with an imagination he lacks. But most of us have infinitely more imagination than we ever use. A blind man, to be sure, cannot learn to see. But it is amazing how much a person with normal eyesight does not see, and how much he can perceive through systematic training of the vision. Similarly, the mind's vision can be trained, disciplined and developed. And the method for this is the systematic search for, and development of, the alternative solutions to a problem.

What the alternatives are will vary with the problem. But one possible solution should always be considered: taking no action at all.

To take no action is a decision fully as much as to take specific action. Yet, few people realize this. They believe that they can avoid an unpleasant decision by not doing anything. The only way to prevent them from deceiving themselves in this way is to spell out the consequences that will result from a decision against action.

Action in the enterprise is always of the nature of a surgical interference with the living organism. It means that people have to change their habits, their ways of doing things, their relationship to each other, their objectives or their tools. Even if the change is slight there is always some danger of shock. A healthy organism will withstand such shock more easily than a diseased one; indeed, "healthy" with respect to the organization of an enterprise means the ability to accept change easily and without trauma. Still it is the mark of a good surgeon that he does not cut unless necessary.

The belief that action on a problem has to be taken may in itself be pure superstition.

For twenty years a large shipping company had difficulty filling one of its top jobs. It never had anyone really qualified for the position. And whoever filled it soon found himself in trouble and conflict.

But for twenty years the job was filled whenever it became vacant. In the twenty-first year a new president asked: What would happen if we did not fill it? The answer was: Nothing. It then turned out that the position had been created to perform a job that had long since become unnecessary.

It is particularly important in all organization problems that one consider the alternative of doing nothing. For it is here that traditional ways of doing things and positions reflecting past rather than present needs have their strongest hold on management's vision and imagination. There is also the danger of the almost automatic growth of layers and levels of management which will be continued unless the decision not to fill a vacant job is always considered as part of the decision how to fill it.

Finding the best solution

Only now should the manager try to determine the best solution. If he has done an adequate job, he will either have several alternatives to choose from each of which would solve the problem, or he will have half a dozen or so solutions that all fall short of perfection but differ among themselves as to the area of shortcoming. It is a rare situation indeed in which there is one solution, and one alone. In fact, wherever analysis of the problem leads to this comforting conclusion, one may reasonably suspect the solution of being nothing but a plausible argument for a preconceived idea.

There are four criteria for picking the best solution.

1. The risk. The manager has to weigh the risks of each course of action against the expected gains. There is no riskless action nor even riskless non-action. But what matters most is neither the expected gain nor the anticipated risk but the ratio between them. Every alternative should therefore contain an appraisal of the odds it carries.

2. Economy of effort. Which of the possible lines of action will give the greatest results with the least effort, will obtain the needed change with the least necessary disturbance of the organization? Far too many managers pick an elephant gun to chase sparrows. Too many others use slingshots against forty-ton tanks.

3. Timing. If the situation has great urgency, the preferable course of action is one that dramatizes the decision and serves notice on the organization that something important is happening. If, on the other hand, long, consistent effort is needed, a slow start that gathers momentum may be preferable. In some situations the solution must be final and must immediately lift the vision of the organization to a

new goal. In others what matters most is to get the first step taken. The final goal can be shrouded in obscurity for the time being.

Decisions concerning timing are extremely difficult to systematize. They elude analysis and depend on perception. But there is one guide. Wherever managers must change their vision to accomplish something new, it is best to be ambitious, to present to them the big view, the completed program, the ultimate aim. Wherever they have to change their habits it may be best to take one step at a time, to start slowly and modestly, to do no more at first than is absolutely necessary.

4. Limitations of resources. The most important resource whose limitations have to be considered, are the human beings who will carry out the decision. No decision can be better than the people who have to carry it out. Their vision, competence, skill and understanding determine what they can and cannot do. A course of action may well require more of these qualities than they possess today and yet be the only right program. Then efforts must be made—and provided for in the decision—to raise the ability and standard of the people. Or new people may have to be found who have what it takes. This may sound obvious; but managements every day make decisions, develop procedures, or enact policies without asking the question: Do we have the means of carrying these things out? and do we have the people?

The wrong decision must never be adopted because people and the competence to do what is right are lacking. The decision should always lie between genuine alternates, that is, between courses of action every one of which will adequately solve the problem. And if the problem can be solved only by demanding more of people than they are capable of giving, they must either learn to do more or be replaced by people who can. It is not solving a problem to find a solution that works on paper but fails in practice because the human resources to carry it out are not available or are not in the place where they are needed.

Making the decision effective

Finally, any solution has to be made effective in action. . . .

If time has to be spent on selling a decision, it has not been made properly and is unlikely to become effective. Presentation of the final results should never be a great concern, though, in line with the oldest and most basic rule of rhetoric, a decision should always be presented to people in language they use and understand.

Though it is a questionable term the emphasis on "selling" the decision points up an important fact: it is the nature of the man-

agerial decision to be made effective through the action of other
people. The manager who "makes" the decision actually does no such
thing. He defines the problem. He sets the objectives and spells out
the rules. He classifies the decision and assembles the information.
He finds the alternative solutions, exercises judgment and picks the
best. But for the solution to become a decision, action is needed. And
that the decision-making manager cannot supply. He can only communicate to others what they ought to be doing and motivate them to
do it. And only as they take the right action is the decision actually
made.

To convert a solution into action requires that people understand
what change in behavior is expected of them, and what change to
expect in the behavior of others with whom they work. What they
have to learn is the minimum necessary to make them able to act the
new way. It is poor decision-making to present a decision as if it
required people to learn all over again or to make themselves over into
a new image. The principle of effective communication is to convey
only the significant deviation or exception—and that in clear, precise
and unambiguous form. It is a problem in economy and precision.

But motivation is a problem in psychology and therefore stands
under different rules. It requires that any decision become "our decision" to the people who have to convert it into action. This in turn
means that they have to participate responsibly in making it.

They should not, to be sure, participate in the definition of the
problem. In the first place, the manager does not know who should
participate until the definition and classification are done; only
then does he know what impact the decision will have and on
whom. Participation is unnecessary—and usually undesirable—in the
information-gathering phase. But the people who have to carry out
the decision should always participate in the work of developing
alternatives. Incidentally, this is also likely to improve the quality of
the final decision, by revealing points that the manager may have
missed, spotting hidden difficulties and uncovering available but
unused resources.

Precisely because the decision affects the work of other people, it
must help these people achieve their objectives, assist them in their
work, contribute to their performing better, more effectively and with
a greater sense of achievement. It cannot be a decision designed
merely to help the manager perform better, do his job more easily or
obtain greater satisfaction from it.

20. LOGICAL ANALYSIS AND
EXECUTIVE PERFORMANCE [1]

M. C. Branch [2]

Introduction

The functions of the executive can be grouped into two general categories. One involves action duties performed through personal contact or communication: leadership, initiation, decision, direction, control, motivation, guidance, inspection, or representation. This operational activity may relate to production, sales, corporate-legal affairs, personnel, public relations, facilities, or any one of a dozen areas of executive concern. The other encompasses responsibilities of an analytical nature requiring careful study: for example, determination of long-range objectives, corporate organization, financial structure and tactics, new product research, or competitive strategies.

Of course, these two categories of activity are by no means mutually exclusive and may be directed toward the same general purposes, but the first emphasizes action, the second analytical thought. One requires the executive to "get up and go" or otherwise act quickly; the other calls for him to "sit down and think" constructively, so he can formulate or approve a solution to a difficult problem, a fundamental policy or strategy, or a longer-range plan for the business. One is extrovertive and more immediate in its emphasis, the other introvertive and longer-range.[3]

Analysis and executive performance

The analytical responsibilities of management become more crucial as business and the socio-economic contexts within which it

[1] From *Journal of the Academy of Management*, Vol. 4, No. 1 (April, 1961), pp. 27-31. Reprinted by permission of the *Journal of the Academy of Management*.

[2] M. C. Branch, Thompson Ramo Wooldridge Inc., Canoga Park, California.

[3] Improvements in analytical method and its increasing application to business affairs are clearly evident in the recent literature. E.g., among the publications of the American Management Association are Felix E. Larkin, "Long-Range Planning at W. R. Grace and Co.," *Management Report No. 3* (1958), pp. 54-60; Paul V. Manning, "Long-Range Planning for Product Research," *Research and Development Series No. 4* (1957), pp. 54-57; and "Return on Investment—Tool of Modern Management," *Improved Tools of Financial Management* (1956). See also H. I. Ansoff, "Strategies for Diversification," *Harvard Business Review*, Vol. 35, No. 5 (September-October, 1957), pp. 113-124.

operates becomes organizationally and technically more complex. Many matters which in times past were appraised quite easily, now require extensive analysis. Witness the enormous increase in tax and other data for various governmental purposes incorporated by business in its operational reporting and influencing most corporate decisions. And as the different aspects of business become more interdependent, maintaining an integrated picture of the company as a whole becomes more difficult, and subject to interpretation, judgment, intent, and statistical subtlety.

New analytical mechanisms are being applied and developed in business. Even today, some executives are called upon to decide between strategies of acquisition expressed in matrix form, choose among different inventory policies derived by linear programming, adopt sales projections developed from multiple-probability assumptions, determine the practical significance of the results of the psychological interview of several executive candidates, or approve research expenditures toward a new product recommended because of estimates of the state of a technical art and scientific sampling of opinion. This type of evaluation employing quantification, mathematics, statistics, and scientific method will be more prevalent in the future.[4]

It is possible to present only the final factual results or conclusions of analysis to the executive for review and decision. But if he does not understand in general the reasoning, methodology, and judgments underlying these results which reach his desk in highly distilled form, he cannot make an intelligent decision. Unless he has sufficient background knowledge to appraise the material critically by asking appropriate questions, he cannot test its accuracy or inclusiveness, request corrections, or suggest constructive improvement. Without this minimum comprehension, he is in effect making decisions to others would, of course, constitute a serious abrogation of his basic responsibility.

At the present time, scientific method can only be applied piecemeal in corporate planning. There are many elements of the business at this level which cannot be quantified reliably, such as employee morale, the success of public relations, most legal situations, or the

---

[4] Cf. Franklin A. Lindsay, *New Techniques for Management Decision Making* (New York: McGraw-Hill Consultant Reports on Current Business Problems, 1958); A. Charnes and W. W. Cooper, "Management Models and Industrial Applications of Linear Programming," *Management Science*, Vol. 4, No. 1 (October, 1957), pp. 38-91.

value of research and development. Even in financial accounting and analysis, with its relatively high degree of quantification attained over the years, there are many aspects as subject to interpretation and subjective judgment as they are to precise calculation. For example, the return on investment of money spent for staff and other indirectly supportive activities cannot be determined with anything approaching the accuracy possible for the direct inputs-outputs of manufacturing.

Although conducted differently by different professional personnel, the diverse elements of a business comprise a single corporate entity or system. A method of comparative measurement which would overcome some of the well-known limitations of the monetary unit (the dollar) would permit a level of analysis now impossible. Since a business organism is constantly changing, a primary value of all analysis is as a basis for projection; even the closing of last year's books is as useful for what it suggests for the future as the legal-operating record it provides. But our methods of applying scientific method to business projections are quite limited. Techniques are needed for coping with constant and unequal change, for determining over-all or composite probabilities.

Because of sum limitations, many of the most vital corporate concerns are decided mainly on the basis of subjective judgment and analysis. For some time to come, it will not be possible or practical to calculate numerically the optimum course of action for such important matters as choice among investment alternatives, long-range strategy of diversification, program of research expenditures, improved personnel policies, or the initiation of foreign operations.[5]

Intuition and subjective appraisal

The time-honored methods of subjective appraisal rely on personal experience. To an extent varying widely with the individual and business situation, the executive may perform his own analytical examination and calculation in reaching his conclusions. More often, he depends on intuitive reaction and discernment. If presented with

[5] Cf. Ernest H. Weinwurm, "Limitations of the Scientific Method in Management Science," *Management Science*, Vol. 3, No. 3 (April, 1957), pp. 225-233; Peter F. Drucker, "Management Science and the Manager," *ibid.*, Vol. 1, No. 2 (January, 1955), pp. 115-126; and *Operations Research Reconsidered—Some Frontiers and Boundaries of Industrial OR*, American Management Association Report No. 10 (1958), 143 pp.

several alternatives, he is more likely to choose one of these specific recommendations than perceive or develop a synthesis solution perhaps preferable from his vantage point to any of the choices submitted. He may consider he does not have the time to resolve the problem himself, believe this can and will be done by others, or is disinclined to spend the time and effort required if he is constitutionally more oriented toward action than analysis. In any event, unless he accepts without question facts, figures, and conclusions as presented to him, he must make some form of quick analytical check for approximate accuracy and content.

Some executives prefer to manufacture logical reasons in an attempt to underpin the intuitive judgment which alone can produce a decision when there is nothing sufficiently definite to analyze meaningfully, or when there is not enough time for conclusive study. And yet, because the greater portion of the mind exists below the surface of immediate consciousness, intuition is far from chance. What is actually occurring is an unconscious or semiconscious utilization of a large mental reservoir which cannot be directly or deliberately tapped; but this accumulation of "forgotten" experiences, conclusions, facts, figures, and impressions absorbed throughout the years is applied nevertheless through intuition. Furthermore, the unconscious mind performs a high degree of effective synthesis between different or conflicting experiences.

The practical value of this intuitive judgment depends on the condition of what might be called the circuitry of the unconscious mind. Significantly crossed emotional wires can short-circuit the mental "computer" in its process of intuitive resolution, and produce a false or uniformly biased answer—not necessarily from the personal point of view of the individual who thinks and acts as he does for some compelling reason but because judgments in the best interest of an institution require as much objectivity as possible. For most businessmen, the condition of his intuitive circuitry is best evaluated by the *post facto* batting average of the sound conclusions it produces and by comparison with other intuitive minds of proven capability. Unfortunately, it is difficult for most of us to admit or even recognize a low batting average in this respect and limit or check our intuitive judgments accordingly.[6]

---

[6] See Melville C. Branch, Jr., "Psychological Factors in Business Planning," *Journal of the American Institute of Planners*, Vol. XXII, No. 3 (Summer, 1956), p. 174; Eugene Randsepp, "Can You Trust Your Hunches—The Role of Intuition in Executive Decision-Making," *Management Review*, Vol. XLIX, No. 4, American Management Association (April, 1960), pp. 4-9, 73-76.

Analytical limitations of the human mind

Although the human mind is a remarkable organism with impressive capabilities, it performs some mental functions less well than others. These relate to what may be described briefly as: scan, correlation, and abstraction.

Most persons do not consciously scan a situation in all important aspects to identify its many different elements and considerations. The frequent assumption that this awareness is widespread ignores our innate tendency to focus on those aspects with which we are most familiar through experience and professional concentration, or toward which we are oriented by our mental-emotional personalities.[7] For most people, the comprehensive view requires deliberate effort or special stimulation. We are also limited in the number of successive correlations we can follow without becoming lost. For example, deriving the outcome of a succession of many different conditional interrelationships is impossible without mathematical knowledge. Confronted with a relatively simple sequence, such as, if $A \leqq B$, $C \geqq A$, $D > B$, and $C < D$, most of us cannot readily derive the relation between A and D. In general, we can retain only a very few elements simultaneously in our minds, resolve their respective interrelationships, and determine their combined effect.[8] The average person is also limited in his capability to comprehend and manipulate abstractions. Our inherent preference is for real-life, concrete images rooted in the vast unconscious storage of experiences we have observed directly. In contrast, a characteristic of analytical method is its dependence on abstraction. Unfortunately, the analytical appraisal increasingly essential in executive business decisions involves these very mental activities we perform less effectively.

In time, our capacity to scan, correlate, and deal with abstractions may improve with educational advances, the effects of our ever-changing environment, and continued evolutionary development of the human mind itself. We know how readily children absorb new concepts with which their parents have great difficulty. It is possible that entirely new methods of conceptualization and analysis may be found which will extend those areas in which we are now cogitatively

---

[7] Insights into the relationship between individual psychology, career selection, and professional performance are provided by Lawrence S. Kubie, M.D., in "Some Unsolved Problems of the Scientific Career," *American Scientist*, Vol. 41, No. 4 (October, 1953), pp. 596-613.

[8] E.g. George A. Miller, "The Magical Number Seven, Plus or Minus Two: Some Limits on Our Capacity for Processing Information," *The Psychological Review*, Vol. 63, No. 2 (March, 1956), pp. 81-97.

relatively weak. But since we can hardly wait for evolution of an uncertain intellectual breakthrough, we must rely at least for some time to come on those aids to our mental functioning now available; and perhaps it is the more efficient utilization of these which will most likely trigger some significant methodological advance.

In our current fascination with the electronic computer, we may be neglecting to employ fully the capabilities of the most impressive cognitive device of all—the intelligent human mental-nervous system. Coupled with intuition, logical analysis is a powerful tool of subjective judgment.[9]

---

[9] In an invited presentation before the Institute of Management Science's College of Planning, at Los Angeles, California on September 12, 1960, the author elaborated upon the prerequisites to logical analysis and discussed some means and methods that might be employed as an aid to logical reasoning. The article above is an excerpt from this presentation.

21. OPERATIONAL TECHNIQUES OF
CREATIVE THINKING [1]

Charles S. Whiting [2]

The following discussion is based on a brainstorming session held at a New England manufacturing company last spring by our research group at the Harvard Business School. In order not to disclose the actual company, the product and circumstances have been disguised.

Chairman: "Gentlemen, today, we want to develop some new ideas to make the display of our paint line more effective at the dealer level. To solve this problem, we're going to use brainstorming, one of the operational techniques of creative thinking. Be sure to remember the two essential brainstorming rules. First, make no evaluation or criticism whatsoever. We only want ideas at this stage of the problem solving process. Second, try for unusual, even impractical ideas. By ranging far and wide, you'll be more apt to come up with a new approach. All set, let's start."

Advertising Manager: "What we need are some action display devices."

Sales Manager: "How about something that lights up—something that flashes on and off. Maybe it could go on and off when you approached it. You might even have a switch that works when someone steps on a certain floor board."

Advertising Agency Account Executive: "You could have a display in the window showing your entire line. Perhaps you could use light effectively to display the colors."

Marketing Director: "I've got an idea! Why don't you tie this in with the current do-it-yourself trend. Set up a film or slides in a machine in the window and show people the proper way to paint a house."

Advertising Manager: "Show them how to do all that kind of thing—lay bricks, paint, even how to hammer a nail properly. First show them a picture—then outline the steps—then give them an ad.

[1] From *Advanced Management* (October, 1955), pp. 24-30. Reprinted by permission of *Advanced Management*.
[2] Charles S. Whiting, associated with McCann-Erickson, Incorporated, New York City.

You might even make them come into the store to get a brochure listing the various steps shown on the slides. That would be a good way to get them into the store—otherwise, they hardly ever come in unless they're ready to buy."

Agency Account Executive: "This do-it-yourself stuff is great! Why don't you get together with other firms in the home improvement field and sponsor do-it-yourself shows in local high school auditoriums. It's already been done in large cities, but I've never seen it done in a small town. You could show films and demonstrate techniques."

Product Designer: "On this do-it-yourself kick again. Why not put a loudspeaker outside the store with a taped instructional spiel on do-it-yourself."

Agency Account Executive: "You know, I'll bet you could make a lot of money just supplying merchants with tape machines and taped advertising messages. Remind me to try that someday."

A little later:

Advertising Manager: "Let's have a minature display—sort of a doll house affair showing painted walls—it could revolve."

Agency Account Executive: "That's not bad, but speaking of miniatures—why don't you have some miniature paint cans made up and send them out as a promotion—they could contain a sample of your paint."

Chairman: "Back to the doll house, I just had a crazy idea—it's no good to us, but what an idea! Have a doll house in which you do-it-yourself. I mean paper the walls, paint it, install miniature plumbing—perhaps even lay miniature bricks. Some toy manufacture should love that idea. It might even bring boys into the doll house market!"

Product Designer: "A minute ago you were speaking of displays. Why not a display in a supermarket with a pitchman or demonstrator. People have to eat so they get to the supermarket every week or so— they hardly ever get into our dealers' stores."

Agency Account Executive: "What an idea I've got—a new advertising medium. Why shouldn't local stores or even national advertisers buy advertising space on supermarket walls? Look at all the blank space behind the meat counter that people could look at while they're waiting to be served."

Sales Manager: "You might even use the ceiling, it's blank."

Marketing Director: "Here's the craziest one yet. Let's paint our different shades on the ceilings of our dealers' stores. You might even have a novelty room upside down on the ceiling."

Chairman: "They'd certainly flock in to see that—and think of the publicity value!"

Company creative programs

Brainstorming, as developed by Alex F. Osborn, is just one of the operational techniques of creative thinking which business organizations are beginning to use in order to enable their employees to produce more new ideas.

The whole field of creative thinking has been drawing a great deal of attention in the last few years although its application to business problems is not exactly new: General Electric has been running a creative engineering program since 1937, and Batten, Barton, Durstine and Osborn has been using brainstorming to solve certain client problems since 1939. More recently companies such as IBM, B. F. Goodrich and the AC Spark Plug Division of General Motors have started various programs designed to teach their employees to be more creative and Ethyl regularly sponsors a presentation of these techniques to its clients, by Charles Clark, one of the experts in the field. Universities too are beginning to experiment with new courses designed to teach students to utilize a more creative approach to problem solving. Professor John Arnold's creative engineering course at MIT is perhaps the best known of these, but Rutgers has a special course combining engineering and creative thinking and Columbia, Boston University, Buffalo University and a host of others offer courses in applied imagination or creative thinking.

Fundamentally, the theory of creative thinking is based on the following premises:

1. Everyone has some degree of creative ability.
2. Certain mental and social factors prevent people from fully utilizing their creative ability.
3. Through proper orientation, use of certain techniques, and through practice, these mental and social blocks can be eliminated and this innate creative capacity can be utilized to a greater extent, and perhaps the level of creative ability may even be raised somewhat by training.

Techniques and programs for stimulating creative thinking can be broken down into two types: educational and operational. Educational programs and techniques are primarily designed to make a person more aware of his creative ability, and through study of the creative process and use of certain imagination exercises, attempt to raise his level of creative ability or at least to teach him how to utilize it more effectively. A great deal has already been written on this aspect of creative thinking, therefore I am going to concentrate on the operational aspects of the subject. Operational creative thinking techniques are perceptual schemes or conference methods which an individual or group can use to produce more new ideas—faster.

Basic operational principles

Two of the basic principles upon which all the operational techniques of creative thinking rely are:

1. A positive attitude is established—criticism or evaluation is delayed until after the ideas have been produced. This elimination of judgment from the idea production stage is one of the strongest causes for the success these techniques have achieved. Since no evaluation is allowed, negative attitudes are eliminated and a climate is created in which the participants feel free to express ideas they might otherwise be reluctant to reveal.
2. Unusual ideas are sought by encouraging many unusual, even obviously impractical, ideas, and individuals or participants in group sessions become accustomed to breaking away from traditional approaches to their problems.

The three types of operational techniques

The operational techniques of creative thinking can be roughly broken down into three categories:

1. Analytical Techniques
2. Free Association Techniques
3. Forced Relationship Techniques

Analytical techniques provide a form in which to attack a problem. They usually also rely heavily on questioning the various elements of the object or problem under consideration. They force you to ask yourself whether this can be changed or eliminated, whether a different type of power might be used, and many similar questions. Three of the commonly used operational techniques that fit into this category are checklists, attribute listing, and the input-output technique.

Free Association techniques are designed to allow any idea that comes to mind to present itself. In these techniques the use of any evaluation whatsoever in the initial idea production stage is strongly discouraged. Included in this category are the brainstorming technique and variations such as Phillips 66 Buzz Sessions, and the Gordon Technique.

Forced Relationship techniques rely on an unnatural or unusual relationship which is forced either by mechanical means or is chosen in an arbitrary manner. Once this forced relationship is established, it is used as the starting point for a series of free associations that can produce a new idea. There are a number of different variations of this type of technique. The ones I will consider will be the listing technique, catalog technique, and the "focused object" technique.

One of the simplest and most commonly used analytical techniques is the checklist. Checklists have been developed for a myriad of special uses and are often very effective when searching for the solution to a specific problem. The principal reason for their effectiveness is that if properly constructed, they recall areas for investigation that might otherwise be neglected. One of the simplest and most effective general checklists is a basic nine category list developed by Alex F. Osborn, one of creative thinking's pioneers. Here it is in its simplest form: [3]

1. Put to other uses
2. Adapt
3. Modify
4. Magnify
5. Minify
6. Substitute
7. Re-arrange
8. Reverse
9. Combine

Checklists however have two rather obvious weaknesses. First, they rely on the historical accumulation of checkpoints; thus they may exclude categories that are important to the new problem being considered. Similarly, they may include many questions that are not necessary and thus may waste the user's time.

Attribute listing

The attribute listing technique was developed by Professor Robert Platt Crawford of the University of Nebraska. Basically, it consists of listing all the attributes or qualities of an object or problem, then systematically considering each attribute or group of attributes in turn, trying to change them in as many ways as possible. An example of a number of variations that could be developed for a common wooden lead pencil through use of this technique is given in Figure 1.

[3] An expanded version of this list appears on page 284 of Osborn's book *Applied Imagination*, Charles Scribner's Sons, New York, 1953.

FIGURE I

Example of Attribute Listing

Attribute	Possible Changes
Lead produces writing	Light might be used to affect photographic paper. Heat might be used to affect a special paper. Could use a solution instead of solid lead or might use a chemical solution that reacted with the paper. (Some of these variations might lead to a pencil or writing instrument that never had to be sharpened or refilled.)
Wooden casing	Could be metal; plastic; entirely made of graphite.
Plain yellow color	Could be any color; carry advertising; or have a design. (Perhaps women would buy pens and pencils carrying the same designs as their dresses.)

The point of the example is only to demonstrate the technique. Clearly most of the ideas are neither new nor very practical, but several of them offer interesting possibilities. Remember, just one good idea can be the basis for an entire new product line or perhaps even a whole new industry.

The input-output technique

The input-output technique has been used in the creative engineering program at General Electric. It is used principally in problems in which energy is involved. The following example quoted from *Imagination-Undeveloped Resource* [4] illustrates this technique very well.

"A dynamic system can be classified according to its (1) input, (2) output, and (3) limiting requirements or specifications. For example in designing a device to automatically shade a room during bright sunlight, the problem can be defined as follows:

Input—Solar energy.
Output—Making windows alternately opaque and transparent.
Specifications—Must be usable on various sized windows, must admit not more than 20 foot-candle illumination anywhere in the room, must not cost more than $100 per 40 square foot window.

"Once the definition is set up, means of bridging the gap between input and output are sought. At each step the question is asked—can this phenomenon (input) be used directly to shade the window (desired output)? Using the above example once again, we observe that solar energy is of two types, light and heat.

[4] Pages 27-28, Imagination-Undeveloped Resource, Creative Training Associates, P.O. 913, Grand Central Station, New York 17, N. Y.

"Step 1: *What phenomena respond to application of Heat? Light?* —Are there vapors that cloud upon heating? Gases expand, metals expand, solids melt. Are there substances that cloud in bright light? Does light cause some materials to move or curl? Light causes photoelectric cells to produce current, chemicals to decompose, plants to grow.

"Step 2: *Can any of these phenomena be used directly to shade the window?*—Vapors that cloud on heating? Substances that cloud in bright light? Bi-metals warp. Slats of a blind could warp shut.

"Step 3: *What phenomena respond to step one outputs?*—Gases expand, could operate a bellows, etc. Photoelectric current, could operate a solenoid, etc. Solids melt, effect on electric conductivity, etc.

"Step 4: *Can any of these phenomena be used directly to shade the window?*—Bellows could operate a blind, etc.

"Step 5: *What phenomena respond to step three output?*—Bellows, solenoid, etc. could operate a solenoid switch or valve, which in turn could operate motors to draw the blind.

"In this manner a number of possible solutions can be developed for evaluation."

For most purposes either attribute listing or the input-output technique are probably more effective than checklists because they are based upon an individual analysis of the product or problem in question rather than on an historical accumulation of checkpoints. However the two techniques are not particularly suited to the same type of problem. Attribute listing is generally most effective when attempting to change or modify an existing object or procedure because it concentrates on the attributes of the object or procedure in question. The input-output technique on the other hand concentrates on the job to be done, thus it is probably best suited for seeking new or alternative ways to accomplish some objective.

Brainstorming

In our society, and throughout our educational process, hard sharp critical judgment has been held out as the mark of the capable man. The basic theory behind the brainstorming method is that many times this worship of critical judgment prevents people from expressing ideas that are a bit unorthodox. Thus, although this unorthodox idea might have been the best solution to the problem at hand, it is not revealed because its originator fears that his reputation for having good judgment may suffer. Furthermore, in many cases it is extremely easy to find fault with even the best idea. Thus in many cases when good ideas are expressed, they are quickly quashed by the exercise of judgment or criticism before they get a real chance.

In a brainstorming session, a climate that is most conducive to the production of ideas is set up. First, no judgment or evaluation is allowed at all. Secondly, the participants are encouraged to produce as many ideas as possible. They are even encouraged to express ideas that are extremely impractical. Who knows, what at first may seem to be a poor idea may stimulate someone else to produce a better idea, or this poor idea itself might even be developed into something useful. In fact, General Electric demonstrates the effectiveness of the brainstorming method by deliberately taking the idea the group members consider the poorest, and developing it into something useful. In one session held at the Harvard Business School for members of the Advanced Management Program by people from General Electric, a toaster was the subject under consideration. Of all the suggested improvements for the toaster, the one the group considered the poorest concerned making toast or toasters mouseproof. Yet, perhaps this idea is not as silly as it sounds. Conceivably, toast or all food for that matter could be treated with some chemical which is offensive to rodents and insects, yet did not affect human beings or the taste of the product. If this process could be developed, the nature of the food preservation business might be drastically changed.

In addition to providing a climate encouraging ideas and freedom of expression, brainstorming works for several other good reasons:

1. Contagion of enthusiasm.
2. Competition, everyone tries to produce more and better ideas than the other participants.
3. It provides the opportunity to improve or change the ideas of others. What may seem absurd to one person, may stimulate someone else to suggest a useful variation.

Brainstorming can also be done on an individual basis. Simply follow the rule of no evaluation and turn off the judicial side of your mind during the idea production stage. After all the ideas have been produced, they can be evaluated, preferably at a later date. This is the time for sharp judgment, after you have the ideas.

A Phillips 66 Buzz Session is often applied to brainstorming with large groups. Basically, a large group is broken down into a number of smaller brainstorming groups. Each group appoints a chairman and proceeds to brainstorm. After they have produced a number of ideas, they select one or more of the better ideas. The chairman of each small group then presents the selected ideas to the entire group.

The Gordon technique

The Gorden technique was developed by William J. J. Gordon of Arthur D. Little, Inc., a research and consulting firm in Cambridge, Mass. This technique is the basic method used by Arthur D. Little's Design Synthesis Group. This group invents new products to order for their clients. So far they have never failed to produce a requested invention. Among the products they have invented are a revolutionary new type of gasoline pump, a new type of can opener, and a new method of building construction.

The objective of a Gordon session is different from that of a brainstorming session. In a brainstorming session, a multiplicity of ideas is sought. In the Gordon method, only one radically new idea is wanted.

The principal characteristic of the Gordon discussion session is that only one man—the group leader—knows the exact nature of the problem to be solved. There are two main reasons why Gordon feels that the other panel members should not know what the problem is. First, he feels that brainstorming produces superficial ideas because solutions are arrived at too soon. He avoids early solutions by not revealing the problem. Secondly, he seeks to avoid "egocentric involvement." In other words, a participant in a brainstorming session may become infatuated with one of his own ideas—perhaps he may even go as far as to consider it the only logical solution. Naturally, such involvement can seriously hamper the participant's effectiveness.

Since the group members do not know the problem being considered, it is extremely important to choose a suitable subject for discussion, one that is related to the actual problem, yet which does not reveal its true nature. Here are a few examples of products and the discussion subject used: toys—play or enjoyment; fishing lures—persuasion; a new can opener—opening.

Here's an example of how a session using the Gordon technique might be conducted. Suppose the problem were to invent a new type of lawnmower. For this problem the subject for discussion could either be cutting or separation. In this case, separation would probably be the best choice because it encompasses a somewhat broader area. Cutting almost implies some sort of mechanical motion employing a blade or blades.

The session would probably open with a discussion of what separation means. The discussion would then probably move on to ways in which things are separated in nature, industry, or the home. A possible solution might be recognized by the group leader when someone talked about the rotary saw blade used in a sawmill to cut lumber. Perhaps a few years ago this idea might have led to the development of the rotary blade lawnmower now on the market. Next, someone might mention welding, and how a flame can be used to cut or separate a piece of metal into two pieces. Possibly this might lead to a solution in which a flame was used to singe the tops of the grass. Another and probably better variation might be a lawnmower that consisted merely of a single heated wire designed to accomplish the same thing. If such a lawnmover could be developed it might have several strong advantages: it would be light and easy to push and there would be no moving parts—thus it might be both safer and longer lasting. The sole purpose of this illustration is to show the kind of possibilities that occur to the group leader as the discussion moves along.

The sessions held at Arthur D. Little usually last three hours. This amount of time is necessary if a thorough discussion of the subject is to be held. After the initial idea is obtained, the group develops the idea into a finished, patented product by more conventional means.

Comparison of systems

The principal weakness of the Gordon method is that so much of the success of the session depends upon the group leader. Unless he has the ability to see relationships quickly, the session can be a failure. Also, if the other members of the group had known the exact nature of the problem, they might have been able to see relationships the leader missed. Very possibly, these relationships might have led to even better solutions for the problem at hand.

Several procedures might be followed to overcome this weakness. In one case, the session would be conducted as at present and the proceedings would be tape recorded. Then, after the session was finished and the problem revealed, the other group members would listen to the recording to see whether there were other possibilities the group leader missed. In the other alternative method, half the group members would know the problem, the other half would not. In this case, three to five people can attempt to see the relationships leading to a solution.

Our research group at Harvard felt that for most purposes, the Osborn brainstorming system is most practical. Its rules are simple and easily understood. Furthermore, many business problems especially in the advertising, sales promotion, and merchandising area call for a wide variety of ideas. The brainstorming session is especially effective in producing a large number of different ideas.

The Gordon system on the other hand probes much deeper than the Osborn system. It goes back closer to natural phenomena and is therefore especially useful for deriving entirely new principles. However, it requires an extremely capable group leader and well-trained participants. Therefore this type of session cannot usually be successfully conducted by novices, whereas brainstorming sessions very often can. A summary of rules and suggestions for both types of group sessions is given in Figure 2 reproduced from *Imagination-Undeveloped Resource.*

Forced relationship techniques

The forced relationship techniques are not particularly suited to solving an existing problem except in the broadest sense. This is because they rely on a chance relationship which is almost impossible to relate to the particular problem at hand. However, they are extremely useful in the artistic or literary fields where the user is often seeking only a new and different idea rather than the solution to a specific problem.

One of the forced relationship techniques consists of making a list of objects or ideas which may or may not have some relationship to each other. The list is then numbered. The next step consists of considering the first item on the list in relationship with each of the other items in order. After item number one has been considered in relationship with each item on the list, item two is treated in a similar manner. This process continues until each item on the list has been considered in relationship with every other item on it. A variation of this technique consists of considering three or more items at the same time.

Catalog technique

One of the favorite methods some cartoonists use to obtain a new idea is to take a Sears Roebuck catalog or a telephone book or any other source containing a large variety of different objects or categories, select two or more objects at random and force a relationship between them. This relation is then used as the basis for a cartoon idea. There are a number of other fields in which this technique or variations on the same theme can be useful.

The technique which I call the "focused object" technique contains elements of both the free association and the forced relationship techniques. It is especially useful for problems such as obtaining ideas for

FIGURE 2

Summary of Rules and Suggestions for Group Sessions

Osborn Brainstorming

   Rules:

   1. Judicial thinking or evaluation is ruled out.
   2. Free wheeling is welcomed.
   3. Quantity is wanted.
   4. Combinations and improvements are sought.

   Suggestions for the Osborn technique:

   1. Length: 40 minutes to one hour, sessions of ten to fifteen minutes can be effective if time is short.
   2. Do not reveal the problem before the session. An information sheet or suggested reference material on a related subject should be used if prior knowledge of the general field is needed.
   3. Problem should be clearly stated and not too broad.
   4. Use a small conference table which allows people to communicate with each other easily.
   5. If a product is being discussed, samples may be useful as a point of reference.

Gorden Technique

   Rules:

   1. Only the group leader knows the problem.
   2. Free association is used.
   3. Subject for discussion must be carefully chosen.

   Suggestions for the Gordon technique:

   1. Length of session: two to three hours are necessary.
   2. Group leader must be exceptionally gifted and thoroughly trained in the use of the technique.

General Suggestions that Apply to Both Techniques

1. Selection of personnel: a group from diverse backgrounds helps. Try to get a balance of highly active and quiet members.
2. Mixed groups of men and women are often more effective, especially for consumer problems.
3. Although physical atmosphere is not too important, a relaxed pleasant atmosphere is desirable.
4. Group size: groups of from four to twelve can be effective. We recommend six to nine.
5. Newcomers may be introduced without disturbing the group, but they must be properly briefed in the theory of creative thinking and the use of the particular technique.
6. A secretary or recording machine should be used to record the ideas produced. Otherwise they may not be remembered later. Gordon always uses a blackboard so that ideas can be visualized.
7. Hold sessions in the morning if people are going to continue to work on the same problem after the session has ended, otherwise hold them late in the afternoon. (The excitement of a session continues for several hours after it is completed, and can effect an employee's routine tasks.)
8. Usually it is advisable not to have people from widely differing ranks within the organization in the same session.

advertising layout or copy. The principal difference between this technique and the other forced relationship techniques is that one object or idea in the relationship is not selected at random, but deliberately chosen. The other object or idea is selected arbitrarily. The attribute or qualities of this second object or idea are then used as the starting point for a series of free associations. An attempt is made to adapt the resulting stream of free associations to the chosen object or problem. In the case of advertising copy and art ideas, the deliberately selected object is usually the product which is to be advertised.

The following example (Figure 3) shows how a common lampshade was used in a forced relationship associated with an automobile. The automobile was the pre-selected object. By focusing on the attributes of the lampshade, a chain of free associations was started, which led to other ideas. The third column shows the applications of the chain of free associations to the problem of obtaining copy and layout ideas for the automobile.

FIGURE 3

Example of Focused Object Technique

Attribute of Lampshade	Chain of Free Association	Application to Automobile
Lampshade is shaped like a peak or volcano	Volcano	
	Volcanic power	
	Explosive power	"Engine has explosive power."
	Peak	"This automobile is the peak of
	Peak of perfection	perfection."
	Steep hill	"It has hill climbing ability."
The lampshade has form	Racing form	Use a layout showing individual
	Horses	horses to dramatize horsepower.
	Horsepower	
	Winner's circle	"This automobile is always in the
	Fine horses	winner's circle."
	Other fine things	"He likes fine horses, he likes fine
	Morocco leather	cars."
	Ivory chess sets	Associate car with fine things.
	Africa	Picture car in use in Africa and all over the world.

Place of these techniques in business

If treated in their proper perspective—as aids for better utilizing native creative capacity, and possibly increasing it somewhat—use of these operational techniques of creative thinking can greatly benefit most organizations. However, they should not be regarded as a panacea—they cannot replace good judgment and hard work.

In addition to providing a greater quantity of ideas, educational and operational programs for stimulating creative thinking provide several other benefits to companies using them. First, they clearly establish the idea in the employees' minds that the company wants new ideas. Secondly, through use of these techniques, employees usually become much more confident of their creative ability—this leads to increased self-confidence that can benefit the organization in many ways. By putting the spotlight on creativity, management itself becomes much more aware of the importance of new ideas and the many factors influencing creative output in an organization. Creativity is encouraged by a permissive atmosphere—that is an organizational climate in which freedom of expression, mutual trust, and respect are present. Once management clearly becomes aware of this more organizations will take steps to see that such an atmosphere exists. Furthermore, by encouraging freer expression of ideas, management may do much to break down the rigid barriers that too often exist between the various echelons in an organization. Thus, flexibility and improved communications may be another side result of the teaching and use of the art of creative thinking.

However, the teaching of creative thinking still faces the problem of gaining industrial and educational acceptance. Part of the reason why some people consider the subject of creative thinking "illegitimate" is due to the way in which it is frequently presented. It is offered as a cure-all with all the fanfare of a medicine show. Naturally, thinking people tend to distrust such proffered panaceas. The net result is that many people are suspicious of and even antagonistic toward the subject. Therefore any company that contemplates using these techniques should be prepared to deal with resistance and perhaps even open antagonism. The proper way to handle this is to move into the area of creative thinking gradually. Be sure you know what you are attempting to do and what the limitations of creative training are. The proper type of program installation is essential. Judge the amount of resistance you expect to encounter and conduct a promotional campaign to overcome it.

Once the difficulties inherent in establishing a program have been overcome, your company can join the ranks of companies such as U. S. Rubber, Carborundum, H. J. Heinz, and Dow Chemical Company, that are already benefiting from their experiences with creative training, not only through a greater number of new ideas, but also in improved employee attitudes and better communication.

22. STIMULATE YOUR EXECUTIVES TO THINK CREATIVELY [1]

Frederic D. Randall [2]

Creativity is important in business. The ability of management to adapt to new or changing conditions, and to make them work for the business, not against it, requires thinking beyond the established areas of past experience. Indeed, an organization may consider a good capacity for creative thinking as one of its most valuable, even though nebulous, assets.

Recognizing the need for imaginative management, the alert company may move to bolster its creative potential. Men who have shown creative capacity may be given opportunities to influence more decisions. Executives of proven imagination may be brought in from other organizations. Some firms have employed experts to teach their executives how to use imagination. Yet frequently, in all the hustle to capture this elusive quality, the organization may tend to overlook a virtually untapped asset—the natural creativity of the *average* executive.

While it is true that some individuals have great creative capacity which is easily recognized in any circumstance, it is also true that almost every person is creative to some degree. Frequently, industry strives primarily to develop the exceptional man, giving him special recognition and special opportunity to function. At the same time, those who display lesser talents in this area are trapped by a system which serves to suppress even the small degree of creativity which they may possess. To be sure, great benefits may be gained by increasing the creative potential of five outstanding individuals each by 10%, and the wise organization will certainly try to do so. But there are also real gains to be achieved by increasing the creativeness of 500 men each by, say, 1%.

Many investigators of creative thinking report discouraging findings. Perhaps this is because they see its development only as an expensive teaching, training, or selection process which can be applied

[1] From the *Harvard Business Review*, Vol. XXXIII, No. 4 (July-August, 1955), pp. 121-128. Reprinted by permission of the *Harvard Business Review*.
[2] Frederick D. Randall, Manager of Merchandising, Industrial Products Division, Eli Lilly and Company, 1955.

just to a very few in key decision-making posts. But the vast natural creative force in the organization need not be developed because it is already there. It needs only an atmosphere in which it may freely emerge and not be stifled. What can management do to stimulate such an atmosphere? That is the problem of this article. I shall try to show that:

> Creativity is the result of a delicate series of mental actions, all of which can be greatly influenced by the business atmosphere in which the executive works.
>
> Creative thinking demands a genuinely free exchange of information among men at different levels of authority. Formal communication programs are not enough.
>
> The "crash" or emergency approach discourages creativity and should not be applied any more than necessary to problems in need of solution, especially those of a vital and long-run effect.
>
> In planning and control, the conditions that stimulate imagination should be taken into account.
>
> A group's understanding about the consequences of failure is an exceedingly powerful force in determining creative potential.
>
> Conditioned thinking, such as may stem from a strict policy of promotion from within, blocks the creative process, unless management takes countermeasures.

CREATIVE PROCESS

How does the mind develop a new thought? Most psychologists would agree that the creative process involves these five fundamental steps:

1. Sensing (recognizing a problem)
2. Preparation (gathering data pertinent to the problem)
3. Incubation (mulling over the data)
4. Illumination (recognizing a possible solution)
5. Verification (testing the proposed solution)

Sensing

The creative person must first be able to sense a disturbing element or a problem. Since he cannot simply set out to "be creative," he first must be able to recognize some area toward which his creative effort may be directed. This starts his mind working in the necessary areas of thought. For example:

> A controller may continue for months preparing a report made obsolete by a change in organization. Unless he senses a wasted effort in his work, he is not likely to originate a report more suited to the changed condition.

In some cases the disturbing problem is overwhelming and quite obvious. In other cases it is much more subtle and requires great sensitivity on the part of the individual. It may be the sensing of something which is out of order in an otherwise orderly mass of information. It may be the recognition of inadequate or obsolete support for an established understanding, or of the lack of explanation for an unexpected event. Whatever the sensation, it seems to be one which can be affected by the emotional environment in which an individual works as well as by the amount and type of information to which he has access.

Preparation

In the second step, the individual assembles in his mind data concerning the problem. He may recall past experience and also study new material. It is important to remember that imaginative work reflects the amount and type of information which he has at his disposal.

A creative idea is not a simple rehashing or rearranging of ideas already known to the conscious mind; it is instead an entirely new and different thing which, as we will see in the next step, comes forth from the subconscious mind as a result of the conscious mind's concentration on known ideas related to the problem. The role of preparation is that of supplying the mind with the necessary collection of information which can be sorted, rearranged, and brought into association to suggest a new hypothesis or solution. As an illustration:

> An industrial engineer, however capable of innovation in production, is not likely to prove creative in, say, organic chemical research. In his mind certain basic information must exist, from which the spark of the new idea may arise. Without this foundation, he can produce little original thought in this new area.

The manner in which information is stored, as well as the amount of it, is important. It is better if the pieces of information are stored not as single units, each separate from the other, but as a part of an associated body of ideas. The individual should have access to the widest possible field of knowledge. With an understanding of other areas which are somewhat associated with his own field of activity, he stores his observations and ideas with a maximum number of "cross references." This affords a greater possibility of recall at a later time when the items are essential in an association with other material to give birth to a new and different idea. To illustrate:

Suppose that, for the first time, two men see a common building brick laid into a wall. The first might simply store the experience with the mental note, "Here is a red building block used in walls."

But the second, with adequate information and a tendency to store cross-referenced experience, might note mentally: "Here is a square red building block used in walls. It is approximately $2'' \times 8'' \times 4''$ and weighs about 4 pounds. It will not burn and is made of fired clay. It is wire cut and has holes to give lightness and improve drying."

Whether the next problem be that of designing a uranium pile or finding a suitable doorstop, the second individual whose store of knowledge consists of a group of related ideas is much more likely to form the mental associations that will lead to solution.

Incubation

This term incubation is applied to the subconscious activity which precedes an insight or inspiration. Very little is actually known of this process, but some such activity is assumed to exist since so much insight appears never to have passed through the entire process of conscious development.

To understand incubation, we must examine two interconnected units, the conscious and the subconscious minds:

> The *conscious* mind is the one with which we are most familiar, and is the center of logical thinking; it is limited, however, because it deals with known ideas and does not create ideas of its own.
>
> The *subconscious* mind directs itself to problems which are of interest to the conscious mind; yet we are not aware of its activity until it creates and submits a new idea to the conscious.

In view of the fact that the output of the subconscious is different from any of the input, and not even a sum of any of the input parts, it seems reasonable to believe that a new idea has probably been created in the subconscious after a certain amount of sorting and manipulating of the multitude of information stored there. To strike the right arrangement may take an instant or a number of years, but once a suitable combination is found which suggests some sort of solution, this solution is presented to the conscious mind in the form of an inspiration or illumination.

In a limited way the process of subconscious mental incubation can be compared to the action of a highly automatic computer:

> In the computer certain input is stored until needed. When a problem is presented, pieces of stored input are manipulated back and forth through the computer until the right combination of data is reached. Then the solution, new and different from any of the data from which it originated, is presented for consideration. The main difference between the characteristics of subconscious incubation and the automatic

computer is that the solution coming out of the computer has a direct or mathematical relation to the data which is stored in the machine.

In mental incubation, by contrast, the solution may be only suggested by the right combination of stored data. Its relation is more nebulous, and there is a less direct or determinable connection with the basic ideas of origin.

Illumination

A great many solutions or inspirations may be presented to the conscious mind during incubation. Most of them may be rejected, others sent back for revision, and a few retained for study and verification. It is interesting to note that the subconscious submits relatively few of these solutions while it is hard pressed by the conscious mind:

> As the conscious mind grapples with a problem, it dominates the action of the subconscious and directs it along the narrow lines of conscious thinking. The subconscious mind may produce during this time, but it is most creative when the conscious mind, after concentration on the problem, is relaxed and not occupied with the matter. During this time, the subconscious does not relax but ranges freely through its stored data, sorting and rearranging until a solution is suggested and transmitted as an illumination.

Evidence of this process is found in the many important inspirations which, after a period of concentrated study and thought, have come to people while they are taking a walk, driving home from work, arising in the morning, or during some other period of mental relaxation. Indeed, this happens so often that some men who are attempting to solve great problems carry pencil and paper at all times, presumably even into the shower, for the inspiration may be fleeting and elusive. If it is not noted down at the time it occurs, the conscious mind may not be able to recall it.

Verification

During verification the mind sets about, perhaps by logical method or by experimentation, to prove or disprove the solution that has been suggested.

This process is essential to sound creative thought, but may work to reduce imaginative output if the individual attaches too much importance to negative test results or is overawed by difficulties and rebuffs. In verification, it is essential to maintain an open mind so as to avoid rejecting an idea only because of previously conditioned thought processes or attitudes resulting from training, experiences, or immediate associations. This is actually a more crucial phase in the creative process than one might first suppose. New ideas are worthless until they come into full form and are available for consideration by those who can use them.

THE RIGHT ATMOSPHERE

From the preceding examination, one can see that the elements of creative thinking can be greatly influenced by the business atmosphere in which an individual works. What are some of the practices, policies, and procedures which make this atmosphere a favorable one?

Certain physical or mechanical factors are, of course, very important. For example:

> The organization should be one that gives the individual free access to associated ideas, both horizontally and vertically, from superiors as well as from peers.
> The group make-up should be one which tends to bring together a variety of backgrounds and experiences so that they stimulate and assist each other in the imaginative process.
> Formal communications should be such as to bring a good volume of associated information to the individual so that he may more effectively orient his knowledge.
> The training should be designed to help him understand his function in correct relation to the work and objectives of the total group.

But while these more or less concrete steps are important in themselves, they cannot assure maximum creativity unless they are present in the correct type of *emotional* atmosphere. Unfortunately, this atmosphere, made up of the thoughts and feelings affecting a group's operation is not easily defined and is extremely difficult to develop or change. It is largely a result of the policies and procedures which have become established—many of them informal and unwritten. Consequently, if management wants to stimulate creativity, it must be prepared to recognize facts and feelings which may or may not have been planned.

There are five key points at which strong influences in the emotional atmosphere can be exercised to bring forth creative thinking, and they have to do with: (a) availability of information; (b) work pressure; (c) rigidity of control; (d) consequences of failure; and (e) conditioned thinking. I shall examine them in order.

Availability of information

As indicated earlier, the mind which has ample information stored and cross-referenced is most likely to come up with creative inspirations. This means that there is a need for a genuinely free exchange of information within the organization. Formal communication programs are not enough.

The example of top executives is very important. Too often it is their custom to consider a great deal of information their exclusive property. They may feel that others will not understand it or be interested in it; or, worse, they may hoard information because to them its possession is a symbol of status in the organization.

In some situations, it is quite common for the leadership all down the line to pass along information in a confidential manner, keeping it from the other members of their groups. No doubt there is a certain amount of material which is best kept confidential. An honest examination is likely to show, however, that the amount is far less than commonly supposed. And if the top executives continually confer on a give-and-take basis with others regarding the problems of work, they will find this practice will tend to be adopted throughout the organization.

Creativity thrives on an understanding that everyone in the group from the newest member up to the leader has some knowledge or experience to enrich the minds of others. This feeling is not built by the use of formal, carefully worded memoranda which carry terse messages in a one-way flow to the receiver, with the implication that no questions should be asked. Nor is it likely to exist where the leadership demands strict stratification and sets itself apart, unapproachable and out of reach. Rather, a less rigid arrangement is desirable, one where individuals at all levels talk over their common problems, where information may be examined and questioned by all those who can use it, and where every individual, feeling a sense of partnership in the total activity, receives pertinent information, good and bad, which may affect the operation.

Another hazard to the free flow of information is the insistence that it flow only through the formal lines of authority as established by the organization chart. Patterns of communication may be quite different from those of authority and responsibility. Information which is helpful in creative thought may remain uselessly contained in a limited area if it is dependent on "channels" for transmittal. The individual must have the greatest possible *opportunity* to seek material from anyone else and to exchange what he knows with any others who may come to him; and the main control should be the *obligation* on each individual's part to pass along information which may be useful in the management of group activity.

Work pressure

Creativity requires long, hard, and diligent preparation so that the mind is filled with material which is related to the solution; at the same time, it is vital to recognize that the solution may *not* come as the result of long, hard, uninterrupted concentration. On the contrary, as noted above, the incubation process may be most effective when the conscious mind is relaxed after a period of concentration and the problem is under consideration in the *sub*conscious mind.

Management should therefore recognize that, while the time needed to study the problems of work can be reduced by good planning and concentration, pressure for action does not always produce the best solutions. I realize that this principle is not entirely compatible with our present pace of business; certain thinking must be done under pressure with minimum preparation and with little or no time for the creative process to run its full course. However, it should be practical to prevent the "crash" or emergency approach from being applied to virtually every problem that is considered, especially those of a vital and long-run nature.

The fact that many creative ideas are presented to the conscious mind during an idle period following tense concentration on a problem gives real meaning to the old quip, "All work and no play makes Jack a dull boy." Many job factors can serve to dull the creative effort. Terrific pressure to reach the solution may so occupy the conscious mind with the consequences of failure that there is little opportunity for possible answers to come to the surface. If the conscious mind is forced down unprofitable channels of conditioned thinking, the subconscious flexibility which might bring solution is lost. As the effort becomes more and more intense, these familiar channels become more and more deeply established, and the possibility of the mind's escape from them becomes less and less likely.

The ideal approach, then, would seem to be developing a good balance between work and relief from work in the executive group. This implies recognition by management that:

> It is proper and desirable to stop and chat with others in the organization, and the scheduled rest periods are useful and productive.
> The man who is chained to a pile of paper work day after day and night after night without a break may be limited in his creative output.
> Vacations are designed to relieve the mind from close concentration on the daily problems and are most valuable if the individual uses them as such.
> A man's mind may make its most important creative contribution on the night that the briefcase full of work is left at the office.

Rigidity of control

In many organizations, planning and control are developed to a high degree of accuracy and efficiency. In the interests of creativity, however, planners should remember that the imagination is not governed by the laws of mechanics or physics. Creativity does not come pouring out like the parts from a punch press when we push the button marked "on." Rather, as study of the basic thought process shows, it is a highly unpredictable operation, dependent on the individual's skill in bringing about an extremely delicate combination in one of mankind's most delicate organisms, the human mind.

Unlike the machine, the mind reacts to all manner of material which surrounds it. The Univac or IBM 705 may function day in and day out without showing the slightest trace of emotion, but in the human mind emotion may be dominant. For this reason, planning and control should be done with some reflection as to the attitudes and emotions of the individuals affected.

Thus, the individual should be allowed as much voice as possible in the planning of his work. The plan should not be one which raises insurmountable emotional barriers in his mind whenever he approaches his assignment. In many cases, it will be enough simply to talk over future planning with the individuals concerned. (In so doing there may be an additional dividend, of course, arising from the fact that those who are to do the work are likely to have valuable ideas as to how it might be done. There is no greater creative incentive for a man than to know that he is working on his own program and that its success or failure is dependent on him.) In other cases, contact, work, conferences, trips, and concentrated study should be mapped out with a view to the personality and needs of the specific executive.

There is also the question of the scope of planning to which the individual should be exposed. In the interest of creativity, it is important that not every item of action is cut-and-dried, and that he see more than the fragmentary, piecemeal parts of the plan which apply immediately to his role. Not only should he be aware of the long-range objectives, but he should know where his contribution is expected to fit into the total program. With this knowledge, he is far better equipped to form the associations and relationships which will make his thinking most productive.

Consequences of failure

Few organizations, if questioned, would report that they have any official policy toward the consequences of individual failure. Yet every group has developed an understanding as to what the result of failure on a problem or project may be. In general, this feeling is based on observation of what has happened in specific cases. While the consequences of failure may never be discussed or even stated verbally, they are an exceedingly powerful force in determining the creative potential of the group.

The reason for all this is that creative thinking, by definition, implies the development of ideas which are different from those already known and hence not proven. Reason may suggest that the new idea which the individual proposes to his superiors will probably work. But the word "probably" must be emphasized; in the consideration of creativity it is essential. Managers should ask themselves: Do we recognize the element of risk which is inherent in the process? Or do we judge a creative hypothesis by the same standards as one which is a safe repetition of some proven practice of the past? The answer may directly reflect the success which the firm will have in keeping up with changing conditions.

In some organizations there exists an overwhelming emphasis on the importance of always being right. Individuals build highly successful careers around the fact that they have never made a mistake. The question is whether the organization is likely to gain anything from such an emphasis. Certainly this might be beneficial *if* the business situation were static. But conditions change and proven practice cannot always show the way. It is rarely possible to let competitors take all the risks of new moves.

The wise policy would seem to be to encourage venturesome thinking, always recognizing that some new ideas will be successful and others (a smaller number, it is hoped) will fail. But the successful ones—because they meet present needs, not the past—will contribute enough to outweigh the cost of the failures and leave a positive balance. Failure of some ideas may be considered as part of the cost of progress.

Consider the pressure upon the individual thinker whose management does not grant him the "freedom to fail":

Faced with a problem situation which should set his mind to work to develop the *best* possible solution, he instead must turn to a search for the *safe* solution. The drive to be right blocks out all creative process, for the element of risk is apparent. Instead of creative process the mind adopts the process of recall, attempting to find a proven rule from the past into which the new problem fits.

If this combination is found, and the fit is a good one, he may possibly expect to do as well as was done in the past, though certainly not much better. And, of course, if the environment has changed sufficiently, he may do much worse. But the important consideration is that he has successfully escaped the possibility of jeopardizing his future with an unknown. He avoids the risk of being called unstable and the possessor of poor judgment.

The situation, then, requires a certain skill in the handling of error. Obviously the approach is not to throw down the bars and invite everyone to abandon reason and strive for the "screwball" solution. Accuracy may still dominate preparation and research prior to the development of the hypothesis. And once the hypothesis is formed, it is in order to insist on the most accurate verification possible and on testing to see where the plan may break down. But when this stage is passed, and the idea is thought to have an extremely high probability of success, it is not reasonable to ask that the originator guarantee its success if adopted and, in effect, stake his future welfare upon it. If this is done, few will be bold enough, or foolish enough, to take the chance.

Needless to say, the creative process again hinges on the concept of mutual confidence which has been discussed previously. If the leader or the company generates an atmosphere of fear and suspicion, creative proposals will be scarce. If, by contrast, there is a feeling that there will be a reasonable understanding should the idea fail, creative attempts will flourish. Almost everyone likes to develop an idea of his own and see it work. The important thing is to make sure that this natural pride in one's product is not overpowered by fear of consequences of failure.

Note, too, that even failure may have a very positive effect in that it may point the way to a further development which will be highly successful. Many problems may be approached only by trial and error, and the management which insists on 100% success may bar its organization from any solution in these areas.

Conditioned thinking

In the study of the general creative process it was pointed out that an individual may possess a certain bias (or conditioned thinking) which prevents him from reaching the best possible hypothesis. In the business organization there may exist a certain bias in policy and procedure which also will hinder creative thought. Not only can this prevent the disturbing observation which starts the creative process, but it can also block effective solution and verification.

Generally the bias exists in some long-time understanding which has been handed along year after year. Probably its origin has been forgotten, and it has come to be accepted as a truth. It has become such a familiar groove in the thought pattern of the group that it seldom occurs to anyone to check its veracity. Such conditional thinking may result from a great many situations:

> It may reflect the views of a person in authority, gained from experience or "pride of authorship." This person may pass the bias along to others as a truth to be used in their thinking, and the situation may not allow them to do other than accept it blindly.
>
> The leader may sense a possible solution by one approach and give such detailed instructions that the subordinate fails to recognize a more fruitful approach when it unfolds.
>
> The source may be an unimaginative system of training, particularly if the material is learned by rote with little opportunity to examine the "why's," or if scant attention is given to related factors outside the field of specialty.
>
> Another cause may be promotion from within. Obviously there are many advantages to such a policy. It gives the work force a feeling of stability and hope for progress. It provides a core of executives whose qualities are well known and who are well schooled in the problems of the business. But because every person in the organization was trained by someone else in the organization and there is no influx of persons with outside experience, ideas may be passed along for generations without anyone's recognizing the possibility that they might be revised.

Reduction of a bias or conditioned thinking depends, once again, on mutual confidence. Every individual must feel free to examine and question, without fear of the consequences, every piece of information which plays a part in his thinking. Unless the practice of questioning is recognized as the normal rather than the abnormal act, there will be little freedom from bias. It is the duty of the top executive not to protect or pamper established ideas, but to see that they are subjected to honest examination and either fall by the way or else emerge the stronger and healthier for the experience.

THE BIG PROBLEM

It may be useful, in conclusion, to look at the problem of creativity in perspective.

For many years, during the early stages of industrialization, business operated in a helter-skelter way. As a holdover from the system of home workshops and self-employed craftsmen, there was little understanding of efficiency in the large-scale organization. Then we learned of "scientific management," and out of it we produced a new breed of managers, disciples of the flow chart, stop watch, and slide rule. The demand was for specialization, systemization, and control. It was felt that man could function most efficiently if his work was narrowly confined so that he could become extremely expert in his segment of the total operation. Business operations were planned and charted with split-second precision as organizations were assembled into smoothly functioning machines.

The idea is a good one and has found a lasting place in the field of business management. With its application, unbelievably complex projects may be completed with certainty and ease. Large numbers of individuals, executives and workers alike, may be brought together and their efforts efficiently applied to the making of useful products. Yet it is disturbing to note that, for all its tremendous potential, the movement conflicts in many ways with business practices which are likely to stimulate creative thinking.

This study has indicated that creativity does not necessarily thrive in the rigid organization. The stimulants for efficiency in the routine and mechanical activities of individuals are quite different from the stimulants for creativity in their mental activities.

Absolute order, systemization, and specialization all tend to restrict the areas of knowledge and interest of the individual. They are designed to confine his energies to a small area so that he may become extremely efficient in it. They preclude the broad understanding and experience which breed new thought associations and imagination. The individual is expected to function according to plan; deviation is not required and may indeed upset the plan. If the activities of a group have been efficiently engineered, the full energies of every member will be needed at all times to complete the scheduled task. No time is available to pursue creative thoughts or activities which are not included in the schedule.

The dilemma of management is obviously a difficult one. Great profits may result from increased efficiency, and equally great profits may result from creativity and inventiveness. Yet the means by which the two are stimulated are not necessarily compatible. Management, therefore, is faced with the need to make a shrewd evaluation of its requirements in each of the two areas, determining the point beyond which the pursuit of specialization, systemization, and control is not necessarily healthy. And the determination of that point must be based on the nature of the individual business and its environment.

The management of a sizable business today must work hard at the task of maintaining a stimulating atmosphere for creative thinking. To succeed it must strike a fine balance between opposing forces, and hold that balance under great temptation to sway either way. This is a key management problem. It may not be successfully side-stepped.

BIBLIOGRAPHY, CHAPTER VI

ALPERT, S. B. "Decision Making, Growth, and Failure," presented at The Institute of Management Sciences, October, 1960.

CYERT, RICHARD M., HERBERT A. SIMON, and DONALD B. TROW. "Observations of a Business Decision," *Journal of Business*, Vol. 29 (1956), 237-248.

EDWARDS, WARD. "The Theory of Decision Making," *Psychological Bulletin* (July, 1954), 380-418.

HENDERSON, ALEXANDER, and ROBERT SCHLAIFER. "Mathematical Programming," *Harvard Business Review* (May-June, 1954), 73-100.

GAUMNITZ, R. K., and O. H. BROWNLEE. "Mathematics for Decision Makers," *Harvard Business Review*, Vol. 34, No. 3 (1956), 48-56.

GUETZKOW, HAROLD, and JOHN GYR. "An Analysis of Conflict in Decision-Making Groups," *Human Relations*, Vol. VII, No. 3 (1954), 367-382.

HODNETT, EDWARD. *The Art of Problem Solving.* New York: Harper & Brothers, 1955.

HURNI, MELVIN L. "Decision Making in the Age of Automation," *Harvard Business Review*, Vol. 33, No. 5 (1955), 49-58.

LARSON, RICHARD L. "How to Define Administrative Problems," *Harvard Business Review* (January-February, 1962), 68-74.

MUTHER, RICHARD. "Techniques for Making Better Decisions," *The Management Review* (October, 1956), 821-822.

OSBORN, ALEX F. *Applied Imagination.* New York: Charles Scribner's Sons, 1953.

SCHMIDT, RICHARD N. "Management and the Electronic Computer," *Journal of the Academy of Management* (December, 1960), 167-173.

SCHULTZ, GEORGE. "Decision Making: A Case Study in Industrial Relations," *Harvard Business Review* (May-June, 1952), 105-113.

SCHWARTZ, CHARLES R. "The Return-On-Investment Concept as a Tool for Decision-Making," *Improving the Caliber of Company Management.* General Management Series, No. 183. New York: American Management Association, Inc.

SYMONDS, GIFFORD H. "Mathematical Programming as an Aid to Decision Making," *Advanced Management* (May, 1955), 11-17.

TANNENBAUM, ROBERT. "Managerial Decision-Making," *Journal of Business*, Vol. XXIII (1950), 22-39.

Chapter VII
Operations Research and
Managerial Decisions

In the preceding chapter the basic groundwork for decision making was presented. The purpose of this chapter is to show how decision making can be furthered by the use of quantitative methods embodied in operations research methods.

In the first article Cyril C. Herrmann and John F. Magee explain the role of operations research within managerial decision making while at the same time pointing out its limitations in use. In a similar view Peter F. Drucker shows what management can expect from the use of operations research and statistical decision methods. He rejects the position that managers are obsolete and, in this respect, takes a somewhat different position than do Leavitt and Whisler in Article 3 of Chapter I.

The last two articles present examples of quantitative methods. In a book such as this it is not possible, of course, to be inclusive with respect to mathematical techniques. Thus, Article 25 was selected for inclusion because it presents a conceptually simple scheduling method that has met with considerable success—the PERT system. Article 26, by contrast, discusses heuristic programming which is just beginning its development, but many believe it to be the next big step in operations research methods.

23. "OPERATIONS RESEARCH"
FOR MANAGEMENT [1]

Cyril C. Herrmann [2]
John F. Magee [3]

There is a new concept in management. It is called operations research. It has helped companies to solve such diverse business problems as directing salesmen to the right accounts at the right time, dividing the advertising budget in the most effective way, establishing equitable bonus systems, improving inventory and reordering policies, planning minimum-cost production schedules, and estimating the amount of clerical help needed for a new operation.

Operations research makes possible accomplishments like these and many others because (a) it helps to single out the critical issues which require executive appraisal and analysis, and (b) it provides factual bases to support and guide executive judgment. Thus, it eases the burden of effort and time on executives but intensifies the potential of their decision-making role. In this sense operations research contributes toward better management.

What is this thing called operations research? How does it work? How does it differ from other services to management? Where can it be used? How should management get it organized and under way? What are its limitations and potentials? These are all questions that we shall try to answer in the following pages.

ESSENTIAL FEATURES

Operations research apparently means different things to different people. To some businessmen and scientists it means only the application of statistics and common sense to business problems. Indeed, one vice president of a leading company remarked that if his division heads did not practice it every day, they would not last long. To others it is just another and perhaps more comprehensive term for existing activities like market research, quality control, or industrial engineer-

[1] From the *Harvard Business Review*, Vol. XXXI, No. 4 (July-August), pp. 100-112. Reprinted by permission of the *Harvard Business Review*.
[2] Cyril C. Herrmann, Assistant Professor of Industrial Management at Massachusetts Institute of Technology.
[3] John F. Magee, on staff of the Arthur D. Little, Inc.

ing. Some businessmen consider it a new sales or production gimmick; some, a product of academic people interfering in the practical world. In truth, operations research is none of these things, as we shall soon see.

It should not be surprising that there has been this confusion. Operations research is not an explicit, easily identifiable concept that developed to meet the specific needs of industry. It was first applied in World War II by groups of scientists who were engaged by the government to help frame recommendations for the improvement of military activities. After the war a few soundly managed companies experimented with it and found that it worked successfully in business operations as well; and it has since gained a secure foothold in industry.

Early attempts by operations analysts to describe their activities, based on the objective of arriving at a precise and comprehensive definition of operations research, tended to be overly generalized, broad, and self-conscious, and suffered from emphasis on military applications. Some of the confusion surrounding the meaning of the term, operations research, has resulted from attempts at identification with special techniques or unnecessarily rigid distinctions between operations research and other management service activities.

Now, let us see if we can cut through some of this confusion.

The first point to grasp is that operations research *is* what its name implies, research on operations. However, it involves a *particular* view of operations and, even more important, a *particular* kind of research.

Operations are considered as an entity. The subject matter studied is not the equipment used, nor the morale of the participants, nor the physical properties of the output; it is the combination of these in total, as an economic process. And operations so conceived are subject to analysis by the mental processes and the methodologies which we have come to associate with the research work of the physicist the chemist, and the biologist—what has come to be called "the scientific method."

The scientific method

The basic premise underlying the scientific method is a simple and abiding faith in the rationality of nature, leading to the belief that phenomena have a cause. If phenomena do have a cause, it is the scientist's contention that by hard work the mechanism or system underlying the observed facts can be discovered. Once the mechanism is known, nature's secrets are known and can be used to the investigator's own best advantage.

The scientist knows that his analogue to nature will never be entirely perfect. But it must be *sufficiently* accurate to suit the particular purposes at hand; and, until it is, he must repeat the processes of observation, induction, and theory construction—again and again. Note that a satisfactory solution must be in quantitative terms in order that it can be predictive—the only accepted fundamental test of being physically meaningful.

The scientific method, in its ideal form, calls for a rather special mental attitude, foremost in which is a reverence for facts. Of course all modern executives are accustomed to using figures to control their operations. But they are primarily concerned with results and only secondarily with causes; they interpret their facts in the light of company objectives. This is a much different attitude from seeking out the relationships underlying the facts.

Thus, when an executive looks at sales figures, he looks at them primarily in terms of the success of his sales campaign and its effect on profits. By contrast, when the scientist looks at these same figures, he seeks in them a clue to the fundamental behavior pattern of the customers. By the process of induction he tentatively formulates a theoretical system or mechanism; then by the inverse process of deduction he determines what phenomena should take place and checks these against the observed facts. His test is simple: Does the assumed mechanism act enough like nature—or, more specifically in this case, does it produce quantitative data such as can be used for predicting how the customers will in fact behave? For example:

> In a company manufacturing specialty products, examination of account records showed that customer behavior could be accurately described as a time-dependent Poisson process—a type of phenomenon found widely in nature, from problems in biology to nuclear physics. This concept yielded the key to establishing measures of the efficiency of the salesmen's work and of the effect of the promotion in building sales. On this basis a new method of directing promotional salesmen to appropriate accounts was constructed—and then tested by careful experiments, to see if sales increases resulted at less than proportionate increases in cost. (The results in this case were spectacular: an over-all sales rise in six figures, and a corresponding gain in net profits.)

Implementation

Through the years mathematical and experimental techniques have been developed to implement this attitude. The application of the scientific attitude and the associated techniques to the study of operations, whether business, governmental, or military, is what is meant by operations research.

Newton was able to explain the apparently totally unrelated phenomena of planetary motion and objects falling on the earth by the simple unifying concept of gravity. This represented a tremendous step forward in helping men to understand and control the world about them. Again, more recently, the power of the scientific method was demonstrated by the ability of the nuclear physicists to predict the tremendous energy potential lying within the atom.

Here are a few summary examples of the way this same kind of approach has been applied to down-to-earth business problems:

*   *   *

A manufacturer of chemical products, with a wide and varied line, sought more rational or logical bases than the customary percentage of sales for distributing his limited advertising budget among products, some of which were growing, some stable, and others declining. An operations research study showed that advertising effectiveness was related to three simple characteristics, each of which could be estimated from existing sales data with satisfactory reliability: (a) the total market potential; (b) the rate of growth of sales; (c) the customer loss rate. A mathematical formulation of these three characteristics provided a rational basis for distributing advertising and promotional effort.

In a company making a line of light machines, the executive board questioned the amount of money spent for missionary salesmen calling on customers. Studies yielded explicit mathematical statements of (a) the relation between the number of accounts called on and resulting sales volume and (b) the relation between sales costs and manufacturing and distribution costs. These were combined by the methods of differential calculus to set up simple tables for picking the level of promotion in each area which would maximize company net profits. The results showed that nearly a 50% increase in promotional activity was economically feasible and would yield substantial profits.

An industrial products manufacturer wanted to set time standards as a basis for costs and labor efficiency controls. The operations research group studied several complex operations; expressed the effect of the physical characteristics of products and equipment and the time required to produce a given amount of output in the form of mathematical equations; and then, without further extensive time study or special data collection, set up tables of production time standards according to product characteristics, equipment used, and worker efficiency, which could be applied to any or all of the production operations.

*   *   *

These examples should serve to give some idea of how the scientific method can be applied. But they represent only a few of the many scientific techniques available (as we shall see when we examine further cases in more detail). Some practitioners even take the rather broad point of view that operations research should include the rather indefinite and qualitative methods of the social fields. Most professional opinion, however, favors the view that operations research is more restricted in meaning, limited to the quantitative methods and experimentally verifiable results of the physical sciences.

Basic Concepts

There are four concepts of fundamental importance to the practice of operations research: (a) the model, (b) the measure of effectiveness, (c) the necessity for decision, and (d) the role of experimentation.

The model

The most frequently encountered concept in operations research is that of the model—the simplified representation of an operation, containing only those aspects which are of primary importance to the problem under study. It has been of great use in facilitating the investigation of operations. To illustrate with some familiar types of "models" from other fields:

1. In aeronautical engineering the model of an aeroplane is used to investigate the aerodynamic properties in a wind tunnel. While perfectly adequate for this purpose, it would hardly do for practical use. It has no seats; it may not even be hollow. It is however, a satisfactory physical model for studying the flight characteristics of the ship.
2. Another, quite different kind of model, with which we are all familiar, is the accounting model. This is essentially a simplified representation on paper, in the form of accounts and ledgers, of the flow of goods and services through a business enterprise. It provides measures of the rate of flow, the values produced, and the performances achieved, and to that extent is useful (though it is hardly a realistic representation of *operations*).
3. Many models are used in physics. Three-dimensional models of complex molecules are probably most familiar to laymen, but the most powerful models in this field are sets of mathematical equations.

There are several different types of operations research models. Most of them are mathematical in form, being a set of equations relating significant variables in the operation to the outcome.

Another type of model frequently used is the punched-card model, where components of the operation are represented by individual punched cards; masses of these are manipulated on standard punched-card equipment. For example, in a study of a sales distribution problem, each customer, of thousands served by the company, was represented by a punched card containing significant information about his location, type of business, frequency of purchases, and average rate of business. The punched cards representing the customers could then be subjected to assumed promotional treatments, with the effects of the promotions punched into the cards. The resulting business could be calculated and an evaluation made of alternative sales promotion campaigns.

Occasionally a model is physical like the ones often used by engineers. For example, the use of a hydrokinetic model has been proposed in the study of a mass advertising problem. The fluid flowing through the model would represent business of various types going to the company or to competitors as a result of various forms of the company's own and competitive promotional efforts (represented in the model by forces acting on the fluids).

Operations research models can also be distinguished as exact or probabilistic:

1. An *exact* model is used in operations or processes where chance plays a small role, where the effect of a given action will be reasonably closely determined. Exact models can be used, for example, in long-range production scheduling problems in the face of known or committed demand. The exact model is sufficiently accurate since it can be assumed that, barring a major catastrophe, over the long run planned and actual production will be reasonably close.

2. The *probabilistic* model, on the other hand, contains explicit recognition of uncertainty. Such models are of great use in the analysis of advertising problems, where the unpredictability of consumers plays a great role. They make extensive use of the highly developed theory of probability, which has come to be of such great value in the physical sciences. One customarily thinks of a physicist as dealing with rather exact concepts and highly predictable experiments. Yet physicists faced a problem equivalent to the advertising problem in predicting atomic activity. Methods developed for physical problems involving behavior under random conditions can be applied with great facility and value to operations.

The model is a major goal of the operations research analyst. In one sense, the construction of the model, or a faithful representation of the operation, is the scientist's primary job. In doing it he develops a theory to explain the observed characteristics of the operation. The investigators link together the salient characteristics of such diverse and complicated operations as sales, promotion, manufacturing, and distribution. The remaining task is to interpret this theory through the manipulation of the model, whether mathematical or physical.

Measure of effectiveness

Related to the concept of a model or theory of operation is the measure of effectiveness, whereby the extent to which the operation is attaining its goal can be explicitly determined. One common over-all measure of effectiveness in industrial operations is return on investment; another is net dollar profit. Measures of effectiveness down the scale might be the number of customers serviced per hour, the ratio of productive to total hours of a machine operation, etc.

A *consistent* statement of the fundamental goals of the operation is essential to the mathematical logic of the model. (It does not matter if the goals are complex.) Just as the model cannot make 2 and 2 add up to 5, so it is impossible to relate fundamentally inconsistent objectives and produce consistent and meaningful results.

Operations research has frequently brought to light inconsistencies in company goals. Take production scheduling for instance. Very often its object has been stated as scheduling production to meet sales forecasts with minimum production costs, with minimum inventory investment, and without customer-service failure. Yet minimizing inventory investment typically requires the use of start-and-stop or at best uneven production plans, resulting in excessive production costs; and eliminating the risk of not being able to ship every customer order immediately requires huge inventories, in the face of fluctuating and at least partially unpredictable demand.

The solution is to combine and sublimate such otherwise inconsistent goals to a higher unified and consistent goal. To illustrate:

> The diverse goals of customer service, production economy, and investment minimization can be expressed in terms of costs—the cost of inefficient production (hiring, training, overtime, etc.), the cost of investment in inventory (the rate of interest the treasurer wishes to charge to conserve his funds or perhaps the return on investment which can be earned through alternative uses of the available funds), and the cost of inability to meet a customer's demand (estimated loss of goodwill and future business). While the latter two costs are primarily policy costs, experience has shown that they are sufficiently determinable and realistic to afford a basis for management decision.
>
> The three component costs can then be cast in an algebraic equation expressing their interrelationships in terms of total scheduling cost; and the minimum total scheduling cost becomes the one, consistent goal.
>
> Note that, once set up, the algebraic equation can be worked in reverse. Thus, the sales manager might be told how much the company can *afford* to pay for an inventory large enough to avoid varying risks of failure to meet consumer demand.

This kind of clarification of goals is particularly important in relating subordinate and over-all company goals—as in the case of a department run efficiently at the expense of other departments or of a promotion budget based on a fixed percentage of sales without regard to the adverse effects on manufacturing budgets.

The statement of a complete and wholly consistent goal of company operations must be recognized as an ideal. Business goals are very complex, and to catch the full flavor of the objectives of an intricate business operation in any simple, explicit statement is difficult. Many business goals remain, and probably ever will remain, at least in part intangible—e.g., efforts to improve employee morale or contribute to the public welfare. To that extent, the objective of operations research must be more modest than the construction of a complete model and the measurement of the extent to which the operation is attaining the complete set of goals established for it. But it still can serve to clarify the interdependency of those intangibles with the company goals which in fact are measurable, thus providing a guide to executive decision.

Necessity for decision

The third concept inherent in operations research is that of decision and decision making. An essential element in all true operations research problems is the existence of alternative courses of action, with a choice to be made among them; otherwise the study of an operation becomes academic or theoretical. This should be clear from the cases already cited.

In sum, the objective of operations research is to clarify the relation between the several courses of action, determine their outcomes, and indicate which measures up best in terms of the company goal. But note that, while this should be of assistance to the executive in making his decision intelligently, in every case the ultimate responsibility still lies with him.

Role of experimentation

The fourth significant concept concerns the role of experimentation. Operations research is the application of experimental science to the study of operations. The theory, or model, is generally built up from observed data or experience, although in some cases the model development may depend heavily on external or a priori information. In either event, the theory describing the operation must always be verifiable experimentally.

Two kinds of experiments are important in this connection:

1. The first kind is designed simply to get information. Thus, it often takes the form of an apparently rather impractical test. In one case the operations analysts directed advertising toward potential customers the company knew were not worth addressing, and refrained from addressing customers the company typically sought—and for a very simple reason. There was plenty of evidence indicating what happened when advertising was directed toward those normally addressed but not enough about its effects upon those *not* normally addressed. To evaluate the effectiveness of the advertising, therefore, it was necessary to find out what happened to those normally promoted when they were not promoted, and what happened to those normally not promoted when they were.
2. The other type of experiment is the critical type; it is designed to test the validity of conclusions. Again, what appear to be rather impractical forms of experimentation are sometimes used. Thus, in the most sensitive experiments of this type, the validity of the theory or model can often be tested most revealingly in terms of the results of extreme policies rather than in terms of the more normal policy likely to be put into practice.

OTHER SERVICES

Now, before going on to discuss in more detail the administrative problems and uses of operations research, it may be well to make clear how it differs from other services to management. Many of these services have been proved of great value to the business community as a result of years of successful application to difficult problems. Are there significant differences that make it possible for operations research to extend the usefulness of these services? Let us examine some of the leading services briefly for comparison:

Statistics. Operations research is frequently confused with statistics, especially as applied to the body of specific techniques based upon probability theory which has grown up in recent years. This statistical approach originally developed in the fields of agriculture and biology but has now been extended into such areas as quality control, accounting, consumer sampling, and opinion polls.

The operations research analyst does use such statistical methods when applicable, but he is not restricted to them. Moreover, there is a difference in basic point of view. Statistics is concerned primarily with the relations between numbers, while operations research is concerned with reaching an understanding of the operation—of the underlying physical system which the numbers represent. And this may make a significant difference in results as well as approach. In a recent advertising study, the operations research team found the key to characterizing the way in which the advertising affected consumers in the results of a series of "split-run" tests. Earlier, these results had been presumed useless after statistical methods such as analysis of variance and multiple regression had failed to show meaningful conclusions.

Accounting. Operations research is also confused sometimes with accounting, particularly with the control aspects of accounting which have developed in recent years. In reality there are several differences. One springs from the fact that the fundamental and historical purpose of accounting methods has been to maintain a record of the financial operations of the company; and this is reflected in the training and attitude of many accountants. The growth of the accounting function as the interpreter of information for control purposes has been a fairly recent development, and the basic methods used and information provided are strongly influenced by the historical accounting purpose.

Accounting information is one of the principal sources of data to support an operations research study. Accounting data, however, require careful interpretation and organization before they can be used safely and efficiently. Businessmen tend to forget that accounting costs are definitions derived in the light of the fundamental accounting purpose, and sometimes they tend to confuse accounting figures with "truth." Operations research, using the same raw data, may make other definitions which serve the special needs of the particular study. One of the great stumbling blocks in the organization and implementation of an operations research study is the disentangling from accounting records of the costs appropriately defined and truly significant to the problem at hand.

It is true, however, that in the analysis and construction of measures of control, the functions of operations research and accounting do tend to overlap. Also, the men working in these functions have strong mutual interests. Accountants have served a useful purpose in bringing the importance of control measures to the attention of business management, while operations research has shown ability in building new methods for developing and implementing these concepts of control.

Marketing Research. This management service is concerned with gathering and analyzing information bearing on marketing problems. Certain marketing researchers do go so far that in some instances they are performing services akin to operations research, but for the most part they are content to measure the market, by the use of questionnaires, interviews, or otherwise, and to gather factual data which management can use as it sees fit.

By contrast, operations research, when applied to marketing problems, seeks to gain a greater understanding of the marketing operation rather than of the market itself. Thus, it may rely heavily on marketing research sources for data; in one retail advertising study, for example, a consumer-interview program was used to obtain information on the frequency with which potential customers purchased outside their own towns. But the objective, even in quantitative studies, is usually to obtain a fundamental characterization of consumers for use in the model. Furthermore, much of operations research in marketing problems is directed toward clarifying the interdependencies between marketing and other company operations. Finally, it draws on a range of techniques and analytical methods that are well beyond the scope of the usual marketing research.

Engineering. Again, the boundary between operations research and engineering is frequently unclear. Some examples may serve to draw it more definitively:

1. During the last war a great deal of effort went into the improvement of the effectiveness and efficiency of depth charges. The objective of engineering and physics research was the construction of a depth charge having the strongest explosive power. Operations research, however, was concerned with the effective use of the depth charges then available for the purpose of sinking submarines.
2. In a recent industrial situation, the engineering problem was to construct a new railway control system which would get control information quickly and clearly to the railway engineer. By contrast, the associated operations research problem was to determine whether increased speed and clarity of control information would help the train engineer in his task of getting the train to its destination safely and quickly.
3. More subtle distinctions can be found in the study of equipment that tends to break down in operation, such as aircraft or chemical-process equipment. The engineering problem may be to find out why the equipment breaks down and how the breakdowns can be prevented. The operations research assignment is likely to be finding the best way to run the operation in view of available information on the relation between breakdown and use.

Industrial Engineering. Perhaps the most difficult distinction to make is that between operations research and modern industrial engineering. The pioneers in the field of industrial engineering did work of a character which operations research analysts would be proud to claim for their field.

In modern practice, however, industrial engineers usually apply established methodologies to their problems. Moreover, their work is generally restricted in scope to manufacturing activities and, in some cases, to distribution operations. Equally important, industrial engineering is not commonly characterized by the mental discipline and techniques of analysis that are commonly associated with the physical scientist; operations research is.

Perhaps the most significant difference marking off operations research from other management services lies in the type of people employed. Operations research people are scientists, not experts. Their value is not in their knowledge or business experience but rather in their attitude and methodology. It is indicative of the influence which the physical sciences have exerted on the people in operations research that they have a self-conscious concern with concepts and first principles and show a desire to generalize from specific examples to all-encompassing theories.

In any event, the important point is that, far from supplanting or competing with other management services, operations research has been shown by experience to be particularly successful in those areas where other services are active and well developed. Indeed, one useful contribution of operations research is frequently that of integrating other information, of using the expert opinion and factual data provided by other services in an organized, comprehensive, and systematic analysis. A soundly organized operations research group should have available the services and counsel of experts in these fields for most effective joint attack on management problems. For example:

> In the continuing research program of one retail store chain operation, marketing research methods are used to provide field observations, opinions, and data on the behavior of consumers.
> The accounting organization provides information on costs and capital requirements.
> In the operations research models these data are combined and interpreted to yield information on cost control, staff incentives, merchandise policies, and credit management.

MANAGEMENT PROBLEMS

The task of establishing operations research in an industrial organization may be broken down into the problems of choosing the initial area for investigation, selecting personnel to conduct the work, and developing organizational plans for future growth. These problems raise many difficult and important questions to which there are no sound answers applicable to all companies, but which must be answered by each firm with particular reference to its own circumstances and needs. However, certain helpful suggestions may be drawn from experience in industrial operations research to date.

Areas for investigation

There are two kinds of starting places: (a) trouble spots where conventional techniques have failed and management feels the need for additional help and a fresh attack; (b) areas deliberately chosen to test the value of operations research because of its possible contribution to the general success of the company, i.e., without particular reference to an immediately pressing problem.

There are certain common characteristics of suitable problems on which to begin operations research.

1. There should be an opportunity for decision between alternative courses of action.
2. There should be a real possibility for quantitative study and measurement. Thus, a preliminary study to provide bases for predicting the acceptance of fabric styles had to be quickly dropped in one case because of the inability to construct within a reasonable period an adequate quantitative description of the complexities of fabric, style, pattern, and color.

3. It should be possible to collect data. In one case, analysis of accounts receivable for the previous two years yielded the key to a knotty marketing problem. But, in another case, a study of maintenance problems was found to be uneconomical because of the lack of available records showing maintenance and breakdown histories on equipment.
4. It should be possible to evaluate results readily. In other words, the problem should not be so large that it is indefinite; there should be some specific aspect which lends itself to solution. Neither the analyst nor the most enthusiastic executive can expect operations research activities to be supported on the basis of faith alone.

The final choice is best made in cooperation with the research team. Executives have found it useful to map out the general area in advance; the research group can then comment on those aspects which are most amenable to study, to clear formulation of the problem, and to likelihood of progress with reasonable effort. On this basis a specific problem can be selected which meets the requirements both of the executive (for importance and us) and of the research group (for suitability of existing data for quantitative study).

Much frustration and dissatisfaction can be avoided when the research team and the executives keep in mind each others' needs. The research team must formulate a sufficiently understandable statement of the problem and method of attack to provide the executives with confidence in giving support. The executives, in turn, must recognize that in research advance specifications for a detailed program including scope and goals are frequently difficult and usually meaningless; they must provide the group with access to the necessary data and people; and they must maintain contact with the work, guiding and redirecting it along the lines of greatest value as it develops.

Selection of personnel

Most reasonably large industrial organizations can either employ operations research people from the outside as needs arise or develop their own team within the company.

Operations research groups attached to reputable consulting research organizations are the principal reservoirs of trained personnel at the present time. There are several advantages in using such consultants. Management is not committed to anyone if it decides ultimately to discontinue the work. Frequently outsiders have been found to have the stature or prestige required to effect necessary changes in internal attitudes or policies. Moreover, they bring a fresh viewpoint to the operation studied, since they are not steeped in the existing internal experiences and conceptions. And they are not so likely to be diverted by pressing but less important day-to-day problems.

With respect to the disadvantages of consulting organizations, there is the matter of fees, though this factor is often overemphasized. Particularly for the smaller corporations, the cost of using a consulting group does not appear to be high relative to the cost of maintaining an internal group of equivalent experience, diversity, and training; professional people have high pay scales, and there is usually a heavy overhead for a group of this type. If the cost of using an outsider is higher at all, it is likely to result from the outsider's lack of acquaintance with the organization and its operations. It takes time to get indoctrinated, and the fees that are charged reflect this fact.

Another possible disadvantage is that regular employees may resent "outsider" investigators dipping into the internal operations of the company. Management can minimize this disadvantage, however, by choosing members of reputable consulting organizations who are trained to approach their work with integrity and tact.

The establishment of an internal operations research group is more feasible for medium-size or large corporations than for small ones. If the large company is able to find the right kind of trained and experienced people (not an easy task these days) and to support a professional group with the associated clerical and computing services, it may realize some definite long-run advantages. The internal group may ultimately become more efficient and less costly, providing an opportunity for closer contact, greater awareness of problems, and deeper acquaintance with management objectives and needs.

A compromise solution has been the use of an outside consulting group to initiate the work and thereafter to provide assistance in getting an internal group organized. This pattern is similar to that frequently followed in the past in physical research. It provides an opportunity for the company to try out operations research before it commits itself permanently and to avoid setting it up on a basis restricted to the thinking of the department in which the first problems studied happen to occur. It also enables the company to draw on the experience of the outside group for the education of its management and analytical personnel.

Organizational plans

In decisions about operations research, as in the case of other important decisions, it is vitally important for management to think ahead about the future implications. This applies with particular force to the question of organization. When the operations research group is organized, what should be its status in the company?

Some analysts have argued that the operations research group should hold a high position, acting in a staff capacity and advising the chief executive. This argument is based on the need for the operations research group to obtain the viewpoint of the company as a whole and to be aware of the objectives of top management. Unfortunately, the same argument can be made with great force for large numbers of other groups and services in the organization. They are all competing for the time of the top executives, and not all of them can have it.

A sounder course is for operations research to start modestly, at a lower point within the organization; and, as it proves itself, to develop and grow to a more prominent position. This has been the common pattern in physical research, where the research group was originally assigned to a rather low level in the organization but where today, as a result of research having proved itself, the chief research executive has risen to the vice-presidential level.

But operations research does have certain minimal requirements with regard to its authority and status even at the outset. It must be established at least at a level where decisions can be made and where there is access to the executives and the data bearing on the problems under study. If successful, the group should be given an opportunity to expand the area of its studies as it proves its case; it should not be shut off or restricted to specific and limited operating areas. Furthermore, the group needs the interest and encouragement of top management if it is to achieve its maximum level of usefulness within the company.

Future growth

If a company undertakes operations research, it should generally do so with the intention of continuing and expanding its use. The investment in knowledge and methodology, no matter how low the initial cost, is too valuable to be thrown away. Experience has shown that the problems first recognized and attacked do not generally turn out to be the most productive ones the group could study. There needs to be full recognition of the fact that operations research is not well suited to sporadic, offhand use.

A company undertaking operations research should be prepared to face the costs, not only the direct costs of the professional group but also the cost in time of executives available to the group. These costs may loom especially large in executives' minds in years to come because the return is not always visible and apparent; while operations research should pay for itself many times over in the end, yet because of the very nature of the work the payoff of specific projects is bound to vary and there will be occasional failures.

Certainly, the operations research group, if it is to realize the full potential of its particular point of view, needs freedom to initiate some problems on its own, to investigate alternative methods, and to elaborate its theories. This means that, from the point of view of the executive, the group must be free to "waste time" on subjects of little immediate or even of doubtful ultimate practical value. The successful case histories in operations research prove that with confidence, freedom, executive support, experienced and capable people, and the appropriate climate and diet of problems, operations research will survive and flourish.

EVALUATION

In perspective, what is the current status of operations research? What are its contributions, its limitations, its future?

Contributions

Case histories show that operations research provides a basis for arriving at an integrated and objective analysis of operating problems. Characteristically, operations research tends to force an expansion in viewpoint and a more critical, questioning attitude. It also stimulates objective thinking, partly because it emphasizes broad purposes and partly because the mathematical nature of the model and techniques limits the influence of personal bias.

The results of operations research studies are quantitative. They provide an opportunity for sound estimates in terms of requirements, objectives, and goals, and a basis for more precise planning and decision making.

The contributions of operations research to business analysis and planning have been important and substantial. Here are two worth singling out:

1. *The application of organized thinking to data already existing within the company*—Frequently a major contribution has been the location, collection, and classification of existing data scattered through widely separated branches of the company. In one recent study, an operations research team found the same fundamental problem cropping up under various guises in a number of different parts of the company.

Each division or section had its own point of view toward the problem, and each had significant information bearing on it that was unavailable to the others. This sort of thing happens despite the most sound and progressive management; operations research tends to rectify it.

2. *The introduction of new concepts and new methods of analysis*—Some of these concepts, such as information theory, control theory, and certain aspects of statistical mechanics have been carried over from other fields; the physical sciences, and in particular modern physics, have been a very fruitful source of transplanted analytical techniques. But there are also certain original contributions, such as the newborn theories of clerical organization and consumer behavior, which suggest the possibility of developing further tools for attacking important business problems. All these techniques make it possible to explore the effects of alternate courses of action before management becomes committed to one of them.

Limitations

Operations research is hardly a cure-all for every business ill; neither is it a source of automatic decisions. It is limited to the study of tangible, measurable factors. The many important factors affecting business decisions that remain intangible or qualitative must continue to be evaluated on the basis of executive judgment and intuition. Often they make it necessary to adjust or modify the conclusions drawn from the quantitative analysis of the researchers. Professional personnel in operations research strongly emphasize this distinction between the operations research responsibility for analysis and the executive responsibility for decision. They point with approval to cases like this one:

> In a recent series of conferences called to implement the results of a long and major operations research investigation, the analysts emphasized that their conclusions were based in part on the assumption that the output of a plant in question could be increased substantially at the existing level of efficiency. The executive responsible for the operation of the plant felt that this assumption was a sound one. The official responsible for the ultimate decision, however, decided to follow a more conservative course of action than the one indicated by the study, primarily because of his estimate of the psychological effect that increases in volume would have on the plant personnel.

The fact that operations research is scientific in character rather than expert means that more time is required to achieve useful conclusions than in the case of normal engineering analyses. As an applied science, the work is torn between two objectives: as "applied" it strives for practical and useful work; as "science" it seeks increasing understanding of the basic operation, even when the usefulness of this information is not immediately clear. The executive who plans to support research work of this character must be fairly warned of the need for restraint. The natural tendency to require that the studies or analyses be "practical" can, if enforced too rigidly, result in the loss of substantial benefits. Also, the results of studies of this type are necessarily somewhat speculative. When operations research is purchased, neither the specific program to be followed, the precise questions to be answered, nor the successful achievement of results can be guaranteed.

Recognition of this difference between operations research and more conventional engineering methods is essential to the satisfaction of both the controlling executive and the analyst.

Problems ahead

Thinking ahead about the future of operations research, the principal internal problem which it faces is the development of a reserve of manpower adequately trained and motivated. There is a serious need at the present time for trained personnel to carry forward even the present limited level of activity. Lack of manpower, even now, threatens the quality of the work. The insufficient supply of adequately trained and experienced men to meet the demand can create a vacuum, drawing in poorly trained persons and making maintenance of standards difficult. The growing interest among mathematicians, physicists, and others is easing this problem somewhat, however, and colleges and universities have taken the first steps in training young men to fill the gap. The problem the academic institutions face is primarily lack of sound case material and the current amorphous state of a subject with uncertain acceptance in industry generally. Industrial support of educational efforts by providing realistic case material and opportunities for field investigations would be of tremendous help.

The most serious problem in external relationships is probably the need to develop efficient means for communicating ideas and results of research to executive users. The more experienced operations research groups have come to realize that explaining or "selling" conclusions is just as important as arriving at conclusions, if they are in fact to be useful. The communication needs are simple: in short, an ability to express clearly and concisely conclusions based on lengthy studies, to organize results in terms of interest to the reader and user, and to recognize that executives' interests are more practical than the researchers'.

If operations research is to have a future, the professional groups and research workers in the field must ultimately establish "operations research" as something more than a catchword, by proving its continued usefulness to management in the solution of important business problems. The year-old Operations Research Society of America will help in establishing the name by circulating case histories and information on methodology among professional workers and, at least implicitly, by establishing professional standards of competence and ethics. It is to be hoped that the activities of the Society will be sufficiently publicized in busness circles to acquaint business executives with the meaning, responsibilities, and standards of the professional operations research field.

There is, unfortunately, already evidence of growing attempts to capture the term, to subordinate it to other established fields in the general areas of statistics or engineering, and to apply it to the activities of operators on the fringes of the established and reputable management and engineering consulting fields. The growth of such tendencies, if unchecked by education and publicity, may well threaten to send the term "operations research" along the way of others, like "efficiency engineering," which sooner or later became victims of undiscriminating acceptance and careless usage.

New horizons

The areas of potential application of operations research appear broad. The future holds possible extensions such as the development of strategic concepts through the applications of the much heralded (but as yet largely untested) theory of games and by the development of a fundamental understanding of the impact of advertising and merchandising methods.

How will operations research help in the future to clarify the role of the executive? Present indications are that it will live up to its expectations of helping executives to make decisions more intelligently, but the decisions will always remain to be made. The possibility of removing all subjective and qualitative factors must be deemed at the present time to be more a hope than a real possibility, and the construction of completely consistent and logical goals, while a reasonable objective in decision making, is probably unattainable. The balancing of the responsibilities to society, consumers, owners, and employees will therefore still be the fundamental task of executives.

24. THE NEW MANAGEMENT TOOLS— AND WHAT THE MANAGER CAN EXPECT OF THEM [1]

Peter F. Drucker [2]

We have all, during the past year or two, seen a tremendous number of articles, reports on speeches, and even books dealing with such new and queer-sounding topics as "operations research," "statistical decision-making," and "linear programming." We have heard a great deal about the "electronic revolution" which the large-scale computer is said to bring about in the office as well as in production work. Now, all these things are, in a way, specific tools for specific purposes. Not one of them, needless to say, is an all-purpose tool; by now we know that there is no such thing and that, just as the carpenter has to know whether he should use a screwdriver or a hammer, we in management have to know what tool to use for what purpose before we use it. But undoubtedly all these tools belong in the same tool kit, and this tool kit is the tool kit of the business manager.

What we are going to call these tools we don't really know yet. Some people call them "operations research"—perhaps the most widely publicized of all the new strange terms. Other people call them simply "management science"; a magazine under this title has just begun to appear in Cleveland. And there are still other names.

The important thing, however, is not what we call this tool kit. It is not even what is in the tool kit—just as the important thing about carpentry is not that its tools are a saw, a hammer, a screwdriver, a plane, and so on. The important thing, as I have said, is that this is *the tool kit of the manager.*

This point is frequently overlooked in discussion—which is not too surprising when most of what we hear about "operations research" or "statistical decision-making" or "large computers" is said or written by technicians in these various fields. After all, a man who is concerned with forging a screwdriver blade is unlikely to be the best man on the use of the screwdriver by the "do it yourself" carpenter.

[1] From *Controls and Techniques for Better Management*, General Management Series No. 176, American Management Association, 1955, pp. 3-15. Reprinted by permission of the American Management Association.

[2] Peter F. Drucker, Author, Consultant, and Lecturer in the field of general management.

He is much too concerned with his own techniques, with the specifications for the steel he uses, the size of the various models. In fact, if such a man were to talk to one of us ordinary screwdriver users, we would probably not understand a word he said. We might even have the greatest difficulty in realizing that he was talking about anything as familiar and simple as the ordinary screwdriver we have down in our basement workshop.

Similarly, most of the discussion in the scientific management field, precisely because it has been left entirely to the technicians and the toolmakers, has been quite incomprehensible—and incidentally most of it, to be blunt, has been quite irrelevant. Operations research has a great many very significant achievements to its credit in the relatively few years in which we have been playing around with it in business. It has succeeded in helping companies solve major problems of production scheduling, of inventory keeping, of financial policy, of sales policy, of pricing, of servicing the customers—to name only a few. It has showed a railroad how to get twice as much use out of its tremendously high investment in freight cars. It has showed a life insurance company how to cut down a 70 per cent turnover rate among newly hired clerical employees. It has shown an electrical company what the right capacity for a new plant is and has thereby saved one-fifth of capital investment. It has shown a metal fabricator how to give twice the service to his customers with half the inventory. Yet, when we read the literature about this subject, we very rarely find a discussion in language that makes sense to a businessman. It is not only that so much of what we read is presented to us in the form of mathematics—for the most part quite unnecessarily, let me add. It is also that the people who discuss operations research are interested not so much in the problem of the businessman as in their own problem, which is the problem of building a better tool.

Here, then, I shall look at these tools from the viewpoint of a manager. I shall talk, not mathematics nor logic, but business. And I shall talk, not about what these tools are and how they can be made or perfected, but about one subject only: What can a manager expect of them? What can they do for him? And what must he do to get the most benefit from them?

Business management as a rational action

I have talked about a "tool kit." But the tool kit that is beginning to be available to us in management is a very different thing from the tool kit of a carpenter. What really underlies all these new tools with their strange names and their mathematical abracadabra is a very simple, not to say elementary, insight: that business management is by its very nature not just irrational, not just "feel" or "experience," but to a very large extent is a rational action. Most experienced businessmen have of course realized this all along. They know that they act not blindly or just by "feel" or "intuition." They know that their actions and decisions are based on certain definite ideas regarding the nature of the business they manage, the nature of the market and economy in which they operate, the nature of the resources at their disposal and their limitations, and the effect of their actions upon the business and upon people outside the business. To use the scientist's term, businessmen act on the basis of a *definite hypothesis* regarding the nature and structure of the business and of the environment in which it operates.

This is, of course, not all there is to business management. I would be the last person to make light of "feel" or "intuition," let alone experience. They are essential, and they will always remain very important. But underlying them is a rational notion of the nature and structure of the business and of the nature and limitations of environment and resources—a rational hypotheses of the business.

Objectives, assumptions, and risks

If we look at this hypothesis a little more closely, we shall see that it has three major parts. First, there are the *definite objectives* of the business, objectives which the manager aims to attain through his actions. These objectives may be clear or confused; they may be tacit or carefully written out. But they are always present.

Second, there are *definite assumptions* which every manager makes, assumptions regarding the world in which he lives, the market in which he sells, the productive organization which turns out his goods, the people who keep the productive organization going, and so forth. If the businessman did not make these assumptions—and again he may make them clearly or confusedly, may imply them, or may spell them out—he could not operate at all. He would be in the position of the centipede in the old Greek fable who, so the story goes, was asked by the fly: "Tell me, centipede, which leg do you move first?" And, the fable says, the centipede has been sitting there ever since, unable to move, pondering deeply the question which of his hundred legs he moves first.

And, finally, there are *risks*, in every action and decision of business management, risks underlying the basic hypothesis which the businessman has to make regarding his business. First, the business-man must have a notion how much risk he can afford. And, second, he must have a notion how much risk is involved in a particular course of action. Economic activity is always risky for the simple reason that it focuses on the future—and the future is always uncertain.

Objectives, assumptions, and risks are the three elements which are always present in the thinking, the decisions, and the actions of a manager in a business. To repeat: the manager may be very confused about all three of them, or he may be quite clear about them. He may imply them, or he may spell them out. But there is always, inevitable and of necessity, a basic hypothesis regarding the structure and nature of the business, the structure and nature of its environ-ment, and the structure and nature of its resources, as the manager sees them. There is always a managerial idea regarding the objectives, the assumptions, and the risks of the business enterprise. In other words, the business enterprise is always a rational system; and business decisions and business actions are always rational decisions on rational action, no matter how important "feel," "intuition," or experience may be.

Purpose of the new tools

The major aim of the new tools of management which are rapidly emerging today, and their major contribution, is to bring out and sharpen this rational system, this rational hypothesis, underlying the business enterprise and underlying managerial decisions and actions.

Their aim is first to find and clearly to define this basic hypothesis, these objectives, these assumptions, these risks. Second, they ask the question: Are these compatible with each other? Does a manager want to attain, at the same time, two objectives which mutually exclude each other? And does he therefore direct his business in two contradictory directions rather than unify all managerial efforts and all managerial resources toward one consistent set of objectives? In other words, are these basic hypotheses rational? Or are they inconsistent and irrational?

Third, the new tools raise—and find the answer to—the question: What will actually be needed to attain these objectives? One can, in other words, use these new tools and methods to unify the business and to bring about *purposeful action* throughout the business. Next, the new tools make it possible to improve the objectives and the assumptions of the business and to *narrow the risks* necessary to attain the objectives and thereby to improve the economic performance of the business.

And, finally, it is possible by means of these new tools to plan *future decisions* more intelligently, with a greater chance of effectiveness and a greater chance of their being the right decisions for the future. That is, it is possible to project systematically and with a fair degree of rationality toward the future.

What I am saying, in effect, is that these new tools are basically the *manager's tool kit for the making of business decisions.*

Seven ways to better management

Specifically, how do these tools do these things? *What, in other words, can a manager expect from them? What do they contribute to the manager?* Let me say again that it is not my purpose here to speak about *how* these tools do these jobs. I am not trying to explain how to use the screwdriver or the hammer. I am only trying to show what the manager can do provided he has these tools and provided he knows what they should be able to do for him. Whether he himself has the skill or whether he hires a carpenter, the important thing— and the thing on which I shall focus—is to make clear what kind of house he can reasonably expect.

There are basically seven ways in which these new tools make better management possible.

1. *They enable a manager in a business to see and understand the whole business in fairly simple terms*—and I don't have to tell any executive how difficult this is. Our economic life and our technology have become so complex as to make it very hard for a man to see the whole of even a simple and small business.

Let me say that we are, of course, not without tools that do this job. Accounting is obviously the oldest and most successful tool for this purpose; indeed, the general accounting system with which we are all familiar is a very good example of a special-purpose tool in this management tool kit. It is, however, as I think most of us know, a special-purpose tool which will do only a few things—though it does those superbly. It is an example, in other words, of the kinds of tools I am talking about, the oldest of the management tools for rational and systematic decision-making, but it cannot do the whole job that modern business management requires.

In essentials, all tools—whether operations research, statistical decision-making, or any other—operate on very similar basic methods: they try to find a simple and universal way of looking at the business as a whole which enables a manager to understand this very complex and very diverse thing that is the modern business enterprise. But these new tools in particular can do one thing which the general accounting system cannot really do—that is, bring into the vision of the manager, the factors outside the business which influence, if not determine, the prosperity and perhaps even the survival of the business. In fact, the most important thing the new tools can do is to give an answer to the manager's question: What factors inside or outside the business determine its survival and the success of this business? What is therefore needed for it to survive and to succeed? This in turn enables a manager both to set the right objectives for the business and to take the right action to attain these objectives, and it also enables him to measure the effectiveness and success of these actions.

2. *The second basic contribution of the new management tools is that they make it possible to take decisions with respect to one area of the business without "sub-optimizing."* We all know that actual action and decision in a business are very rarely taken for the whole business. Of necessity a business, except the very smallest, is organized in functions, in departments, in divisions, or what have you. Most of the problems with which people in management deal are problems within one area of the business, problems of manufacturing or of selling, of labor relations or of purchasing.

Now, all of us know—indeed, we know it so well that it really should not have to be said—that the only reason why we have these functions is that they contribute to the business. They are not ends in themselves. And we all recognize that, properly speaking, there are very few actions or decisions in any one of these areas which do not have real impact on other areas. It is this fact that the business is an integrated whole, while managerial action by necessity is mostly concerned with a part, that causes most of our problems.

To express this in fancy language, I would say that we are forced to optimize the operations in one area of the business at the expense of performance in other areas; in other words, we continuously "sub-optimize." I have good reason for bringing in this term—and it is not that I want to dazzle the reader with my erudition. On the contrary this term "sub-optimize" is one which we are going to hear more and more in the years to come, and we might as well become familiar with it.

When I say, therefore, that the new tools available to management make it possible to take decisions with respect to one area without "sub-optimizing," I mean that it is possible to take decisions which are right for one area—which are, for instance, the right decisions on warehousing, on inventory, on pricing, on production schedules, or on the maintenance of machinery and which, at the same time, are the right decisions for the business as a whole. At the very least, it is becoming possible now to spell out fairly simply the consequences of a certain decision or action in one such area on the rest of the business.

It is also possible—and this may well be even more important—to spell out in advance what other areas have to do to make such a decision on, let us say, production scheduling effective and successful. What is needed from the sales manager for the best production scheduling? What does the purchasing agent have to contribute? What will it mean for the employment of people, the kind of people needed, their hours, their shifts—all the things which employee relations or personnel people have to work on, and so forth?

In other words, we now have tools that enable us to operate functionally or in a decentralized fashion yet know all the time what a decision in a certain area of the business means for the other areas and for the business as a whole.

3. *The next contribution of the new tools, the next thing the manager should expect and demand of them, is that they present to the manager all the alternatives of action possible in a situation.* Full knowledge of these alternatives, and of their risks and implications, is probably the most important factor in sound decision-making. All of us, inevitably, tend to see one course of action as "obvious." Our experience has conditioned us this way. It is the decision we have thought of first—and the more we think about the problem, the more sense it makes to us. This tendency of the human mind to see one or at the most two courses of action is, however, a real danger in decision-making. Most wrong decisions are not made because people are stupid. They are made because people fail to see the alternatives. Without conscious effort, and without strict methods of approaching each decision, alternatives are very hard to find.

*   *   *

To see the full range of alternatives, obviously, is essential. That the new methods, the new tools, offer for management a way of seeing the full range of alternative courses of action, the assumptions underlying each course of action, the risks which each course of action involves, and the efforts which will be needed to make each of them successful is therefore a tremendous contribution—and particularly to the small business. For one of the things which the staff people can do in a large business is to bring alternatives of action to the attention of management; whereas the smaller businessman who has to run a business alone or with a few associates, and who usually finds it impossible—or at least very difficult—to think through the full range of alternatives and all that they imply, may need to do this most.

4. *The manager should expect—and demand—of these new tools that they show him what risks there are in each course of action, what assumptions underlie it, and what efforts and resources will be needed to carry it out successfully.* He should, in other words, demand of the new tools that they show him exactly what it is he is being asked to decide.

Within its limitations—that is, within a strictly financial frame— this is, of course, what we expect our accounting system to do for us. This is what our controller should do when it comes to a question of capital investment, for instance. All I am saying is that, while the general accounting system is only one tool, we now have additional tools which, while they too have limitations, can do things which a general accounting system cannot do.

5. *These new tools can determine what measurements are appropriate to a certain decision and to a certain area of the business.*

Let me give one simple example. Anybody who has ever had anything to do with the management of people in a shop—whether as a personnel or a manufacturing man—knows, for instance, that a very small number of people, very rarely more than 10 per cent of the plant, account for 90 per cent of the absenteeism. He knows that a very small number of people account for the majority of accidents and sickness. He also knows that a very small number of jobs usually account for 90 per cent of the turnover in the plant, or that practically all the turnover occurs during the first six months of a man's employment. Yet, while all this is known, we continue to measure turnover, accidents, absenteeism, or sickness in terms of so many days lost or so much per thousand employees. This means that our figures are based on the assumption of a normal distribution of accidents, absenteeism, turnover, and so forth, whereas the distribution is not normal but is, in fact, highly abnormal. Here is one of the major reasons why we find it so very difficult to do anything really effective in respect to turnover, accidents, sickness, or absenteeism. Our figures, while statistically quite correct, mislead us totally. They do not show us where the problem is, nor do they make it possible for us to find out what it is.

The greatest limitation of accounting as a tool of management, lies precisely in its rigid and conventional concept of measurements—a concept which is necessary if accounting is to do its financial job but which greatly limits its use as a management tool. An accountant must assume that the dollar is stable; yet we all know that the dollar has a very unstable purchasing power and that to compare 1929, 1937, and 1955 dollars is very much like comparing Diesel engines, pears, and women's dresses. The accountant must assume that dollars and cents—that is, money—is the right measure for everything. Yet it is clear that this is not quite correct and that, when it comes to such things as customer service, product quality, employee relations, capital investment, research and so forth, the dollar is only one and a fairly limited measurement.

Again, the accountant must assume that the calendar year is the right time span of measurement. But we all know that the calendar year is purely arbitrary, is purely a fiction as far as economic activity is concerned—at least unless one happens to be a wheat farmer with an annual harvest—and that we have to find out what the time span really is. To the extent to which we move toward automation and the fully mechanized factory, this time span problem will become very much more serious. In an automatic factory, for instance, cost per unit—which is the cost accountant's traditional cost concept—will be meaningless. The only thing that will be meaningful is cost per time span of production compared to the number of units we turn out and sell during the same time.

But perhaps the area in which we need measurements most is the area in which our most important daily management decisions lie. We have, by and large, little control over expenses that are directly geared to the volume of production. Such things as direct labor costs and direct raw material costs change only when we change the basic ways we do the work—and that does not happen every day. We have even less control over the costs that relate to the decisions we made yesterday or the year before—the expenses on past capital investments, for instance. But we do have control over the expenses on research and sales promotion, on personnel development and a host of other things—the things the accountant calls "controlled" or "administered" expenses. Everyone knows that the decisions with respect to these expenses have the greatest immediate impact on immediate profits. Almost any company can convert a profit into a loss or a loss into a profit if it changes the depreciation basis, the research budget, or the machine maintenance schedule. Yet, at the same time, these expenses—all of them—are not incurred for the sake of current production; they have to do with the future. And the decision made today on these expenses very largely determines whether the business will have a future or not. In other words, the center of these daily managerial expenses is the decisions on the controllable expense budget. (Only basic long-range capital investment decisions are more important, and they are much less frequent.) Yet, on these expenses, we almost entirely lack measurements of what is the right expense and what is too little or too much.

It is in this area that the new tools of the manager can therefore make a tremendous contribution. They can identify and define the measurements that are appropriate to an area. They can show the time span that underlies the measurements, the time span over which a certain decision or activity should be measured. And they can work out what is relevant, the criteria of measurements for such areas as advertising, promotion, research, personnel and management development, and all the other areas of "controllable expense"—not only the areas which are decisive for both the present profit and future prosperity of the business but the areas which are a growing part of the budget and of the expenses of every business.

One example would be my own experience in determining the direction and size of the research activity in a pharmaceutical company and measuring its effectiveness and results. What we did here was not to eliminate the large area of judgment but, on the contrary, to bring out what judgments must be made, what consequences they would have, and what risks they carried. What used to be pure "guess" is now informed judgment. As a result, the company knows what research results it needs to survive. It knows how much to spend, when to spend, and how much in the way of results to expect when.

6. *The new tools can help the manager to find out who should know about decisions and about things that go on; who should have information, when he should have it, and in what form.* They can greatly help, therefore, with the communication problem of a business, especially the communication within management—which, as we all have learned, is the really important and decisive aspect of this problem. Let me again say that the closer we come toward automation, the more important this will be. For automation depends above all on really good and effective internal communication within management.

7. *Finally, these new tools can tell the manager what to look out for in the future.* They can show him what things he does not know when he makes a decision, what facts he just guesses at, and what things he had therefore better look out for. They can also show him what he expects to happen in such a way that he notices right away when

it does not happen—early enough, perhaps, to change a decision before it has become the wrong decision, before it has really done harm. The new tools can, in other words, give the manager guideposts for the un-charted future. They cannot tell him what the country will look like, but they can tell him exactly on what expectations of the country ahead he has to base his decisions: what kind of terrain he must anticipate in building his car, how long a trip he must plan for when filling his gas tank, and so forth. And they can flash a warning to the manager as soon as any of these expectations prove to have been unfounded.

Role of specialist assistance

At this point I should answer a question which I know a great many executives will immediately ask: In order to do all this, do I have to get a doctorate in mathematics? Or do I have to hire myself a whole stableful of mathematicians, physicists, and graduate statisticians?

The answer to the first question is definitely "no." You do not have to become a mathematician, a logician, or any other kind of scientist. All you have to do is to be a business manager—which is what you are already. For these are tools of the manager; they are not substitutes for the manager.

Whether you have to hire specialists to do the job is another question, to which there is really no one answer. What these tools do for you can in a way be compared to the building of a bridge. If you have a small brook to span, and if all you want is just a way to walk across it, you can lay two planks across yourself. You do not need any specialist help for that. On the other hand, if your problem is to span San Francisco Bay, you'd better get yourself some expert bridge-designers and bridge-builders. But—and this is the important "but"—these bridge-builders and bridge-designers can only design a bridge on the basis of the specifications you give them. It is not their job to tell you that you need a bridge. It is not their job to tell you where you need a bridge. And it is not their job to tell you how much traffic the bridge should bear. These decisions are not within the competence of the bridge-designer or bridge-builder. They are the basic decisions that have to be made before he can work.

Similarly, you may need specialists to do certain of these jobs. Whether you want to bring them into your own business or whether you want to farm out the work is immaterial—both ways will undoubtedly be used successfully. But, no matter how highly specialized the job which you have to do, it will be up to you to ask the basic questions; it will be up to you to tell the specialist what you demand and expect that he do.

In handling a great many of your problems, you will not need a specialist. You will indeed be perfectly capable of being your own "operations research" specialist or your own "management scientist." All you have to do is to ask the questions which I have tried to spell out in this paper: What are the objectives, the assumptions, and the risks on which I operate my business? Are they consistent, are they valid, are they sound? What do I have to do to attain these objectives—and am I actually doing it or am I doing something else? What are the alternative courses of action in a given situation? What are the impacts of action in one area of the business on all the others? What are the risks, the assumptions, and the objectives of each possible alternative course of action? What is the right measurement, and what is the right time span? Who has to know this decision and when? And what have I assumed in making it, what do I expect to happen—and what should I therefore look out for?

Summary and conclusions

Let me repeat that I do not say business is entirely a logical, systematic, scientific process. Business is very much like medicine or law, in both of which you need experience, you need intuition, you need "feel." And it is probable, if not certain, that these intangible things make the difference between a first-rate doctor and a competent doctor, between a first-rate lawyer and a competent lawyer. But it is the rational, the systematic, the logical discipline of medicine or law which makes the competent doctor and the competent lawyer. Without it, even the medical or legal genius would be a sorry quack.

Similarly, it will increasingly be the rational, the systematic, the methodical discipline of business management that will make the competent business manager—though to be a first-class manager will probably always require a plus value of intuition, experience, and "feel."

To achieve this competence—and, without first achieving it, experience, intuition, and "feel" are useless and futile—management will need more and more an understanding of these tools of management—whether you call them "management science" or "operations research" —and knowledge of the concepts of business and management on which they are based.

25. PROGRAM EVALUATION AND
REVIEW TECHNIQUE [1]

David G. Boulanger [2]

Since the first management "principles" were introduced, most planning and control methods have been predicated on using historical data. Early shop practitioners sought the most efficient utilization of time by employing timestudy and task-setting methods based on stopwatch measurement of "past" processes that were physical and finite in character. Few useful techniques have been offered facilitating forward planning of management activities for which empirical information was not available.

Current industrial activities, however, can be summarized as heavily oriented toward research and development. A "one best way" of planning and pursuing R & D projects in terms of most efficient use of time presents some intangibles that cannot conveniently be measured. This growing condition, particularly in defense industries, has prompted the development of a prognostic management planning control method called Program Evaluation and Review Technique, or PERT.[3] This article intends to briefly present the idea of the PERT method in a manner permitting the reader to ascertain its potential usefulness. . . .

The PERT technique was developed as a method of planning and controlling the complex Polaris Fleet Ballistic Missile Program for Special Projects Office (SP) of Bureau of Ordnance, U. S. Navy. The team consisted of members from SP, the contractor organization, and Booz, Allen and Hamilton, Chicago.[4] Over-all, PERT appears to be a manifestation of the program concept of management with

[1] From *Advanced Management*, Vol. 26, Nos. 7 and 8 (July-August, 1961), pp. 8-12. Reprinted by permission of *Advanced Management-Office Executive*.
[2] David G. Boulanger, Specialist—Engineering Budgets and Measurements in the Missile Production Section, Missile and Space Vehicle Department, General Electric Company.
[3] Various acronyms are coined (*e.g.*, PEP, PET, etc.) to describe modifications from the PERT method described here.
[4] See bibliography Item 5. [Malcolm, D. G., J. H. Roseboom, C. E. Clark, and W. Fazar. "Application of a Technique for Research and Development Program Evaluation," *Journal of Operations Research*, Vol. 7, No. 5 (September-October, 1959), pp. 646-669.]

emphasis on "management by exception," in that potentially trouble-some areas in R & D programs can be spotted and action taken to prevent their occurrence.

PERT, as a dynamic program tool, uses linear programming and statistical probability concepts to plan and control series and parallel tasks which appear only remotely inter-related. Many tasks involve extensive research and development which itself is difficult to sched-ule, least of all to find a "one best way" of doing it. PERT's objective is to determine the optimum way by which to maximize the attain-ment, in time, of some pre-determined objective that is preceded by a number of constraints—hence its linear programming feature. A measure of the degree of risk is predicted in probabilistic terms to foretell the reasonableness of accomplishment on scheduled time—hence its statistical probability feature.

Program network development

The bar chart, presumably derived from Gantt and still widely used, serves to plan the occurrence of entire phases of tasks in series and parallel groups over a time period. Figure 1 illustrates a sample.

PROGRAM BAR CHART

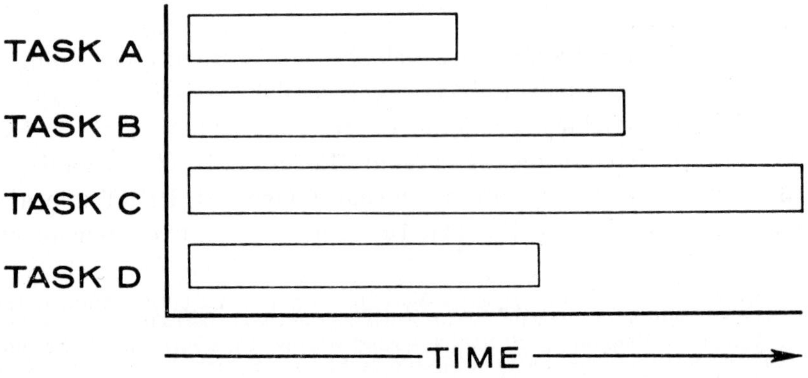

FIGURE 1

An outgrowth of the simple bar chart, called a "milestone chart," indicates significant event accomplishments as illustrated in Figure 2.

PROGRAM MILESTONE CHART

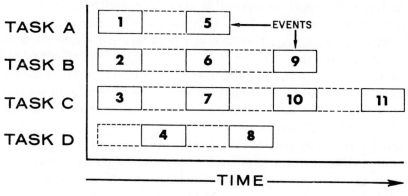

FIGURE 2

Neither technique ties together interdependencies between tasks and significant events. Series and parallel paths should indicate the inter-relationship constraints between events and tasks as shown by the arrows in Figure 3.

PERT NETWORK

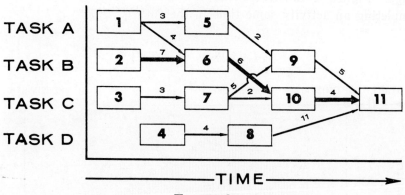

FIGURE 3

A network *event* describes a milestone, or checkpoint. An event does not symbolize the performance of work, but represents the point in time in which the event is accomplished. Each event is numbered for identification.

Arrows connecting events are *activities,* and represent performance of work necessary to accomplish an event. No event is considered accomplished until all work represented by arrows leading to it has been completed. Further, no work can commence on a succeeding event until the preceding event is completed.

If we include in Figure 3 the estimated weeks to accomplish each activity, e.g., ⟶³⟶, the earliest time objective Event 11 above can be accomplished is the sum of the longest path leading to it. This is the *critical path*, and is identified by the heavy lines connecting Events 2, 6, 10, and 11 totaling 17 weeks. The critical path contains the most significant *and* limiting events retarding program completion in less than 17 weeks.

But the time required to complete a future task is more realistically stated in terms of a likelihood rather than a positive assurance. To apply this likelihood in a probabilistic sense, three time estimates are stated as a future *range of time* in which an activity may be accomplished. The three time estimates are called *optimistic, most likely,* and *pessimistic.* They serve as points on a distribution curve whose mode is the most likely, and the extremes (optimistic and pessimistic) whose spread corresponds to the probability distribution of time involved to perform the activity. It is assumed there would be relatively little chance (*e.g.,* 1 out of 100) the activity would be accomplished *outside* the optimistic or pessimistic time estimate range. Figure 4 illustrates the estimating time distribution for completing an activity some time in the future.

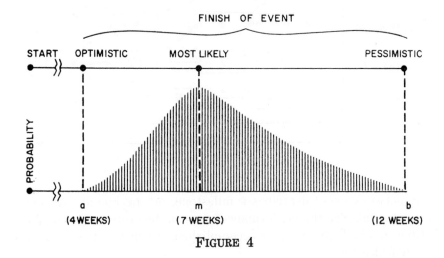

FIGURE 4

From the three time estimates (a, m, b above), a statistical elapsed time (t_e) can be derived by solving $t_e = \dfrac{a+4(m)+b}{6}$

for each activity.[5] Following this, a statistical variance (σ^2) can be derived by solving $\sigma^2 = \left(\dfrac{b-a}{6}\right)^2$ for each activity.[6] Variance may be descriptive of uncertainty associated with the three time estimate interval. A large variance implies greater uncertainty in an event's accomplishment and *vice versa*, depending whether the optimistic and pessimistic estimates are wide or close together. This facilitates evaluating risks in a program network, and using trade-offs in time and resources to minimize risk and maximize more efficient use of "factors of production."

Program network analyses

The analytical value derived from any PERT network depends on the configuration and content of the network. Every network should contain events which, to the program team's best knowledge, serve to significantly constrain the achievement of the end objective event. Next, events are inter-connected with "activities" to illustrate their flow and interdependencies. After the network of events and activities is defined, three time estimates for each activity are made.

PERT NETWORK
VEHICLE ARMAMENT SYSTEM

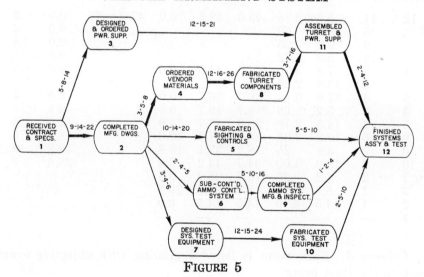

FIGURE 5

[5] The elapsed time formula is based on the assumption that the probability density of the beta distribution $f(t) = K(t-a)\alpha \, (b-t)\gamma$ is an adequate model of the distribution of an activity time.

[6] The statistical variance formula assumes the standard deviation as $\dfrac{1}{6}$ (b-a).

To illustrate network development and analyses, a hypothetical R & D program is assumed specifying contract completion 11 months (47 weeks) after order. Fixed resources are allocated to the program: *e.g.*, 40-hour work week, given personnel, budgeted money, *etc.* Management now is interested in:

1. What's the one best way of conducting effort toward completion?
2. What's the earliest expected time we can complete the program?
3. What are our chances of completing within the contract limitations of 47 weeks?

The network in Figure 5 is a simplified analogue of our plan to develop a "vehicle armament system." Events are described with a verb in the past tense to indicate their end accomplishment at a fixed point in time.

The analyses of the network is next performed and explained below.

PERT ANALYSES

A	B	C	D	E	F	G	H	I	J	K
Event	Pre. Ev.	t_e	σ^2	T_E	T_L	T_L-T_E	T_S	P_R	T_L-T_E	Event
12	11	5.0	2.78	49.5	49.5	0.0	47.0	.28	0.0	2
	5	5.8	.69						0.0	4
	9	2.2	.25						0.0	8
	10	5.3	1.78						0.0	11
11	8	7.8	4.70	44.5	44.5	0.0			0.0	12
	3	15.5	2.25							
8	4	17.0	5.44	36.7	36.7	0.0			9.5	7
4	2	5.2	.69	19.7	19.7	0.0			9.5	10
5	2	14.3	2.78	28.8	43.7	14.9			14.9	5
9	6	10.2	3.36	28.5	47.3	18.8			18.8	6
6	2	3.8	.25	18.3	37.1	18.8			18.8	9
10	7	16.0	4.00	34.7	44.2	9.5			20.5	3
7	2	4.2	.25	18.7	28.2	9.5				
3	1	8.5	2.25	8.5	29.0	20.5				
2	1	14.5	4.70	14.5	14.5	0.0				
1	—	—	—	—	—	—				

Column A. Each event is listed beginning with objective event back to the start event.

Column B. The preceding event(s) is (are) listed beside each event. Hence, there is a succeeding and preceding event for each activity.

Column C. Statistical elapsed time (t_e) for each activity is found by substituting optimistic, most likely, pessimistic estimates for a, m, b and solving $t_e = \dfrac{a+4(m)+b}{6}$.

Column D. Variance (σ^2) for each activity is found by substituting optimistic and pessimistic estimates for a and b and solving $\sigma^2 = \left(\dfrac{b-a}{6}\right)^2$.

Column E. Earliest expected time (T_E) of accomplishment for each *event* is found by adding the elapsed time (t_e) of each activity to cumulative total elapsed times through the preceding event, staying within a single path working from "start to finish." When more than one activity leads to an event, that activity whose elapsed time (t_e) gives the greatest sum up to that event is chosen as the expected time for that event. For example, the earliest expected time to *accomplish* Event 5 below is 10 weeks.

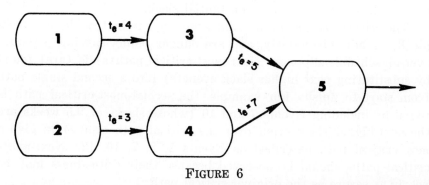

FIGURE 6

Column F. Latest Time (T_L) for each event is found by first fixing the earliest time of the objective event as its latest time. Next, the objective events corresponding elapsed time in Column C (*i.e.*, 5.0 weeks) is subtracted to find the latest time of the preceding event, staying within a single path working backward from finish to start. When more than one activity leads from an event (while working backwards to determine latest time), the activity which gives the *least* sum through that event is selected.

Some events may be accomplished later than expected time and have no effect on meeting the objective event. Knowledge of "slack" time in a network (*i.e.*, how much and where located) is of interest in determining program effects of "trade-offs" in resources from high-slack to low-slack areas.

Since linear programming theory says "negative slack" is not admissible (*i.e.*, not technically feasible at the objective event assuming fixed resources), we commence from an objective viewpoint to compute "positive" (or non-negative) slack. In spite of theory, a latest time derived from a fixed contractural date *less* than earliest expected time must be recognized to determine how much network "compression" is necessary to meet a scheduled date with reasonable assurance. The theory simply recognizes time is not reversible; therefore, to alleviate "negative" slack one must either extend contractual dates or employ added resources like overtime, more funds, personnel, *etc.* We assume in our analyses that resources are fixed at inception of program to maintain profit potentials.

Column G. Slack time for each event is found by subtracting Expected Time from Latest Time ($T_L - T_E$). The purpose is 1) to locate the critical path in the network designated here by events having zero slack and 2) to determine next-most-critical paths, as well as those events having substantial slack.

The critical path contains events most apt to be troublesome technically or administratively, and are danger points causing potential over-all schedule slippage. Next-most-critical path(s) is (are) found by substituting next higher slack event(s) into a second single path from start to finish. For example, the second-most-critical path is found by including Events 7 and 10 (whose slacks of 9.5 weeks are the next-higher slack event over the critical path events) to give a new critical path described as Events 1, 2, 7, 10, 12. Next-most-critical paths should be observed because their criticalness may be nearly as severe as the original critical path.

By locating events having substantial slack time, it becomes possible to effect trade-offs in resources to those events having little or zero slack. For example, Events 6 and 9 each have 18.8 weeks slack, meaning their expected time of completion could be intentionally delayed 18.8 weeks without causing slippage in over-all program schedule. A point of optimization in network development is approached when the greatest possible number of events have the smallest possible range in slack from the lowest to highest slack value.

Column H. Schedule Time (T_S) is the contractual date of completion. A scheduled time may also exist for major events within a network, which later facilitates evaluating the range of risks throughout a program plan.

Column I. Probability (P_R) of meeting a scheduled time is calculated to determine feasibility of program accomplishment under the constraints in the network. Generally, probability values between .25 and .60 indicate an acceptable range to proceed with a program as depicted in the network. Probability values less than .25 assume the schedule time, T_S, cannot reasonably be met with the given resources. Values higher than .60 may indicate excess resources "built in" the network, and may warrant consideration for their use elsewhere. Probabilities need not be computed where schedule time —T_S and expected time—T_E are equal, as this assumes .5 or 50 per cent probability of completing on schedule.

Probability of events are computed as follows:

1. Solve for each event which has a schedule time (in our example, the objective event):

$$\frac{T_S - T_E}{\sigma\epsilon\sigma^{2}*} = \frac{47.0 - 49.5}{\sqrt{18.31}} = \frac{-2.5}{4.279} = -.584$$

2. Refer answer to Area Under the Normal Curve Table and compute probability P_R.

The value —.584 refers to —.584 standard deviations from the mean under a normal curve. Referring to a normal curve table, we find its corresponding per cent of area under the normal curve to be about —.21904. Thinking of area under the normal curve and probability as synonymous, we subtract —.21904 from .50000 (the mean of a normal curve) to derive a probability of .28906, or 28 per cent. Explained, there is a 28 per cent chance of meeting the schedule time of 47.0 weeks, and hence may be "acceptable" to proceed with the program under plans and resources factored in the network. Any standard of "acceptability" in probability terms should be flexible according to the importance of a program and the consequences if schedule time should not be met. Therefore, any probability value attached to a program plan should be viewed and used cautiously.

Diagrammatically, 28 per cent probability is roughly represented by the shaded area under the normal curve below. [Figure 7, page 320]

Columns J and K. Under Column J is the ascending order of slack, and under Column K their corresponding event numbers. This

---

* Read as "standard deviation of the sum of the variances." In our example, this is solved by: 1) finding the sum of variances ($\Sigma\sigma^2$) for the events in the Critical Path, that is 4.70 + .69 + 5.44 + 4.70 + 2.78 = 18.31; 2) finding the square root of 18.31 = 4.279. Probability for *any* event in a network can be computed if a T_S and T_E value is known, and by finding that event within a single network path.

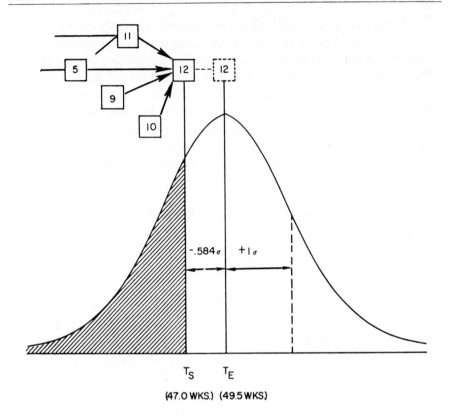

T_S T_E

(47.0 WKS.) (49.5 WKS)

FIGURE 7

brings out the Critical Path as 0.0 slack events, next-most critical path(s), and those events or paths with high slack from which resources and time may be deployed to events having zero or low slack. This facilitates locating the "one best way" of reaching the objective event in relation to time.

Re-evaluation and optimization

A potential value from PERT at inception of an R & D program is the opportunity it affords to introduce revised constraints into the plan and then simulate its outcome. If repeated, the optimum network can be sought, its troublesome areas located, and various tasks set under optimum conditions before time, cost, and performance were expended. Computer programs are available to expedite this, but manual methods are economical for networks up to 200 events depending on complexity of event inter-relationships. Various schedules and performance reporting formats can be developed from the analyses for team use and management analysis.

Two advantages from PERT are 1) the exacting communications it offers to participants in a program and 2) its use as a planning foundation to support bid proposals. Each participant can see his relative position and understand the timing and relationship of his responsibilities to other participants on the program team. Often the intangibles and assumptions that plague accurate bid proposals are brought out when supported with a PERT network and analyses

Using PERT for resources planning, cost analyses [7]

Considerable study is reported with PERT applied to resources (manpower and facilities) planning. Introducing a second variable to create a simultaneous two dimensional model whose objective functions are to be optimized—while their preceding constraints are being manipulated (at the same time satisfying various restrictions placed on potential solution)—will be more difficult to perform, and probably involve more elaborate procedures.

Some work is reported with PERT applied to cost analyses of a program (presumably assuming a three or N-dimensional model with variables of time, resources, cost, *et al*). It appears the object would be something analogous to predetermining that point on an average total cost curve where marginal cost intersects marginal revenue— hence, maximization of profits. Some suggestions have been offered relative to the "assumed" linearity between time and cost, in the duration of a program, but this needs clarifying before concrete methods of planning costs by PERT can be formulated.

[7] Notes from American Management Association Meeting, Saranac Lake, New York, March 27-29, 1961.

26. THE USE OF HEURISTIC PROGRAMMING IN MANAGEMENT SCIENCE [1]

Fred M. Tonge [2]

INTRODUCTION

This paper is a partial survey of the present and potential use of heuristic programming. It is intended as a study guide to the use of heuristic programming in management science.

HEURISTIC PROGRAMMING

By heuristics we mean (after Newell, Shaw, and Simon [20]) principles or devices that contribute, on the average, to reduction of search in problem-solving activity. Heuristic programming is the construction of problem-solving programs organized around such principles or devices.

Several implications of this definition should be emphasized.

First, we are concerned with exploiting *partial information* in a problem situation where we have no guaranteed way of using that information to find a best solution (or even, in some cases, any solution).

Second, by heuristic programming we mean preparing a procedure expressed as a *computer program* to make effective use of this partial information. At present this use of digital computers is our only means of making explicit the behavior of a complex heuristic procedure.

Third, heuristic programming is an *art*. It has advanced to date through the construction of particular programs, the examination of those programs and their behavior, and the construction of better programs based on the insight thus gained. Increasing effort is being spent on formalizing methods of integrating heuristics into problem-solving procedures. But at present this is a body of knowledge built up through experience with specific examples, lacking as yet an underlying analytic framework.

[1] From *Management Science*, Vol. 7, No. 3 (April, 1961), pp. 231-236. Reprinted by permission of *Management Science*.
[2] Fred M. Tonge, The Rand Corporation.

Problem Characteristics

Simon and Newell [32] suggest three general characteristics of the ill-structured problems for which heuristic programming techniques have proven appropriate.

1. Interest in non-numerical variables and their interrelations—in variables subject to other than purely arithmetic manipulations.
2. Interest in non-numerical criteria of performance and of an acceptable solution.
3. Lack of an optimal algorithm that is computationally feasible in the interesting cases.

Using these characteristics as a guide, we can restate our definition of heuristic programming.

1. Lack of a feasible guaranteed method of reaching "the best" solution; or even,
2. a description of "the solution" in terms of acceptability of characteristics rather than by optimizing rules;
3. some knowledge of interesting and useful things to do; and
4. sufficiently many possibilities to make complete trial-and-error infeasible.

Heuristic programming is concerned with constructing decision models (stated as computer programs) for such situations, emphasizing the use of *selectivity* rather than pure computational speed.

Heuristic Programming and Behavioral Science

While management scientists may be concerned for the most part with heuristic programs dealing with "applied" problems, much of the emphasis for this work comes from research in the simulation of human cognitive processes and the study of artificial intelligence [9, 16, 20, 23].

Heuristic programs have been undertaken for the following problems: proving theorems in one phase of symbolic logic [18, 19, 22], proving theorems in geometry [8, 9], memorizing nonsense syllables and making simple discriminations [6], predicting human behavior in a two-choice situation [7], and playing chess [21].

This research should be studied, independent of interest in the particular subject matter, because it faces the same questions of pattern recognition, organizing hierarchies of heuristics, symbolizing the results of experience, and so forth, that arise in constructing heuristic programs to deal with any ill-structured problem.

Management Science Applications of Heuristic Programming

Several problem-solving procedures reported for management science problems embody the heuristic approach of interest here.

(Not all would claim to be examples of heuristic programming; some might even deny it. But we feel they illustrate this approach.) We mention these briefly, indicating the particular features of interest.

Assembly line balancing

A heuristic program has been prepared to balance production assembly lines, as in an appliance factory [33]. Balancing a line is the act of assigning jobs to workers so that a given production rate can be met with minimum men. This heuristic program first constructs a series of simpler line balancing problems by aggregating several jobs into a single, compound job, and then uses that series of simpler problems as a guide in applying limited exhaustive analysis to find a balance. The acceptance criterion used by this program is an aspiration level mechanism, sensitive to the effort required to achieve a satisfactorily small number of men. If grouping jobs into work stations is too easy, the program will reduce the acceptable number of men; if too difficult, it will increase the number.

Simulation of a department store buyer

The Behavioral Theory of the Firm Project at Carnegie Institute of Technology is developing a simulation of the price and quantity decisions of a department store buyer [5]. This simulation can be extended to include such factors as: when the buyer will seek new alternatives (new sources of supply, for example), when he will re-evaluate sales forecasts, or when he will employ various hedging actions (such as sending stock to the bargain basement, or changing the mix of high and low margin items on display) in order to present the external performance (average return on inventory, say) that he desires. Thus, such a decision procedure not only can specify price-quantity decisions in terms of cost, inventory, sales expectations, and so forth, but also can specify how and in what order these factors are reconsidered if the apparent implications of the decision are not satisfactory. (An earlier study [4] develops a similar model for price-quantity decisions by firms in a duopoly.)

Investment decisions

A heuristic program is now being prepared to simulate investment activity under a trust fund [3]. This program infers from the statement of the trust what the purpose of its investment activities must be—relative preference for yield versus risk, for example. It infers from such documents as the financial journals information about the financial world. From this information the program first directs its attention to specific industries and then, within those industries, makes specific buy and sell decisions. Note two interesting properties of this program. First, the data to be abstracted from the pertinent documents is both numerical and non-numerical. Both "IBM up 4½ to 498" and "Most analysts foresee a noticeable increase in railroad yields over the next six months" are statements of interest. Second, the program must be relatively stable in the face of changing data. It must react to day-by-day market movements in terms of larger patterns.

Simulation of the individual executive

Those parts of the SDC Business System Simulation Project determining how the individual executive is represented are in many ways good examples of this approach [12]. Fragments of empirical evidence—such as observations of how executives actually spend their time—and pieces of analytic technique—such as a queueing theoretic analysis of relations with subordinates as total time available for interaction changes—are combined to produce a model of the executive that performs reasonably well for purposes of this simulation.

Job shop scheduling

While no formal results have yet been published, two separate attempts to construct heuristic programs for the job shop scheduling problem are underway [11, 34]. This work will be of particular interest in offering comparisons between the heuristic approach and the numerous formal, analytic attempts to deal with this problem.

THE NEXT DEVELOPMENTS

In what ways will the next heuristic programs differ from those described above? At least two different aspects are indicated.

There will be integration of present research in such related fields as pattern recognition and information retrieval [15, 28]. Many of the programs mentioned above have incorporated ad hoc solutions to such problems. Inclusion of more general techniques developed and tested for that purpose should have a beneficial effect on heuristic problem-solving programs.

There will be formal developments of immediate importance to all applications of heuristic programming. By this we mean both 1) conscious efforts to unite various activities in this field in a common framework and 2) the explicit development of generalized problem-solving procedures, which can be applied to many content areas. A recent survey paper by Minsky [16] is an excellent example of the former. Such problem-independent procedures as the General Problem Solver [22] or the Advice Taker [13] are examples of the latter.

Advances in Computer Techniques

Wide application of this approach to constructing problem-solving procedures depends not only on advances in heuristic programming techniques but also on advances in general computer programming capabilities and hardware.

Programming

What characteristics must programming languages have so that the heuristic programs described here become easy and natural to express—so that each instance of utilizing this approach is no longer a major undertaking? Rather than attempt an exhaustive listing, we mention but two points.

First, the primary goal is to make possible for all problems an easy, direct correspondence between the concepts the user has in mind and the data organization within the machine; between the methods by which he would manipulate the data and the machine processes.

This is not unreasonable to expect of the programming art in the immediate future. It is close to true already for those problems centering around algebraic manipulation. The newer symbol-manipulation, list-processing programming systems are first steps in this direction [10, 14, 24, 25, 26].[3]

Competent researchers are studying the logical nature of programming languages and trying to develop appropriate tools for analyzing them.

Present investigations demand these advances, and so they will be accomplished at least in an ad hoc form.

Second, the appropriate programming system for handling heur-

---

[3] However, several large and interesting problem-solving programs have been constructed without use of intermediate symbol-manipulation languages [2, 27].

istic procedures will contain some measure of ability (we should even say, intelligence) in the translator processing the program.

Both the user and the problem-solving system must expect and accept a common base of knowledge. It must be possible to construct, and operate in, a meaningful context of implied information.

Hardware

What characteristics should computer hardware have to meet these needs? The needed advances seem to be in machine organization as much as pure increases in speed and size [17, 29]. There are currently many investigations into this general subject. We mention but one.

There is underway at The RAND Corporation an Information Processor Project. This is a joint investigation, by both programmers and hardware people, into the nature of a system truly designed for information processing. There is no commitment that this effort end in a hardware design; a programming system on one of our present high-speed computers may be the final as well as an intermediate result. Whatever the outcome, it is clear that enough experience has been gathered in symbol manipulation problems to undertake this next development in the appropriate languages in conjunction with competent engineers looking at the hardware implications.

Long Term Implications

In viewing the long term implications of heuristic programming in management science, one's attention shifts from the construction of specific problem-solving procedures to consideration of the automation of what are commonly called "management decisions" [30].

Thinking machines, in the popular sense of the word, are imminent, and (the author feels) these machines will be constructed in large part following the approach under discussion here. Questions of the degree to which such capabilities will be introduced into the management scientist must consider what his attitude to such developments will be, and to what extent management science can and will enter into these developments [1].

Conclusion

Heuristic programming is, at present, a useful tool for the management scientist. The body of literature cited here offers sufficient food for thought to support anyone wishing to try this approach. Like all artisan's tools, the use of heuristic programming requires skill. The need to design models carefully, to weigh which factors to include and which to ignore, which relationships to focus on, has not been lessened. And for some time to come most significant uses of this technique will of necessity contribute to the development of heuristic programming itself. But our scope in designing decision procedures has been, and will be even more in the future, considerably widened.

References

1. Armer, Paul, Attitudes Toward Intelligent Machines, The RAND Corporation Paper, P-2114, September 1960.
2. Bernstein, A., et al., "A Chess-Playing Program for the IBM 704," *Proceedings of the 1958 Western Joint Computer Conference*, IRE, May 1958.
3. Clarkson, G. P. and A. H. Meltzer, "Portfolio Selection: A Heuristic Approach," *Journal of Finance*, December 1960.
4. Cyert, R. M., E. A. Feigenbaum and J. G. March, "Models in a Behavioral Theory of the Firm," *Behavioral Science*, April 1959.
5. Cyert, R. M. and J. G. March, *A Specific Price and Output Model*, Behavioral Theory of the Firm Working Paper No. 23, Graduate School of Industrial Administration, Carnegie Institute of Technology, November 1960.
6. Feigenbaum, E. A., *An Information Processing Theory of Verbal Learning*, The RAND Corporation Paper, P-1817, October 1959.
7. Feldman, J., *Analysis of Predictive Behavior in a Two-Choice Situation*, unpublished doctoral dissertation, Carnegie Institute of Technology, 1959.
8. Gelernter, H., "Realization of a Geometry Theorem Proving Machine," *Proceedings of the International Conference on Information Processing*, UNESCO, Paris, 1959.
9. Gelernter, H. and N. Rochester, "Intelligent Behavior in Problem-Solving Machines," *IBM Journal of Research and Development*, October 1958.
10. Gelernter, H., J. R. Hansen, and C. L. Gerberich, "A FORTRAN-Compiled List Processing Language," *Journal of the Association for Computing Machinery*, April 1960.
11. Gere, William S., Jr., *Heuristics in Job Shop Scheduling*, O.N.R. Memorandum No. 70, Graduate School of Industrial Administration, Carnegie Institute of Technology, June 1960.
12. Greene, R. M., Jr., *Representation of Human Functions in Business System Simulation*, System Development Corporation field note, FN-3745, 1960.
13. McCarthy, J., "The Advice Taker," *Proceedings of the Symposium on the Mechanization of Thought Processes*, Her Majesty's Stationery Office, London, 1959.
14. McCarthy, J., "Recursive Functions of Symbolic Expressions and Their Computation by Machine, Part I," *Communications of the ACM*, April 1960.
15. Maron, M. E. and J. L. Kuhns, "On Relevance, Probabilistic Indexing and Information Retrieval," *Journal of the Association for Computing Machinery*, July 1960.
16. Minsky, Marvin, "Steps Toward Artificial Intelligence," *Proceedings of the IRE*, January 1961.
17. Newell, A., "On Programming a Highly Parallel Machine to Be an Intelligent Technician," *Proceedings of the 1960 Western Joint Computer Conference*, IRE, May 1960.
18. Newell, A., J. C. Shaw and H. A. Simon, "Empirical Explorations of the Logic Theory Machine," *Proceedings of the 1957 Western Joint Computer Conference*, IRE, February 1957.

19. NEWELL, A., J. C. SHAW and H. A. SIMON, "Programming the Logic Theory Machine," *Proceedings of the 1957 Western Joint Computer Conference*, IRE, February 1957.
20. NEWELL, A., J. C. SHAW and H. A. SIMON, *The Processes of Creative Thinking*, The RAND Corporation Paper, P-1320, August 1958.

BIBLIOGRAPHY, CHAPTER VII

ALDERSON, WROE. "Operations Research and Management Problems," *Advanced Management* (April, 1955), 1-17.

BAKER, C. T., and B. P. DZIELINSKI. "Simulation of a Simplified Job Shop," *Management Science* (April, 1960), 311-323.

CALHOUN, S. REED, and PAUL GREEN. "Simulation: Versatile Aid to Decision-Making," *Advanced Management* (April, 1958), 11-16.

CHURCHMAN, W., R. L. ACKOFF, and E. L. ARNOFF. *Introduction to Operations Research*. New York: John Wiley & Sons, 1957.

CRAWFORD, ROBERT W. "Operations Research and Its Role in Business Decisions," *Planning for Efficient Production*, Manufacturing Series No. 206. New York: American Management Association, Inc. 1953, 3-15.

EMERY. "Heuristic Models of the Marketing Process," *Human Relations* (February, 1962), 63-76.

FORRESTER, JAY W. "Industrial Dynamics, a Major Breakthrough for Decision Makers," *Harvard Business Review* (July-August, 1958), 37-66.

GEISLER, MURRAY A. "Logistics Research and Management Science," *Management Science* (July, 1960), 444.

————————————. "The Simulation of a Large-Scale Military Activity," *Management Science* (July, 1959), 359.

GOETZ, B. E. "Mathematical Models of Management Significance," *Advanced Management* (February, 1957), 21-24.

MARTING, ELIZABETH (Ed.), *Operations Research, A Basic Approach*. New York: American Management Association, Inc. 1952, 3-6.

MILLER, ROBERT W. "How to Plan and Control with Pert," *Harvard Business Review* (March-April, 1962), 93-104.

MORSE, PHILIP M. "Operations Research: Past Present and Future," *Advanced Management* (November, 1954), 10-15.

SALVESON, MELVIN E. "High Speed Operations Research," *Harvard Business Review* (July-August, 1957), 89-99.

SWAN, A. W. "Industrial Operations Research," W. G. IRESON, and E. L. GRANT (Eds.), *Handbook of Industrial Engineering and Management*. New York: Prentice-Hall, Inc., 1955, 1015-1071.

SECTION B. PLANNING

Planning decisions are those which guide the course of future action in organizations. Some planning decisions are semipermanent in nature and form a continuing framework within which other decisions and actions are channeled. These plans include organization objectives and policies, examined in the two chapters immediately following.

Planning decisions applicable to actions peculiar to specific time periods include short- and/or long-run plans. Such plans are restructured for each time period to which they apply. The final chapter in this section is devoted to them.

Chapter VIII
Setting Objectives

If the members of the organization know the objectives, they have a goal at which to shoot and a guide for carrying out their activities. It is helpful, therefore, to set forth specifically in written form the objectives of the organizational unit whether it be a company or a subdepartment of a company.

In Article 27 Peter F. Drucker criticizes the utilization of a single objective, such as profit, for a business and offers eight "key areas" in which objectives need to be set in order for a business to survive in the long run. In the next article John F. Mee surveys the growing trend in American business to predetermine objectives. He then develops the "principle of the objective."

The lack of coordinated planning is a reason for lower efficiency in business organizations. Alfred N. Watson gives some examples of these inconsistencies and the results that they cause in Article 29. The last article by Peter F. Drucker discusses what the objectives of a manager should be and how these objectives should be established.

27. THE OBJECTIVES OF A BUSINESS [1]

Peter F. Drucker [2]

Most of today's lively discussion of management by objectives is concerned with the search for the one right objective. This search is not only likely to be as unproductive as the quest for the philosopher's stone; it is certain to do harm and to misdirect.

To emphasize only profit, for instance, misdirects managers to the point where they may endanger the survival of the business. To obtain profit today they tend to undermine the future. They may push the most easily saleable product lines and slight those that are the market of tomorrow. They tend to short-change research, promotion and the other postponable investments. Above all, they shy away from any capital expenditure that may increase the invested-capital base against which profits are measured; and the result is dangerous obsolescence of equipment. In other words, they are directed into the worst practices of management.

To manage a business is to balance a variety of needs and goals. This requires judgment. The search for the one objective is essentially a search for a magic formula that will make judgment unnecessary. But the attempt to replace judgment by formula is always irrational; all that can be done is to make judgment possible by narrowing its range and the available alternatives, giving it clear focus, a sound foundation in facts and reliable measurements of the effects and validity of actions and decisions. And this, by the very nature of business enterprise, requires multiple objectives.

What should these objectives be, then? There is only one answer: *Objectives are needed in every area where performance and results directly and vitally affect the survival and prosperity of the business.* These are the areas which are affected by every management decision and which therefore have to be considered in every management decision. They decide what it means concretely to manage the business.

[1] From *The Practice of Management* (New York: Harper & Brothers). Copyright, 1954, by Peter F. Drucker; English copyright by William Heinemann Ltd. Reprinted by permission of Peter F. Drucker, Harper & Brothers, and William Heinemann Ltd.

[2] Peter F. Drucker, Author, Consultant, and Lecturer in the field of general management.

They spell out what results the business must aim at and what is needed to work effectively toward these targets.

Objectives in these key areas should enable us to do five things: to organize and explain the whole range of business phenomena in a small number of general statements; to test these statements in actual experience; to predict behavior; to appraise the soundness of decisions when they are still being made; and to enable practicing businessmen to analyze their own experience and, as a result improve their performance. It is precisely because the traditional theorem of the maximization of profits cannot meet any of these tests—let alone all of them—that it has to be discarded.

At first sight it might seem that different businesses would have entirely different key areas—so different as to make impossible any general theory. It is indeed true that different key areas require different emphasis in different businesses—and different emphasis at different stages of the development of each business. But the areas are the same, whatever the business, whatever the economic conditions, whatever the business's size or stage of growth.

There are eight areas in which objectives of performance and results have to be set:

Market standing; innovation; productivity; physical and financial resources; profitability; manager performance and development; worker performance and attitude; public responsibility.

There should be little dispute over the first five objectives. But there will be real protest against the inclusion of the intangibles: manager performance and development; worker performance and attitude; and public responsibility.

Yet, even if managing were merely the application of economics, we would have to include these three areas and would have to demand that objectives be set for them. They belong in the most purely formal economic theory of the business enterprise. For neglect of manager performance and development, worker performance and public responsibility soon results in the most practical and tangible loss of market standing, technological leadership, productivity and profit—and ultimately in the loss of business life. That they look so different from anything the economist—especially the modern economic analyst—is wont to deal with, that they do not readily submit to quantification and mathematical treatment, is the economist's bad luck; but it is no argument against their consideration.

The very reason for which economist and accountant consider these areas impractical—that they deal with principles and values rather

than solely with dollars and cents—makes them central to the management of the enterprise, as tangible, as practical—and indeed as measurable—as dollars and cents.

For the enterprise is a community of human beings. Its performance is the performance of human beings. And a human community
must be founded on common beliefs, must symbolize its cohesion in
common principles. Otherwise it becomes paralyzed, unable to act,
unable to demand and to obtain effort and performance from its
members.

If such considerations are intangible, it is management's job to
make them tangible by its deeds. To neglect them is to risk not only
business incompetence but labor trouble or at least loss of worker
productivity, and public restrictions on business provoked by irresponsible business conduct. It also means risking lack-luster, mediocre, time-serving managers—managers who are being conditioned to
"look out for themselves" instead of for the common good of the
enterprise, managers who become mean, narrow and blind for lack of
challenge, leadership and vision.

How to set objectives

The real difficulty lies indeed not in determining what objectives
we need, but in deciding how to set them.

There is only one fruitful way to make this decision: by determining what shall be measured in each area and what the yardstick of
measurement should be. For the measurement used determines what
one pays attention to. It makes things visible and tangible. The things
included in the measurement become relevant; the things omitted are
out of sight and out of mind. "Intelligence is what the Intelligence
Test measures"—that well-worn quip is used by the psychologist to
disclaim omniscience and infallibility for his gadget. Parents or
teachers, however, including those well aware of the shakiness of its
theory and its mode of calculation, sometimes tend to see that precise-
looking measurement of the "I.Q." every time they look at little Susie
—to the point where they may no longer see little Susie at all.

Unfortunately the measurements available to us in the key areas
of business enterprise are, by and large, even shakier than the I.Q.
We have adequate concepts only for measuring market standing. For
something as obvious as profitability we have only a rubber yardstick,
and we have no real tools at all to determine how much profitability is
necessary. In respect to innovation and, even more, to productivity,
we hardly know more than what ought to be done. And in the other

areas—including physical and financial resources—we are reduced to statements of intentions rather than goals and measurements for their attainment.

For the subject is brand new. It is one of the most active frontiers of thought, research and invention in American business today. Company after company is working on the definition of the key areas, on thinking through what should be measured and on fashioning the tools of measurement.

Within a few years our knowledge of what to measure and our ability to do so should therefore be greatly increased. After all, twenty-five years ago we knew less about the basic problems in market standing than we know today about productivity or even about the efficiency and attitudes of workers. Today's relative clarity concerning market standing is the result not of anything inherent in the field, but of hard, concentrated and imaginative work.

In the meantime, only a "progress report" can be given, outlining the work ahead rather than reporting accomplishment.

28. PRINCIPLE OF THE OBJECTIVE [1]

John F. Mee [2]

In current thinking and writing, the starting point for either a philosophy or the practice of management seems to center around predetermined objectives. The entire management process concerns itself with ways and means to realize predetermined results and with the intelligent use of people whose efforts must be properly motivated and guided. Objectives may be general or specific; they may concern the organization as a whole, a segment of it within a decentralized unit, or even a particular function such as production, sales, or personnel.

What are or should be the objectives of management in our industrial economy? A study of current management literature and the published objectives of business firms provide some revealing and interesting concepts from recognized authorities. Here are some selected statements:

> The goal of the organization must be this—to make a better and better product to be sold at a lower and lower price. Profit cannot be the goal. Profit must be a by-product. This is a state of mind and a philosophy. Actually an organization doing this job as it can be done will make large profits which must be properly divided between user, worker and stockholder. This takes ability and character. [3]

> If we were to isolate the one factor, above all others, that transformed the tiny company of 1902 into the industrial giant of 1952, while hundreds of competitors failed and are forgotten, I should say that it has been Texaco's settled policy of thinking first of quality of product and service to the customer, and only second to the size of its profit. To some of you, this may sound somewhat trite. But it is the starkest kind of business realism. In a highly competitive industry such as ours, the highest rewards are reserved for those who render the greatest service. [4]

[1] From "Management Philosophy for Professional Executives," *Business Horizons*, Bureau of Business Research, School of Business, Indiana University (December, 1956), pp. 5-11. Reprinted by permission of *Business Horizons*.
[2] John F. Mee, Head of the Department of Management at Indiana University. Author, Lecturer, and Consultant.
[3] James F. Lincoln, *Intelligent Selfishness and Manufacturing* (Bulletin 434; New York: Lincoln Electric Co.).
[4] Harry T. Klein, *The Way Ahead* (New York: The Texas Co., 1952), p. 14.

To make and sell quality products competitively and to perform those functions at the lowest attainable cost consistent with sound management policies, so as to return an adequate profit after taxes for services rendered. As a corollary objective, the corporation must be the low-cost producer of the product it offers for sale. (United States Steel Corporation statement of general company objectives.)

The mission of the business organization is to acquire, produce and distribute certain values. The business objective, therefore, is the starting point for business thinking. The primary objectives of a business organization are always those economic values with which we serve the customer. The principle objective of a businessman, naturally, is a profit. And a profit is merely an academic consideration, nevertheless, until we get the customer's dollar.[5]

Numerous further examples of published and stated objectives of modern business management could be presented. However, all of them could be summarized with the conclusion that: (1) *Profit* is the motivating force for managers. (2) *Service* to customers by the provision of desired economic values (goods and services) justifies the existence of the business. (3) *Social responsibilities* do exist for managers in accordance with ethical and moral codes established by the society in which the industry resides. The economic values with which customers are served include increased values at lower costs through innovation and creativity over a period of time.

In formulating and developing a modern management philosophy for successful practice, a combination of the above objectives in the correct proportion is required. Every decentralized organization unit and essential function must contribute to the realization of the general objectives by attaining the organizational, functional, and operational objectives. Unless predetermined objectives are set and accepted, little or no basis exists for measuring the success and effectiveness of those who perform the management functions.

The importance of predetermining the objectives desired has resulted in the formulation of the management principle of the objective. This principle may be stated as follows: Before initiating any course of action, the objectives in view must be clearly determined, understood, and stated.

---

[5] Ralph C. Davis, "What the Staff Function Actually Is," *Advanced Management*, XIX (May, 1954), p. 13.

29. INCONSISTENCIES OF COMPANY
GOALS AND OPERATIONS [1]

Alfred N. Watson [2]

I should like to expand for a moment on this thought about operating policy and company goals. It is all too easy to encourage departments to strive for goals which are inconsistent with the company goal. For example, one company has a formula for paying commissions on a product line which has many products but is dominated by one, a low-margin item. Commission is figured on a two-way table, of which one side is total dollars of all products sold and the other side is number of units of the dominant product. Now, the salesman can make the same commission either by selling many units of the dominant product and fewer total sales or by selling more total dollars and fewer units of the dominant product.

To the salesman, the incentive and reward are the same in either case. To the company, the method which the man uses to make his commission can make quite a difference in rate of return. This should not and need not happen.

Management is charged with setting the goals and incentives of its operating units. If management has as its own goal the maximization of rate of return on investment of the total company, then the department manager's operations should be judged by yardsticks which reach their maximum at the same time that company return on investment is maximized.

Let me cite just a few other examples of how operating policies can be out of line with company goals.

The October 31, 1952, issue of *Research Institute Recommendations* suggests that asking the question about departmental goals can open the door to real savings in many firms. The article cites a life insurance company which started a drive on cleaner typing of policies but which actually geared its typist pool arrangements to the number of

[1] From *Operations Research and Financial Planning, Techniques and Data for Planning Financial Policy*, American Management Association, 1952, pp. 3-12. Reprinted by permission of the American Management Association, Inc.

[2] Alfred N. Watson, staff, Arthur D. Little, Inc., Cambridge, Mass. and staff member of the School of Industrial Management, Massachusetts Institute of Technology.

policies turned out each week. In another instance, where it was important for the company to hold existing business, the sales force was rewarded primarily for new business brought in.

We have all seen the situation where a great drive is put on to reduce overtime in all departments. To the extent that this results in improved scheduling and greater productivity, it is a good thing. However, when the pressure becomes sufficiently great, each department will tend to hold down its own overtime regardless of the effect on the overtime of succeeding departments. If the departments which follow have relatively higher skills or more capital equipment involved, one hour of overtime saved in Department No. 1 may reduce company revenue if it causes even a half-hour delay in Department No. 2.

A proper goal-setting activity of management is to see to it that the low-cost departments have the proper incentive to do those things which lower total company costs even though it may raise their own. This takes extraordinary budgeting skill and a close control of operations. But the rewards are there for those who can see the total company picture. Those in charge of financial planning for a company are certainly in an ideal position to perform this function.

We need not go into more detail about this subject of departmental goals and incentives. It is sufficient to say that consistency should be practiced all the way through the organization down to the man on the bench and the salesman in the field. The kind of analysis which normally develops from Operations Research provides a suitable basis for the establishment of consistent goals throughout the organization. It is a logical consequence of a minute examination of cause and effect.

30. MANAGEMENT BY OBJECTIVES
AND SELF-CONTROL [1]
Peter F. Drucker [2]

What should the objectives of a manager be?

Each manager, from the "big boss" down to the production fore-man or the chief clerk, needs clearly spelled-out objectives. These objectives should lay out what performance the man's own managerial unit is supposed to produce. They should lay out what contribution he and his unit are expected to make to help other units obtain their objectives. Finally, they should spell out what contribution the man-ager can expect from other units toward the attainment of his own objectives. Right from the start, in other words, emphasis should be on teamwork and team results.

These objectives should always derive from the goals of the busi-ness enterprise. In one company, I have found it practicable and effec-tive to provide even a foreman with a detailed statement of not only his own objectives but those of the company and of the manufacturing department. Even though the company is so large as to make the distance between the individual foreman's production and the com-pany's total output all but astronomical, the result has been a signifi-cant increase in production. Indeed, this must follow if we mean it when we say that the foreman is "part of management." For it is the definition of a manager that in what he does he takes responsibility for the whole—that, in cutting stone, he "builds the cathedral."

The objectives of every manager should spell out his contribution to the attainment of company goals in *all areas* of the business. Obviously, not every manager has a direct contribution to make in every area. The contribution which marketing makes to productivity, for example, may be very small. But if a manager and his unit are not expected to contribute toward any one of the areas that significantly affect prosperity and survival of the business, this fact should be

[1] From *The Practice of Management* (New York: Harper & Brothers). Copyright, 1954, by Peter F. Drucker; English copyright by William Heinemann Ltd. Reprinted by permission of Peter F. Drucker, Harper & Brothers, and William Heinemann Ltd.
[2] Peter F. Drucker, Author, Consultant, and Lecturer in the field of general management.

clearly brought out. For managers must understand that business results depend on a balance of efforts and results in a number of areas. This is necessary both to give full scope to the craftsmanship of each function and specialty, and to prevent the empire-building and clannish jealousies of the various functions and specialties. It is necessary also to avoid overemphasis on any one key area.

To obtain balanced efforts the objectives of all managers on all levels and in all areas should also be keyed to both short-range and long-range considerations. And, of course, all objectives should always contain both the tangible business objectives and the intangible objectives for manager organization and development, worker performance and attitude and public responsibility. Anything else is shortsighted and impractical.

Management by "drives"

Proper management requires balanced stress on objectives, especially by top management. It rules out the common and pernicious business malpractice: management by "crisis" and "drives."

There may be companies in which management people do not say: "The only way we ever get anything done around here is by making a drive on it." Yet, "management by drive" is the rule rather than the exception. That things always collapse into the *status quo ante* three weeks after the drive is over, everybody knows and apparently expects. The only result of an "economy drive" is likely to be that messengers and typists get fired, and that $15,000 executives are forced to do $50-a-week work typing their own letters. And yet many managements have not drawn the obvious conclusion that drives are, after all, not the way to get things done.

But over and above its ineffectivenes, management by drive misdirects. It puts all emphasis on one phase of the job to the inevitable detriment of everything else.

"For four weeks we cut inventories," a case-hardened veteran of management by crisis once summed it up. "Then we have four weeks of cost cutting, followed by four weeks of human relations. We just have time to push customer service and courtesy for a month. And then the inventory is back where it was when we started. We don't even try to do our job. All management talks about, thinks about, preaches about, is last week's inventory figure or this week's customer complaints. How we do the rest of the job they don't even want to know."

In an organization which manages by drives people either neglect their job to get on with the current drive, or silently organize for collective sabotage of the drive to get their work done. In either event they become deaf to the cry of "wolf." And when the real crisis comes, when all hands should drop everything and pitch in, they treat it as just another case of management-created hysteria.

Management by drive, like management by "bellows and meat ax," is a sure sign of confusion. It is an admission of incompetence. It is a sign that management does not know how to plan. But, above all, it is a sign that the company does not know what to expect of its managers—that, not knowing how to direct them, it misdirects them.

How should managers' objectives be set and by whom?

By definition, a manager is responsible for the contribution that his component makes to the larger unit above him and eventually to the enterprise. His performance aims upward rather than downward. This means that the goals of each manager's job must be defined by the contribution he has to make to the success of the larger units of which he is a part. The objectives of the district manager's job should be defined by the contribution he and his district sales force have to make to the sales department, the objectives of the project engineer's job by the contribution he, his engineers and draftsmen make to the engineering department. The objectives of the general manager of a decentralized division should be defined by the contribution his division has to make to the objectives of the parent company.

This requires each manager to develop and set the objectives of his unit himself. Higher management must, of course, reserve the power to approve or disapprove these objectives. But their development is part of a manager's responsibility; indeed, it is his first responsibility. It means, too, that every manager should responsibly participate in the development of the objectives of the higher unit of which his is a part. To "give him a sense of participation" (to use a pet phrase of the "human relations" jargon) is not enough. Being a manager demands the assumption of a genuine responsibility. Precisely because his aims should reflect the objective needs of the business, rather than merely what the individual manager wants, he must commit himself to them with a positive act of assent. He must know and understand the ultimate business goals, what is expected of him and why, what he will be measured against and how. There must be a "meeting of minds" within the entire management of each unit. This can be achieved only when each of the contributing managers is expected to think through what the unit objectives are, is led, in other words, to participate actively and responsibly in the work of defining them. And only if his lower managers participate in this way can the higher manager know what to expect of them and can make exacting demands.

This is so important that some of the most effective managers I know go one step further. They have each of their subordinates write a "manager's letter" twice a year. In this letter to his superior, each manager first defines the objectives of his superior's job and of his own job as he sees them. He then sets down the performance standards which he believes are being applied to him. Next, he lists the things he must do himself to attain these goals—and the things within his own unit he considers the major obstacles. He lists the things his superior and the company do that help him and the things that hamper him. Finally, he outlines what he proposes to do during the next year to reach his goals. If his superior accepts this statement, the "manager's letter" becomes the charter under which the manager operates.

This device, like no other I have seen, brings out how easily the unconsidered and casual remarks of even the best "boss" can confuse and misdirect. One large company has used the "manager's letter" for ten years. Yet almost every letter still lists as objectives and standards things which completely baffle the superior to whom the letter is addressed. And whenever he asks: "What is this?" he gets the answer: "Don't you remember what you said last spring going down with me in the elevator?"

The "manager's letter" also brings out whatever inconsistencies there are in the demands made on a man by his superior and by the company. Does the superior demand both speed and high quality when he can get only one or the other? And what compromise is needed in the interest of the company? Does he demand initiative and judgment of his men but also that they check back with him before they do anything? Does he ask for their ideas and suggestions but never uses them or discusses them? Does the company expect a small engineering force to be available immediately whenever something goes wrong in the plant, and yet bend all its efforts to the completion of new designs? Does it expect a manager to maintain high standards of performance but forbid him to remove poor performers? Does it create the conditions under which people say: "I can get the work done as long as I can keep the boss from knowing what I am doing?"

These are common situations. They undermine spirit and performance. The "manager's letter" may not prevent them. But at least it brings them out in the open, shows where compromises have to be made, objectives have to be thought through, priorities have to be established, behavior has to be changed.

As this device illustrates: managing managers requires special efforts not only to establish common direction, but to eliminate misdirection. Mutual understanding can never be attained by "communications down," can never be created by talking. It can result only from "communications up." It requires both the superior's willingness to listen and a tool especially designed to make lower managers heard.

BIBLIOGRAPHY, CHAPTER VIII

ANTHONY, ROBERT N. "The Trouble with Profit Maximization," *Harvard Business Review* (November-December, 1960), 126-134.

COLLACOTT, ROBERT H. "An Accent on Aims," *Dun's Review and Modern Industry* (October, 1953), 209-218.

"Company with a One-Track Mind," *Business Week* (June 22, 1957), 77-84.

DALE, ERNEST. *Planning and Developing the Company Organization Structure.* New York: American Management Association, Inc., 1952. Stage I.

GOTT, RODNEY C. "Meshing Defense Work with Corporate Objectives," *The Management Review* (January, 1960), 10-15, 78-82.

HOLDEN, PAUL E., L. S. FISH, and H. L. SMITH. *Top-Management Organization and Control.* New York: McGraw-Hill Book Company, Inc., 1951. 4 f.

HOUSTON, CHARLES LUKENS, JR. "Setting Corporate Objectives," *Targets for Management,* General Management Series No. 17. New York: American Management Association, Inc., 1955, 3-14.

SPIELVOGEL, CARL. "Old Stores Die If They Stay Old," *New York Times* (February 17, 1957), Section 3, 1.

SULLIVAN, M. R. "Setting and Achieving Management Objectives," *Assuring the Company's Future Today,* General Management Series No. 175. New York: American Management Association, Inc., 1955, 3-10.

URWICK, LYNDALL F. "The Purpose of a Business," *Dun's Review and Modern Industry* (November, 1955), 51, 52, 103-105.

Chapter IX
Policy Formulation and Control

Policies provide a broad guide as to how the objectives of a business are to be achieved. Company policies, if followed, implement company objectives. Departmental policies implement departmental objectives. The logic of this arrangement implies, further, that not only are departmental objectives subject to company objectives but they also should be consistent with company policies. Plans at subordinate organization levels are dependent upon and should complement higher-level plans. This is the familiar means-ends-means chain concept.

The first article examines the question of why policies are needed to maintain an efficient operation. In addition, Robert H. Johnson shows the different characteristics of sound policies for providing consistency and effectiveness. Finally, he examines the impact of poor policy formation upon the results which a retail store is able to achieve. Although this selection was originally written specifically for retail stores, the principles that are expounded can be applied with equal effectiveness to almost any organization.

In the second article Ernest C. Miller discusses the problems of developing and implementing policies. Like Johnson, Miller's presentation is applied to a particular area (in this case, the personnel function), but the basic ideas have a much wider applicability.

31. RETAIL POLICIES: THEIR SELECTION
AND APPLICATION [1]

Robert H. Johnson [2]

THE NEED FOR POLICIES

Establishing and operating a retail business is a complex undertaking. It involves the coordination of numerous and varied activities requiring special knowledge and skills.

Before a new store is ready to receive customers, the prospective proprietor must consider many factors which determine the proper location, the type of store he should operate, the kinds and amount of equipment and fixtures needed, the legal form of organization, and the most suitable methods of selling. Then, he must analyze his market to learn where his potential customers are located and who they will be, what goods and services they will demand, when they will want them, and how and where they will wish to buy them.

After the store has been opened for business, management involves the continuing tasks of selecting merchandise and displaying and selling it, and collecting payment. In addition to the basic functions of buying and selling, the operator of a retail store usually finds it necessary to advertise, extend credit, make deliveries, and carry on many other activities which facilitate the sale of consumers' goods.

To successfully perform all of these tasks, the proprietor must know something about many fields, such as market analysis, business law, accounting, display, and salesmanship. And, of course, he must have a knowledge of the particular goods which his store handles. Also, he must be able to make skillful application of the knowledge at his disposal.

But the ability to take care of the day-to-day problems involved in retail trade does not, in itself, constitute effective management. There is need for a basic underlying guide which the owner can follow in directing all activities toward the same goal, and by means of which the various operations can be integrated.

[1] From Washington: *Department of Commerce*, Office of Domestic Commerce (1946), pp. 1-9.
[2] Robert H. Johnson, U. S. Department of Commerce, Office of Domestic Commerce, 1946.

For example, for effective management, the retailer must have an efficient plan for selecting merchandise and granting credit. Moreover, the type of credit must be related to the merchandise being sold, and both must be related to the demands of consumers and to their abilities to pay. This coordination of the various phases of retail store operation is facilitated by the selection and application of policies—those settled courses of business procedure designed to lead to the attainment of specified objectives.

In the absence of clear-cut objectives and related business policies, most retailers—particularly new proprietors—are prone to become lost in the maze of details to the extent that their over-all management of the enterprise is impaired. Frequently, retail failures attributed to inadequate management or insufficient capital, for example, occur because the capital and efforts of the proprietor have been dissipated in inconsistent, conflicting practices which were not properly related to the goals of the business.

In other instances, proprietors spend a disproportionate amount of their personal time and energy on details which could be handled by employees following an explicit policy. If, for example, the proprietor of an apparel store establishes a policy requiring a 20-percent deposit on all "lay-away" or "will-call" transactions, his salespeople need not question him each time a sale of this type is made. Thus, the proprietor can devote just that much more of his time to the problems which really require managerial judgment. Furthermore, there will be no inconsistencies in the treatment of customers, because each one will be required to deposit the same percentage of the purchase price.

The proprietor's capital, too, is conserved by the adoption of specific objectives and policies. The merchandise policy, which is the most important single policy to be formulated by a retail firm, should be a means for controlling the investment in stocks, as well as a device for saving the time spent in purchasing.

For example, if a firm decides to handle complete assortments in a few lines of goods, the buyer is relieved of the task of considering all the other lines that might conceivably be handled were there no definite policy with respect to the composition of the merchandise inventory. At the same time, the capital of the concern is protected by the limitation imposed on the buyer.

Even where the proprietor does all the purchasing, there is need for a general guide to control the tendency to buy without proper consideration for the way in which the goods will fit into the merchandising plan of the store. Buying without specific objectives in mind is a certain invitation to slow-moving and dead stock, such as is found on the shelves of most retail failures.

It is not enough, however, for the retailer to formulate policies on the buying of merchandise. Other features of the business should also be covered. If, for example, a firm plans to cater to a group of customers who will demand delivery service, its activities will include delivery as a matter of general policy. To render this service in the most effective manner consistent with other features of the store, the proprietor needs to establish a delivery policy which will specify the scale of charges, if any, for the service, the minimum size of orders for delivery, the areas in which and the times at which deliveries will be made, the emphasis to be given to this particular service, and other general regulations governing its use.

Although the need for explicit policies is more frequently recognized in large retail stores, it is not confined to the larger organizations. Irrespective of type, size, location, or form of organization, definite guides for selecting and performing the various retail functions are necessary. In fact, because of the limited financial and managerial capacities of the small proprietor, it is imperative that he relate his activities directly to specific aims.

CHARACTERISTICS OF SOUND POLICY

Naturally, the policies selected for a retail store should be based on circumstances peculiar to that firm and the economic environment in which it will operate. That is, the decisions to carry high-priced or low-priced goods, offer few or many services, and sell for cash or on credit must be related to the conditions under which the particular business will operate. There are certain characteristics of sound policies, however, which are universally applicable.

Relationship to business objectives

A sound retail policy should facilitate the attainment of the firm's objectives. But as each retail outlet caters to a specific group, its policies should be designed to guide management in meeting the needs of that group. Certainly, there is no one type of merchandise policy, for example, which would be equally well suited to all firms. And in the formation of the general store policy, those functions or activities which do not facilitate attainment of the stated objectives should be eliminated. For instance, while credit and delivery would be necessary in a store selling large electrical appliances, they would be unnecessary and uneconomical in most variety stores.

Planned development

Second, to be sound, the retail policy must be a planned development rather than the result of opportunistic decisions made on the spur of the moment. Naturally, not every problem arising in the operation of the store can be foreseen, or solved on the basis of established policy. But although there will usually be a very large and important area in which the judgment of management will be the only guide, routine activities should be carried on in a manner dictated by policy.

Clarity

Third, policies should be clear and definite. They should be so formulated that they cannot possibly be misinterpreted. They should minimize the number of situations in which decisions must be based on personal opinion and hastily collected information. And regardless of the size of the firm, policies should be reducible to the point where they have significance for each individual in the organization.

Clear-cut policies are more easily formulated and applied if they are reduced to writing. For the person responsible for store policies will be forced to delve more deeply into their implications by putting them in writing than if they remain only nebulous ideas in his mind.

Moreover, an explicit, written statement of policy reveals the intent of management to all employees and to actual and potential customers. A few retail stores which have developed clear-cut, distinctive policies have given these statements of principles wide publicity in their promotional activities. While some features of store policy may not interest the customers, others such as those covering merchandising and credit, should be made known to both customers and the employees who are responsible for the application of the policies.

Consistency

Fourth, policies should make for consistency in the operation of the business. In other words, the functions and activities called for in the general policy of the store must be in agreement. For example, the retailer who desires to develop a reputation for low prices cannot consistently offer free credit and delivery services. Furthermore, both general and specific policies must result in stability over a considerable period of time. If the store is to develop a clear-cut personality, the goods and services offered in one period must be comparable to those offered in another.

The principles of consistency should also be followed in selecting and training employees. In choosing salespeople, for example, the proprietor should hire individuals who not only know the merchandise they will sell, but also have a faculty for meeting and being at ease with the customers. Then all employees should be trained in such a way that customers may receive substantially the same type of treatment from every representative of the firm with whom they come in contact, whether he be credit manager, salesperson, or deliveryman. A brisk, impersonal attitude on the part of a deliveryman, for instance, can destroy an impression of friendly service which the customer has received from the salespeople and the general atmosphere of the store.

Individuality

Fifth, the general policy of a store should lead to the development of a clear-cut character, or personality, for the establishment. Having individuality offers several competitive advantages. For one thing, it enables the store to build up a steady clientele whose patronage does not depend on a constant promotional barrage.

Furthermore, it tends to reduce the vulnerability of the store to direct price competition, although individuality may be acquired through a policy of low and competitive prices. In fact, many operators have chosen policies designed to appeal to customers in the lower income brackets, selected the best merchandise available at prices which these customers can pay, and—with these policies publicized— have maintained satisfactory earnings over a period of years.

Actually, it is possible to operate a store successfully with almost any type of policy, as long as the provisions of that policy are related to the needs of a specific group of customers, and the various phases of the store's operations are generally consistent.

A certain degree of character is achieved, of course, when the proprietor selects the merchandise he will handle and the specific group to which he will cater. Something more is necessary, however, if the concern is to attain a special meaning in the eyes of the customers. One way for a retail store to acquire individuality is to build its activities around a specfic theme which is set up as a matter of policy.

Flexibility

Finally, retail policies must have a certain degree of flexibility. The adoption and application of policies impose certain limitations on retail operations which are conducive to profitable performance as long as the social and economic environment remains stable. But management must be able to modify policies when basic economic and social conditions change, and such adjustment is a most important task. If it is to be performed successfully, there must be constant study of the economic trends within and without the community, and of the effects of changes on the suitability of policies.

EFFECTS OF INADEQUATE POLICIES

Retail policies are inadequate to the extent that they do not meet the requirements presented above. The effects of such inadequacies, as well as of the absence of policy, become apparent in many ways. Eventually, they cause unprofitable operation and subsequent failure. Retail mortalities attributed to insufficient capital, poor location, over-buying and competition in many instances actually result from the adoption of improper policies for the particular business situation—or from the lack of a definite policy.

32. PERSONNEL POLICIES—FRAMEWORK FOR MANAGEMENT DECISIONS [1]

Ernest C. Miller [2]

Personnel policies are unnecessary restrictions on our freedom of action. . . . It's a waste of money to have written personnel policies; everyone around here knows how to handle personnel situations. . . . I don't want to commit myself in advance; I think each personnel problem must be handled on its own merits.

These are a few of the statements one might hear in a management discussion of personnel policies. They represent the attitudes of experienced and sincere managers faced with the daily problems of managing a business. Such attitudes are still prevalent—are they justified?

To begin with, let's get a working definition of a policy. A policy is a statement or a commonly accepted understanding of decision-making criteria or formulae, prepared or evolved to achieve economy in operations by making decisions relatively routine on frequently occurring problems and, consequently, facilitating the delegation of such decisions to lower management levels.

By providing decision-making criteria, a policy gives assurance that decisions made will be consistent, fair, and in keeping with the objectives and interests of the business. A policy permits decisions to be made on similar problems without repetition of the closely reasoned and expensive analysis required initially to state the policy or make the decision.

The detailed manner of applying a policy to a particular administrative context is a *procedure*. Policies are general instructions; procedures are specific applications.

The development of personnel policies becomes important to a company when:

1. The organization has reached a size that requires many decision-making centers that will act consistently.

[1] From *The Management Review* (January, 1960), pp. 20-26. Reprinted by permission of the American Management Association.
[2] Ernest C. Miller, Hellwig, Miller & Associates.

2. Situations requiring decisions occur frequently.
3. A record of decision-making criteria is needed to evaluate the effectiveness of the criteria as the results of decisions become known.

One company—many policies

Lacking written statements of personnel policy, a large organization may have different decisions being made on similar problems in different organizational units. Rather than having no policy in such circumstances, as you might first assume, you will almost invariably find you have as many different policies as you have organizational units. Whether this plethora of policies is a problem in itself will depend on how important the policy decisions are and how extensive is the communication among members of the various organizational groups.

Approaching the question from another point of view, issuing a written statement of personnel policy does not automatically make it policy. For a policy to be issued is one thing; for it to be accepted, understood, and used as a guide to decisions and actions is another. The emphasis is on action: only when actions taken are consistent with the provisions of the written policy can the policy be said to exist.

Developing personnel policies

Generally speaking, policies are developed through making decisions and taking action on the day-to-day problems of the organization. In making decisions we analyze the problem against criteria, values, or other expressions of results to be achieved by the organization and decide on the solution that gives the optimal combination of gains and losses. As we decide more and more of these problems, all similar in general outline but different in detail, we generalize a principle that becomes a basis for future decisions. The principle, abstracted and generalized from the mass of specific decisions, constitutes the experience basis for policy statements.

The process of developing a personnel policy involves assessing its appropriateness to the organization. It must be acceptable in all the situations in which it might be used as a basis for decision— tested against each of the organization's major functions to make certain that all operating, legal, financial, marketing, and public relations considerations have been taken into account.

The policy should also be tested against community practice to assure that the reputation of the firm is being maintained at as high a level as its business and financial situation will permit. The maintenance of a competitive position in the community in these matters can assist the organization with its employees, its public, its bankers, its stockholders, and its customers, and thereby facilitate the survival and growth of the organization.

Participation in policy-making

Personnel policies should be recommended by those closest to the point of decision and use—those in face-to-face contact with the employees. It is this group who, lacking a prepared policy, have been making the daily decisions that have defined the policy that already exists informally in the organization. These are the people who can best provide the information needed to draft the policy and who can best help to introduce the change in method of operation that almost inevitably accompanies the formalization of policy.

For reasons of efficiency, the personnel unit of the organization should be assigned the task of collecting information from both inside and outside the organization as a basis for the draft statement. They should also prepare the draft statement of policy for the criticism of the line managers and employees. Employees can well participate in the criticism of the personnel policies applicable to their units. This is now the case for unionized groups, but even in non-unionized areas, participation by employees can do much to insure the acceptance of the formalized policies.

Line managers act as the equivalent of a legislative body—they review, criticize, and amend the policy drafts presented to them by their staff group. The staff group does research and drafts suggested statements, but it should not set the final provisions of any policy.

Participation is the keynote to policy formulation—participation by those who will use the policy and live with the results of its application. Whether we realize it or not, our personnel policies are to a considerable extent written by the needs and desires of our employee groups. Management may attempt to guide or channel the expression of these needs and desires, but beyond that it can only delay their introduction into the organization's life. The values expressed in the policy and represented by management in its actions are values that have come from, or at least are acceptable to, the employees and the community.

A policy can only be said to exist to the extent that it guides action. Experience in countless areas has shown that changes in action or approach to situations, since such changes only come after changes in the individual, can best be accomplished by having those who must change help to determine the direction and amount of change. This is the essence of participation.

Issuing the policy

Because a personnel policy is a total commitment of the organization to act in specified ways, it can be issued only by the highest line executive of the organization. In issuing the policy he is really only approving it as drafted by the managers and employees of the organization, but since the policy will be executed by people directly and indirectly responsible to him, it must go out with the support of his authority. In this sense, if the members of the organization play a legislative role, the chief executive officer assumes what would be the executive role of government.

Personnel policies must be known and understood before they can be fully effective as guides to action and as aspects of "company atmosphere." This means that personnel policies should receive a sufficiently broad distribution so that anyone who wishes may review the policy. If the values represented in the policy are positive reflections of the values of employees, the community, and management, there will be no hesitancy about preparing written statements to be distributed to those who will apply the policy and those to whom it will be applied.

If the values represented in the policy statement are negative or less favorable than employees or the community have indicated as acceptable, many organizations think that they can successfully hide this shortcoming by not issuing a written policy. It is unlikely that this approach will be successful; it is more likely that it will lead to accusations of management deceit. Policies become known through actions; even under ideal conditions, we can hide what we are only for a very brief period, particularly when we must continue to decide and act each day.

The form that written policies take is of consequence only so far as it helps or hinders their use. If they are gathered in one book, numbered in a way that permits revision, and indexed, the audit activity that is necessary to keep the policies current will be facilitated.

Room for exceptions

Exceptions to policy must be permitted, since problems will arise for which an equitable solution will require a variance from policy. One objective of policies is to achieve consistency and fairness of action; we cannot permit rigid adherence to restrictive terms of a policy to prevent us from achieving equity.

To say that exceptions are permitted, however, does not mean that they should be easy to make. Exceptions should require the approval of an executive at least three levels removed from the person to whom the decision will be applied or, lacking three levels, by the chief executive. This assures flexibility with proper control.

The nature of each exception should be stated in writing, with the circumstances that led to the exception clearly and completely stated. This makes it possible to consider all valuable experience when the policy is revised and insures that the decision has been arrived at only after thorough documentation, careful analysis, and objective reasoning.

Application and revision

The application of policy is very similar to the judiciary function of governmental organization. In business organizations, the executive and judiciary functions are often in the same man. This is true even for unionized groups, at least at the lowest step of the grievance procedure. In non-unionized groups, appeals from the unfair application of a policy or for exceptions to the policy, when realistically possible at all considering the sanction system of the authority structure, are only to a higher level of authority than involved in the original decision.

In unionized groups, an appeal to an impartial arbiter is usually permitted. Perhaps, for non-unionized groups, a jury of managers or peers not in the line of authority should be considered to make more real the right of each individual to appeal an unfair decision or request a previously denied exception to a policy. Where this check on managers is not available, executives must carry out their responsibility with integrity of the highest order.

Since policies represent values and decision-making criteria, they must change as our objectives, values, and decision-making criteria change. Comments from the users, requests for exceptions, audits of policy application, and a review of the results obtained in the areas in which the policies were designed to be of assistance all help to signal a need for revision. A request that a policy be reviewed can be initiated at any level in the management structure. Administrative reasonableness, of course, requires that policies only be reviewed every three years, or after some other reasonable period.

Just as with the initial formulation of the policy, policy revisions should be participative. All those who have used a policy should be asked to criticize it and to suggest revisions they think will improve it. A policy should not be revised piecemeal; each revision should be based on a complete review.

A framework for decisions

Personnel policies, whether written or unwritten, exist in all organized activity. To adopt a procedure for the systematic development and communication of personnel policies adds an important degree of control over the form and substance of an organization's policy. Written personnel policies can help an organization to achieve consistency and fairness in its treatment of its employees and can make possible the economy of operations that results when the broadest possible range of decisions are made routine and easily delegated.

BIBLIOGRAPHY, CHAPTER IX

ANSHEN, MELVIN. "Price Tags for Business Policies," *Harvard Business Review* (January-February, 1960), 71-78.

BELLOWS, E. H. "Administrative Arrangements and Policy Objectives," *Advanced Management* (March, 1957), 14-15.

CASSELS, LOUIS, and RAYMOND L. RANDALL. "The Company Policy Manual: Guide to Efficient Management," *Management Review* (March, 1960), 61-63.

COIL, E. J. "Administrative Organization for Policy Planning," *Administration—The Art of Organization and Management.* Albert Lepawsky (Ed.), New York: Knopf, 1949, 530-533.

CULLMAN, W. ARTHUR. "Policy Reappraisal and Maintenance," *Business Horizons* (Winter, 1959), 68-73.

DAVIS, RALPH C. *The Fundamentals of Top Management.* New York: Harper & Brothers, 1951. Chapter 6.

DEAN, RICHARD F. "Foremen Should Participate in Policy Formation," *Personnel Journal,* Vol. 28, No. 3 (July-August, 1949), 91-93.

MITCHELL, DON G. "The Challenge Facing Management," *Advanced Management* (December, 1958), 5-8.

Progressive Policies for Business Leadership, General Management Series 156. New York: American Management Association, Inc., 1952.

SEYBOLD, GENEVA. *Written Statements of Personnel Policy,* Studies in Personnel Policy No. 79, National Industrial Conference Board, Inc., 1947.

Top Management Policies and Philosophies, General Management Series 133. New York: American Management Association, Inc., 1945.

Chapter X
Long- and Short-Range Planning

Objectives and policies constitute the semipermanent framework within which the managers will operate. There is the remaining question of just what activities the firm should undertake in order to achieve the objectives within the policy framework. Specific operating plans need to be developed so that specific and realistic action can be taken.

In order for a manager to know what he should do today, he needs to know what the firm should be doing five years from today. Perhaps he ought to be ordering a survey of possible locations for a retail outlet so that a selection can be made next year, a building can be finished three years hence, and the store can furnish goods five years from today. But in order to know that the site survey should be made today, he needs to have a long-range plan which shows that customers will exist for a profitable store five years hence.

In order to have long-range planning, economic forecasting is required. Consequently, the arrangement of this chapter undertakes the study of forecasting, long-range planning, and the relation of long- and short-range planning to each other.

In the first selection, Ewing W. Reilley brings the interrelationships of objectives, policies, and long- and short-range planning into focus in discussing the strategy of a business.

In the article by Murray L. Weidenbaum, methods of economic forecasting are examined in a wider interdisciplinary context. Additionally, he explains the role of the economist in the business firm.

In the following example of forecasting within a particular company, J. J. Curran shows how this information is used to develop specific financial, marketing, and production policies for a product. The use of forecasting data in long-range planning and short-range planning, although less than perfect, is still highly useful as this selection shows.

The concept of planning and its concomitant, control, are discussed by James L. Peirce in the last selection in this section on planning. Not only is the relationship between planning and control explained but also their relationships to organization and reporting.

33. PLANNING THE STRATEGY
OF THE BUSINESS [1]

Ewing W. Reilley [2]

The challenges of our dynamic economy require strategic planning by top management similar in many respects to that done by the General Staff of an army. It used to be that wars could be won by brilliant field generals who operated on the basis of genius, experience, and hunch. Today *battles* may be won by such generals. But *wars* are won by strategic planning based on a careful estimate of the total situation.

Similarly in business short-term success can be achieved through shrewd intuitive decision making, successful opportunism, personal sales ability, leadership and drive, and the like. But, increasingly, long-term success in adjusting to changing conditions and continuing growth and profitability are dependent on careful strategic planning and then diligently carrying out the plan.

We have all asked ourselves why some companies consistently come up with more and better new products, more and better jobs, better relations with the community and government, and increasingly larger profits than others. Also, why is it that many of the companies that were leaders twenty-five or fifty years ago have now sunk into relative oblivion, while many that were unknown then are leaders today? But even more important, what caused some companies which were leaders *then* to still be leaders today?

Observation of many companies has convinced me that the answers to these questions lie in the way a company goes about planning its business strategy. To be successful, business strategy must be based on:

A *searching look within* to identify the strengths of the business that can be capitalized on and the limitations that must either be overcome or recognized in realistic planning.

A *broad look around* to be sure that planning takes cognizance of the external factors affecting business success and adequately balances the

[1] From *Advanced Management* (December, 1955), pp. 8-12. Reprinted by permission of *Advanced Management*.
[2] Ewing W. Reilley, Partner, McKinsey and Co., and President of the Mc-Kinsey Foundation for Management Research.

company's obligations to customers, employees, owners, suppliers, and the community. Those businesses that have geared their policies to the dynamics of the economy, the market and social trends have made the best adjustments to stresses and to opportunities for expansion.

And finally, while far-sighted planning has always paid off, today the increasingly long-term nature of business commitments also makes a *long look ahead* almost a necessity.

The success of strategic business planning depends further on management's recognition of the importance of these critical jobs: setting objectives; establishing policies within which to work toward objectives; organizing to assign responsibilities and provide for coordinated action; selecting and developing key personnel; helping them adjust to change; motivating them, and stimulating them to think creatively; and measuring progress and evaluating results.

The heart of strategic business planning is defining and setting up the proper objectives.

In this connection, the first job of top management is to decide what kind of business the company wants to have and the place in the market to which it aspires.

Does it want to specialize or diversify? Does it want to grow, or is it content with its present size?

In general, the broader the company's base is in terms of range of products offered and markets served, the better are its chances of success. However, some companies have become highly successful by finding a unique role and specializing in it. For example, the dyestuffs industry is generally characterized by huge companies which have large capital investments but which must be satisfied with modest returns. Yet there is a moderate sized dyestuffs company which has enjoyed a remarkable growth and consistently made more than a fifty percent return on invested capital. It does this by specializing in dyes which involve difficult problems, but which are of such small volume that large companies do not wish to invest the technical ability required to solve them. Also, it is fast to sense new trends and ingenious in capitalizing on them.

Is growth one of the company's goals? Few things in life, including businesses, stand still. They either grow or decline. However, not all companies are equipped to grow. Recently an outstanding specialty manufacturer decided against acquiring another company in its own industry because its management recognized that, while they were outstandingly successful in their own narrow field, they were untrained for the administrative responsibilities needed to become a big factor in the industry.

Factors in sound growth

The most valuable growth is not necessarily the most rapid, but rather the most persistent. This characteristically results from successful research into many new fields, continuously creating new markets for old products and new and better products to add to the line. There is convincing evidence of the importance of industrial research —for example, a recent study which indicated that there was a direct correlation between the relative amounts of money companies in a certain industry spent on research and their relative market position four years later.

In deciding how to achieve its goals of diversification and growth, top management should assess the strengths on which it can capitalize as well as the limitations that must be recognized. For example, a leading chemical company will go into a new field only if it is one where its outstanding research and technical skill will give it an important competitive advantage. Another leading company is only interested in products where the mass production techniques in which it is pre-eminent will give it cost advantages. A third seeks only products on which a consumer franchise can be built by capitalizing on its advertising skills. Thus, by building on strength, these companies avoid products and fields which they are not well equipped to handle.

Product planning

Having set its objectives regarding the kind of a business and market position it wants to have, top management must next assay the product line's adequacy to meet these objectives.

Most products have a profit life like human beings, including a period of growth, a period of stability, and a period of decline. The top management of a leading chemical company recognizes this by periodically appraising the economic health of its products. Managerial and financial resources are then targeted on those having the most promising outlook. Those in the declining phase are rigorously weeded out if return on investment falls below a certain level. This pruning process helps top management to concentrate on the need to develop healthy growing products to take their place.

Product planning should also take into account external economic and social developments. A dramatic example of the importance of such planning was the decision reportedly faced some years ago by a major automobile company concerning its low-priced line of cars. Top management had these alternatives: to concentrate on building the cheapest automobile possible, or, instead, to give the consumer a better product at approximately the same cost in terms of purchasing power. They decided to follow the latter course because they recognized the underlying trend in this country toward a higher standard of living. As a result, the company's low-priced cars are today a better automobile than its highest-priced ones were a relatively few years ago.

As further illustration, strategic product planning enabled the top management of a relatively small company to turn a loss into a profit. They recognized that the dominant companies in their industry had tremendous advantages in engineering, production, advertising, and sales, but only in their high-volume products. By studying what constituted an economic unit in the industry, they found that their own company could make a very handsome return on its investment if it got only 4 to 5 percent of the total market. So instead of trying to compete for the mass market on a "me too" basis, they decided to use consumer research to identify the desires of buyers who wanted "something different." This market was not economical for the big fellows, but a small company could do very well by getting only one buyer out of twenty.

Top management marketing decisions cannot be profit decisions without superior strategic planning. A classic example of this was the decision some years ago by the top management of a company that held a leading position in the high-priced prestige car field to "trade down" by bringing out models bearing the same name in the medium-priced field. Top management hoped by so doing to tap a much larger segment of the potential market. However, they failed to recognize that the marketing and other management skills which could be successful in the high-priced car field were not necessarily adapted to doing a volume job. They also failed to recognize that, by trading down on their name, they would impair the prestige which had given them a leading position in the high-priced field.

Not too many years ago the sales of another company—a major packaged consumer goods producer—declined sharply because top management did not recognize the growth in importance of chain stores and super markets and continued to base its marketing strategy primarily on appealing to the independent grocer.

Economic production

Top management strategy must also consider how it can produce most economically with a proper regard for stabilization of employment and return on invested capital.

Recent developments leave little doubt that increasing emphasis on stabilized employment will tend to convert direct labor from a variable to a more nearly fixed cost. This will require top managements to look further ahead to be sure that the continuing demand for a given product or operation will justify incurring these fixed labor costs. There will be more need to see whether the company can add new products or subcontract work to level out peaks and valleys. Finally, there will be a need to make sure that the company is doing everything it can to *plan* for stabilized employment and to build greater versatility into its work force.

Facilities decisions

Long-term facilities planning requires that top management analyze the probable future market for its products, determine what percentage of the market they think they can get and translate these into plant requirements. If they overestimate they end up with excess capacity and unnecessary capital investment and fixed charges. If they underestimate they incur the added costs and inefficiencies of overtime to meet peak demands.

Facilities decisions also involve considering the plans of competitors. For example, some companies may find that, whereas the outlook for growth in demand is good, the aggregate of all of the expansion planned by the industry may create overcapacity for some years to come, as has happened in the case of DDT, penicillin, beer, and many other products.

Strategic facilities planning also requires study of the impact of automation, electronics, atomic energy, new product competition, and new techniques on manufacturing operations. A few years ago a large woolen manufacturer ordered several million dollars' worth of looms made to a prewar design. A radically new loom was being introduced by a European manufacturer at the time this contract was signed. By the time the old-design looms were put in position in the factory, the new design loom had demonstrated cost savings of 47 percent. So before the electricity was turned on, a $3 million investment had been obsoleted.

The failure to base facility plans on a searching look within was costly to a medium-sized company that hired a top production executive from a very much larger competitor. This executive was accustomed to large-volume operations that justified a high degree of automation. Without thinking through the differences in the nature of the two businesses, he introduced a degree of automation that could really not be justified by the company's volume. Thus, he tied up capital that was sorely needed for other purposes and also incurred unnecesary fixed charges.

The tremendous importance of management in our society underlines the necessity for top management to have ethical and moral considerations in mind in setting its objectives and managing its business. This involves consideration of the impact of management decisions on employees, customers, suppliers, the industry, the community, and—where applicable—the nation. No discussion of strategic planning would be complete without emphasizing the importance of these considerations. However, the limited amount of space that we can devote to any single aspect of strategic planning will not permit us to do full justice to it here.

The foregoing examples illustrate the strategic approach to top management planning of the objectives of the business. The same approach must be applied to designing the organization structure; selecting, developing, and motivating the people through whom these objectives must be accomplished; and measuring the results of their efforts.

Planning the organization

In planning its organization structure, top management must take a searching look within to determine whether it has identified and provided for all essential activities.

Even if these activities are now being performed, there may be no provision for clear-cut responsibility for results and the necessary authority to achieve them. For example, in reviewing its organization, a leading airline recognized that the loyalty of air travelers to a given line is directly related to the way they are handled when they call for a reservation, get tickets, wait for baggage, or when flights must be delayed or rerouted, etc. They found that responsibility for these activities was divided among several departments. Therefore, the organization was changed so that responsibility for all aspects of customer service was placed under a single executive in the company's headquarters, and at each location where the company operates.

Strategic organization planning also involves taking into account all of the factors which determine how the work should be organized. For example, the above-mentioned airline recognized that the need for fast, coordinated decision-making on a nationwide basis required central direction of all flight activities. On the other hand, customer and plane servicing required on-the-spot coordination and decision making.

Therefore, the latter activities were decentralized under local and regional managements.

Freeing top management

Furthermore, the organization plan must make it possible for top management executives to concentrate on basic planning, policy making, and evaluation of results. This can be achieved by delegating as much decision-making authority as practical to lower levels of management.

In this connection, the advantages of a decentralized divisional type of organization are well recognized today as a means of freeing top management for overall corporate planning and at the same time providing profit centers and focal points for coordinated planning and action for individual segments of the business.

But a number of companies have found that this type of organization would increase their management costs by anywhere from 15 to 30 percent because of the need to duplicate certain activities. Therefore, in deciding how far they could go in decentralizing, these companies have had to weigh whether the advantages to be gained were likely to enable them to increase gross profits enough to justify these increased costs.

One of the primary considerations in designing the top management structure is to provide for strategic planning. This involves seeing that activities like research and development, commercial and market research, organization planning and operations research are provided for where applicable. It also includes building coordinated strategic planning into top management processes. Some companies have assigned a top management executive specific responsibility for assisting the chief executive in coordinating and programing corporate planning and provided staff to assist in this process.

Strategic organization planning, short-term at least, must also take into consideration the informal relationships between key individuals and groups. No matter how good it looks on paper, a plan that has not taken these into account is likely to run into trouble.

The plan of organization that is best for a company at any given time will depend on the state of its own evolution. For example, during the Twenties, a number of packaged consumer goods companies were merged on the strength of the advantages that would come from selling through a common sales force. Initially the business was organized on a functional basis with all sales activities reporting to a

Vice President for Sales, all plants reporting to a Vice President for Manufacturing, and the like.

Conditions during the depression of the Thirties and World War II shortages encouraged the establishment of strong central control. But shortly after the war top management felt that the number of products had become so great that centralized planning and coordination was no longer effective. So they decided to divisionalize. However, after costing it out, they decided to continue to sell through a common sales force, which acted as the distribution agency for all divisions. But the company's growth of late has been such that a salesman could no longer do justice to the entire line of products. So the company recently merged several smaller divisions and gave each of the remaining divisions its own sales force.

Planning personnel strategy

No matter how good the objectives and organization structure may be, in the last analysis results depend on the capabilities of people. Therefore, an extremely important aspect of strategic planning is the selection and development of the kind of people needed to meet long-run objectives.

For example, in planning to expand, companies often overlook the important fact that different businesses require different skills and temperaments. This is illustrated by the case of a successful manufacturer of industrial goods whose research department developed a product for the consumer market which was judged to have outstanding possibilities. A new division staffed with the company's own people launched the new product. But the predicted profits shortly turned out to be staggering losses. It was first assumed that the product was poor, then that the decision to launch it had been based on faulty staff work. More careful investigation showed that the real problem was people. The new division's staff had been entirely competent in the parent company's engineering type of business. But the new product had been launched in a highly speculative market, where success depended largely on shrewd, entrepreneurial decisions and fast action. Certain key positions in the division were then staffed from outside the company, with executives who had demonstrated their ability to make money in this market. The division soon moved solidly into black ink for the first time.

Organization changes—for example, the decision to decentralize on a divisional basis—can also pose some serious personnel problems.

Experience demonstrates that most executives rise to the challenge of decentralized management. However, unfortunately some do not. Frequently most candidates for division managership will have little knowledge of a number of the functions they will be directing or experience in being over-all businessmen as compared with functional specialists. Also, many have not been trained to make their own decisions, and to live with them after they have made them. This can have serious consequences for the newly-divisionalized company. One company reports that one-third of its original division managers had to be replaced within five years. Equally difficult are the problems of former top management operating executives who must shift over from line to general management functional jobs.

Since it takes a long time to develop people, strategic personnel planning involves anticipating future requirements for managers and making sure that they are developing. The most important factors affecting the development of managers are the way the business is run and challenging opportunities in the work they do. In addition, some important techniques now emerging, such as automation and operations research, will require a higher order of analytical and planning skill, not to mention technical knowledge, than is possessed by many present managers.

These problems highlight the need for management training, discussed below.

Change is one of the few certainties of our modern society. So just as mobility is important in military strategy, present trends are increasing the premium on management's ability to help the organization to adjust to change.

Adjusting to change

Changes can be accomplished more fully, quickly, and smoothly and casualties such as those referred to above can be minimized if the management planners bear in mind that results must be accomplished through people. There are a number of guidelines that can help in this connection.

It would be hard to overemphasize the top man's role in effecting change. Therefore, the plan must be one that he can work with. It would be unrealistic to set goals that require a price higher than he is willing to pay. For example, an executive approaching retirement may be unwilling to undertake certain things a younger man who is "on the make" would do. It is also essential to be sure that the top man understands and is prepared to do what he must do to help carry out the program. Otherwise, when he comes up against something difficult or unpleasant, he may say, "No, I don't want to go that far. I hadn't realized I would have to do this. I would rather struggle along with what I have." And if the top man is not prepared to carry out his part, the resistance and inertia down the line will increase immeasurably.

People can change only if they understand what is expected of them. Therefore, it is important to spell out concretely at each level in the organization what people are supposed to learn in order to perform effectively. It is also important to provide teaching aids to assist them in actually absorbing and learning new skills.

Change can be facilitated by making people aware of the benefits to be derived and providing assurances on points on which they have misgivings. Frequently they are so accustomed to their former ways of doing things that they do not recognize the disadvantages. So the proponents of change need to stress the drawbacks of the present approach as well as the advantages that will accrue to each individual as well as to the business as a result of the change.

Finally, means must be provided for determining how the plan is progressing so that problems can be recognized and dealt with quickly. No one can foresee the entire future. So it is necessary to check on how the plan is really working so that problems can be recognized and dealt with promptly.

However, results will also depend on top management's ability to motivate people, to stimulate the creative thinking required by leadership in today's changing world, and to integrate their efforts toward the achievement of company goals.

Management climate

An important source of motivation comes out of the satisfaction the individual gets out of his job. This depends in part on how work is organized. It also depends on a management climate which emphasizes delegation of authority, encouragement of innovation, freedom of action, teamwork, and uncompromising insistence on high standards of performance.

Perhaps the most important factor influencing management climate is how well top executives can formulate basic concepts in their own minds, communicate them to the organization, and stimulate lower level executives to think creatively, make their own decisions, and stand on their own feet. Incidentally, most top management executives underestimate the extent to which their leadership and example, like a stone dropped into a pool, fans out and affects the entire organization.

In this connection, many operating executives who are promoted into top management positions find the transition extremely difficult. They miss the satisfactions of feeling in direct control, of making decisions, issuing orders, getting things done, and seeing quick, frequent, and tangible results. Frequently they tend to revert to their former ways of managing and, in one way or another, to intervene in the work of their subordinates. This not only diverts top management's own attention from strategic planning. It also consumes an enormous amount of time of lower levels of management in preparing justifications and explanations, time which could better be directed toward more constructive work.

Measuring results

The motive power of the management machine is also greatly influenced by the approach top management takes to judging and rewarding performance.

The Chairman of the Board of one of our leading manufacturing companies recently cited a dramatic example of this. This company had been quite drastically reorganized. One of the changes was installation of a modern cost control system and a supplemental compensation plan. But much to management's surprise, little or no improvement followed these innovations. So they called a meeting of several hundred of their top people, at which they analyzed and compared the profit performance of each unit, showing each man how his performance was reflected in the supplemental compensation fund. Each man in turn held similar meetings of his own supervisors and the process continued on down the line, with meetings held at regular intervals. The direct relationship between the results for which they were responsible and their own compensation caused all members of management to determine to put their houses in order.

As a result, direct labor costs were reduced from an off-standard of 65 percent to 10 percent *under* standard in seven years. Manufacturing overhead was also drastically reduced. Top management is convinced that these achievements would have been impossible without the combination of a system for measuring performance tied to real incentives.

Return on investment is, of course, both widely used and highly effective for measuring results where integrated divisions are concerned, but is not adequate by itself. For example, one large company had considered the managers of two of its divisions to be equally competent. Quite accidentally, during the course of a study of these two divisions it became clear that one manager was far more able than the other. To be sure, each division's volume and profits had increased at approximately the same rate. However, when the shares of market enjoyed by these two divisions over a period of years were analyzed, it was found that one had been losing position—although increasing its volume—while the other division had been increasing its share of market.

This is but one evidence that top management needs to learn much more about measuring results in order to improve its strategic planning. Growing recognition of the limitations of financial measurements alone is causing more and more companies to take a searching look at all the major factors essential to success and to seek ways of measuring results on each. Among the factors receiving increasing consideration are share of market enjoyed, new products introduced, productivity, development of key personnel, and employee and community attitudes. Short and long term considerations should be balanced since there are many ways that a manager can improve his short-term showing at the expense of the future.

Goals

In addition we must not overlook the motivating force of integrating corporate and individual objectives and of company-wide communication of clearly defined goals and plans to achieve them. . . .

It seems inevitable that strategic planning, which integrates all aspects of the business and is based on a searching look within, a broad look around, and a long look ahead will play an increasingly important role in meeting the challenges and problems of our dynamic economy. This approach enables top management to be sure that its energies are devoted to really profit-building activities, rather than to day-to-day emergencies. It also ensures that in so doing management will not overlook its important obligations tc customers, employees, owners, suppliers, its industry, or the community. Equally important, this approach enables top management to define its goals so that all members of management can see them clearly and can thus coordinate their individual efforts toward the attainment of these goals, measure their results, and derive motivating satisfactions from group achievement.

34. THE ROLE OF ECONOMICS IN
BUSINESS PLANNING [1]

Murray L. Weidenbaum [2]

An economist may make a number of contributions to business planning, particularly in relating the external economic environment to company operations. This article briefly describes the business planning process and then discusses some of the more important contributions that economics and economists can make to that process. It is a synthesis of available information on industrial economics and is not limited to the experience of any single company.

The literature on business planning is sufficiently voluminous without adding to the available descriptions of techniques to be used in preparing planning documents or in organizing the planning operation. However, the repetition of a few fundamentals of planning may be beneficial both to those who participate in the process and those outside of it who wish to understand it.

Fundamentally, business planning is not, or at least should not be, merely a collection of estimates of future sales, profits, manpower, or other statistical forecasts. To cite the obvious, Webster's *New International Dictionary* informs us that to plan is "to devise or project as a method or course of action." Here we have the essence of business planning: it is a process which is designed to provide a *course of action* for a business enterprise. The statistical data merely furnish a basis for decisions. The present article is primarily concerned with the overall planning of a diversified business enterprise rather than the planning performed by an individual division or department. Much of the approach and methodology is equally pertinent.

Economics and business planning certainly are not synonymous, although many people may take them to be so or would like them to be so. Business planning properly is a multi-disciplinary field,

[1] From *Business Topics* (Summer, 1962), pp. 46-54. Reprinted by permission of *Business Topics*.
[2] Murray L. Weidenbaum, Corporate Economist, The Boeing Company.

utilizing economics, accounting, engineering, marketing, and many other specialties.

It should be acknowledged, perhaps with some pride, that a goodly number of directors of business planning are economists. By rough count, approximately a dozen members of the National Association of Business Economists are planning directors. Their titles range from the simple Director of Planning to Economist and Director of Planning and Coordination.

In many other instances, the planning directors have come up through the financial or marketing routes. In any event, the planning organization must contain or draw upon men with all of these capabilities as well as others.

The following are some of the major phases of the business planning process, especially those to which economists may contribute. Each phase will be discussed in turn.

1. Setting forth the external environment in which the business enterprise will be operating during the planning period.
2. Establishing goals and objectives for the enterprise.
3. Analyzing the capability and resource availability of the enterprise.
4. Developing the specific programs to be undertaken.
5. Evaluating the projected performance of the enterprise.

FORECASTING THE EXTERNAL ENVIRONMENT

Most business plans, particularly those of a long-range nature, begin with or are prepared on the basis of an evaluation of the external environment in which the company will be operating. This is the area in which business economists may make their most important contribution. All available surveys of the role of company economists indicate that forecasting is the predominant activity which they have in common.

A survey of economic staffs of American industry conducted by the National Industrial Conference Board revealed that "periodic forecasting is reported by respondents to be the most important single activity of staff economists." [3] A similar survey conducted by the Socony Mobil Oil Company concluded:

> If there is a single activity common to all the company economists surveyed . . . it is forecasting long- and short-term trends in the national economy and relating them to sales and profits. [4]

---

[3] "Sources of Economic Intelligence," *Conference Board Business Record* (September, 1960), p. 28.
[4] C. S. Teitsworth, "Growing Role of the Company Economist," *Harvard Business Review* (January-February, 1959), p. 100.

It was reported that such forecasts are of value to management in preparing sales objectives and planning inventories, procurement, production, and capital expenditures for periods from five to twenty years in the future.

Types of forecasting

Company planning may utilize different types of economic forecasting. These vary from sophisticated models of the gross national product (and other items in the national income and product accounts) to a naive assumption à la Sewell Avery that the storm cellar is the most likely symbol of the economic outlook.

Almost all of the long-term economic forecasts used by business firms which have come to the attention of the writer in recent years are based, with varying degrees of sophistication, on the following simple formula:

$$G = E \times H \times P$$

G stands for the gross national product; E is the average number of persons employed during the period; H is the average hours worked per employee; and P represents the output per man-hour or productivity. This, of course, is the projection of potential supply of gross national product.

Employment estimates

The employment estimates are generally based on Census Bureau and Labor Department projections of population and labor force. Given the population forecast—and the Census Bureau obligingly provides several alternatives, based primarily on different assumed fertility rates—the estimate of the labor force primarily is a question of determining participation rates among the groups of working age. For forecasts up to about fifteen years in the future, the relevant population distributions involve little guesswork, except for in- and out-migration and mortality rates, which are factors of lesser order of magnitude than fertility.

Assumptions are then necessary as to the portions of the labor force not involved in civilian employment: the members of the armed forces and the unemployed. A 4 percent unemployment ratio seems to be the most popular assumption. The estimate of hours is generally based on the historical experience of a declining secular trend in the average workweek—usually a reduction of less than 1 percent a year.

Productivity

Productivity is estimated to increase as the result of expanded research and development, new business investment, and increasing application of new technologies such as those spawned by the entire field of electronics. The differences in assumed rates of productivity can be crucial to the GNP figures finally obtained. A rise in the annual increase in productivity from 2½ to 3 percent, assuming the same employment and hours, may raise the GNP in 1970 by $50 billion.

As would be expected, the various estimates of GNP obtained by different forecasters cover a broad range, although there is virtual unanimity that the trend of GNP is upward sloping. Table 1 contains some representative forecasts of GNP in 1970 which have been used by business firms.[5] The range is striking—from $675 billion to $803 billion, in terms of 1959 dollars.

TABLE 1

PROJECTIONS OF GROSS NATIONAL PRODUCT IN 1970
(In Billions of 1959 Dollars)

SOURCE OF PROJECTIONS	AMOUNTS
National Planning Association .... (judgment model)	803
American-Marietta Company	750
Stanford Research Institute	725
McCann-Erickson, Inc.	700
B. F. Goodrich (conservative)	675

NOTE: Some of the projections were originally made on the basis of "1957" or "1958" dollars and were converted to 1959 dollars by the author, using the implicit deflators of GNP contained in the January 1961 issue of *Economic Indicators*.

Models of the economy

Many long-term forecasters cross-check these projections of supply of GNP against a more complete model of the economy. Such

---

[5] National Planning Association, *Long-Range Projections for Economic Growth*, Planning Pamphlet No. 107 (October, 1959); American-Marietta Company, *The Years Ahead: 1960 to 1975*, 1960; Stanford Research Institute, *Indications of Tomorrow* (November, 1958); McCann-Erickson, Inc., *A Marketing Profile of "The Big Sixties"*; J. W. Keener, President, B. F. Goodrich Company, "Marketing's Job in the 1960's" (Keynote address to the 42nd National Conference of the American Marketing Association, June 17, 1959).

a model may show, on the one hand, the demand for output by consumers and others, and, on the other hand, the cost of producing the output (national income, by component, plus the adjustment factors between national income and GNP). Table 2 shows an example of this type of approach, based on the actual data for 1959. Such a model provides a useful cross-check of the internal consistency of the estimates used.

TABLE 2

NATIONAL INCOME AND PRODUCT ACCOUNT, 1959

(In Billions of Dollars)

Compensation of employees	277.8
Proprietor's income	46.5
Rental income of persons	12.4
Corporate profits	46.6
Net interest	16.4
National Income	399.6
Business transfer payments	1.8
Indirect business tax liability	42.6
Current surplus of government enterprises less subsidies	—.6
Capital consumption allowances	40.5
Statistical discrepancy	—1.8
Gross National Product	482.1
Personal consumption expenditures	313.8
Gross private domestic investment	72.0
Net exports of goods and services	—1.0
Government purchases of goods and services	97.1
Gross National Product	482.1

NOTE: Details may not add to totals shown due to rounding.
SOURCE: *Survey of Current Business* (July, 1960), p. 12.

In many cases, much detailed analysis of economic history and a very considerable amount of judgment and insight goes into the preparation of these forecasts. Also, the spelling out of the basic assumptions underlying the forecast serves as a description of much of the external environment in which the enterprise will be operating. Typical assumptions include the following:

1. The current state of international tensions—the cold war—will continue. No major war will occur during the forecast period, nor will a workable disarmament program be adopted.
2. Scientific and technological advances will continue at the current rate or higher.

3. The federal government will take necessary action to avoid major depressions or runaway inflations.
4. Prices will rise at the average rate experienced during the 1950's (or, alternatively, all estimates are prepared in "constant" dollars).

Projections of the overall performance of the economy are in the nature of a starting point and need to be related to specific industries and geographical areas. For military producers, for example, the forecast of GNP is used in projecting the military budget, which is the basic market research task for that industry and central to long-range planning.

Methodology

A widely used methodology for military market forecasts is based on a three-fold process: [6]

1. A long-term projection of GNP.
2. A projection of the military budget on the basis of the economic forecast.
3. A statistical analysis of the composition of the military budget.

Figure 1 shows the relationships between steps (1) and (2). The simplest method is to take military expenditures as a constant percentage of GNP. A slightly more sophisticated approach, somewhat in line with recent experience, is to estimate the military expenditure level as a declining precentage of GNP.

FIGURE 1

THE RELATIONSHIP BETWEEN GNP AND MILITARY SPENDING

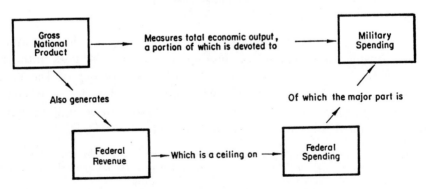

[6] Murray L. Weidenbaum, "The Military Market in the 1960's," *Business Horizons* (Spring, 1961).

However, as Figure 1 illustrates, the situation is more complex than that. In the post-World War II period, military expenditures have been a major part, but only a part, of the federal budget and certainly a much smaller proportion of GNP. Within the constraint of a budget which is approximately in balance over the cycle, the GNP, and its growth, is far more of a limitation on federal revenues than on military spending directly. A model of the federal budget is needed, which is built up from both the revenue side and the expenditure side, which encompasses the various non-defense programs as well as defense programs, and possibly, tax and debt reductions over the period.

The economist's contribution to projecting the future composition of defense spending is two-fold: Through even the simplest of statistical analyses of historical data, he may bring to light emerging trends in military procurement and research and development which may have escaped others in the planning process who are less familiar with economic statistics. Figure 2 is an example of such

FIGURE 2

THE CHANGING MIX OF MILITARY R AND D

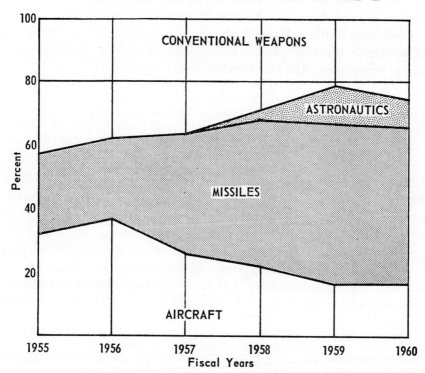

an analysis of shifts in the product mix of military R & D. Incidentally, we have here a "lead" indicator, for the shifts in R & D from aircraft to missiles, for example, herald future shifts in the same direction in the larger category of procurement. Figure 2 shows an emerging shift to astronautics. Significantly, expenditures for military space programs have not yet shown up in the procurement statistics.

GOALS AND OBJECTIVES

The second phase of the business planning process mentioned earlier is related to goals and objectives. It is problematical whether, in this area, economic theory may necessarily make a practical or acceptable contribution. Economists have generally been nurtured on the doctrine of profit maximization as the rational mode of conduct for entrepreneurs. The transition is almost instinctive from the belief that profit maximization should be the desired goal to the certainty that it must "obviously" be the accepted goal of entrepreneurs. Profit maximization may be the dominant goal of a business enterprise, but that is not necessarily the situation. A large business organization may have a diversification of goals.

Professor William Baumol is the rare example of an outstanding economic theorist with a substantial amount of business consulting experience. He has concluded:

> . . . most oligopolistic firms aim to maximize not profits, but sales volume (measured in money terms; sales are what the economist in his jargon calls "total revenue"). So long as profits remain at a satisfactory rate, management will devote further effort to increasing its sales rather than its profits.[7]

In practice, there are many forms which the goals and objectives of an enterprise may take. Management may wish to maintain—or increase—the historical growth in sales or earnings. It may wish to attain a given percentage rate of return on investment. A certain diversification of the product line or market served may be desired. Some or all of these objectives may be aimed at. In fact, they may be interrelated and many of them may be derivatives of an explicit or implicit profit maximization goal. The economist

---

[7] William Baumol, "Price Behavior, Stability, and Growth," *The Relationship of Prices to Economic Stability and Growth*, Compendium of Papers Submitted by Panelists Appearing Before The Joint Economic Committee (Washington: Government Printing Office, 1958), pp. 54-55.

may aid both in selecting the type of goal to be followed and in providing statistical measuring sticks for gauging attainment.

Sales goals

In the case of sales goals, the economist can point out the historical and projected rates of growth in the economy as a whole, in the industry or industries in which the company is operating, and for other companies of comparable size or market position. Similar data can be obtained for profit rates.

Sales objectives can be set in the form of maintaining or improving market shares. Here, knowledge of the historical trend of the pertinent industries and markets, as well as usable economic forecasts can play an important role. In some cases, the identification and measurement of the market or industry may be no simple task. The electronics "industry," to cite an important example, still has not come into its own in the Standard Industrial Classification which underlies the data of the Census Bureau and many other governmental agencies. Bits and pieces of electronics production are contained in a dozen or more SIC codes. The case of missile production would be even more difficult, were it not for the fact that the customer is in position to make comprehensive reports available.

RESOURCES AND CAPABILITIES

The economist can make a contribution to the analysis of an enterprise's resources and capabilities during the planning period by stressing the element of futurity. For example, financial and engineering personnel may be in the best position to estimate the basic costs of future programs. Yet, they may or may not need to be reminded that price levels may change, and possibly at different rates than those that obtained in the recent past. Some simple analyses of overall supply and demand factors for the commodities involved may prove to be quite helpful. This is illustrative of a general function of the industrial economist, to relate the activities of his individual company to broader trends in the national, and increasingly the international, economy.

Statistical data

Personnel management may perform the basic projections of manpower requirements. Yet, they may or may not need to be advised concerning future trends in national or regional labor force availability. In this connection, the U. S. Department of Labor's studies of the future composition of national employment can be extremely useful.[8] Figure 3 is an example of the kind of economic statistical data that can be helpful to management in relating the problems that a company may consider peculiar to its operations to fundamental developments in the national economy. The anticipated shift from relatively unskilled workers to professional and technical personnel is striking.

FIGURE 3

PROJECTED SHIFTS IN NATIONAL EMPLOYMENT REQUIREMENTS

Percent Change in Employment 1960-1970

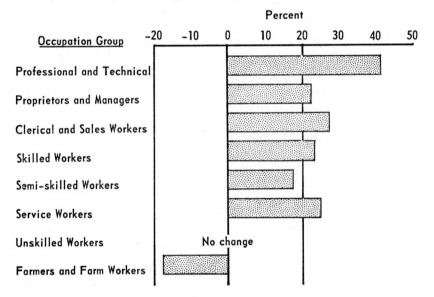

In the short run, the analyses of the external business environment may be required by treasury officials concerned with estimating the cost and availability of corporate funds and the preferences among stock issues, bonded indebtedness, and bank debt.

In some cases, the proposed capital asset portion of the business plan may usefully be related to the outlook for business investment generally and to sales-investment ratios for specific industries. Types of economic data and guidance required in developing the resource aspects of business planning vary with the individual firm.

[8] U. S. Department of Labor, *Manpower—Challenge of the 1960's* (Washington: Government Printing Office, 1960).

Development of Programs

The development of specific programs to utilize the enterprise's resources in meeting established goals is generally a function of line or divisional management. Here, too, the role of the economist is essentially that of advice or review.

The most apparent utilization of economic analysis is in connection with sales forecasting. Forecasts of the sales of specific products need to be checked against appraisals of the market potential. Hopefully, the sales estimates were prepared on the basis of a comprehensive market research job in the first place, which included use of the analyses and forecasts of the national economy and of the specific industries in which the firm is operating.

In a more fundamental way, continuing analysis of the various segments of the national economy may yield selected "growth" markets which the enterprise might wish to penetrate with new products or adaptations of existing products. Conversely, information on differential growth and profit rates can be useful in selecting, among the various possibilities, products to be developed and marketed.

Evaluating Performance

A critical aspect of business planning is the evaluation of the adequacy of the individual divisional and departmental plans as well as that of the company total. The evaluation itself is a proper function of management. The economist and other staff specialists mainly provide the materials for making the evaluation, such as the quantifications of the performance of the larger group of which the enterprise is a part: the industry or the economy as a whole. The goals and objectives described earlier can play a crucial role in evaluating performance.

Here we close the loop. The reasonableness of the goals and targets set earlier are checked against the likely accomplishments of the enterprise in view of its resources and capabilities in the expected environment. Necessary modifications may then be made in the goals and targets as well as in the programs to accomplish them.

Conclusions

In planning, as in the other phases of business operations, the economist must be guided by the special problems being faced by the company, its particular history and outlook, and the stated needs of its management for staff work. The role of the economist, or of any staff specialist, is not to identify the most intellectually stimulating problems to work on or necessarily to use the most advanced and sophisticated techniques. His function is to make, on the basis of his special training and capability, the most useful contribution to his management. This contribution certainly is not to talk down to management or to put some intellectual window dressing on the most fashionable current opinion.

This contribution consists of bringing to bear on business problems the tools of economic analysis, the results of economic research, the findings from economic statistics and, in a generalized way, the value of professional objectivity. The role of the business economist might be considered to be the furnishing of a window through which the firm can see aspects of the outer world it may otherwise ignore or not fully comprehend. Sir Dennis Robertson, in an address to the Royal Economic Society entitled, "On Sticking to One's Last," stated,

> I do not want the economist to mount the pulpit or expect him to fit himself to handle the keys of Heaven and Hell . . . I want him to be rather humble . . . I like to think of him as a sort of Good Dog Tray. . . .

35. COORDINATING BUDGETS WITH
FORECASTING [1]

J. J. Curran, Jr.[2]

*   *   *

Forecasting and budgeting contrasted

Forecasting is to business what courtship is to a man. While he is pursuing the lady of his choice, a man still keeps a sharp eye open for other girls. He can change speed and direction rather quickly or even stop running if conditions change.

Budgets, on the other hand, are to business what an engagement is to a man. The scouting and the pursuit are over, the plans are set, and the engagement determines rather definitely whom the man will marry, where, when, and how. Society does not encourage us to change these rather fixed plans. Similarly, after the goal of a business has been set, the budget programs where, when, and how it will be achieved.

Forecasting and budgeting are not things separate from the day-to-day operations of business. They are not functions performed by bearded prophets in ivory tower offices.

To me, forecasting and budgeting are the basis of "operations planning," which in turn is the essential basis of efficient management. Forecasting and budgeting together are like the agenda for a meeting. They outline the desired goals of the business and program the managerial decisions by which the goals shall be achieved.

Two types of forecasting

Forecasting in the business world involves two major activities:

First, there is forecasting of general business conditions. This type of forecasting is familiar to us all. It is done by government agencies, banks, economists, and professors. The monthly letters issued by the National City Bank and the Guaranty Trust Company are good examples.

[1] From *Charting the Company's Future*, American Management Association, 1954, pp. 32-43. Reprinted by permission of the American Management Association.
[2] J. J. Curran, Jr., Director, Budget Analysis, General Foods Corporation, 1954.

· 383 ·

Second, there is a more specific kind of forecasting. It has to do with estimating the potential of an industry or a product or the trend of customer preference. This type of forecasting involves the study of many factors: population growth and movement, national income, age distribution, and so on. It requires study of the motives which cause people to buy or to switch brands. It requires knowledge of trade inventories and geographic markets.

It is characteristic of a forecast that it is as often expressed in words as in figures and deals with matters which are beyond the control of an individual business and, indeed, often beyond the control of governments.

Long or short-term "guesstimates"

Forecasts may be said to represent the best "guesstimate" of a situation that can be made at the time of preparation. And, even though forecasts can never be as accurate as a watch, they represent assumptions which are prerequisite to good budgeting.

Business forecasts may be for a short-term or a long-term period, dependent upon the business. For example, a hot dog vendor has to forecast what the weather will be like for tomorrow's game if he wants to budget or plan his operations. Business can be ruined if he orders too few or too many weenies and buns.

Often a forecast is made for years ahead. Far-sighted businessmen tried during the war to gauge the economic climate which would prevail after the war. Would there be boom, or bust, or both in quick succession? The fact that much of the forecasting, when done, was inaccurate is not discreditable. If we wish to control and guide our destiny, we must make forecasts and assumptions.

The length of time for which a forecast is prepared should be determined by the needs of the business and by how far ahead it is possible to forecast. In utility companies 10- and 15-year forecasts are not unusual, while for most other companies one- or two-year estimates are probably typical. Forecasts should be revised as often as new information or better judgment indicates.

Forecasts are like a doctor's prescription. They should be used only by the person and at the time for which they were made. For example, assume that a good business climate over the next five years is forecast for a machine tool manufacturer. It could be the height of folly for a toy manufacturer to plan his next season's operations on the basis of that forecast.

The "profit plan"

We do not use the term "budget" at all in General Foods. We prefer to use the term "profit plan" because it is a descriptive phrase which tells what the budget is—a plan for profitable operation.

Profit-planning is a term which denotes life and activity. On the other hand, the term "budget" is one which has connotations of penny-pinching, wage-freezing, and long dreary lists of figures. Profit-planning, too, is a concept which is readily understood by marketing, production, management, and other non-accounting personnel.

A profit plan represents the actual plan for the operation of a business. Because it is intended to be followed day by day, so far as is possible, it should be prepared for a definite period of time, as close as possible to the beginning of the period. The plan should be prepared periodically—monthly, quarterly, or annually, according to the needs of the business.

It is important that profit plans be detailed enough to indicate a course of action clearly. It is also important that the plans be the expression of the goals and intentions of all levels of management and that they be approved by top management.

Profit plans should be used as a bench mark to appraise actual results of operations. Management can thus see how well the plans were prepared and how well they were followed.

Needless to say, this comparison of actual against plan is a great incentive for better planning.

Road map for all management levels

There are four ways in which forecasts and profit plans together assist a business in maintaining a sound, healthy financial condition.

In the first place, forecasts and profit plans are a means of detailing and formalizing the plans and goals of every segment of a business. No business ever operates without a plan. The businesses which grow and prosper and seemingly run themselves, though, are those businesses where the plans are written down. When the plans are written, they can be studied and reviewed by all personnel who can make a contribution—and this includes just about everyone in the shop. By formalizing the plan, I mean clothing it in a uniform and familiar garb and expressing all parts of the plan in a common denominator—dollars.

The second thing forecasting and profit-planning do is to coordinate the plans of all segments of the business and to ascertain that together they offer the best opportunity to achieve—without undue risk—the dollar profit goal and a return on investment the company considers adequate.

Forecasting and profit-planning also provides a basis for "management by exception." If an executive wishes to keep abreast of competition and the economy, he cannot spend much of his time looking over daily operations. In a company the size of General Foods, it is physically impossible for management to see everything that happens.

The profit plan allows top management to look at operations periodically with a view to whether the plan is realistic and satisfactory. Once that is settled, the division manager has full authority to go ahead, and only a change in plan will have to be approved by top management.

The forecast and profit plan therefore provides a sort of road map which all levels of management can refer to. If actual results differ materially from the plan, management is alerted in time to take corrective action.

In General Foods, we issue a monthly "Operations Review" which, in a few words and a few charts, tells management how we are progressing and spotlights those divisions or products which are doing better or worse than plan. This report is prepared by my Budget and Analysis group and is a most important phase of our work.

Introducing a new product

Forecasting and profit-planning played an important role in introducing a major postwar General Foods product and making it welcome in the American home. This product is Instant Maxwell House, which has been described as "the most marvelous merchandising success ever seen in the food business."

Instant, or soluble, coffee is a classic example of a convenience product. It's a powder obtained by brewing coffee in the factory and then extracting the water from it. It offers many advantages in that you can prepare one cup as easily as 10 cups, it keeps fresh longer than ground coffee, and it is quick—you can make a cup as quickly as water can be made to boil.

These advantages would justify a premium price over regular coffee. But instant coffee has the added advantage of economy—it is cheaper than regular coffee on a cup-for-cup basis, and it is less wasteful.

The first instants contained carbohydrate additives which gave the drink a slight off-coffee flavor. Now the instants are pure, and they make a good cup of coffee.

Creation of a market

Instant coffee has an interesting history. Almost a hundred years ago, soldiers of our Civil War experimented with tablets of coffee powder which were dropped into hot water like Alka-Seltzer pills. The stuff was pretty bad. However, it is surprising that instant coffees were little heard of for half a century after.

Then, in 1910, a man named George Washington, who died in 1954, marketed a coffee powder in individual cup containers. The product was successful, but because of its high price it was luxury or specialty item.

It was not until just before the war that the outline of a mass market for instant coffee became apparent. When the war came, production for the armed services was stimulated and civilian supplies were curtailed. The mass sampling of thousands of servicemen and civilians because regular coffee was not available undoubtedly helped create a peacetime market for instant coffees.

General Foods, as a major principal in the coffee business, realized that it must keep up with developments in the instant field. We produced instant coffee for the government during the war, and in 1946 our product appeared on grocery shelves.

Our first marketing experience was like that of some of our competitors—we were getting millions of people to buy our product once or twice, but repeat demand was weak. We knew the answer was in product acceptability and therefore directed our research toward improvement.

Research paid off in 1949 when we found ourselves with a new process which gave us 100 per cent pure coffee. We believed it was better than anything else on the market and had great promotional possibilities.

A look at past experience

What did we do with this advantage, and what part did forecasting and profit-planning play in the steps we took?

We first made a long-range forecast. To do so, we made a careful appraisal of our progress to date and took a good look at our then current situation.

Why did we look back to the past when we wanted to move forward? My answer is that business forecasting does not operate with formulas which are mathematical and infallible and for that reason must rely largely on what has happened before.

While history does not exactly repeat itself, it is nevertheless true that like causes tend to have like effects. Wise marketing and management practice therefore normally includes a continuing effort to build a comprehensive "book of experience," so to speak.

So we examined the *sales history* of our first instant coffee. We wanted to find out where it had sold best; through what type of outlet, chain or independent; and in what sizes and containers.

We found that our sales had not been growing fast even though most of the 20-odd manufacturers who had entered the business since the war had dropped out. By 1948, four companies controlled 90 per cent of the market, and Instant Maxwell House was a poor third in the race.

Continuing our examination, we found that our *distribution* was national but that retailer and wholesaler stocks were low—while our competitors seemingly had more abundant supplies.

Then we looked at our past *marketing activity*. We studied the effect of couponing, trade dealing, and media advertising on volume, on profits, and on our competitors. We found that our marketing had been unable to capitalize on any outstanding *quality* or *packaging advantage*. Sales records indicated no outstanding consumer preference for Instant Maxwell House.

Assessing future possibilities

Having looked at what had happened, we then had to forecast the future of Instant Coffee. This is the point where we had to *assess* the *limits of the market* and our ability to penetrate that market.

The big questions were:

1. How big was the instant coffee market?
2. How fast was the market growing?
3. How much would it grow?

We found that there was a large existing market for instant coffee and ample evidence that there was room for great expansion. We found that no company had yet produced an instant coffee which matched the taste of regular brewed coffee. However, we believed that our new process gave our instant a superiority over all our competitors.

We next projected the consumption of coffee for a period of years, taking into account population, income, and coffee consumption trends. Then we had to forecast how much of this coffee would be sold in instant form—and where it would be sold.

Having made the forecast, or assumption, of the size of the instant market and its location, we proceeded to make a *long-term profit plan*.

Factors in setting volume objectives

The first task and the most difficult was to set *volume objectives* for our new instant coffee for a period of years.

This first basic step in profit-planning-setting volumes is much like the first instruction in a famous English recipe for rabbit pot pie: "First catch a rabbit." Overcome that hurdle and the rest is easy.

We set volumes after checking these questions or determining factors:

1. Was our product as good as we thought it was?
2. Would the housewife share our enthusiasm?

To find out, we made many consumer surveys, one of which I shall describe.

An independent testing organization went into 3,500 homes in Washington, D. C., with a coffee pot and a pound of regular Maxwell House Coffee. The tester said he wanted to compare the brand of coffee used by the housewife and brewed in her own way with regular Maxwell House brewed in his way. So the housewife and the tester each brewed a pot of coffee. Then the housewife was asked to leave the room, but her husband or another member of the family was asked to stay.

When the woman left, the tester poured the regular Maxwell House Coffee he had brewed down the sink and quickly mixed an equal quantity of Instant Maxwell House. The husband then called his wife back into the kitchen, and she was asked to taste the two coffees—her own favorite and Instant Maxwell House. By a two-to-one vote the housewife preferred our instant to her regular!

It was a remarkable demonstration, and it convinced us *we really had something!*

Miscellaneous decisions

With our new product, we could now advertise 100 per cent pure coffee. How effective would this claim be?

Our product was less bulky than the old one. Should we pack in two-ounce, or six-ounce sizes? We decided on two and six ounces.

Should we pack in glass jars or in tin cans? We decided the glass jar was a better selling package.

Was the name Maxwell House, which was associated with regular coffee and with our old, relatively unsuccessful "filled" instant, an asset or a liability for our new product? We decided to retain the name, but to use a distinctive redesigned label for the new instant.

After considering all these questions, we set volume goals for each of our sales regions. The cost of production at varying volume levels was then projected, using cost accounting and engineering skills.

The marketing strategy

The profit plan next had to set forth the marketing strategy which would be used to introduce the new product. This involved many difficult decisions.

How could we exhaust all of the old label stock and introduce the new?

Should we strive for immediate national distribution, or should we introduce the new product region by region?

What media should be used—TV, newspapers, magazines, billboards, or what combination of these?

What deals or incentives should we use to get retailers to stock, and consumers to buy, the new Instant Maxwell House?

To get answers to these questions, we set up a test market. In three cities we introduced Instant Maxwell House with one marketing approach, and in three similar cities we used a different approach. Each group of cities showed surprisingly uniform results. In both cases, consumers bought our product and remained loyal to it after they used it. The second marketing approach, however, gave the most dramatic results.

These test cities were in the East, where instant coffee was already well accepted. To check the marketing plan in an area where instant coffee was not used extensively, we tried this second marketing approach in Kansas City. The approach was even more successful there, so we planned accordingly.

Plant capacity and location

To repeat, our volume projection was made by regions. We next made a study to determine when we would need new plant capacity and—considering freight rates, regional markets, and other factors—where new plants should be built.

As a result, plans were made to expand in New Jersey and to build in Florida, California, and Texas.

Responsibility for planning

This long-range planning which I have described was done under the supervision of the general manager of the Maxwell House Division and with the knowledge of the operating vice president concerned. The work was done by the division which had profit responsibility.

After the plan was complete and the projected profits were carefully examined, it was approved by the general manager and by the operating vice president, who, in turn, passed it on to corporate management for approval. Approval was necessary because the plan, to be executed, would require millions of dollars for bricks, mortar, and machinery and more millions for accounts receivable and inventories.

Short-term profit-planning

Only when we had settled by means of a long-range forecast where we were going and how we were going to get there could we make more specific profit plans for the immediate future. When the long-term course for Instant Maxwell House was set and approved, we could make short-term profit plans as we would for any established product.

The methods used in short-term profit-planning and forecasting are similar to those already described in connection with long-term forecasting and profit-planning. Throughout the corporation, we make profit plans on a fiscal year basis. The year's plan is composed of four quarterly plans.

A final profit plan for each quarter is prepared just before it begins. When we make up this revised quarterly profit plan, we look ahead to see what effect our latest planning will have on the year's result. The final quarterly profit plan embodies the promises and expectations of the general manager, the product managers, the purchasing organization, the advertising agency, the production manager, etc., to their supervisors and to General Foods. They must be in harmony with one another, and they must add up to a profit acceptable to top management.

The quarterly and annual profit plans of all divisions eventually end up in my office. My group consolidates them into a corporate plan, analyzes them, and writes interpretive comments for the administrative staff, which spends about two days each quarter reviewing the division profit plans and the corporate summary. Changes are sometimes made.

When the administrative staff approves a plan, the general manager has a green light to go ahead and is held accountable for variations.

Summary

In conclusion, let me state these three principles of forecasting and profit-planning:

1. They should be tailored to fit the needs of the business.
2. They should be based on good organization with clear-cut and distinctly defined lines of responsibility and authority.
3. Each executive, department head, and supervisor should prepare the forecast and plan for the operation he is responsible for. The top forecast or plan should represent the best judgment of all members of management as to what can be accomplished.

Forecasting and budgeting based on these principles give direction to a business. Just as important, their intelligent preparation and application give top management a chance to really steer the business and to take corrective action to avoid the pitfalls which lie before all of us.

36. THE PLANNING AND
CONTROL CONCEPT [1]

James L. Peirce [2]

A discussion of the planning and control idea might be started by saying that it is synonymous with management itself. Certainly no business can exist without some form of this twin concept, and it might perhaps be demonstrated that success in business is proportionate to the astuteness of its planning and the skill with which it is controlled.

This sweeping statement, however, would dodge the important issues. Although business has lived through many decades of history with marked success, the full planning and control principle is only now emerging and gaining acceptance. This concept can now be reduced to precepts and rules, which may be followed with predictable results. As a consequence, planning, deliberate and detailed, has assumed a new priority among the duties of management at all levels; and controllership, which is the orderly practice of control in business, has become a profitable branch of the science of management.

Definition of planning

It may be useful at the outset to define "planning" (as the word is understood in the concept we are discussing) and to place it in relation to the control function. Planning, of course, is carried on during every hour of the business day, and sometimes during many other hours besides. It may exist with or without control—that is, with or without disciplined efforts to follow the plan or to explain deviations from it. On the other hand, control cannot exist without planning, and therefore the planning must be designed to fit the specifications of control.

In the modern sense of an integrated planning and control system, then, planning refers to the construction of an operating program, comprehensive enough to cover all phases of operations, and detailed enough that specific attention may be given to its fulfillment in con-

---

[1] From *The Controller* (September, 1954). Reprinted by permission of the *The Controller*.
[2] James L. Peirce, Vice President and Controller, A. B. Dick Company, 1954.

trollable segments. It may therefore be reiterated that the planning process must be conducted in direct relation to the needs of control.

Definition of control

An examination of this word "control" shows that, like many another word in the English language, it has a number of meanings. It is absolutely necessary to have a clear understanding of its definition in the specialized sense in which it will be used herein.

Perhaps the easiest approach to this shade of meaning is to mention some of the things that the word "control" in this usage does not include. It does not signify the kind of control over a business enjoyed by a majority shareholder. It does not refer to any part of the control centered in a board of directors or a president. It does not include line authority for making or carrying out policy or operating decisions.

What then is "control" in the sense to be used here? It is defined as the presence in a business of that force which guides it to a predetermined objective by means of predetermined policies and decisions. Every business executive can identify this control force in his company. It operates quite apart from the mass of operating decisions and instructions constantly emanating from the line organization. It does not steer the course, but it informs operating management at once of any significant deviation from it. It does not take action, but it frequently impels action by turning a spotlight on the pertinent facts.

Organization aspects

The practice of this variety of control may be referred to as controllership. When delegated, it is exercised by an executive properly called a controller, although he may not actually carry that title. His title may be, for example, vice president and treasurer and his controllership assignment intermingled with financial and other administrative duties. Nevertheless, regardless of title, because he performs the controllership function, he will be referred to here as the controller.

The problem of assignment and performance of duties in the organization structure will be touched upon at a subsequent point in this paper. For the purpose of delineating the planning and control concept, it may be summarized in this way: Planning is the primary duty of the president, assisted by all line and staff executives. The control function is exercised by the same group, but may be centered functionally in the controller. The objective of controllership is to assist all levels of management in controlling to the plan. It never issues orders, but it coordinates the machinery of planning, records and reveals the facts and makes plain to those in charge what they must do to achieve the prescribed aim.

The control formula

The control process, like all effective modes of management, rests on a simple principle. It may be stated as a three-part formula:

> The first component is the adoption of a plan.
> The second is reporting actual performance as compared with the plan.
> The third is making decisions and taking action.

This pattern is repeated as many times as there are units of responsible supervision in the company, and the whole is assembled as a grand plan which directs the company's operations and controls its course. As time goes on, experience sometimes dictates alterations in the plan. Action taken as a result of reporting performance against plan reaches forward to new and better plans.

It should be evident that the three phases of the formula are operating concurrently—that a management following this system will be constantly planning, reporting and taking action. The important thing to note is that the decisions reached and the actions taken will be directly related to a master plan. They will not be spasmodic nor will they be consummated without adequate reference to the fundamental objectives of the business. No decision or action will be taken which is out of harmony with actions in other departments of the business, because all are governed by a universal plan.

To accomplish this atmosphere of controlled power requires diligent effort by men who are both fully conscious of the importance of this technique and willing to accept the self-discipline that it requires.

The adoption of the plan

The initial step, the adoption of a plan, is perhaps the most difficult. Even after the habit of planning has become ingrained, it is not easy to induce a group of executives to set aside pressing matters and think into the problematical future. Perhaps this step can only be accomplished through the firm insistence of the president, combined with the monotonous persistence of the controller.

First, consider the form in which the planning is to be stated. The common denominator, of course, is money. All planning must ultimately be translated into dollar figures, which is the language in which business operates. The ultimate form of the programming therefore is, typically, a planned profit-and-loss statement for a forthcoming period of, say, 12 months, supported in detail by sales budgets or forecasts, expense budgets and so on, and also supplemented with detailed explanations. The assumptions, bases and computations upon which the budget figures are predicated all should be recorded because they will later serve a vital purpose.

These figures are not the plan itself. They are only the external expression of the plan, in a language understandable to all. The statements are a mere vehicle with which to inform, appraise and perchance readjust. The substance of the plan itself is in the minds of its creators.

It would hardly be necessary to emphasize this self-evident truth if it were not ignored so often. It is of no value whatever to budget a given amount for advertising, for instance, without clear advance knowledge on the part of the advertising manager of the media to be used, the markets to be reached, the products to be advertised. In fact, the advertising budget does not qualify as a segment of a true operating plan unless the sales manager also understands the exact degree of support it will afford him in selling his forecast volume.

Let no one be satisfied with a mere estimate, offered without detailed study and based on nothing more than last year's expenditures. Though purporting to be an advertising budget, it is actually only a guess, lacking in supporting reasoning, subject to manipulation and devoid of responsibility.

To be effective, planning cannot be superficial. It depends on a firm statement of principles by the top executive, a clear understanding by each man of the contribution his division or department is expected to make to the enterprise, and a willingness to plan with care and to stand back of the plan. An expense budget, for example, reflecting the planning of an individual unit of the business, must be prepared with utter sincerity, and with a commitment to follow the charted course or stand accountable for any substantial deviation.

What the plan covers

Anyone who has taken part in the preparation of a plan of operations for an industrial company is aware that the undertaking is far more comprehensive than it may first appear. No activity of the company is exempt; every segment must be fitted into a master program.

Consider for a moment the implications of preparing a sales budget, sometimes referred to as a sales forecast, for a period of a year ahead. All products must be budgeted, including those which have not yet been introduced. Due weight must be given the general economic outlook and its bearing on the demand for the company's products. The effect on volume of proposed changes in merchandising methods must be considered. Both volume and selling prices must be planned, and this involves an advance determination of the quantities to be sold in each market or through each sales outlet.

Bear in mind that creative sales budgeting will not tolerate retrospection, astrology nor guesswork. The penalties are too severe. For example, the sales promotion budget will lean heavily on the planned sales volume. What is perhaps even more significant, so will factory production levels, purchase commitments and the ever-critical acquisition and layoff of production workers. Planning is a company-wide process of integration, in which no man can stand alone. All depend upon each other.

When the volume of planned sales has been established, the manufacturing division is in a position to plan production levels and times, as well as inventories. Manufacturing costs must then be fitted into the program, including material purchase prices, wage levels and even manufacturing efficiency. The planning process then fans out to include factory administration costs, research objectives, selling strategy and general administration. The spotlight is turned on the future course of each activity and each is reduced to budgeted figures.

Finally, when all this planning has been done and translated into the language of dollars—after financing decisions have been made and estimates of money costs and income taxes prepared—it is possible to arrive at the planned net profit. It is this figure which determines return on the capital invested in the business and willingness on the part of investors to provide more capital as required by its growth.

It is this figure also which has such a marked effect on the prosperity of the business that it becomes the key point in the planning process. If it is deficient, it must be raised. And it can only be raised, normally, in one of two ways: an increase in planned sales income or a decrease in budgeted outgo. The adjustment at this critical point may involve major revision of important segments of the plan, reaching back once more into the deep recesses of the thinking of all elements of management.

Planning is a man-sized job

We have skimmed lightly over a process which sometimes taxes the capacity and judgment of every executive in the business. It is not an easy task to make major operating decisions for 12 months ahead and place them neatly on a timetable. Yet this is what must be done if the company is to operate under the kind of control that produces satisfactory results.

Suppose, for example, that you are a general sales manager. You are asked by the controller for a budget of sales volume and expense for the coming year—the first three months separately and the remainder of the year by quarters. This is a fairly common way to make a budget. You pinpoint the period immediately ahead but are not asked to be quite so accurate in timing the remainder of the year.

You know from experience that you have to do a good job in preparing this plan—not because you will be fired if you do not meet it, but because the actions of so many other people are geared to your planning. You also know that there are going to be a lot of explanations to make if your actual performance is not according to plan. So you resolve to plan very carefully and insist that your subordinates do likewise with respect to their parts of the process.

But the first thing you stumble on is a new product shortly to be released by the research division. You explain to the controller that the research director does not know exactly when the item will be ready; it may be in six months or it may be in 12, depending upon what priority can be given it in the research division program. So, of course, your first inclination is to feel that you cannot be responsible for a sales forecast under these circumstances.

Furthermore, the ripples from this problem affect the timing of your space advertising insertions. Not until you have definite knowledge on a release date for the product will you be in a position to turn loose a barrage of direct mail promotion. Then you discover that certain traveling and sales training expenses also depend directly on the introduction date of this product. As a result your entire budget is tentative and uncertain.

You explain all this to the controller, but he is not very sympathetic. He simply says that you will be held responsible for your forecast and budget, and if you have no definite information on release dates for new products, it will be necessary to get them. But, he offers to help you to find the answers. This results in a conference with the president and the research director, in which agreement is reached as to completion date for the project; but you then discover that the manufacturing group will require additional time for production of tools and rearrangement of factory layout before the first units can be finished, and that purchasing requires time to obtain material commitments.

Dividends from the difficulties

After a difficult series of conferences, during which all product planning is given a searching review, a conclusion is reached, in which all concur, as to a release date for the new product. You then proceed to complete your budget.

Perhaps this typical incident will afford a hint of the constructive power released by the planning and control mechanism. Nothing short of a conscious policy and formal channels for the process to follow could force the hard thinking which leads to advance decisions on such knotty problems as the one described. To paraphrase a familiar anecdote—"Many decisions which are impossible to make simply take a little longer."

Sometimes these advance determinations are subject to subsequent revision. The planning process should accommodate this need. If decisions must be made subject to probable change, all concerned should understand the assumptions on which they are based and the extent to which the plan may have to be altered. Flexibility, not rigidity, is a characteristic of dynamic planning.

The dividend from this process is proportionate to the magnitude of the hurdles surmounted. First, there is time for deliberation on the problems appearing on the horizon, as contrasted with solving them at the last minute in an atmosphere of crisis. And second, the kind of interchange described in the foregoing illustration yields a mutual understanding of the basics of the business which could not be obtained in any other way. There is no comparable training course for executives.

Capital expenditures planning

Planning of the company's operations cannot be considered complete unless it is integrated with a plan for providing required new buildings, machinery, equipment, tools and so on. The needs of the organization in this area should be assembled as carefully as are the departmental operating budgets.

In this case, however, the term of planning is usually a little longer —say three years, as compared with the customary 12-month projection of sales and expenses. Capital requirements must be prepared on a long-range basis because of the time requirement for construction and procurement and because these items are largely charged against the income of future years.

Furthermore, such expenditures will largely govern the planning for financing. The logical outcome of this thinking is a phase of planning which is far broader than capital expenditures alone, and which might be referred to as a financial program.

In constructing such a program, estimates must be made of required operating cash, accounts receivable and inventories, as well as plant and equipment items for the planned period. In fact, every item on the company's balance sheet receives scrutiny in this process, and the resulting financial program may be expressed in terms of pro forma balance sheets for each of the succeeding three years. Obviously, borrowings, net profits, dividends and enlistments of new equity capital must be planned in order to accomplish this result.

The process of constructing a financial program is perhaps even more difficult than that of creating an operating plan for a one-year period. It requires that proposed major moves be frozen into at least tentative decisions, which can usually be made only by boards of directors.

The benefits of such programming are proportionate to its cost, however, and correspond to those adduced to operating planning. Objectives are defined. Decisions are reached in advance. A course is set. Furthermore, it is a comfortable feeling to know that so long as the company is able to follow the plan, it will not suddenly be faced with a shortage of cash some morning, with little or no warning.

Reporting on performance

It will be recalled that the control formula consists of (1) the adoption of a plan, (2) reporting actual performance as compared with the plan, and (3) making decisions and taking action. The second of these steps merits a brief discussion.

Probably the simplest known form of reporting performance against plan is the typical expense report issued by the accounting department, showing itemized expenses for the month, compared with budget figures. Too often the reporting ends there. It should add two other features: a written explanation of the figures where it would be helpful, and sympathetic consultation with the recipient of the figures. The latter should only be lengthy enough to ascertain that the man responsible really understands the meaning of the figures.

The same principle, of course, applies to profit-and-loss statements and to reporting on the performance of any unit of the business. The reporting cannot be perfunctory. It must be based on an intimate knowledge of the operation and of the plan itself, rather than merely on the figures. For instance, it is far more significant to point out a deviation from a planned expansion of the sales force than to report only that salaries are so many dollars less than the amount budgeted.

In all cases, the controller must get at the essential facts. He must report the same story to all levels of supervision involved. And he must take the responsibility for seeing that the facts are not only reported but understood. The hard core of the reporting is comparison of actual with planned performance, in sufficient detail that every fraction of the operation, and thereby the whole, may be controlled.

Decision and action

The final step in the control formula is decision and action. When the planning has been done properly and adequate reporting has been made on performance against the plan, the ensuing decisions sometimes become surprisingly clear. The action is frequently indicated in the reporting itself.

Assume, for example, a failure of actual manufacturing cost to match the planned cost for a given month. The result, of course, shows up in a deficient net profit. The excess of actual over budgeted or planned cost has been traced to its source. It is relatively easy to do this if the plan has been constructed in adequate detail by the manufacturing organization. Whether the reason be low production volume, high material prices, heavy waste losses, or any of the myriad of other happenings which push costs upward, management is faced at once with a clear-cut decision. Either the condition must be corrected, or, if this is not possible, other changes in the plan must be made to compensate for it. Planned expenses, costs or sales volume must be improved, or planned net profit must be reduced.

The decision should be reached in an atmosphere of participation by everyone concerned. If an adjustment is made in the plan itself, each responsible executive and supervisor accepts the full impact of the change on the performance expected of him.

In practice, an orderly method is required for revision of the operating plan and reflection of the change in the projected operating figures. For example, it may be advisable to give effect to new planning and changes in plan only at three-month intervals, in the course of a complete revision of budgets. Interim deviations, meanwhile, are made conspicuous, in harmony with the best management-by-exception tradition.

By these devices of control, all units of the business are coordinated. The simple triad, planning-reporting-action, becomes the guiding principle of the business. When this state of thinking has permeated the organization—when this modus operandi has become second nature—management potential reaches a new altitude and the business responds with superior performance.

Who is responsible?

It is a long step from the resolution to have better planning and control to its actual realization. As in every other advance in management method, responsibility must be fixed at the outset. In this case, however, the assignment of responsibility is decidedly complex.

Fundamentally, every manager or supervisor in charge of a unit of the business well enough defined to have a budget of its own must be made responsible for the planning and control of that unit. By implication, the responsibility travels up the organization line all the way to the top.

The president, of course, is ultimately charged with the obligation of success in this field, as in all others, and he therefore must undertake to see that the control mechanism is constructed and maintained and that the entire organization is educated in its use.

Because this multiple task is so time-consuming, experience has proven the wisdom of assigning it to a staff executive who may be referred to as the controller. The latter, if he is alert to the immense possibilities of the planning and control concept, and aware that he is the executive in the most advantageous position to carry out the assignment, will need to reorganize his thinking, and perhaps his entire department. He will need to subordinate all accounting, cost and budget activities to the needs of the greater sphere of planning and control.

Essentially the burden of installation, education and follow-up falls on the president and the controller. The respective areas of action of these two executives require a little further comment.

The president's responsibility

It is axiomatic that all policies of management must enjoy the unqualified support of the top man in the business. Planning and control techniques are no exception. The company's president must understand them, use them himself and furnish the required leadership in their application.

This philosophy permeates through the organization only when the president gives it being and vitality. If his allegiance to it is luke warm, his adherence tentative and his concept hazy, he cannot expect his controller to keep it alive and vigorous. It might be possible to operate a passable control system without a controller, if the president were equal to the task. The reverse, however, is not true. No controller can accomplish it without the wholehearted and intelligent collaboration of the chief executive of the business.

It is probably self-evident that the same comments apply, in degree, to executive vice presidents, division and department managers and others. The acceptance and use of the planning and control concept must be commensurate with the authority invested. It is the president's task to create an understanding of these points in his immediate subordinates, who in turn are held accountable for transmitting this understanding and making control effective throughout their respective spheres of activity.

The controller's responsibility

It should be re-emphasized that the control function, within the concept we are discussing is not always assigned to an executive with the title of controller. It is frequently found to reside in a top financial or administrative officer, and sometimes remains in the hands of the chief executive. Perhaps it would be clearer to refer to the duties of controllership, regardless of where they are vested.

Nevertheless, more and more business management is turning to a concept which provides a controller for the business, delegates to him the duties of controllership in the modern sense, and relieves him of operating duties. It does not relieve him of various functions traditionally associated with that office, such as those of chief accounting officer or the responsibility for tax administration, internal auditing and sometimes credit, insurance and office management. Nevertheless, these duties should be subordinate to the compelling task of providing effective controls for the business. Accounting in particular, long considered the major concern of controllers, fits into its proper place as a tool of control.

Definition of controllership

As defined by the Controllers Institute of America, the functions of controllership include establishing, coordinating and maintaining an integrated plan for the control of operations, but it is specified that this must be done through authorized management. Such a plan, it is stated, would provide cost standards, expense budgets, sales forecasts, profit planning and programs for capital investment and financing, together with the necessary procedures to effectuate the plan. The important words in this assignment are "through authorized management" and this little phrase sets the keynote for the controller's peculiar mode of getting things accomplished. He himself should never establish a single standard or budget (except his own), nor a single sales forecast. The plan must be constructed, under his helpful guidance, by the operating executives who will have to accept the responsibility for performance.

The Institute's definition then assigns to the controller the duty of measuring performance against approved operating plans and standards, and of reporting and interpreting the results of operations to all levels of management. It is within this assignment that he finds the need for designing, installing and maintaining accounting and cost systems, and records, determining accounting policy and compiling statistics.

Other parts of the definition equip the controller with power to measure, interpret and report on almost anything—even the validity of the objectives of the business—and to consult with all responsible segments of management on any phase of the operation of the business. He is also charged with the duty of interpreting economic and social influences in their impact on the business. He is free, in fact, to offer his constructive thinking wherever he feels that it will contribute to more effective planning, direction, control.

A discreet controller can exercise this wide latitude without offense to his fellow executives, provided he heeds the ground rules of controllership. These include a fastidious abstention from taking on operating responsibilities or making operating decisions; reporting consistently to all concerned; insisting that the line organization determine their own budgets and standards of performance; and above all, reporting and interpreting without exaggeration, bias or regard for the preconceptions of others.

In particular also, he must not take operating people to task for failure to meet the standards, and he must not be placed in the position of making negative decisions on spending money. It is a familiar myth that these unpleasant attributes are the characteristics of a controller. The penalty for permitting this misconception to be accepted among his associates is the sacrifice of controllership effectiveness.

The particular state of mind that the controller ought to impart to the organization is a sense of balance, stability and direction.

The road ahead

It would be unfortunate to leave the impression that planning and control solve all the problems of running a business. Planning and control simply facilitate the solution of these problems very materially and open up possibilities of achievement which could not be realized otherwise. In a word, it represents thinking forward instead of meeting each daily crisis when it arises. It represents detailed knowledge of where and why we are going astray, as contrasted with a tardy awakening to development which have been buried for too long in the debris of current affairs. Its fruition is a priceless sense of knowing where we are going rather than steering a blind course.

The question may be asked: What do you do when your planning has all been carefully arranged, your control system is working smoothly, and you suddenly encounter some unforeseeable disaster, such as a strike? Plans are completely upset, decisions made hand-to-mouth. The situation is analogous to that of a ship in a storm. You do not dispense with the instruments of navigation. You simply reconcile yourself to the fact that they are momentarily less effective, and re-establish your course as soon as possible. There is nothing about an emergency that lessens the need for planning and control. On the contrary, the effect of the crisis, the means for meeting it and the measures required to repair the damage are all appraised more accurately and quickly in relation to an established plan.

If clear direction is needed to surmount the difficulties of the years to come, then there must be orderly thinking. All units of the business must be brought into harmony. The complex specializations demanded of the various departments must be syncronized so that the whole may move forward together more confidently.

This is a present possibility. We are just beginning to learn the unlimited benefits of wisely conducted planning and of control constructively applied. New and better methods will constantly improve the practice of planning and control, but its unchanging principles, symbolized by the planning-reporting-action formula, are the eternal possession of business management from the time of their discovery.

BIBLIOGRAPHY, CHAPTER X

ANDERSON, RICHARD C. "Organization of the Planning Process," *Advanced Management* (May, 1958), 5-11.

BRIGHT, JAMES R. (Ed.), *Technological Planning on the Corporate Level.* Boston: Harvard University Graduate School of Business Administration, 1962.

Business Forecasting: A Survey of Business Practices and Methods. New York: Controllership Foundation, Inc., 1950.

EWING, DAVID W. "Looking Around: Long-Range Business Planning," *Harvard Business Review*, Vol. 34, No. 4 (1956), 135-146.

GILMORE, FRANK F., and RICHARD G. BRANDENBURG. "Anatomy of Corporate Planning," *Harvard Business Review* (November-December, 1962), 61-69.

HASSLER, RUSSELL H. "Performance Measurement," E. Bursk and D. Fenn, Jr. (Eds.), *Planning the Future Strategy of Your Business.* New York: McGraw-Hill Book Company, Inc., 1956, 119-128.

MOORE, GEOFFREY H. "Analyzing the Economic Cycles," *Dun's Review and Modern Industry* (October, 1953), 64-66, 117-124.

PAYNE, BRUCE. "Steps in Long-Range Planning," *Harvard Business Review* (March-April, 1957), 95-106.

PEIRCE, JAMES L. "Budgets and People: A Positive Approach," *Guides to Modern Financial Planning*, Financial Management Series No. 104. New York: American Management Association, Inc., 1953, 3-12.

PLATT, HENRY M. "Economic Indicators—How to Use Them in Business Forecasting," *Management Review* (April, 1959), 9-13, 67-72.

PLATT, WILLIAM J., and N. R. MAINES. "Pretest Your Long-Range Plans," *Harvard Business Review* (January-February, 1959), 119-136.

Practical Techniques of Forecasting, Planning and Control, Manufacturing Series No. 216. New York: American Management Association, Inc., 1954.

REDFIELD, J. W. "Elements of Forecasting," *Harvard Business Review*, Vol. 29, No. 6 (November, 1951), 81-91.

WRIGHT, WILSON. *Forecasting for Profit.* New York: John Wiley & Sons, Inc., 1947.

SECTION C. DIRECTING

Decisions forming the basis for the direction of subordinates are made to guide activity toward achieving organization and individual goals. In Chapter XI the theoretical foundation underlying individual and group behavior as a basis for better decisions on leadership methods is examined. These leadership methods and their choice are examined in Chapter XII.

Chapter XI
Individual and Group Behavior

As background to the methods and approaches that a manager decides to employ in issuing instructions to subordinates, a knowledge of the motivation bases and the effect of the group upon the individual is important. The purpose of this chapter is to introduce these concepts. Closely related to these ideas are the articles presented in Chapter III.

In Article 37 Charles D. McDermid places economic motivation within the same framework of needs that McGregor utilized in Chapter III. Rensis Likert relates the history of motivation research and describes some of the elements of the superior-subordinate relationship that tend to enhance organization performance in Article 38.

Article 39 reviews the work of Solomon E. Asch. Asch discovered wide variability in individual conformity to group pressure. These results imply that managers should approach each individual working with or for him in different ways if he expects to obtain optimum performance from them.

In the last article Leonard R. Sayles reviews the wide range of research dealing with work groups. Since there remains a degree of uncertainty as to the direction and importance that the several variables in group behavior have upon individual and group performance, the theoretical explanation of organization behavior remains an important area for further research. Similarly, it leaves managers with less than perfect knowledge or understanding of a complex subject.

37. HOW MONEY MOTIVATES MEN [1]

Charles D. McDermid [2]

For many corporations, payroll represents the major cost of doing business. More than 50 per cent of our gross national product is paid each year to employees for their time and effort. And yet the expenditure of this vast sum of money, presumably to motivate men, has been subjected to surprisingly little research, and to even less theoretical discussion. Those studies that have been made of compensation are generally of the survey variety; they emphasize *what* is being done, not *why* it is being done, or what *should* be done. How to get the most out of each payroll dollar is seldom studied.

Modern management is deeply concerned with the motivational impact of financial incentives. It no longer trusts the attitude of the old-line foreman who told me, "But money does work. Just put an extra dollar in that guy's pay check—or take the dollar away—and you'll see what effect it has." In too many companies—companies with high wages, profit sharing, elaborate benefit programs, and incentive systems—money has not worked. Consequently, responsible managers are asking:

1. Is our wage and salary level adequate? And what determines an "adequate" level?
2. How about our sales bonus—what effect does it have?
3. Is our management incentive plan paying off?
4. What is the value of a stock option plan?
5. Will profit sharing work for us?
6. Just how motivational is our benefit program?
7. And how about our entire compensation package? Does it have an optimum balance of base salary, incentive payments, protective provisions, benefit plans, and perquisites?

To tackle questions such as these, one must have a basic understanding of what money means and how it motivates men. With this

[1] From *Business Horizons* (Winter, 1960), pp. 94-100. Reprinted by permission of *Business Horizons*.
[2] Charles D. McDermid, Consulting Psychologist, Humber, Mundie & McClary, Evanston.

understanding, a compensation program can be designed so as to achieve maximum motivation at lowest possible cost—in both human and financial terms. In this way, the needs of employees can best be met and the attainment of corporate objectives best ensured.

HUMAN MOTIVATION

Traditionally, compensation practices have been based on the classic economic theory that man is a rational animal motivated by the desire to maximize his economic gains. This premise has given rise to the belief that employees can automatically be motivated to produce more by the promise of additional money. As a theory, this economic concept of man has often been decried; its limitations have repeatedly been exposed (for example, even under piecework incentive systems output is often restricted); yet it still forms the basis for most of our compensation practices today.

A psychological theory of motivation, first advanced by Maslow,[3] provides better insight into the dynamics underlying human behavior. The essence of this theory is well illustrated in the famous anecdote about Samuel Gompers, for a long time president of the American Federation of Labor. When Gompers was asked, "Just what do the trade-unions want?" he replied, "More!" His answer goes beyond union philosophy; it sums up all human motivation. *Man always wants, and wants more.* As Maslow has phrased it, "Man is a wanting animal."

Two further principles are of basic importance in Maslow's theory. One is that man's wanting depends completely on what he already has. *Satisfied needs do not motivate behavior.* Only needs not yet gratified exert any considerable force in influencing what we do. The other principle is that *needs and wants are arranged in a hierarchy of importance.* As soon as needs on a lower level are fulfilled, those on a higher level emerge and demand satisfaction. When man operates at these higher levels, classic economic theory gives a very incomplete picture of human motivation.

The hierarchy of needs is arranged in a pyramid of five levels, from basic physiological drives at the bottom to the desire for self-realization, the highest expression of the human spirit, at the apex. Graphically, these need levels can be arranged thus:

[3] For a more complete presentation of this theory, together with considerations and qualifications that must be omitted here, see A. H. Maslow, *Motivation and Personality* (New York: Harper & Brothers, 1954), especially pp. 80-106.

To fill out this diagram, a brief description follows for each need level.

Physiological needs

The physiological needs are the needs for oxygen, food, drink, elimination, sexual satisfaction, rest, activity, and temperature regulation; these are the basic drives of human behavior. If a person is really deprived of any of them (with the possible exception of sexual activity), he will bend every effort to satisfy this need. The starved man thinks only of food, wants only food, perhaps hallucinates about food, and so directs all his behavior to obtain food. Similarly, the drowning man wants only to breathe; an overworked executive yearns for sleep; the consuming public buys air-conditioners during a heat wave. Even the sexual needs, which from the standpoint of survival are comparatively mild, can completely dominate the behaving organism.

Once these needs are satisfied, however, they cease to be important motives for behavior. How many people think about their need for air except when they are deprived of it? Food and drink, sleep and activity needs, at least in American civilization, are so readily satisfied that they do not often dominate our goal-seeking. On the other hand, sex receives so much emphasis in our culture because it is the one physiological need not always satisfied. To the extent, then, that basic needs are satisfied, they cease to motivate behavior, and new and higher needs emerge, demanding satisfaction in their turn.

Safety needs

The safety needs are directly above the physiological in this hierarchy. These include the need for protection from physical danger (fire, accidents, criminal assault, and so forth); for economic security (by means, for example, of various social insurances); for the familiar rather than the unfamiliar; and for a religious, philosophic, or scientific ordering of the chaotic into a meaningful whole. R. K. Burns [4] has described these as needs for economic security and emotional surety.

The healthy adult in our society feels at least a minimal satisfaction of his safety needs, and consequently their motivating force is a diminished one. But we have only to turn to the child or the neurotic to see how all-important safety needs can be. A child confronted with a new or strange situation may panic and cling to his mother for security. The neurotic, threatened by anything unexpected or unfamiliar, will go to great lengths to hedge his world in with familiar symbols of safety. And even with healthy adults, to judge by collective bargaining demands, protection against the risks of old age, sickness, and unemployment are important motives for behavior—once a living wage, that is, provision for food and drink and shelter, has been provided.

Social needs

Love, affection, and "togetherness" seem most important to the individual who has satisfied his physiological and safety needs. Now he wants to belong, to find acceptance, to be part of a group. Deprived of family and friends, he will feel the need for them with all the intensity of a hungry man for food.

Unlike physiological and safety needs, social needs are not readily satisfied in our culture. The flight from the family farm and small town community, often to impersonal urban centers, and our traditional taboo on tenderness have helped to prevent fulfillment of these needs. Consequently, social needs have become a dominant motivating force in the United States. Incentive workers who restrict output in accordance with group pressures are motivated by this powerful need to belong. For the same reason, some young people develop a loyalty to their gang that yields to no outside pressure.

These instances are relatively new expressions of ways in which Americans are trying to compensate for the loss of social roots that

[4] Robert K. Burns, "Management and Employee Motivation," *Public Personnel Review*, I (April, 1959), pp. 122-127.

once gave them their sense of belonging. Social needs, comparatively unsatisfied, have become primary motives for much of our behavior.

Esteem needs

Next in the hierarchy of needs are those relating to esteem, both self-esteem and the esteem of others. The need for self-esteem includes the desire for personal worth and dignity, for strength, for competence, achievement, and mastery, for independence and freedom. The need for the esteem of others includes desires for attention and recognition, for status, prestige, and reputation, for importance and power.

These needs are obviously important determinants of behavior. The very real need of "keeping up with the Joneses," of joining the best club, of getting the better office, of driving the right car, or of having a socially acceptable address—all these are manifestations of needing the esteem of others. Self-esteem, too, takes various forms: for example, the need to feel the importance of one's work or to take a stand on some moral issue.

Esteem needs are capable of satisfaction in the American culture, but generally a good deal of effort is required to ensure their gratification. Accordingly, fulfilling the needs for esteem is today an important motivating force in our behavior.

Need for self-realization

Self-realization is the ultimate in the hierarchy of needs. In the language of philosophy, it entails the fulfillment of one's highest potential. It refers to doing or being what one can do or be; it requires making use of all one has, to become everything that one is capable of becoming.

As human potentials vary from individual to individual, so must self-realization. Advancing nuclear theory, writing poetry, playing golf, managing an enterprise, or being an ideal mother can all be expressions of self-realization. The one characteristic underlying all these activities is fulfillment of capacity, whether that capacity is large or small.

Examples of self-realization are rare. We may conclude, I am sure, that no human being has ever fulfilled all his potential. Maslow cites Abraham Lincoln and William James, among others, who have come relatively close to self-realization. As more people have their lower needs more and more satisfied, it can be predicted that a greater number will work towards fulfilling their potential. This, in fact, may be considered the ultimate test of any civilization: To what extent does it give its citizens the opportunity for self-realization?

QUALIFYING FACTORS

Multiple motivation

Activity generally involves several sources of driving power; often many needs interact to bring about a given bit of behavior. An act of love, for example, may be motivated by needs for affection, for dominance, for self-realization, as well as for sexual release. The discussion of a need hierarchy, therefore, should not be taken to imply that a lower need level is the sole motive for all behavior until completely satisfied, at which point the next need emerges and dominates behavior until in turn it is satisfied. Need levels are indications of relative, not absolute, importance. To quote Maslow: ". . . if prepotent need A is satisfied only 10 percent, then need B may not be visible at all. However, as this need A becomes satisfied 25 percent, need B may emerge 5 percent, as need A becomes satisfied 75 percent, need B may emerge 50 percent, and so on." [5] Behavior is effected by multiple and interacting needs, arranged in a rough hierarchy of prepotency.

Frustration

The motivation theory we have described so far is essentially a positive one. We have considered only goal-directed behavior, that is, activity oriented *towards* a goal. Goal-seeking of this simple type calls forth relatively rational and logical behavior to achieve the desired end result.

But it should be noted that seldom is human activity so neatly ordered. Generally, something complicates our goal-seeking. This barrier calls forth two basic types of behavior: ingenious attempts to solve the problem, or frustration. In human affairs, the latter is frequently the case; in fact, most theories of human motivation, including Freud's theory, have dealt largely with frustration-instigated behavior.

[5] *Motivation and Personality*, p. 101.

Frustration evokes the emotional reactions of aggression, regression, fixation, and assorted defense mechanisms. Behavior that was formerly orderly and rational becomes disorganized and emotional; instead of bending his behavior towards a goal, the individual must cope with emotions aroused by fleeing from the barrier. If the attempt to cope with these emotions is radically unsuccessful, neurosis or psychosis may result. Eventually, psychotherapy may be needed to probe beyond the emotional reactions of the individual, reach the original barrier or barriers, help to resolve it or them, and so set the behaving organism on the positive road to goal-seeking once again.

While such extremes as these are not the common experience of industrial organizations, modified forms of frustration-instigated behavior do occur. One form is responsible for a militant union's fighting for more money and bigger benefits when it has already secured the best pay in the area. Frustrated in satisfying higher needs, the men (and their union) have regressed to a previously satisfying form of behavior—that is, the original satisfaction of their physiological and safety needs. As labor history so pointedly illustrates, no additional amount of money will satisfy them now, though they will continue to expend their efforts in this direction. Instead, the frustrating barriers to the satisfaction of social and esteem needs must be removed in order to cancel out these negative expressions of militant unionism.

As Likert's modified theory of management [6] points out, these patterns of negative behavior exist throughout the echelons of management too. Frustrating an executive's need for status by, for example, a reduction in office appointments or window space, can be just as damaging as cutting his pay. He will react negatively and emotionally. But to take a less obvious example, consider the frustration of such a need as pride in the significance of one's job; if this need is not fulfilled, the resulting vague discontent may motivate the executive to seek a higher salary as an indication of his worth, while the true cause of his discontent remains unallayed. Instances of this sort are too numerous to list. But the main point deserves emphasis: Money substitutes in an imperfect way for the satisfaction of certain higher needs. A man who has these needs frustrated cannot be truly satisfied or motivated by a raise in pay since money cannot buy what he wants.

[6] For a popular presentation of this theory, see the interview with Rensis Likert, "How to Raise Productivity 20%," *Nation's Business*, XLVII (August, 1959), pp. 30-32, 40, 42-44.

Functional autonomy

Another aspect of human motivation that has special relevance to money is the curious phenomenon known as functional autonomy. Briefly stated, this is the idea that goals once desired as means to an end can become goals desired for their own sake. A miser, for example, may once have valued money for the physiological and safety needs it satisfied, but eventually he came to regard money as valuable in its own right.

This concept helps explain why a Rockefeller, a Carnegie, or a Getty may work to his death accumulating wealth that he can never spend. Money no longer serves as an exchange symbol for such men; it has become functionally autonomous, divorced from the original reason for its value.

In most organizations there are employees, especially in the upper echelons, for whom money and money-making have become functionally autonomous. For such individuals, money has a direct significance not dependent upon its purchasing power. It is in itself the most powerful incentive, for it directly satisfies their dominant needs.

Employee surveys

Psychologists in industry have conducted many studies asking workers what they want from their jobs.[7] Such surveys typically produce the following results: In order of importance the items most wanted are steady work; opportunity for advancement; good supervision; desirable work group or companions; good pay; and desirable type of work, working conditions, hours, and benefits.

According to the theory proposed in this paper, those needs at the bottom of the ranking, hours and benefits, are relatively well satisfied, whereas those at the top of the list, such as steady work, are not. Such surveys, in other words, indicate those needs that are dominant because they are not fulfilled.

Obviously, certain factors will affect these surveys. Results will vary from organization to organization, from echelon to echelon; age and sex may influence them. The manager interested in meeting the needs of his workers will take an individual reading on the

---

[7] See, for example, C. E. Jurgensen, "What Job Applicants Look for in a Company," *Personnel Psychology*, I (Winter, 1948), pp. 433-435.

deprivations that his work force feels and adjust his employee relations program accordingly.

Wage and salary administrators, too, need to be aware of these factors. As Meiklejohn has pointed out,[8] different financial needs are characteristic of different employee levels in an organization. Attempting to meet these needs with uniform compensation practices makes inefficient use of money-motivation. Ideally, needs should be identified for each group through such a technique as a depth survey; then the compensation package should be adjusted to meet these needs. The results may range from supplemental unemployment benefits for the rank and file to stock options for top management. Maximum motivation at lowest cost is the desired end result.

The Meaning of Money

How does all this theory relate to the role of money in motivating behavior? What does compensation represent to its recipients? What needs does it fulfill?

Obviously, the first meaning of money lies in its power to buy satisfaction of the basic physiological needs—food, clothing, and shelter. Closely allied to these basic needs are certain acquired needs with a physiological basis, such as the need for tobacco. It is only after these fundamental drives have been relatively well satisfied that any major amount of money will be diverted towards other goods.

Next in the hierarchy of needs is the category termed safety, a major expression of which, in today's culture, is the need for financial security. Here money represents insurance against physiological deprivation and against the financial hazards of poor health, old age, and unemployment. Collective bargaining demands for security, as well as such common phenomena as buying life insurance and "putting away for a rainy day," are obvious examples of using money to satisfy safety needs.

Money can also facilitate satisfaction of the social needs, the third level in the hierarchy, but only indirectly. Thus one can purchase membership in a country club, but the actual exchange of friendship and love does not necessarily result. The biggest benefit of money at this level lies in freeing the individual from the insistent clamor

[8] Robert P. Meiklejohn, "Financial Incentives Beyond Base Pay," *Management Record* (May, 1958), pp. 165-170.

of his physiological and safety needs so that he can attend to his social wants.

The situation is different in the case of the esteem needs. The American way of life has stressed money as the measure of status and achievement. Hence it has become most important to the satisfaction of esteem needs. The extent to which this is ingrained in our sense of values can be seen not only in one man's evaluation of another on the basis of his financial show, but even in the dependence of his concept of himself on the amount of money he makes. Many men, in other words, are willing to accept their salary as the indication of their worth. Compensation has become important on this level not only for what it buys, but also for what it means, both in judging one's self and one's neighbor.

What about self-realization at the peak on the need pyramid? Money is of little importance in gaining fulfillment at this level; it can do no more than remove obstacles to self-realization. Here the role of money is to satisfy the physiological and other needs so that the individual is free to devote his efforts to fulfilling his potential.

From the preceding paragraphs it can be seen that money is efficient in satisfying needs at the lower levels since it can be quickly and directly converted into ways and means of satisfying individual wants. A great variety of foods, clothes, and shelter arrangements can be bought. But at higher levels in the hierarchy, the situation is more complicated. Man's striving for money, once his basic needs are satisfied, often becomes a substitute for the true satisfaction of his higher needs. It might be instructive at this point to examine how this happens, and what can be done about it.

Offering a money wage to an employee is based on much the same principle as dangling a carrot in front of a donkey. High wages are a reward for productive work. Conversely, withholding money by demoting or firing the employee is a form of punishment for poor work, much like the cancellation of a child's treat. This system of rewards and punishment is effective at lower need levels since the gratification of physiological and safety needs is largely dependent on buying outside sources of satisfaction. When a man is motivated by these needs, he can be controlled by the granting or withholding of money. But the source of satisfaction for higher needs lies within each individual. The man motivated by social or esteem or self-realization needs is not easily controlled by external rewards and punishments; consequently, money per se is a relatively weak motivating force. As D. M. McGregor puts it: ". . . direction and control are useless methods of motivating people whose physiological and safety needs are reasonably satisfied and whose social, egoistic, and self-fulfillment needs are predominant.[9]

People in many walks of life are motivated to work by incentives other than money. The dollar-a-year men in Washington, religious leaders, scientists and academicians, dedicated trade-unionists, and creative artists take pride in the significance of their work; they attach personal and social values to it. Within the large corporation, too, there are many who will respond as readily to work of intrinsic interest and value as to financial rewards, which are always extrinsic to any job.

This means two things to management:

1. Do *not* rely exclusively on further increases in wages and security benefits to motivate employees, once adequate wages and benefits have been established.
2. *Do* create conditions conducive to a man's satisfying his social and esteem and self-realization needs on the job.

For management the important conclusion to be drawn from the whole theory is that no one incentive is the only answer to motivating men on the job. Money is powerful, but its power is limited. Aiding group activities, creating opportunities, recognizing worth, encouraging growth, and fostering individual expression can also promote employee effort, in some cases more effectively than money. It is the responsibility of management to understand those factors that motivate their men, and to arrange conditions and methods of work so that employees can best achieve their own goals by directing their efforts toward organizational objectives.

PRACTICAL APPLICATION

This money-motivation theory can be used to evaluate any compensation device and to help determine how to maximize its motivational impact. Let us take, as an example, a management incentive plan. The questions basic to our study are:

1. How well is this management incentive plan attracting, retaining, and motivating superior men?
2. Is it successful? Are its returns greater than its costs to the corporation?

[9] D. M. McGregor, "The Human Side of Enterprise," in *Adventure in Thought and Action* (Cambridge: Massachusetts Institute of Technology, 1957), p. 28.

3. How can this management incentive plan be improved?

Specific hypotheses may be formulated from the money-motivation theory set out in the preceding paragraphs. It is obvious from the following list that all these hypotheses cannot be true at one and the same time. The aim here is to cover every possibility.

1. Positive motivation.
   a. Incentive awards primarily represent purchasing power to recipients (physiological need level).
   b. Incentive awards primarily represent financial security to their recipients (safety need level).
   c. Incentive awards primarily indicate the participants' belonging or participating or contributing to the corporate welfare (social need level).
   d. Incentive awards primarily confirm one's own sense of achievement for a job well done (self-esteem need level).
   e. Incentive awards primarily indicate recognition of one's contribution to the corporation (other-esteem need level).
   f. Incentive awards primarily encourage the recipient to fulfill his potential (self-realization need level).
2. Negative motivation.
   a. Reducing or withholding incentive awards (for mediocre performance) increases the intensity of positive need gratification.
   b. Reducing or withholding incentive awards (for mediocre performance) produces frustration effects inimical to the accomplishment of the plan's objectives.

It should be clear from the first part of the article that a given hypothesis might be true for one group—stratified according to executive level, job function, salary, and so on—and not for another. Accordingly, data to test the truth or falsehood of the hypotheses must be collected in sufficient depth and breadth to permit detailed analysis in every dimension.

Three stratified random samples of management personnel, distinct but comparable, should be selected for depth interviews, survey questionnaires, and projective sentence-completion forms, respectively. These techniques should be designed so that they indicate how participants feel about their management incentive plan, how they think it affects their behavior and the behavior of their superiors, peers, and subordinates, and what they suggest to improve it.

All three investigatory techniques should be so ordered as to yield information pertinent to the hypotheses listed above. In this way each hypothesis could be supported or denied by the data, and the degree of support or denial indicated. In addition, the validity of each hypothesis could be determined for specific groups of participants stratified according to such dimensions as age, income, echelon, and function within the corporation.

As a result of all this information, the management incentive plan could be tailored to the express needs of management personnel—and of the corporation. In this way, both personal and corporate objectives could be more perfectly realized, with profit for both parties.

Results from the research outlined above could help shed light on one of the questions raised in the introduction to this article: "Is a given management incentive plan paying off?" Similarly, this approach could be used to structure research on other questions related to money and motivation; the efficiency of any compensation device could be studied in this way.

The prototype described in the previous section could, moreover, serve as a model in the study of an entire compensation program. All elements in the package—base pay, incentive plans, protective provisions, benefit programs, and perquisites—could be evaluated in their relationship one to another. Then if it were found that a given level of employees was primarily motivated by physiological needs, great emphasis could be placed on base pay; by safety needs, on protective provisions; by esteem needs, on perquisites.

Thus, through an understanding of what needs were motivating men and how money could be used to satisfy them, the compensation program could be so ordered as to achieve maximum motivation at lowest possible cost; the needs of each individual would best be met, and the attainment of corporate objectives best ensured.

38. MOTIVATION AND INCREASED PRODUCTIVITY [1]

Rensis Likert [2]

Human relations research has great potential value for modern management. Many of its findings can serve as the basis for sound principles of management and good leadership. It is my purpose at this time to talk to you about some of the major conclusions that are emerging from this research.

As a background for stating these conclusions, it will be useful to consider the problem historically by examining two important trends.

The first of these two trends began almost a century ago, and has had by far the greater influence upon both management practices and industrial productivity. I refer to the whole movement in which Frederick W. Taylor and his colleagues provided pioneering leadership. For purposes of brevity, I shall use the term "scientific management" to refer to this whole movement.

Generally speaking, scientific management has brought about a very great improvement in productivity. But associated with these gains have been some serious problems and adverse effects.

Setting production goals through the use of time standards has often been accompanied by an expectation of higher levels of productivity. And, therefore, there has been increased pressure on the workers to produce more. Workers resented and resisted this; and the "speed-up" was and still is a major source of conflict and bitterness. Another aspect of this method of managing which caused resentment was the attitude that workers could contribute nothing of value to the organization of their jobs and to the methods of work to be used. As Henry Ford expressed it, "all that we ask of the men is that they do the work which is set before them."

These and similar adverse effects of scientific management were recognized more and more clearly during the second, third, and fourth decades of this century. The speed-up and "efficiency engineering" were sources of much hostility between workers and their supervisors.

[1] From *Management Record*, Vol. XVIII, No. 4 (April, 1956), pp. 128-131. Reprinted by permission of the National Industrial Conference Board.
[2] Rensis Likert, Director, Survey Research Center, University of Michigan.

And these hostilities manifested themselves in a variety of ways, such as widespread restriction of output (even under incentive pay) and a demand for protection through unions, which eventually led to the Wagner Act.

The second trend which I wish to examine started at the end of the First World War when a few business leaders and social scientists began to appreciate some of the problems that were the consequence of scientific management. More general recognition of these problems, however, was brought about dramatically by the famous Western Electric studies. These studies showed conclusively and quantitatively that workers were responding to the methods of scientific management by restricting their production to levels which they felt were appropriate. Moreover, neither group nor individual incentive methods of payment prevented this restriction.

These studies also revealed that the workers had developed an "informal organization" which differed from the "formal." And it was found that this informal organization exercised an important influence on the behavior of the workers, often effectively countermanding the official orders of the formal organization. The Western Electric studies also showed that when the hostilities, resentments, suspicions and fears of the workers were replaced by favorable attitudes, a substantial increase in production occurred, just as it was clear that unfavorable attitudes exerted an appreciable restraining influence upon productivity.

Mathewson, Houser, and others, in a modest number of studies during the Thirties, showed that conditions existing in the Western Electric Company were relatively widespread in American industry. Morale and motivational factors were generally found to influence production. Restriction of output was common, and "informal organizations" were found to exist in most of the companies studied.

During the past decade this second trend, which might be called the human relations trend, has gained greater impetus. The volume of research is still small but it is growing. The findings are consistent with the earlier studies and have important implications for the future trend of management theories and practices.

Some of the results of this more recent research can be shown by briefly presenting a few findings from studies conducted by the Institute for Social Research.

Orientation of Supervision. When foremen are asked what they have found to be the best pattern of supervision to get results, a substantial proportion—usually a majority—will place primary emphasis on getting out production. By this, they mean placing primary emphasis on seeing that workers are using the proper methods, are sticking to their work, and are getting a satisfactory volume of work done.

But other supervisors, who we have called employee-centered, report that they get the best results when they place primary emphasis on the human problems of their workers. The employee-centered supervisor endeavors to build a team, whose members cooperate and work well together. He tries to have people work together who are congenial. And he not only trains people to do their present jobs well, but tends to train them for the next higher jobs. In other words, he is interested in helping them with their problems, both on and off the job. He is friendly and supportive, rather than punitive and threatening.

Higher levels of management, however, tend to place greater emphasis than do foremen on the production-centered approach as the best way to get results.

But which orientation actually yields the best results? A variety of studies in widely different industries show that supervisors who are getting the best production, the best motivation, and the highest level of worker satisfaction are employee-centered rather than production-centered.

However, there is an important point to be added to this finding. Those employee-centered supervisors who get the best results tend to recognize that high production is also one of their major responsibilities.

Closeness of Supervision. Related to orientation of supervision is closeness of supervision. Close supervision tends to be associated with lower productivity, while more general supervision seems to be related to higher productivity.

Low productivity, no doubt, at times leads to closer supervision, but it is also clear that close supervision causes low productivity. In one of the companies involved in this research program it has been found that when managers of high- and low-production divisions are switched, the high-production manager raises the productivity of the low-production division faster than the former high-production division slips under the low-production manager. Supervisors, as they are shifted from job to job, tend to maintain their habitual attitudes toward the supervisory process and their subordinates.

Both general supervision and close supervision are also related to how workers feel about their supervisors. Workers under foremen who supervise closely, or are production-centered, have a less favorable attitude toward the boss than do workers who are under foremen who supervise more generally or are employee-centered.

As we have seen, the research findings indicate that close supervision results in lower productivity, less favorable attitudes, and less satisfaction on the part of the workers, while more general supervision achieves higher productivity, more favorable attitudes, and greater employee satisfaction. These results suggest that it should be possible to increase productivity in a particular situation by shifting the pattern of supervision so as to make it more general. To test this, we conducted an experiment involving 500 clerical employees in a large company. The work these employees did was something like a billing operation; there was just so much of it, but it had to be processed as it came along.

Briefly, the experimental procedure was as follows. Four parallel divisions were used, each of which was organized in the same way, used the same technology and did exactly the same kind of work, with employees of comparable aptitude. For the purpose of our experiment, certain changes were initiated. In two of the divisions, decision-making was introduced at lower levels; general supervision of the clerks and their supervisors replaced close supervision; workers were given more information about matters that affected them; and their ideas and suggestions were sought before decisions were made. In addition, the managers, assistant managers, supervisors, and assistant supervisors of these two divisions were trained in group methods of leadership. The experimental changes in these two divisions will be called Program I.

We faced many problems in attaining the desired changes. Pushing downward the level at which decisions were made proved difficult. Managers and supervisors seemed to feel that such action was an admission that they were not essential. Therefore, they made virtually no changes. However, when the general manager asked the managers under him if they would help him with some of his work, they responded favorably. He then asked them if there was work that they could turn over to their subordinates in order to free them to assist in his work. The managers then readily found work which their subordinates could handle. A similar process was used all down the line to get supervisors to turn over work to subordinates, and thereby push decision levels down.

In order to provide an effective experimental control for Program I, in the other two divisions the closeness of supervision was increased and decision-making was pushed upward. This will be called Program II. These changes were accomplished by a further extension of scientific management. One of the first steps was to have the jobs timed by the methods department, and standard times computed. This showed that these divisions were overstaffed by about 30%. The general manager then ordered the managers of these two divisions to cut staff by 25%. This was to be done by transfers and not by replacing persons who left. No one was to be dismissed.

The four divisions participating in the experiment were assigned on the basis of one high- and one low-productivity division to Program I, and one high and one low to Program II.

The experiment at the clerical level lasted for one year. Several months were devoted to planning before the experimental year, and there was also a training period of approximately six months just before the experiment began. Throughout the period of the experiment, productivity was measured continuously and computed weekly. Employee and supervisory attitudes and related variables were measured just before and after the experimental year.

Productivity Reflected in Salary Costs. In Program II, where there was an increase in the closeness of supervision, productivity increased by about 25%. In this group, it will be recalled, the general manager had ordered a 25% cut in staff.

But a significant increase in productivity was also achieved in Program I, where supervision was modified so as to be less close and no reduction in work force was ordered. Although the increase in productivity in Program I was not so great as in Program II, it was nevertheless a little more than 20%. And one of the divisions in Program I increased its productivity by about the same amount as each of the two divisions in Program II. The other division in Program I, which historically had been the poorest of all the divisions, did not do so well.

Productivity and Workers' Responsibility. Although both programs were alike in increasing productivity, they were significantly different in the other changes which occurred. The productivity increases in Program II, where decision levels were moved up, were accompanied by adverse shifts in attitudes, interest, involvement in the work, turnover, and related matters. The opposite was true in Program I. Here it was found that when more general supervision was provided, the employees' feeling of responsibility to see that the work got done increased. In Program II, however, this work responsibility decreased. In Program I, when the supervisor was away, the employees kept on working. When the supervisor was absent in Program II, the work tended to stop.

Effect of Employee Attitudes. The experiment changed the workers' attitudes toward their supervisors. In Program I all the shifts were favorable; in Program II all the shifts were unfavorable.

This very brief description of the experiment, I hope, has made clear the pattern of results. Both experimental changes increased productivity substantially. In Program I this increase in productivity was accompanied by favorable shifts in attitudes, interests, and perceptions. The girls became more interested and involved in their work. They accepted more responsibility for getting the work done. Their attitudes toward the company and their superiors became more favorable. And they accepted direction more willingly. In Program II, however, all these attitudes and related variables shifted in an unfavorable direction. All the hostilities, resentments, and unfavorable reactions which have been observed again and again to accompany extensive use of scientific management manifested themselves.

This experiment with clerical workers is important because it shows that increases in productivity can be obtained with either favorable or unfavorable shifts in attitudes, perceptions, and similar variables. Further application of classical methods of scientific management did substantially increase productivity, but it was accompanied by adverse reactions upon the part of the workers involved. With the other approach used in the experiment, a substantial increase in productivity was also obtained, but here it was accompanied by favorable shifts in attitudes and similar variables. A fundamental conclusion from this experiment and other similar research is that direct pressure from one's superior for greater production tends to be resented, while group pressure from one's colleagues is not.

Thus, though scientific management has clearly demonstrated its capacity to get high production, this productivity is obtained at a cost which tends to have serious consequences in the long run.

People will produce at relatively high levels when the techniques of production are efficient, the pressure for production is great, the controls and inspections are relatively tight, and the economic rewards and penalties are sufficiently large. But such production is accompanied by attitudes which tend to result in high scrap loss, lowered safety, higher absences and turnover, increased grievances and work stoppages, and the like. It also is accompanied by communication blocks and restrictions. All these developments tend to adversely affect the operation of any organization.

The critical weaknesses in the scientific management approach, of course, are the resentments, hostilities, and adverse motivational and attitudinal reactions which it tends to evoke. In my judgment, these hostilities and unfavorable attitudes stem from powerful motives which scientific management has ignored in its theoretical basis as well as in the day-to-day operating procedures it has developed. But although scientific management has ignored these powerful motives, it has not been able to avoid the substantial impact of their influence in daily operations.

The fundamental cause, therefore, of the adverse reactions produced by scientific management is the assumption that all persons are simple economic men; that it is only necessary to buy a man's time and he will then willingly and effectively do everthing which he is ordered to do. Management textbooks emphasize authority and control as the foundation of administration. They either take for granted the power to control or they hold that the relationship of employer and employee in an enterprise is a contractual obligation entailing the right to command and the duty to obey. The critical weakness of scientific management occurs at precisely the point where the human relations research approach has its greatest strength: motivation.

The power of human relations research findings lies in the understanding and insight which they provide into:

1. The character and magnitude of the powerful forces which control human behavior in working situations;
2. And the manner in which these forces can be used so that they reinforce rather than conflict with one another.

The fundamental problem, therefore, is to develop a management theory, as well as the supervisory and managerial practices needed for operating under this theory, which will make use of the concepts of scientific management while fully utilizing in a positive manner the major forces which influence human behavior in work situations. And, I believe, we are developing just such a theory which effectively combines the resources of scientific management and the findings of human relations research. There is not time here to examine it fully, but one or two aspects can be considered.

A basic condition of the theory is that all attempts to influence the behavior of subordinates in an organization should be of such a nature that there is a maximum probability that the subordinates will react favorably. When all of the influence attempts are reacted to favorably by a subordinate, the motivational forces acting upon him will be reinforcing, cumulative and maximized, rather than being minimized by being in conflict.

Two conditions appear to be necessary for a subordinate to react favorably to his superior's attempts to influence his behavior. First the influence attempts should be ones which he has reacted favorably to in the past—that is, they need to be familiar. Second, the influence attempts, as seen by the subordinate, should be supportive rather than threatening. And he will see them this way when they contribute to his sense of importance and personal worth; he will see them as threatening when they decrease his sense of personal worth.

From these conditions it is possible to derive a modified theory of management and the day-to-day operating procedures required to implement it.

Thus, for example, it is possible to state the following principle based on this theory: Any attempt to produce a change in an organization will work best when the people whose behavior needs changing want themselves to change. An attempted change, therefore, will work better when management creates a situation in which people can see the possibility and desirability of change and even initiate the change, rather than merely being ordered to change.

Research findings show that supervisors improve in their handling of human relations much more when provided with objective measurements about their operation and then stimulated to discuss these measurements with their subordinates as a group, than when they are merely given a supervisory training program. A supervisory training program is, after all, just another way of ordering a foreman to change his behavior.

Another operating principle based on this modified theory is also related to the best way to bring about changes and improvements. This principle indicates that an organization will perform more effectively when it functions as a network of integrated and coordinated teams, each of which has a high team spirit, high performance goals related to its part of the total job, favorable attitudes toward its supervision and management, and confidence and trust in them. These teams are knit into an integrated and coordinated organization by supervisors, managers and staff, who hold overlapping memberships in two or more teams or groups. . . .

39. UNDER PRESSURE [1]

Social pressure often breeds conformity; the individual's decisions are influenced by what has been called, at different times and by different people, environment, group pressure, or propaganda. In a recent issue of *Scientific American*, Dr. Solomon E. Asch describes a series of experiments conducted at a number of universities to measure the degree to which contrary group opinion can cause an individual to amend his personal judgment. Put more succinctly, the experiments studied the "engineering of consent."

In the current experiments, seven to nine young men compared, by eye, the lengths of vertical black lines drawn on two large white cards—one bearing a standard line, and the other bearing three lines, one of which was identical to the standard. Each subject was asked to report which line on each of several test cards matched the standard. At first, all went well; in the first two comparisons the subjects all agreed. But then, one man (the real subject of the experiment) found himself disagreeing with his colleagues, who by prearrangement had been instructed to give wrong answers. The built-in schism continued; further line-matching measured the subject's ability to resist the pressure of the contrary opinion of the group.

The experiments were so conducted as to keep the subject from suspecting his position. Sometimes the majority would agree with him, according to plan. Sometimes the disagreement was slight; here the subject had to weigh the evidence of his senses very carefully against the opinion of his group. But in any event, the subject had to state his opinion in public, in the face of majority and equally public opinion to the contrary. The position of the majority was frequently the wrong one; out of 18 trials in each series of experiments, the majority gave 12 wrong answers.

Under these circumstances, the average individual tested lost his self-confidence. Whereas he would normally err less than one per cent of the time in matching the lines, he swung to the position of the

[1] From the *Industrial Bulletin* of the Arthur D. Little, Inc. (February, 1956). Reprinted by permission of the *Industrial Bulletin*.

majority, and voted wrong 36.8 per cent of the time under group pressure. There was considerable spread, however; about one-quarter of the subjects tested never lost their independence of judgment, while conversely, some were never able to break free from the herd.

To test the effect of the size of the majority, the "opposition" was varied from one to fifteen persons. With only one contradiction to face, subjects almost always answered correctly, but when the opposition increased to two persons, the "margin of error" jumped to 13.6 per cent, and to 31.8 per cent for three persons. Beyond three persons, there was little additional effect.

Whenever the subject was provided with a supporting partner, his tendency to err decreased to one-fourth its previous level. But it appeared that if the partner was a "moderate" dissenter—choosing a line only slightly different from the standard—the subject followed his colleague's opinion; if the partner was an "extremist"—making grossly erroneous choices—the subject expressed even more freedom in his opinion.

Dr. Asch's conclusions

Dr. Asch concludes his article with some remarks that deserve quotation: "Life in society requires consensus as an indispensable condition. But consensus, to be productive, requires that each individual contribute independently. . . . That we have found the tendency to conformity in our society so strong that reasonably intelligent and well-meaning young people are willing to call white black is a matter of concern. . . ." That is an understatement justified only by the limited scope of the experiments.

As consolation, Dr. Asch observes: ". . . those who participated in this challenging experiment agreed nearly without exception that independence was preferable to conformity." The most important result of these tests may be the discovery that 25 per cent of the subjects did in fact refuse to knuckle under.

40. WORK GROUP BEHAVIOR AND THE LARGER ORGANIZATION [1]

Leonard R. Sayles [2]

The individual's most immediate and meaningful experiences of work are obtained in the context of the work group and his work associates. The larger organization is experienced by indirection, but membership in the small group contributes directly to the shaping of attitudes and behavior toward the entire world of work. For this reason of potency, therefore, the contribution of the small group to the total organization has been a subject of substantial research by those interested in human relations in industry.

CONCEPTIONS OF THE WORK GROUP

As Whyte observes, the individual is *not* a member of a single group within a larger structure.[3] Rather, he typically interacts in a variety of settings within the organization. It is the task of the researcher to identify those interaction patterns which are focused and concentrated so that it is reasonable to speak of a "group."

If we follow all the members of the organization through their hours on the job, or find some "high" vantage point and observe the total of all interactions, we are likely to be impressed with this proliferation of memberships. Most apparent is membership, except for that unique individual, the president, in some *command group;* that is, the employee shares a common supervisor with a number of colleagues. Distinguishable from this group, but closely related, is a *functional* or *task group*—those employees who must collaborate in some fashion if the work task defined by the organization is to be accomplished. In fact, both of these groups are rather well defined

[1] "Work Group Behavior and the Larger Organization" by Leonard R. Sayles in *Research in Industrial Human Relations* by Conrad M. Arensberg, *et al.* Copyright © 1957 by Harper & Row, Publishers, Incorporated. Reprinted by permission of the publishers.

[2] Leonard R. Sayles, Professor of Management, Graduate School of Business, Columbia University.

[3] William F. Whyte, "Small Groups in Large Organizations," in *Social Psychology at the Crossroads*, John Rohrer and Muzafer Sherif, Eds. (New York: Harper, 1951), pp. 303-304.

by the larger organization, and the group typically retains those boundaries.

However, there are two other kinds of clusterings that tend to overlap and penetrate the organization in unexpected ways. They are not defined by the formal organization and are often included under the general term, informal organization. One has received much attention from researchers: the *friendship clique*. The other is less well studied, but equally important. That is the *interest group*. This is comprised of employees who share a common economic interest and seek to gain some objective relating to the larger organization.

Memberships in these groups are not exclusive; often they will overlap considerably. However, the motivations of the members, and, more important, their behavior, are distinctive; and we have no reason to believe that the boundaries will be perfectly coincident.

The command group

Perhaps the most obvious kind of small group in the large organization is composed of the supervisor and his immediate subordinates. As Jacques observes, the entire organization is composed of interconnected *command groups*, the subordinates in one group being the superiors in their own command group, with the exception of the first level.[4] While we might expect that research would have emphasized this unit of the organization, if we exclude the manifold studies of leadership styles dealt with elsewhere in this volume, there are relatively few systematic explorations of the relationship between the leader and his subordinates as a group, as individuals, and among the subordinates themselves. Jacques' volume is a notable exception.[5] His examination of the command group has a strong psychiatric flavor. He stresses the leader's ambivalence: his *authority* over his subordinates and *dependence* upon them, his sense of isolation, the problem of integrating pair relationships (leader and individual subordinates) with cohesiveness among subordinates, and the

---

[4] Elliot Jacques, *The Changing Culture of a Factory* (New York: Dryden Press, 1952), pp. 273-297.

[5] There are two other noteworthy recent exceptions. Argyris devotes a small volume to the relationship between a plant manager in a medium-sized factory and his immediate subordinates. (Chris Argyris, *Executive Leadership* [New York: Harper, 1954]). Two researchers at the Harvard Business School provide us with a very revealing study of the day-to-day changes in the relationship between a first-line supervisor and assembly-line girls during a period of technological changes—Harriet Ronken and Paul Lawrence, *Administering Changes* (Boston: Graduate School of Business Administration, Harvard University, 1952).

mixed feelings of the subordinates as a group who find the leader both expendable and indispensable (one to be protected or exposed?).

The friendship clique

This has been conceived as the elementary building block of human organization. As Mayo writes, "Man's desire to be continuously associated with his fellows is a strong, if not the strongest human characteristic." [6]

At the workplace we find a multitude of friendship groups representing the diverse interests of the workers placed there by the organization. The boundaries of these clusterings appear to reflect the employees' off-the-job interests and associations or previous work experience. Age, ethnic background, outside activities, sex, marital status, and so on, comprise the mortar that binds the clique together.

The friendship group has emerged as the agency which welds the individual to the organization. Loyalty, even attachment, to the total organization with its impersonality, extended hierarchy, and social distance becomes ambiguous. However, attachment to the immediate and easily perceived face-to-face group is the predominant reality of organization experience. For the individual it provides a source of personal security in an impersonal environment.

Where cliques are largely nonexistent, as in the rapidly expanding aircraft plants of California, turnover can be enormous. The presumption is that stable social groups take time to crystallize; during the period of formation many potential members will leave voluntarily because they do not find an established unit with which they can affiliate. This in turn inhibits the formation of permanent groups; the process is self-defeating.

Thus Lombard and Mayo conclude that the naive administrator who seeks to break up these cliques because of the inefficiency and wasted motion of the purely social activities involved is actually doing a disservice to the organization. [7] In fact, they find that it takes skillful leadership to encourage their formation, at least in organizations undergoing rapid expansion. A recent well-received

[6] Elton Mayo, *Social Problems of an Industrial Civilization* (Boston: Graduate School of Business Administration, Harvard University, 1945), p. 111.
[7] Elton Mayo and George F. Lombard, *Teamwork and Labor Turnover in the Aircraft Industry of Southern California* (Boston: Graduate School of Business Administration, Harvard University, 1940).

text [8] in the field of public administration comes out strongly on the side of encouraging on-the-job social life, concluding that production increased when social conversation was allowed. However, a study employing methods of precise interaction observation is unique in casting some doubts as to the positive correlation between social interaction and productivity.[9]

More serious criticism of the universal efficacy of friendship cliques, however, involves considerations of personality and work structure differences. A study of "rate busters" disclosed a significant majority who were indifferent to, if not hostile to, the social groupings they found on the job.[10]

A recent examination of British longshoremen finds that approximately half of the longshoremen on the docks studied have consciously avoided social entanglements of work group membership. Given an opportunity to join semipermanent gangs, they prefer random work assignments that leave them free to come and go at will, with no group responsibility.[11]

Formation of social groups also appears to be a function of the structure of the work situation itself. Argyris, in his Bank study, finds that incidence of informal social groupings among tellers is less than for bank employees who have less interaction with customers.[12] This conclusion would confirm a basic hypothesis of Chapple, that individuals seek some equilibrium in their rate and range of interaction.[13]

From this theoretical approach, we would expect that the whole range of group activities, not just social life, would be influenced by the interaction pattern fostered by the job. The previously cited study by the University of Liverpool researchers, for example, notes that dockworkers who were members of semipermanent crews were rarely found among the informal leaders of the longshoremen or

---

[8] Herbert Simon, Donald Smithburg, and Victor Thompson, *Public Administration* (New York: Knopf, 1950), pp. 113-114.

[9] A. B. Horsfall and Conrad Arensberg, "Teamwork and Productivity in a Shoe Factory," *Human Organization*, VIII (Winter, 1949), pp. 21 ff.

[10] These men tended to have a rural background emphasizing individualism. Orvis Collins and Donald Roy, "Restriction of Output and Social Cleavage in Industry," *Applied Anthropology*, V (Summer, 1946), pp. 1-14.

[11] University of Liverpool, *The Dock Worker* (Liverpool: University Press of Liverpool, 1954), pp. 61 ff.

[12] Chris Argyris, *Organization of a Bank* (New Haven: Labor and Management Center, Yale University, 1954), p. 129.

[13] Eliot D. Chapple, "Applied Anthropology in Industry," in *Anthropology Today*, A. L. Kroeber, Ed. (Chicago: University of Chicago Press, 1953), pp. 819-831. Many of the observations in this section are based on the theoretical work of Chapple.

among the active participants in the union.[14] Moving in the other direction, Lipset concludes that because some jobs handicap workers in maintaining adequate off-the-job relations with other friends (e.g., unusual working hours as among printers, actors, and policemen), they tend to form more closely knit "fellow worker" groups, as evidenced by their record of high participation in local union activities.[15]

Similarly, George Strauss has observed an unusually high degree of membership participation in certain occupational groups involving relative isolation from fellow workers, like insurance salesmen, utility meter readers and substation operators.[16]

Such studies add to the trend toward considering the *need for social relations* as a variable worth studying in itself. It would be interesting to know, for example, whether industrial occupations in which there is high inter-worker dependence in the work process, such that almost constant interaction is required, show less social life than groups characterized by relatively independent operations.

The task group

Perhaps one of the most important aspects of small group behavior in large organizations is their relation to the work process itself. The formally designated task builds a group structure, just as do individual social needs and the organizational authority structure.

More specifically, the work process stimulates group controls of (a) work method, (b) output standards or productivity, and (c) relative compensation and prestige relationships.

Impact on work method. The experience of working in close proximity on a day-to-day basis induces methods that may depart from the organization's original conception of the job, or at least "fills in" the specific details of the operation not specified in the formal work plan. Thus, employees may exchange repetitive jobs, although such trading is illegal; one worker may do two jobs while a colleague rests; or, as Whyte [17] found, they may change the sequence of the operations to reduce tensions and provide short cuts. Roy

---

[14] University of Liverpool, *op. cit.*, p. 72.
[15] Seymour M. Lipset, "The Political Process in Trade Unions: A Theoretical Statement," in *Freedom and Control in Modern Society*, Monroe Berger, Theodore Abel, and Charles Page, Eds. (New York: Van Nostrand, 1954), pp. 101-102.
[16] Personal correspondence, Professor Strauss, University of Buffalo.
[17] William F. Whyte, "The Social Structure of the Restaurant," *The American Journal of Sociology*, LIV (January, 1949), pp. 306-307.

observed similar "adjustments" in relations among toolroom clerks, job setters, and machinists where the objective was maximizing piece rate earnings.[18]

Some of these informal, or unplanned for, work methods may decrease worker output. For example, workers' machinations in Roy's machine shop tended to overstate make-ready time during job changes. However, other worker innovations, such as those described by Whyte, undoubtedly increase the total output. Gross found that radar teams, through communication circuits set up during off-the-job social periods, were compensating for deficiencies in the information provided by the formal organization.[19]

Similarly researchers have analyzed the initiative exhibited by a group of department store salesmen in evolving a new work pattern that solved a serious internal morale problem created by a new incentive system.[20]

However, the work structure can be designed so that elaborations of the informal group necessarily work in opposition to the major objectives of the organization. Recent studies of changes in the method of mining coal, conducted by the Tavistock Institute in Great Britain, illustrate such organization.[21] The change from jobs completed by small groups of miners in one shift to successive operations carried out by three shifts resulted in reduction of interaction and communication and a consequent decrease in the miners' recognition of their total responsibility for the operation.[22]

Thus the Tavistock studies suggest that the goal of the engineer in designing the technological organization is to provide the work group with a relatively autonomous task so that responsible *internal* leadership can develop. This kind of organizational structure, is, in fact, the very essence of decentralization:

> A primary work organization of this type has the advantage of placing responsibility for the complete . . . task squarely on the shoulders of a single, small, face-to-face group which experiences the entire cycle

[18] Donald Roy, "Quota Restriction and Goldbricking in a Machine Shop," *The American Journal of Sociology*, LVII (March, 1952), pp. 427-442.

[19] Edward Gross, "Some Functional Consequences of Primary Controls in Formal Work Organizations," *American Sociological Review*, XVIII (August, 1953), pp. 370-371.

[20] Nicholas Babchuck and William Goode, "Work Incentives in a Self-Determined Group," *American Sociological Review*, XVI (October, 1951), p. 686.

[21] E. Trist and K. Bamforth, "Some Social and Psychological Consequences of the Long Wall Method of Coal-Getting," *Human Relations*, IV, No. 1 (1951).

[22] The same problem can arise even though the employees are not separated into different time shifts. A study of a textile mill provides us with an example of the impact of worker-machine allocations. Cf. A. K. Rice, "Productivity and Social Organization in an Indian Weaving Shed," *Human Relations*, VI, No. 4 (1953).

of operations within the compass of its membership. For each participant the task has total significance and dynamic closure.[23]

The development of mutually convenient methods of conducting the work process can extend to the "job" of collective bargaining. We have ample evidence that union-management relationships at the work group level often depart radically from established practices and attitudes prevailing at higher levels, and may in fact contradict these other, more "formal" relationships.[24]

Aside from evolving methods which seem most convenient to work group members, the pattern of doing the job is fitted to the status system of the group. Those members with most prestige, if at all possible, receive the best jobs. Where possible, working location and equipment are similarly "assigned." And where these are not under group control, helping and trading can be adjusted to the status system. The exchange-of-favors system readily responds to the prestige hierarchy. Of course, the evaluation placed on jobs is itself a product of group interaction.

The methods evolved within the group for task completion become firmly established. Where outside forces (e.g., technological change) threaten to induce changes, the ranks close and resistance is applied. In part, of course, this may be the natural reaction of the culprit fearing punishment for rule infractions. A more reasonable explanation of the informal group's resistance to change, however, is the intimate relationship between the task group as an entity and the work methods they have evolved. A threat to one is a real threat to the other.

Impact on output standards. Probably more attention has been given to this aspect of task group behavior than to any other. Starting with the work of Mathewson, and extending through the Western Electric studies, a long and distinguished line of studies indicate that work groups often formulate quite specific output standards and obtain close conformity from their members in *maintaining* these standards. Productivity itself is increasingly conceived as a group phenomenon.

Several reasons have been advanced as to why output control occupies a place of such importance in the life of the group. Work standards are one of the most important aspects of the job, which

---

[23] Trist and Bamforth, *op. cit.*, p. 6.
[24] Cf. Melville Dalton, "Unofficial Union-Management Relations," *American Sociological Review*, XV (October, 1950), pp. 611-619.

can in some fashion be influenced by worker action. The energy expenditure required by the job is largely determined by the number of units required, rather than by the nature of the job itself. Presumably without group control management would be able to utilize individual differences, and competition for promotion and greater earnings, to obtain higher and higher standards. This would penalize particularly the slower worker and the older employee. It might, however, penalize all workers by cutting piece rates, where such exist, and/or reducing the number of employees required by the operation. "Run away" output might have internal ramifications. We have observed situations where group controls were weak, and younger, low-prestige employees exceeded the production and earnings records of their "betters." The results were calamitous for the status hierarchy of the department and ultimately for the effectiveness of the formal organization.

Output control is a basic objective of group action as well as an essential element in maintaining group stability. Not only the relationship of the members to one another, but the durability of the worker relationship to his job depends on the efficacy of this process. Again we need to note that the resultant is not always unfavorable to management. We have many instances on record where the group has sanctioned increasingly high productivity,[25] rejected fellow workers who could not maintain high output, and resisted threats to existing high quality standards.

Evidently a great deal of the interest in "informal group relations" is the result of this presumed relationship between output standards evolving within the group and actual worker productivity. Wilensky in an earlier chapter reviews some of the efforts to find the magic formula to convert group norms from "low" to "high."

Some of the earliest research on productivity was based on the assumption that internal harmony in the work group would produce higher performance records. Increasingly researchers have become disillusioned with the relationship between social satisfaction and worker effort. Perhaps one of the most telling blows to the impetus to devote substantial energies to building work groups that are "sociometrically sound" is the provocative study by Goode and Fowler in a low morale plant. They found "the informal relationships which developed were such as to maintain pressures toward

---

[25] Cf. George Strauss, "Group Dynamics and Intergroup Relations," in William F. Whyte and others, *Money and Motivation* (New York: Harper, 1955), pp. 90-96.

high production in the face of considerable *animosity* toward the owners and *among the workers themselves.*" [26] While their findings are severely limited by the somewhat unique environment they chose, it has become recognized that the relationship between friendship and output is a complex one.

More recently, Seashore finds in a study in a large "heavy equipment manufacturing company" that highly "cohesive" work groups are more likely to have output records that diverge *in either direction* from plant averages.[27] By implication, then, tightly knit work groups are almost as likely to have notably *poor* production records as outstandingly *good* ones.

The present author is inclined to believe that these inconsistencies in research results are due to an overemphasis on output as a part of informal group equilibrium. Control over output is also a major weapon in the arsenal of the group engaging in conflict with management, other work groups, and even the local union. We need to know more about the *total situation* facing a given work group, including these external factors, before predicting its work performance.

The evolution of the method of *group decision* for gaining acceptance for changes in production methods and output standards is recognition of the potency of group standards. The theory presumes that leadership methods that involve the entire work group in the change process have two major advantages:

1. They can eliminate the major barrier of existing group standards which militate against any change, per se.
2. More positively, they commit the individual to new efforts in the context of his group membership. In a sense, the individual "promises" his fellows to accomplish some change in his behavior. Valuing the opinions of his associates, he feels bound to maintain his agreement.

Ideally the "decision" itself becomes the new standard or norm of conduct for the task group. Similarly efforts to develop plant-wide incentive systems are premised on the assumption that output and effort are dependent on the relation of the work group to the total social system of the plant.[28]

---

[26] William Goode and Irving Fowler, "Incentive Factors in a Low Morale Plant," *American Sociological Review*, XIV (October, 1949), p. 624; italics added by author.

[27] Stanley Seashore, *Group Cohesiveness in the Industrial Work Group* (Ann Arbor: Institute for Social Research, University of Michigan, 1954), p. 98.

[28] Cf. William F. Whyte and others, *Money and Motivation, op. cit.*, p. 225.

Impact on relative compensation and prestige relationships. The fact that jobs take on a significant social meaning can be seen in the importance attached to wage differentials within the group itself. For example, we have many instances on record when management assigned an equal value to each job and the group found significant distinguishing characteristics. Jobs ranked by employees as *more important or desirable* are expected to have higher earnings than jobs ranked below. The established hierachy is reinforced over time by the gradual perfection of the correlation between esteem accorded particular workers and prestige accorded to their jobs. The "more important" workers have moved to the "more important" jobs. (The importance attached to the job is not only a function of the earning capacity but also the quality of the surroundings, equipment, the tempo of the work required, etc.) Problems occur only when changes are introduced which violate the established hierarchy.

A persistent problem has been that jobs which the group evaluates as relatively undesirable may need to be compensated at a higher rate than the "desirable" jobs, in order to attract adequate personnel. However, this differential may be contrary to the status system of the work group. Similarly, jobs evaluated (by the group) as desirable may lack characteristics which would bring them a high rating under the organization's formal ranking plan. These contradictions between the group and the organization's ranking system become more important during periods of relative labor shortage, when new recruits are difficult to obtain and when the group undergoes aging.

While these several concepts of the "informal group" are not identical, and in some cases not even complementary in their basic dimensions, they do have one common feature. All stress equilibrium, the development of a system of interpersonal relations which stabilizes the work situation (among subordinates and between superior and subordinates), an interconnected series of friendship linkages, work flow relationships, output levels, and status-income relations. The objectives are the maintenance of individual and group stability by insuring a predictability of day-to-day events and effecting a *modus vivendi* as between individual on-the-job needs and the requirements of the formal organization.

As such, the *informal group* in any and all of its meanings is serving well-recognized and accepted human needs. Its existence and continued preservation are hardly matters for surprise. The building up of routines, of established methods of accomplishing tasks, of predictable social relationships, of group roles—these are all elements of structuring which social scientists have found typical of the human group. In fact, the elements define the group.

Particularly through the setting and maintenance of group standards, informal groups have protected their memberships from possible indiscretions that might reflect adversely on them all; also they have provided support for the individual, by acting as a buffer to outside organizations and by sustaining him through the provision of *known and acceptable* routines of behaving within the face-to-face work group.

Thus the informal group, as perceived in such studies, *reacts to* the initiations of other organizations, particularly management. Being defined in equilibrium terms, the reaction is always an attempt to *regain* the previous undisturbed state—to protect work methods, social relationships, and output levels incorporated in the norms of the group.

Concerted interest as the focus

Workers also band together into *interest groups*. These are formed not only to protect their members but also to exploit *opportunities* to improve their relative position. Improvements can take the form of "looser standards," a preferred seniority position, more overtime, more sympathetic supervision, correction of "inequities," better equipment, and countless other less tangible goals that make the job a better one and that often serve to substitute for the more traditional kinds of promotions and mobility.

Distribution of these benefits may be much influenced by pressures of united and determined informal groups. What management feels is "equitable," just as what the union determines is in the "members' interest," is determined to a large extent by attitudes expressed by those individuals who can support their demands by group reinforcements. Those work groups which for one reason or another are unable to exercise similar power in the market place of the plant are penalized.

This is not the traditional concept of the informal group seeking conformity with established norms of conduct. These are much more "free enterprise" units, interacting in a struggle for maximization of utility. All are not equally aggressive in the struggle for self-improvement or equally well equipped with the wherewithal to do battle via the grievance procedure and the more direct pressure tactics on union and management. Some lack the spirit of combat, others the means, while only a restricted few are endowed with the characteristics associated with sustained "activity" and progress toward the goals they seek.

Much of what we say implies a degree of dual or even treble *disloyalty*. Other groups, management, the union, and fellow workers, are perceived as either barriers or sources of assistance. From the point of view of the interest group, it is not high identification or loyalty that counts, but rather the right tactics in using or ignoring these other aggregations.

Thus, management is neither "good" nor "bad," liked or disliked as such. In fact, this approach suggests that it may not always be fruitful to think in pro-management and pro-union terms. It may well be that a group which is satisfied with *itself*, with its ability to protect and improve its own interests, is more favorable to *both* union and management.[29]

The results for the larger plant may not be a system tending toward equilibrium at all. We might expect that certain combinations of pressure groups actually involve the organization in increasing instability—a trend toward disequilibrium. We have observed plants where the interaction of these groups involves increasingly greater discontent, turmoil, and nonadaptive behavior. That is, their behavior tends to reinforce the very problems it was designed to solve.

Similarly, the internal structure of these groups is much more responsive to changes in its external environment than is often implied in the concept of the informal work group as a relatively durable, impervious entity. Literally overnight, technical changes introduced by management can convert a cohesive task force into a disunited, apathetic "rabble," squabbling over internal differences. Similarly, we have observed a group of weakly-united employees become a force of some magnitude in the social system of the plant within a brief period, with no changes in personnel.

The existence of these *interest group* types suggests that greater attention should be given to matching supervisory "types" with group "types." We have tended to think of effective supervision as being the product of a relationship between a good leader and his group, on the assumption that the group of subordinates was a con-

---

[29] These areas will be further elaborated in the author's forthcoming study, *Technology and Work Group Behavior* (Ann Arbor: Bureau of Industrial Relations, University of Michigan, 1956).

stant. In fact, variations in the effectiveness of supervision may be as much due to inherent differences in the group itself as to the leadership practices exhibited by the supervisor.

The Internal Dynamics of the Work Group

We have concentrated primarily on the relationship of the small group to the larger organization, the functions served, the "compatibilities" and "incompatibilities." Therefore, we have failed to explore much of the research that stresses the intriguing inner processes of these groups, as semiautonomous organizations. This means neglecting the processes of self-selection and exclusion developed in the work of Moreno and his colleagues in the field of sociometry. We have also omitted the prolific findings of the "group dynamics school" with its emphasis on leadership patterns and role differentiation, factors contributing to cohesiveness, and the impact of the group itself on membership perceptions and attitudes. Bales and his associates at Harvard have probed deeply into the "ebb and flow" of the problem-solving process within the group. The sequential member roles have been analyzed effectively.

For our purposes it would seem appropriate at least to make specific reference to the work of George Homans. His work places substantial emphasis on the relationship of the internal life of the group to the outside environment (primarily the attitudes, organizational structure, and work method induced by management).[30] "Elaborations" of behavior and sentiment induced in the small group in turn modify the larger organization. While we believe an overemphasis on the concept of *equilibrium* may be misleading, Homans' theorizing does provide a framework within which to relate the small group to the larger organization of which it is a part.

Conclusion

Clusterings of workers-on-the-job all have these characteristics: They stem from the uniqueness of individual personality, which refuses to combine into larger "wholes" without changing those entities. The sum of a group of individuals is something more than the total of the constituents; it is a new organization, because most of the members (there are significant exceptions as we have noted) obtain

---

[30] George Homans, *The Human Group* (New York: Harcourt Brace, 1950).

satisfaction in gaining acceptance as a part of the group, and the group itself yields an influence over its members. Put in another way, there are pressures toward *conformity* within the group. These pressures result in the establishment of accepted ways of living together. The way of life of the group includes a complex system of customs and rules, vested interests, and interaction patterns which govern the relationship of members of the group to one another and to the larger environment of which it is a part.

This observance of group-sanctioned behavior and attitudes "fills out" the rationally conceived organization. What is on paper an organization becomes a "living, breathing" social organism, with all the intricacies, emotions, and contradictions we associate with human relations. While no organization would long persist which did not provide its members with this opportunity for spontaneous "human relations," a major problem of the larger organization becomes one of successfully incorporating the small group.

BIBLIOGRAPHY, CHAPTER XI

BERWITZ, CLEMENT J. "Beyond Motivation," *Harvard Business Review* (May-June, 1960), 123-125.

BRADLEY, NELSON. "The Work Addict," *Sales Management* (July 7, 1961), 39-41.

DOUTT, JOHN T. "Management Must Manage the Informal Groups Too," *Advanced Management* (May, 1959), 26-28.

"Employee Discipline: Problems and Policies," *Management Review* (October, 1960), 49-52.

HALL, R. L. "Group Performance Under Feedback that Confounds Responses of Group Members," *Sociometry,* Vol. 20, 297-305.

HERSHEY, ROBERT. "Individualism vs. Teamwork," *Management Review* (November, 1957), 4-9.

LASSER, J. K., and V. H. ROTHSCHILD. "Deferred Compensation for Executives," *Harvard Business Review,* Vol. 33, No. 1 (1955), 89-102.

LEARNED, EDMUND P. "Getting the Organization to Work Effectively as a Team," BURSK and FENN (Eds.), *Planning the Future Strategy of Your Business.* New York: McGraw-Hill Book Company, Inc., 1956. 71-84.

MAGOUN, F. ALEXANDER. "Misconceptions of Cooperation," from *Cooperation and Conflict in Industry.* New York: Harper & Brothers, 1960.

SCHAFFER, ROBERT H., and PHILIP WOODYATT. "New Horizons for Personnel Management," *Personnel* (March-April, 1962), 42-52.

SMYTH, RICHARD C. "Bonus Plans for Executives," *Harvard Business Review* (July-August, 1959), 66-74.

TANNENBAUM, ROBERT, *et al. Leadership and Organization.* New York: McGraw-Hill Book Company, Inc., 1961.

"The Meaning and Maintenance of Discipline," *Factory Management and Maintenance* (July, 1950), 130-132.

TOWER, JAMES W. "Incentive Patterns of Executive Compensation," *Addresses on Industrial Relations, 1960 Series.* Ann Arbor: Bureau of Industrial Relations, The University of Michigan.

WHYTE, WILLIAM F., *et al. Money and Motivation.* New York: Harper & Brothers, 1955.

ZAJONC, ROBERT B. "The Effects of Feedback and Probability on Individual and Group Performance," *Human Relations,* Vol. 15 (1962), 149-162.

ZALEZNIK, A., C. R. CHRISTENSEN, F. J. ROETHLISBERGER. *The Motivation, Productivity, and Satisfaction of Workers.* Boston: Harvard University, Division of Research, Graduate School of Business Administration, 1958.

Chapter XII
Leadership Methods

Although our theory of human behavior is incomplete, managers must do and act in spite of this limitation. The purpose of this chapter is to explore the differing possibilities or approaches that managers employ in their relations with subordinates. These approaches range the continuum from highly autocratic authoritarianism to extreme latitude in the direction of subordinate activity. These ranges are exemplified by the selection of articles in this chapter.

In Article 41 George V. Moser shows how managers are able to achieve success by employing relatively unstructured direction. He explains consultative management in which there is a high degree of subordinate participation in the operation of the organization.

Chris Argyris shows the difficulty encountered in achieving high degrees of use of participative managerial approaches in his first article. Argyris's second article illustrates the high degree of success that an autocratic manager was able to achieve in a plant which had theretofore shown fairly low productivity. Argyris goes on to suggest that the economic success of the autocratic manager was achieved at the expense of human dignity and maturity.

The problem of how the modern manager can be "democratic" in his relations with subordinates and at the same time maintain the necessary authority and control in the organization for which he is responsible is discussed in Article 44 by Robert Tannenbaum and Warren H. Schmidt. The final selection by Harold J. Leavitt attempts to place the role of the human factor in perspective with the spectrum of variables influencing managerial decisions.

41. CONSULTATIVE MANAGEMENT [1]

George V. Moser [2]

Consultative management is a philosophy and a method of administration. It involves explanation and consultation, at all levels, between a supervisor and the people who report to him. The supervisor practices consultative management on all matters of mutual interest, and he does this before he makes a decision.

This kind of management has always existed to some degree. But in the past twenty years it has been steadily replacing the fast-fading dictator type of manager.

Those who fully grasp consultative management say it is based on genuine respect for the personality and dignity of the individual. They say it goes hand-in-glove with the belief that all men are endowed with intelligence, free will and the responsibility to think for themselves. They say that consultative management unleashes productive forces that can only emerge through the cooperation of free men working as a team. They also say that consultative management is most effective when it is so habitual as to be automatic, when a manager has absorbed the idea to such an extent that he cannot think of operating in any other way.

To get a better idea of how consultative management works, consider what happened in the production department of the mythical Whiteside Manufacturing Company.

Jake Morgan, foreman, leaned back in his swivel chair. He was thinking hard. One drill press had to be moved and he had to decide where it should go. After examining the possibilities, he decided that the best place was on the other side of the electric switches. Jake picked up the phone and ordered the machine moved that night. Then he went to Tony, the operator.

[1] From *Management Record*, Vol. XVII, No. 11 (November, 1955), pp. 438-439, National Industrial Conference Board. Reprinted by permission of the National Industrial Conference Board.

[2] George V. Moser, Division of Personnel Administration, National Industrial Conference Board, Inc.

"Tony," he said, "your machine has to be moved. We're putting it over there on the other side of the switches. When you report to work tomorrow your machine will be there ready for you. You understand?"

"Okay, boss, I got it," said Tony. But the more Tony thought about this, the madder he got. "How come they gotta move my machine? Why not somebody else? I got plenty seniority around here. Over by the switch is not good. The boss says move, I move, but, by God, I don't have to like it." Tony went back to work with a chip on his shoulder and with lead in his feet and heart.

Six months later Jake was up against the same problem. Tony's drill press had to be moved back near where it had been before. But this time Jake handled it differently. He had just completed a company course on how to be a better supervisor.

"Tony," he said, "I have to move your machine back near where it was before. Do you see any objections to that?"

"No, boss, I got no objections to that."

"Well, Tony, do you see any place your machine ought to be moved to that would be better?"

"No, boss, I think you got it doped out about right."

"All right, Tony, but don't forget we want your ideas."

The more Tony thought about this the madder he got. His reaction could be summed up in one word, Nuts! "Who," he asked his pal, "does this guy think he's kidding? Why ask me what I think? He already decided. Nothing I'd say would change anything. I'd be crazy to say anything but Yes, Yes, Yes. Human relations, Ha! These guys make me sick with their cute tricks." Tony went back to work with a chip on his shoulder and with lead in his feet and heart.

A year later Jake Morgan had to talk to Tony again about the machine. Jake had learned a lot in this year. And this time he started by explaining to Tony why the machine had to be moved. "But before I decide where your machine ought to go, Tony," Jake continued, "I need your ideas on where the best place might be. Can you help me?"

Tony did have some ideas. And together they talked over the advantages and disadvantages of three locations. During the discussion Tony brought up a point that Jake had not considered. The result was that the third location, which neither Tony nor Jake had favored at first, now seemed the best place to put the machine. Then, and only then, did Jake decide.

That day, Tony ate his lunch without danger of indigestion as he reflected on the fact that he had had the chance to have his say when it really counted. His boss had made the decision, sure, but that's what bosses are for. And even if Jake had not decided on what Tony wanted, Tony would still have felt the same glow of pride because he knew that he had had a part in the decision.

An analysis of these situations between Jake and Tony can be summed up in the findings of much of the current research in the field of human relations. This research demonstrates the superiority of consultative management over other philosophies and methods of administration; it demonstrates the greater effectiveness of the boss as a leader as contrasted with the boss as a driver; it demonstrates the greater will to work and the greater productivity that result from cooperation as contrasted with coercion. Countless studies have shown that consultative management succeeds in raising the level of morale and productivity, and therefore lowers costs.

How does consultative management achieve such outstanding results?

Consultative management is a vital element of teamwork. Employees whose ideas are constantly sought by their supervisors and who are "in the know" because their supervisors keep them informed automatically take their places as members of the team, rather than as interested, or even disinterested, bystanders.

As members of the team, the employees know that there are goals to be reached and, more important, they know what the goals are. As they work toward these goals, they have the inner assurance that they will be kept informed of their progress and that they will be consulted when problems or obstacles arise that stand in the way of achieving the goals. An obstacle may take the form of a machine in the wrong place, or of too much absenteeism, or of too many rejects, or of a thousand and one other things. In every case affecting them, the employees' ideas will be solicited and, in the process of working out a solution, they learn more about the company's problems and its goals.

The manager who can view the over-all situation from this vantage point is strengthened through the pooled ideas of everyone on the team. And so long as the manager is earnestly seeking help, and has an open mind, the decision that he eventually makes is likely to be better than if he had decided on his own. No less important is the great surge of the group's determination and effort that can emerge because the team members have played a part in arriving at the decision.

Executives who have used consultative management over a long period of time hasten to clear up a widespread misunderstanding.

They know that many managers shy away from this philosophy and practice because of the mistaken belief that consultative management means "management by ballot box"—that is, the manager surrenders his authority and responsibility for decision-making to the group.

Nothing could be further from fact. In any position, responsibility and authority must be commensurate. The authority to make any decision and the responsibility for it must be delegated to a single individual. Thus, the manager may count noses to find out how many members of the team favor this and how many favor that, but it is the manager, and no one else, who is accountable for what is done. And his final decision, after weighing all of the available facts and ideas of his team, may be quite different from the views expressed by any or even all members of the group.

When this occurs, it is unlikely that those who disagree with the final decision will suddenly change their minds. But as team members, their ideas have been asked for, they understand the problems involved and the reasons for the decision. As in Tony's case when his opinions were finally sought out with sincerity, any disappointment or resentment is likely to be more than counterbalanced by a willingness to go along with the decision and to try to make it work.

One word of warning comes from the experienced managers and also their employees who are regularly invited to participate in decision-making. Don't try to use this method of administration unless you really want to know and make use of the opinions and ideas of the people on your team. The manager who uses it as a clever gimmick is immediately labeled by the group for what he is—a phony.

42. ORGANIZATIONAL LEADERSHIP AND
PARTICIPATIVE MANAGEMENT [1]
Chris Argyris [2]

* * *

Importance of participation

"Participative management" and "democratic leadership" are phrases that are currently in the limelight in most management circles. These phrases are taken to mean that the subordinates should be given an opportunity to participate in the various decisions that are made in their organization which affect them directly or indirectly. Many executives, consultants, and research scientists, including the author, have written and continue to write about the advantages of participative management. These people encourage supervisors and executives to increase the employees' participation in various organizational activities, especially in the decision-making process. They point out that, among other things, studies show that participative management tends to (1) increase the degree of "we" feeling or cohesiveness that participants have with their organization; (2) provide the participants with an over-all organizational point of view instead of the traditionally more narrow departmental point of view; (3) decrease the amount of conflict, hostility, and cutthroat competition among the participants; (4) increase the individuals' understanding of each other which leads to increased tolerance and patience toward others; (5) increase the individual's free expression of his personality, which results in an employee who sticks with the organization because he (i.e., his personality) needs the gratifying experiences he finds while working there; and (6) develop a "work climate," as a result of the other tendencies, in which the subordinates find opportunity to be more creative and to come up with ideas beneficial to the organization.

Although these trends are admittedly desirable, many supervisors and executives ask, "Exactly how far can this notion of participation

[1] From *The Journal of Business*, Vol. XXVII, No. 1 (January, 1955, University of Chicago), pp. 1-7. Reprinted by permission of *The Journal of Business*.
[2] Chris Argyris, Research Project Director at the Yale University Labor and Management Center.

and democracy be carried out?" Lately we have been asking ourselves the same question. Although we cannot answer it completely within the space of this paper, we would like to present for the reader's consideration some preliminary thoughts on the matter.

FACTORS INFLUENCING THE SUCCESSFUL INTRODUCTION OF PARTICIPATIVE MANAGEMENT IN AN ORGANIZATION

Much attention has been given and continues to be given to (1) the executives' feelings and attitudes about participative management; (2) the small informal groupings within the organization; and (3) the personnel policies of the organization. The assumption is that these are the three crucial factors in making participative management work.

We agree that these three factors are crucial, but we would like to add another. It seems to us that the kind of organizational structure within which these factors operate is also crucial. It is this factor that we propose to examine further.

How may we characterize the nature of most modern industrial and business organizations? One way to answer this question is to note the underlying rules or principles used by administrators to create and administer these organizations.

Simon defines some of the more common principles of administration upon which organizations are based as:

1. Administrative efficiency is increased by a specialization of the task among the group. (Specialization.)
2. Administrative efficiency is increased by arranging the members of the group in a determinate hierarchy of authority. (Unity of Command.)
3. Administrative efficiency is increased by limiting the span of control at any point in the hierarchy to a small number. (Span of Control.)

These principles serve as the basis for the definition of organizational structure. They point out the kind of organization within which we usually try to introduce participative management programs. The question arises, "What problems can we predict will tend to arise when we try to introduce participative management to such an organization?"

In order to answer this question, we find it necessary first to re-examine and perhaps to redefine exactly what we mean by "organization."

A Concept of Organization

We may begin by defining an organization as an aggregate of parts (e.g., individuals, departments) integrated into an organized "whole."

How do these parts (e.g., individuals) become integrated into an organized whole? Research at the Yale Labor and Management Center indicates that the following *organizational processes* must be performed if an aggregate of individuals is to become an organization:

1. A *Work-flow Process* to define the behavior sequence that the parts of the organization must accomplish to achieve the objective (e.g., in a shoe factory a series of behavior sequences must be set up which people must perform in order to produce shoes)
2. A *Reward and Penalty Process* to induce people to do the work the organization assigns to them (in other words, the Reward and Penalty Process "taps" human motivation by rewarding or penalizing according to the acceptability of the actions performed)
3. An *Authority Process* to direct the employees in order that the organizational requirements be met
4. A *Perpetuation Process* to maintain and replenish the basic resources of organization (men, materials, and ideas)
5. An *Identification Process* to select and define clearly understood emotionally toned symbols, concepts, or other such aspects which will help individual employees identify with the organization as a whole, which in turn automatically helps to point out the uniqueness of the organization in the larger environment in which it is imbedded
6. A *Communication Process* to provide media and paths for communication

In other words, according to this scheme, we assume that an organization cannot exist unless someone performs at least these essential (but not sufficient) processes. We may now begin to understand how the principles of specialization and unity of command affect the possibilities of successfully initiating "participative management" in organizations.

Let us assume that we have a plant all set up to manufacture shoes. We have purchased the plant, the equipment, and the materials necessary to produce our product. We now need only "labor" to make the shoes. We hire these employees, and, if we administer our organization according to the modern management principle of task specialization, we will assign them to the specific task (or set of tasks) of making shoes. In terms of our outline this means that we assign them to tasks in the work-flow process.

But, according to our definition of organization above, these employees cannot be welded into an organization because they lack the remainder of the organizational processes (e.g., authority, reward and penalty, etc.). In order to provide these processes and thus create an organization out of this aggregate of people, we create a new job containing the missing processes. We give the person who takes this job control over the authority, reward and penalty, perpetuation, and other processes. We call this person the "organizational leader." Now, the employees who are making the shoes can be welded into an organized unit. But, to do so, they must by definition become dependent upon the organizational leader for the missing processes of organization. They must turn to him for their authority, reward and penalties, perpetuation, etc. Thus the principle of unity of command is now "translated" into the principle that the subordinates are to report to one leader and are to be dependent upon him for certain crucial activities.

In other words, the scheme suggests that what is customarily called "the principle of unity of command" is actually the principle of inducing the subordinates to follow the leader by making them dependent upon him and by paying them to accept this dependence. There is, therefore, a "built-in" sense of dependency of the subordinates upon the organizational leader. This dependency, we suggest, is inevitable if we follow the principles of task specialization and unity of command.

Do Dependence and Participation Go Together?

The question arises, "How truly participative (i.e., how spontaneous and free) can subordinates be if they are to be dependent upon their leader?" "How much democracy can we have if the power lies in the one who leads and not in the ones who are led?" Or, if we take the leader's point of view, "How democratic can he be if his job *is* to control the processes of organization?" Unfortunately, these and other similar questions are not answered by the many interesting and provocative studies in small-group dynamics from which so much of our information about the value of participation stems. The reason is that most of the research is based upon experimentally created or actual groups whose basic purpose is *not* to give any one leader a "life-or-death grip" (to quote an employee) on the members of the group. Leadership in these groups seems to arise at any given time from the individual's ability to fulfill the needs of the other members of the group. It does not arise because of any predetermined power of any one member over the other members of the group.

Although we also do not have a clear-cut answer to the question of "How much participation is possible?" there are some implications in our analysis which might be useful in eventually helping us to arrive at an answer. We discuss some of these implications below.

A Basic Conflict Between Organization Development and Personality Development

If the modern management principles (e.g., unity of command, task specialization, span of control, etc.) are to obtain *ideal* expression in an organization, the management would have to assign non-supervisory employees to a job which tends to (1) permit them little control over their work-a-day world; (2) place them in a situation where their passivity rather than initiative would frequently be expected; (3) lead them to occupy a subordinate position; (4) permit them a minimum degree of fluidity (variety) and emphasize the expression of one (or perhaps a few) of the agent's relatively minor abilities; and (5) make them feel dependent upon other agents (e.g., the boss).

The problems that would tend to arise if we assign people to such jobs can be seen by asking the following questions, "What sorts of personality characteristics do people in our culture tend to exhibit?" Or, to put it another way, "What needs do relatively normal adults in our culture have?" "Would these needs be able to find some such expression in a job situation as the one we describe above?"

A somewhat detailed analysis of much of the material available on the development of the human personality suggests that people in our culture (1) tend to develop from receiving and incorporating aspects of culture as an infant to controlling, using, redefining, and helping others incorporate these aspects of culture as an adult; (2) develop from a state of being passive as an infant (i.e., having other people initiate action for them); (3) develop from being capable of behaving only in a few ways and in a rigid manner as an infant to being capable of behaving in many different ways and behaving in a flexible manner as an adult; (4) develop from being in a subordinate position in the family and society as an infant, to occupying a more equal and/or superordinate position in the family and society as an adult; and (5) develop from a state of high dependence on others as an infant to a state of independence and finally to a state of interdependence in their society as an adult.

If we assume, for a moment, that the people who come to work for us are relatively normal, then may we not conclude that these people will tend to desire to find work which will help them fulfil some combination of the above trends? (The exact combination naturally depends on the individual.) In order to accomplish this, an individual would require a job in which he can (1) define for himself a ratio of activity (initiation of action) to passivity where activity is greater than passivity (passivity defined as others initiating action for the individual); (2) define for himself a position equal and/or super-ordinate to the other people with whom he interacts; (3) define for himself tasks where he is able to provide expression for the many learned ways of behaving that are important to him (this includes the expression of important abilities, needs, sentiments, and personal goals); (4) define for himself a sense of fluidity and flexibility that is comparable to his personality fluidity and flexibility; (5) express feelings of independence and interdependence in relation to the other people in the organization; (6) feel that he has the respect of other individuals who are important in his life; and (7) obtain from his job a degree of creature sufficiency he desires.

Thus, relatively normal individuals are characterized as "having built into them (through the process of growing up) tendencies to be active, to be independent, to be flexible, and to express their many and varied abilities," etc. Job situations, on the other hand, are described as requiring an individual to be passive, to be dependent, and to express only one or two abilities.

The job requirements are clearly different from, and in some cases antagonistic to, the requirements of relatively normal individuals. However, they *are* substantially similar to the requirements of an infant in our culture.

Thus, we are led to conclude that it would be difficult for the organization to place relatively normal adult individuals in "ideal" job (i.e., from the organization's point of view) situations without creating difficulties. Similarly, it would be difficult for the individual to obtain ideal personality expression without blocking the efficient expression of the organizational principles.

There are a number of ways out of such a dilemma for both the employees and the management. For example, some recent research at the Yale Management and Labor Center indicates that employees may adapt to their working situation in various ways. Individuals may (1) leave the organization; (2) accept the frustration on the assumption that if they work hard they will eventually be raised to a leadership position; (3) become apathetic and not "give a damn" about their work; (4) create informal activities and informal groups to help them adapt (if the groups are found to be effective, the individuals may desire to stabilize them and make certain that these groups will always exist; this might be accomplished by the individuals bringing to bear upon the work situation power which is inherently theirs (i.e., that which comes from the political, social, and economic privileges given to all people in this country; thus, the groups may be stabilized in the form of trade unions); and (5) come into the organization prepared (through culture training) to expect no high degree of personality expression; this expectation tends to act to reduce the negative effects of the actual lack of personality expression obtained on the job.

Management, on the other hand, may act to minimize the difficulties by decreasing the employees' dependence upon the organization leader. This is one of the main objectives of increased employee participation in decision-making. The point we would make is simply that, if we are to use participation to decrease dependency, then we may also have to change the nature of our organization. Our organization is no longer being administered by the principles described above. In short, participative management implies a different set of organization principles.

If what we have said to date makes sense, then clearly there are some interesting implications for executive training. First, is there not a need for a re-examination of the basic structure of organization as defined by traditional administrative principles? Perhaps a different type of organization structure is necessary if "participative management" is really to work. Until such basic changes are made, might it not be more realistic to teach participative management principles to executives *after* they have been helped to understand the effects that this basic dependency relationship has upon the employees? We could teach them to understand the nature of a dependency relationship and point out how it conflicts with normal personality needs. This would help the supervisors gain more insight into the "why" of the often-observed apathetic, disinterested behavior on the part of employees. It would help the supervisor to understand the *adaptive value* of the many informal activities that employees create but which management may dislike. For example, what would happen if the supervisor is helped to realize that apathy may be a healthy way to adapt to the type of work situation in which a person is usually placed? Would it not lead the supervisor to ask himself, "How can I minimize this dependency relationship and reduce the number of personality-blocking aspects of the organization without detracting from the efficient management of the organization?" He would do this *before* he spent hours making "morale" speeches.

Moreover, would not this knowledge help us learn to set realistic limits to participative management, thereby making the supervisors more secure in its use? It seems to us that one reason many supervisors resist participative management is that they feel that there are no limits to its use. Also, would it not help to alleviate, or at least to decrease, the often-produced feelings of inadequacy and perhaps guilt that supervisors have after listening to how democratic they ought to be?

We close with this point. Let nothing in this paper be construed to mean that we are implying that modern management principles are "bad" or that apathy and indifference on the part of members of organizations are "good." We are simply trying to spell out what *is*. It seems to us, if we all (employees and executives) understand the basic difficulties inherent in organization, there should result a greater tolerance for and patience and understanding of the organization's problems, our own problems, and the problems of others.

43. LEADERSHIP PATTERN
IN THE PLANT [1]

Chris Argyris [2]

This article describes some of the methods used by a brilliant man
—the Leader—to administer a deteriorating organization so that in
a few years' time it became, according to the management, the best
division, moralewise and profitwise, in the entire corporation. Focused as it is on the relationship between the Leader and his 20
middle-management supervisors, the article should be of particular
interest because the findings disclosed run counter to many conventional "human relations" ideas.

Note that I say "Leader" with a capital "L." Because of the confidential nature of the data, that is the only name and title he can be
given here. Moreover, I want to remind readers continually that a
particular individual is being discussed, and that this must be taken
into account when they try to apply the findings, as I hope they will,
to other administrators operating under similar conditions.

My objective is to describe concretely and accurately the Leader
in action. This I shall try to do on the basis of interviews and observations made over a two-year period—intensively, almost constantly, for
one year; intermittently for another year.

My objective is *not* to pass judgment on the man's *leadership pattern*—meaning by that simply the way he leads people, whether expressed as a "style," a "method," or a "set of rules" of leadership, and
whether derived from his experiences with other people or stemming
from his own personality needs. In fact, I want to avoid *any* evaluation which suggests that I am against the ultimate aims of human
relations. I believe strongly that employees must have all the opportunity that can be given them to work under leadership which provides
room for individual creativity, happiness and growth.

Further, I suggest that readers also refrain from making immediate judgments. Let us, for the time being, not concern ourselves with
whether this man's leadership pattern is inherently "good" or "bad."

[1] From the *Harvard Business Review*, Vol. XXXII, No. 1 (January-February,
1954), pp. 64-75. Reprinted by permission of *The Harvard Business Review*.
[2] Chris Argyris, Research Project Director at the Yale University Labor
and Management Center.

All we need to know at this point is that it *works* and in that sense is successful. This way we shall avoid the misleading prejudgments which might otherwise be caused by lack of understanding of the situation in which the Leader operates—particularly, the condition of the organization as it was when he came to it and of the tactics he used to meet the problems he found there.

The Particular Situation

The division which the Leader heads turns out custom-made and standard products for an increasingly competitive market. The plant is multistoried. There are about 650 employees, most of whom belong to a union.

When the Leader was assigned to his position, he found that the plant was many thousands of dollars in the red. It had been losing money consistently. The organization had previously been administered loosely by a benevolent, kindhearted man. To quote one of the employees, it had been run like a "corner drugstore." Anyone could go directly to the top man with any kind of trouble. In this situation, the morale of workers was relatively good, but the supervisory positions had been undermined. In fact the point had been reached where people preferred never to become supervisors.

One of the Leader's first decisions was to rejuvenate the supervisors and raise the status of their positions. He worked hard with the supervisors and continually encouraged them to better themselves and their departments. In short, the Leader felt compelled to use some pressure to instill motivation, raise efficiency, and increase the overall effectiveness of the organization. And there is abundant evidence that he secured the desired results.

Use of pressure

The Leader's use of "pressure" deserves special comment—if only to emphasize further the danger of making value judgments without full understanding of what is actually going on. In this case pressure means such behavior as when the Leader (a) repeatedly coordinates and controls others in a directive manner, (b) repeatedly checks on supervisors to make certain they follow directions, and (c) repeatedly sets supervisors' goals just high enough to present a challenge but low enough to be achievable by hard work.

The Leader is not alone in his use of pressure. Many line executives in highly competitive industries recognize that they use pressure to motivate people to improve their performance. Furthermore, the fact that pressure is not *necessarily* bad is supported by some recent findings on the motivation of individuals. In some experiments on frustration with children, scientists have found that mild frustration increases the effectiveness of the children's activities.[3] Therapists believe that one of their primary tasks is to utilize and, at times, create tension within a patient in order that he will feel a need to change. Psychologists inform us that some of this country's most creative men are motivated by deep internal tension.

At the same time, experienced line executives recognize that the application of pressure, beyond a certain point, is likely to give rise to frictions within the organization, with subordinates trying to duck out of the pressure by passing the buck or hiding their errors. More extreme pressure can even destroy the individual's motivation to do a job.

Understanding what is the appropriate balance is not an easy task. Only by examining actual cases where pressure is being applied can some sort of conclusion be developed. Our Leader seems to be very careful in applying pressure. He is always on the lookout for the effects of his actions on the supervisors being motivated. Moreover, to quote one supervisor, "If he bawls you out, you know that he forgets about it. He never holds it against you."

One cannot help but see some similarity between this behavior and some recently discovered notions about discipline. The suggestion is that discipline is most effective, and has least negative effects upon individuals, if the individual receiving it feels that his behavior at that particular moment is the only thing being criticized. In other words, he is not made to feel that he is being hurt or rejected as a person.

THE LEADERSHIP PATTERN

Let us now turn our attention to the leadership pattern. I shall begin by describing it from my point of view—an outsider's. In so doing, I will use actual concrete examples of situations in which I observed the Leader in action. Then, I shall give the Leader a chance to give us his own picture of his leadership pattern, his view of himself, and his beliefs about effective executive leadership. Following the presentation of both points of view, I shall describe some of the effects of the leadership pattern on the Leader's subordinates.

[3] Roger G. Barker, Tamara Dembo, Kurt Lewin, *Frustration and Regression; an Experiment with Young Children*, Studies in Child Welfare, Vol. 18, No. 1 (Iowa City, University of Iowa, 1941).

Outsider's viewpoint

1. *The Leader is constantly interacting and constantly commanding.* One of the strongest and most frequent characteristics of the Leader's leadership pattern is his constant interaction with the supervisors. He is continually "on the floor," talking with them, giving them his views, listening to theirs, and making on-the-spot decisions. Even when he becomes tired and leaves the floor to go to his office, he immediately calls in some individual or some group of supervisors to discuss one of the many current production problems.

Moreover, in the majority of his contacts with the supervisors, the Leader is continually taking the lead, interjecting new ideas, asking important questions, and usually coming up with some decision before any of the supervisors begin "to see the light."

Consider the following illustrative incident—one out of many—a meeting between the Leader and Supervisor A:

> A few minutes before he was called to the Leader's office, Supervisor A was having an early-morning meeting with some of his "subforemen" regarding a knotty production problem. Supervisor A was doing his best to consider all aspects of the case before making a decision. Suddenly the loudspeaker interrupted with "Supervisor A . . . Supervisor A." He dropped his pencil with an air of disgust and remarked: "Damn these interruptions. Well, that's it, boys. I've got to see the boss. Now what the hell did I do with those production reports on that faulty stuff that was sent to us? . . . Oh, yes, here they are. I'll see you fellows later."
>
> As he started to leave his office, the phone rang. Supervisor A rushed over, jerked the phone to his ear, and said hurriedly, "Yes . . . , speaking." The voice on the other side of the line said something which made Supervisor A red in the face. He replied, "All right, I'll be right there. I just heard it over the speaker!"
>
> He hurried to the Leader's office door, suddenly slowed his pace, and knocked softly.
>
> *Leader:* "Come in, come in, I've been waiting for you. . . . Glad to see you. How are things going today?"
>
> *Supervisor A:* "Fine."
>
> *Leader:* "About that material. What's the beef that your gang has?"
>
> *Supervisor A* [very cautiously and slowly]: "It's this material—this material that I mentioned last week. We've been having trouble with it. The trouble is it is not our usual quality. Don't you think it's the purchasing department's fault? Well, you know, he ought to take care of getting us the stuff we asked for."
>
> *Leader:* "Why certainly, that's his job! You tell him I told you that's his job. Now, look here, you know what to do. Why don't you really do a job on this? I mean a real job."
>
> *Supervisor A* [visibly upset]: "Well . . . you see . . . it's . . ."
>
> *Leader:* "I mean a job. Take it over to number two. Lay it out right. Put a few men on it. Get the thing out right away. You know what to do about poor material."

Supervisor A: "Well, we're catching up on it."

Leader: "Do you have men working on it?"

Supervisor A: "No, not . . ."

Leader: "Why not?"

Supervisor A: "Well, we don't have any extra . . ."

Leader: "What do you mean? What the hell are you doing with Joe?"

Supervisor A: "He has to take care of bags that we . . ."

Leader: "Now wait a minute. I spoke to Supervisor C just a little while ago. He said that he was taking care of that problem. Look, let's do a job on this. Come on now. You'd better see Supervisor C on this and get this thing straightened out right away."

2. *The Leader's personal goals, values, and feelings are all organizationally centered.* His primary concern in life is the organization. He literally thinks, eats, and sleeps his job. And as a result of his own emphasis on the welfare of the organization, the Leader also insists that the supervisors exhibit equal loyalty. Loyalty, in the Leader's eyes, requires that the supervisors reshape their personal goals and feelings to the organization's requirements.

An example of this attitude was taken from a management "bull session" between the Leader and some of the supervisors. The supervisors were discussing the problem of informal restriction of production:

Supervisor E: "But I still say the new supervisor has to overcome the locker-room talk where somebody comes up and says, 'Look, what do you want to do, kill the job?' The new supervisor is doing an outstanding job, but he has to decide whether he wants to adjust his work to the group and be accepted by the group, or whether he's going to say, 'To hell with the group.' Now, how does a supervisor handle this? How does he adjust to this group idea of what is good production?"

Leader: "I think a good leader can get in there and talk with the boys. I don't believe he has to say, 'To hell with the group.' But I do think he should be a leader to the extent that he'd say, 'We've got to get the best production possible.' He'd get the group to go along, no matter what, and still be on good terms with his group."

3. *The Leader makes the organization a part of his self-picture.* Not only is the Leader completely oriented toward the organization; he goes one step further and makes the organization a part of his self-picture—meaning by that his conception of himself, including all his feelings, prejudices, needs, goals, values, abilities, and so on.[4] This is much further than most people go in loyalty to an organization.

---

[4] See Carl R. Rogers, *Client-Centered Therapy* (Boston, Houghton Mifflin Company, 1951), pp. 497-500.

Once a person forms a picture of the self, it serves him as a guide for evaluating his experiences. All future experiences, therefore, are (a) accepted by the person and integrated with the picture he already has of himself, (b) ignored because the experiences do not make sense to the person, or (c) denied or distorted because the experience is inconsistent with the picture of himself. In other words, a man tends to adopt those ways of behaving which are consistent with the picture that he already has of himself.

Perhaps in this case there is a basic agreement between the Leader's personality needs and the organization's demands. If the Leader's personality actually requires that he command others and be the focus of attention among others, and if his organizational job is defined to permit these needs to be fulfilled, then it is understandable why the Leader can make the organization part of himself. The fact that he has done so helps to explain the complete loyalty which he exhibits toward the organization; that loyalty of course provides him with important personality satisfactions.

The Leader in his everyday evaluations and in the yearly merit ratings of supervisors does his best to be as fair as possible. But his evaluations are affected by his conception of himself. If a supervisor tends to be like him, the supervisor receives a high evaluation; if he is different from the Leader, then the supervisor has something to learn. During a conversation with me, the Leader stated:

> "Do you want to know a good man? There's Supervisor F. He's going to get somewhere. Of course, this is because he's been around me. I can see him use my kind of thinking all the time. Supervisor F is close to me because I've been able to guide him.
> "On the other hand, take Supervisor B. I'm having trouble with him. He's a nice fellow, but he's not like Supervisor F. He's a long way off. He's got to go quite a ways before he ever gets to my thinking."

4. *The Leader handles the supervisors as individuals rather than as members of a group.* The Leader treats each supervisor differently from the way he treats the others. If he is to reprimand three supervisors, he usually calls them into his office one by one and reprimands each according to his conception of that supervisor's "human nature." The Leader shows little insight into the fact that the supervisors are actually part of a total social system and that as such they may interact with each other concerning their relationships with the boss.

The Leader's practice of handling his supervisors as individuals continues even when he meets them as a group. The primary patterns of interactions seem to be from the Leader to a supervisor or vice versa. Little interaction occurs among the supervisors. About the only occasions when these men speak directly with each other are when they are contradicting each other, trying to place the blame on each other, trying to give each other some information, or simply reinforcing something that the Leader has already stated.

Consequently, these meetings of Leader and supervisors are characterized by competition for the Leader's praise. This serves to align the supervisors against each other, which in turn tends to emphasize the importance of the Leader and the dependence of the supervisors on him, and this in turn helps maintain the Leader's perception of the necessity for his leadership pattern. Moreover, he senses the supervisors' dependence on him and thus becomes more assured of his importance.

The crucial question is what the chances are for an effective team to be built up among the supervisors if they are kept ignorant of their fellow supervisors' relationships with the Leader and if they require the Leader to solve their quarrels for them.

5. *The Leader controls the transmission of important information.* By the very nature of his position, the Leader is placed in control of receiving and transmitting the communications that emanate from above. He makes it a point to communicate any important information that is designed for the entire plant first to the supervisors and then to the employees. Receiving the information before the employees emphasizes to the supervisors that they are "on the management team."

In most cases the Leader transmits important information as soon as he is able. There are times, however, when he temporarily withholds information, either on instruction from top management or on his own decision. For example, it may be that he knows a new plant is being built and that some of his subordinates are to be considered for transfer and promotion. The trouble is that in the meantime the supervisors hear of the possible changes through the grapevine and then have to go to the Leader to try to obtain further information.

Of course, the fact that the supervisors view the Leader as their source of important information and continually turn to him for it reinforces their realization that they need the Leader.

6. *The Leader emphasizes the present.* The Leader seems to care little about the past; and even less about the future, which he considers is for the "long hairs" and the research workers. In short, he

sees his security as lying in day-to-day living. He is constantly making statements like these:

> "We just can't wait in business."
> "The fundamental results are what count, and these results occur today, not tomorrow."
> "Time is valuable in business; it costs money."

Since the Leader controls the information channels, and since his emphasis is upon the present, the information transmitted is primarily in terms of what is important in the present. Here again, we get that reinforcing effect. Since the supervisors know little of the future, they need to turn to the Leader for future guidance. Similarly, since the Leader must keep the supervisors informed from day to day, he tends to find further reason for his constant interaction with them. Such interaction, in turn, tends to increase the Leader's importance in his own eyes as well as in the eyes of the supervisors.

7. *The Leader sets goals realistically.* The Leader sets his goals just high enough so that effort is required to achieve them, but not so high that they are unattainable. Over and over again, the Leader emphasizes in supervisory meetings that one should not try to aim for a job that is two or three rungs up the ladder; one should aim for the next rung. Similarly, he cautions his supervisors about committing themselves or their workers to unrealistic production goals. For example, during one supervisory meeting he told the supervisors:

> "It seems to me that a supervisor could help a girl get more enjoyment from her work if he told her to start in the morning of her first day and set a realistic goal. Keep track of how much she makes. Once she has met this goal, then she would be asked to try to better her record all of the time. I think that this is one of the problems in industry. Many supervisors try to set goals too high, and the result is that their workers don't meet them and consequently feel terrible."

This rounds out the picture of the Leader's leadership pattern as it appears to the outsider. His own picture follows in the next section; it is what he calls his philosophy, adding the comment, "My leadership philosophy is very close to my heart."

The leader's viewpoint

1. *I believe firmly; I defend doggedly.* The Leader feels that, whatever a man's beliefs are, he should believe in them firmly and he should be willing to defend them against "all comers" and "all odds." As he says:

"All my dealings with people have been with these principles in mind. If a leader believes in something, and if he really knows that something is right, he should stick to his beliefs. He should be able to defend his beliefs in front of anyone."

Coupled with firmness of position, however, the Leader suggests there should be fairness. More specifically, he believes (a) that a leader must make certain that he has all the important facts regarding any problem and (b) that he must weigh them carefully and decide only after he is certain he has examined all the facts. When asked whether any person can ever have all the facts, the Leader retorts, "A good leader *always* has *all* of the facts." Moreover, when he is questioned about the possibility of two different people having two equally plausible but antagonistic sets of facts, the Leader is quick to point out that an effective leader can always show that only one set of facts, in the final analysis, can be correct.

2. *I work hard; I am bold; I always get the job done.* The next aspect of leadership that is important to the Leader is concerned with his deep desire to work hard and to get the job done in the best possible manner. If he does this, he is a realist, and "all leaders must be realists." In his view:

"The primary job in life is to get your job done. I just can't see how some of the fellows in this plant expect to get ahead if they don't work hard in their job. I can't figure these guys out who spend all their spare time in sports or something like that."

Getting the job done may take more than hard work; a leader must often show boldness too. He should "pull no punches"; he cannot afford to. An effective leader should be "straightforward," "honest," and permit the "chips to fall where they may." After all, suggests the Leader, it is not he who dictates where the chips should fall; the job dictates such things.

If a leader creates a few enemies in getting the job done, then he should be careful to discuss this with the persons involved. An effective leader never "holds grudges," never leaves people with "hurt feelings." If necessary, he keeps them in his office and talks to them until he is certain that they no longer feel hurt. But, the Leader is quick to point out, such "smoothing over" discussions, necessary as they are, should come *after* the job is done. Nothing should stand in the way of completing the job. He goes on to point out:

"The boss is the man that counts, so you might as well work hard for him. You know, some people think they can change the boss. I wonder. Seems to me, more like it, he will change you."

3. *I keep my eyes open for opportunities to get ahead.* The Leader feels that a man without a burning desire continuously to raise his sights is not much of a man, and even less of a leader. He says:

"I can't see how some fellows live without having some goals in life. The fellow who is going to get ahead is the one who wants to get ahead— the man who has the push in him.

"Now, to Bill over here, money and advancement don't mean much. To him, opportunity means doing his same old work. To me, opportunity would mean the possibility of getting ahead and making more money. Maybe it's not everything, but money is important. I'd like to have the opportunity to double my salary."

The Leader is quick to add that advancement is hastened (a) if the person develops "contacts" and (b) if the person has the ability to be a good leader. If he has both these attributes, then he should have little difficulty in "selling himself" to the proper people.

4. *I keep my supervisors close to me.* One of the points the Leader keeps repeating is that he feels that the supervisors must be close to him and on the management side—and that, conversely, he must always back up his supervisors. The Leader seems to be suggesting that his leadership pattern could not be effective unless the supervisors were "on his side." He says:

"The worst thing a management leader can do is to by-pass his supervisors. You've got to have them behind you, or else you're licked. The supervisors are the backbone of management.

"I believe that sincerely. I've worked hard with my boys. I think I've made some of them topnotch men. Together we will get somewhere. Together we'll work on the other employees."

(One almost obtains a sense of "about-face" as he listens to the Leader describe his need for the supervisors. Here is a man who insists that an effective leader can "stand on his own two feet," and yet now he is equally insistent that he cannot get far without good subordinates. Could it be that the Leader has, as the psychologists would tell us, a sense of insecurity which, not unnaturally, he overcomes by gathering his subordinates close to him?)

5. *I make supervisory positions highly respected in the organization.* This characteristic follows directly from the previous one. If

supervisors are important, and if they are to be respected, then it follows that their positions in the organization must be respected. The Leader insists that the first step an effective leader takes when he gets into a top position is to build up the prestige of his supervisors. He says:

> "I want to get the supervisor's position so that a fellow will strive to be a supervisor rather than avoid it. We have people in our plant who avoid a supervisory job. All plants have that. I think one thing you've got to do is to give the supervisors the authority they deserve and require."

Effects on Supervisors

Let us turn now to an examination of some of the effects of this leadership pattern on the supervisors. More specifically, we are going to examine what happens to the supervisors when the Leader is not present—in other words, their informal activities.

Informal activities are responses that people make when they are trying to adapt to a certain set of circumstances. These activities arise from at least three different causes: (a) the supervisors' need to express their pent-up feelings due to the frustration and conflict that they experience in their working world, (b) their need to behave, at times, in an independent manner, and (c) their need to express normal feelings of antagonism that are bound to arise when men work closely, under the conditions described so far.

A crucial problem immediately arises, since the behavior required to fulfill the needs listed above is different from that which the Leader rewards. Thus at times the supervisors feel that they want "to tell each other off." At other times they "wish the Leader would leave them alone." Conflict and tension loom on the horizon because this sort of behavior is at odds with the picture the Leader paints of a "cooperative team" working together, with him as the quarterback; hence there is fear on the part of the supervisors that the Leader may discover the antagonistic nature of their informal activities.

The supervisors try to "resolve" this problem by simply keeping any antagonistic informal activities secret from the Leader. However, their attempts to keep such activities secret are undermined by various members of their own group. The Leader knows that the supervisors will not tell him everything, and he has a few supervisors who, in order to gain his favor, act as "information gatherers" for him and keep him posted on the informal activities. At the same time, even these information gatherers have their own limits as to what information they will convey.

Interestingly enough, the supervisory group seems to have a pretty good idea of the identity of these men, and is tolerant of them. In fact, the supervisors sometimes plant rumors with these "informers" in order to communicate certain information to the Leader which they do not want to communicate directly. Thus, in some respects the information gatherers become a two-way communication link between the Leader and his supervisors.

Barrier of secrecy

Placing a barrier of secrecy between the Leader and the supervisors can only cause a weakening of the organization. It prevents upward communication of the important human problems that are creating difficulties. An interesting example arose at the end of some intensive human relations training, when the supervisors were considering the possibility of sending a report to the Leader listing the major problems that had been discussed during the session. This would mean that the negative data concerning the Leader, the pent-up feelings of the supervisors, and the hostility that existed in the intersupervisory relationships which had come out into the open during the course would become known to the Leader.

According to the analysis above, the supervisors would not be expected to agree to such a report. If they did agree, it would probably be only after considerable argument. Here is what actually happened:

> The supervisors discussed the possibility of a report for two hours. They all agreed that it was a good idea for the Leader to know about their problems, but there was complete lack of agreement as to what problems should be sent to the Leader. Every time a topic was suggested, it was voted down because it might have "bad" effects. Here are some of the remarks made during the second hour:
>
> *Supervisor L:* "If we don't make a report, it's sort of like admitting that we haven't solved anything."
>
> *Supervisor K:* "If we don't bring a report to him, how the hell is he going to do anything about our changes?"
>
> *Supervisor C:* "We should have a general over-all report. Not a specific report."
>
> *Supervisor A:* "Can't we summarize some of those weekly reports and use that? That's general enough."
>
> *Supervisor I:* "Well, we have to talk about the boss. Maybe we can throw a few stones at the boss."
>
> *Supervisor R:* "You can't get away with it."
>
> *Supervisor A* [desperately]: "Can't we say anything good about him?"
>
> *Supervisor F:* "I don't think we should mention the boss."
>
> *Supervisor G:* "Why not? The plant would run without him."
>
> *Supervisor M:* "All kidding aside, I think we ought to leave him alone."

Supervisor A: "It's not his needle that we're worried about; it's his sledgehammer." [The whole group roared with laughter.]

Supervisor F: "Hell, the boss is like anyone else."

Supervisor E: "That's right; he drinks, he sleeps, and he eats."

Supervisor L: "As soon as he reads this report and wants to know something about it, he'll find out about it anyway."

Supervisor E: "Well, hell, fellows . . ."

Supervisor A: "Are we men or mice?" [The group again broke into laughter.]

The group never reached a decision as to what should be in the report. Finally, in the last few minutes they agreed to "allow" the research people to write a report and submit it to them for their approval before it was submitted to the Leader. They gave instructions that no specific problems, people, or incidents could be mentioned. As the meeting came to a close one of the supervisors said, "Just one thing; I'd like you research people to give us a 24-hour lead on him, because once he gets it, *he'll start popping questions!*"

Some days later, in the management smoking room after lunch, a group of supervisors and a research man were talking about the lack of cooperation in the plant, when another revealing incident occurred:

The discussion had reached the point where the various supervisors were citing examples of just how bad the cooperation was. Suddenly the Leader walked into the meeting. Everybody said hello to the Leader. Then a silence ensued; everybody waited for the Leader to say something. The wait was a short one. The Leader began to talk about the plant and some production problems. After a while the Leader turned to the research man and said: "You've been here for a long time. Tell me, and tell these other fellows, what you've learned, if you've learned anything."

The research man suggested that there might be room for improvements at certain spots. The Leader retorted: "What do you mean? We have good cooperation, don't we? Now you fellows be honest. Tell him, don't we have good cooperation?" The result was as expected. Not one supervisor answered in the negative.

The Leader left the scene convinced that the research man was "all wet." As soon as he left, all the supervisors left behind him. None seemed to "stick around" to continue talking with the research man. A little later one of the supervisors saw the Leader and told him that what the research man really was getting at was lack of coordination, not cooperation, and maybe what was needed was a planning coordinator

Not only were these supervisors keeping the real problems in the plant concealed from the Leader, but one of them in doing so tried to turn a basically human problem into a technical problem. One wonders how often that happens in industry.

Cooperation among supervisors

Previously we have seen instances of the lack of cooperation among the supervisors. Let us examine this problem more carefully so that we can relate it to the leadership pattern.

The Leader is directly in control. The supervisors learn to compete "diplomatically" with each other for the scarce rewards the Leader offers. Furthermore, the Leader continually emphasizes that each supervisor should worry about his own and primarily his own department. This policy is reinforced by the kind of accounting production, and other control records utilized by the organization.

As a result, the supervisors learn to become centered around the problems of their own department. They worry little about the over-all organizational problems. It is not difficult to see how the supervisors, working under such conditions for many years, find it difficult to work cooperatively. For example:

> *Supervisor B:* "Last week we had a government order, and in five days which included Saturday and Sunday they wanted the whole thing done. The order was duck soup to us, but it was tough. A lot of the other boys had problems with it."
>
> *Supervisor A:* "It was a dead duck—to us. That's the trouble around here; no one particularly gives a damn about the next guy."
>
> *Supervisor S:* "It wasn't my fault the order got messed up. So I try to pass the buck on to somebody else. The point is, where do you become a heel, and where don't you?"
>
> *Supervisor E:* "Are you complaining? We all got the same problems, haven't we?"

Not all the relationships among supervisors, however, exhibit a lack of cooperation. There are times when the supervisors work cooperatively and with a minimum of hostility. But the point is that these instances usually have nothing to do with achieving an organizational purpose. They are related to the supervisors' needs to know the disposition of the Leader. For example, there is an informal agreement among the supervisors that whoever "visits" with the Leader first in the morning will contact the others and inform them how the Leader feels and "what he's hot on today." Needless to say, this supervisor achieves quick communication to the rest of them.

Once each supervisor receives the information, he will check with his own subordinates. If the Leader seems to be worried about errors, all the supervisors emphasize the reduction of error in production; if they think the Leader is worried about production rates, they try to step up production; and so on.

The supervisors' dependence

One of the crucial results of the leadership pattern is the dependence of the supervisors on the Leader. The Leader is an indispensable link in the management of the organization. He is the sun; the supervisors are the satellites. Without him the cohesiveness and effectiveness of the supervisory group are greatly diminished. Here is an example:

The supervisors were attending a meeting called by the Leader. The Leader, in his usual manner, informed the supervisors that a drastic error had been made. As a result of the error, the customer was returning all of the merchandise. The plant had to rework the order.

A supervisor, with an eye to the Leader's desires, suggested that since the error budget was "way over," the supervisors themselves ought to work on the order. If they did, the plant would not have to pay overtime to the employees. The Leader agreed and requested volunteers. The supervisors as a group pledged a few evenings a week and Saturday all day for as long as needed to rework the order.

The first meeting of the supervisors was on the following Saturday. All were there. The task they had to perform was not difficult; it involved nothing more than sorting out the work, and the engineering department had set up some simple measuring devices. *But the Leader was not present.*

There was so much disagreement as to the best method for going about the job that hardly any work at all was done that day. The supervisors became irritated with each other. Each tried to tell the other, "Let's get at this; the earlier we begin, the earlier we finish." One supervisor remarked later: "I'll tell you why no work was done. It's because these supervisors are *independent* people. They're not used to taking orders. If we want results, we should say, "Okay, here it is, you guys; do it this way; don't ask any questions!"

On Monday, when the report of the lack of production reached the Leader, he instructed all supervisors to come to the plant that evening. That evening, he told the supervisors that he was sorry things didn't work out. He pleaded with them to work together as a team. He announced that he would work with "the gang" and the firm would buy them all a big steak dinner as soon as the job was done. The supervisors responded with a few loud cheers; and with the Leader "in the lead," they worked steadily for the succeeding four hours.

The next few evening sessions were extremely productive. Suddenly, on Saturday morning, the Leader announced that he had to fly to Washington for a new government order and therefore would not be able to work with them the following week. He reminded them of the fine work they had done as a team and ended by recalling the steak awaiting them "at the end of the road."

The inevitable happened. The first meeting after the Leader left was attended by only three-fourths of the supervisors. Two sessions later the attendance had dwindled down to two supervisors. All supervisors, except these two, suddenly found themselves with "sick wives," "sick children," "wife's folks in town," or "just plumb beat out."

It is interesting to note who the two faithful attenders were. One was a man who was doing his best to make a good impression so that he could climb the organizational ladder. The other perceived himself as the most "needled" supervisor in the plant; he hoped that the Leader would now realize who *really* was loyal to the company and proceeded to prepare a secret attendance report to present to the Leader upon his return.

Relations with employees

Are supervisor-employee relationships affected by the leadership pattern? Do the supervisors try to lead their employees in the same way as the Leader leads them? We might expect that they would, since the Leader rewards and perpetuates those supervisors who tend to express a leadership pattern similar to his own, and since it is a well-established psychological fact that if people cannot give vent to their pent-up feelings in relation to their superiors, they tend to do so in relation to their subordinates.

But actually things do not work out that way. There appear to be four reasons why:

1. The supervisors have so many employees under them that the constant, close interaction required in such a leadership pattern is not possible.
2. The supervisors are directly dependent on their employees to achieve the goals of the work-flow process. They cannot encourage the same kind of informal activities that they use themselves to express their pent-up feelings. Moreover, the employees, unlike the supervisors, have a union to turn to if they are dissatisfied.
3. For a leader to make his supervisors as dependent as they are requires substantial authority over the reward-and-penalty process. Although the Leader has such control over supervisors, the supervisors do not have it over their workers because of (a) the centralization of hiring, firing, and salary increases in the personnel department and (b) the rise of the union in the plant.
4. The conditions characteristic of the Leader's relations with the supervisors are completely against the union's philosophy. For example, the union through its contract does not permit complete unilateral control of all the formal processes by management. Moreover, it refuses to permit the employees to be treated individually and secretly; a shop steward must always be present. Placing the employees in competition with each other is also outlawed. Furthermore, the union attempts to obtain the employees' loyalty to the union goals, values, and demands; sole and complete loyalty to management is fought by every possible means. Finally, one of the union's battle cries has been the necessity for individual personality expression on the part of the workers.

Even so, there is ample evidence that the supervisors *on occasion* behave as the Leader does. If an employee has a poor production record, or if he is a trouble-maker, or if he is simply "a nuisance," the supervisors can be observed to "tear into him."

The fact remains, however, that for the most part the supervisors are careful and cautious lest they have a grievance on their hands. Many of the supervisors have stated spontaneously at some time, "You can't be like the boss and get the work out of the boys on the line."

Supervisors' morale

The picture presented of the supervisors' world might make us believe that no one would want to be a supervisor in this company. Conflict, tension, frustration, aggression seem prevalent. The question may be asked, "How do the supervisors feel about the situation—are they unhappy, do they dislike the Leader?"

The answer to this question is definitely *no*. As a matter of fact, the supervisors express admiration for the Leader. They believe he is an excellent administrator—"one of the best in the business," to quote a typical comment. While they realize that his leadership pattern cannot be used by them with the front-line employees, nevertheless they seem to feel the Leader must act the way he does. At times, some express resentment over the fact that the Leader may take their ideas and make them his own, but even these supervisors are quick to suggest that this may indeed be the test of a good administrator. An effective leader listens to ideas, picks the best ones, and puts them into action.

How can the supervisors have such an opinion of a leader who, from their point of view, places them in some very unhappy situations? In the next few pages, I shall attempt to outline several important explanations (still tentative, pending further controlled research).

DEFENSE MECHANISMS

The supervisors are unconscious of the effects the leadership pattern has upon them. They do not realize that many of their tensions arise from the leadership pattern and the plant conditions related to the pattern.

This does not mean that the supervisors are insensitive to the world around them. I am not implying that they are blind to the Leader's disadvantages. What I am suggesting is that these negative conditions have become so much a part of their world that they are unable to see clearly the causes for these conditions. This is not unusual. In fact, it is a technique frequently used by people to adapt to a negative situation.

All healthy personalities are able to adapt to negative conditions by a device known as a "defense mechanism." [5] Defense mechanisms are psychological processes which the person can use to defend his picture of himself. By putting them into action, the person (a) distorts reality in such a way that it does not affect him too seriously and (b) is able to "drain off" a lot of inner conflict, tension, and frustration rather unconsciously. Four of the most often used defense mechanisms found to be operating among the supervisors here are repression, rationalization, projection, and sublimation.

Repression

Briefly, repression is the forcing down into our unconscious of those conflicts, tensions, and frustrations (and usually their causes) that annoy us very much.

An indication that the supervisors repress their underlying tensions is shown by the many times each has been recorded as stating he is "fed up" and wishes he could "get away for a few days." In this case the inner tensions that prevented expression are beginning to accumulate within, and the person feels "down and out."

Another indication of repressed feelings is the fact that some supervisors "blow up" at the slightest provocation. After they have "blown their top," they admit that they "can't see why they got so excited" and usually close the matter with, "Well, who cares, I feel better now." These men have less control over their deeper feelings than those who hold their feelings back until they become "tired" and "fed up"—and have to take a day off. They let the "breaking point" creep up on them to such a degree that even a "little" occurrence makes them explode. But the fact that they do not take as many days off shows that they have released their tensions.

An interesting by-product is that, since the majority of the supervisors repress rather than express their feelings, they tend to be cautious in their interactions with the "touchy fellows." Consequently, much direct and straightforward communication is inhibited.

Rationalization

Another often-used defense mechanism is rationalization. Rationalization occurs when we invent some excuse (acceptable to our own

[5] Chris Argyris, *Personality Fundamentals for Administrators: An Introduction for the Layman* (New Haven, Yale Labor and Management Center, 1952), Chapter VI.

personality) to cover up our failure in a situation or to cover up our inability to accept something. For example, many supervisors remark, "Life is tough, but isn't that true all over?" or, "Such is life; this atomic age is going to send us all to hell." Thus the supervisors excuse their own conflicts and tensions by saying that this is the way life is.

As a result of these constant rationalizations, an interesting development takes place. Since tension is "natural," one begins to expect it. As a supervisor builds up more and more expectation of tension, the existing tension becomes seemingly less. This is true because his tolerance for tension is now higher. Thus, for a supervisor to sense as much tension as he is accustomed to, the existing tension would have to increase. Similarly, when people who expect to be disappointed are disappointed, the disappointment seems less than expected. Here is another reason why the tension in the plant is less noticeable to the supervisor than to an outsider.

Moreover, since tension is "natural," it no longer produces an urge on the part of the supervisors to want to change the situation. This resignation to tension naturally helps maintain the status quo—tension—and this leads to another rationalization relating to the necessity for strong leadership. Since the world is full of troubles, there is a need for strong leadership. Thus we have a situation where an acceptable reason for strong leadership arises from the tension and conflict which, in the first place, is partially created by that strong leadership!

Projection

The third defense mechanism is projection. By projection I mean avoiding blame or ascribing responsibility to other persons or things, while ignoring one's own part in the problem.

Here, for example, many of the problems we have seen are projected on the salesmen; it is their fault that so many problems occur, since they are interested in only one thing—more sales. The production control and the cost and budget control people also receive a substantial part of the projection. Production control people, according to the supervisors, are always "bungling up the planning," while the budget and cost personnel are simply disliked people who have their "clutches of death" on all.[6]

Another factor blamed for all the supervisors' troubles is that some of the products they manufacture are custom-made and extremely

[6] For a more detailed discussion of the human problem created by budgets see Chris Argyris, *Impact of Budgets on People* (New York, Controllership Foundation, 1951); or, in more condensed form, "Human Problems with Budgets," *Harvard Business Review*, January-February, 1953, p. 97.

complicated. Custom-made products, the supervisors explain, are extremely difficult, since the customers' personal idiosyncrasies and desires affect almost all the stages of production.

Sublimation

The fourth mechanism is sublimation. This occurs when the individual unconsciously channels his negative feelings into other forms of expression. These tensions are then permitted to return to the conscious self, but are now expressed in a different and usually more acceptable manner. Thus some of the supervisors give vent to their tensions by working extremely hard and trying to manifest aggressive and dominating leadership. Still others express the tension by being completely passive and withdrawn.

Those who adjust by taking on a more aggressive leadership pattern insist that the reason they are aggressive is because they "have to be or the work would never get done." They further insist that the employees are inherently lazy and only the supervisors really work hard on the job. No one, they continue, worries as much about the department as they do. (Note the similarity of this rationalization to the one used by the Leader as one of his reasons for the necessity of a "needling" leadership pattern.)

Those who adjust by becoming passive and withdrawn, on the other hand, tend to complain of the "damn tension in the business." Once this first feeling is expressed, they usually continue by complaining about "some of the apple polishers who run around hell-bent-for-election acting as if they run the whole outfit." Then they will admit confidentially that they are beginning to wonder if all this pressure really is necessary. In other words, they have become psychologically tired of the plant situation and have taken on a passive role simply to prevent it from affecting them further.

I ought to add that the existing interdepartmental "cold wars" also offer unusually good opportunity for the supervisors unconsciously to channel and express their negative feelings.

BUILT-IN DEPENDENCY

The point is that somehow the supervisors are able to think very highly of their Leader. They admire him, emulate him, and unhesitantly admit that he is responsible for many of the improvements in the plant. Moreover, they are not glum; they do not go around with long faces; they do not continually gripe. Their plant, they proudly proclaim, is as good a place to work in as any they know of. If tension is great, or even damaging, they are not worried about it. They are doing a good job. Their plant has the best profit and efficiency record in the entire organization. There is little question in their minds but that, all things considered, "We're working in the best damn place in the world, under the greatest guy in the world."

Perhaps all modern industrial organizations based upon such principles as "unity of command" and "task specialization" automatically place subordinates in a dependency relationship with their leader. In other words, no matter what type of personality an administrator has, perhaps his subordinates would always feel a certain degree of dependence on him.

I am at the moment conducting new research in another organization and with another leader. This leader's pattern of leadership is quite different from the one discussed in this article. But the type of organization is the same. I find that subordinates there also report that they feel dependent on their leader and, even though they have learned to hide it from him, they feel leader-centered. Finally, they admit that there exists hostility, competition, and buck passing among themselves.

Because of the possibility (still not proved) that dependency of the subordinates toward an administrator may be a built-in feature of modern industrial organization generally, I would like to suggest that *part* of the dependence on the Leader that the supervisors feel here is created by the make-up of the organization. Certainly, as we have seen, the supervisors do not blame the Leader; in fact, all of them feel that the Leader's leadership pattern is inevitably the kind that is rewarded by management in general. Although they do not feel they can be as go-getting, needling, active, and energetic as the Leader, they *wish* they could. They definitely state that in their experience it is this type of leadership that will help them advance in the kind of world in which they work.

Conclusion

This article is based upon the study of one leader. I do not know, nor am I claiming, that this leadership pattern is typical of a substantial number of executives. But I do say that to the extent executive leadership in America is as we describe it, then it seems wise to ask ourselves some questions. In doing so, we must keep in mind that, by all conventional efficiency standards, our Leader is extremely successful. A substantial share of the high profits, the low production errors, the low production waste, the high production efficiency, and the relatively low absenteeism may all be clearly attributed to him. He has created a financially healthy organization; he continues to maintain it that way.

These are the questions I would raise:

1. Should we not be more careful in our insistence that subordinates show creativity, initiative, and individualism if the very make-up of the organization tends to lead them to experience dependence and submissiveness? Whom are we fooling when we *write* and *talk* about "creative management" as long as our employees *experience* a different state of affairs?

2. What about the great emphasis on democratic or participative management? Can we really expect our subordinates to be spontaneously and freely participative in groups if, by the very nature of the situation in which we place them, they are led to be dependent and leader-centered?

3. In view of the high morale and financially healthy organization that developed under our Leader, would the "milk-toast" human relations methods advocated by some writers have effected the same favorable situation? Does this mean it is preferable for administrators to be swift and to the point and sometimes even ruthless, rather than to be easy and considerate?

4. Was the top executive right who one time told me that he picked his executives on the basis of ulcers (those who have them get the jobs; those who don't wait until they do)?

5. What kind of organization and what kind of leadership do we need to minimize submission, dependence, and leader-centeredness and to maximize organizational growth and individual expression and creativity?

I certainly do not have the answers to these questions. I am uncertain about the questions themselves. But I do feel strongly that there is something basically tragic about the response these hardworking supervisors gave when they asked themselves whether they were "men or mice." They just laughed.

44. HOW TO CHOOSE A
LEADERSHIP PATTERN [1]

Robert Tannenbaum [2]
Warren H. Schmidt [3]

❦ *"I put most problems into my group's hands and leave it to them to carry the ball from there. I serve merely as a catalyst, mirroring back the people's thoughts and feelings so that they can better understand them."*

❦ *"It's foolish to make decisions oneself on matters that affect people. I always talk things over with my subordinates, but I make it clear to them that I'm the one who has to have the final say."*

❦ *"Once I have decided on a course of action, I do my best to sell my ideas to my employees."*

❦ *"I'm being paid to lead. If I let a lot of other people make the decisions I should be making, then I'm not worth my salt."*

❦ *"I believe in getting things done. I can't waste time calling meetings. Someone has to call the shots around here, and I think it should be me."*

Each of these statements represents a point of view about "good leadership." Considerable experience, factual data, and theoretical principles could be cited to support each statement, even though they seem to be inconsistent when placed together. Such contradictions point up the dilemma in which the modern manager frequently finds himself.

[1] From *Harvard Business Review* (March-April, 1958), pp. 95-101. Reprinted by permission of Robert Tannenbaum, Warren H. Schmidt, and *Harvard Business Review*.
[2] Robert Tannenbaum, Professor of Personnel Management, Institute of Industrial Relations, University of California at Los Angeles.
[3] Warren H. Schmidt, Professor of Personnel Management, Human Relations Research Group, University of California at Los Angeles.

New Problem

The problem of how the modern manager can be "democratic" in his relations with subordinates and at the same time maintain the necessary authority and control in the organization for which he is responsible has come into focus increasingly in recent years.

Earlier in the century this problem was not so acutely felt. The successful executive was generally pictured as possessing intelligence, imagination, initiative, the capacity to make rapid (and generally wise) decisions, and the ability to inspire subordinates. People tended to think of the world as being divided into "leaders" and "followers."

New focus

Gradually, however, from the social sciences emerged the concept of "group dynamics" with its focus on *members* of the group rather than solely on the leader. Research efforts of social scientists underscored the importance of employee involvement and participation in decision making. Evidence began to challenge the efficiency of highly directive leadership, and increasing attention was paid to problems of motivation and human relations.

Through training laboratories in group development that sprang up across the country, many of the newer notions of leadership began to exert an impact. These training laboratories were carefully designed to give people a first-hand experience in full participation and decision making. The designated "leaders" deliberately attempted to reduce their own power and to make group members as responsible as possible for setting their own goals and methods within the laboratory experience.

It was perhaps inevitable that some of the people who attended the training laboratories regarded this kind of leadership as being truly "democratic" and went home with the determination to build fully participative decision making into their own organizations. Whenever their bosses made a decision without convening a staff meeting, they tended to perceive this as authoritarian behavior. The true symbol of democratic leadership to some was the meeting—and the less directed from the top, the more democratic it was.

Some of the more enthusiastic alumni of these training laboratories began to get the habit of categorizing leader behavior as "democratic" *or* "authoritarian." The boss who made too many decisions himself was thought of as an authoritarian, and his directive behavior was often attributed solely to his personality.

New need

The net result of the research findings and of the human relations training based upon them has been to call into question the stereotype of an effective leader. Consequently, the modern manager often finds himself in an uncomfortable state of mind.

Often he is not quite sure how to behave; there are times when he is torn between exerting "strong" leadership and "permissive" leadership. Sometimes new knowledge pushes him in one direction ("I should really get the group to help make this decision"), but at the same time his experience pushes him in another direction ("I really understand the problem better than the group and therefore I should make the decision"). He is not sure when a group decision is really appropriate or when holding a staff meeting serves merely as a device for avoiding his own decision-making responsibility.

The purpose of our article is to suggest a framework which managers may find useful in grappling with this dilemma. First we shall look at the different patterns of leadership behavior that the manager can choose from in relating himself to his subordinates. Then we shall turn to some of the questions suggested by this range of patterns. For instance, how important is it for a manager's subordinates to know what type of leadership he is using in a situation? What factors should he consider in deciding on a leadership pattern? What difference do his long-run objectives make as compared to his immediate objectives?

EXHIBIT 1

CONTINUUM OF LEADERSHIP BEHAVIOR

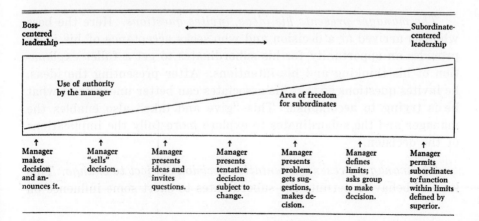

Range of Behavior

Exhibit I presents the continuum or range of possible leadership behavior available to a manager. Each type of action is related to the degree of authority used by the boss and to the amount of freedom available to his subordinates in reaching decisions. The actions seen on the extreme left characterize the manager who maintains a high degree of control while those seen on the extreme right characterize the manager who releases a high degree of control. Neither extreme is absolute; authority and freedom are never without their limitations.

Now let us look more closely at each of the behavior points occurring along this continuum.

The manager makes the decision and announces it. In this case the boss identifies a problem, considers alternative solutions, chooses one of them, and then reports this decision to his subordinates for implementation. He may or may not give consideration to what he believes his subordinates will think or feel about his decision; in any case, he provides no opportunity for them to participate directly in the decision-making process. Coercion may or may not be used or implied.

The manager "sells" his decision. Here the manager, as before, takes responsibility for identifying the problem and arriving at a decision. However, rather than simply announcing it, he takes the additional step of persuading his subordinates to accept it. In doing so, he recognizes the possibility of some resistance among those who will be faced with the decision, and seeks to reduce this resistance by indicating, for example, what the employees have to gain from his decision.

The manager presents his ideas, invites questions. Here the boss who has arrived at a decision and who seeks acceptance of his ideas provides an opportunity for his subordinates to get a fuller explanation of his thinking and his intentions. After presenting the ideas, he invites questions so that his associates can better understand what he is trying to accomplish. This "give and take" also enables the manager and the subordinates to explore more fully the implications of the decision.

The manager presents a tentative decision subject to change. This kind of behavior permits the subordinates to exert some influence on the decision. The initiative for identifying and diagnosing the problem remains with the boss. Before meeting with his staff, he has thought the problem through and arrived at a decision—but only a a tentative one. Before finalizing it, he presents his proposed solution for the reaction of those who will be affected by it. He says in effect, "I'd like to hear what you have to say about this plan that I have developed. I'll appreciate your frank reactions, but will reserve for myself the final decision."

The manager presents the problem, gets suggestions, and then makes his decision. Up to this point the boss has come before the group with a solution of his own. Not so in this case. The subordinates now get the first chance to suggest solutions. The manager's initial role involves identifying the problem. He might, for example, say something of this sort: "We are faced with a number of complaints from newspapers and the general public on our service policy. What is wrong here? What ideas do you have for coming to grips with this problem?"

The function of the group becomes one of increasing the manager's repertory of possible solutions to the problem. The purpose is to capitalize on the knowledge and experience of those who are on the "firing line." From the expanded list of alternatives developed by the manager and his subordinates, the manager then selects the solution that he regards as most promising.[4]

The manager defines the limits and requests the group to make a decision. At this point the manager passes to the group (possibly including himself as a member) the right to make decisions. Before doing so, however, he defines the problem to be solved and the boundaries within which the decision must be made.

An example might be the handling of a parking problem at a plant. The boss decides that this is something that should be worked on by the people involved, so he calls them together and points up the existence of the problem. Then he tells them:

> There is the open field just north of the main plant which has been designated for additional employee parking. We can build underground or surface multilevel facilities as long as the cost does not exceed $100,000. Within these limits we are free to work out whatever

[4] For a fuller explanation of this approach, see Leo Moore, "Too Much Management, Too Little Change," *Harvard Business Review* (January-February, 1956), p. 41.

solution makes sense to us. After we decide on a specific plan, the company will spend the available money in whatever way we indicate.

The manager permits the group to make decisions within prescribed limits. This represents an extreme degree of group freedom only occasionally encountered in formal organizations, as, for instance, in many research groups. Here the team of managers or engineers undertakes the identification and diagnosis of the problem, develops alternative procedures for solving it, and decides on one or more of these alternative solutions. The only limits directly imposed on the group by the organization are those specified by the superior of the team's boss. If the boss participates in the decision-making process, he attempts to do so with no more authority than any other member of the group. He commits himself in advance to assist in implementing whatever decision the group makes.

Key Questions

As the continuum in Exhibit I demonstrates, there are a number of alternative ways in which a manager can relate himself to the group or individuals he is supervising. At the extreme left of the range, the emphasis is on the manager—on what *he* is interested in, how *he* sees things, how *he* feels about them. As we move toward the subordinate-centered end of the continuum, however, the focus is increasingly on the subordinates—on what *they* are interested in, how *they* look at things, how *they* feel about them.

When business leadership is regarded in this way, a number of questions arise. Let us take four of especial importance.

Can a boss ever relinquish his responsibility by delegating it to someone else? Our view is that the manager must expect to be held responsible by his superior for the quality of the decisions made, even though operationally these decisions may have been made on a group basis. He should, therefore, be ready to accept whatever risk is involved whenever he delegates decision-making power to his subordinates. Delegation is not a way of "passing the buck." Also, it should be emphasized that the amount of freedom the boss gives to his subordinates cannot be greater than the freedom which he himself has been given by his own superior.

Should the manager participate with his subordinates once he has delegated responsibility to them? The manager should carefully think over this question and decide on his role prior to involving the subordinate group. He should ask if his presence will inhibit or facilitate the problem-solving process. There may be some instances when he should leave the group to let it solve the problem for itself. Typically, however, the boss has useful ideas to contribute, and should function as an additional member of the group. In the latter instance, it is important that he indicate clearly to the group that he sees himself in a *member* role rather than in an authority role.

How important is it for the group to recognize what kind of leadership behavior the boss is using? It makes a great deal of difference. Many relationship problems between boss and subordinate occur because the boss fails to make clear how he plans to use his authority. If, for example, he actually intends to make a certain decision himself, but the subordinate group gets the impression that he has delegated this authority, considerable confusion and resentment are likely to follow. Problems may also occur when the boss uses a "democratic" facade to conceal the fact that he has already made a decision which he hopes the group will accept as its own. The attempt to "make them think it was their idea in the first place" is a risky one. We believe that it is highly important for the manager to be honest and clear in describing what authority he is keeping and what role he is asking his subordinates to assume in solving a particular problem.

Can you tell how "democratic" a manager is by the number of decisions his subordinates make? The sheer *number* of decisions is not an accurate index of the amount of freedom that a subordinate group enjoys. More important is the *significance* of the decisions which the boss entrusts to his subordinates. Obviously a decision on how to arrange desks is of an entirely different order from a decision involving the introduction of new electronic data-processing equipment. Even though the widest possible limits are given in dealing with the first issue, the group will sense no particular degree of responsibility. For a boss to permit the group to decide equipment policy, even within rather narrow limits, would reflect a greater degree of confidence in them on his part.

Deciding How to Lead

Now let us turn from the types of leadership that are possible in a company situation to the question of what types are *practical* and *desirable*. What factors or forces should a manager consider in deciding how to manage? Three are of particular importance:

1. Forces in the manager.
2. Forces in the subordinates.
3. Forces in the situation.

We should like briefly to describe these elements and indicate how they might influence a manager's action in a decision-making situation.[5] The strength of each of them will, of course, vary from instance to instance, but the manager who is sensitive to them can better assess the problems which face him and determine which mode of leadership behavior is most appropriate for him.

Forces in the manager

The manager's behavior in any given instance will be influenced greatly by the many forces operating within his own personality. He will, of course, perceive his leadership problems in a unique way on the basis of his background, knowledge, and experience. Among the important internal forces affecting him will be the following:

1. *His value system.* How strongly does he feel that individuals should have a share in making the decisions which affect them? Or, how convinced is he that the official who is paid to assume responsibility should personally carry the burden of decision making? The strength of his convictions on questions like these will tend to move the manager to one end or the other of the continuum shown in Exhibit I. His behavior will also be influenced by the relative importance that he attaches to organizational efficiency, personal growth of subordinates, and company profits.[6]
2. *His confidence in his subordinates.* Managers differ greatly in the amount of trust they have in other people generally, and this carries over to the particular employees they supervise at a given time. In viewing his particular group of subordinates, the manager is likely to consider their knowledge and competence with respect to the problem. A central question he might ask himself is: "Who is best qualified to deal with this problem?" Often he may, justifiably or not, have more confidence in his own capabilities than in those of his subordinates.
3. *His own leadership inclinations.* There are some managers who seem to function more comfortably and naturally as highly directive lead-

    [5] See also Robert Tannenbaum and Fred Massarik, "Participation by Subordinates in the Managerial Decision-Making Process," *Canadian Journal of Economics and Political Science* (August, 1950), pp. 413-418.
    [6] See Chris Argyris, "Top Management Dilemma: Company Needs vs. Individual Development," *Personnel* (September, 1955), pp. 123-134.

ers. Resolving problems and issuing orders come easily to them. Other managers seem to operate more comfortably in a team role, where they are continually sharing many of their functions with their subordinates.

4. *His feelings of security in an uncertain situation.* The manager who releases control over the decision-making process thereby reduces the predictability of the outcome. Some managers have a greater need than others for predictability and stability in their environment. This "tolerance for ambiguity" is being viewed increasingly by psychologists as a key variable in a person's manner of dealing with problems.

The manager brings these and other highly personal variables to each situation he faces. If he can see them as forces which, consciously or unconsciously, influence his behavior, he can better understand what makes him prefer to act in a given way. And understanding this, he can often make himself more effective.

Forces in the subordinate

Before deciding how to lead a certain group, the manager will also want to consider a number of forces affecting his subordinates' behavior. He will want to remember that each employee, like himself, is influenced by many personality variables. In addition, each subordinate has a set of expectations about how the boss should act in relation to him (the phrase "expected behavior" is one we hear more and more often these days at discussions of leadership and teaching). The better the manager understands these factors, the more accurately he can determine what kind of behavior on his part will enable his subordinates to act most effectively.

Generally speaking, the manager can permit his subordinates greater freedom if the following essential conditions exist:

1. If the subordinates have relatively high needs for independence. (As we all know, people differ greatly in the amount of direction that they desire.)
2. If the subordinates have a readiness to assume responsibility for decision making. (Some see additional responsibility as a tribute to their ability; others see it as "passing the buck.")
3. If they have a relatively high tolerance for ambiguity. (Some employees prefer to have clear-cut directives given to them; others prefer a wider area of freedom.)
4. If they are interested in the problem and feel that it is important.
5. If they understand and identify with the goals of the organization.
6. If they have the necessary knowledge and experience to deal with the problem.
7. If they have learned to expect to share in decision making. (Persons who have come to expect strong leadership and are then suddenly

confronted with the request to share more fully in decision making are often upset by this new experience. On the other hand, persons who have enjoyed a considerable amount of freedom resent the boss who begins to make all the decisions himself.)

The manager will probably tend to make fuller use of his own authority if the above conditions do *not* exist; at times there may be no realistic alternative to running a "one-man show."

The restrictive effect of many of the forces will, of course, be greatly modified by the general feeling of confidence which subordinates have in the boss. Where they have learned to respect and trust him, he is free to vary his behavior. He will feel certain that he will not be perceived as an authoritarian boss on those occasions when he makes decisions by himself. Similarly, he will not be seen as using staff meetings to avoid his decision-making responsibility. In a climate of mutual confidence and respect, people tend to feel less threatened by deviations from normal practice, which in turn makes possible a higher degree of flexibility in the whole relationship.

Forces in the situation

In addition to the forces which exist in the manager himself and in his subordinates, certain characteristics of the general situation will also affect the manager's behavior. Among the more critical environmental pressures that surround him are those which stem from the organization, the work group, the nature of the problem, and the pressures of time. Let us look briefly at each of these.

Type of organization. Like individuals, organizations have values and traditions which inevitably influence the behavior of the people who work in them. The manager who is a newcomer to a company quickly discovers that certain kinds of behavior are approved while others are not. He also discovers that to deviate radically from what is generally accepted is likely to create problems for him.

These values and traditions are communicated in many ways— through job descriptions, policy pronouncements, and public statements by top executives. Some organizations, for example, hold to the notion that the desirable executive is one who is dynamic, imaginative, decisive, and persuasive. Other organizations put more emphasis upon the importance of the executive's ability to work effectively with people—his human relations skills. The fact that his superiors have a defined concept of what the good executive should be will very likely push the manager toward one end or the other of the behavioral range.

In addition to the above, the amount of employee participation is influenced by such variables as the size of the working units, their geographical distribution, and the degree of inter- and intra-organizational security required to attain company goals. For example, the wide geographical dispersion of an organization may preclude a practical system of participative decision making, even though this would otherwise be desirable. Similarly, the size of the working units or the need for keeping plans confidential may make it necessary for the boss to exercise more control than would otherwise be the case. Factors like these may limit considerably the manager's ability to function flexibly on the continuum.

Group effectiveness. Before turning decision-making responsibility over to a subordinate group, the boss should consider how effectively its members work together as a unit.

One of the relevant factors here is the experience the group has had in working together. It can generally be expected that a group which has functioned for some time will have developed habits of cooperation and thus be able to tackle a problem more effectively than a new group. It can also be expected that a group of people with similar backgrounds and interests will work more quickly and easily than people with dissimilar backgrounds, because the communication problems are likely to be less complex.

The degree of confidence that the members have in their ability to solve problems as a group is also a key consideration. Finally, such group variables as cohesiveness, permissiveness, mutual acceptance, and commonality of purpose will exert subtle but powerful influence on the group's functioning.

The problem itself. The nature of the problem may determine what degree of authority should be delegated by the manager to his subordinates. Obviously he will ask himself whether they have the kind of knowledge which is needed. It is possible to do them a real disservice by assigning a problem that their experience does not equip them to handle.

Since the problems faced in large or growing industries increasingly require knowledge of specialists from many different fields, it might be inferred that the more complex a problem, the more anxious a manager will be to get some assistance in solving it. However, this is not always the case. There will be times when the very complexity of the problem calls for one person to work it out. For example, if the manager has most of the background and factual data relevant to a given issue, it may be easier for him to think it through himself than to take the time to fill in his staff on all the pertinent background information.

The key question to ask, of course, is: "Have I heard the ideas of everyone who has the necessary knowledge to make a significant contribution to the solution of this problem?"

The pressure of time. This is perhaps the most clearly felt pressure on the manager (in spite of the fact that it may sometimes be imagined). The more that he feels the need for an immediate decision, the more difficult it is to involve other people. In organizations which are in a constant state of "crisis" and "crash programing" one is likely to find managers personally using a high degree of authority with relatively little delegation to subordinates. When the time pressure is less intense, however, it becomes much more possible to bring subordinates in on the decision-making process.

These, then, are the principal forces that impinge on the manager in any given instance and that tend to determine his tactical behavior in relation to his subordinates. In each case his behavior ideally will be that which makes possible the most effective attainment of his immediate goal within the limits facing him.

Long-Run Strategy

As the manager works with his organization on the problems that come up day by day, his choice of a leadership pattern is usually limited. He must take account of the forces just described and, within the restrictions they impose on him, do the best that he can. But as he looks ahead months or even years, he can shift his thinking from tactics to large-scale strategy. No longer need he be fettered by all of the forces mentioned, for he can view many of them as variables over which he has some control. He can, for example, gain new insights or skills for himself, supply training for individual subordinates, and provide participative experiences for his employee group.

In trying to bring about a change in these variables, however, he is faced with a challenging question: At which point along the continuum *should* he act?

Attaining objectives

The answer depends largely on what he wants to accomplish. Let us suppose that he is interested in the same objectives that most modern managers seek to attain when they can shift their attention from the pressure of immediate assignments:

1. To raise the level of employee motivation.
2. To increase the readiness of subordinates to accept change.
3. To improve the quality of all managerial decisions.
4. To develop teamwork and morale.
5. To further the individual development of employees.

In recent years the manager has been deluged with a flow of advice on how best to achieve these longer-run objectives. It is little wonder that he is often both bewildered and annoyed. However, there are some guidelines which he can usefully follow in making a decision.

Most research and much of the experience of recent years give a strong factual basis to the theory that a fairly high degree of subordinate-centered behavior is associated with the accomplishment of the five purposes mentioned.[7] This does not mean that a manager should always leave all decisions to his assistants. To provide the individual or the group with greater freedom than they are ready for at any given time may very well tend to generate anxieties and therefore inhibit rather than facilitate the attainment of desired objectives. But this should not keep the manager from making a continuing effort to confront his subordinates with the challenge of freedom.

CONCLUSION

In summary, there are two implications in the basic thesis that we have been developing. The first is that the successful leader is one who is keenly aware of those forces which are most relevant to his behavior at any given time. He accurately understands himself, the individuals and group he is dealing with, and the company and broader social environment in which he operates. And certainly he is able to assess the present readiness for growth of his subordinates.

---

[7] For example, see Warren H. Schmidt and Paul C. Buchanan, *Techniques that Produce Teamwork* (New London: Arthur C. Croft Publications, 1954); and Morris S. Viteles, *Motivation and Morale in Industry* (New York: W. W. Norton & Company, Inc., 1953).

But this sensitivity or understanding is not enough, which brings us to the second implication. The successful leader is one who is able to behave appropriately in the light of these perceptions. If direction is in order, he is able to direct; if considerable participative freedom is called for, he is able to provide such freedom.

Thus, the successful manager of men can be primarily characterized neither as a strong leader nor as a permissive one. Rather, he is one who maintains a high batting average in accurately assessing the forces that determine what his most appropriate behavior at any given time should be and in actually being able to behave accordingly. Being both insightful and flexible, he is less likely to see the problems of leadership as a dilemma.

45. UNHUMAN ORGANIZATIONS [1]

Harold J. Leavitt [2]

The purpose of this article is to urge that we take another look at our beliefs about the place of people in organizations. They are beliefs that have matured, even oversolidified, in the 1940's and 1950's. And they are beliefs which, until the last couple of years, have seemed as safe and inviolate as the moon.

Let me emphasize from the start that although this article is a critique of our "human relations" emphasis on people, I am not worried about "manipulation," "group-think," "softness," "conformity," or any of the other recent criticisms. In fact, most theories and techniques of human relations are, to my mind, both sound and progressive. *The theme here is not that human relations theory is either incorrect or immoral. My argument is that it is simply insufficient. It is too narrow a perspective from which to analyze the management of organizations.* But I am not suggesting that we turn back to the earlier and even narrower beliefs of "tough" management. What we have to do is to push beyond the plateau of present beliefs, which are becoming too deeply ingrained among managers and social scientists. Such beliefs now hold:

1. That organizations are and ought to be in their essence *human* systems.
2. Therefore, that the management of organizations is and ought to be in its essence a process of coordinating human effort.
3. Implicitly, that the best organization is the one in which each member contributes up to his "full potential"; and that the best individual manager is he who has set up conditions which maximize the creativity and commitment of his people.
4. And that management is a *unified* rather than a *differentiated* process; i.e., that good management at one level or in one locale of an organization ought to be essentially the same as good management at any other level or locale in that or any other organization. This idea is so implicit, so seldom said aloud, that I cannot be perfectly sure it is really there.

[1] From *Harvard Business Review* (July-August, 1962), pp. 90-98. Reprinted by permission of the *Harvard Business Review*.
[2] Harold J. Leavitt, Professor of Industrial Management and Psychology, Graduate School of Industrial Administration, Carnegie Institute of Technology.

Incidentally, this fourth belief in some unifying essence was, I think, held to by earlier theorists about management, too. To early Taylorists, for example, "rationalization" of work was the pure essence of good management and was, in theory, applicable anywhere and everywhere from president to sweeper.

Participative Beliefs

For simplicity, let me refer to the first three of the above as "participative beliefs." They have one common integrating element —the idea that organizations are essentially human. It follows that we should begin our descriptions and analyses of organizations in human terms. They have a value element in common, too—a very strong one; i.e., not only are organizations best described in human units; they *ought* to be human. It is right, many of us believe, to think about organizations from a human point of view, because people *are* more important than anything. Moreover, we are blessed (according to these beliefs) by the happy coincidence that managerial practices which place human fulfillment first also happen to be the most efficient and productive practices.

I can offer no definitive evidence to prove that these beliefs are not straw men. It may be they are not really widely shared by social scientists, managers, consultants, and personnel people. If that should be the case, and they are only fat red herrings, then our re-examination may help to destroy them.

Reasons for re-examination

I urge that these beliefs be re-examined not so much because they are wrong, in any absolute sense, and certainly not because the beliefs that preceded them, especially the Tayloristic beliefs, were right. Essentially, the participative beliefs ought to be re-examined for two reasons.

1. *In so eagerly demolishing Taylorism we may have thrown out some useful parts of the baby with the bath water. We may even be repeating some of the mistakes of Taylorism that we have taken such pains to point out.*

Incidentally Taylor made himself almost too clear a target for those who came later. He had no trouble at all organizing all sorts of humanistic people against him by making statements like this:

Now one of the very first requirements for a man who is fit to handle pig iron . . . is that he shall be so stupid and so phlegmatic that he more nearly resembles . . . the ox than any other type. . . . he must consequently be trained by a man more intelligent than himself.[3]

Such antidemocratic pronouncements probably contributed back-handedly to the oversolidification of the participative beliefs. For while part of the participative target was to improve management practice, part of it was also to win the war against "inhuman" scientific management.

Though it is clear that Taylorism has had some large and unforeseen costs, it also seems clear that present-day Taylorism, i.e., the ideas and techniques of industrial engineering, continue to be viable and almost invariably present in American firms. Human resistance to the techniques has been a real problem, but not always an insurmountable or economically intolerable one. And partially with the naive help of social scientists, the costs of Taylorism (the slowdown, for instance) have often been eased enough by psychological palliatives (like suggestion systems) to warrant their continued use.

Moreover, we may have overshot, in condemning Taylorism, by *appearing*, at least, to be condemning any *differentiation* of organizations that separates out planning functions from performing functions. We have urged more participation, more involvement, but we have not been very explicit about how far we want to go toward the extreme of having everyone participate in everything all the time.

2. *We have new knowledge both from the information and communication sciences and the social sciences that may be applicable to organizational problems; and if we freeze on our present beliefs, we may not be able to incorporate that knowledge.*

Two relevant sets of ideas have been emerging over the last few years. One is the development of information technology, a science in which human beings need *not* be the fundamental unit of analysis. We cannot examine that in detail here.[4] The other set is the emerging findings from recent research on individual and group problem solving. This research in which human beings have indeed been the fundamental unit will be the subject of the rest of this discussion.

---

[3] Frederick W. Taylor, *Scientific Management* (New York: Harper & Brothers, 1911), p. 59.

[4] See Harold J. Leavitt and Thomas L. Whisler, "Management in the 1980's," *Harvard Business Review* (November-December, 1958), p. 41; or H. A. Simon, "The Corporation: Will It Be Managed by Machines?" in *Management and Corporations, 1985*, edited by M. L. Anshen and G. L. Bach (New York: McGraw-Hill Book Company, Inc., 1960).

Self-programming people

Some remarkably similar findings keep turning up in a number of different places. They look irrelevant at first, but I think they are really quite to the point. For instance, given a problem to solve, people try to develop a program that will solve not only the specific problem at hand but other problems of the same "class." If we give a true-false test, the subject not only tries to answer each question properly; he almost invariably sets up and checks out hypotheses about the order of true and false answers. If he hits the sequence "True, False, True, False," for example, he guesses that this is "really" an alternating series and predicts a "True" for the next one. This is a commonplace finding, known to baseball fans (i.e., the next pitch is "due" to be a fast ball) and gamblers and school kids, and even to social scientists.

The point, which I believe is as fundamental as many other points psychologists have made about the nature of man, is that humans have strong and apparently natural tendencies to program themselves. In many cases a "solution" to a problem is really a program for solving all problems of that class.

The second finding is that the challenge, the puzzle, the motivational impetus for the problem solver also stems in part from this same need—the need to develop a general program. Moreover, when such a general program is discovered, then any particular task within the program is likely to become trivial and uninteresting. When we "understand" tick-tack-toe, the game stops being much fun.

Here is an example from an experiment that will come up again later:

> Suppose we ask three people to play the "Common Target Game." [5] The three players are blindfolded and not allowed to talk with one another. At a signal from an instructor each is asked to put up any number of fingers. If each man puts up zero fingers, the sum of the three will of course be zero; and if each man puts up his maximum of ten, the total shown by the three will be 30.
>
> Given these rules, we now set up the following task. The instructor will call out some whole target number between zero and 30. The cooperative objective of the three players (without knowing what the

[5] Research with this "Common Target Game" was started by Alex Bavelas of Stanford University. For a recent paper on its use see Harold J. Leavitt, "Task Ordering and Organizational Development in the Common Target Game," *Behavioral Science* (July, 1960). Bavelas also inspired the communication experiment described later.

others have done) is to put up enough findings so that the sum of the fingers will add up exactly to the target number. Thus, if the instructor calls out the number 16, each player tries to hold enough fingers such that the three together hold up a total of 16. They are then told what they actually hit; and if they miss, they try again until they hit that target. Then they are given a new target.

If we play this game for a while and tune in on the players' thoughts, it turns out that each player is busily thinking up general systems for deciding how many fingers to hold up. Usually he says something like this to himself: "There are three of us. Therefore it is probably sensible to start by dividing each target number by three. If the target is 16, we should each take five to begin with. Then we will have to decide who will take the extra one that is left over." He then goes on to think up additional sets of rules by which these leftovers can be allocated.

But what he has done in effect is to say this: "Let us not treat each new target as a brand new problem. Let us instead classify all possible targets into three simple categories: (a) *targets evenly divisible by three*, e.g., 15; (b) *targets divisible by three with one left over*, e.g., 16; (c) *targets divisible by three with two left over*, e.g., 17." Our subject has now simplified the world by classifying all possible targets. No target is any longer novel and unique. It is now a member of one of these three classes.

Moreover, if the players can agree on one general program that permits them to hit targets on one trial, then they rapidly lose interest in the game—well before all targets have been tested. It is exciting, challenging, and disturbing only until a general program has been developed. Once they have developed it, the players can very easily instruct other people, or machines, to play the game according to the system they have developed.

These dual findings—programing oneself out of a challenging and novel situation, and then losing interest—keep showing up. And they keep reiterating the probably obvious point, so clearly observable in children, that people tend to reduce complexity to simplicity, and having done so find that the game isn't so much fun any more.

These findings lead me, very tentatively, to the generalization that high interest, high challenge, may be caused as much by the job at hand (is it already programed or not?) as by "participation." The players in our game participated fully—but they got bored when required routinely to operate their program, despite the fact that it was their own baby. The fun was in the making.

If we make a big jump, we can then ask: Is it reasonable to

think that we can, in the real world, maintain a continuously challenging "unprogramed" state for all members of an organization? . . . especially when members themselves are always searching for more complete programs? . . . and while the demands made upon the organization call for routine tasks like making the same part tomorrow, tomorrow, and tomorrow that was made today?

The answer to this question is not obvious. In fact we have all witnessed the frequent demand of groups of workers for more and more highly detailed job definitions, on the one hand, accompanied by more and more complaints about "deskilling," on the other. For instance, the airline pilot wants more and better ground-control programs to deal with increasing traffic; but once he gets them, he finds that the new programs also reduce the autonomy, the freedom, and the exercise of human judgment that make flying interesting.

Unhuman teachers

Consider next the development and application of teaching machines—those simple, unsophisticated, mechanical gadgets which ignore the complexities of people, and which use feedback principles that are almost primitive in their simplicity.

With them, if the evidence is correct, we can teach spelling faster than most human teachers can, and perhaps languages too. We can instruct workers in complex machine operation, and often thereby enlarge their jobs. And girls can be taught to wire complex circuits as well as experts do simply by providing them with a sequential series of diagrams projected on a screen at the work place. The girl can control the diagram, moving back two pictures or forward four. Teach her to solder, give her the materials, and she can do the job —fast.

Her job has been enlarged, for she now wires the whole circuit (50 or 60 hours' worth) instead of one small piece. But there is no human interaction here—no patient human teachers; no great involvement; not even very much learning. For the crutch of the teaching machine stays there—always. She can lean on the diagrams next year if she should still want to, and she probably will.

It is beguilingly easy to demean or disavow such gadgets, to relegate them to low-class teaching of routines. It is especially easy to sweep them aside if we have been raised in the tradition of the participative beliefs. For even more than in management these beliefs prevail in education. "Real" teaching is, by current definition, a *human* process. How then can we take seriously devices which completely bypass the human teacher, which are not even in the same ball park with those problems that are believed to be at the very center of the teaching process, i.e., teacher-student rapport, teacher understanding of student personality, student dependency on the teacher?

It is not so much that teaching machines directly threaten present beliefs about teaching; it is rather that they simply bypass large parts of those beliefs. By treating teaching, naively perhaps, as something other than a human relations process, one simply does not face problems, that arise as a consequence of human relationships.

Taking this view of things, one begins to wonder how many of the problems of teaching have been *caused* by the human teacher.

Which kind of structure?

A little over 12 years ago another area of research got under way at the Massachusetts Institute of Technology which dealt with communication nets and their effects on problem solving by groups. As this body of experimentation has built up, it too has added reason for uneasiness about the unshakability of the participative beliefs.

Let me review the experiments very quickly. They are quite simple in their conception and purpose. They ask how the structure of communication among members of a group affects the way that group solves a given problem.

Suppose, for example, we connect up groups of five men so that they may communicate *only* through the two-way channels represented by the lines shown below. We can then ask whether comparable groups, working on the same problem, will solve it "better" in Network I than in Network II or Network III.

The men are put in booths so that they cannot see one another, and then given this simple problem to solve:

Each man has a cup containing five marbles of different colors. Only *one* corresponding color marble appears in *all* of the cups. The

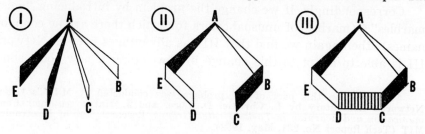

problem is to discover what that single color is, and to do it as fast as possible. Only written communications are allowed—only along the channels open in the particular network being tested. The job is not considered solved until all five men know what the common color is. The problem is used again and again for the same group in the same net, each time with new sets of marbles.

We can then measure the "efficiency" of each net by such factors as speed of problem solving, number of messages sent, number of errors made, clarity of organizational form, specificity of each job in the organization, and clarity of leadership. It turns out that on these simple tasks Network I is far more efficient than II, which in turn is more efficient than III. In other words, groups of individuals placed in Network I within a very few trials solve these problems in an orderly neat, quick, clear, well-structured way—with minimum messages. In Network III, comparable groups solve the same problems less quickly, less neatly, with less order, and with less clarity about individual jobs and the organizational structure—and they take more paper, too.

However, if we now ask members of these three networks to indicate how *happy* they are in their jobs, we get the reverse effect. Network III people are happier, on the average, than II or I people (though the *center* man in Network I is apt to be quite happy). But since we are concerned with effectiveness, we may argue that happiness is not very important anyway. So let us go on to some other possible criteria of organizational effectiveness: creativity and flexibility.

We find two interesting things. First, when a bright new idea for improvement of operations is introduced into each of these nets, the rapid acceptance of the new idea is more likely in III than in I. If a member of I comes up with the idea and passes it along, it is likely to be discarded (by the man in the middle) on the ground that he is too busy, or the idea is too hard to implement, or "We are doing O.K. already; don't foul up the works by trying to change everything!"

Correspondingly, if we change the problem by introducing "noisy marbles" [6] (marbles of unusual colors for which there are no common names), then again we find that III has advantages over I. Network III is able to adapt to this change by developing a new code, some

---

[6] Research on this part of the problem was conducted at M.I.T.'s Group Networks Laboratory by L. Christie, D. Luce, and J. Macy; see their *Communication and Learning in Task Oriented Groups*, Research Lab of Electronics, MIT (Tech Report No. 231, May, 1952).

agreed on a set of names for the colors. Network I seems to have much greater difficulty in adapting to this more abstract and novel job.

So by certain industrial engineering-type criteria (speed, clarity of organization and job descriptions, parsimonious use of paper, and so on), the highly routinized, noninvolving, centralized Network I seems to work best. *But* if our criteria of effectiveness are more ephemeral, more general (like acceptance of creativity, flexibility in dealing with novel problems, generally high morale, and loyalty), then the more egalitarian or decentralized Network III seems to work better.

What shall we conclude? Using the common "efficiency" criteria, the Taylorists are right. But these are narrow and inhuman, and if we use creativity and morale as criteria, modern participative beliefs are right. But are we also to conclude that the criteria of creativity and flexibility and morale are somehow *fundamentally* more important than speed and clarity and orderliness?

Or shall we (and I favor this conclusion) pragmatically conclude that if we want to achieve one kind of goal, then one kind of structure seems feasible? If we want other criteria to govern, then another structure may make sense. Certainly it is reasonable to guess that in the real (as distinct from the laboratory) world, there will be locations and times which might make one set of criteria more important than the other even within the same large organization.

But participative managers, myself once included, will immediately go back to the happiness issue that I treated so cavalierly a few paragraphs ago. They will counter by arguing that Network I cannot work long—for the growing resistance and low morale it generates in its members will eventually cause it to burst.

The evidence is negative. The *relative* importance of this resistance is apparently small. There seem to be fairly cheap ways of compensating for the low morale, yet still keeping the organization going efficiently. To the best of my capacity to speculate, and also the best of my knowledge from extended runs (60 trials) of Network I,[7] it can keep going indefinitely, highly programed and unchallenging as it is to most of its members. Moreover, we could probably automate Network I rather easily if we wanted to, and get rid of of the human factor altogether.

[7] A. M. Cohen, W. G. Bennis, and G. H. Wolkon, "The Effects of Continued Practice on the Behaviors of Problem Solving Groups," *Sociometry* (December, 1961).

Planned decisions

In the Common Target Game mentioned earlier—the little game in which three players hold up fingers to try to sum to a target—some other interestingly odd results turn up. For one thing, we find that the game is solved better with an asymmetric system of rewards. If we offer only one player in the group a personal bonus depending on the number of fingers he contributes, groups seem to perform better than if we offer no rewards to anybody or equal rewards to everybody. In fact, if we offer everyone a personal payoff (1 point per finger, say), so that each man gets a reward in accordance with the size of his contribution, performance is not very good but *learning* is very fast. There is evidence, in other words, that competitive groups learn how to solve the problem very quickly, but then refuse to solve it that way because they are so busy competing.

One more finding: If groups simply play the game cooperatively, without any special payoff system, they almost never come up with the one cleanest and simplest solution to it. If, however, we ask them to sit down and plan *how* to play it, they almost always do come up with that neat and elegant system. (The simple, neat solution: A takes everything from 0 to 10; B adds everything from 11 through 20; and so on.)

Tentatively, then, we have these mildly disturbing findings:

1. Differentiated groups (ones in which some members are rewarded differently from others) can perform better than undifferentiated groups—whether they be rewarded cooperatively only, or both cooperatively and competitively.
2. Competitively motivated groups learn faster than cooperative ones; but their corresponding performance is dampened by their competition.
3. Groups that "evolve" by working together directly on the problem come up with different, less clean, and less simple solutions than groups in which the planning and the performing phases of their activity are separated.

These results do not directly contradict any present ideas; but they suggest that manipulation of variables like competition or differentiation of roles may yield results we cannot easily fit into our well-organized and perhaps overly rigidified beliefs about the universal effectiveness of self-determination, wholehearted cooperation, and bottom-up planning.

What kinds of teams win?

Finally, in some research we have been doing recently with the complex year-long business game that has been developed at Carnegie Institute of Technology, another similar finding has turned up.[8] We found that those teams had the highest morale and also performed best in which there was the greatest *differentiation* of influence among team members. That is, teams whose players saw themselves as all about equally influential were less satisfied and made smaller profits than teams whose players agreed that some particular individuals were a good deal more influential than others.

Now bringing the influence problem in at this point may be another red herring. But the optimal distribution of influence, and of power that produces influence, has been one of the problems that has plagued us industrial social scientists for a long time. Does participative management mean, in its extreme form, equal distribution of power throughout the organization? If not, then how should power be distributed? What is a "democratic" distribution? What is an autocratic one? I fear that none of us has satisfactorily resolved these questions. We have made some soft statements, pointing out that participation does not mean that everyone does the same job, and that the president ought still to be the president. But our specifications have not been clear and consistent, and we have never made a very good theoretical case for any optimal differentiation of power within an organization.

Again the finding is antiegalitarian, and in favor of differentiation. Yet egalitarianism of both communication and of power is often assumed to produce, through the participative beliefs, involvement, commitment, and morale.

IDEA OF DIFFERENTIATION

So it is developments in these two areas—the information sciences and bits and pieces of organizational research—that should, I submit, stimulate us to start re-examining our beliefs about the role of people in organizations. Together these developments suggest that we need to become more analytical about organizations, to separate our values from our analyses more than we have up until now; that we need

---

[8] W. R. Dill, W. Hoffman, H. J. Leavitt, and T. O'Mara, "Experiences with a Complex Management Game," *California Management Review* (Spring, 1961), pp. 38-51.

also to take a more microscopic look at large organizations and to
allow for the possibility of *differentiating* several kinds of structures
and managerial practices within them.

Changes in this direction are, of course, already taking place
but mostly at the research level (as distinct from the level of applied
practice). In practice, participative management and the beliefs
that accompany it are clearly very much on the rise. Efforts to
promote more open communication across and up and down the
organization are visible everywhere. There is not a first-rate business
school in the country that does not place heavy emphasis on human
relations in industry, with its implicit assumption of the essential
role of people in problem solving. Although groups and committees
are still dirty words in some industrial quarters, they are not nearly
as dirty as they used to be. And certainly *decentralization* is an
acceptable idea for almost every educated American executive.

But it is worth pointing out that, even at the level of current
practice, participative ideas do not seem to be sweeping into the
organization uniformly. In general, we have been concentrating more
effort on developing participation at middle-management than at
hourly levels—the Scanlon plan notwithstanding. We train supervisors, study R & D groups, counsel top management, and run sensitivity training programs for management groups, all on a large
scale. Except for the Scanlon plan, it is not clear that we have moved
very much beyond the suggestion system on the hourly worker front.
But this is not because social scientists have not tried. They have tried
very hard to bring the hourly worker into such activities. Sometimes
they have been rebuffed by the workers or their unions, sometimes
by managerial unwillingness to indulge in such "risky" experiments.

This differential emphasis on middle management as opposed to
hourly workers is probably not a temporary accident. It represents, I
believe, a general trend toward differentiating management methods
at different organizational levels, roughly in accordance with the
"programedness" of the tasks that those levels perform. It represents
a new third approach to the problem of routinization and programing
of work.

The first approach was Taylor's: to routinize all work and, by
routinizing, to control it. The second, the participative approach, was
to strive to eliminate routine—to make all jobs challenging and novel.
I suggest that the third approach—the one we are drifting into—is
to do both: to routinize and control what we can; to loosen up and
make challenging what we cannot. In so doing we may end up being

efficient, and at once human and unhuman, depending on where, within the large organization, we choose to focus.

Consider, for example, recent thinking about the administration of research and development activities. Many observers have pointed up the growing tendency to free researchers, to deprogram them, to loosen their administrative bonds. Certainly the typical large and enlightened firm has moved in this direction, from a punch-the-time-clock attitude toward R & D (especially R) to looser controls and a freer environment.

What Does Change Mean?

I think most social scientists and personnel people have interpreted the change as a large breakthrough in the war against the whole tightly run autocracy of industrial organization. Loosening up of R & D, many feel, is just the first step toward loosening up the whole show. For our goal is not to eliminate the time clock in the lab; it is to eliminate all time clocks. The emancipated researchers is thus not a special case, but a model of the freedom that all members of an organization will ultimately enjoy.

This is a pleasant, democratic vision, but I don't believe it. Top management's willingness, under duress, to allow the R & D prima donna to behave like a prima donna can have another meaning. It can mean movement toward a more *differential* organization, with some parts of it very much loosened up while other parts become increasingly tight. While the creative researcher is being left free to create, the materials purchasing clerk must conform more tightly than ever to the new computer controlled program he has been handed.

I submit that the facts we have all observed fit together better when thus interpreted as signals of increasing differentiation.

By this third interpretation, we are not seeing in R & D the growth of participative management as such, but the growth of management-according-to-task; with the use of those administrative tools, participative or otherwise, that seem best adapted to the task at hand.

If this interpretation is correct, we should be seeing less and less uniformity in managerial practice; more of a class system, if you like—though a fluid one—in which the rules governing everything from hours of work to methods of evaluation to systems of compensation may vary from one group to another within the same parent organization. And, further, the many variations will be understandable in large part if one looks first at the tasks that each group is trying to accomplish, and secondly at the tools, psychological and technical, that are at the moment available for working on those tasks.

By this interpretation, too, growing differentiation should create some nasty problems in its own right. Differentiation should make for more problems of communication among sets of subgroups each governed by different rules. Mobility from one subgroup to another should become more difficult. And so on.

Let us, if you will permit me to press the point, suppose such problems do arise. What might we do to solve them? If we jump off from our participative beliefs, we move almost naturally toward a search for ways of increasing communication among groups, and opening mobility pathways as widely as possible. Jumping off from a more analytic base, however, we might stop and ask: Is communication among these groups useful? How much? For what? And how much mobility?

Perhaps only a thread of communication will be needed—perhaps no mobility across groups at all. But without further speculation I suggest that more and more we are differentiating classes and subclasses of tasks within organizations, so that questions about how much we use people, the kinds of people we use, and the kinds of rules within which we ask them to operate, all are being increasingly differentiated—largely in accordance with our ability to specify and program the tasks which need to be performed and in accordance with the kind of tools available to us.

CONCLUSION

The main purposes of this article, then, have been to ask for a re-examination of the "participative beliefs" about management, and to urge a consideration of the idea of differentiation.

In asking for a second look at the participative beliefs, I have tried not to associate myself with some others who are asking for the same thing but for quite different reasons. I do not want a return to tough management. Nor am I worried about groups replacing individuals. In my opinion the participative beliefs represent a great advance in management, one that needs now only to be placed in perspective.

In our eagerness over the last couple of decades to expand and test our new and exciting findings about participation, we may have made two serious but understandable and correctable mistakes: we have on occasion confused our observations with our values; and we have assumed that our participative beliefs represented the absolute zero of management—that there was no more basic level.

But though I believe in the values associated with the participative beliefs and in their great practical utility for solving huge present and future problems of human relationships, I ask that we try to fit them into the still broader perspective on organizations that is being generated out of the communication and systems sciences, and out of our rapidly growing understanding of the processes of thinking, organizing, and problem solving.

One way of setting these beliefs into a different perspective may be, I submit, by viewing large organizations as differentiated sets of subsystems rather than as unified wholes. Such a view leads us toward a management-by-task kind of outlook—with the recognition that many subparts of the organization may perform many different kinds of tasks, and therefore may call for many different kinds of managerial practices.

BIBLIOGRAPHY, CHAPTER XII

ARGYRIS, CHRIS. *Interpersonal Competence and Organizational Effectiveness.* Homewood, Illinois: The Dorsey Press, Inc., 1962.

DALTON, MELVILLE. *Men Who Manage.* New York: John Wiley & Sons, Inc., 1959.

HECKMAN, I. L., and S. G. HUNERYAGER. *Human Relations in Management.* Cincinnati: South-Western Publishing Co., Inc., 1960.

JENNNGS, E. E. *An Anatomy of Leadership.* New York: Harper & Brothers, 1960.

————————————. "Elements of Democratic Supervision," *Advanced Management* (October, 1954), 19-22.

LAWRENCE, PAUL R. "How to Deal with Resistance to Change," *Harvard Business Review* (May-June, 1954), 49-57.

LIKERT, RENSIS. *New Patterns of Management.* New York: McGraw-Hill Book Company, Inc., 1961.

McGREGOR, DOUGLAS. *The Human Side of Enterprise.* New York: McGraw-Hill Book Company, Inc., 1960.

MOORE, LEO B. "Too Much Management Too Little Change," *Harvard Business Review,* Vol. 34, No. 1 (January-February, 1956), 41-48.

ODIORNE, GEORGE S. "How Do Managers Make Things Happen?" *Michigan Business Review* (November, 1961), 25-29.

PRENTICE, W. C. H. "Understanding Leadership," *Harvard Business Review* (September-October, 1961), 143-157.

SCOTT, WILLIAM. *Human Relations in Management.* Homewood, Illinois: Richard D. Irwin, Inc., 1962.

SUMMER, CHARLES E., JR. "The Managerial Mind," *Harvard Business Review* (January-February, 1959), 69-78.

WALKER, CHARLES R. *Modern Technology and Civilization.* New York: McGraw-Hill Book Company, Inc., 1962.

SECTION D. CONTROLLING

Decisions to initiate changes in operations on the basis of information relating to these operations are control decisions. In the first chapter of this section, the nature of control decisions is examined in greater detail. Since these decisions depend upon feedback of information, setting standards and measuring performance are then examined. Finally, since management can be considered as an open system, data external to the system must be considered as influencing internal operations. These questions are examined in the final chapter of this section.

Chapter XIII

Management Control

In the first article Douglas S. Sherwin distinguishes control from some other common management activities and, at the same time, clarifies the role of the manager in the control process.

The Small Business Administration has been active in showing how to adapt modern management practices to small firm operations. An example of such an adaptation is given in the article by Edward L. Anthony.

In the next article John R. Curley points out some of the control limitations in the commonly available accounting data. He describes the criteria which a control system must meet in order to relieve the manager from "crisis" reviews and dependence on luck.

A balance of administration to accomplish all the objectives of the organization, not just one or a few, is needed. Chris Argyris shows how control on the basis of budgets impinges upon people.

Raymond Villers examines (1) how control can be exercised within a decentralized organization and still continue a true decentralized operation, (2) the relative advantages of participation in setting standards against which one will be measured, and (3) the importance of relevant reporting.

In the last article Clement J. Berwitz presents methods of control to achieve consistency in decision making.

46. THE MEANING OF CONTROL [1]

Douglas S. Sherwin [2]

"What exactly do you mean by management control?" When this question was asked of a number of managers, in both Government and industry, the answers showed a surprising lack of agreement—surprising, since in a field for which theory has been developed to the extent it has in business management, terms should be precise, specific, and unambiguous. The literature, as one might expect, reflects about the same variety of views as entertained by management men themselves, and so does little to clarify the situation.

Is it important that managers have a clear understanding of this concept? The question almost answers itself. A manager who does not understand management control cannot be expected to exercise it in the most efficient and effective manner. Nor can staff men whose duty it is to design systems and procedures for their organizations design efficient systems unless they possess a clear understanding of management control. And certainly (though the truth of this is seldom sufficiently appreciated) anyone who is subject to control by others has to understand clearly what that means if he is to be contented in that relationship.

Indeed, when management control is *not* understood, good management is a very improbable result. This is especially true when—as frequently it is—control is identified with management, or is confused with certain devices of management, such as objectives, plans, organization charts, policy statements, delegations of authority, procedures, and the like. The manager who believes managing and controlling are the same thing has wasted one word and needs a second to be invented. And one who believes he has provided for control when he has established objectives, plans, policies, organization charts, and so forth, has made himself vulnerable to really serious consequences. A clear understanding of control is therefore indispensable in an effective manager.

[1] From *Dun's Review and Modern Industry* (January, 1956), pp. 45, 46, 83, 84. Reprinted by permission of *Dun's Review and Modern Industry*.
[2] Douglas S. Sherwin, Assistant Coordinator, Rubber Chemicals Division, Phillips Chemical Company, 1957.

Understanding control really means understanding three principal things about it: What is control? What is controlled? And who controls? By proposing answers to these questions, I will try to frame a concept of control that will be useful to practitioners of the managerial art.

The conception of control which I advocate can be simply and briefly stated as follows:

The essence of control is action which adjusts operations to predetermined standards, and its basis is information in the hands of managers.

We have a ready-made model for this concept of control in the automatic systems which are widely used for process control in the chemical and petroleum industries. A process control system works this way. Suppose, for example, it is desired to maintain a constant rate of flow of oil through a pipe at a predetermined, or set-point value. A signal, whose strength represents the rate of flow, can be produced in a measuring device and transmitted to a control mechanism. The control mechanism, when it detects any deviation of the actual from the set-point signal, will reposition the valve regulating flow rate.

Basis for Control

A process control mechanism thus acts to adjust operations to predetermined standards and does so on the basis of information it receives. In a parallel way, information reaching a manager gives him the opportunity for corrective action and is his basis for control. He cannot exercise control without such information. And he cannot do a complete job of managing without controlling.

As mentioned earlier, some students of management have defined control as what results from having objectives, plans, policies, organization charts, procedures, and so forth; and they refer to these elements of the management system, consequently, as controls or means of control. It is not difficult to understand why these devices of managing are so described by proponents of this point of view. Without objectives, for example, we all know results are likely to be other than desired, so it is assumed they function to control the results. And so it is with the other elements of the system.

Nevertheless, these elements are neither controls nor means of control. They do have, however, as we shall see later, an important role to play in a control *system*, and we can therefore examine them now in a little detail.

Certainly, to accomplish a task except through accident, people must know what they are trying to do. Objectives fulfill this need. Without them, people may work quite industriously yet, working aimlessly, accomplish little. Plans and programs complement objectives, since they propose how and according to what time schedule, the objectives are to be reached.

But though objectives, and plans and programs are indispensable to the efficient management of a business (or, for that matter, to the management of almost any human endeavor) they are not means of control. Control is checking to determine whether plans are being observed and suitable progress toward the objectives is being made, and acting, if necessary, to correct any deviations.

Policy is simply a statement of an organization's intention to act in certain ways when specified types of circumstances arise. It represents a general decision, predetermined and expressed as a principle or rule, establishing a normal pattern of conduct for dealing with given types of business events—usually recurrent. A statement of policy is therefore useful in economizing the time of managers and in assisting them to discharge their responsibilities equitably and consistently.

Policy Verification

Nothing in these advantages, however, makes policy a means of control. Indeed, by their very nature, policies generate the need for control; they do not fulfill that need. Adherence to policies is not guaranteed, nor can it be taken on faith. It has to be verified. Without verification, there is no basis for control, no control, and incomplete managing.

Organization is often cited as a means of control. This detracts both from its own significance and from the concept of control.

Organization is part of the giving of an assignment. The organization chart, for example, is a first crude step in the defining of assignments. It gives to each individual, in his title, a first approximation to the nature of his assignment, and it orients him as accountable to a certain individual. But it is not in a fruitful sense a means of control. Control is checking to ascertain whether the assignment is being executed as intended—and acting on the basis of that information.

The relation between "internal check" and "internal control" is likewise not well understood. The two terms refer to quite different

aspects of the managerial system. "Internal check" provides in prac-
tise for the principle that the same person should not have responsibility for all phases of a transaction. This makes it clearly an aspect
of organization, rather than of control. For how do we provide for
internal check? We provide for it through segregating the duties of
recording and those of custodianship and assigning them to different
employees or groups of employees.

Assigning duties is, of course, the very essence of organizing, and
thus internal check is simply organizing in a special way in order to
realize special objectives. Internal control, on the other hand, observes
the actual performance of duties as against the assigned duties and
acts, where necessary, to correct deviations of the actual from the
assigned.

Internal check and internal control are obviously both very necessary in an enterprise. But they operate differently. The objective of
internal check is to reduce the opportunity for fraud or error to occur.
The objective of internal control is to restore operations to predetermined standards. Internal check is thus static or built-in; it is
provided before-the-fact; and its operation is preventive in its effect.
Internal control, in contrast, is active and continual; it is exercised
after-the-fact; and its operation is corrective in its effect.

Assignments are far from defined, however, by the preparation of
an organization chart. Among the ways we have for supplementing
the titles and lines of authority of an organization chart are delegations of authority. Delegations of authority clarify the extent of
authority of individuals and in that way serve to define assignments.
That they are not means of control is apparent from the very fact
that wherever there has been a delegation of authority the need for
control increases, and this could hardly be expected to happen if
delegations of authority were themselves means of control.

Manager's Responsibility

Control becomes necessary whenever a manager delegates authority to a subordinate, because he cannot delegate, then simply sit back
and forget all about it. A manager's accountability to his own superior
has not diminished one whit as a result of delegating part of his
authority to a subordinate. It is therefore incumbent upon managers
who delegate authority to exercise control over actions taken under
the authority so delegated. That means checking results as a basis for
possible corrective action.

The question whether budgets are a means of control does not yield a straightforward answer because budgets perform more than one function. They perform three: they present the objectives, plans, and programs of the organization and express them in financial terms; they report the progress of actual performance against these predetermined objectives, plans, and programs; and, like organization charts, delegations of authority, procedures, and job descriptions, they define the assignments which have flowed down from the chief executive.

In expressing the objectives and plans of the organization, budgets are of course not means of control, for reasons examined earlier when objectives and plans were considered. Nor do budgets qualify as means of control in their function of defining assignments. Though this service of budgets is frequently overlooked, defining an assignment is neither a means of control nor the exercise of control.

Budgets are a means of control only in the respect that they report progress of actual performance against the program—information which enables managers to take action directed toward bringing actual results into conformity with the program.

In the previous paragraphs I have tried to show that objectives, plans and programs, organization charts, and other elements of the managerial system are not fruitfully regarded as either "controls" or "means of control." They nevertheless do bear a very important relationship to the control function. They are the pre-established standards to which operations are adjusted by the exercise of management control.

It may seem unfamiliar to some to view these devices of management in that light. Perhaps "standards" is not the very best word. Yet these elements of the system are standards in a very real sense, for they have been laid down by competent authority as models or standards of desired performance.

These standards are, of course, dynamic in character, for they are constantly altered, modified, or revised. But for a moment let us give our attention to their static quality.

An objective is static until revised; a plan or program is static until it is abandoned. They possess a kind of temporary durability or limited permanence. They are in force until superseded. This same static quality inheres also in the other elements of the managerial system we spoke of. Policies, organizational set-up, procedures, delegations, job descriptions, and so forth, are, of course, constantly altered and added to. But, like objectives and plans, they retain their force until they are either abandoned or revised.

Suppose, for convenience, we use the phrase "framework of management" to mean all the elements of the managerial system taken together—objectives, plans and programs, policies, organization, and the like. Doubtless, a more descriptive phrase could be invented, but this one at least suggests the notion that there is something of a semi-permanent nature in the managerial system. Now we can in a new way identify what is controlled. Managers control adherence to the objectives, plans, policies, organizational structure, procedures, and so forth, which have been laid down. In brief, managers control adherence to a predetermined "framework of management."

Now we can turn to the very important question that must be answered: "Who should act?"

It has become almost axiomatic as a management principle (which is unfortunately not always given effect in practice) that that person should act who is responsible for the results. "Results" has to be interpreted here in a broad sense. For results include not only profits and costs—obvious items—but the conformity of all operations with all standards. Hence, whoever had responsibility for specifying and establishing a particular standard has to be ultimately responsible for controlling adherence to it and responsible, therefore, for such corrective action as is necessary. Of course, those below him in the chain of command may help him, but they cannot relieve him of final responsibility for control. Therefore, authority for managers to establish standards should be delegated as far down in the organization as practical wisdom permits. It then becomes their responsibility to control adherence of operations to the system they establish.

It is not only a responsibility, but a right; and it is asking for trouble to place in anyone else's hands the responsibility for controlling results in the operating manager's sphere of responsibility.

If the basis of control is information in the hands of managers, "reporting" is elevated to a level of very considerable importance. Used here in a broad sense, "reporting" includes special reports and routine reports; written, oral, and graphic reports; staff meetings, conferences, television screens, and any other means whereby information is transmitted to a manager as a basis for control action. Even the non-receipt of information, as where management is by exception, can be informational and imply the existence of control.

We are often told that reports should be timely and designed to meet the needs of managers. We are in a better position to appreciate this when we realize the important role that reporting plays in the control function. Certainly if it is to be the basis for control, information should be assembled with that objective in view. It should exclude material extraneous to the problem of control and must be placed at the disposal of managers quickly so that operations do not deviate any further from the desired norm—or for a longer period—than can be avoided.

That control occurs after the fact is a point that sometimes troubles managers. It should not—since this is simply part of the nature of the concept. The situation is entirely comparable in the process control system described earlier. In that system the detecting device continuously evaluates results and transmits them back to the control mechanism, which, sensing the difference between the actual and the desired results, acts to restore results to the desired value. The results, just as in management control, precede the exercise of control. Control systems, human or mechanical, deal with transfers of energy and a transfer of energy takes time. We learn from this—and it underscores the importance of speed in reporting—that all we can do for the management problem is to minimize the time lag between results and action.

CONTROL SPECTRUM

There is another sometimes troublesome aspect of control, namely, that control over some things must be relinquished as successively higher echelons of management are reached. This again we must simply face. Managers in the first echelon require certain information as their basis for controlling. But in the next higher echelon, the character of required information changes; some information is dropped, some is added. There is thus a kind of "control spectrum." For the process of fading out and shading in of information is continued as you move up the pyramid until, just as in the visible spectrum the colors at one end are wholly unlike those at the other, the information reported to the top is wholly different from the information reported to first line managers.

This would hardly be worth pointing out except that some managers are burdened with a persistent sense of insecurity which undermines their self-confidence and ability to do the job, because they are unable to keep track of all the details under their management. Of course, they should not be able to keep track of all the results, or more accurately, should not allow themselves to do so. Relinquishing control over some operations is a calculated risk, taken so that managers can assume more important tasks.

It will bear mentioning that information serves other purposes than as the basis for control. The notion of a "framework of management," which we suggested earlier, is helpful in describing one of these purposes. This "framework," we said, is constantly undergoing change in one or another of its aspects. Such change takes place, not accidentally, but following conscious decisions for change by those responsible for such decisions. And decisions for changes in the framework are based on information that is conceptually different from information used for controlling adherence to the framework.

Where Forecasts Fit

Forecasts and projections, for example, have no place in the problem of control (since control is after-the-fact while forecasts are before) but they are very important for setting objectives and formulating plans. Of course, information for aiming and for planning does not have to be before-the-fact. It may be an after-the-fact analysis proving that a certain policy has been impolitic in its effect on the relations of the company with customer, employee, or stockholder; or that a certain plan is no longer practical; or that a certain procedure is unworkable. The prescription here certainly would not be "control" (since in these cases control would simply bring operations into conformity with obsolete standards), but the establishment of new standards—a new policy, a new plan, and a new procedure—to be controlled to.

Besides furnishing evidence of a need for reconstructing the managerial framework, information is, of course, the basis of all communication. But since that subject is one of the most discussed in the management field today, there is no need to discuss it further here.

Control, we have seen, means something quite specific in the managerial art. This is certainly as it should be in an area of thought as well developed as business management. For in any field for which theory has been developed to an appreciable extent, terms should be precise and unambiguous. Control, when used in a management context, should mean one thing and one thing only. I have suggested that it means action directed toward bringing operations into conformity with predetermined standards and goals; that it is exercised by managers; and that its basis is information in their hands after-the-fact.

In addition to being a specific part of managing, control is also, quite evidently, an extremely important part of managing. In organizations, therefore, where the responsibility for control is not placed in the hands of managers, or not accepted by them, difficulties are certain to arise. Managers must control. Staff members of the organization may, by furnishing information, help a manager discharge this responsibility, but may not share in it. Where this philosophy is adopted by top management as the policy of the organization, the probability is enhanced that the energies of the organization will be channeled in fruitful directions.

TERMINOLOGY

Control is admittedly a term with emotional connotations. The denotation of the term, however, suffers from no such objection. Control is not supervision. Experienced managers perceive that as their authority is broadened, their superiors must place increased reliance on control as a means of safeguarding their own accountability. But at the same time, supervision of their activities by superiors become less close. There seems every reason to believe, therefore, that as the real nature of control becomes better understood, managers will come to recognize that their being subject to it in increasing measure is as sure a sign as any of their progress in the organization and in the fulfillment of their position.

47. EFFECTIVE CONTROL
FOR BETTER MANAGEMENT [1]

Edward L. Anthony [2]

The term "control" means something affording a standard of comparison, a means of verification, or a check. In small business management, control can be illustrated by these three situations:

A sales manager dictates a letter acknowledging receipt of an order and promising shipment before a certain date. He then asks his secretary to send a copy of that letter to the shipping room with a note: "Please date and return to me when order goes out." That's a control system.

A plant superintendent knows that to meet production requirements, he needs a reserve supply of about 100 small metal castings which go into his product. He buys in lots of 500 whenever his stock drops to 100. To relieve himself of this detail he has the storage bin divided into a small section which holds just 100 units, and a big section which will take up to 500. Then he assigns the job of keeping tabs on the castings to a stock clerk. The clerk is told to put through a reorder requisition for 500 castings as soon as the last one is removed from the big section of the bin. Production workers are told to hand in a parts-withdrawal chit for each unit they need to take out. Along with the requisition, the clerk is to send to the purchasing agent all the parts-withdrawal chits he has collected. When the new stock comes in, he is to see that the small section of the storage bin is completely filled. Periodically the superintendent inspects the 100-part section to see that there are no empty spaces. That's a control system, too.

A new president takes charge of a small company which produces four separate product lines. The president divides the company into semi-autonomous divisions, each one charged with a specific share of the total invested capital. Each division is also held accountable for earning a 10-percent return on that investment. A system of internal records and reports is set up by which the president can see regularly how each division is making out in terms of earnings as a percentage of sales and turnover—the factors which produce the return. That's also a control system.

TWO BASIC PROBLEMS

In devising effective controls in your small business, you must cope with two basic problems. First, to be of practical value, your system

[1] From *Management Aids for Small Manufacturers,* Small Business Administration (January, 1957), pp. 1-4. Reprinted by permission of the Small Business Administration.

[2] Edward L. Anthony, Managerial Assistance Division, Small Business Administration.

cannot be very costly because a small company cannot afford to be burdened with excessive personnel and overhead charges. This means that your control system should be simple and sparing of manpower.

Second, you must face the fact that almost everybody not only resents the idea of being controlled, but also objects to being judged. More often than not, the targets of a control system are regarded as personal report cards. According to studies made by the Controllers Institute, standards and budgets can be highly unpopular. Many supervisors hate them. They feel, for example, that standards put more and more pressure on employees, and more and more emphasis on past performance. Furthermore, these supervisors add, while standards don't show why the goal wasn't reached, they do strengthen the idea that supervisors have to be constantly goaded into greater efficiency. Those points are clear evidence that your control system should be installed with patience and tact so as to be accepted by those who will operate under it. Otherwise, it may not have much success.

The foregoing remarks will, of course, not surprise readers who have been plant supervisors. They will remember well that production men normally think in *unit* figures rather than in *dollars* or *percentages*. Many will also recall how they kept their own brand of back-of-an-envelope data—sufficient to show whether they were making out well enough to satisfy "the front office." Some will even be reminded of the suspicion with which they regarded the findings of statistical experts who depended upon "tabular views and colored charts for analyzing operations they'd never done."

This lack of a genuine meeting of the minds can be a significant road-block to control—particularly in a small plant where single individuals have a big influence on overall performance. In getting rid of this obstacle, plant owners are finding it is the figure man, not the operating man, who must shift his approach.

PRACTICAL BENEFITS

Despite its difficulties, there are practical benefits from control. There *are* ways to make it work better. For example, control often works best where the accounting man works directly with, and reports directly to the production boss. In this way "control" gets the feel of actual "operations" in the shop and reports them with a production viewpoint.

To be sure, many a control person resists this concept because he thinks that its effect is to demote him. On the one hand, the control man may have to turn over much of his authority to the production chief. On the other hand, he may be expected by the top manager to change from a figure specialist to a kind of consultant who knows the score on the whole business. This, of course, is precisely the objective. It may be a trying matter while the changes are being made, but moving from narrow statistical reporting to broad, company-wide figure interpretations can make for effective control and better management.

The payoff may come slowly, but the experience of successful companies proves that it *will* come. To be sure, control by itself will not produce profit; other elements, even good or bad luck, always influence earnings records. But control can help materially to reduce losses where they are occurring and to obtain profits where they are being missed.

Time Needed to Develop Control

At this point you may well say: "All right, that makes sense as far as it goes. We could use a better control setup. But you say the payoff may be slow. How much time do you really need to get an adequate system working?"

The answer depends on how much control you already have. If your company can build on an existing foundation of good basic records plus some experience with various kinds of budgets, you don't have so far to go. In that case, you can usually expect useful results in a matter of months. If, however, your company must have practice in recordkeeping and reporting, must build up a backlog of historical information, and must gain experience in forecasting, some authorities say you shouldn't expect the new system to be very effective until the third year.

This shouldn't be considered an insurmountable handicap. Everyday you work at it you're a little better off than the day before. The key to the problem is to start at once by making some attempt, somewhere. Plan to make adjustments as you go along, and watch developments very closely during the first year.

Whether you set your sights on a 6-month or a 3-year shakedown period, don't attempt too ambitious a program at the start. Undoubtedly, control of individual activities does not have the same benefits as company-wide control. Nevertheless, the best approach is to insist that some progress be made constantly, but that innovations be adopted at a rate which lets your organization absorb each new technique.

You should recognize, too, that the picture brought into focus during the first few weeks by the control system may be disconcerting. There is something merciless about the way a control system shows up failures to reach planned goals. The shock is usually sufficient to produce immediate action on the part of those whose operations fell short. When that happens, watch out for two things: ill-considered, desperate action, and personal resentment. You're bound to get some of both.

Moreover, when goals are not met—especially when a control system is new—review carefully your company's available resources in money, personnel, and so on. If they are not adequate for the goal you set (and cannot be made so) each individual target should be re-analyzed, and your entire plan should be recast.

When you start with a definite idea of what you want to control and what results you want to get, you don't have to wait until all the groundwork is done before seeing evidence of progress. You can set tentative goals and check movement toward them within 60 days after the basic decisions are made.

The Control Process

One of your main jobs as a manager is to give responsibility and authority to assistants who are capable of using it, but still to retain for yourself the means of assuring that performance is satisfactory. If you are to function effectively as the top man you should spend most of your time on planning, directing, and coordinating. Therefore, you need to be freed as much as possible from routine and detail work.

When they think about it carefully, many managers realize that they often get bogged down in too many authorizations, reviews, and approvals. Much of this sort of thing could be delegated to various subordinates if they were allowed to make final decisions on certain assignments. But much of it *isn't* delegated. Why? Typically, because the top man doesn't dare. He frequently feels that if he wants something done right he must do it himself. Or he frequently believes that he can't safely delegate authority because if a mistake were made, things might get out of hand. This reasoning indicates inadequate control.

What is needed is a simple system of rules and limits for action so that things don't get out of hand. The starting point could be any recurring and bothersome task; for example, making out purchase requisitions such as might develop in the parts-reordering situation cited earlier.

Control always involves three ingredients:

The goal, which states what is to be done.

The procedure, which specifies (1) how and when something is to be done, (2) who is to do it, and (3) what makes up satisfactory performance.

The checkup, which indicates how well the job was carried out.

In the parts reordering situation, the goal was to have a reserve inventory of about 100 castings on hand. The procedure comprised setting up a method for recognizing when there were only 100 castings left, putting a clerk in charge of the stock, and telling him to reorder as soon as the last casting was removed from the big section in the storage bin. The checkup was made through typing in the parts-withdrawal chits, the purchase requisition, and the superintendent's inspection. This is a simple case, of course, but even so, all of the essential elements are present.

To set up effective control, you have to decide, first, what you want to accomplish in the long run. Second, you have to figure out how to obtain that result. In this connection, techniques are available which can be adapted to conditions in your individual plant.

For example, to control *wages*, the technique combines sound job evaluation, pay ranges for each classification established in proper relation to outside wage rates, careful review of any proposed exceptions or changes, and regular appraisals of actual performance.

To control *costs*, the technique involves comparing the results of actual operations with standard costs based on optimum conditions in the plant. This, in turn, presupposes some kind of cost accounting to reveal what the actual costs are, and to provide some basis for determining what they should be.

To control *methods and manpower*, the first step is to find out what is now being done, how it is being done, and by whom. Once those facts are established they can be studied to determine the activities that are necessary, the best methods for performing them, the number and type of people required, the proper pattern of organization, and the expected cost.

To control *overall profitability*, the return-on-investment concept is often used. This involves deciding—partly on the basis of past company experience, and partly on estimates of the future—what return the enterprise should make on the capital invested in it.

Here's how that works. Say you have a business worth $1,200,000 and you want to net a return on that capital of 10 percent. This goal means that you must earn profits at the rate of $10,000 each month in order to end the year with your budgeted $120,000. But profits as such are often hard to judge accurately as you go along. Sales figures are much easier to watch. Therefore, you might decide to figure your profits as a percentage of sales for a first step, and then as a second step to relate this figure to return on investment. By that procedure you might find that to earn your budgeted $10,000 profit each month, you needed a monthly sales volume of $200,000—because your net profit on sales consistently ran around 5 percent.

Thus, sales figures of less than $200,000 in any one month would be a signal to look into the causes of the shortage and to intensify efforts to make up for it in future months.

CONTROL BY EXCEPTION

Following out this line of reasoning, you might next break down your goal, say, in terms of individual products. Say you make five items, each of which accounts for about 20 percent of your total revenue. Each then would have to develop a sales volume of $40,000 in every month. You could then ask your bookkeeper to call to your attention *only* those situations where the monthly sales were, say, below $38,000 or above $42,000. In the first case, you would want to find out what the trouble was as soon as possible so that you could take corrective action; in the second case, you would want to see if something could be learned from that success to apply to the other products. This approach is called managing by exception.

TOO MUCH CONTROL?

Much has been said about the evils of insufficient control. A related point also should be raised: Is there a danger of having too much control? The answer is yes.

Not long ago a zealous and methodical manager got interested in controlling the replacement parts his company made and sold for the servicing of equipment which it manufactured. A system was devised and duly inaugurated. To test its merit, only a few large items were included at the beginning. Soon opportunities for savings were revealed. Fired by early success, the manager then insisted that every part be subject to the system. He reasoned that if control was good on a few parts it would be better on all of them.

But trouble was not long in developing. Delays in getting parts (caused by the extra recordkeeping) began to occur much to the annoyance of customers. In addition, such an intensive system was very expensive; in fact, the control cost more than many of the parts being controlled. Ultimately the manager realized that he had built up too much of a good thing and that many small parts should be provided to customers without charge on a service and public-relations basis.

Control can also generate too many reports and records. One good example is the case of the unwanted overhead figures. The boss had decided that "full information" about job costs, including figures on both direct labor and overhead, should be circulated to all his executives. But the overhead figures produced by the control system often involved the use of different rates for estimating, for pricing, and for bidding on various jobs. These differences soon caused confusion and disputes in the engineering section. Furthermore, the cost sheets were seen by some in the shop who could not understand why the final figures on some jobs showed up in red ink, even though the production people had met the estimates on direct labor and materials.

After a period of such misunderstanding, the boss decided that the overhead figures should be eliminated from the cost sheets distributed to the engineering, production, and purchasing sections. The staff members in those sections who formerly saw the overhead figures seemed entirely satisfied not to be bothered with such information.

One production man, for example, said, "The new system is better because we have a straight target to hit. You can't explain overhead control to most shopmen, and they shouldn't be burdened with those figures. They just don't have the background to understand them."

These situations add up to a noteworthy conclusion for small business operators: Keep your control system appropriate and keep it simple.

The Payoff

Effective control will pay off, profitably. In the first place, by showing the owner-manager where his company is heading profit-wise, control can forewarn of danger while there is still time to do something about it. In the second place, control can provide a means to larger, steadier returns on investment. In the third place, a control system which works, is a real asset when new money—either borrowed funds or equity capital—is sought. As Abraham Lincoln put it: "If we could first know where we are and whither we are tending, we could better judge what to do and how to do it."

48. A TOOL FOR
MANAGEMENT CONTROL [1]   John Richard Curley [2]

Faced with a never-ending pattern of change in current-day operations and long-range plans, the heads of today's industrial concerns are seeking a better answer to the complex problem of control over their organizations. Whatever the correct definition of the word "control" may be, it must be practiced as a dynamic rather than a static concept, one which primarily involves people rather than things. And while plans can be made in the undisturbed quiet of paneled offices, not the slightest degree of control can actually be exercised from that vantage point, either before or after the day-by-day operations (which of course must be right the first time) have taken place. Herein lies the challenge of modern executive leadership.

Keenly aware of this challenge, business executives are devising methods to make themselves and their key subordinates more efficient, so their companies will emerge from whatever situation lies ahead in a healthy, profitable position. Many of the control methods currently practiced are very informal; they still depend primarily on the unique backgrounds and abilities of key executives who are justifiably proud of their good average in making decisions, even though in many instances these are often based on but scanty factual data. There are, on the other hand, an increasing number of executives, particularly in large corporations, who are finding that their personal qualities of leadership and business know-how are far from the whole answer and who have developed and formalized methods for the establishment and maintenance of efficiency tools which serve as aids and guides to management direction.

No system yet developed has been so skillfully designed as to eliminate the necessity for the presence of superior executive talent in every major business decision. Indeed, the very nature of competitive industry is such that no system can ever do that. The tools which

[1] From the *Harvard Business Review*, Vol. XXIX, No. 2 (March, 1951), pp. 45-59. Reprinted by permission of the *Harvard Business Review*.
[2] John Richard Curley, Assistant to the Vice President, Engineering Products Department, Radio Corporation of America, 1951.

have been devised, however, have in most cases proved themselves to be valuable supplements to superior executive knowledge and leadership, thus tending to insure a greater percentage of correct and timely business decisions.

It is the purpose of this article to discuss and analyze one method —though by no means the only method—of accepting the challenge of the times, drawing from the experience of one of the major departments of the RCA Victor Division for a great deal of the information presented. The method adopted at RCA is not new, nor, let it be emphasized, does it accomplish any more than to formalize systems already practiced by many executives in an informal way. In one sentence, it can be described as a system which achieves decentralized, effective control by combining regular operational review meetings with a series of status and trend charts and graphs which highlight current problems and provide the basis for group discussion and management decisions.

During the period 1947-1948 significant improvements in internal operations were brought about in the Engineering Products Department of RCA. In the short space of a year, for example, the ability of the manufacturing activity to meet its schedules showed a 20% improvement, with an attendant reduction in in-process inventories. Other activities, such as sales, purchasing, standardization, quality control, and plant engineering, also showed comparable improvements in this period. Just how much of that improvement can be directly attributed to the control tools used is frankly a matter of conjecture. Careful analysis of all factors involved indicates that just as certainly as one cannot attribute *all* of the improvement realized to this control approach, neither can one eliminate it as a major source of the progress made. Moreover, experience since 1948 at RCA has shown that as a tool for continuing control and improvement this method is fully (though less dramatically) as valuable during periods of relative stability as it was during the 1947-1948 period of postwar change.

Although many of the specific techniques applied with success at RCA are not applicable to all industrial concerns, the basic philosophy as well as the general mechanics of the method can unquestionably be of benefit to every business organization.

Necessity for new tools

As a prelude to the RCA experience, an analysis of common business practice disclosed that in a majority of industrial concerns existing accounting statements and reports are utilized by top managers as the basis for their informal and formal "control" activities—despite the fact that historically accounting records were not devised for control purposes at all but, rather, were fashioned into the form which they still essentially retain for legal and tax, i.e., "status" or "record," purposes.

The conclusion reached at RCA was that it is incorrect to associate static financial reports or charts or graphs directly with the dynamic concept of "control," in its connotation as a force which deals chiefly with motivation and persuasion of people. Financial statements, budgets, organizations, procedures, and the like, it was decided, are really being used by industry as vehicles for control, but neither do they provide control themselves nor are they necessarily the best tools with which to attempt to bring about better control.

In starting out from this point to discover or develop the right kind of tool for its internal control activities, the RCA management quickly concluded that there is a paucity of practical information on the general subject of control methods. The specific tools which are used most widely have very little in common with each other. It was found that, in an effort to make existing reports more amenable to the control task they had not been designed to handle, most companies had dressed them up in form as well as substance in one way or another.

"Actual" versus "Budget." Nearly every company issues some kind of statement showing on a monthly basis "actual" versus "budget." All else being equal, this is an excellent way to measure progress against a goal. The trouble at RCA in 1947, a trouble probably shared by every other industrial concern in the country, was that all else was *not* equal, rendering this tool for control inadequate.

Additional considerations resulted in the conclusion that from a control viewpoint existing records and reports themselves, rather than their application, were basically at fault. For example, in some companies budgets are made up once a year, or perhaps every six months, and remain fixed during that period irrespective of changes in markets, products, and so forth. How else is a hard-hitting, farsighted management going to demonstrate to the board of directors that it makes and executes solid business plans? It is much more acceptable to all concerned to explain variations from budget to the board of directors after the fact than it is to rush into their presence every month or two with a revised schedule of sales, expenses, and profits. Under current American business organization practice, this is perfectly understandable and as it should be, for few members of the board require or expect anything else. The existence of this underlying purpose of the budget, however, makes it very difficult for management to use these semifixed statements as springboards to continuing internal control.

Another reason for long-term budgets is the necessity for doing an intelligent job of cash and expenditure planning. So long as the total of all individual budgets is more or less realized, there is no serious upheaval within the company. This, again, is as it should be from the limited standpoint of cash planning; but for managers to turn around and attempt to control their businesses on the basis of these long-term "guestimates" is a tremendously difficult task in the face of ever-changing, hard-to-anticipate business conditions.

Looking into the content of long-term budgets reveals that a great many companies' budgets, particularly those which are turned over to boards of directors, are usually on the conservative side, for there is nearly always a temporary expression of heroic accomplishment awaiting the manager who goes over his sales budget or under his expense or inventory budget, whereas the manager who sets for himself a truly stiff goal and misses is rarely complimented in any way for his noble efforts.

In a few companies it was found that managements have developed duplicate sets of budgets: (1) The first set is used for the information and guidance of the board of directors, stockholders' reports, cash planning, auditors from within and without, taxes, etc. This set of books is the conservative one which sets down in budget form what management thinks will happen with a 50-50 operation of "breaks," and shows results in standard accounting form. There is no compelling management urgency to publish this accounting record promptly. (2) The other set is the one which management looks on as its own, for internal use only. It always shows a stiffer, more optimistic goal—one which assumes better than 50-50 chances with the "breaks" and depends to a great extent upon better than average performance by all members of the firm. It often varies in its form from standard accounting practices so as to permit management to use it for control purposes. It has very definite advantages with respect to internal control, but it is objectionable from several standpoints, particularly expense, time of issuance, and incompleteness.

Internal Accounting Reports. As a very natural addition to the "paper" comparison month by month of "actual" versus "budget," many top managers have developed additional columns of numbers on their financial sheets to aid them in evaluating performance of the various elements of their businesses. Nearly all internal accounting reports include a cumulative "year-to-date" column which at least gives the top executive a set of numbers of significance so long as he goes through the following mental steps, which may appear too simple to mention but which nonetheless do demand a fair proportion of the executive's limited time:

1. Divide number of months so far this year into "year-to-date" total.
2. Compare with "this month."
3. Decide whether the most logical reaction should be "How come?" or "Is this good or bad?" or "Isn't this terrific!"
4. Dig further to confirm the initial reaction and determine what the numbers really mean.

Quite a few variations of the systems outlined above are in use, of course. Some companies, for example, use a "same month a year ago" column, particularly where the business is seasonal, to provide a better basis for comparison than "year-to-date" gives. Others show an "average year-to-date" figure which is of great assistance to the reviewing and controlling executive though it fails to give him a real notion of the trend of the business.

It is obvious that the addition of columns, such as "year-to-date," "average this year," "same month last year," to the "actual versus budget" statement of a company is an outgrowth of the determination of most managements to make a single set of accounting books with no supplements save narrative and verbal reports do the whole job, be it tax computation or internal control. The consolidated summary statements which naturally develop from this condition are usually highly complex, very incomplete, and completely confusing to all save the accountants who prepared them and those few managers who have participated in their growth. Internal control meetings which use these sets of numbers as the basis for discussion and decision are often pathetic affairs where the top brain of the firm does all of the work of piecing together for himself and his staff those facts which are needed for intelligent appraisal of the progress and problems of a portion of the business. Conversation at one of these meetings very often develops as follows:

President (seeing $18,212.14 sales for month of March and $39,394.15 year-to-date): "Poor month last month, eh?"

Reporting sales manager: "No, sir. If you remember, I told you at our last meeting that I was billing in February some equipment originally scheduled for March delivery. On year-to-date, you will note, we are practically even with our budget."

President: "Hmm, so you are. I thought we decided at the beginning of the year to sell $300,000 in your line this year. Even if last month was unusually low, at a going rate of, let's see, $13,000 a month, we'll never make it, will we?"

Reporting sales manager: "Well, as you know, we put on two extra salesmen in January, and in our line a new salesman doesn't start producing overnight. If you'll let me get my back reports—oh, here they are—in January we billed $8,000—January is always a low month—and in February we billed $15,000, $2,000 of which was originally scheduled for March delivery. If you add that $2,000 to the March total, you have a gradually increasing billing figure reflecting the gradual breaking-in of the new salesmen."

President: "Then you think we'll hit $300,000 for the year?"

Reporting sales manager: "Well, as I see it, we should get up to a going rate of $10,000 per salesman, or $30,000 total in a month or in a couple of months and then level off as the new salesmen reach their saturation points, and then—let's see, nine months to go at $30,000 per month, that's $270,000 for the balance of the year. Adding the $39,000 we have so far, that'll give us around. . . ."

President: "That's about $310,000, isn't it?"

Reporting sales manager: "That's right. We should have no trouble making $300,000 if everything goes right."

The above is an abbreviated and deliberately extreme illustration of how some busy executives in their review of operations do not quickly, or in some cases at all, get to the subject with which they really should be concerned. How much better, for example, would this conversation have been if the discussion had centered around the extent of the market potential and the possibility of adding one or more additional salesmen *now*? As we shall see later, this could have been accomplished very simply and effectively through the use of better control tools.

Basic Flaws. The conclusion reached at RCA was that in all of the attempted control methods which depend upon accounting statements and reports there are several very basic flaws, the sum total of which prove the need for different tools for dynamic control:

1. *Time of issuance is too late for effective control*—Usually business accounting reports arrive on the desks of top managers around the fifteenth of the month following the month of activity; rarely, if ever, are they available before the tenth. Management control sessions are normally conducted sometime after the reports are issued, which leads to the following contradictory conditions:
   a. Discussion, particularly with sales personnel, is likely to revolve around what's going on this month rather than the month on the record. The month under review, therefore, does not always get the analysis it deserves.
   b. Decisions reached cannot effectively be put into operation during the current month, which is already at least half gone.
2. *Absolute precision of accounting statements is not needed for control purposes*—The average accounting mind is trained to be precise and

accurate even if it does take a little longer. The average executive mind, on the other hand, doesn't need or want to know whether sales last month were $4,521.73 or $4,521.93, to the last penny. The executive wants to know whether $4,500 is high, low, or average, and in any case, "What can we do *now* to improve this performance?"

3. *Accounting statements give only a portion of the information needed for control*—Unless the executive can visualize a trend pattern, he is unable to exercise any control at all. His mind automatically seeks a picture showing a line going up, down, or staying on a level and always in relation to some other line which to him means "what it ought to be." Under present accounting systems we force our highest paid corporate talent to translate a set of numbers—usually a very incomplete set—into the picture he has trained his mind to paint, and without which he cannot make an intelligent decision or plan.

4. *Accounting statements usually hide the elements requiring control in the business*—Lower than budgeted sales volume does not really tell the executive anything about the under-the-surface state of his business. Neither do higher than expected manufacturing or engineering costs. To do a control job the executive must see what the plan for raising sales or lowering costs is and how well the sales department is making out in relation to that plan. If the plan to increase sales involves the appointment of new or additional distributors or salesmen, that is what he wants to hear about. Toward assisting executives in their control activities, accounting reports frequently do nothing more than offer a lump of sugar or wave a red flag with the challenge. "From here on in you're on your own." Too often control meetings turn out to be battles of wits instead of mutual understandings and joint solutions of problems.

Basic Requirements. What, then, are the features which we at RCA determined to be essential to a good control tool? Seven in number, they may seem at first glance to be too obvious to mention or discuss, but actually human nature is such that we often lose sight of the obvious in our far too complex world. This is particularly true, we have found at RCA, in the field of management control, where existing reports and records force the manager to work toward the simple from a highly complex starting point.

1. *It must be timely*—The business mind, particularly where time is involved, is stimulated to exert and properly receive pressure to a lesser and lesser degree the farther it is away from the activity it is reviewing. Realizing this human weakness, many reporting managers take advantage of it by throwing into an already cloudy picture such confusing information as orders received during the past ten days, distributors' inventory changes last week, etc. Not unlike other firms, we had at RCA right after the war one product manager who appeared late for scheduled monthly review meetings as a regular practice, each time contending that he had been detained by a phone call which virtually closed the biggest deal of his career, the details of which he would always be more than willing to relate.

All such current information is most interesting and essential though it has nothing to do with the period under review. So interesting is it that usually the top executive spends the bulk of his limited review time discussing it and too small a portion of his time analyzing the cold facts of the previous month. A proper control tool is therefore one which is available immediately following the period to be reviewed for control purposes.

2. *It must be simple*—Psychologists differ with respect to many aspects of the mind, but they all agree that the unaided mind cannot cope with more than two or three elements at the same time. The mass of numbers appearing on most financial statements make logical comparison a very difficult task. As pointed out above, the executive mind is trained to form a mental picture showing him comparisons and trends from a sheet of numbers though the mental process is time- and energy-consuming. Normally, the picture visualized by the reviewing executive requires description and explanation before other parties to the conversation are in a position to assist the executive in evaluating its significance, or to understand his evaluation.

All of this preliminary mental activity could be avoided if the tool used in the review reduced the problems of the business to a simple, clear-cut presentation which at a glance provided everyone with an unquestioned basis for discussion.

3. *It must show the essence of the problems to be controlled*—Too frequently, financial statements submitted to top management are oversimplified by the custom of netting various quasi-common elements under a single heading. For example, at RCA we have an over-all category called "manufacturing variance" into which, accounting-wise, we lump production variances from standards, underliquidations or overliquidations of overhead, purchased parts variances from quoted prices, excess material handling expenses, etc. It frequently happens that a very favorable performance in any one of these categories obscures on our summary statements poor performance in one or more of the others.

From accounting summaries alone these below-the-surface facts are not clearly indicated to top management, which discovers their existence either by insight, accident, or by a meticulous study of the detailed financial statements on which the summary is based—or not at all. A proper tool for management control therefore must be one which shows the essence of the problems requiring control.

4. *It must show trends as well as status*—How a product, line, or function fared last month against its budget or on an average year-to-date basis often has little if any relation to the increasing or decreasing efficiency or value of that product or function. The only way an executive can go about the task of control over the activity is by obtaining somehow, somewhere, a "feel" of how things are going. To force him to probe about with a series of verbal questions, or search into the detail of previous months' accounting statements, not only wastes time which might otherwise be devoted to the application of his experience, advice, and counsel to the manager directly responsible, but too often results in confusion as to what the trend really is. In many instances, as the dialogue above indicates, realignment of figures is necessary before it is possible to utilize accounting statistics as trend indicators.

A good control tool is therefore one which reflects the results of all of the spade work necessary to show realistic trends undistorted by the many elements which accounting statements normally embody.

5. *It must permit establishment of clear-cut goals*—Establishment of mutually developed, clear-cut goals, and measurement of performance against these goals, is one of the most basic control techniques available to industrial management. Nearly all top-flight executives automatically think in terms of progress against goals and endeavor to permeate their organizations with this spirit of shooting against par. Records generally in existence, however, do not ideally lend themselves to this desire of the executive, who seeks to accomplish two ends in his goal-establishing process:

a. He wants to set up attainable goals which are not vague or easily misunderstood. Normally his goals are stiffer than the average manager is expected to achieve but not too stiff for an exceptional manager to reach.

b. He tries to set up goals in such a way that measurement against them will eliminate the possibility of "smart aleck" maneuvers or changes in definition which will make for "paper" success regardless of real progress of the operating manager.

A good control tool must therefore be one which serves as the basis for the establishment of clear-cut goals and which can be used for accurate measurement of progress against those goals. We have found at RCA a universal acceptance of, and response to, this psychological tool toward better performance, even among those who for one reason or another did not initially accept our over-all control method.

6. *It must be flexible*—The only certain pattern in present-day competitive endeavor is one which spells uncertainty. This is, of course, a more drastic condition in times such as these, when government activities affecting all industry are the rule rather than the exception. No matter how solid the product or the market looks, estimates into the future are by their very nature uncertain. The present national emergency with its almost daily changes of serious and far-reaching consequences is a forceful example.

Control over modern business enterprise must accordingly keep pace with the perpetually changing pattern, or it will fail at the start. Measurements against semifixed budgets are inadequate from a flexibility standpoint. Yet executives and managers too frequently strive to make the times fit their preplanned budgets; too often they postpone the revision of plans beyond the earliest indication that some internal or external condition, unexpected in nature, requires a different approach from the one originally decided upon.

A good control device, therefore, is one which is flexible enough to permit change as soon as change is required, irrespective of the passage of some arbitrary period of time.

7. *It must be the tool of the reviewing manager himself*—Accounting statements and records are rarely, if ever, accepted by either top management or operating managers as the goals or records of the top executive himself. Rather, they are accepted as the product of a third, a side-line party to the direct challenges of running the business. It is not uncommon for a clever salesman or plant manager to shift the trend of a control discussion by capitalizing on the obscuri-

ties with which summary accounting statements are necessarily loaded. The basic difficulty is, of course, the attempt to make accounting statistics serve more than one purpose.

The solution is obviously one which would furnish to the top executive his own exclusive control tool; one which is associated by everyone with his own unique personality; one which he and only he establishes or discontinues; and one which he consistently uses as his springboard to discussions concerning the state of the business.

Suggested Solution. As stated previously, there is in existence no tailor-made solution to the problem of adequate control tools—tools which permit more than just a measurement of past performance—nor is it likely that there will ever be any standard devices with universal application. The experience at RCA, however, indicates that it is possible to develop control systems which have distinct advantages over customary methods. As is the case with organization and procedures, this system of control must be custom-tailored to fit individual businesses, but its general philosophy is adaptable to any business large or small. This system adds virtually nothing to the administrative expenses of a company and has numerous benefits other than control. Essentially it embodies two basic elements:

1. Issuance, between the first and fifth of each month, of the top executive's personally developed booklet of control charts and graphs.
2. Strict adherence to a regular schedule of management control meetings shortly after the booklet is issued, with the booklet serving as the basis for all discussion.

At RCA the installation of this type of control system was accomplished by selecting initially the eight or ten major problems of the business—the ones which were most in need of regular top-level review and assistance. These were selected solely from the standpoint of areas where operations were obviously not functioning so smoothly and efficiently as they should be under ideal conditions. Whether or not the activity could be readily translated into chart form had nothing to do with the initial selection by the top executive.

The first booklet of charts included graphic presentations of such aspects of the business as net sales, unfilled customer orders, customer cancellations, manufacturing variance (i.e., difference between actual unit cost to build and estimated unit cost, expressed in per cent), inventory, ability to meet production schedules, and direct labor costs. By the end of 1948 all but four of the subjects included in the initial booklet (February 1947) were dropped because they had ceased to be of over-all significance *as probelms.* These four—sales, inventory, unfilled orders, and manufacturing variance—are of such persistent importance to any business that they continue to receive their deserved top-management attention. It is interesting to note, however, that the charts and graphs covering these four subjects are today entirely different presentations from the pictorial offerings in the initial booklet, which in retrospect was at best a very crude attempt at graphic presentation.

* * *

Conclusion

In nearly every business enterprise there is in existence all of the information and talent required for a thorough review of a product, a group of products, or a function at the time such review can be of tremendous control advantage. This information, however, is often in such a scattered condition that it is useless for "crisis" reviews (such as all businesses have recently undergone and can expect to undergo many times in the immediate future) until it has been specially gathered and analyzed on a one-time project basis. Sometimes the crisis is or appears to be so imminent that top managers cannot wait for detailed and specific analyses. So they do the next best thing by issuing arbitrary orders, depending more upon their highly developed "feel" than on the facts they do not have at hand. At other times top management, though hard pressed by an impending crisis, waits from 30 to 60 days while special analyses are prepared in an effort to arrive at a more intelligent course of action. In these cases the 30- to 60-day delay may well prove to be the worse of the two evils for the business.

A solution to the dilemma exists, of course, and is found in the case of those managers who are so well informed about all internal aspects of their business that the firm experiences no delay from the date of crisis awareness to the date of decision, but rather is in a position to execute a well-planned, gradual, anticipatory program.

There is no question but that the last postwar period has been economically more stable than that which followed the previous war chiefly because of the improved caliber of managers which the intervening period of time demanded and the management tools these men have developed. The ideas expressed in this article and the system described represent just one specific example of the manner in which this new type of management has found expression. Through such techniques we now look into the future with an attitude of "it ought to happen" rather than of "with the help of God." This is because our tools have been changed as well as sharpened, with the result that our ability to utilize the past and the present as guide for the future has vastly improved.

As a method of improving operations through the development of decentralized self-control and thereby aiding top management to keep pace with the increasingly heavy burden of the modern business world, the system described in this article has been thoroughly tested and has proved itself. All of the other benefits derived from the system, a number of which have been mentioned, are secondary and subsidiary to that primary accomplishment. There is little doubt but that the *philosophy* which *underlies* this particular approach to management control exemplified by the experience of the RCA Victor Division will be broadly accepted throughout the whole of American industry within the next decade.

49. HUMAN PROBLEMS
WITH BUDGETS [1]

Chris Argyris [2]

Budgets are accounting techniques designed to control costs through *people*. As such their impact is felt by everyone in the organization. They are continuously being brought into the picture when anyone is trying to determine, plan, and implement an organizational policy or practice. Moreover, budgets frequently serve as a basis for rewarding and penalizing those in the organization. Failure to meet the budget in many plants invites much punishment; success, much reward.

Because budgets affect people so directly, it seems appropriate to ask ourselves some questions about them. What are the effects of budgets on the human relationships in the organization? How well are budgets accomplishing their practical purposes? How can the use of budgets be improved to make them more effective? This article reports some of the results of a pilot study designed to suggest answers to questions like these.

Background Information

To keep the research problem within manageable limits, it was decided to focus primarily on the effects of *manufacturing* budgets (e.g., production, waste, and error budgets) upon the *front-line supervisor*. To this end our research group made a field study of three small plants (i.e., with less than 1,500 employees) manufacturing both "custom made" products and products "for stock"—all three of them unionized and covering the full range from highly skilled to nonskilled workers. (None of the plants, it should be noted, has a supervisory incentive system as part of its budget system.) In one plant we interviewed a 100% sample of front-line supervisors, in another a 90% sample, and in the third a 25% sample, using non-directive questions; and in addition we observed many of the same supervisors in action.

[1] From the *Harvard Business Review*, Vol. XXXI, No. 1, pp. 97-110. Reprinted by permission of the *Harvard Business Review*.
[2] Chris Argyris, Research Project Director at the Yale University Labor and Management Center.

Just in case my observations suggest that I have little sympathy for budgets, let me say that any such impression stems from the negative reactions which the interviews themselves produced. This is perhaps inevitable, when one keeps the following points about budgets in mind:

1. Budgets are, first of all, evaluation instruments. Because they tend to set goals against which to measure people, they naturally are complained about.
2. Budgets are one of the few evaluation processes that are always in writing and therefore concrete. Thus, some of the supervisors tend to use budgets as "whipping posts" in order to release their feelings about many other (often totally unrelated) problems.
3. Budgets are thought of as pressure devices. As such they produce the same kind of unfavorable reactions as do other kinds of pressure regardless of origin. In fact, the analysis I shall make of the effects of management pressure upon supervisors is not necessarily limited to budgets. For example, a company "saddled" with a domineering executive but which has no budget may well be affected by the same factors as those reported herein.

Preparation of budgets

The process of preparing a manufacturing budget is much the same in all plants:

It usually starts with a meeting of the controller, the assistant controller, and a group of top-management members to determine over-all financial goals for the company in the forthcoming year. The controller's staff then translates the financial goals into the detailed breakdowns required for departmental budgets. This preliminary budget is then sent to all superintendents, who are asked to scrutinize it carefully and report any alterations they wish to make.

During their period of scrutiny, the superintendents (middle management) discuss the budget with their own supervisory group in a series of meetings. The first-line foremen do not usually take part in these discussions, although their ideas are requested when the superintendents deem it desirable.

Once the superintendents have their budget modifications clearly in mind, a meeting is held with the controller and his staff. Both parties come to the meeting "armed to the teeth" with "ammunition" to back their demands. After the disagreements are resolved, all parties sign the new budget proposal. The superintendents return to their offices, awaiting the new budget and the expected drive to "put it over."

So much for background information. Now, let us turn to a discussion of some of the effects budgets seem to have upon people. This discussion will be limited to five major areas: (1) the problem resulting from the fact that budgets are used as a pressure device, (2) the problem of the budget supervisor's success and the factory supervisor's failure, (3) the problem of department-centered supervisors,

(4) the problem resulting from the fact that budgets are used as a medium for personality expression, and (5) a case example of human problems related to budgets. In conclusion, some lines of action for management to follow in meeting these problems will be suggested.

As a Pressure Device

One of the most common of the factory supervisors' assumptions about budgets is that they can be used as a pressure device to increase production efficiency. Finance people also admit to the attitude that budgets help "keep employees on the ball" by raising their goals and increasing their motivation. The problem of the effects of pressure applied through budgets seems to be at the core of the budget problem.

Causes of pressure

Employees believe that pressure from above is due to top management's assumption that most workers are basically or inherently lazy. Employees also believe that top management thinks the workers do not have enough motivation of their own to do the best possible job. And first-line supervisors have the same beliefs.

Interviews with top-management officials revealed that these employee beliefs were not totally unfounded, as a few quotations from some of the top management (both line and finance) make clear:

> "I'll tell you my honest opinion. About 5% of the people work, 10% of the people think they work, and the other 85% would rather die than work!"
>
> "I think there is a definite need for more pressure. People have to be needled a bit. Man is inherently lazy, and if we could only increase the pressure, I think the budget system would be more effective."
>
> "There are lots of workers in this plant, hundreds of them, who don't have the capacity to do things other than what they're doing. And they're lazy! They might be able to develop some capacities, although I think there are a lot of them who couldn't even if they wanted to. But *they don't even have the desire.*"

Such feelings, even if never openly expressed to the employees, filter through to them in very subtle ways. Once they sense that feelings of this kind exist in top management, they may become very resentful. Some supervisors, who apparently felt that budgets reflected this situation, expressed warnings like the following:

> "The employees have an established conception of a fair output. Now, if you believe, like most financial people do, that the average worker is out to cheat the company all the time, I give up."

"Managements ought to change their attitudes that employees are out to get them."

"Well, I guess they think that we need this needling. But *I* don't think so."

Effects of pressure

How do people react to pressure? In the three plants studied factory supervisors felt they were working under pressure and that the budget was the principal instrument of pressure. Management exerts pressure on the work force in many ways, of course; budgets are but one way. Being concrete, however, budgets seem to serve as a medium through which the total effects of management pressure are best expressed. As such they become an excellent focal point for studying the effect of pressure on people in a working organization.

To help clarify what happens when management "puts on the pressure" let us think of a situation in specific terms:

> For the sake of illustration, assume that the technical efficiency of a plant is at a maximum and that human efficiency, or effort, has to be increased if production is to be raised. The work force of the plant is producing at 70% of its efficiency. Since the level of efficiency is 70%, there must be certain forces which keep it from falling below 70% and certain forces which prevent it from going above 70%.
>
> Some of the forces which keep it from falling below 70% are: (a) budget talks to foremen; (b) red circling of poor showing of the departments in the budget results; (c) production drives; (d) pep talks by supervisors using budgets as evidence; (e) threat of reprimand if the budget is not met; and (f) threat of feelings of failure if budget is not met.
>
> Some of the forces which prevent efficiency from going above 70% are: (a) informal agreements among employees not to produce more; (b) fear of loss of job if efficiency increases; (c) foreman (union) agreements against "speedups"; (d) abilities of individual employees; (e) abilities of work teams as a whole.

In our example the level of production is stable; therefore both sets of forces are equal in strength. Suppose that top management decides to increase production. Usually, thought is immediately given to adding more factors to those that help increase production. The logic is that if these forces can be strengthened, they overcome the forces which tend to prevent efficiency from rising, and thereby increase production.

Budgets play an important part in this new "push." Finance people are usually asked to scrutinize all budgets carefully. They are directed to cut out all "the lace and niceties" and "get down to essentials." In short, a new pressure upwards is expressed somewhere in the new budgets in terms of a "tighter" figure.

The results may be as expected. Human efficiency rises, say, 10%, and production is increased. A new level of efficiency is stabilized at 80%.

But actually something else has occurred concurrently with this new push—something which management may not perceive. Since the level of human efficiency has now been stabilized at 80%, presumably factors that keep production down also have increased until they equal the factors that tend to increase production. Therefore, coupled with an increase in production, the plant also acquires an increase in forces directed in the opposite direction. People and groups are now trying harder (consciously or unconsciously) to keep production at this new level and prevent it from rising again.

It is not difficult to see what happens. Tension begins to mount. People become uneasy and suspicious. They increase the informal pressure to keep production at the new level. Any new increase will have to be "paid for" by management in "free" tickets to football games, slowdowns, strikes, etc.[3]

Moreover, management has to work harder to keep the new strength of the forces which tend to drag down efficiency from overwhelming the forces which resulted in increased production. It will find itself constantly looking for new ideas, new methods to keep the production at the present level. Any slight decrease in pressure on its part will result in an immediate reduction in production.

Finally, this constant increasing pressure from top management for greater production may lead to long-term negative results. People living under these conditions tend to become suspicious of every new move management makes to increase production, particularly budgets.

Creation of groups

An increase in tension, resentment, suspicion, fear, and mistrust may not be the only result of ever stronger management pressures transmitted to supervisors and, in turn, to employees. We know, from psychological research, that people can stand only a certain amount of pressure. After this point is passed, it becomes intolerable to an individual. We also know that one method people use to reduce the effect of the pressure (assuming that the employees cannot reduce the

---

[3] See Kurt Lewin, "Group Decision and Social Change," *Readings in Social Psychology*, edited by Theodore Newcomb and Eugene L. Hartley (New York, Henry Holt and Co., 1947), especially p. 342.

pressure itself) is to join groups, which help absorb much of the pressure and thus relieve the individual personally.

The process of individuals' joining groups to relieve themselves of pressure is not a simple one. The development of a group on such a basis seems to go through the following general stages:

1. First, the individuals sense an increase in pressure.
2. Then they begin to see definite evidences of the pressure. They not only feel it; they can point to it.
3. Since they feel this pressure is on them personally, they begin to experience tension and general uneasiness.
4. Next, they usually "feel out" their fellow workers to see if they too sense the pressure.
5. Finding out that others have noted the pressure, they begin to feel more at ease. It helps to be able to say, "I'm not the only one."
6. Finally, they realize that they can acquire emotional support from each other by becoming a group. Furthermore, they can "blow their top" about this pressure in front of their group.

Gradually, therefore, the individuals become a group because in so doing they are able to satisfy their need to (a) reduce the pressure on each individual; (b) get rid of tension; (c) feel more secure by belonging to a group which can counteract the pressure. Now, let us take a look at an actual example of the way this works out:

One of the plants we studied was under the "iron rule" of a top management executive known to the employees as "old thunder and guts" or "the whip." Many of the people interviewed in this plant mentioned what a terrible place it was in which to work. The pressure from above was high, and no one, reported the interviewees, knew exactly why it was high. Furthermore, they saw no sign that it would "let up."

As the pressure became intolerable for these people, some interesting things began to happen. Informal meetings between employees occurred with the pressure as the main topic of conversation. At first it was mentioned through jokes and "friendly gripes," but it soon became an increasing source of grievance. The private meetings expanded, and the groups became as high as eight in number. When asked why they attended these meetings, the interviewees answered: "It made me feel good to know I wasn't the only one." "If you're going through hell, it's nice to know that the others are also." And so on.

In due time the informal group feelings grew stronger, and the friendships created began to expand from the locker room to the members' homes, the local bars, and other social situations. Thus, out of these contacts there developed strong bonds which, although they were originally created by the pressure from management, had by now become re-enforced and stabilized by many other social activities.

The end result, judging by the interview material, was that the new groups became extremely cohesive and "well-knit." This high degree of solidarity had the effect of permitting these people to feel that they were now free to gripe against management because they had the support and sanction of their group.

In short, new cohesive groups developed to *combat* management pressure. In a sense, the people had learned that they could be happier if they combined against it.

Suppose now that top management, aware of the tensions which have been generated and the groups which have been formed, seeks to reduce the pressure. The emphasis on budgets is relaxed. Perhaps even the standards are "loosened." Does this then destroy the group? After all, its primary reason for existence was to combat the pressure; and now that the pressure is gone, the group should, according to common sense, disintegrate.

But apparently the group continues to exist. Just why this is so cannot be stated conclusively. In matters like this, we must make use in part of inference. Conceivably one or more of these three factors could operate to keep the group in existence:

1. There may be a "time lag" between the moment management announces the new policy and the time the workers put it into effect. However, no direct evidence was obtained to substantiate this possibility.

2. The individuals have made a new and satisfactory adjustment with one another. They have helped to satisfy each other's needs. They are, as the social scientist would say, "in equilibrium" with each other. Any attempt to destroy this balance will tend to be resisted even if the attempt represents an elimination of a "bad" or unhealthy set of conditions. People have *created* a stable pattern of life, and they will resist a change in this pattern.

    This resistance to change is not unusual. Experimental evidence suggests that cohesive groups will tend to resist attempts which may destroy their solidarity regardless of where these attempts originate (i.e., whether they come from the members themselves or from people outside the group).

    The top executives in two of the plants studied presented us with some vivid evidence of this factor. Under the influence of "high-pressure" leadership in these plants the employees seemed to become more suspicious of all management executives and at the same time more rigid and "harder to get along with." Issues which had never previously erupted were channeled through the organizational ladder as being "red-hot" grievances. Moreover, employees seemed to show great fear of any new changes. This was true even when they were assured that such changes would not occur until all their arguments had been heard and appropriate steps taken wherever possible.

    The top executives summed up the situation with such phrases as: "Things weren't like they used to be." "We weren't as close as we used to be." "To be honest with you something smelled somewhere, but I was not sure what." When asked if they felt the union might be the cause of their problem, they were quick to reply that the plants were organized long before these unhappy developments.

3. The individuals in the group may fear that pressure will come again in the future. Because of this feeling they will tend to create unreal

conditions or to exaggerate existing conditions just so they can rationalize to themselves that pressure still exists and therefore that the need for the group also exists.

Here again we found substantiating evidence. Some of the employees admitted in their interviews that, while management had officially announced a new policy of less pressure and more participation, they were suspicious about the participation and considered it a new way to cover up the old pressure. Others admitted freely that they spread unverified rumors about management intentions. In short, employees were doing their best to create *in their own minds* the conditions that would permit them to feel that pressure was still present and the need for the group still strong.

Pressure on supervisors

But what about the supervisor, particularly the front-line supervisor or foreman? Strong pressures also converge upon him. How does he protect himself from these pressures?

He cannot join a group against management, as his work force does. For one thing, he probably has at least partially identified himself with management. For another, he may be trying to advance in the hierarchy. Naturally, he would not help his chances for advancement if he joined an antimanagement group.

The evidence obtained from our study seems to indicate that the line supervisor cannot pass all the pressure he feels along to his workers. Time and time again factory supervisors stated that passing the pressure down would only create conflict and trouble, which in turn would lead to a decrease in production.

The question thus arises: Where does the pressure go? How do the supervisors relieve themselves of at least some of it? There is evidence to suggest at least three ways in which pressure is handled by the supervisors:

1. *Interdepartmental strife*—Some foremen seek release from pressure by continuously trying to blame others for the troubles that exist. In the three plants observed, much time was spent by certain factory supervisors in trying to lay the blame for errors and problems on their fellow supervisors. As one foreman put it, "They are trying to throw the cat in each other's backyard."
2. *Staff versus factory strife*—Foremen also try to diminish pressure by blaming the budget people, production-control people, and salesmen for their problems.
3. *"Internalizing" pressure*—Many supervisors who do not complain about the pressure have in reality "internalized" it and, in a sense, made it a part of themselves. Such damming up of pressure can affect supervisors in at least two different ways:
   a. Supervisor A is quiet, relatively nonemotional, seldom expresses his negative feelings to anyone, but at the same time he works

excessively. He can be found at his desk long after the others have gone home. He often draws the comment, "That guy works himself to death."

b. Supervisor B is nervous, always running around "checking up" on all his employees. He usually talks fast, gives one the impression that he is "selling" himself and his job when interviewed. He is forever picking up the phone, barking commands, and requesting prompt action.

One type "A" supervisor made the following remark:

"I'm just about sick and tired of the damn pressure in industry. It isn't human; moreover it's unnecessary. I've learned my lesson. I'm going to do my job as well as I can and not let things bother me. Some of the men around here work with the speed of a man 'hell bent for election.' Not me. And to be quite honest with you, I think I get as much done as they do."

After some further questioning, the same supervisor admitted that he would "like to tell a few people off around here. Believe me, at times I'd like to tear into. . . ." With a smile he speculated, "I wonder what they would think of me. I bet I'd surprise the daylights out of them." (There is little doubt that this supervisor would surprise those he threatens to attack. In fact, he would probably also surprise himself.)

Although we found quite a few examples of type "A" in our study, there were even more of type "B." One budget man of the "B" variety, after substantial clinical interviewing, admitted that he was working too hard. But he quickly added that he *had* to overwork himself; and that, if he didn't, the organization would not be in as sound a financial position as it is now. He sadly lamented the "fact" that there was no subordinate capable of replacing him. He said that he didn't think any of the likely candidates would worry about the job as he does. Yet, interestingly enough, he seemed greatly relieved when, after his admission that he really did want to take it easy, the interviewer did not respond with astonishment.

Both of these types are expressions of tensions and pent-up emotions that have been internalized. People working under too much pressure finally are forced to "take it easy," or they find themselves with ulcers or a nervous breakdown.

But that is not the end of the problem. Constant tension leads to frustration. A person who has become frustrated no longer operates as effectively as he used to.[4] He finds that he tends to forget things he used to remember. Work that he once did with pleasure he now

---

[4] Roger G. Barker, Tamaro Dembo, and Kurt Lewin, "Frustration and Regression," *University of Iowa Studies in Child Welfare*, Vol. 18, No. 1, 1941, p. 314.

delegates to someone else. He is not able to make decisions as fast as previously. Now he finds he has to take a walk or get a cup of coffee—anything to "get away from it all."

When times are bad

Most finance people agreed that budgets are used with greatest force when times are bad. In their experience, as soon as sales and profits decrease and the economic future begins to look black, budgets are immediately emphasized and strengthened.

What happens in such a situation? The foreman, who is already living in a pressure-laden and tension-filled world, suddenly finds himself (with others) in a bad economic period. All the stresses and strains (at home as well as in the plant) which are associated with poor economic conditions are added to the already existing tension-creating factors in his life. To make matters worse, management usually adds a third set of such factors by applying all sorts of pressure on him through budgeting.

The results are immediately evident. Extreme application to work or extreme aggression become "natural"—part of the "human nature" of the supervisor. His consequent attempts to alleviate some of the factors causing the tension may lead to quick, ill-conceived, confused, or violent action.[5]

Withdrawal, apathy, indifference are other results of such stresses and strains. Rumors begin to fly; mistrust, suspicion, and intolerance grow fast. In short, conflict, tension, and unhappiness become the key characteristics of the supervisor's life.

Another way to raise production

We have seen how, in order to increase human efficiency from 70% to 80%, pressure was applied through the medium of the budget. Adding to the forces which increase efficiency also strengthened the forces which decrease efficiency. Employees sought to relieve themselves of increased tension by combining into groups. Front-line supervisors, prevented from grouping, either "took it out" on other foremen or on the budget people, or else bottled it up within themselves. It seems possible that by such a procedure management has mortgaged the future to bring about an immediate increase in efficiency. This raises the question: Is there any other way to increase production?

[5] Alexander Leighton, *The Governing of Men* (Princeton, Princeton University Press, 1946) ; see especially the appendices.

The necessity for constantly increasing efficiency is a basic fact of business life. Yet increasing efficiency generates forces which in the long run decrease efficiency, and the problem is still unsolved; it may be worse than ever. So perhaps more can be gained by concentrating on weakening those forces which tend to decrease efficiency, rather than strengthening the forces which tend to increase efficiency. Basically, the only way out is to obtain the participation of the employees themselves in alleviating the factors that they have created to help keep production down.

To this end, conferences and interviews can be conducted where the employees have an opportunity to express their fears of increased production and their reasons for preventing production from rising. Needless to say, the executives in charge of such meetings should be sensitive to and aware of the facts that can cause resistances to changes. They should also be skilled in conference technique. For example, they may find it more profitable to prevent any vote by the group on a new idea, even a majority vote in acceptance. A vote in any group simply points up the fact that the group is divided. And since there may be employees who, as a result of the vote, are forced to do more than they consider a fair day's work, they are likely to have inner resistances to the changes and be the cause of further trouble. A more fruitful and lasting objective would be for the executives to help the group members define an objective upon which they all can agree.

In other words, the primary aim of such participation is to attempt to obtain acceptance of a new idea or change by removing the resisting forces within the individuals rather than by applying outside pressure.

Success and Failure

Students of human relations agree that most people want to feel a sense of achievement. We observe people constantly defining social and psychological goals, struggling to meet them, and, as they meet them, feeling successful.

Budget and factory supervisors are no exception. The typical budget or finance supervisor does his work as best he can. He hopes and expects just praise of his work from *his superior*. It is the "boss" who will eventually say "well done," or recommend a promotion. Most of his success comes, therefore, from his superior's evaluation. The situation is the same for the factory supervisor. He also desires success; and like the finance supervisor, much of his success also derives from the comments and behavior of the "boss." In short, both finance and factory supervisors are oriented toward the top for an evaluation of how well they are doing their jobs.

But here is where the trouble comes in: success for budget supervisors means failure for factory supervisors.

Role of budget supervisors

Our interviewers suggested that the budget people perceive their role as being "the watchdog of the company." They are always trying to improve the situation in the plant. As one finance supervisor said, "*Always* there is room to make it better." Or as a controller said, when describing a successful budget supervisor, "The budget man has made an excellent contribution to this plant. He's found a lot of things that were *sour*. You might say a good budget man . . . lets top management know if anything is *wrong*."

In other words, the success of the finance men derives from finding errors, weaknesses, and faults that exist in the plant. But when they discover such conditions, in effect they also are singling out a "guilty party" and implicitly, at least, placing him in failure. Naturally, any comment that "things aren't going along as well as they could in your department" tends to make the particular foreman feel he is deficient.

To be sure, such an occurrence will not make every factory supervisor feel he has failed. Some of the foremen we studied apparently do not worry much about their jobs. The one who really feels the failure is the foreman who is *highly interested in doing a good job*.

The implications of this phenomenon are interesting. It means that management people need to think twice when they discipline their supervisors; they need to study the differential effects of discipline upon supervisors. Otherwise they may create a situation in which the supervisor who "doesn't give two hoots" about his job will be unaffected while the supervisor who is loyal will suffer unduly.

Methods for rewarding supervisors may also need to be re-examined. The same objective increase in salary may tend to have different effects upon those receiving this increase. Thus a hard-working supervisor may feel hurt when he realizes that his "excellent" raise has also gone to supervisors who show in their work that they have no loyalty to the company.

Reporting foremen's shortcomings

The way in which foremen's shortcomings are reported also is important.

Let us assume that a finance man discovers an error in a particular foreman's department. How is this error reported? Does the finance man go directly to the factory foreman? In the plants studied the answer, usually, is no.

The finance man cannot take the "shortest" route between the foreman and himself. For one reason, it may be a violation of policy for staff personnel to go directly to line personnel. Even more important (from a human point of view), the finance man achieves his success when *his boss* knows he is finding errors. But his boss would never know how good a job he is doing unless he brought attention to it. In short, perhaps because of organizational regulations but basically because the measure of success in industry is derived from above, the finance man usually takes his findings to his own boss, who in turn gives them to his superior, and so on up the line and across and down into the factory line structure.

Taking the long way around has at least one more positive value for finance people. Those in middle and top management also derive some success in being able to go to the plant manager and point to some newly discovered weaknesses in the factory. Therefore, all the interested people up the entire finance structure obtain some sense of satisfaction.

But how about the factory people? The answer seems evident. In such a situation, the foreman experiences the negative feelings not only of being wrong but also of knowing that his superiors know it, and that he has placed them in an undesirable position.

Finally, to add insult to injury, the entire incident is made permanent and exhibited to the plant officials by being placed in some budget report which is to be, or has been, circulated through many top channels.

Effects of failure on people

One might ask: What effects has this kind of failure upon an individual? If the results were insignificant, obviously we would not be concerned. Unfortunately, such is not the case. Feelings of failure can have devastating effects upon an individual, his work, and his relationships with others.

Lippitt and Bradford, reporting on some ingenious scientific experiments conducted on the subject of success and failure, state that people who experience failures tend to:

1. Lose interest in their work,
2. Lower their standards of achievement,

3. Lose confidence in themselves,
4. Give up quickly,
5. Fear any new task and refuse to try new methods or accept new jobs,
6. Expect failure,
7. Escape from failure by daydreaming,
8. Increase their difficulty in working with others,
9. Develop a tendency to blame others, to be overcritical of others' work, and to get into trouble with other employees.[6]

We found many instances of supervisors who were experiencing failure and who exhibited these characteristics. Some of them were apathetic and did not care much for their work; they would, however, break out into a smile when they talked about fishing, vacations, the company recreational events, or any other activity which took place *outside* the plant environment. Other supervisors blamed everyone but themselves for their problems and insisted that in the industrial world one had to "look out for himself, for it was dog eat dog." Still others expressed little confidence in themselves or their subordinates; they claimed they could trust no one, and that life in the plant was a pretty dismal affair. (Of course other factors than a sense of failure were also contributing to these attitudes, but the failure aspect was clearly important.)

Wall between finance and factory

At least two more factors operate to place the finance people in the peculiar position which they hold:

1. Since the budget people are always looking for faults, they begin to develop a philosophy of life in which their symbol for success is not the error discovered but the very *thought* of the discovery of a possible new error.

2. The realization of the peculiar position in which they are placed leads budget people into a tendency to become defensive about their work. Though basically they may not like putting people in embarrassing positions, they have to. So they react negatively to queries about their methods, their language, their books. Sometimes they even use their technical know-how and jargon to confuse the factory people. As one budget man suggested, "After all, if the foremen don't know anything about budgets, how can they criticize them?"

   Thus, the ignorance of the factory people concerning budgets may serve as a wall behind which the finance people may work unmolested, and one of the major causes of insecurity among factory supervisors concerning budgets (i.e., "we can't understand them") becomes one of the primary factors of security for the budget people.

[6] Ronald Lippitt and Leland Bradford, "Employee Success in Work Groups," *Personnel Administration*, December 4, 1945, pp. 6-10.

There seems little doubt that the problem of success and failure is a major one. It needs further study. Present research has served merely to identify it.

DEPARTMENT-CENTERED SUPERVISORS

We have already shown that supervisors are partially evaluated by budget records. The factory supervisor who desires to be known as efficient and effective must make certain that his daily, weekly, monthly, and quarterly results compare favorably with the predicted results defined by the budgets. In short, a factory supervisor will feel successful, other things being equal, when he "meets his budget."

This idea of meeting the budget is crucial. For the budget, measuring the effectiveness of a supervisor as it does, continually emphasizes to each supervisor the importance of *his*, and *primarily* his, department. The budget records he receives show *his* department's mistakes, *his* department's errors, and *his* department's production—all *against* the other departments.

Interviews with the factory supervisors left little doubt that they were department-centered in outlook rather than plant-centered. Typical comments were:

> "The other day, I received an order to do a job, but no requisition. I called up production control and asked what was going on. I said to them, 'Why didn't I get the requisition on that order?' They started to give excuses. Sure, they didn't worry. *This was my job, just like I don't have to worry when the other departments stand still.*"

> "Each one of us gets *his* own picture when we get the budget results. Even if we got the total picture, it wouldn't mean much to us. We go right for our sheet. . . . As I said, we might get the whole plant picture, *but we're primarily interested in our own department.*"

> "I don't get a picture of the other people's budgets in this place, and I don't think I need or even want one. My main responsibility is in this here outfit of mine. *Nowhere else.* So, let them worry about their problem, and I'll worry about mine."

The philosophy which budgets foster may be expressed this way: if every supervisor worries about his own department, there will be no trouble in the plant. Therefore, if each supervisor is made primarily responsible for the production aspect of his part of the whole picture, no problems will arise.

Such a philosophy overlooks an extremely important point. An organization is something different from the sum of the individual parts. The parts of an organization exist in certain *relationships* with each other, and it is these relationships which create the difference. One cannot conceive of "adding" together the parts of an organization any more than adding together the hundreds of pieces that make up a watch in order to make it run. The crucial problem is to place the parts in correct relationship to each other.

Without laboring the point it seems clear that important relationships between departments are disregarded by overemphasizing the individual departments. If everyone does his utmost to make certain that his own department is functioning correctly, but at the same time pays no attention to the functioning of his department in relation to others, trouble will still arise. And then, particularly in plants which make forceful use of budgets, with the supervisors trying to blame someone else so their departments are not the ones to be penalized, the conflict begins.

Controlling conflicts

But does not control of the relationships among departments rest with the plant manager or some higher authority? Is he not able, from his high position, to control the conflict among departments? The crux of the matter is that this *is* all the leader can do—*control* conflict. (He is unable to eliminate it, since its deep-rooted causes are not within his reach.) And because the supervisors know he controls conflict, they increasingly look to him to break up a fight or settle a dispute. Furthermore, the more successful the top leader is in this respect, the less the supervisors need to worry about cooperation. They soon learn that the leader will solve any interdepartmental problem, and become dependent on him.

Here is an example of the kind of situation that can develop:

> In one of the plants studied a mistake was made on a customer order. The customer returned the material to the plant, where the error was corrected, and the material was then sent back to the customer.
>
> The cost of making the correction was nearly $3,000. The error, especially since it was so large, had to be entered in the budget records. Some department had to be charged with the error. But which department? That was the problem.
>
> For two months supervisors of the departments most likely to be blamed waged a continuous campaign to prove their innocence. Each blamed the others. No one wanted the error on *his* record. They spent hundreds of man-hours arguing and debating among themselves. Emotions were aroused; people began calling each other names. Finally, two of the supervisors stopped talking to each other.
>
> By this time the division manager was also in hot water. To charge any supervisor with such an error would certainly invite hostility from that supervisor—hostility which might have further effects in the future. Naturally, the division manager did not want to risk a weakening of his relationships with any of his supervisors. But he had to make a decision.

A meeting was held with the interested supervisors. The problem was discussed, and blame was placed on just about everybody and everything possible. The division manager finally gave up; he decided to charge the error to no department but rather to let the plant as a whole carry the stigma. As he himself explained it, "I thought it might be best to put the whole thing under general factory loss. Or else someone would be hurt."

This case shows that budget records, as administered, foster a narrow viewpoint. They serve as a constant reminder that the important aspect to consider is one's own department, not the over-all good of the plant.

LEADERSHIP PATTERNS

The final problem to be discussed became evident only after a series of interviews with various controllers and top factory officials indicated that the ways in which people express their interest in budgets, and the ways in which they describe and use them, are directly related to the pattern of leadership they use in their daily industrial life. For example, when a rather domineering, aggressive, "go-getting" top executive was interviewed, his presentation of the problem tended also to be made in a domineering, aggressive, "go-getting" manner.

Therefore, although it is accurate to state that budgets are composed of "cold, nonhuman symbols" (i.e., figures), it is equally valid to state that once human beings use these "nonhuman figures," they project on to them all the emotions and feelings at their command. An incident which occurred in one of the plants studied may illustrate this point:

At the close of a particularly violent budget meeting in which a top executive had flayed his subordinates needlessly, he ended by saying, "Now, fellows, I'm sorry I got hot. But it's these budget figures—well, you know, I worry about them." The subordinates all nodded their heads to indicate that they understood. They left the meeting room thinking, "Those damn budgets again. *They get the boss all upset.*"

But this kind of interpretation, although highly prevalent when such instances occur, is not at all accurate. It was *not* the budgets that got the boss "all upset." The budgets were merely a medium through which the boss could *express* the fact that he was upset. Obviously budgets per se can do nothing. It is the people who use them that cause the behavior observed. Budgets, then, can be used to express one's pattern of leadership.

Because budgets become a medium of personality and leadership expression, and since people's personalities and leadership patterns are different, our research study found a number of methods with which top factory executives used budgets. A few of these methods are illustrated by the following comments made by top factory supervisors:

> "I go to the office and check that budget every day. I can then see how we're meeting it. If it's O.K., I don't say anything. But if it's no good, then I come back here and give the boys a little—well, you know, I needle them a bit."
>
> "I make it a policy to have close contact, human contact, with the people in my department. If I see we're not hitting the budget, I go out and tell them I have $40,000 on the order. Well, they don't know what that $40,000 means. They think it's a lot of money so they get to work. The human factor, that's what is important. If you treat a human being like a human being, you can use them better and get more out of them."
>
> "You know it's a funny thing. If I want my people to read the budget, I don't shove it under their nose. I just lay it on my desk and leave it alone. They'll pick it up without a doubt."

Note how the different ways in which these men use budgets express different patterns of leadership.

A Case Example

A case example may serve to illustrate the use of budgets as media through which the factory executive expresses his personality, and at the same time point up the problem of department-centered supervisors previously discussed.

A top factory executive called a meeting to discuss the problem of waste in his organization, especially the waste in two departments. Present at the meeting were the supervisors of the two departments in question, the supervisor of another department supplying the material to these two departments, two budget people, and the top executive whom we shall call the leader.

> *Leader:* "I've called you fellows down to get some ideas about this waste. I *can't* see why we're having so much waste. I just can't see it. . . . Now, I've called in these two budget men to get some ideas on the subject. Maybe they can tell us how much some of the arguments you're going to give are worth."
>
> *Budget man* [slightly red, apparently realizing he is putting the supervisors "on the spot"]: "Well, uh, we might be wrong, but I can't see how. There's an entire 0.1% difference, and that's a lot."
>
> *Supervisor X to Supervisor Y* [trying to see if he can place the blame elsewhere]: "Well, maybe—maybe—some of your boys are throwing away the extra material I sent back to your department."

Supervisor Y [quickly and curtly]: "No, no. We're reworking the extra material and getting it ready to use over again."

Supervisor X [changing his tack]: "Well—you know—I've been thinking, maybe it's those new trainees we have in the plant. Maybe they're the cause for all the waste."

Leader: "I can't understand that. Look here—look at their budget—their waste is low."

The meeting continued for another twenty minutes. It was primarily concerned with the efforts of supervisors X and Y to fix the blame on someone besides themselves. The leader terminated the meeting by saying, "All right, look here, let's get busy on this—all of you—all of *us*, let's do something about it."

Supervisor X left the meeting, flushed, tense, and obviously unhappy. As he passed through the door, he muttered to himself, "Those . . . budgets!"

Supervisor Y hurried down to his area of the plant. He rushed into the office and called his subordinates abruptly, "Joe, Jim, all of you, get over here. I want to speak to you; something is up."

The subordinates came in, all wondering what had occurred. As soon as they had all assembled, the supervisor started: "Look, we've just *got* to get at this waste. It makes me look like hell. Now let's put our heads together and get on the ball."

His subordinates then set to work to locate the causes for the waste. Their methods were interesting. Each one of them *first* checked to see, as one of them put it, "that the group in the other departments aren't cheating us." A confidential statement finally came to Supervisor Y's desk from one of the subordinates to the effect that he had located the cause in Department X.

Supervisor Y became elated, but at the same time was angry at the fact that he had been made to look "sick" at the meeting with the leader. He warned, "I'm going to find out why they are making the waste. I don't mind the short end of the stick as long as it's me that's doing the trouble."

Supervisor Y roared out of his office and headed straight for the office of Supervisor X. The latter saw him coming and braced himself for the onslaught. Y started in, "I found out that it's your boys causing the waste. You . . . , I want to know why. . . ."

"Don't get your blood up," cut in X. "I'll tell you. . . ."

And so it went. In this cost-conscious plant, six people on the supervisory level spent many hours trying to place the blame on someone else.

IMPLICATIONS FOR MANAGEMENT

This explanatory research has led to the tentative conclusion that budgets and budgeting can be related to at least four important human relations problems:

1. Budget pressure tends to unite the employees against management, and tends to place the factory supervisor under tension. This tension may lead to inefficiency, aggression, and perhaps a complete breakdown on the part of the supervisor.
2. The finance staff can obtain feeings of success only by finding fault with factory people. These feelings of failure among factory supervisors lead to many human relations problems.
3. The use of budgets as "needlers" by top management tends to make each factory supervisor see only the problem of his own department.
4. Supervisors use budgets as a way of expressing their own patterns of leadership. When this results in people getting hurt, the budget, in itself a neutral thing, often gets blamed.

Now, in the light of these findings, what lines of action should management take? Though the problems obviously are complex, and the research into them exploratory, there do appear to be two areas in which management action may prove fruitful.

Participation in making budgets

The first is in the problem of getting an acceptance of budgets. Interviews with controllers suggest that this area is a crucial one. Time and time again our research group was told that the best way to gain acceptance is to have the supervisors all participate in the making of the budgets that affect them. In particular the controllers emphasized the need for participation of all key people in instituting any *changes* in budgets, plus the willingness on the controllers' own part to revise their budgets whenever experience indicates it necessary.

The typical controller's insistence on others' participation sounded good to us when we first heard it in our interviews. But after a few minutes of discussion it began to look as if the word "participation" had a rather strange meaning for the controller. One thing in particular happened in *every* interview which led us to believe that we were not thinking of the same thing. After the controller had told us that he insisted on participation, he would then continue by describing his difficulty in getting the supervisors to speak freely. For example:

> "We bring them in, we tell them that we want their frank opinion, but most of them just sit there and nod their heads. We know they're not

coming out with exactly how they feel. I guess budgets scare them; some
of them don't have too much education. . . . Then we request the line
supervisor to sign the new budget, so he can't tell us he didn't accept it.
We've found a signature helps an awful lot. If anything goes wrong,
they can't come to us, as they often do, and complain. We just show
them their signature and remind them they were shown exactly what
the budget was made up of. . . ."

Such statements seem to indicate that only "pseudo-participation"
is desired by the controller. True participation means that the people
can be spontaneous and free in their discussion. Participation, in the
real sense of the word, also involves a group decision which leads the
group to accept or reject something new. Of course, organizations
need to have their supervisors accept the new goals, not reject them;
however, if the supervisors do not really accept the new changes but
only say they do, then trouble is inevitable. Such halfhearted acceptance makes it necessary for the person who initiated the budget or
induced the change, not only to request signatures of the "acceptors"
so that they cannot later on deny they "accepted," but to be always on
the lookout and apply pressure constantly upon the "acceptors"
(through informal talks, meetings, and "educational discussions of
accounting").

In other words, if top-management executives are going to use
participation, then they should use it in the real sense of the word.
Any dilution of the real thing "will taste funny," and people will not
like it.

Of course employees cannot participate in all phases of the plant
budget. In the typical plant most of the over-all goals of a plant or
even a department cannot be set by the members of the plant or the
department. But the ways in which these goals are to be accomplished
can be decided upon cooperatively by the interested employees. In
other words, if top management has set down a profit goal for the
year, then there is not much sense in saying the people actually participated in setting that goal. Nor should management try to get them
to feel this is *their* goal in the sense that they created it. But top
management can try to make them feel that this is *their* goal in the
sense that they participated in a decision to accept it.

We have found that goals are most often accepted if the individual
members can come together in a group, freely discuss their opinions
concerning these goals, and take part in defining the steps by which
these goals will be accomplished.

Training in human relations

The second area in which management action may attack these budget problems is that of training in human relations.

Our interviews with the top controllers constantly brought out the "figure conscious," narrow-minded rigidity of most finance people. Here are some typical criticisms of accountants:

> "Most of them are warped and they have narrow ideas. That, incidentally, is one of the failures of our educational system. We give the fellows all the textbook stuff, but we never teach them how to 'sell' accounting."
>
> "Most of our accountants are narrow and shortsighted. They have a narrow breadth of view. They are what I call 'shiny pants bookkeepers.' They're technicians. They don't know how to handle people."
>
> "I might add, right here and now, that I think one of the worst human problems we have is the poor job of 'selling' that is done with cost records and budgetary control. I think our accounting people are very, very poor in ability to get along with people and to sell them correctly. In fact, I'd go as far as to say that the better the accountant, the poorer he is in human relations. I feel quite strongly about this."

Our findings indicate that, first of all, more instruction in human relations need to be given to students of cost accounting and budgeting at the college level. We are not prepared to say in what form this instruction can best be integrated into the curriculum, though it appears that such instruction could well be fitted into the traditional case approach of accounting instruction. The accounting and cost-control cases usually present to the student some major technical problems for solution. At the end of each case the student is asked to answer certain questions, and these could well include some issues involving the human relations implications of the problem.

As far as industry's role in training is concerned, I doubt that its main function is to make budget people familiar with the factory people's tasks. To do such a job thoroughly would require a lengthy and extremely expensive training program. Moreover, wherever plants have attempted to have the finance people visit the factory departments and learn some of the factory people's problems, this training has helped but does not seem to have solved the underlying problem.

Rather, the training should be focused on the underlying problems, not on the superficial difficulties. In line, then, with the major problems identified by our analysis up to this point, the following specific suggestions seem appropriate:

1. The training should be focused to help the finance staff perceive the human implications of the budget system.
2. The training should help show the finance staff the effects of pressure upon people. Thorough discussions seem necessary to understand the advantages and disadvantages of applying such pressure.
3. The training should also include discussions concerning the effects of success and failure. The accounting staff should be helped to perceive their difficult position, namely, that of placing others in failure. They should also be taught the symptoms of people who feel they have failed. Most important, the course should include practical techniques which the finance staff can use to get along better with the factory people. Knowing full well that they may place these factory people in failure.
4. Again, the human relations training should include thorough discussions of the human problems related to the department-centeredness of supervisors that is caused by budgets. The finance people should be helped to perceive this department-centeredness as a defense on the part of the factor supervisors rather than as the "narrow-mindedness" which many of them seem to think it is.
5. Finally, there needs to be some instruction in the basic content of human relations as a field of study. This includes the concepts of informal and formal organizations, industrial organizations as social systems, status systems in industrial organizations, and such subjects as interviewing, counseling, and leadership.

Throughout such training the emphasis should be placed upon these supervisors' learning to understand themselves (e.g., their feelings, their values, their prejudices). Once they have been helped to evaluate themselves as human beings, then they are better able to understand their human effects on the others with whom they deal as experts in their particular field.

As for training methods, it follows that the trainer should keep lecturing to a minimum. Case discussion,[7] role-playing,[8] and the member-centered conference [9] are examples of methods which may be profitably used. The conference sessions should be so designed that the leader helps the trainees help themselves. Since the group members are to be the center of their own problem-solving conferences, the leader will take only such roles as a "summarizer of opinions," "clarifier of feelings," and "instigator of free creative thinking." [10]

---

[7] F. J. Roethlisberger, "Training Supervisors in Human Relations," *Harvard Business Review*, September, 1951, pp. 47-57; also in the same issue see Kenneth R. Andrews, "Executive Training by the Case Method," pp. 58-70.
[8] Chis Argyris, "Role-Playing in Action," N.Y.S.S.I.R.L. Bulletin (Ithaca, Cornell University, April, 1952).
[9] Chris Argyris, "Techniques of 'Member-Centered' Training," *Personnel*, November, 1951, pp. 236-241.
[10] *Ibid.*

50. CONTROL AND FREEDOM
IN A DECENTRALIZED COMPANY [1]   Raymond Villers [2]

Industrial management today faces a strange dilemma. Half a century of experience has shown conclusively that planning and control are the basic requirements of economical manufacturing. But a decade or so of intensive research in human relations shows with equal conclusiveness that our large organizations and our methods of planning and control are, more often than not, antagonistic to good human relations, so essential to the successful management of an industrial enterprise. Reliable studies indicate that our methods of planning and control may even tend to deprive the members of our industrial organizations of one of man's basic needs—a sense of purposeful and worthwhile accomplishment. [3]

PRACTICAL PROBLEM

Planning and control are nevertheless as necessary today as ever; large organizations are here to stay—and will continue to develop further. The practical problem, therefore, "is that of building large organizations and of retaining, at the same time, the quality and strength of small, well-integrated work groups." [4] How can this be done?

An increasing number of companies are endeavoring to find the answer in a policy of decentralization of decision making; that is, they are trying to spread the responsibility for final decisions. The methods followed in implementing this policy vary greatly from one company to another. Some companies have decentralized along geographical lines, others by products manufactured, others by management functions, and so on; sometimes these various factors are combined.

[1] From the *Harvard Business Review*, Vol. XXXII, No. 2, pp. 89-96. Reprinted by permission of the *Harvard Business Review*.
[2] Raymond Villers, Visiting Associate Professor of Industrial Engineering at Stevens Institute of Technology and Lecturer, Columbia University, 1954.
[3] See, for instance, Chris Argyris, "The Impact of Budgets on People," *Harvard Business Review* (January-February, 1953), p. 97.
[4] Burleigh B. Gardner and David G. Moore, *Human Relations in Industry* (Chicago: Richard D. Irwin, Inc., 1950), p. 402.

In every case, however, certain functions or activities are kept centralized. At General Motors, for instance, the divisions are decentralized both geographically and by products, but the financial and legal functions have remained centralized. At Koppers, where decentralization is also the general rule, the purchasing function is centralized for most products. And in many other companies the personnel function has remained centralized.

Regardless of the specific approach used, all companies face the same two major obstacles to success in their efforts:

1. The difficulty of decentralizing down to a sufficiently small unit. (The decentralized unit of a large corporation is generally of substantial size, often including many plants and several thousand employees. There is little or no decentralization *within* such a unit.)
2. The difficulty of controlling the decentralized unit. (Simplified controls, such as those based essentially on the well-known criterion of "return on investment," often prove to be deceptive and can be applied successfully only to decentralized units of substantial size.)

Useful Concept

It is the purpose of this article to describe the concept of centralized planning and control associated with decentralized authority and responsibility which management can use to overcome these obstacles. This concept reconciles the organization's need for coordinated action with the legitimate aspirations of individuals; and it is applicable to large, small, and medium-size companies alike. Although it is comparatively new, it has gained increasing acceptance in recent years, no doubt due in large part to the results it has secured.

After a brief description of its basic features, three case studies will show how it works in the hands of executives who are under pressure to solve everyday business problems. This will give us a realistic idea of the difficulties and the benefits which can be expected when the concept is applied.

Four essential features

There are four essential features of the concept of centralized planning and control in conjunction with decentralized authority and responsibility:

Management must functionalize planning and control, centralizing it in a separate department.

Management must make a precise determination of the lines of authority and responsibility.

Management must define clearly the methods by which the various division and department heads can participate in planning.

Management must develop methods of control which are adapted to the need of coordinated action in a decentralized organization.

Now let us examine these points in a little more detail.

Centralized control

In the process of planning and controlling the complex activities of such specialized departments and functions as purchasing, marketing, engineering, personnel, accounting, and so on, modern management has developed techniques which have themselves become so complex that they have to be handled by specialists. When this need is recognized, general management retains the full responsibility for high policy decisions, for giving directives, for rewarding or penalizing; but the technical activities involved in planning and control are entrusted to a specialized department. Some companies call it the "control department," others the "administrative controls department," and still others merely extend the regular duties of the controller's office to include the new function.

Although the details vary greatly among individual companies, a planning and control department usually has these general functions:

1. It collects the data necessary to general management at the time decisions of high policy are being made—sales estimates, marketing policy, size of inventory, level of employment, financing needs, and so on.
2. It translates high policy decisions into specific assignments. The department heads who receive such assignments are given an opportunity to express their views and may under specified conditions request a change in the scope or the timing of the assignments.
3. It compares the quantity, quality, timing, and costs of actual performance with the specifications in the assignment, and prepares managerial reports based on the comparison. The reports are addressed to the department which has received and accepted the assignment, as well as to executives at higher levels of management who are responsibile for coordinating action in the organization. Under this centralized approach, in turn, such reports can be kept together in an up-to-date "control book."

Lines of authority

The translation of high policy into specific assignments for departments or individuals obviously means that someone must make decisions with respect to lines of authority and responsibility. The planning and control department is *not* responsible for decisions of this sort. Rather, they should be made by the top operating executives in the form of permanent operating procedures for the whole organization.

Much has been said about the dangers of specialization. The reader is no doubt familiar with the picture often presented of the conditions prevailing in the average modern plant where no member of management supervises a wide variety of jobs but instead each is restricted to a narrow field of activity. Instead of being left alone with a crew of men as in the "good old times" (which incidentally were not very pleasant times in terms of human relations), the modern foreman sees his activity limited by many specialists—the engineer, the inspector, the personnel director, and so forth. He tends to feel like a small cog in a big wheel.

To some extent this picture is true. Supervisors do often feel frustrated in this way. But in another respect it is misleading. The popular assumption about the cause of the dissatisfaction is not justified. It is not specialization so much as the *lack of communication* that causes supervisors to feel the way they do.

Moreover, it is futile to try to solve the problem by "turning the clock back." Specialization is the unavoidable consequence of our industrial civilization. It will get us nowhere to be nostalgic; rather, we must think in terms of constructive adjustment to the needs of today's industrial life. Most certainly we should not ignore the human problem, but we should consider it in the light of the requirements of modern industry.

In sum, we do not need to be afraid of drawing lines of authority and responsibility to meet the needs of specialization if at the same time we keep the lines of communication between the various functions wide open. Then each specialist can visualize in its proper perspective the part he plays in the whole organization, even though his field of authority and responsibility is clearly and, if need be, narrowly defined. Instead of feeling like a cog in a wheel, he can feel like a member of a team—a specialized but eminently useful member.

Participation in planning

The specialist's feelings of being part of a team are reinforced if he is called upon to participate in the planning of his activities and is given complete independence of action within his field of specialization. These purposes are served and encouraged within the framework of planning and control when the following principles are observed:

1. The planning and control department acts as a service department only. It does not issue orders, but simply translates general decisions into specific assignments. It does not tell each department *how* a certain goal should be reached but defines *what* should be accomplished and *when* it should be done, in order to implement decisions of policy made at a high management level.

2. These specific assignments are initially *proposals*. In actual practice they take the form, for example, of a schedule of material requirements addressed to the purchasing department, or of a schedule of production of finished items addressed to the plant superintendent, or of a schedule of preparation of blueprints for tools addressed to the manager of the tooling department.

   Each department manager who receives such an assignment has the privilege of declining it for any valid reason, such as that the time allowed is too short or the quality is unobtainable. If the department concerned cannot agree with planning and control on a substitute assignment, the matter is referred to a higher level of management as in the case of any controversy between departments in a well-managed organization.

3. To expedite matters and avoid unnecessary meetings, it has been found advantageous to establish the general rule that if the department head who receives the assignment raises no objections to it within a given period, say three or four days, he becomes fully responsible for the performance. At the same time he and his associates are free to choose their own ways and means as long as the goal assigned is reached at the right time, at the right cost, and in accordance with the terms of the assignment or standard specifications.

Methods of control

The risk involved in the foregoing practices is obvious. A department or an individual is entrusted with a given assignment and left alone in accordance with the principle of decentralization of authority and responsibility. That is fine if he succeeds, but what happens if he fails? Obviously, this is a crucial question.

A partial answer is that the members of the organization should be given the proper training and should have opportunities to develop their ability to handle responsibility. If they can judge wisely what assignments they can fulfill and what they cannot, failures to perform will be rare. Furthermore, they can be asked to give a warning as soon as they have a serious reason to doubt that they will be able to perform as expected. Through this procedure the damaging consequences of an eventual failure can be minimized.

Nevertheless, it is a fact that failure will occur from time to time. A policy of decentralization of authority, based on the concept that individuals may be entrusted with the full responsibility for certain assignments, is acceptable only if the risk entailed by failure is not of excessive magnitude. It is essential, therefore, for control to be exercised at such frequent intervals as is necessary to prevent excessive damage in the case of a failure to perform. This means that there is a limit to how far decentralization can go. To illustrate:

> If new tools are required for certain production run six months hence, the assignment issued to the tool engineer might be broken down into these five stages:
>
> 1. Preliminary report and proposed design
> 2. Cost estimate
> 3. Blueprint and ordering of materials
> 4. Test run
> 5. Delivery of tools to toolroom.
>
> The planning and control department assigns a deadline to *each* of these steps, using the final deadline set up by top management for a guide, and allowing for a certain safety cushion in the timing. If a delay occurs in the test runs, for instance, it is reported immediately. Proper managerial action by a higher authority can then be taken in time to prevent the whole production program from being jeopardized because tools are not available.

Finally, it is in some cases possible and desirable to evaluate in dollars and cents the consequences of a failure to perform. If, for instance, an undue delay occurs in the delivery of materials, the cost of this delay, in terms of dollars of direct labor representing the time lost in the plant, may be recorded in a special report which reflects the responsibility of the purchasing agent in the matter.

THREE CASE STUDIES

Now let us turn to three actual cases [5] which illustrate, in narrative form, some of the difficulties and advantages of applying the concept of planning and control associated with decentralized authority and responsibility.

Plant superintendent

This is the case of a plant superintendent in a plant employing over 700 workers.

Prior to the creation of a planning and control department, the organization of planning was very much neglected. The plant superintendent was accustomed to regulating production on the basis of orders received by the company from its customers and of indications

---

[5] Adapted from the author's book, *The Dynamics of Industrial Management* (New York: Funk & Wagnalls Company, 1954).

given to him in an informal way by the sales department. He would request the services of the maintenance department when needed; his assistant would "keep an eye" on the materials in the warehouse; he would anticipate his needs in personnel in time of seasonal peaks and give instructions for future hiring to the personnel department; and so forth. While he complained about being forced into such an exhausting activity, and while he was sincere in his complaint, he actually found it gratifying in many respects.

Then a planning and control department was established. He learned that in the future this department would tell him what items should be produced and when, and that no longer would he have responsibility for materials, tools, personnel, and so on. Instead, he would merely have to requisition from the warehouse; tools would be ready for use the day an item was scheduled for production; and personnel needs would be anticipated on the basis of future production programs without requiring his intervention. Quite naturally, he felt as if he had been demoted.

It soon became apparent that his area of authority had in fact decreased; to this extent his first reactions were confirmed. Granted, his authority was more clearly defined. But he was no longer negotiating with the sales department about a rush order, or with the tooling department about urgent requirements, or with the purchasing department about needed materials. He was told what to produce and when.

Yet if his authority had decreased in *surface*, it had increased in *depth*. He soon noticed that, within his own field of responsibility, he had more stature as a manager than before. No one at a higher level would suggest to him that he should, for instance, instruct his foremen to watch more carefully the quality of production or the productivity of their workers—subjects which had in the past been a frequent source of controversy between him and his vice president. He was shown the results obtained in his plant in more detail than he had ever known in terms of cost, rejects, sales returns, absenteeism, turnover, and so on; but this was information rather than interference, for it was left to him to improve the situation, as needed, in his own way.

In turn, he learned to apply similar principles in his relationships with his foremen; and, thanks to the planning and control department, he had more data with which to control their performance objectively.

After about a year this plant superintendent came to the conclusion that he had gained in independence of action and that his real responsibility had increased. He concentrated willingly and with sincere satisfaction on his newly defined assignment. In retrospect, that things turned out this way seems to be due in large part to two factors, which experience indicates are essential to the successful centralization of planning and decentralization of responsibility:

1. Centralized planning was limited to a service activity; it did not operate as an order-issuing agency.
2. Informal relationships developed between specialized functions—e.g., between the plant superintendent and the head of the tooling department—which made it possible for them to work together despite the fact that neither had authority over the other.

Purchasing agent

In this case (all names disguised), Richards was the purchasing agent in a highly centralized company, the Rigid Corporation. The president of the company was in the habit of checking every move of his executives. He would call Richards at any time of the day, and sometimes in the evening at his home: "Have you written to the supplier about that problem we discussed this morning?" Or, "Don't write; go and see him." Or, "Don't tell him this; rather, take it from that angle. . . ." He would also make remarks implying that his executives were not punctual, such as, "I called you half an hour ago, but you had not yet arrived."

Richards' salary was good and his job secure, but after ten years he finally decided that the situation was hopeless, and he quit at the first opportunity. He went to the Hart Manufacturing Company as purchasing agent. His predecessor there had been transferred prior to his arrival and was not available to instruct him about the details of his new job.

The Hart Manufacturing Company had been reorganized two years before. A planning and control department had been created, and a policy of decentralization of authority had been adopted. Having served as an adviser to the company, the writer was asked to initiate Richards. The initiation went much as follows:

"From what you tell me, I would say that you will find that the methods of management at the Hart Manufacturing Company are almost exactly the opposite of those you have been used to at the Rigid Corporation. You will find that no one here will check how you are doing your job.

"Ralph, whom you met this morning, is the head of the planning and control department. He will tell you what materials are needed for production and when. Every six months he will give you a general purchasing program and you will place the orders. You get the specifications from the engineering department. You select the suppliers yourself. You decide yourself about what prices you want to pay.

"You will find that for most materials used we have standard prices. The variance between the price you pay and the standards are carefully followed up by Ralph's department and reported both to you and to your vice president, who keeps in touch with the market and will step in if he feels that the prices you are paying are too high. Incidentally, if you find a way of getting lower prices, he will step in, too—to congratulate you.

"But, in any case, he will step in *after* you, under your own responsibility, have placed the purchase order, not before—unless you turn to him for advice, which you may do at any time. In some exceptional cases, he may take the initiative; but you will find this a very rare occurrence.

"For planning purposes the weeks of the year are designated by consecutive numbers. Every week you will receive a release schedule which will tell you what materials, on order but not yet delivered, are needed for production during each of the following eight weeks. As you know, we are short of materials. [This was a few months after the outbreak of the war in Korea.] This release schedule is therefore a very important matter. Check it carefully when you receive it. If you do not call Ralph within a few days after you have received it, you are considered as having accepted it.

"It then becomes your responsibility to supply the materials on time. Any delay will disrupt production. The cost of the disruption will be evaluated by the planning and control department and will be charged against your department."

At this point, Richards asked two questions and received the following answers:

Question: "You know how suppliers are. They may say 'yes' and yet they don't deliver. They may just say 'perhaps.' What do you want me to tell Ralph, when I receive his release schedule, in a situation where I am 50-50 sure?"

Answer: "Your position is fully appreciated. But you must realize that, in the whole organization, you are *the one* who is in the best position to evaluate the situation. Now, someone has to take responsibility. As you know, a plant cannot have a 'perhaps' production schedule or 'perhaps' tools on hand or a 'perhaps' machine setup. It has to be 'yes' or 'no.' Sometimes we will be disappointed. Everyone agrees that it can happen that you will say 'yes,' and yet the material will not be there on time. But that doesn't lessen your responsibility.

"The real issue is how often it will occur and what the damage will be. At the end of the year, two accounts will tell the whole story. The price-variance account will show how active you have been in getting good prices. The time-lost account will show how reliable your deliveries to the production department have been.

"In addition, of course, we expect that your materials will be up to specifications—and that you will not systematically protect yourself by refusing to accept Ralph's release schedules."

Question: "What do I do if I think that I cannot get the material in time?"

Answer: "You call Ralph and tell him so. Nine times out of ten, even more often than that, you will settle the matter between yourselves by changing the production schedule. Your release schedules are issued weekly for an eight-week period. As a rule, this gives you at least four weeks' advance notice, inasmuch as we avoid changing the coming four weeks unless it is absolutely necessary. Now, if you and Ralph cannot see eye to eye, the matter will have to be referred to the executive committee, but you will find that Ralph is pretty good at solving problems.

"By the way, let me make this clear to you. Ralph is no more your boss than you are his. If the foreman of the tool room needs to purchase anything, you know that he is not permitted to go and buy it outside. He must send *you* a requisition. Now, this does not make you his boss. You are the head of a service department, available to service him. Ralph is the head of another service department. The release schedule he sends you is a service he renders to you and to the whole organization. It is important for you to understand the spirit in which his department functions.

"You will find that the control you are submitted to is very detailed, but it is objective. You receive an assignment. You may accept it or reject it. But if you accept, you must perform. There is no excuse for a failure—no argument, either. If you fail, the damage is evaluated. We all make mistakes. The important point is to avoid making too many mistakes and also to understand fully that this extensive control is the necessary balance to the great freedom of action you are being given.

"No one will ask you what time you arrive in your office, why you did not show up last Thursday, or whether you have neglected to write to this or that supplier. You are your own boss as far as your function is concerned."

Failure and Resentment. About three months elapsed. Richards was delighted. A new life had started for him. He felt like himself again—no fears, a real feeling of independence. He worked harder than ever, but he worked really for himself.

During Week No. 24 he was advised that Part No. 1234—a critical part—would be needed for assembly on Tuesday morning, Week No. 32. He found that the regular supplier could not deliver. He called everywhere, finally found a supplier in the Middle West, and accepted the commitment.

He followed up by mail. Yes, the supplier assured him, the part would be ready. The matter was so important that on Thursday of Week No. 31 he checked by phone. Yes, the shipment had left in time. Richards was reassured and did not check further. But on Tuesday of Week No. 32 the part was not in the warehouse. Inquiry revealed that the shipment had been misdirected by the railroad company and was still in Chicago.

The writer was asked to "arbitrate" the case and decided that the time lost in the plant should be charged to the purchasing department.

Certainly the plant manager could not be asked to underwrite a loss due to failure of delivery over which he had no supervision.

Richards listened attentively and smiled politely as the decision was explained. But obviously he felt that an injustice had been committed; he was bitterly disappointed. He said that he thought he had done all he possibly could. It did no good to remind him that he had performed very well in the past and would certainly perform well again in the future.

From that point on Richards' attitude was changed.

New Understanding. Some time later, while teaching his course in industrial engineering at Columbia University, the writer was describing to his students the advantages of centralizing planning and control in conjunction with decentralizing authority and responsibility. In all fairness to the students, he felt they should be told that at least in one specific case the plan had not worked well. He invited Richards to come as a guest lecturer and present the other side of the picture. Here is what happened:

> Class time was 9:00 a.m. Shortly before, Richards entered the writer's office. He was smiling and looking forward to the chance to let off steam. "Don't hesitate to tell them how you feel," he was told. Don't beat around the bush."
>
> Richards smiled; he certainly would take full advantage of the opportunity. He said he would tell them that he liked the idea in general, but that you should not go too far with it. Suddenly he stopped talking and looked worried.
>
> "May I use your phone to place a long-distance call to the office?" he asked. "I just forgot to tell them I would not be in today."
>
> It was the writer's turn to smile. "I should like to ask you one question. In your previous job, at the Rigid Corporation, would you have forgotten to tell them that you were not coming?"
>
> "Certainly not," he said. "I would have requested permission three weeks in advance, and most probably the permission would have been refused."
>
> The suggestion was made: "Why don't you tell that to the class, too?"
>
> Richards' face changed. He was obviously thinking deeply. "Oh," he said, "I think I see the point."
>
> The session in class was rather different from what had been expected. The students were surprised to hear a guest lecturer who, contrary to their expectation, was not at all critical of the concept they were studying!

Plant variance

In a certain organization, objections were being made to a report which the planning and control department was putting out.

This report was a weekly analysis of the variance between the actual direct labor payroll in the assembly department and what the payroll would have been if all goods had been produced at standard cost. The planning and control department was in charge of assigning to each department concerned the responsibility for a portion of the variance. The maintenance department would be responsible for breakdown, the purchasing department for lack of material, the sales department for rush orders, the plant management for time lost, and so on. Virtually the whole variance could thus be accounted for.

The cost of this report was considered excessive by some executives. It required, at that time, almost the whole attention of two clerks and about eight hours of IBM equipment. For a certain period, the report was issued without bringing any return; and some executives remarked sarcastically, "What is the use of knowing where we are losing money, if we lose it anyway?"

After a few months, however, their attitude changed. The first beneficial effect of the report was that it eliminated a source of friction that had for years cast a shadow over the relationships between sales and production, namely, requests for rush orders. It is the rare executive who is not familiar with this kind of problem:

> The sales department requests a rush production. The plant scheduler argues that it will disrupt his production and cost a substantial though not clearly determined amount of money. The answer coming from sales is: "Do you want to take the responsibility of losing the X Company as a customer?" Of course the production scheduler does not want to take such a responsibility, and he gives up, but not before a heavy exchange of arguments and the accumulation of a substantial backlog of ill feeling.

Analysis of the payroll in the assembly department, determining the costs involved in getting out rush orders, eliminated the cause for argument. Henceforth, any rush order was accepted with a smile by the production scheduler, who made sure that the extra cost would be duly recorded and charged to the sales department—"no questions asked." As a result, the tension created by rush orders disappeared completely; and, somehow, the number of rush orders requested by the sales department was reduced to an insignificant level.

Even more spectacular was the virtually total elimination of a "plant variance" of almost $1,000 a week. Everyone in the organization knew that the labor expense in the assembly department was much higher than the standard; but the causes were so numerous and their relative impact so undetermined that every executive or supervisor was sincerely convinced that he was *not* the one who could help. But when the head of the assembly department was shown that $1,000 a week was attributable to time lost in his department, he realized that this was really his responsibility. So he reorganized entirely his procedures of job assignment and made it a point every week to study the payroll analysis report at a meeting he held with his foremen.

After six months the plant variance had virtually disappeared. The savings resulting from that factor alone more than compensated for the cost of the whole analysis.

CONCLUSION

As the foregoing cases indicate, neither specialization nor control presents insurmountable obstacles to the free development of human personality in our modern industrial organizations. It is true that specialization narrows the *area* of responsibility of each executive, but it does not necessarily lessen the *depth* of his authority. Within his field, he may have more responsibility and leeway than his predecessors of earlier years. Much the same applies to control. Contrary to a widespread prejudice, born of the many abuses that have been committed in the past, control is not by itself a hindrance to individual freedom. Rather, control is in fact a prerequisite to decentralization, and without decentralization there can be no real freedom.

The high-ranking executive who is responsible for the operations of large sections of an industrial organization and who is not in a position to make use of effective controls, tends to be tyrannical because he is worried. He will give much greater independence to his subordinates if he knows that their mistakes will be detected before any irreparable damage results. That is a key function of the concept described in this article—centralized planning and control in conjunction with decentralized authority and responsibility.

This concept is not, however, a substitute for good management. It is only a tool of management. Like any other tool, it may be misused; and precisely because it is effective, it may become dangerous. It may become an instrument of oppression if excessive emphasis is placed on "control"; or it may become the source of serious disruptions if, on the contrary, "decentralization" is overemphasized.

At the same time, experience shows that this concept, if applied with skill and moderation, provides a solution to the strange dilemma in which industrial management finds itself today. Management can use the concept to reconcile the technical necessity for planning and control with the pressing need for good human relations in industry.

51. SECURING UNIFORM DECISIONS IN SIMILAR JUDGMENTAL SITUATIONS [1]

Clement J. Berwitz [2]

Several years ago, after I finally caught up with my favorite relative, the head of a well-known manufacturing and distributing organization in a highly competitive industry, I asked:

"Jim, why do you spend so much time in the field? I followed you all over the country, through your secretary. She never knew exactly where you'd go after your next scheduled stop. Were you putting out fires, or just sampling grass roots' pressures?"

"Not precisely," he answered. "You know we've got a fine organization. Our men have plenty of initiative, are loyal, and responsive. Their accomplishments are very satisfactory; their reports nail everything down, perhaps too much so. That's not the real problem. I'm worried because we find it so difficult to get consistent decisions and actions in the same, or related, situation, either within a city or among cities. Sometimes I wish all of our men had one-track minds —and yet, that's the one type we can't hire because there are so many variables in our business; we cannot operate unless our men use independent judgment all day long. For example, a special deal given to one of our distributors in Toledo causes a disturbance in St. Louis with repercussions in Kansas City and Indianapolis. Yet, after I leave each of those towns, everybody's happy and still our loyal customer. I'm not referring to clandestine or "package" deals. We improvise on the spot to meet a competitive situation the instant it arises. Our men don't seem to know how far they can go on their own in a new situation even though we've set the limits of discretion in general terms. If I could lick this, if I could find a way to get a uniform decision in a given situation, I wouldn't travel a third as much as I do."

"It's strange," my former boss once said to me "that Casualty Insurance Company A's local office in Syracuse is respected for its

[1] From *Advanced Management* (January, 1957), pp. 10-13. Reprinted by permission of *Advanced Management—Office Executive*.
[2] Clement J. Berwitz, Chief, Methods & Procedures for Field Operations Divisions of Unemployment, New York State Labor Department.

toughness in adjusting claims, but its Buffalo office is soft as butter. On the other hand, Casualty Insurance Company B's Buffalo office is tough but its Syracuse counterpart is easygoing. I know the heads of the two companies. Both want a uniform policy of adjustment based on the facts—paying claims promptly and fully where warranted. Yet, their adjusters in different cities can't seem to act as if they belong to the same company. How do you account for it?"

The problem of securing uniform decisions or end products in judgmental situations, where the facts are substantially similar, is doubtlessly as old as human life itself. It is the root of justice. It is an exacting discipline which cannot be prescribed definitively in advance because one unforeseen variable in a given situation may affect the end product differently under differing conditions. It has nothing to do with the fetish of uniformity for uniformity's sake. There are virtues, even where options exist, in organizing certain types of entities into fully homogeneous units, each mimicking the other, each having the same sized staff with the same titles, each utilizing the same procedure routines in the same static situation. There is obviously more virtue, however, in such organizations in permitting local discretion in certain areas to meet local competitive conditions within a broad framework of predetermined policy.

The uniformity with which this article is concerned is the type which would obtain if one individual, with a consistent sense of logic, with unswerving fidelity to a set of tested guiding principles, was able to handle personally every case which required a judgmental determination. Thus, were it possible for Jim's staff to refer to him the case folder for each contingency as it arose, Jim wouldn't have to travel, but he would have to stay up twenty-five hours in each twenty-four, with an ice bag tied to his fevered brow and an electrocardiograph attached to his chest.

Consider the Employment Security System, with its millions of adjustment interviews to determine if claimants are eligible for this week's benefit. Consider the effect on public confidence if inconsistent determinations were made in different cities for former employees of the same company all of whom were separated for the same reason. Consider the havoc to be wrought to any company if personnel efficiency rating plans, sales promotion campaigns, bank loans, leasing policies, retail store adjustments on returns, failed to operate with the same intended end product to each person served, and the persons involved compared notes. Most fair-minded people will accept an adverse determination, or refusal of service, or denial of credit, or failure to be accepted by their dream college, or will wait their turn equably if everyone else in their group were given the same hard consideration on the basis of the facts, within the elements of a consistent policy. What's sauce for the goose must be sauce for the gander.

What seems to be needed is that each decision maker, or person responsible for creating an end product, must be so permeated with the purpose, objectives, and policies of his company that he is able to carry out the administrator's intention in the absence of specific instruction in a new situation. What seems to be needed is that 100 decision makers, operating in 100 different cities, with a hundred different sets of facts, select the same course of action, thereby making decision making as interchangable a part as a Ford brake-band! The following excerpt from "The Elements of Administration" by L. Urwick (pp. 68-69) illustrates the point:

> Marshall Foch once said that active obedience always presupposes understanding. "There can be no collective harmony in the active sense in any organization unless each and every one concerned knows what the purpose is!" This definition of the objective is the primary meaning of doctrine. But in all forms of coordinated effort there is also a doctrine of procedure of some kind. It is essential that every member of the organization should not only know its doctrine, but should feel it and absorb it. Provided the objective be desirable and legitimate, there can be built a unity of doctrine which translates itself into a unity of spirit, a moving force ensuring the maximum of continuous and coordinated efficiency.
>
> One of the surest methods of securing this uniformity of doctrine is identity of training. Sir Ian Hamilton has given a dramatic example of the way such identity of training works in war: "At a Staff College . . . we find . . . selections out of a great service in the first flower of their prime; eager, impressionable, retentive. Upon this plastic, fiery stuff the Commandant puts his stamp. If he is worth his salt, the whole of the Staff Officers passed into the Army during his tenure will have digested his doctrine. Suppose that long afterwards, in some battle the Generalissimo's plan goes wrong; the enemy are weak where they were expected to be strong; there is heavy firing from directions supposed to be clear; the telephones are dumb; the aeroplanes do not return; the fog of war descends. Now, a certain Staff College graduate is commanding a British Corps; a man of his year has the Corps on his right, whilst a man of a later batch, but taught by the same Commandant, is Chief of Staff on his left; *each of these three will know what the other two will do, and what they will expect him to do!*"

We've heard from the military. Let's see what government practice has to offer. Government techniques have evolved over a period of years, one agency cheerfully borrowing from another, and from industry. The distillate of industrial and governmental experience should provide the most rewarding, ultimate techniques.

I. Reducing knowledge to writing

Every government agency has its five-foot shelf of manuals: Organizational, Policy, Procedural, Interpretations or Precedent, and, of course, the Forms Manuals; some agencies integrate them into one or two; others like to keep them separate, for some perfectly valid reasons indigenous to the agency. But there they are, formidable, even silly, to the uninitiated; invaluable as bible and arbiter to the sincere operator, though he hates every laboriously written word of it; hates it because it strait-jackets his freedom to do the job *his* (the best) way.

Let's concentrate on policy-procedural manuals. These ordinarily describe the job to be done, the methods to be used, the qualitative standards to be achieved. They start with the objectives of the agency which are implicit in the statute they implement. Thus, the objective of unemployment compensation is to pay benefits promptly, when due, to eligible claimants. Every agency or private organization has its objective or aims. It's remarkable how quickly they are forgotten, or how far afield a policy of procedure can wander until some one redirects attention to the written objectives, upon which everybody once agreed.

Policies, of course, are the by-laws, or "rules," under which objectives are to be achieved. *Everyone legally entitled to service shall be interviewed*, or *Only students in the top 10% of their class can qualify for admission.*

The policies obviously shape the procedures and their component routines: *Instruct applicant for operator's licenses to fill out tripartite Form "A"; review it for completeness; detach applicant's copy (section 1) and hand it to him; detach section 2 and route to alphabetic file; route section 3 to the numeric file.*

Objectives, policies and procedures comprise the basis for statements of qualitative performance standards. For example: *The claimant is to be given an opportunity to present all pertinent facts, either on his own initiative, or in response to questions.* Or, *The interview should be controlled throughout, and be terminated when its objectives have been accomplished.* And *Each letter requesting information is to be answered within 72 hours of its receipt.*

Precedent case manuals, unique to those government agencies involved in adjudications, follow their legal prototypes. They utilize both the case and textbook approach. Significant cases are digested and indexed by subject. Interpretative statements based upon appeal board or court decisions provide specific courses of action in situations four-square with the facts presented.

The foregoing types of written material are basic in achieving uniformity in judgmental situations. They comprise some, but not all, the ingredients. Before examining the other techniques, let's review the depth to which instructions should be prepared to stimulate uniform courses of action in judgmental situations.

II. The depth of instructional writing

This subject is troublesome, controversial, complicated; the solution is largely dependent upon the state of organizational maturity, i.e., the level of development or "depth" of "doctrine" attained, the degree of competence of the staff, and the character and depth of its training department. This article, however, is not concerned with these particular problems, instead, it will delimit only those aspects which specifically and directly affect securing uniform end products in judgmental situations.

Consider, for example, an instruction to be prepared for a unit which handles complaint letters from the public; assume that twenty-five correspondents, decentralized in three operating units, are employed in this activity. The following represent some of the alternative instructions which might guide this unit in the effective performance of its task.

Possible Depth of Instructional Statements to Staff

1. Prepare reply to each letter of complaint; mail promptly.
    or
2. Prepare reply. Include the following elements:
    a. Acknowledge receipt of the complaint.
    b. Select from list of "pattern" paragraphs (see Form 200) the specific one which best fits the specific complaint under review.
    c. Conclude with paragraph No. 15 from Form 200 which expresses the agency's appreciation to the complainant for his letter.
    or
3. Prepare reply to embody the following:
    a. Summary of the nature of the complaint.
    b. Agency policy on this specific contingency; if none exists, see supervisor.
    c. A brief statement of the decision.

d. Appreciative statement to complainant for bringing this to the agency's attention.

Obviously, not one of the foregoing alternatives, as written, reveals to the staff the specific policy or attitude of the agency toward the reaction to be created *within the complainant*. More specifically, does the agency welcome complaints because they reveal areas of strength or weakness? Or, does it regard complaint letters as a necessary nuisance the writers of which are to be placated as promptly as possible? How far is it willing to go to improve public understanding and acceptance?

Similarly, does the agency want the complainant to *believe* from the reply to his letter that he *has* received *individualized consideration*, that his hurts have been fully explored, that remedies are in process, that this sort of thing will never happen again to him or to anyone else? Does the agency want the complainant to have renewed confidence, to feel free to come in again for service, or, does it want the complainant to feel that its harsh policy is applicable to all, and the customer can "take it or leave it?"

This in a sense is the core of the problem. How often has an executive listened in on an interview, say, concerning a customer's complaint to a department store adjuster, only to be bewildered by the statements made by his employee on his behalf? Unless everyone in the agency concerned knows, and feels, and is permeated with agency policy toward complainants, and the attitudes to be created in them, any uniformity which occurs will be strictly fortuitous.

The remedies are relatively simple. Procedural statements, of course, can be written to include statements of purpose, policies, and guiding principles. Training classes, too, can be created to cover this kind of guiding material. Perhaps the most desirable method of all is to create statements of qualitative standards—in writing—to be issued to each staff member for his continuing reference. These supplement instructional statements.

These standards [3] (statements of the conditions that will exist if the job is well done, to paraphrase Lawrence Appley) are developed most effectively by a work committee [4] comprising representation from the operating unit involved, its supervisor, and any other line

---

[3] See Dickson Reck, "The Role of Company Standards in Industrial Administration" in *Advanced Management* (April 1954), for an excellent discussion of substantive and procedural standards and their role in decision making.

[4] See article by the author in the *Harvard Business Review* (January-February, 1952), on the subject of organizing and operating work committees.

or staff, or "program" representation known to be able to contribute. The task involves the determination of the specific qualitative-end products to be achieved, and recording them in terms specific enough to be utilized as guiding principles by the users.

The creation of guiding principles or standards, however, merely sets the stage; they give the agency a fighting chance to obtain uniformity in judgmental situations—but they do not guarantee results. Let's look at a few additional techniques.

III. Gaining acceptance prior to installation

This method embraces securing staff participation either during the developmental stages of formulating a policy, standard, or procedure, or soliciting it during the "clearing" stage.

Let me be didactic for a moment. Few procedures are popular. They give the over-worked operator something extra to do when he is sure his cup is already running over; nothing adds more to his indignation than a carelessly conceived procedure. Give him a crack at it during the developmental, or clearance stage, and the chance for willing adherence is measurably improved. Who knows better, within limits, of the operational feasibility of a proposal, than the man who will perform it? Yes—it is a "tension relieving" technique, and ministers to the need for "personal" acceptance. But, how else does one get teamwork—belief in the desirability of the goal—the will to win? How better can one achieve staff responsiveness later on, when it's necessary to get the bugs out of something everyone "bet" would work?

IV. Performance evaluation

These techniques are useful in determining the extent of uniformity achieved in judgmental determinations. Two methods are ordinarily used:

1. Review of records or end products.
2. Auditing, where oral interviews or oral communication is part of the process.

The basis for the review are written, qualitative standards. Evaluation consists in ascertaining the extent to which standards are being achieved. Areas of weakness become exposed and are subjected to remedial action: closer supervision, coaching, formal training, improved procedures to close gaps, etc.

Some government agencies use "analysis sheets" for "reviewing records." These identify in the "Y" axis, the accompanying written standards established (either by abbreviation, or by number) ; the stub, or "X" axis lists the specific cases either by name or case number. Narrative comments are entered on the reverse, for specific cases or elements.

Case No.		STANDARDS							
		1	2	3	4	5	6	7	8
Totals	√								
	X								
	0								
Legend:	Enter "√" if performance meets standard; "X" if below standard; "0" if omitted though pertinent.								

The items reviewed may be selected at random from the file, thus providing a cross section of production, or may comprise, say, a day's production of an individual employee.

For conducting audits, a form or blank sheet is used with the specific, written standards serving as criteria for the evaluation. These enable the auditor to enter comments on specific elements, while still fresh in his mind, and, also to enter specific phrases deemed objectionable or questionable, for subsequent discussion with the employee.

V. Centrally directed review

Two approaches are often utilized:

1. Reviewing end products in the field by Central Office inspection teams, sometimes called "Administrative Inspectorate."
2. Requiring the submittal of a random sampling of "completed" cases to be sent to a central office unit for analysis and evaluation.

Both methods assume the use of identical, qualitative written standards by the operating and evaluation staff.

Under the first approach, a team of two experts visit each local installation, say, once per year. They review records and audit interviews or other operation, using guide lists to ascertain adherence to policies, standards or procedures. On completion of the evaluation, they discuss their findings with the local management and recommend remedial action. The emphasis is on local improvement, not fault-finding, or report writing.

An invaluable by-product is that the teams determine the adequacy of centrally prepared policies, procedures, standards and techniques. Suggestions for improvement are relayed to headquarters and correction is initiated promptly. Central units, too, can be wrong!

The second method (central office review of cases) requires each local installation to submit a specified number of cases, selected at random, usually for specific types of contingencies. The Central Unit reviews the cases, compares performance and the degree of uniformity *among* local installations, as well as *within* a single installation.

VI. Case conferences

These are problem solving meetings held at the local, district or regional level. The participants include line and staff representatives. Actual problem cases are presented, for consideration by the group. The objective is staff training, and indoctrination with respect to approach, content, and security uniformity in similar cases in the future.

VII. Grass roots visits

In many organizations, the line expert who accepts a staff job loses his field expertness quickly. Conditions change, new personnel, new procedures, new policies quickly alter the original pressures which created our expert and he becomes a novice among his old associates. Frequent visits to the grass roots is a good palliative. It is more than that. It is a vital medium for giving and getting information. The field must know continuously what headquarters is thinking if it is to carry out its intention, and similarly, headquarters will quickly stub its toe if it wanders too far afield from the firing line.

Grass roots visits should have specific objectives; that's at least as important as checking on the health and well-being of the district man's wife and kiddies.

VIII. Coordination

Every "good" organization down to the lowliest clerk shares information; no one "pinches" it off in the interest of empire building. Everyone in the company has a stake in imparting any pertinent information to enable it to permeate everyone thoroughly, thereby creating a "oneness" of thinking.

IX. Administrative analysis or statistics

This method is useful when quantitative records are kept of workload produced, complaints received, actions taken for specific contingencies, or similar items. It involves the maintenance of data and the use of ratios or percentages comparing one item with others.

The first step is to draw up a list of the ratios to be maintained; the second step is to obtain and record the figures, daily, weekly, or monthly; the third step is to analyze the data; the fourth step is to establish "working norms" for each; the fifth step is to go behind the figures when significant deviations appear; and the final step is to take remedial action, where indicated. "Working norms" are ratios which are used as yardsticks: For example, in a well-supervised unit handling applications for service, 7.5% have been rejected consistently. Thus, 7.5% can be used as the "working norm" and any deviation by any staff member in the unit should be explored to determine if the employee is unduly harsh, or lenient. Working norms can also be established through the use of an experimental group.

X. Pilot or "stipulated" cases

This method is limited to those jurisdictions in which repetitive situations occur, or where a single set of facts applies to many individuals or cases, and a decision in one pilot or "stipulated" case will be applicable to all.

This method is particularly useful where the activity involves legal, or quasi-legal activity. It is used extensively in certain types of government agencies, where referees, or review boards are utilized, or the statute permits appeal to the courts. One test case is referred through the usual channels. The decision is applied to all in the group where the facts are similar.

XI. Interpretation units and program consultants

Some government agencies use Central Interpretations Units, where legal or quasi-legal facts are involved. The practice is to permit local installations to contact such central units directly, or through the District Supervisor, to obtain clarification, or advice, concerning the course of action to be taken in a specific set of local facts, within the framework of established policy.

Another device embraces the use of "Program Consultants"; these consultants are usually responsible for planning the content of their technical program; assisting in developing policies, procedures, and training materials; installing the program in the field; examining and appraising performance to secure uniformity of concept and application; recommending on request, actions to be taken in specific situations; and testing the adequacy of the program content and procedures.

Program Consultants are ordinarily available on a direct contact basis to local installations.

BIBLIOGRAPHY, CHAPTER XIII

BUDIN, MORRIS. "Reports: A Problem in the Control Function of Management," *Advanced Management* (June, 1958), 14-17.

EDWARDS, NATHAN D. "Performance Analysis," *Advanced Management* (January, 1958), 24-25.

EMICH, ARNOLD F. "Control Means Action," *Harvard Business Review* (July-August, 1954), 92-99.

FOLLETT, MARY PARKER. "The Process of Control," Gulick and Urwick (Eds.), *Papers on the Science of Administration.* Institute of Public Administration, 1937.

HASSLER, RUSSELL H. "Performance Measurement," Bursk and Fenn (Eds.), *Planning the Future Strategy of Your Business.* New York: McGraw-Hill Book Company, Inc., 1956. 119-128.

How the duPont Organization Appraises Its Performance. Financial Management Series 94. New York: American Management Association, Inc., 1950.

JASINSKY, FRANK J. "Use and Misuse of Efficiency Controls," *Harvard Business Review* (July-August, 1956), 105-113.

LARKE, A. G. "Management Self-Audit for Smaller Companies," *Dun's Review and Modern Industry* (March, 1955), 40-42.

McLEAN, JOHN G. "Better Reports for Better Control," *Harvard Business Review* (May-June, 1957), 95-105.

McQUIE, ROBERT. "The First Law of Management Audits," *Advanced Management* (July-August, 1961), 22-27.

MERRIHUE, WILLARD V., and R. A. KATZELL. "ERI—Yardstick of Employee Relations," *Harvard Business Review* (November-December, 1955), 91-100.

NEUSCHEL, RICHARD F. "Overhead Cost Control: How to Get Results and Make Them Last," *Management Review* (March, 1958), 14-18.

OXENFELDT, ALFRED R. "How to Use Market-Share Measurement," *Harvard Business Review* (January-February, 1959), 59-68.

RATHE, ALEX W. "Management Control," *Advanced Management* (May, 1955), 23-25.

ZIEGLER, RAYMOND J. "The Application of Managerial Controls in Selected Business Firms," *Advanced Management* (August, 1958), 10-12.

Chapter XIV
Standards of Measurement for Control

When a student enters college, a minimum objective for him is to graduate. His course grades are the yardsticks of performance which he uses to evaluate his progress toward his objective. He controls his study activity by periodic comparison of his actual grades to the standard required for graduation.

There are two elements to these standards of measurement for control: (1) what is the yardstick that is to be used to measure performance, and (2) what relative value of this yardstick is required to indicate whether excellent, good, mediocre, or poor performance has been achieved. These two elements exist in problems that managers face in developing standards to measure and control performance so as to meet the objectives.

Paul Kircher presents a review of the general problem of measurement. He then describes some of the newest techniques available to assist in the measurement process. The fact that Professor Kircher feels the need to get down to "fundamentals" emphasizes the crude state of the measurement process.

In the next selection Robert W. Lewis brings an example of how standards of measurement have been established to evaluate how well the manager has met or not met the objectives of his organization. The difficulty of setting quantitative measurements to objectives which lend themselves to primarily qualitative evaluations is an ever-present problem, as Mr. Lewis' presentation implies. In a similar way, the article shows that there are no pat answers to the problem of what measurements should be applied to an organization nor what the level of such measurement ought to be in order to indicate good performance or bad.

52. FUNDAMENTALS OF MEASUREMENT [1]

Paul Kircher [2]

Measurement has always been an important factor in providing information to serve as the basis for solving business problems. But as business management has become more and more interested in using scientific tools to aid in making decisions, it has become increasingly evident that present methods of measurement in the business field frequently are inadequate.

For this reason the Management Sciences Research Project at UCLA (sponsored by the Office of Naval Research) has undertaken a research study of the general problem of measurement.

Preliminary analysis has shown that the fundamentals of measurement, as such, have never been clearly defined, even by scientists. Each discipline or science has developed its own techniques and methods, with few attempts at coordination with others. This is true in spite of the fact that it is difficult to evaluate the effectiveness of any system of measurement, or of any other logical activity, from criteria which are part of the system itself. If the system can be viewed from "outside," from a more fundamental point of view, it often is easier to correct mistakes and to obtain insights which lead to new and better methods.

There is a limit to this search for fundamentals, it must be admitted. One of the interesting aspects of modern mathematics is the discovery that as yet we cannot prove that the ultimate logical structure of mathematics is consistent. The most ambitious attempt to do this, by Hilbert, was shown by Godel to have the form of a proposition which could neither be proved or disproved. It merely could be accepted, if one chose to do so.

[1] From *Advanced Management* (October, 1955), pp. 5-8. Reprinted by permission of *Advanced Management*. This article was prepared while the author was under contract to the Office of Naval Research, Logistics Branch, and employed on the Management Sciences Research Project, University of California, Los Angeles.

[2] Paul Kircher, Associate Professor of Accounting in the School of Business Administration, University of California at Los Angeles.

There are many aspects of business logic which rest on indefinable terms or unprovable propositions. In the past these assumptions have been so numerous and so important that business has been characterized as an art. There have been few precepts of general significance —each problem the manager encountered was seen as being a brand new one, at least in some respects. As Vatter has said, "Business is an experiment."

Whereas, we can expect that much of this indefinability will continue, nevertheless there are many relationships which can be measured in business. Especially in situations where methods such as linear programming have proven useful, businessmen are coming to recognize that decision-making can be moved to a higher plane. In these situations, it can be seen that when certain objectives are clearly defined, and the factors of the situation are objectively measured, then decisions are already made. Scheduling the operations becomes mechanical—it can be done on an electronic computer.

As a simple example, suppose a manager makes the decision that he will choose the course which earns the highest profit. He has three courses open to him (such as shipping routes). If he can measure the profitability of each of the three routes, then the policy decision in effect makes the operating decision.

We are still a long way from being able to put policy-making on a scientific basis. Policies are always set in an atmosphere of much uncertainty. Indeed, a major difference between the human brain and the so-called "electronic computer brain" is that the former can operate with partial information. A computer must have a complete program, or it will stop or give inaccurate results.

However, policy-making can be improved with experience, since certain situations do tend to repeat themselves. But lessons can be learned only if the important factors in each situation are measured, so they can be compared and correlated with the results of the decisions.

The structure of the measurement process

The major effort of the present research study is directed toward the attempt to establish the basic structure of the measurement process. It is hoped that by dividing the process into important elements, each of these may be studied with more precision, and the relationships between them can be seen more clearly.

As indicated in the paper presented by the author to the 1955 national meeting of the Operations Research Society of America, [3] the following elements of the measurement process have been identified:

1. Determination of the objective of the business entity, the purpose which is to be served in a particular situation.
2. Determination of the types of factors which might serve to attain the objective.
3. Selection of the key aspects of the factors, the aspects which are to be measured.
4. Choice of (a) a measuring method, (b) a measuring unit.
5. Application of the measuring unit to the object to be measured—the central action of measurement.
6. Analysis of the measurement—relating it to other measurements (other in time or in kind).
7. Evaluating the effectiveness of the measurement by determining the extent to which it assisted in the attainment of the objective.

Each of these needs investigation and is being studied in some detail. Since it is impossible to describe all the various considerations within the scope of a single article, an attempt will be made to indicate something of the direction and purpose of the research by relating each of the above elements to a few specific problems. Examples will be given from:

a. highly developed and effective systems, such as the measurement of length.
b. highly developed but less effective systems, such as accounting,
c. moderately developed systems, such as job evaluation, and
d. areas where systems hardly exist, as yet, such as selection and evaluation of executives.

The first and most obvious step is to define the objective. Obvious as it is, however, it is not always easy to do.

Executives have struggled with the problem of objectives ever since companies grew from the single proprietor stage. Now that social consequences are a major consideration, many executives spend a great deal of their time attempting to establish policies which exhibit business statesmanship, and which will lead to stability and continuation of earnings, as well as immediate gains.

Unless these problems are solved, it is not possible to develop the objectives in terms that will be susceptible of some sort of quantification. In other words, it is necessary to set the stage for measurement.

[3] Held in Los Angeles, California, August 15-17, 1955.

Without a clear understanding of the purposes which a to-be-hired executive is to serve, it is difficult to establish standards by which to select him, and later, to judge his performance.

Determination of relevant factors

The second step is to determine which factors may be employed to attain the objective.

In physical problems this step is often clearly definable. When it is, the measurement process may become relatively easy, unless certain factors are physically inaccessible, or unless methods have not been sufficiently developed to handle the particular type of problem. For example, if the purpose is to provide a means of travel across a river at minimum cost, certain obvious alternatives are present— a bridge, a ferry, or a tunnel. (Of course, every such problem also presents an opportunity for the "genius" who can by-pass the problem, e.g., by finding a better route that does not go near the river, or by using helicopters.) Excepting the unusual solutions, the problem then becomes one of measuring the expected flow of traffic, measuring the cost of construction and operation of the various alternatives, and expressing the costs and capacities in comparable terms.

With a problem such as the selection of an executive the "factor" choice is considerably more difficult. In the first place, though the company organization chart may appear to offer a "slot" which is to be filled, it is not possible with present knowledge to describe the position in terms comparable to those which can be used to describe the quantity of traffic flow—such as the expected weights of the vehicles.

Even if it were possible to define the job narrowly, at the executive level the individual capabilities of the manager chosen will soon start reshaping the responsibilities and activities concerned.

Moreover, it is at least theoretically desirable that each vacancy should be the occasion for a re-examination of the company organization to see whether the position should be re-defined, or perhaps even eliminated. Such considerations add considerably to the difficulty of the measurement problem.

Selection of key aspects

Once it has been determined what the purpose is, and the objects to be measured, it is necessary to select those aspects, which can and should be measured. These are the aspects which are themselves quantifiable, and are related in some way to the quantifiable aspects of the purpose or objective of the entity involved.

An example can be drawn from accounting. Various types of assets and liabilities are measured in order to obtain information concerning the revenue and expense flows, and the financial position of the firm. These are indicative of the degree of attainment of the profit-making objectives of the business.

The illustration from accounting is especially interesting since accountants have deliberately chosen to restrict their activities to those measurements which they believe can be made within a certain standard of accuracy. This means that certain other items, vital to the well-being of the firm, are resolutely omitted. For example, the company's investments in advertising its products, or in developing its executives, are not considered to be assets, but are written off in the period of expenditures, as a rule. Goodwill as such has almost disappeared from company statements.

In certain types of job evaluation, it is possible to quantify some of the key aspects. For example, a stenographer should be able to take shorthand at so many words per minute and type at a given rate, in order to perform the duties of a given job. Other important attributes, however, such as the ability to get along with others, are harder to quantify.

In choosing an executive the problem is much more difficult. There is little knowledge as to the particular abilities which are required for a manager to act successfully in a specific situation. Even where certain abilities have been ascertained as desirable, it is seldom that they can be expressed in terms which are quantifiable. They are seldom established on the basis of what the man can *do*; rather they are usually expressed in terms of what he *is*—e.g., sincere, capable, loyal, patient, trained, experienced, etc. These attributes are difficult to express quantitatively, and thus are difficult to relate to later performance, however measured.

Choice of measuring method and unit

The act of choosing a measuring method and a measuring unit has been given considerable attention throughout history, but so far not much of the theoretical work is helpful to businessmen. Mathematics, "the Queen of the Sciences," is a logical process whose object, in the words of Comte, is "the indirect measurement of magnitudes," and "it constantly proposes to determine certain magnitudes from others by means of the precise relations existing between them."

Most of theoretical mathematical work, however, has deliberately avoided the problems of application, especially to anything so "crass" as business problems. The essence of mathematics is deductive reasoning from explicitly stated assumptions. Only since World War II have many mathematicians discovered, much to the surprise of most of them, that business problems are difficult, challenging, and can be as intellectually interesting as the act of contemplating abstract "Number."

In recent years, however, activity in the application field has increased tremendously. In addition to increased activities in this field in many societies nationwide, three societies have been formed— "The Institute of Management Sciences," "The Operations Research Society of America," and the "Society for Industrial and Applied Mathematics," whose objectives express this interest.

Development of scales

Perhaps the most advanced work in the field of measurement of a type useful for choosing executives has been done by the applied psychologists. In their attempts to measure such things as intelligence, men like Thurstone have had to develop scales where zero could not be fixed, nor could absolute intervals be specified. In several works Stevens has shown how various types of scales are possible depending upon the type of manipulation which can be performed on the measurements—the nominal, ordinal, interval and ratio scales.

Further developments have been hampered, however, by lack of clear-cut definitions of the relationship between the concepts we call "qualitative" and those we call "quantitative." Following the mathematicians, most writers appear to treat "quantity" as referring to an abstraction which somehow has almost a physical significance of its own.

It would appear to be more useful to firmly establish the concept that quantities are measurements of qualities. For example, the quality "length" occurs in various physical objects. By choosing some standard unit, and determining the number of repetitions of the unit in the object, the length can be expressed as a quantity. Then, following Stevens, the manipulations of arithmetic—addition, etc.— can be attempted to see what type of scale is involved.

In this process of measurement the problem for the observer is to identify certain characteristics in the object to be measured, characteristics which appear similar to those in the measuring unit, and which also have some identifiable relationship to the purpose of the measurement. These characteristics should be invariant, in the sense that they can be identified and seen to persist. Basically, of course, every object and every event in the universe is unique, and it is constantly changing through time. To find invariant characteristics, then, requires the human process of abstraction.

In measuring an executive, for example, the objective desired may be the organization of a research program. It is necessary to determine which types of ability are required for this, then to find a means of measuring these types of ability in the alternative men available. Each type of ability must be defined in such a way that it can be seen as a distinct part of a complicated personality. It must also be comparable to a part of the complicated personalities of the other candidates.

We are far behind the physical sciences in our ability to accomplish this. So far behind, in fact, that many people consider any effort in this direction to be useless. However, it does appear to offer the best hope for eventual improvement over present intuitive methods, so research in this direction probably will continue.

The importance of invariance can be seen in the difficulties which arise when the measuring unit chosen has varying characteristics. The dollar, the measuring unit of accounting, is an example. Changes in purchasing power not only create difficulties of evaluation, but can lead to serious inequities. An appreciable part of the "income" taxed by our government in recent years is really the result of the diminished value of the dollar unit.

Application of the measuring unit

The simplest method of measurement is to identify the unit characteristics in the object to be measured, and then merely to count the recurrences. Almost equally simple are the cases where the unit can be directly compared, as in measurement of length or weight. More advanced measurements, such as in astronomy, require the construction of chains of relationships.

Most business measurements involve quantity of performance in given time periods, since business is a dynamic process. The time factor introduces many complications.

Another major factor in business measurements is the force of custom. Even when systems are demonstrably weak, the difficulties of retraining and reeducating the users of data, to say nothing of the problem of development of a better system, frequently operate to hinder improvements.

On the other hand, custom does offer some advantages. Most businessmen are familiar with the major elements of the accounting system, and so can interpret results even when these are not as precise as one might wish.

In newer fields, such as measurement of executive abilities, there are several systems in use. They exhibit few attributes in common. The result is that acceptance of the systems is correspondingly more difficult to achieve.

Analysis of the measurements

The area of analysis of measurements in business has seen startling advances in recent years, and there is reason to hope that even greater improvements can be achieved. Primary interest has centered on attempts to relate various measurements into integrated systems that reflect the business operations. These attempts usually involve the construction of mathematical models of the operations.

Developments in linear programming, game theory, communication theory, etc., have shown that complicated situations can be resolved by the use of models if the relevant data can be obtained, and if the relationships are of certain types. While the use of some of these models requires advanced training in mathematics, others are simpler and yet very effective. Examples are the method for studying investment decisions (developed by Markowitz, see article by Weston and Beranek in the *Analysts Journal*, May, 1955) or for forecasting working capital needs (article by Rothschild and Kircher, *Journal of Accountancy*, September, 1955), or inventory control in production (Vazsonyi, *Management Science*, June, 1955).

One of the pioneers in the field of management improvement is General Electric. In a speech to the Controllers Institute, M. L. Hurni of General Electric's Management Consultation Services Division, gave a summary of the management problem which indicates how measurements are used and evaluated.

"The examination of an operation, or a situation within an operation, as a problem in logic consists in doing fundamental research upon the operation itself. It is not providing quick isolated solutions to current problems as they arise on the basis of readily available means.

"First, it consists of systematic examination of the environment in which the business exists for such things as the possible structure, range, and probability of specific demands upon the business, the recurrence or lack of recurrence of particular aspects of the environment, the drift in the environment from a given known position.

"Such examination includes not only a qualitative examination of characteristics of this type, but also application to them of strict methods well known in other disciplines, for the purpose of determining units of measure through which such phenomena or characteristics may be increasingly quantified or expressed in numbers.

"Second, it includes the systematic examination of the resources of the business for the purpose of determining quantitatively the identifying characteristics of such resources—for example, characteristics of performance, or probable malfunctioning, and the balances, limitations and restraints that may exist within the resources.

"Lastly, it includes the development and testing of models of action that give a description of the relation between the environment and the resources and which will define needs for performance and contribution, the information which must be communicated to make such performance or contribution possible, units of measure of the resultant performance, and the statement of possible risks that will result from a range of probable courses of action.

"In short, the purpose of the problem in logic is not the taking of specific action but the attainment of more complete understanding so that increasingly purposeful action may be taken with greater assurance." [4]

Conclusions

The material given in this article may serve to indicate that the problems of measurement in business are increasingly being investigated, and also that some progress is being achieved.

However, much more remains to be accomplished. The author would hesitate to present such limited results if it were not for the fact that this affords an opportunity to let people know of the research and to contribute criticisms and suggestions.

It does seem certain that progress in the directions indicated can be no more rapid than is permitted by our methods of measurement. This is a field in which business can carry on a great deal of basic research and discussion with some assurance that the payoff can be considerable.

[4] M. L. Hurni, "Planning, Managing and Measuring the Business," Part 6, *Future Horizons in Business Management*, Controllership Foundation, Inc., New York City, Jan., 1955.

53. MEASUREMENT, REPORTING, AND APPRAISING RESULTS OF OPERATIONS WITH REFERENCE TO GOALS, PLANS AND BUDGETS [1]

Robert W. Lewis [2]

Over the years, many companies have expended considerable effort on the developing of procedures for establishing objectives and measuring the results of operations of their businesses. However, within General Electric the evolution of our organizational philosophy and the establishment of our decentralized management structure indicated a need to take a fresh look at the measurements we had been using to determine two things—first, whether our existing measurements could be improved upon and, second, whether our measurements program was sufficiently broad in scope.

Guiding principles

Early in our research activity, we developed the following set of principles by which we believed our Measurements Project should be governed:

1. Measurements within the scope of the Project are designed to measure the performance of *organizational components*, not of *individuals*.
2. The Project is concerned with formulating common *indexes* of performance but is not concerned with developing common *standards* of performance. For example, rate of return on investment is an *index* common to all businesses but the *standard* in terms of this index might be ten per cent for one product business, twenty per cent for another, and thirty per cent for a third.
3. Measurements are designed to supplement, not supplant, judgment. Measurements provide a valuable tool to help management make decisions based on a greater amount of factual knowledge, but they cannot be substituted for judgment.
4. Measurements must be so constructed as to be useful in appraising both current results and future projections in order that a proper balance may be maintained between immediate results and long-term objectives.
5. Measurements must be kept to a minimum at each level of the organizational structure.

[1] Taken from the report, *Planning, Managing, and Measuring the Business: A Case Study of Management Planning and Control at General Electric Company* (New York: Controllership Foundation, Inc., 1955), pp. 29-41. Reprinted by permission of the Controllership Foundation, Inc.
[2] Robert W. Lewis, Manager, Measurements Services, Accounting Services Division, General Electric Company, 1955.

Division of overall project into sub-projects

With these ground rules defined, the Project was then segregated into three major sub-projects:

1. Operational measurements—for example, profitability and market position.
2. Functional measurements—engineering, manufacturing, marketing, finance, employee and plant community relations and legal.
3. Measurements of the work of management—planning, organizing, integrating and measuring.

In approaching the problem of developing operational measurements, we asked ourselves this question: What are the specific areas for which measurements should be designed, bearing in mind that sound measurements of over-all performance require a proper balance among the various functions and among the aspects (planning, organizing, for example) of managing? In seeking an answer to this question, a careful analysis was made of the nature and purposes of the basic kinds of work performed by each function, with the purpose of singling out those functional objectives which were of sufficient importance to the welfare of the business as a whole as to be termed "key result areas."

Key result areas

To check whether a tentative area was sufficiently basic to qualify as a key result area, this test question was applied:

"Will continued failure in this area prevent the attainment of management's responsibility for advancing General Electric as a leader in a strong, competitive economy, even though results in all other key result areas are good?"

The result of this evaluation produced the following eight key result areas:

1. Profitability.
2. Market position.
3. Productivity.
4. Product leadership.
5. Personnel development.
6. Employee attitudes.
7. Public responsibility.
8. Balance between short-range and long-range goals.

Key Result Area Number 8 is, of course, essentially different in nature from the other seven. The decision to segregate it initially as a separate area is simply to recognize that its significance is so basic that we prefer to risk over-emphasis rather than under emphasis.

In summary, these eight key result areas constitute the operational measurements sub-project and, in addition, represent the foundation on which we hope to build sound measurements of both functional work and the work of managing.

Now I would like to review briefly our preliminary thinking on each of the key result areas constituting the operational measurements portion of the Project.

Profitability

I believe we all recognize that profitability is the ultimate measure of business performance in a free competitive economy. Profits alone make possible the funds for expansion of physical facilities, for research, for product development, for the development of a distributive organization and for the many other elements that are the seeds of growth.

Our study of profitability indexes included an evaluation of conventional indexes, such as rate of return on investment and per cent profit to sales and a number of possible other indexes, such as per cent profit to value added. Rate of return on investment, today probably the most widely used index of profitability, is generally considered to be the most significant yardstick available to measure the effectiveness with which capital has been employed. We do not quarrel with this as an abstract principle. If capital has been committed to a given operation, we agree that it makes sense to look at rate of return, and specifically at the elements that contribute to it, to get an indication as to whether operating costs are getting out of line or segments of investment are not being turned over as rapidly as they should be. Or, looking at the future, if you have a list of investment proposals of equivalent risk involving expenditures in excess of the amount available to spend, it makes sense to select those promising the highest rates of return.

Weaknesses of rate of return index

However, we have tentatively concluded that in a company as decentralized as General Electric, rate of return possesses several shortcomings which preclude establishing it as the *primary* profitability objective of each of our businesses. It seems to us that the acid test of an index should be its effectiveness in guiding decentralized managment to make decisions in the best interests of the company overall, since operating managers' efforts naturally will be to improve the performance of their businesses in terms of the index used for evaluation. This test points up the particular weakness of rate of return and of other ratio indexes, such as per cent profit to sales. This weakness is the tendency to encourage concentration on improvement of the *ratios* rather than on improvement in *dollar* profits. Specifically, the business with the better results in terms of the ratios will tend to make decisions based on the effect the decisions will have on the particular business's current *ratios* without consideration of the *dollar* profits involved. This tends to retard incentive to growth and expansion because it dampens the incentive of the more profitable businesses to grow.

What I am saying in brief is that in a decentralized organization it is important to consider the motivating influence of an index. In a centralized organization with control concentrated at the top, or in a small owner-type company where the decisions are made by the owner-general manager, there is no particular need to consider the motivating influence of an index. In a decentralized structure, however, where operating management is given a substantial degree of autonomy, the motivating factor becomes important.

To summarize then, we are seeking in the profitability area to develop an index which will meet the following criteria:

1. Recognize the contribution of capital investment to profits;
2. Recognize the contribution of human and machine effort to profits;
3. Recognize the corporate "facts of life," in the sense that the index is realistic, understandable, equitable and in accord with our organizational philosophy;
4. And, finally, guide operating management's decisions in the best interests of the whole company.

Market position

Market position measures the acceptance of a company's products and services by the market and thus reflects the value placed by the market on the quality and prices of the company's products, its distributing and promotional policies and its technological contributions. Sound measurements of market position will provide the best indicators of the success of a business in attaining its twin objectives of growth and leadership.

The first major consideration in designing market position measurements is a determination of what constitutes a product line and what constitutes the market for each product line of a business.

A product line may be defined as a grouping of products in accordance with the purposes they serve or the essential wants they satisfy. The definition is somewhat misleading in that a product line may be a broad classification, such as clocks, or it may be a narrow classification, such as alarm clocks, kitchen clocks, or mantle clocks. In addition, product lines may overlap so that a particular product could be included in several product lines. Hence, the actual grouping of products by product lines must be accurately identified.

There may be wide variations in the interpretation of what constitutes the market for a given product line. Therefore, it is important that for each of their lines, our product departments identify such things as:

1. Whether the market includes not only directly competing products but also indirectly competing products (electric ranges vs. electric ranges; electric ranges vs. all types of ranges—electric, gas, oil, and others).
2. Whether the market includes sales by all domestic competitors or only those reporting to trade associations.
3. Whether the market includes imports, if foreign sellers are competing in the domestic market.
4. Whether the market includes export sales.
5. Whether the market includes captive sales.
6. Whether the market is considered to be represented by sales to distributors, or to retailers, or to ultimate users.

In other words, in establishing measurements of market position there should be a clear understanding of precisely what comprises the product line and what comprises the market. The purpose of having sharp definitions of these two items is, of course, to avoid being misled into thinking we are doing better than we actually are simply because of failure to identify the nature and extent of our competition.

After the market has been defined, the second major undertaking becomes measuring performance in that market, based on our relative status in terms of:

1. Sales to the market.
2. Customer satisfaction with our service performance and the quality of our products.

With respect to sales to the market, it appears that our present measurement index—per cent of available business—is as good an index as can be devised. "Market" in this sense is generally expressed in terms of dollars or in terms of units, KVA, or other meaningful terms.

In studying market position in terms of customer satisfaction with our service performance and the quality of our products, we have not been able to design a precise method of expressing the measurement. It appears that the survey technique is the best means of obtaining a reading on service performance and product quality. The mechanics of making the survey would vary depending upon the nature of the business, but the objective in any case would be to determine what the customer expects in the way of quality and service, how we compare with competitors in the areas of quality and service and what the customer would like to have that he does not now get.

Productivity

In a broad economic sense, productivity may be defined as the utilization of men, capital, and natural resources in creating goods or services to satisfy human wants. A measurement of productivity, therefore, is a measurement of the ability of a business to utilize its human, capital, and material resources to the best advantage and in the best balance.

In general, productivity may be measured by relating the *output* of goods and services to the *input* of human effort and of the other factors of production. Accordingly, an improvement in productivity means that *output* is increased without a corresponding increase in *input*.

The indexes of productivity developed for the economy as a whole are computed by relating derivatives of gross national product to total man-hours worked. In developing an index of productivity for a specific business, rather than the economy as a whole, we may consider that sales billed is the counterpart of gross national product (or output) and that productivity of an individual business may be expressed as the relationship between its sales billed and the number of man-hours worked by its employees. There are many other factors, however, that may be used to express productivity and, in developing an index for our product business, we propose to examine the merits of all the possible combinations. A listing of these factors includes the following:

OUTPUT	INPUT
Sales billed.	Man-hours worked.
Units sold.	Payroll dollars.
Value added.	Equivalent man-hours.
Manufacturing cost.	Floor space.
Units produced.	First cost of plant and equipment.

We have not completely explored the possible indexes, but in our preliminary look we have not been satisfied with the factors commonly used to express either output or input.

We have been seeking to develop an index which will do two things: (1) measure improvement in the productivity of our operations as distinguished from improvement contributed by our suppliers of materials, and (2) broaden the input base so as to recognize that capital as well as labor contributed to improvement in productivity.

In reviewing the factors that might be used to express productivity, we have considered several possibilities. In lieu of sales billed as an expression of output, we have been studying the possibility of using "value added," which may be defined as sales billed less the cost of goods and services purchased from other producers whether incorporated in the end product or consumed in the operation of the business. Another possibility is "contributed value," which is sales billed less only the cost of goods or services actually incorporated in the end product. While "value added," in theory, would reflect the more realistic evaluation of the contribution of the product business, "contributed value" would be easier to compute and would be less subject to differences in definition. On the input side of the ratio we have thought about using payroll dollars plus depreciation dollars as the input factor and, hence, expressing productivity as the ratio of contributed value to the sum of these two items. The use of payroll dollars, rather than hours, is to give effect to differences in the labor skills employed, and the use of depreciation dollars is an attempt to factor in machine effort. Since productivity indexes computed from dollars of output and input would be affected by changes in price and cost levels, it would be necessary to express both output and input in dollars of constant value.

Product leadership

Product leadership is the ability of a business to lead its industry in originating or applying the most advanced scientific and technical knowledge in the engineering, manufacturing and marketing fields to the development of new products and to improvements in the quality or value of existing products.

In our first attempt at measurements of performance in this area, we have tentatively concluded that the measurements most applicable at this time are more of a qualitative than quantitative nature. By this we mean that we cannot readily place numbers on the factors involved in product leadership but we can measure performance by appraising our existing products to determine:

1. How they compare with competitors' products and with General Electric standards;
2. The source of the research on which the products are based; and
3. Whether the basic product and subsequent product improvements were first introduced by General Electric or by competition.

Each business would conduct an annual product review for the purpose of analyzing its products both intrinsically and in direct comparison with competitors' products. In making this analysis the viewpoints of the engineering, marketing and manufacturing functions would be brought to bear in order to get a balanced evaluation. From such a review, an overall appraisal could be made to determine whether the product has held its own or has lost ground as compared with competitors' products. In addition, the review would provide a convenient occasion to evaluate the opportunities and need for product improvement and to stimulate thinking in terms of the need for new products to replace those that are subject to obsolescence because of engineering advances, changes in manufacturing processes or equipment or changes in the market.

The sources of the research on which the products of our businesses are based may include competitors, universities, the Government, other nations and company components. We think it important that our measurement structure provide for determination of the source of such research. Factual knowledge with respect to sources of research would result in a greater awareness of research status and research needs and stimulate more effective and efficient planning for the future.

The number of new products and product improvements first introduced by the product business as compared with competition would be a significant indicator of product leadership. A listing of "firsts" would include a wide range of products or product improvements, some of which would be much more significant than others. By means of a weighting system, a "first" which did not add appreciably to the volume and stature of a business, or which was marketed before it had been adequately developed, would receive limited or "minus" recognition, whereas one which made a substantial contribution to the growth and prosperity of a business would receive extensive recognition.

In order to bring into focus short-range and long-range objectives, each product business would prepare a projection of new products and product improvements that may be required for the succeeding five or ten-year period together with a program to satisfy these requirements. Such a projection would be facilitated by the three-fold appraisal of our existing products along the lines I have just described because these appraisals would promote a greater awareness of our own deficiencies, the need to provide for overcoming them and the need to be planing ahead to avoid a recurrence in the future. These projections and programs would then be useful as yardsticks for additional measurements in this area. Current performance could be measured by comparing actual accomplishments with planned objectives and with competitive advances as disclosed by the annual product review.

Personnel development

We define personnel development as the systematic training of managers and specialists to fill present and future needs of the company, to provide for further individual growth and retirements and to facilitate corporate growth and expansion. It includes programs in each field of functional endeavor, such as engineering, manufacturing, marketing and finance, and broad programs aimed at developing an understanding of the principles of managing. Such programs must be designed to provide a continuous flow of potentially promotable employees in sufficient numbers to permit proper selection and development of individuals for each position. And, at the same time, these programs must encourage competition and initiative for further individual growth.

One approach to measuring the effectiveness of personnel development programs consists of inventorying managers and functional specialists to determine the nature of their training background, that is, whether they were graduates of company-sponsored programs, were hired from outside the company or attained their position without the benefit of a company-sponsored program. Such data if collected on a year to year basis would yield a broad measurement of the success of company-sponsored educational programs and could be used to measure progress over a period of time.

A more direct measurement of the effectiveness of personnel development programs would be the degree of progress achieved by employees as evidenced by promotions within the department, transfers to higher positions in other components and the number of qualified individuals made available for promotion to higher positions either within the department or in other components.

In order to achieve a proper balance between short and long-range objectives, it would be necessary to forecast annually the immediate and long-range needs of each department and of the company at all levels and for each function. Such a projection would represent in effect a master timetable of manpower requirements and would take into consideration the department's responsibility for developing managers and technical specialists not only for its own needs but for other company components as well. This forecast of requirements could also be used as a basis for an additional measure of performance in the sense that a comparison of actual accomplishments with the projection would provide an indication as to how accurate a department forecast its needs and how well the needs were met.

A personnel development program is essentially long-range in nature. There is no quick and easy way to measure its effectiveness; our suggestions on possible measurements are not intended to imply otherwise.

Employee attitudes

Employee attitudes may be defined as the disposition of the employees to discharge their duties voluntarily to the full extent of their ability and in the best interests of the business. Although employee attitudes are ultimately reflected in productivity and profitability measurements, they are not discernible from the numerous other factors which also contribute to the overall result. Consequently, it is necessary to consider other indicators in order to develop measurements in this area.

In considering measurements of employee attitudes, we have tentatively concluded that two different approaches are required. The first is concerned with those objective factors which are generally accepted as indicators of employee attitudes—labor turnover, absenteeism, safety, and suggestions. The second involves a direct approach to the employees themselves, utilizing surveys which request the answers to specific questions.

In order to use labor turnover rates to measure employee attitudes, it would first be necessary to establish turnover standards based on the optimum turnover desired. The optimum turnover would be determined by the nature of the work, the nature of the work force and other considerations, such as the condition of the labor market. The variation between actual and standard turnover could then be interpreted in terms of employee attitudes. Similarly, in order for absenteeism data to be meaningful, the actual rate must be compared with the normal rate to be expected for the nature of the work force employed. Safety records and suggestion systems may also be useful in measuring employee attitudes. The value of statistics on these items lies in the trends disclosed over a period of time, rather than in the absolute numbers.

As these objective measurements do not show management where action is needed and what it should be, they must be supplemented by a series of employee attitude surveys, focusing on management policies and practices. In order to be effective, such surveys must be conducted with the primary objective of building attitude. Management must convince the employees that it really wants to know their thoughts and opinions and that it is committed to do something about legitimate complaints. It would be necessary for management to report back the results of the survey to the employees, acknowledge legitimate criticisms and tell the employees what was being done to alleviate just complaints. The survey would have to be repeated periodically for an extended period to obtain maximum benefits.

Public responsibility

In a broad sense, the corporation's obligations to society are three-fold: to render a worthwhile service; to make a profit so that it may continue to render that service; and, while fulfilling these obligations, to conduct its affairs in a manner becoming a good citizen. We feel that the corporation's obligations with respect to rendering service and earning a profit are covered in other key result areas and that in Key Result Area Number 7, *Public Responsibility*, we may confine ourselves to the third obligation of the corporation: to conduct itself as a good citizen within society.

Society is a broad classification and we must identify the elements which comprise it if we are to construct meaningful measurements. For this purpose we have considered that society includes shareowners, customers, employees, vendors, the plant community, the business community, educational institutions and all areas of government.

In considering how we might measure our conduct with respect to each of these elements of society, we have tentatively concluded that responsibilities to shareowners, educational institutions and areas of government are best measured from an overall company viewpoint rather than from the viewpoint of the individual product businesses. In addition, we believe that there would be little point in trying to measure relationships with customers under the heading of "public responsibility." While customers are a social group with which we are vitally concerned, the effectiveness of the way in which the product businesses fulfill their responsibility to their customers is best measured by "market position," which we have set apart as one of the key result areas.

From the viewpoint of the individual product businesses, then, the elements of society for which measurements must be developed are employees, vendors, the plant community and the business community. I will review very briefly specific indicators that might be used to measure performance with respect to these social units.

Significant indicators for evaluating the economic relationship existing between a product business and its *employees* as a social group might include stability of employment, improvement in standard of living, job opportunities and family security. These could be expressed in quantitative indexes prepared from statistical data on such factors as average number of hours worked per week, average number of employees and hourly wages in terms of what they will buy.

The conduct of a product business as it affects its *vendors* could best be determined by means of an attitude survey which would request the vendor's appraisal of the product business as an individual customer and also as compared with its principal competitors.

Comprehensive reaction surveys are probably the most effective device for measuring the effect of the actions of a product business on the *plant community*. These reaction or opinion surveys could be supplemented by quantitative indexes developed from various types of data such as community rate surveys, number of employment applications, volume of local purchases, contributions to local charities and participation of leading employees in civic, church and business organizations.

In considering measurements of a product department's responsibility to the *business community*, we are thinking in terms of its relationships with all components of the business society without regard to geographical location. Suggested measurements of the conduct of a product business with its customers and vendors have been mentioned previously. We believe that qualitative measurements might be developed to appraise the reasonableness of the product business in its dealings with its distribution and dealers and competitors.

Balance between short-range and long-range goals

The balance between short-range and long-range goals has been set out as a separate area in order to emphasize its significance as a factor to be considered in developing any measurements program. The survival and growth of our businesses five, ten and fifteen years hence depend on the major management decisions made today, and the impact of these decisions on the future must not be overlooked.

As a practical matter, we have decided that our approach will be to consider the "balance between short-range and long-range goals" as an integral part of the development of measurements in each of the first seven key result areas, rather than as an area separate and distinct in itself. Upon completion of the measurements program in the other seven areas, we plan to summarize the specific recommendations which relate to the proper balance between goals in order to assure ourselves that consideration has been given to this important factor.

The foregoing material represents our preliminary thinking on measurements in each of the key result areas constituting the operational measurements portion of our Project. These key result areas also represent the foundation on which we hope to build sound measurements of functional work and the work of management in the product businesses of the General Electric Company.

BIBLIOGRAPHY, CHAPTER XIV

CARROLL, PHIL. "Measurement of Management," *Advanced Management* (October, 1955), 9-12.

Controlling Capital Expenditures, Studies in Business Policy, No. 62, National Industrial Conference Board, Inc., 1953.

GRIMES, L. E. "A Comprehensive System of Performance Reports," *Tested Approaches to Capital Equipment Replacement*, Special Report No. 1. New York: American Management Association, Inc., 1954, 86-94.

HABERSTROH, CHADWICK T. "Control as an Organization Process," *Management Science* (January, 1960), 165-171.

HEITMAN, CHARLES E. "Using Standards as Controls in Factory Management," *Advanced Management* (July, 1954), 12.

LUCK, W. S. "Now You Can Really Measure Maintenance Performance," *Factory Management and Maintenance* (January, 1956), 81-86.

MOORE, LEO B. "Industrial Standardization," W. G. Iresom and E. L. Grant (Eds.). *Handbook of Industrial Engineering and Management*, 1955. New York: Prentice-Hall, Inc., 619-651.

PETERSEN, D. N. "Pace—A New Industrial Engineering Technique for Management," *Journal of Industrial Engineering* (July-August, 1960), 304-312.

"Return on Investment—Tool of Modern Management," *Improved Tools of Financial Management*. Financial Management Series No. 111. New York: American Management Association, Inc., 1956, 3-30.

RIDGWAY, V. F. "Dysfunctional Consequences of Performance Measurement," *Administrative Science Quarterly* (September, 1956), 240-247.

RUBENSTEIN, ALBERT H. "Setting Criteria for R & D," *Harvard Business Review* (January-February, 1957), 95-104.

TRUEHAFT, WILLIAM C. "Experience with Executive Standards of Performance," *Improving the Caliber of Company Management*. General Management Series No. 183. New York: American Management Association, Inc., 1956, 3-11.

Chapter XV
External Control

In carrying out the duties of his position, a manager not only is subject to control from above and within the organization in the form of its objectives, policies, and directives, but he also is influenced and controlled by the demands and pressures of external forces. The purpose of this chapter is to present examples of the types of influences outside of the management proper to which managers need to direct a portion of their attention.

In the first article Erwin H. Schell presents a list of criteria against which the management of a business is judged by an investment company. Since a majority of medium- and large-sized corporations are likely to find a need for capital over a period of years, the views of investment companies exert a perceptible influence upon company managements. The criteria for the evaluation of a business presented by Schell are worthy ones. A management team might well adapt them for self-evaluation.

In Article 55 a wider perspective of managerial responsibilities is considered. Fred H. Blum is concerned not only with economic performance of business organizations but also considers noneconomic attainment as relevant activity for which management is accountable. In this view work should possess a meaning beyond the paycheck. This view is shared by Ohmann (Article 4, Chapter II).

54. INDUSTRIAL ADMINISTRATION THROUGH THE EYES OF AN INVESTMENT COMPANY [1]

Erwin H. Schell [2]

The attempt by investment houses to measure the effectiveness of administrative or managerial ability in a manufacturing enterprise, apart from the technical approach of the security analyst is nothing new. As long ago as 25 years, the president of our oldest American investment trust stated that, in judging a security, he gave 50 per cent weighting to the statistical report, and an equal amount to information gained from personal contacts with directors, executives, vendors, customers and community.

The justification for this paper, then, is less because of any innovational qualities, than because of the somewhat unusual objectives that it seeks to describe.

The investment company on whose board I serve as a representative of the public, offers to the buyers of securities a spectrum of ten Certificates of Participation, based upon an equal number of investment funds ranging in degree of conservatism from high-grade bonds to appreciation common stocks. The portfolios of each of these ten funds contain securities selected according to their consistent tendency to reflect the characteristics of their particular class.

The service rendered the investor is the assurance that he is buying what he thinks he is buying. Decisions as to *what* type of investment he should buy are his to make, with the aid of dealer counsel if he should so desire.

This investment company therefore is concerned chiefly with the selection and classification of securities into groups which may be depended upon to behave in a truly representative fashion in terms of their class. Moreover, it is important that this representation be a distinguished one; that the securities selected be leaders in their respective fields; and that this leadership be dependable. Clearly, this requirement of *consistent leadership* demands a choice of securi-

[1] From *Appraising Managerial Assets—Policies, Practices and Organization,* General Management Series No. 151. American Management Association, 1950, pp. 3-9. Reprinted by permission of the American Management Association.
[2] Erwin H. Schell, Member of the Board, Keystone Custodian Funds, Inc.

ties on a long-range basis—a quality which is provided only through long-term administration.

To a surprising degree the questions asked by this investment company are, therefore, the identical questions which an alert top executive will find valuable in assessing the quality and effectiveness of his long-term administration. For this reason I have asked permission of the president of my organization to present its procedure here.

Some years ago, the following question was put to us as directors:

> Assuming that you are personally considering investment in the securities of a given company, and that you have access to balance sheets, income statements and other statistical data, *what five questions would you ask*—over and above those which may be answered by analysis of statistical reports—in obtaining an objective measure of the quality of management of the company?

This question engendered a wide variety of responses which were classified and incorporated in part in the field questionnaire which forms a portion of the selective procedure employed.

It should go without saying that, whereas this form of managerial investigation is viewed as the most important of the several analyses undertaken, yet it is but one aspect of the economic, industrial and financial studies which also contribute their share to the final judgment.

Criteria for Evaluating Management

Obviously, each manufacturing enterprise calls for a different type of leadership. Someone has said with considerable truth that a successful business requires the application of good standard practice to routine functions and the application of genius to the key activities. While we may not agree with this statement in full, we cannot evade the fact that businesses *are* different and call for varying talents in their administration.

Nevertheless, there are certain criteria that appear to apply to so broad a field that they may be said to be generally indicative.

In the Management Evaluation Questionnaire, the more than 60 queries are arranged for convenience in the making of individual interviews. I have regrouped them under twelve headings in the order in which they would normally follow in preparing a final report.

Managerial personnel

Here we refer to the executive staff—the principal officers and department heads. We are careful to obtain their respective ages, length of service with the company, nature of previous business experience, compensation and stock interest, if any. We are happy when we have a preponderance of upper-level executives in the middle-age group, with length of service sufficient to reflect stabilization, receiving compensation in accordance with an objectively designed salary plan, and with the further stimulus of a stock interest, where possible.

We have also discovered that the outside interests of these men throw considerable light on the probable depth and trend of their personal application to the business.

Casting this specific information against our previously prepared background of general business trends and special conditions in the industry of which this company is a part, enables us to assess whether, in general, the company is staffed with "men of the hour" as well as "men who have what (specifically) it takes."

Additional calipers will be applied to this group under subsequent headings.

Administration

We are particularly interested in the composition and activities of the board of directors; who are the principal directors; their major interests and abilities, and to what extent they are members of executive or other board committees; on what other boards they serve.

We are hopeful of finding in this group men of sufficient competence, experience and judgment to make a direct and continuing contribution to the establishment of long-term company policy. We are hopeful that these men, in addition to their industrial or professional ability, will be "men of parts" having wide and varied contacts, including service on other boards. We are hopeful that the board will contain men representing management, stockholders and the public; that it will be a diversified group capable of making a directors' discussion broadly constructive.

We believe that boards of directors will be called upon in the future to play an even more active role in the conduct of a business than heretofore and we are gratified when we find a committee structure or other device in operation to implement and stimulate these activities. It is pleasing to discover a scattering of young men on these boards. They can be expected to bedevil the oldsters, but they do add precious leaven to the loaf.

Objectives

We are eager to learn what objectives are given highest priority by the company. This, we find, is a hard thing to get at. Searching as we are for establishments that provide distinguished leadership in their field, we anticipate that the basic problem of making a profit has been under control for some time, thus enabling other objectives to be given important and attentive consideration. The way we approach this matter is to inquire what are the most important problems that the company faces today, for important objectives always meet important difficulties and it is in overcoming such difficulties that important problems are born.

To paraphrase an old saying: "Management is known by the problems it keeps."

It delights us when a company president can tell us precisely what he is shooting for (rifle, not shotgun); how he is organizing to accomplish his purpose; how far advanced he is on his program; and how he thinks he is getting along. Such information enables us more effectively to judge of his probable future success or failure and its effect upon the business which he directs.

Organization

While we have suggested to our field investigators several leading questions regarding organization—having to do with such matters as definite and clean-cut responsibilities and attending authority, and the presence of up-to-date manuals, charts and the like—yet we are chiefly interested to learn whether the top executive is convinced of the fact that in any establishment of reasonable size, current changes are so frequent as to make organization a continuing problem.

We look forward to the possibility that he not only believes this to be true, but has set up some sort of permanent committee, staff group, or outside counsel to assure the presence of this continuing scrutiny and adjustment to new needs.

As we make our constant round of investigations of the securities in our ten portfolios, it affords us no little satisfaction to find that progressive changes in organization are made apace with the changes in process, personnel or product.

The days when organizations received only periodic refurbishings, like spring housecleaning, are gone. Constant evolutional change is the order of the day.

Plans

The long depression and the subsequent war were for many concerns periods of crisis-management rather than of long-term planning. We believe that tomorrow the far look ahead will become increasingly essential for any company which aspires to consistent and continuing leadership in its field.

Modern forecasting and planning techniques make use of Confucius' admonition: "We should make plans so that we may have plans to discard."

The fields of procurement of materials, distribution of product, financing, labor and executive requirements, plant growth and equipment purchase, long-term estimates reaching far forward at half-yearly intervals and subject to semi-annual revisions until the future becomes the present—all these enable industry to plan intelligently, explain the bases for alteration of plans as time passes and thus gain a firmer mind-hold upon what is to come.

Our questions relating to the presence of out-reaching devices for this dimensioning of the future are, in reality, designed to measure the degree to which top management is already dedicated to a program of planned rather than of fortuitous progress.

Control

An industrial analyst of earlier days once told me that the first thing he set about doing was finding the person in the company— whether executive, director or stockholder—who was in position to say "no," to mean it, and to enforce it.

Such people are rightfully still extant in industry, but we use the term somewhat more broadly. We feel that any management which aims at long-term distinction must of necessity have developed objectives, standards, supervision, evaluation and reward for the control of output, quality, materials, facilities, processes, costs, finances and indeed every active function of the business.

To put it bluntly, we welcome the presence of these control activities as proof that the operating executive is really running the business, rather than vice versa. We are pleased when we find such procedures long established and, in fact, taken for granted as inescapable elements of competent managerial operation.

Our questions here, therefore, are somewhat general in character and serve mainly to assure us that a long-accepted principle of good management has not been allowed to atrophy.

Nevertheless, these inquiries do, from time to time, reveal informal control structures that do not appear on the organization chart.

Upkeep

In our evaluation of management we are definitely and deeply concerned with management's policies and practices regarding upkeep. In today's industrial world, where obsolescence is increasingly outdistancing the effect of depreciation due to wear and tear, the problem of maintaining technical parity with the advancing state-of-the-art has become a major issue for well-nigh every manufacturer.

The problem is especially severe in areas of productive facilities. Most plants today have within their walls an assortment of equipment dating from the days of World War I to the present. Only a few have managed to keep the entire plan reasonably up-to-date. It is these latter organizations whose securities are apt to impress us favorably, for we have learned by experience that the greatest bulwark of competition is the continuing presence of modern facilities, irrespective of the age of the establishment.

Auxiliary areas of upkeep such as external plant appearance, housekeeping, and building maintenance reveal the presence or absence of standards of management which are vital to long-term leadership, as we see it.

Our questions are useful, then, in determining the *attitude* of management no less than the *action* of management with respect to upkeep as it exists in a rapidly advancing technology.

In this area, we also direct questions to those responsible for personnel and executive training. Upkeep of human resources is no less a managerial responsibility than the maintenance of physical equipment. We view continuing industrial training programs as the prime method by which obsolescence in workmen and managers may be combatted. Executive techniques no less than worker skills are experiencing marked changes as time passes. The state-of-the-art here is no less eruptive than in the more technical areas of equipment and process.

Improvement

It goes without saying that consistent long-term leadership today demands the presence of constant improvement in materials, processes, products, personnel and indeed all the active functions of management, if the position is to be maintained. Moreover, this improvement must be over and above that required to obtain parity with the general advancing state-of-the-art.

Our questions here are directed to determine the degree to which management has actually taken steps to insure and assure such progress. We ask, for example, about the presence of adequate provision for product research and development; how the research organization rates in the field of the industry; how research expense ratios compare with those of other progressive organizations; the extent to which current sales volume stems from past research and development. We ask about the status of market research; of the nature of current demand for company products. We ask whether management has ever summarized and evaluated its own management; whether management has made use of consultants in areas where improvements may be hastened through benefit of professional advice. We ask whether the company has been a leader in adopting the newest production methods; whether it has shown aggressive adaptability to meet changing conditions.

We view this section of our evaluations most importantly and want full assurance that the implements, engineering procedures and skilled personnel for the making of constant improvement are at hand.

Morale

So many people have confused morale with group enthusiasms or excitements that I hesitate to use the word out of its precise context. By morale we mean that temper of spirit which causes organizations to drive patiently, unromantically and inceasingly through difficulty and disappointment; the quality of loyalty that causes older employees to try to get their sons and daughters jobs in the same organization; the kind of support that gives full obedience with a grin although honest differences of opinion still exist.

We want particularly to know whether there is a good working team upstairs. For example, it is an old banking rule in New England that no money is loaned to a business where a family row is in progress. We respect the soundness of this tradition. We want to know whether employees, in general, are sold on the company; whether they think it is a "good place to work."

We are interested in the history of the company's labor relations but we do not necessarily view past difficulties as diagnostic of current or future weakness. Often these early encounters when fairly adjudicated build for subsequent mutual respect and regard.

No area that we examine is more intangible than this. No area is more important.

Attitude

We are convinced that the personal attitudes of top executives toward their employees, their stockholders, their community, the public and the government, directly determine the success or the failure of these varied staff activities as conducted by subordinates farther down the line. We view it as vital to the managerial evaluation of any company that the attitudes of top management toward these five groups of interest be obtained.

To support and confirm responses to our questions, we also look at the record. We want to know whether the attitude as expressed has been put to use in a practical way. In each of these categories we ask whether there is any evidence that the record of the company in its chosen field has been outstanding; whether definite and clear-cut operating policies have been developed; organization problems solved; personnel appointed and programs designed, supervised and evaluated.

In this area of managerial attitude we rely heavily on the Biblical adage: "By his works shall ye know him."

Competitive resource

The competitive position of the company in its industry is subject to statistical measurement and therefore not germane to these inquiries.

The nature and extent of competitive power, however, is a topic with which we are definitely concerned here. For example, we think it important to know why customers buy of the company under study in preference to competitors. Is it price, quality, delivery, or what? We think it important to know whether this competitive strength resulted from planned developments within the company or from chance. We should like to know whether these competitive resources are the result of environmental advantages that will be permanent, or whether they are in current danger as a result of competitive research and development, patent termination or other causes.

Every going company produces a good to which its customers give preference over competitive goods. Too often, top management is not aware of exactly what its advantage consists, and does not recognize its loss until too late.

Reputation

Last in this company report, I put the topic of reputation. From the point of view of the field investigator, it again will be the last factor to be scrutinized. Too early knowledge of the opinions of others regarding a company may cause us unwittingly to develop prejudgments which may later color the facts as found.

Again, the nightmare of the investment analyst is the company which to all outward appearance is well managed, but which is undeservedly living on its reputation while dry-rot and senescence are at work within.

With these precautions in mind, our investigator turns to the company's competitors, customers, bankers, to other investment and underwriting houses, cooperating analysts, insurance companies and other sources, for comments and counsel. When these statements are at odds with his findings, the investigator returns to the company for recheck.

The final report, when combined with other studies of general business, of the industry in question, of the company's financial structure and condition, earnings and dividends, of internal market action, and certain other factors, permits of decision as to the precise position on the waiting list of our company's future purchases; or continuance in, or elimination from, current portfolios.

CONCLUSION

When we review the nature and purpose of our inquiries in these twelve fields—management, administration, objectives, organization, plans, control, upkeep, morale, improvement, attitude, competitive resource and reputation—we find that the times are requiring us to apply new yardsticks to managerial competence.

The depth and rapidity of economic and industrial change; the growth of application of democratic principles (I do not refer to politics here); the widening of active relationships with employees, stockholders, community, public and government—these three basic trends appear to be responsible for new and greater stress upon:

vigor and versatility in operating management; breadth and variety of viewpoint in administration; vigilance in matters of organization; clarity and definiteness of long-term objectives; dependency upon far-reaching plans; maintenance of integrated controls; upkeep in harmony with an advancing art; improvement as a normal expectancy; effective (result-getting) managerial attitudes; creativeness through high morale; resources for increasing competition; reputation for consistently distinguished, long-term leadership in a specific industry.

In our field studies thus far, only a small proportion of the companies analyzed are rated as superior in terms of all these requirements.

Finally, investment analysis cannot be held to be scientific as we speak of science and technology. Intangible factors are difficult to get at, particularly difficult to measure and therefore susceptible to underemphasis.

We are continuing to discover revealing criteria in this nebulous area. You have been presented with our most recent thinking and procedures.

55. SOCIAL AUDIT OF THE
ENTERPRISE [1]

Fred H. Blum [2]

Most businessmen would say that humanitarian ideals often conflict with efficient operations. Which should come first if the two
collide? Can they be reconciled?

The idea that workers are to be respected as individual human
beings with a sense of dignity may come easily or instinctively, or
slowly and perforce because it is expected; but every businessman
feels it. Also, taking pride in being practical, every businessman
recognizes an apparent (though not automatic) cause-and-effect relationship between the human or social side and the dollars-and-cents
side of his enterprise.

This well-accepted concept, however, dodges the real issue because
it clearly sets the company's goals—efficiency, profit, share of the
market—as of the highest priority, and simply considers people as
one of the tools to be used to reach those goals. If the development
of the people in the company and the fulfillment of their human
needs were made a primary or coordinate objective, along with
financial success, would we see them differently than we now do—
and perhaps act differently toward them?

New Purpose

A survey which I recently conducted brought this problem into
sharp focus. It was a "social audit" of a company, which differed
from the usual "morale survey" with which management is familiar,
in that it was concerned with the workers as people in their own
right rather than as functional parts of the organization. We wanted
to find out how well—or how poorly—the company was doing in
satisfying the basic human needs of its employees; and, for the

[1] From *Harvard Business Review* (March-April, 1958), pp. 77-86. Reprinted by permission of *Harvard Business Review*.
[2] Fred H. Blum, Co-Chairman, Social Science Program, Department of
Interdisciplinary Studies, College of Science, Literature, and the Arts, University
of Minnesota.

sake of industry generally, which organizational factors are the significant ones for this purpose and what their implications are for action.

The framework for the survey was well expressed by Howard R. Bowen in his book, *Social Responsibilities of the Businessman*, which was sponsored by the National Council of Churches as a part of its series on "Christian Ethics and Economic Life." Said Mr. Bowen:

> Another possible institutional change which might help to strengthen the social point of view in business management would be the *social audit*. Just as businesses subject themselves to audits of their accounts by independent public-accountant firms, they might also subject themselves to periodic examination by independent outside experts who would evaluate the performance of the business from the *social* point of view.[3]

The attitude survey which I conducted in the course of my study is, as far as I know, the first actual implementation of the social-audit idea.

It adds meaning to the whole project to realize that the opportunity for making such a study was supplied by a Quaker businessman—Walter Lamb, president of Robert E. Lamb, Inc., a medium-size industrial engineering and construction firm in Philadelphia. It is typical of the Quaker philosophy to think of moral-ethical ideals and profit goals as consistent parts of the same effort. Mr. Lamb's company has been cooperating since 1955 with a number of other Quaker companies in an industrial relations project under the auspices of the Friends' Social Order Committee in Philadelphia, in an attempt to assess the basic problems of industry as a first step toward experimentation with new ideas that could serve as models for industry as a whole.

Mr. Lamb's idea is that if a business thinks it worthwhile to have a yearly audit of its operations in financial terms, it is equally important to have a yearly audit of "progress in human relations." This is what makes the study different—its explicit purpose, i.e., to measure the success of the company in meeting its social responsibilities.

Particular focus

Thus, the specific procedures that I used—basically not different from the advanced techniques worked out by such organizations as

---

[3] New York: Harper & Brothers, 1953, p. 155.

the Research Center for Group Dynamics at the University of Michigan, and the Tavistock Institute of Human Relations in London —were selected, combined, and applied with a particular focus. For example, the interview procedure was one I developed and tested in the course of a major research project at Geo. A. Hormel & Company in Minnesota: a combination of interviewing and exchanging information, designed not only to obtain insight but also to meet people as people rather than as guinea pigs.[4] Perhaps even more significant, a basic distinction was made between two kinds of measurement:

1. *Organizational scores* measure the extent to which the company has succeeded in achieving its objectives (a) by evoking general attitudes among employees which support the purposes of the organization and which are in harmony with the means used to achieve these purposes, and (b) by identifying the aspirations of the employees with the goals of the organization.
2. *Individuation scores* measure the extent to which the company satisfies the personal needs and aspirations of the individuals who are part of the company. The Quaker conception of basic needs and aspirations —namely, individual self-expression and creative development of the personality—is the basis for the evaluations reported in the study and hence for the individuation scores.

In effect, the survey is designed to learn the feelings and attitudes of workers as a measure of the company's success in attaining both objectives: adjusting the workers to the company's needs *and* adjusting the company to the workers' needs. In the original report of the study the difference between the two kinds of scores is explained as "an expression of the fundamental conviction that human needs and values are primary and that the organization has to be adjusted to these needs."

All office workers and full-time field supervisors (i.e., not including construction gangs) were interviewed, and with only one exception cooperated fully—"glad of the opportunity to talk."

Separate scores have been reported for the two areas. (Exhibit I is a summary of the tabulation.) For each there is an over-all score and a more specific breakdown. The maximum is 100; a figure of less than 100 indicates how far the situation falls short of the ideal. Clearly, the usefulness of such figures is not in their absolute values (which cannot be precise), but in the opportunity they provide for determining relative achievement from year to year or company to company.

---

[4] For a detailed account of this interview technique, see Fred H. Blum, "Getting Individuals to Give Information to the Outsider," *Journal of Social Issues,* Vol. VIII, No. 3 (1952), p. 35.

Exhibit I
SUMMARY OF SCORES

Organizational scores

Over-all attitude toward the company	95
Competence of top management	95
Satisfaction with position in the company	70
Fairness of earnings distribution	85
Adequacy of information	60
Effectiveness of organization as a whole	60

Individuation scores

General satisfaction of working for the company	70
Satisfaction with personal relations	90
Present use of abilities	60
Satisfaction with pay	65
Basic work satisfaction	60

KEY TO SCORES: 80-100, very good; 60-80, good; 40-60, medium; 20-40, inadequate.

The point of the survey, of course, is to put into focus those areas in which the company can improve, and it is obvious that the specific problems of the Lamb company will not be those of another firm. Consequently, for purposes of this article, I shall discuss only those results which are of a more general nature and which bring the basic feelings that *any* employee may have about his company.

COMPANY GOALS

As the tabulation above shows, the score for the over-all attitude toward the company is very high—indicating a much more favorable attitude, in fact, than I have found in other industries and other localities. Perhaps such a result is to be expected in view of the company's unusually high degree of interest in human relations problems. More is needed, however, than favorable responses by employees to such a demonstration of interest by management. The balance of the organizational scores are mixed and include some that are much less satisfactory. In other words, there is still plenty for management to do to improve organizational relationships—but now it has a background against which to measure progress from year to year.

Over-all attitude

The main factors determining the favorable over-all attitude toward the company are:

1. *The immediate work environment.* The modern office building was mentioned repeatedly as a factor making work more enjoyable. For example: "It is lovely to work in. I don't know where to find as pleasant an office." This response shows that comparisons with alternatives known to the employee play an important role in his feelings of satisfaction. A reference to "ample parking facilities" may have the same origin.

2. *The people in the work group.* "They are a very nice group of people," or "You work with exceptionally talented people," may suffice to indicate the importance of human contacts as an element determining the feeling about the company.

3. *The general atmosphere.* Many of the employees commented spontaneously on "the informal atmosphere," which is expressed in the freedom given to employees in regard to lunch hours and the confidence shown in them by not keeping any close check on when they come to work and what they do during working hours. This general atmosphere created by the company's policy and executives is an expression of a basic underlying attitude of trust on the part of management toward the employees, demonstrated not only by financial allowances and loans in case of need due to special circumstances, but by a conscious attempt to assign employees individual tasks which involve a little more responsibility than the actual position in the company may call for.

Top management

Respect for the character and ability of top management was expressed in various ways. A typical comment:

> This company has a young head. I think he is ambitious. Others are not that way. He uses every possible tool he can think of to make the company better. . . . He is not afraid to take a chance, . . . not afraid to take a gamble to back up his convictions.

Related to these convictions are the good feelings of being in a company "with a future." This is not just a matter of personal opportunity, of being in a company "in which one can work oneself up," but of the company's policies, methods, and reputation in the field of construction. The employees find satisfaction in the external reflection of the company on the minds of other people, as well as in the extrinsic quality of the company that they experience themselves in their work.

Position in company

Employees' satisfaction with their positions in the company is partly a matter of internal organization—especially the managerial or supervisory hierarchy—and partly a matter of the job content.

A comparison of questions on (a) to whom employees actually report, (b) to whom they would like to report, and (c) to whom they would not like to report indicates (along with some other questions) a high level of satisfaction with personal supervisory relationships. In particular, employees feel free to raise questions and to make suggestions: "This company gives you credit for having a brain. You are more on your own. If you prove yourself, you get more leeway to do your job."

Attitudes about job content reflect the relationship between the actual work done and the abilities or potentialities of the individual employees. "Enjoyment of the work" was mentioned repeatedly as a positive factor. "The opportunity to use imagination and initiative, personally and through the type of work" is another typical expression of the same theme.

Satisfaction was also expressed in more general form: "You have a feeling of belonging and not just of being a cog in the wheel." "You are treated as an individual, not as a number." "You have a more essential part in the company rather than being one in a thousand." Particularly significant was the repeated and spontaneous indication that the company allowed employees to have "integrity as a person."

Distribution of earnings

Favorable feeling about the amount of money earned and the fairness of distribution is an important element in the general attitude of the employees toward the company. When asked to classify the specific advantages derived from working for this company, most employees listed "money" first. This bread-and-butter theme came up consistently; and it is too obvious to need much elaboration. However, its strength is indicated by the fact that it came ahead of "development and growth" and "the people with whom we work," which in this company are unusually strong sources of satisfaction.

INDIVIDUAL VALUES

Even in this company, with its highly developed sense of human relations and social responsibilities, the tabulation of scores shows that the needs of the workers are being served far less well than the traditional needs of the company; presumably morale can be favorable organizationally (and thus productive of efficiency, sales, and profits) without being equally rewarding in terms of individual values.

The scores in this area all tend to run lower, but to appreciate the nature of the differences note particularly the discrepancy between the scores indicating (a) "fairness of earnings distribution," an organizational score that shows the degree of satisfaction with company policy in regard to earnings, including profit sharing, and (b) "satisfaction with pay," an individuation score that shows the degree of personal satisfaction derived from the earnings.

While the "fairness of earnings distribution" score was very high, personal satisfaction with the pay proved to be distinctly lower. The response of one employee to the question "Are you pretty well satisfied with the amount of pay you are now getting?" throws some light on the reasons for this difference:

> No, but I am not dissatisfied to the point where I beat my brains out. I think within a reasonable amount of time the company will realize it. I am just normally underpaid, not to the point where it worries me—partly because I do not have a demanding wife.

This expression, "I am just normally underpaid," is illustrative of the feelings of many employees. A man who is satisfied with his pay is often considered to be unambitious. "Everyone thinks he should get more salary" is a typical response. We are confronted here with a "normal" expectation of a steadily rising pay scale. A blockage of this expectation is experienced as a dissatisfaction with the pay.

General satisfaction

Now let us take a broader look at job satisfactions. Employees are, on the whole, well satisfied with their work. The overwhelming majority feel that they have enough freedom to do their jobs in their own way: "They tell you to do it the way you think best."

Practically all employees feel that the days are varied: "Every day is tremendously different. . . . "It is the same pattern . . . yet on different days you solve different problems." It is, therefore, not astonishing to hear that as a rule time passes fast on the job: "It passes too fast. There is never enough time to get enough done." Not too many employees, when at work, wish that "something would happen." Only a small fraction of the employees ever feel bored on the job: "No, I can't remember being bored. I may be perplexed, but not bored."

This general satisfaction still does not produce a score indicative of all-out contentment—perhaps because it also reflects the result of several contradictory factors:

Fatigue and tension. Physical fatigue is still frequent. More than nine out of ten employees feel "certainly" or "occasionally" tired. But fatigue no longer seems to prevent people from being active after working hours.

In any case, complaints about physical fatigue were far outnumbered by complaints about mental strain, tensions, or the speed of work. This may seem perfectly natural in view of the nature of the work performed by these employees—largely office tasks. These feelings, however, cannot be explained on this ground only—as we shall see presently. Asked what about the job makes him tired, one employee said: "Boy, that's another nice one, to draw the line between physical and mental fatigue." Another employee was more explicit: "That's a question I often ask myself when I come home at night. I'm usually fagged out, though I'm sitting all day. It isn't the physical effort. Is it completely the mental effort or is it tension? If I work physically all day, I'm less tired. . . . In this job I can't really relax. . . ."

There is no doubt that time pressure plays an important role in mental strain. A large number of employees feel uncomfortable because "too much is left over," or they "can't forget the job." Or, as one employee put it: "There are days when I feel a little tense, when I can't completely drop the job. After that I have a bottle of beer, relax, and forget about the job." The need for "relaxation" and for "a change" is a dominant theme, often noticed in other studies of work, and does not need much elaboration here.[5]

The desire to work. No matter what problems work may bring, however, the employees would rather return to their jobs the next day than stay at home. An overwhelming majority wanted a balance between work and off-work: "I wouldn't want to work seven days; still I wouldn't want to stay idle seven days a week. A balance of the two is the ideal situation." Though there is only a minority who would say, "I think I like working better than all the rest," work remains the most important activity which in the best of circum-

[5] See Georges Friedmann, *Où Va Le Travail Humain* (Paris, 1950), pp. 254 ff; also Fred H. Blum, *Toward a Democratic Work Process* (New York: Harper & Brothers, 1953), pp. 94 ff.

stances gives meaning to the life of the employees, or which at least "keeps you occupied."

Approximately half of the employees would like to work all their lives rather than retire. One man put it this way: "I hope to work until the day I die. People who retire are well-educated vegetables. They make a career out of little things. I know some people who inherited money. They don't have to work. Their life is pretty meaningless. You can travel just so long; have hobbies just so long. Professional people who can retire gradually are fortunate."

About every four out of five employees would want to continue working even if they "inherited enough money to live on without working." One employee stated sharply: "Sure, I would want to work. I would go crazy, drink myself to death worrying what to do. I get nuts doing nothing."

These quotations highlight the kinds of satisfaction derived from work. They definitely show how central the job is in the lives of most people. While remaining central, work creates personal tensions which permeate an employee's whole life. It could easily be shown that these tensions figure among the most important factors that lower the satisfactions employees derive from working for this, and for any other, company. A number of surveys undertaken among blue- and white-collar workers in different companies substantiate this point. Moreover, they show that the tension differences between the firm's factory workers and its office personnel are not as great as one might expect—and they will become less and less significant as automation becomes more widespread.

Use of abilities

It cannot be emphasized too strongly that one of the most frequently mentioned ingredients of an interesting and satisfactory job was the degree to which an employee could carry through a complete assignment and the extent to which he could see the results of his efforts: "Your satisfaction comes from a completed job. You want to start something and complete it." Another employee liked his work because he could see "the job from start to finish, watching it grow." This is true not only for employees who have to do with the physical building operations; as an accountant said:

> I can see something accomplished, come up with an end result. . . . Everyone concerned is interested in that figure, and there is a certain amount of contentment when you are through and it comes out right.

Inability to see the whole picture as well as interruption on a particular task were given repeatedly as reasons for dissatisfaction with the work. It must be noted, furthermore, that feelings of partnership with the company were impaired whenever the nature of the job was such that it did not enable an employee to use and develop his abilities and/or to perform a task which gave him a feeling of completion.

UNDERLYING VALUES

The relationship between personal satisfaction with work and the way the work is organized can be understood only if we know the system of values held by the individual employees and the degree to which they can realize these values.

The approach used in this survey—specifically the distinction between organizational and individuation scores—facilitates evaluative analysis of the meaning of work because differences between scores often make it *necessary* to examine underlying values. Thus, in exploring the question of satisfaction with pay, which showed such a discrepancy with fairness of earnings distribution, we were led on to a series of interrelated factors revolving around the need for success and meaning.

Because of the strength of the underlying value system, it deserves special attention by all managements.

Need for success

The significance of ambition and the desire to be successful is well known. For many of the employees interviewed, these values manifest themselves in a very concrete desire: to have a business of their own. This is a general desire which has been found not only in offices but in factories as well.[6] "To have somebody work for me," "to be managing somebody or something," "to start my own business" —these are the typical statements made again and again and in the most varied contexts. One employee, who was most articulate, said:

> What people want most is to be on their own; or, to the extent to which this is not possible, to have a feeling of independence and of control in the organization.

[6] Among more recent studies see Robert H. Guest, "Work Careers and Aspirations of Automobile Workers," *American Sociological Review* (April 1954), p. 161.

Feelings of partnership with the company are decisively influenced by the extent to which this need for success and independence is satisfied. The survey showed that employees could be divided into three groups:

1. *Those at the top levels of management who have realized this basic goal or who are close to its realization.* In this group we find the largest proportion of satisfied people. "I am satisfied because I take part in major policy decisions." The area in which these decisions are made has a magnetic attraction for many employees. "I want to go where the decisions are made" is a typical expression of their feelings.

2. *Those employees who are next to the top levels of management and who are striving to get into the circle of the chosen few.* These employees give their best to the company because they can achieve their goal only if they give evidence of unusual abilities and drive. As a rule, this group identifies its interests strongly with those of the company. But at the fringe of this group, some doubts do arise. When asked "What comes to your mind when you see the words Robert E. Lamb, Inc.?" one employee answered: "I just had it happen over the weekend. I had a mixed reaction. I am very proud to be a member of the company, but I sometimes wonder how much of a member I really am. Or, to put in the vernacular, what's in it for me?"

3. *Those employees, the largest group, who either have given up the hope of ever becoming part of the control group or who never had such aspirations.* "I take the path of least resistance because I'm not far enough to be in control of the company" is a statement which highlights these feelings. Another person answered the question as to his sense of partnership by saying: "That implies a little more significance than I feel. . . . I have decided after having worked for a number of companies that there is only one driving force in a company, only one individual—the company. Though many people feel that they are working toward the goal of becoming part of the management team, they really are not."

So it is not surprising that feelings of partnership become weaker as we "descend" in the hierarchy of business until we find employees who limit themselves "to doing what we are told to do."

Need for meaning

Before examining some of the broader implications of these findings it is important to realize that wanting to be close to the top, to participate in the decision-making process, cannot be explained exclusively in terms of the desire for power. It is greatly influenced by the desire to have an interesting, meaningful job, as the survey has shown so clearly.

References to this need have been included in the interview material just presented. Its full significance emerges clearly in the case of the Lamb company because the firm is in a peculiar stage of development. Until recently, personal relationships were a decisive factor in creating a satisfying job situation, and employees were pleased with the large and varied scope of their assignments. The new organization, on the other hand, requires formal channels of communication, and the more complex work tasks do have a tendency to get split up, even though new opportunities are opening. This period of transition brings out sharply the whole problem of participation in the company and of meaningful work tasks.

We could again observe three groupings of employees:

1. *Those to whom the change has made little difference.* In effect, they still enjoy the benefits of a small organization.
2. *Those for whom the larger organization creates new opportunities.* Particularly during the period of transition, when organizational lines are still fluid, the enterprising, daring, and imaginative person has many chances to advance or, sometimes, literally to create his own job. People in this group feel most positive about both their work and the company.
3. *Those for whom the possibilities of direct contact with top management become increasingly limited.* For a while they console themselves with a vicarious participation in control and leadership. But as the tasks become redivided along lines different from those typical for a smaller organization and as jobs that formerly were a unit are broken up, dissatisfaction arises: "Work has lost a good deal of its meaning for me since I am not any more working directly with——," said one employee. Others, aware of the problem, look for new solutions: "The job is too split up . . . I want the company to experiment with the idea of . . . one person being responsible for a whole job." Another employee looks in a different direction to restore a sense of integrity and unity: "I don't see how any one individual can produce a completed product in a reasonable amount of time. . . . But we do try to have him see the whole job and his relation to the whole."

The real criterion

The three groups of employees classified according to the satisfaction of the desire for being "successful" in the sense of participating in the decision-making process do not correspond exactly to the three groups classified according to the satisfaction of the desire for a meaningful and unified work task. Yet the two categories intermingle. As already pointed out, the desire to be a success in the company is often accompanied by—if not determined by—the desire for a meaningful job. Status strivings, the desire for recognition of all kinds, are intimately related to the need for self-esteem and recognition as a human being.

It would be a grave mistake, however, to mix up these two needs or to subsume one in the other. It is quite possible to be highly "successful" without having a humanly satisfying experience of work, without experiencing any unity and wholeness of personality— as a number of studies on management show.[7] Several surveys which I undertook in different companies substantiate these findings. But my criterion is neither success in the usual sense of the word nor a vague, comfortable feeling of belonging; it is the deeper satisfaction of the human need for unity and integrity. Here is the ultimate criterion with which to evaluate the performance of business.

Larger Concepts

The data just presented show that the meaning of work is decisively influenced by the way in which the work is organized. More particularly, they have shown a clash between the aspirations of the people and the current form of corporate organization. Such a clash of values is not new. What *is* new in the situation is that the appeal to the old virtues of success, of getting ahead and getting more pay, can no longer be relied on to lead to strong partnership feelings with the company or, to put it differently, to strong company identifications. It is this situation which underlies the present widespread interest in the various human relations areas. There is no question that industry as a whole is moving in that direction.

But there remains a serious question as to the extent that the need for a meaningful work task will be recognized in the trend toward the group and "group thinking." [8] There is a real danger that this new trend is a thinly veiled attempt to maintain, if not to strengthen, a type of purely organizational thinking that does not satisfy the deep need for unity and integrity of personality. I feel that the significance of this need was revealed in the Lamb company survey.

Broaden human relations

It is undoubtedly true that a concern with human relations is profitable for most companies. Human values have been neglected to

---

[7] See Richard Austin Smith, "The Executive Crack-Up," *Fortune* (May, 1955), p. 108; and also William H. Whyte, Jr., "The Wives of Management," *Fortune* (October, 1951), p. 86, and "The Corporation and the Wife," *Fortune* (November, 1951), p. 109; also relevant is Whyte's book, *The Organization Man* (New York: Simon and Schuster, Inc., 1956), Chapter 21, "The Transients."

[8] See William H. Whyte, Jr., "Group-think," *Fortune* (March 1952), p. 114; also Whyte's book, *The Organization Man, op. cit.*, Chapter 5, "Togetherness."

such an extent that productivity has often been impaired. There are vast untapped possibilities of improving productivity, and thus reducing costs, while applying the insights of all the research on group dynamics. It is true that there is simply not enough "room on the top" in the bureaucracy of a large-scale organization; but many businessmen have recognized this and are trying to introduce an increasing measure of democratic control into their organizations—in order to tap the abilities of those who will never enter the circle of the chosen few on top and in order to give to these employees a feeling of belonging.

While the value of these efforts must be fully recognized, and while they may at least partially solve some of the problems emerging from the discussion of the three groups in the preceding section, their manipulative dangers cannot be overlooked so long as the basic frame of reference is the *organization* rather than the *people*.

The basic value of the social audit is that it focuses attention on the people. This orientation has emphasized the point made by a number of observers of the industrial scene, namely that the central problems which American business faces do not lie in the human relations field as it is usually defined (in terms of relationships between different levels of management and the work group). These relationships are of great importance, but they derive their importance from the problem that is really central: the extent to which work satisfies not only the need for success in the traditional sense but even more the need that the individual feels for purpose and unity in his life.

Add to cost items

At present, technical efficiency remains the primary concern of most business organizations. This is a human value to the extent that it produces goods and services which satisfy human needs most efficiently; technical efficiency has, therefore, a human value for all of us as consumers. For those who work in factories, offices, and farms, it may have positive meaning—for example, by reducing toil. But it may also mean monotony, inability to develop initiative and thought. Instead of satisfying the basic needs for unity and integrity, it may inhibit their fulfillment. By emphasizing technical efficiency as an exclusive or predominant value, business considers *in fact* the needs of individuals as secondary or incidental.

The social audit seeks to increase the values for which business takes responsibility by including human values as "cost items" in its cost accounting system and giving them a central place in that system. This, and only this, is a realistic and practicable way of meeting men's demands. It must be a gradual process of expansion, in tune with the competitive needs of the business, yet nonetheless systematic enough to restore human values to that key position lost during the nineteenth century.

It should be mentioned that these values for measuring the performance of business are not brought from "the outside." They are deeply ingrained in the people who work in the factories and offices, as the survey has demonstrated. They are so deeply ingrained because our culture is at least partially molded by the Judaeo-Christian heritage and influenced by our Western democratic tradition—both of which stress the dignity of the individual. It is also undeniable that certain individual values are fundamental and universal, transcending the peculiarities of any one culture.

It is true that, generally speaking, people are more articulate in expressing the need for success or comfort than they are in expressing the need for unity and integrity. In a culture that stresses "success" as much as ours does, this is not surprising. What is surprising is *the frequency with which this deeper need has in fact been expressed by the employees included in the survey.* Granted that the survey was focused on this particular need, it remains, nevertheless, highly significant that people give clear evidence of their desire to satisfy a need which is fundamental, according to the Quaker ideal of self-expression.

Reform time-cost theories

It is because efficiency has become industry's principal concern that the social audit has its essential contribution to make. It challenges the effectiveness of the prevailing concept of productivity (the cost concept). It demands a broadening of this concept in such a way as to make human values *central* and to relegate all technical-mechanical considerations to a *secondary* role.

It is interesting to note that a similar challenge has been addressed recently to business from other quarters.

Adam Abruzzi, in his *Work Measurement, New Principles and Procedures,* has shown that the mechanical subdivision of tasks on which practically all time and motion studies are based is scientifically shaky because "each worker organizes operation elements into an integrated total pattern." [9] His work—based on elaborate mathe-

---

[9] New York: Columbia University Press, 1952, p. 146.

matical techniques that were found valuable in quality control—weakens the whole philosophical concept of time underlying current time and motion studies.

This is a glaring example of how an incomplete philosophical concept can vitiate important aspects of business enterprise. The purely mechanical conception of time—corresponding to our mechanical concept of productivity—must be replaced by an "existentialist" conception of time, which focuses attention on man, on natural rhythms and "integrated work patterns." The neglect of such a concept not only does immeasurable harm to the integrity of the personality; it may also lower productivity.

A scientific approach and a religious approach merge at this crucial point. Both lead to the necessity of a revaluation of the *basic* assumptions on which business is based, and this means a philosophical revaluation. Philosophy is not an abstract, impractical pursuit that refuses to come to grips with the harsh realities of everyday life (though some philosophical systems are of such a nature). Whether or not we are conscious of it, all our activities, our whole way of life, and every system of business enterprise are determined by some basic philosophical category such as "reality," "time," or "space." We may or may not be aware of them, but they are always with us—and they are always part of a "theory." This is why Keynes said: "Practical men who believe themselves to be quite exempt from any intellectual influences are usually the slaves of some defunct economist." [10]

Conclusion

At this point the businessman may say: "This is all fine. I may agree with the principle that man should be central, and his needs should be a stated objective of my firm, but how can this be accomplished and what should be done?"

Every businessman who is confronted with the problem of reorganizing an established business or with the problem of organizing a new or expanding business has to operate within a market and a general economic environment that he does not determine himself; they are "external" to his business. He must, furthermore, build up a profitable enterprise that can withstand competitive pressures and demands. These objectives are taken for granted in this article.

[10] John Maynard Keynes, *The General Theory of Employment, Interest and Money* (London: Harcourt, Brace and Company, 1936), p. 383.

Yet American business genius has developed more than one form of internal organization. A few illustrations may suffice to show that there is room for a wide range of action within the accepted limitations of a free competitive economy:

1. Lincoln Electric Company has developed the idea of "efficiency management" and has for all practical purposes abolished the traditional supervisory hierarchy.[11]
2. Nunn-Bush Shoe Company has worked out a form of partnership in the distribution of rewards.[12]
3. Geo. A. Hormel & Company has worked out a new formula to distribute what it considers "joint earnings" and has experimented with a completely new form of joint consultation.[13]

All such experiments and the insights that they have yielded are relevant to the reorganization suggested here, since all move toward making human values central. Yet none of them is sufficiently concerned with the problem of a meaningful work task, with the unity and integrity of the individual as the *central* problem in the organization of work.

During the past decade or two American business has striven to pay the highest possible wages and to introduce liberal fringe benefits. Yet neither managements nor unions, both of whom are responsible for these achievements, are sufficiently aware of the problem of giving meaning to work. Rising wages, profit sharing—all the attention given to benefits of this kind is inadequate. Indeed, under certain circumstances, it may be desirable to spend some money for changes in the organization of the work process instead of paying out the money for direct financial benefits to the employees. Changes in layout, introduction of new types of machinery, shifts from one job to another—these are only a few examples of changes that are designed to enhance the satisfaction of the deeper needs. Much knowledge of the factors which determine work satisfaction is already available. There is a growing literature on "job enlargement" that is most relevant here.[14]

[11] See James F. Lincoln, *Intelligent Selfishness and Manufacturing* (Cleveland: The Lincoln Electric Company, 1943); also "A Discussion of Incentive Management," *Partners* (June, 1953), p. 20.

[12] Joseph L. Snider, *The Guarantee of Work and Wages* (Boston: Division of Research, Harvard Business School, 1947), Chapter III, p. 30.

[13] *Ibid.*, Chapter II: also Fred H. Blum, *Toward a Democratic Work Process, op. cit.*, particularly pp. 31 ff.

[14] See, for example, Charles R. Walker, "The Problem of the Repetitive Job," *Harvard Business Review* (May, 1950), p. 54. The Institute of Human Relations, Yale University, has a special bibliography on "Job Enlargement."

It is not possible, within the scope of this article, to deal with specific problems of reorganization. Conditions differ from company to company, and many experiments are required. A great deal of further research is necessary. The mere fact that we are only beginning to know the *human* effects of different construction of machinery, different layout of the plant, and so forth, shows how long this area has been neglected and how imperative it is to bring it into focus. The social audit is one method of investigation that can be used with good effect.

A realistic answer

A practical step would be for each company *to set aside a certain percentage of its profits for research and action in regard to the work factors influencing the satisfactions of men's need for unity and integrity.* Although some companies may not be competitively strong enough to finance this project, a large number *are* in a position to do so. Larger firms can add a person to their personnel staffs to explore systematically the situation from the point of view of satisfaction of human values. Smaller firms may have to pool their resources and wait before they act until present knowledge is systematized and further developed. But few, if any, firms will be unable to find a positive course of action once they begin to think primarily in terms of human values.

Without a broadening of the traditional concept of "cost" this cannot be achieved. Once the basic attitude in this area has changed, the ingenuity of American businessmen will find many ways of implementing the more inclusive concept.

The particular kind of social audit, then, is not the real point. The crucial question is: Are we interested in individuals *for their own sake?* In the language of the businessman this means: Is a narrow technical concept of productivity, and a corresponding concept of cost, the ultimate criterion for business decisions (as it now usually is)? Or is the ultimate criterion a broadened concept of "productiveness" which includes human values?

Businessmen who are willing to reorient their thought along these lines and who think concretely in terms of the individual's need for unity and integrity become the kind of businessmen whom Alfred North Whitehead may have had in mind when he said: "A great society is a society in which its men of business think greatly of their functions." [15]

BIBLIOGRAPHY, CHAPTER XV

BEAL, EDWIN F. "Co-Determination for Unions—Miracle or Mistake?" *Factory Management and Maintenance* (November, 1953), 222-232.

Company Guide to Effective Stockholder Relations. New York: American Management Association Research Report 21, 1953.

GLOVER, JOHN D. "The Attack on Big Business," Bursk and Fenn (Eds.). *Planning the Future Strategy of Your Business.* New York: McGraw-Hill Book Company, Inc. (1956), 232-246.

GOMBERG, WILLIAM. "Should Labor Have a Voice in Management," *The Union's Role in Production Management,* Production Series No. 189. New York: American Management Association, Inc., 1950, 13-16.

"Improving the Company's Relations with Stockholders and the Financial Community," *Coordination and Communication Problems of the Financial Executive,* Financial Management Series No. 109. New York: American Management Association, Inc., 1954, 22-40.

SCHEEL, HENRY. "Measuring the Efficiency of Management from a Society's Viewpoint," *Advanced Management* (September, 1959), 4-7, 11-13, 30.

SCHELL, ERWIN H. *Technique of Administration.* New York: McGraw-Hill Book Company, Inc., 1951. Part 5.

SOLOMON, HERBERT. "Mathematical Thinking in the Measurement of Behavior," *The Free Press.* Glencoe, Illinois: 1960.

---

[15] Alfred North Whitehead, "Foresight," Introduction to W. B. Donham, *Business Adrift* (New York: McGraw-Hill Book Company, Inc., 1931), p. xxvii.

SECTION E. ORGANIZING

Decisions which establish the organization structure determine the power and communication structure within which other decisions with respect to the firm and its operations are made. In this section consideration is given first to alternate theories of organization behavior, power, and authority as a basis for organizing decisions. Attention is given next to the application of these concepts to centralized and/or decentralized organizations. Finally, organization methods are examined in detail.

Chapter XVI
Organization Theory

Several problems in explaining and prescribing organization structure exist. For example there are several different theories of organization or organization behavior. Each of these approaches examines, to some extent, a different aspect of the organization or its workings.

In the first article of this chapter William G. Scott surveys these several approaches to organization theory, pointing out their differences and similarities. Within this perspective, the principles of organization are presented by S. Avery Raube. Following these articles is a criticism of the classical approach to organization through principles by Rocco Carzo. The last article presents the views of Herbert A. Simon, a "modern" innovator in organization theory.

This chapter forms the basis for the examination of power and authority in Chapter XVII and its delegation and decentralization in Chapter XVIII. The final chapter in this section is devoted to the examination of methods employed to apply these theoretical concepts in actual organizations.

56. ORGANIZATION THEORY: AN OVERVIEW AND AN APPRAISAL [1]

William G. Scott [2]

Man is intent on drawing himself into a web of collectivized patterns. "Modern man has learned to accommodate himself to a world increasingly organized. The trend toward ever more explicit and consciously drawn relationships is profound and sweeping; it is marked by depth no less than by extension." [3] This comment by Seidenberg nicely summarizes the pervasive influence of organization in many forms of human activity.

Some of the reasons for intense organizational activity are found in the fundamental transitions which revolutionized our society, changing it from a rural culture, to a culture based on technology, industry, and the city. From these changes, a way of life emerged characterized by the *proximity* and *dependency* of people on each other. Proximity and dependency, as conditions of social life, harbor the threats of human conflict, capricious antisocial behavior, instability of human relationships, and uncertainty about the nature of the social structure with its concomitant roles.

Of course, these threats to social integrity are present to some degree in all societies, ranging from the primitive to the modern. But, these threats become dangerous when the harmonious functioning of a society rests on the maintenance of a highly intricate, delicately balanced form of human collaboration. The civilization we have created depends on the preservation of a precarious balance. Hence, disrupting forces impinging on this shaky form of collaboration must be eliminated or minimized.

Traditionally, organization is viewed as a vehicle for accomplishing goals and objectives. While this approach is useful, it tends to obscure the inner workings and internal purposes of organization itself. Another fruitful way of treating organization is as a mechanism having the ultimate purpose of offsetting those forces which

[1] From *Journal of the Academy of Management*, Vol. 4, No. 1 (April, 1961), pp. 7-26. Reprinted by permission of *Journal of the Academy of Management*.
[2] William G. Scott, Associate Professor of Management, DePaul University.
[3] Roderick Seidenburg, *Post Historic Man* (Boston: Beacon Press, 1951), p. 1.

undermine human collaboration. In this sense, organization tends to minimize conflict, and to lessen the significance of individual behavior which deviates from values that the organization has established as worthwhile. Further, organization increases stability in human relationships by reducing uncertainty regarding the nature of the system's structure and the human roles which are inherent to it. Corollary to this point, organization enhances the predictability of human action, because it limits the number of behavioral alternatives available to an individual. As Presthus points out:

> Organization is defined as a system of structural interpersonal relations . . . individuals are differentiated in terms of authority, status, and role with the result that personal interaction is prescribed. . . . Anticipated reactions tend to occur, while ambiguity and spontaneity are decreased.[4]

In addition to all of this, organization has built-in safeguards. Besides prescribing acceptable forms of behavior for those who elect to submit to it, organization is also able to counterbalance the influence of human action which transcends its established patterns.[5]

Few segments of society have engaged in organizing more intensively than business.[6] The reason is clear. Business depends on what organization offers. Business needs a system of relationships among functions; it needs stability, continuity, and predictability in its internal activities and external contacts. Business also appears to need harmonious relationships among the people and processes which make it up. Put another way, a business organization has to be free, relatively, from destructive tendencies which may be caused by divergent interests.

As a foundation for meeting these needs rests administrative science. A major element of this science is organization theory, which provides the grounds for management activities in a number of significant areas of business endeavor. Organization theory, how-

---

[4] Robert V. Presthus, "Toward a Theory of Organizational Behavior," *Administrative Science Quarterly* (June, 1958), p. 50.

[5] Regulation and predictability of human behavior are matters of degree varying with different organization on something of a continuum. At one extreme are bureaucratic type organizations with tight bonds of regulation. At the other extreme are voluntary associations, and informal organizations with relatively loose bonds of regulation.

This point has an interesting sidelight. A bureaucracy with tight controls and a high degree of predictability of human action appears to be unable to distinguish between destructive and creative deviations from established values. Thus the only thing which is safeguarded is the *status quo*.

[6] The monolithic institutions of the military and government are other cases of organizational preoccupation.

ever, is not a homogeneous science based on generally accepted principles. Various theories of organization have been, and are being evolved. For example, something called "modern organization theory" has recently emerged, raising the wrath of some traditionalists, but also capturing the imagination of a rather elite *avant-garde*.

The thesis of this paper is that modern organization theory, when stripped of its irrelevancies, redundancies, and "speech defects," is a logical and vital evolution in management thought. In order for this thesis to be supported, the reader must endure a review and appraisal of more traditional forms of organization theory which may seem elementary to him.

In any event, three theories of organization are having considerable influence on management thought and practice. They are arbitrarily labeled in this paper as the classical, the neo-classical, and the modern. Each of these is fairly distinct; but they are not unrelated. Also, these theories are on-going, being actively supported by several schools of management thought.

The Classical Doctrine

For lack of a better method of identification, it will be said that the classical doctrine deals almost exclusively with the *anatomy of formal organization*. This doctrine can be traced back to Frederick W. Taylor's interest in functional foremanship and planning staffs. But most students of management thought would agree that in the United States, the first systematic approach to organization, and the first comprehensive attempt to find organizational universals, is dated 1931 when Mooney and Reiley published *Onward Industry*.[7] Subsequently, numerous books, following the classical vein, have appeared. Two of the more recent are Brech's, *Organization*[8] and Allen's, *Management and Organization*.[9]

Classical organization theory is built around four key pillars. They are the division of labor, the scalar and functional processes, structure, and span of control. Given these major elements just about all of classical organization theory can be derived.

---

[7] James D. Mooney and Alan C. Reiley, *Onward Industry* (New York: Harper and Brothers, 1931). Later published by James D. Mooney under the title *Principles of Organization*.

[8] E. F. L. Brech, *Organization* (London: Longmans, Green and Company, 1957).

[9] Louis A. Allen, *Management and Organization* (New York: McGraw-Hill Book Company, 1958).

(1) *The division of labor* is without doubt the cornerstone among the four elements.[10] From it the other elements flow as corollaries. For example, *scalar* and *functional* growth requires specialization and departmentalization of functions. Organization *structure* is naturally dependent upon the direction which specialization of activities travels in company development. Finally, *span of control* problems result from the number of specialized functions under the jurisdiction of a manager.

(2) *The scalar and functional processes* deal with the vertical and horizontal growth of the organization, respectively.[11] The scalar process refers to the growth of the chain of command, the delegation of authority and responsibility, unity of command, and the obligation to report.

The division of the organization into specialized parts and the regrouping of the parts into compatible units are matters pertaining to the functional process. This process focuses on the horizontal evolution of the line and staff in a formal organization.

(3) *Structure* is the logical relationships of functions in an organization, arranged to accomplish the objectives of the company efficiently. Structure implies system and pattern. Classical organization theory usually works with two basic structures, the line and the staff. However, such actvities as committee and liaison functions fall quite readily into the purview of structural considerations. Again, structure is the vehicle for introducing logical and consistent relationships among the diverse functions which comprise the organization.[12]

(4) *The span of control* concept relates to the number of subordinates a manager can effectively supervise. Graicunas has been credited with first elaborating the point that there are numerical limitations to the subordinates one man can control.[13] In a recent statement on the subject, Brech points out, "span" refers to ". . . the

---

[10] Usually the division of labor is treated under a topical heading of departmentation, see for example: Harold Koontz and Cyril O'Donnell, *Principles of Management* (New York: McGraw-Hill Book Company, 1959), Chapter 7.

[11] These processes are discussed at length in Ralph Currier Davis, *The Fundamentals of Top Management* (New York: Harper and Brothers, 1951), Chapter 7.

[12] For a discussion of structure see: William H. Newman, *Administrative Action* (Englewood Cliffs, New Jersey: Prentice-Hall, Incorporated, 1951), Chapter 16.

[13] V. A. Graicunas, "Relationships in Organization," *Papers on the Science of Administration* (New York: Columbia University, 1937).

number of persons, themselves carrying managerial and supervisory responsibilities, for whom the senior manager retains his over-embracing responsibility of direction and planning, co-ordination, motivation, and control." [14] Regardless of interpretation, span of control has significance, in part, for the shape of the organization which evolves through growth. Wide span yields a flat structure; short span results in a tall structure. Further, the span concept directs attention to the complexity of human and functional inter-relationships in an organization.

It would not be fair to say that the classical school is unaware of the day-to-day administrative problems of the organization. Paramount among these problems are those stemming from human inter-actions. But the interplay of individual personality, informal groups, interorganizational conflict, and the decision-making processes in the formal structure appears largely to be neglected by classical organi-zation theory. Additionally, the classical theory overlooks the contributions of the behavioral sciences by failing to incorporate them in its doctrine in any systematic way. In summary, classical organi-zation theory has relevant insights into the nature of organization, but the value of this theory is limited by its narrow concentration on the formal anatomy of organization.

NEOCLASSICAL THEORY OF ORGANIZATION

The neoclassical theory of organization embarked on the task of compensating for some of the deficiencies in classical doctrine. The neoclassical school is commonly identified with the human relations movement. Generally, the neoclassical approach takes the postulates of the classical school, regarding the pillars of organization as givens. But these postulates are regarded as modified by people, acting inde-pendently or within the context of the informal organization.

One of the main contributions of the neoclassical school is the introduction of behavioral sciences in an integrated fashion into the theory of organization. Through the use of these sciences, the human relationists demonstrate how the pillars of the classical doctrine are affected by the impact of human actions. Further, the neoclassical approach includes a systematic treatment of the informal organiza-tion, showing its influence on the formal structure.

[14] Brech, *op. cit.*, p. 78.

Thus, the neoclassical approach to organization theory gives evidence of accepting classical doctrine, but superimposing on it modifications resulting from individual behavior, and the influence of the informal group. The inspiration of the neoclassical school were the Hawthorne studies.[15] Current examples of the neoclassical approach are found in human relations books like Gardner and Moore, *Human Relations in Industry*,[16] and Davis, *Human Relations in Business*.[17] To a more limited extent, work in industrial sociology also reflects a neoclassical point of view.[18]

It would be useful to look briefly at some of the contributions made to organization theory by the neoclassicists. First to be considered are modifications of the pillars of classical doctrine; second is the informal organization.

Examples of the neoclassical approach to the pillars of formal organization theory

(1) The *division of labor* has been a long standing subject of comment in the field of human relations. Very early in the history of industrial psychology study was made of industrial fatigue and monotony caused by the specialization of the work.[19] Later, attention shifted to the isolation of the worker, and his feeling of anonymity resulting from insignificant jobs which contributed negligibly to the final product.[20]

Also, specialization influences the work of management. As an organization expands, the need concomitantly arises for managerial motivation and coordination of the activities of others. Both motivation and coordination in turn relate to executive leadership. Thus, in part, stemming from the growth of industrial specialization, the neoclassical school has developed a large body of theory relating to

[15] See: F. J. Roethlisberger and William J. Dickson, *Management and the Worker* (Cambridge: Harvard University Press, 1939).

[16] Burleigh B. Gardner and David G. Moore, *Human Relations in Industry* (Homewood, Illinois: Richard D. Irwin, 1955).

[17] Keith Davis, *Human Relations in Business* (New York: McGraw-Hill Book Company, 1957).

[18] For example see: Delbert C. Miller and William H. Form, *Industrial Sociology* (New York: Harper and Brothers, 1951).

[19] See: Hugo Munsterberg, *Psychology and Industrial Efficiency* (Boston: Houghton Mifflin Company, 1913).

[20] Probably the classic work is: Elton Mayo, *The Human Problems of an Industrial Civilization* (Cambridge: Harvard University, 1946, first printed 1933).

motivation, cordination, and leadership. Much of this theory is derived from the social sciences.

(2) Two aspects of the *scalar and functional* processes which
have been treated with some degree of intensity by the neoclassical
school are the delegation of authority and responsibility, and gaps
in or overlapping of functional jurisdictions. The classical theory
assumes something of perfection in the delegation and functionalization processes. The neoclassical school points out that human
problems are caused by imperfections in the way these processes are
handled.

For example, too much or insufficient delegation may render an
executive incapable of action. The failure to delegate authority and
responsibility equally may result in frustration for the delegatee.
Overlapping of authorities often causes clashes in personality. Gaps
in authority cause failures in getting jobs done, with one party
blaming the other for shortcomings in performance.[21]

The neoclassical school says that the scalar and functional processes are theoretically valid, but tend to deteriorate in practice. The
ways in which they break down are described, and some of the
human causes are pointed out. In addition the neoclassicists make
recommendations, suggesting various "human tools" which will facilitate the operation of these processes.

(3) *Structure* provides endless avenues of analysis for the neoclassical theory of organization. The theme is that human behavior
disrupts the best laid organizational plans, and thwarts the clean-
ness of the logical relationships founded in the structure. The neoclassical critique of structure centers on frictions which appear
internally among people performing different functions.

Line and staff relations is a problem area, much discussed, in
this respect. Many companies seem to have difficulty keeping the
line and staff working together harmoniously. Both Dalton[22] and
Juran[23] have engaged in research to discover the causes of friction,
and to suggest remedies.

Of course, line-staff relations represent only one of the many
problems of structural frictions described by the neoclassicists. As
often as not, the neoclassicists will offer prescriptions for the elimi-

---

[21] For further discussion of the human relations implications of the scalar
and functional processes see: Keith Davis, *op. cit.*, pp. 60-66.
[22] Melville Dalton, "Conflicts Between Staff and Line Managerial Officers,"
American Sociological Review (June, 1950), pp. 342-351.
[23] J. M. Juran, "Improving the Relationship Between Staff and Line," *Personnel* (May, 1956), pp. 515-524.

nation of conflict in structure. Among the more important harmony-rendering formulae are participation, junior boards, bottom-up management, joint committees, recognition of human dignity, and "better" communication.

(4) An executive's *span of control* is a function of human determinants, and the reduction of span to a precise, universally applicable ratio is silly, according to the neoclassicists. Some of the determinants of span are individual differences in managerial abilities, the type of people and functions supervised, and the extent of communication effectiveness.

Coupled with the span of control question are the human implications of the type of structure which emerges. That is, is a tall structure with a short span or a flat structure with a wide span more conducive to good human relations than high morale? The answer is situational. Short span results in tight supervision; wide span requires a good deal of delegation with looser controls. Because of individual and organizational differences, sometimes one is better than the other. There is a tendency to favor the looser form of organization, however, for the reason that tall structures breed autocratic leadership, which is often pointed out as a cause of low morale.[24]

The neoclassical view of the informal organization

Nothing more than the barest mention of the informal organization is given even in the most recent classical treatises on organization theory.[25] Systematic discussion of this form of organization has been left to the neoclassicists. The informal organization refers to people in group associations at work, but these associations are not specified in the "blueprint" of the formal organization. The informal organization means natural groupings of people in the work situation.

In a general way, the informal organization appears in response to the social need—the need of people to associate with others. However, for analytical purposes, this explanation is not particularly satisfying. Research has produced the following, more specific determinants underlying the appearance of informal organizations:

1. The *location* determinant simply states that in order to form into groups of any lasting nature, people have to have frequent

[24] Gardner and Moore, *op. cit.*, pp. 237-243.
[25] For example: Brech, *op. cit.*, pp. 27-29; and Allen, *op. cit.*, pp. 61-62.

face-to-face contact. Thus, the geography of physical location in a plant or office is an important factor in predicting who will be in what group.[26]

2. *Occupation* is key factor determining the rise and composition of informal groups. There is a tendency for people performing similar jobs to group together.[27]

3. *Interests* are another determinant for informal group formation. Even though people might be in the same location, performing similar jobs, differences of interest among them explain why several small, instead of one large, informal organizations emerge.

4. *Special issues* often result in the formation of informal groups, but this determinant is set apart from the three previously mentioned. In this case, people who do not necessarily have similar interests, occupations, or locations may join together for a common cause. Once the issue is resolved, then the tendency is to revert to the more "natural" group forms.[28] Thus, special issues give rise to a rather impermanent informal association; groups based on the other three determinants tend to be more lasting.

When informal organizations come into being they assume certain characteristics. Since understanding these characteristics is important for management practice, they are noted below:

1. Informal organizations act as agencies of *social control*. They generate a culture based on certain norms of conduct which, in turn, demands conformity from group members. These standards may be at odds with the values set by the formal organization. So an individual may very well find himself in a situation of conflicting demands.

2. The form of human interrelationships in the informal organization requires *techniques of analysis* different from those used to plot the relationships of people in a formal organization. The method used for determining the structure of the informal group is called sociometric analysis. Sociometry reveals the complex structure of interpersonal relations which is based on premises fundamentally unlike the logic of the formal organization.

3. Informal organizations have *status and communication* systems peculiar to themselves, not necessarily derived from the formal systems. For example, the grapevine is the subject of much neoclassical study.

4. Survival of the informal organization requires stable continuing relationships among the people in them. Thus, it has been observed that the informal organization *resists change*.[29] Considerable atten-

---

[26] See: Leon Festinger, Stanley Schachter, and Kurt Back, *Social Pressures in Informal Groups* (New York: Harper and Brothers, 1950), pp. 153-163.

[27] For example see: W. Fred Cottrell, *The Railroader* (Palo Alto: The Stanford University Press, 1940), Chapter 3.

[28] Except in cases where the existence of an organization is necessary for the continued maintenance of employee interest. Under these conditions the previously informal association may emerge as a formal group, such as a union.

[29] Probably the classic study of resistance to change is: Lester Coch and John R. P. French, Jr., "Overcoming Resistance to Change," in Schuyler Dean Hoslett (editor) *Human Factors in Management* (New York: Harper and Brothers, 1951) pp. 242-268.

tion is given by the neoclassicists to overcoming informal resistance to change.

5. The last aspect of analysis which appears to be central to the neoclassical view of the informal organization is the study of the *informal leader*. Discussion revolves around who the informal leader is, how he assumes this role, what characteristics are peculiar to him, and how he can help the manager accomplish his objectives in the formal organization.[30]

This brief sketch of some of the major facets of informal organization theory has neglected, so far, one important topic treated by the neoclassical school. It is the way in which the formal and informal organizations interact.

A conventional way of looking at the interaction of the two is the "live and let live" point of view. Management should recognize that the informal organization exists, nothing can destroy it, and so the executive might just as well work with it. Working with the informal organization involves not threatening its existence unnecessarily, listening to opinions expressed for the group by the leader, allowing group participation in decision-making situations, and controlling the grapevine by prompt release of accurate information.[31]

While this approach is management centered, it is not unreasonable to expect that informal group standards and norms could make themselves felt on formal organizational policy. An honestly conceived effort by managers to establish a working relationship with the informal organization could result in an association where both formal and informal views would be reciprocally modified. The danger which at all costs should be avoided is that "working with the informal organization" does not degenerate into a shallow disguise for human manipulation.

Some neoclassical writing in organization theory, especially that coming from the management-oriented segment of this school, gives the impression that the formal and informal organizations are distinct, and at times, quite irreconcilable factors in a company. The interaction which takes place between the two is something akin to the interaction between the company and a labor union, or a government agency, or another company.

The concept of the social system is another approach to the interactional climate. While this concept can be properly classified as

---

[30] For example see: Robert Saltonstall, *Human Relations in Administration* (New York: McGraw-Hill Book Company, 1959), pp. 330-331; and Keith Davis, *op. cit.*, pp. 99-101.

[31] For an example of this approach see: John T. Doutt, "Management Must Manage the Informal Group, Too," *Advanced Management* (May, 1959), pp. 26-28.

neoclassical, it borders on the modern theories of organization. The phrase "social system" means that an organization is a complex of mutually interdependent, but variable, factors.

These factors include individuals and their attitudes and motives, jobs, the physical work setting, the formal organization, and the informal organizations. These factors, and many others, are woven into an overall pattern of interdependency. From this point of view, the formal and informal organizations lose their distinctiveness, but find real meaning, in terms of human behavior, in the operation of the system as a whole. Thus, the study of organization turns away from descriptions of its component parts, and is refocused on the system of interrelationships among the parts.

One of the major contributions of the Hawthorne studies was the integration of Pareto's idea of the social system into a meaningful method of analysis for the study of behavior in human organizations.[32] This concept is still vitally important. But unfortunately some work in the field of human relations undertaken by the neoclassicists has overlooked, or perhaps discounted, the significance of this consideration.[33]

The fundamental insight regarding the social system, developed and applied to the industrial scene by the Hawthorne researchers, did not find much extension in subsequent work in the neoclassical vein. Indeed, the neoclassical school after the Hawthorne studies generally seemed content to engage in descriptive generalizations, or particularized empirical research studies which did not have much meaning outside their own context.

The neoclassical school of organization theory has been called bankrupt. Criticisms range from, "human relations is a tool for cynical puppeteering of people," to "human relations is nothing more than a trifling body of empirical and descriptive information." There is a good deal of truth in both criticisms, but another appraisal of the neoclassical school of organization theory is offered here. The neoclassical approach has provided valuable contributions to lore of organization. But, like the classical theory, the neoclassical doctrine suffers from incompleteness, a shortsighted perspective, and lack of integration among the many facets of human behavior studied by it.

---

[32] See: Roethlisberger and Dickson, *op. cit.*, Chapter 24.
[33] A check of management human relations texts, the organization and human relations chapters of principles of management texts, and texts on conventional organization theory for management courses reveals little or no treatment of the concept of the social system.

Modern organization theory has made a move to cover the shortcomings of the current body of theoretical knowledge.

MODERN ORGANIZATION THEORY

The distinctive qualities of modern organization theory are its conceptual-analytical base, its reliance on empirical research data and, above all, its integrating nature. These qualities are framed in a philosophy which accepts the premise that the only meaningful way to study organization is to study it as a system. As Henderson put it, the study of a system must rely on a method of analysis, ". . . involving the simultaneous variations of mutually dependent variables." [34] Human systems, of course, contain a huge number of dependent variables which defy the most complex simultaneous equations to solve.

Nevertheless, system analysis has its own peculiar point of view which aims to study organization in the way Henderson suggests. It treats organization as a system of mutually dependent variables. As a result, modern organization theory, which accepts system analysis, shifts the conceptual level of organization study above the classical and neoclassical theories. Modern organization theory asks a range of interrelated questions which are not seriously considered by the two other theories.

Key among these questions are: (1) What are the strategic parts of the system? (2) What is the nature of their mutual dependency? (3) What are the main processes in the system which link the parts together, and facilitate their adjustments to each other? (4) What are the goals sought by systems? [35]

Modern organization theory is in no way a unified body of thought. Each writer and researcher has his special emphasis when he considers the system. Perhaps the most evident unifying thread in the study of systems is the effort to look at the organization in its totality. Representative books in this field are March and Simon, *Organizations*,[36] and Haire's anthology, *Modern Organization Theory*.[37]

[34] Lawrence J. Henderson, *Pareto's General Sociology* (Cambridge: Harvard University Press, 1935), p. 13.
[35] There is another question which cannot be treated in the scope of this paper. It asks, what research tools should be used for the study of the system?
[36] James G. March and Herbert A. Simon, *Organizations* (New York: John Wiley and Sons, 1958).
[37] Mason Haire (editor), *Modern Organization Theory* (New York: John Wiley and Sons, 1959).

Instead of attempting a review of different writers' contributions to modern organization theory, it will be more useful to discuss the various ingredients involved in system analysis. They are the parts, the interactions, the processes, and the goals of systems.

The parts of the system and their interdependency

The first basic part of the system is the *individual,* and the personality structure he brings to the organization. Elementary to an individual's personality are motives and attitudes which condition the range of expectancies he hopes to satisfy by participating in the system.

The second part of the system is the formal arrangement of functions, usually called the *formal organization.* The formal organization is the interrelated pattern of jobs which make up the structure of a system. Certain writers, like Argyris, see a fundamental conflict resulting from the demands made by the system, and the structure of the mature, normal personality. In any event, the individual has expectancies regarding the job he is to perform; and, conversely, the job makes demands on, or has expectancies relating to, the performance of the individual. Considerable attention has been given by writers in modern organization theory to incongruencies resulting from the interaction of organizational and individual demands.[38]

The third part in the organization system is the *informal organization.* Enough has been said already about the nature of this organization. But it must be noted that an interactional pattern exists between the individual and the informal group. This interactional arrangement can be conveniently discussed as the mutual modification of expectancies. The informal organization has demands which it makes on members in terms of anticipated forms of behavior, and the individual has expectancies of satisfaction he hopes to derive from association with people on the job. Both these sets of expectancies interact, resulting in the individual modifying his behavior to accord with the demands of the group, and the group, perhaps, modifying what it expects from an individual because of the impact of his personality on group norms.[39]

---

[38] See Chris Argyris, *Personality and Organization* (New York: Harper and Brothers, 1957), esp. Chapters 2, 3, 7.

[39] For a larger treatment of this subject see: George C. Homans, *The Human Group* (New York: Harcourt, Brace and Company, 1950), Chapter 5.

Much of what has been said about the various expectancy systems in an organization can also be treated using status and role concepts. Part of modern organization theory rests on research findings in social-psychology relative to reciprocal patterns of behavior stemming from role demands generated by both the formal and informal organizations, and role perceptions peculiar to the individual. Bakke's *fusion process* is largely concerned with the modification of role expectancies. The fusion process is a force, according to Bakke, which acts to weld divergent elements together for the preservation of organizational integrity.[40]

The fifth part of system analysis is the *physical setting* in which the job is performed. Although this element of the system may be implicit in what has been said already about the formal organization and its functions, it is well to separate it. In the physical surroundings of work, interactions are present in complex man-machine systems. The human "engineer" cannot approach the problems posed by such interrelationships in a purely technical, engineering fashion. As Haire says, these problems lie in the domain of the social theorist.[41] Attention must be centered on responses demanded from a logically ordered production function, often with the view of minimizing the error in the system. From this standpoint, work cannot be effectively organized unless the psychological, social, and physiological characteristics of people participating in the work environment are considered. Machines and processes should be designed to fit certain generally observed psychological and physiological properties of men, rather than hiring men to fit machines.

In summary, the parts of the system which appear to be of strategic importance are the individual, the formal structure, the informal organization, status and role patterns, and the physical environment of work. Again, these parts are woven into a configuration called the organizational system. The processes which link the parts are taken up next.

The linking processes

One can say, with a good deal of glibness, that all the parts mentioned above are interrelated. Although this observation is quite cor-

---

[40] E. Wight Bakke, "Concept of the Social Organization," in *Modern Organization Theory*, Mason Haire (editor) (New York: John Wiley and Sons, 1959) pp. 60-61.

[41] Mason Haire, "Psychology and the Study of Business: Joint Behavioral Sciences," in *Social Science Research on Business: Product and Potential* (New York: Columbia University Press, 1959), pp. 53-59.

rect, it does not mean too much in terms of system theory unless some attempt is made to analyze the processes by which the interaction is achieved. Role theory is devoted to certain types of interactional processes. In addition, modern organization theorists point to three other linking activities which appear to be universal to human systems of organized behavior. These processes are communication, balance, and decision making.

(1) Communication is mentioned often in neoclassical theory, but the emphasis is on description of forms of communication activity, i.e., formal-informal, vertical-horizontal, line-staff. Communication, as a mechanism which links the segments of the system together, is overlooked by way of much considered analysis.

One aspect of modern organization theory is study of the communication network in the system. Communication is viewed as the method by which action is evoked from the parts of the system. Communication acts not only as stimuli resulting in action, but also as a control and coordination mechanism linking the decision centers in the system into a synchronized pattern. Deutsch points out that organizations are composed of parts which communicate with each other, receive messages from the outside world, and store information. Taken together, these communication functions of the parts comprise a configuration representing the total system.[42] More is to be said about communication later in the discussion of the cybernetic model.

(2) The concept of *balance* as a linking process involves a series of some rather complex ideas. Balance refers to an equilibrating mechanism whereby the various parts of the system are maintained in a harmoniously structured relationship to each other.

The necessity for the balance concept logically flows from the nature of systems themselves. It is impossible to conceive of an ordered relationship among the parts of a system without also introducing the idea of a stabilizing or an adapting mechanism.

Balance appears in two varieties—quasi-automatic and innovative. Both forms of balance act to insure system integrity in face of changing conditions, either internal or external to the system. The first form of balance, quasi-automatic, refers to what some think are "homeostatic" properties of systems. That is, systems seem to exhibit built-in propensies to maintain steady states.

[42] Karl W. Deutsch "On Communication Models in the Social Sciences," *Public Opinion Quarterly*, 16 (1952), pp. 356-380.

If human organizations are open, self-maintaining systems, then control and regulatory processes are necessary. The issue hinges on the degree to which stabilizing processes in systems, when adapting to change, are automatic. March and Simon have an interesting answer to this problem, which in part is based on the type of change and the adjustment necessary to adapt to the change. Systems have programs of action which are put into effect when a change is perceived. If the change is relatively minor, and if the change comes within the purview of established programs of action, then it might be fairly confidently predicted that the adaptation made by the system will be quasi-automatic.[43]

The role of innovative, creative balancing efforts now needs to be examined. The need for innovation arises when adaptation to a change is outside the scope of existing programs designed for the purpose of keeping the system in balance. New programs have to be evolved in order for the system to maintain internal harmony.

New programs are created by trial and error search for feasible action alternatives to cope with a given change. But innovation is subject to the limitations and possibilities inherent in the quantity and variety of information present in a system at a particular time. New combinations of alternatives for innovative purposes depend on:

1. The possible range of output of the system, or the capacity of the system to supply information.
2. The range of available information in the memory of the system.
3. The operating rules (program) governing the analysis and flow of information within the system.
4. The ability of the system to "forget" previously learned solutions to change problems.[44] A system with too good a memory might narrow its behavioral choices to such an extent as to stifle innovation. In simpler language, old learned programs might be used to adapt the change, when newly innovated programs are necessary.[45]

Much of what has been said about communication and balance brings to mind a cybernetic model in which both these processes have vital roles. Cybernetics has to do with feedback and control of all kinds of systems. Its purpose is to maintain system stability in the face of change. Cybernetics cannot be studied without considering

---

[43] March and Simon, *op. cit.*, pp. 139-140.
[44] Mervyn L. Cadwallader "The Cybernetic Analysis of Change in Complex Social Organization," *The American Journal of Sociology* (September, 1959), p. 156.
[45] It is conceivable for innovative behavior to be programmed into the system.

communication networks, information flow, and some kind of balancing process aimed at preserving the integrity of the system.

Cybernetics directs attention to key questions regarding the system. These questions are: How are communication centers connected, and how are they maintained? Corollary to this question: what is the structure of the feedback system? Next, what information is stored in the organization, and at what points? And as a corollary: how accessible is this information to decision-making centers? Third, how conscious is the organization of the operation of its own parts? That is, to what extent do the policy centers receive control information with sufficient frequency and relevancy to create a real awareness of the operation of the segments of the system? Finally, what are the learning (innovating) capabilities of the system? [46]

Answers to the questions posed by cybernetics are crucial to understanding both the balancing and communication processes in systems.[47] Although cybernetics has been applied largely to technical-engineering problems of automation, the model of feedback, control, and regulation in all systems has a good deal of generality. Cybernetics is a fruitful area which can be used to synthesize the processes of communication and balance.

(3) A wide spectrum of topics dealing with types of decisions in human systems makes up the core of analysis of another important process in organizations. Decision analysis is one of the major contributions of March and Simon in their book *Organizations*. The two major classes of decisions they discuss are decisions to produce and decisions to participate in the system.[48]

Decisions to produce are largely a result of an interaction between individual attitudes and the demands of organization. Motivation analysis becomes central to studying the nature and results of the interaction. Individual decisions to participate in the organization reflect on such issues as the relationship between organizational rewards versus the demands made by the organization. Participation decisions also focus attention on the reasons why individuals remain in or leave organizations.

March and Simon treat decisions as internal variables in an organization which depend on jobs, individual expectations and mo-

---

[46] These are questions adapted from Deutsch, *op. cit.*, 368-370.

[47] Answers to these questions would require a comprehensive volume. One of the best approaches currently available is Stafford Beer, *Cybernetics and Management* (New York: John Wiley and Sons, 1959).

[48] March and Simon, *op. cit.*, Chapters 3 and 4.

tivations, and organizational structure. Marschak [49] looks on the decision process as an independent variable upon which the survival of the organization is based. In this case, the organization is viewed as having, inherent in its structure, the ability to maximize survival requisites through its established decision processes.

The goals of organization

Organization has three goals which may be either intermeshed or independent ends in themselves. They are growth, stability, and interaction. The last goal refers to organizations which exist primarily to provide a medium for association of its members with others. Interestingly enough these goals seem to apply to different forms of organization at varying levels of complexity, ranging from simple clockwork mechanisms to social systems.

These similarities in organizational purposes have been observed by a number of people, and a field of thought and research called system theory has developed, dedicated to the task of discovering organizational universals. The dream of general system theory is to create a science of organizational universals, or if you will, a universal science using common organizational elements found in all systems as a starting point.

Modern organization theory is on the periphery of general system theory. Both general system theory and modern organization theory studies:

1. The parts (individuals) in aggregates, and the movement of individuals into and out of the system.
2. The interaction of individuals with the environment found in the system.
3. The interactions among individuals in the system.
4. General growth and stability problems of systems.[50]

Modern organization theory and general system theory are similar in that they look at organization as an integrated whole. They differ, however, in terms of their generality. General system theory is concerned with every level of system, whereas modern organizational theory focuses primarily on human organization.

The question might be asked, what can the science of administration gain by the study of system levels other than human? Before

[49] Jacob Marschak, "Efficient and Viable Organizational Forms" in *Modern Organization Theory*, Mason Haire, editor (New York: John Wiley and Sons, 1959), pp. 307-320.
[50] Kenneth E. Boulding, "General System Theory—The Skeleton of a Science," *Management Science* (April, 1956), pp. 200-202.

attempting an answer, note should be made of what these other levels are. Boulding presents a convenient method of classification:

1. The static structure—a level of framework, the anatomy of a system; for example, the structure of the universe.
2. The simple dynamic system—the level of clockworks, predetermined necessary motions.
3. The cybernetic system—the level of the thermostat, the system moves to maintain a given equilibrium through a process of self-regulation.
4. The open system—level of self-maintaining systems, moves toward and includes living organisms.
5. The genetic-societal system—level of cell society, characterized by a division of labor among cells.
6. Animal systems—level of mobility, evidence of goal-directed behavior.
7. Human systems—level of symbol interpretation and idea communication.
8. Social system—level of human organization.
9. Transcendental systems—level of ultimates and absolutes which exhibit systematic structure but are unknowable in essence.[51]

This approach to the study of systems by finding universals common at all levels of organization offers intriguing possibilities for administrative organization theory. A good deal of light could be thrown on social systems if structurally analogous elements could be found in the simpler types of systems. For example, cybernetic systems have characteristics which seem to be similar to feedback, regulation, and control phenomena in human organizations. Thus, certain facets of cybernetic models could be generalized to human organization. Considerable danger, however, lies in poorly founded analogies. Superficial similarities between simpler system forms and social systems are apparent everywhere. Instinctually based ant societies, for example, do not yield particularly instructive lessons for understanding rationally conceived human organizations. Thus, care should be taken that analogies used to bridge system levels are not mere devices for literary enrichment. For analogies to have usefulness and validity, they must exhibit inherent structural similarities or implicity identical operational principles.[52]

[51] *Ibid.*, pp. 202-205.
[52] Seidenberg, *op. cit.*, p. 136. The fruitful use of the type of analogies spoken of by Seidenberg is evident in the application of thermodynamic principles, particularly the entropy concept, to communication theory. See: Claude E. Shannon and Warren Weaver, *The Mathematical Theory of Communication* (Urbana: The University of Illinois Press, 1949). Further, the existence of a complete analogy between the operational behavior of thermodynamic systems, electrical communication systems, and biological systems has been noted by: Y. S. Touloukian, *The Concept of Entropy in Communication, Living Organisms, and Thermodynamics*, Research Bulletin 130, Purdue Engineering Experiment Station.

Modern organization theory leads, as it has been shown, almost inevitably into a discussion of general system theory. A science of organization universals has some strong advocates, particularly among biologists.[53] Organization theorists in administrative science cannot afford to overlook the contributions of general system theory. Indeed, modern organization concepts could offer a great deal to those working with general system theory. But the ideas dealt with in the general theory are exceedingly elusive.

Speaking of the concept of equilibrium as a unifying element in all systems, Easton says, "It (equilibrium) leaves the impression that we have a useful general theory when in fact, lacking measurability, it is a mere pretense for knowledge."[54] The inability to quantify and measure universal organization elements undermines the success of pragmatic tests to which general system theory might be put.

Organization theory: quo vadis?

Most sciences have a vision of the universe to which they are applied, and administrative science is not an exception. This universe is composed of parts. One purpose of science is to synthesize the parts into an organized conception of its field of study. As a science matures, its theorems about the configuration of its universe change. The direction of change in three sciences, physics, economics, and sociology, are noted briefly for comparison with the development of an administrative view of human organization.

The first comprehensive and empirically verifiable outlook of the physical universe was presented by Newton in his *Principia*. Classical physics, founded on Newton's work, constitutes a grand scheme in which a wide range of physical phenomena could be organized and predicted. Newtonian physics may rightfully be regarded as "macro" in nature, because its system of organization was concerned largely with gross events of which the movement of celestial bodies, waves, energy forms, and strain are examples. For years classical physics was supreme, being applied continuously to smaller and smaller classes of phenomena in the physical universe. Physicists at one time adopted the view that everything in their realm could be dis-

---

[53] For example see: Ludwig von Bertalanffy, *Problem of Life* (London: Watts and Company, 1952).

[54] David Easton, "Limits of the Equilibrium Model in Social Research," in *Profits and Problems of Homeostatic Models in the Behavioral Sciences*, Publication 1, Chicago Behavioral Sciences (1953), p. 39.

covered by simply subdividing problems. Physics thus moved into the "micro" order.

But in the nineteenth century a revolution took place motivated largely because events were being noted which could not be explained adequately by the conceptual framework supplied by the classical school. The consequences of this revolution are brilliantly described by Eddington:

> From the point of view of philosophy of science the conception associated with entropy must I think be ranked as the great contribution of the nineteenth century to scientific thought. It marked a reaction from the view that everything to which science need pay attention is discovered by microscopic dissection of objects. It provided an alternative standpoint in which the centre of interest is shifted from the entities reached by the customary analysis (atoms, electric potentials, etc.) to qualities possessed by the system as a whole, which cannot be split up and located—a little bit here, and a little bit there. . . .
>
> We often think that when we have completed our study of *one* we know all about *two*, because "two" is "one and one." We forget that we have still to make a study of "and." Secondary physics is the study of "and"—that is to say, of organization.[55]

Although modern physics often deals in minute quantities and oscillations, the conception of the physicist is on the "macro" scale. He is concerned with the "and," or the organization of the world in which the events occur. These developments did not invalidate classical physics as to its usefulness for explaining a certain range of phenomena. But classical physics is no longer the undisputed law of the universe. It is a special case.

Early economic theory, and Adam Smith's *Wealth of Nations* comes to mind, examined economic problems in the macro order. The *Wealth of Nations* is mainly concerned with matters of national income and welfare. Later, the economics of the firm, microeconomics, dominated the theoretical scene in this science. And, finally, with Keynes' *The General Theory of Employment Interest and Money*, a systematic approach to the economic universe was reintroduced on the macro level.

The first era of the developing science of sociology was occupied by the great social "system builders." Comte, the so-called father of sociology, had a macro view of society in that his chief works are devoted to social reorganization. Comte was concerned with the inter-

---

[55] Sir Arthur Eddington, *The Nature of the Physical World* (Ann Arbor: The University of Michigan Press, 1958), pp. 103-104.

relationships among social, political, religious, and educational institutions. As sociology progressed, the science of society compressed. Emphasis shifted from the macro approach of the pioneers to detailed, empirical study of small social units. The compression of sociological analysis was accompanied by study of social pathology or disorganization.

In general, physics, economics, and sociology appear to have two things in common. First, they offered a macro point of view as their initial systematic comprehension of their area of study. Second, as the science developed, attention fragmented into analysis of the parts of the organization, rather than attending to the system as a whole. This is the micro phase.

In physics and economics, discontent was evidenced by some scientists at the continual atomization of the universe. The reaction to the micro approach was a new theory or theories dealing with the total system, on the macro level again. This third phase of scientific development seems to be more evident in physics and economics than in sociology.

The reason for the "macro-micro-macro" order of scientific progress lies, perhaps, in the hypothesis that usually the things which strike man first are of great magnitude. The scientist attempts to discover order in the vastness. But after macro laws or models of systems are postulated, variations appear which demand analysis, not so much in terms of the entire system, but more in terms of the specific parts which make it up. Then, intense study of microcosm may result in new general laws, replacing the old models of organization. Or, the old and the new models may stand together, each explaining a different class of phenomenon. Or, the old and the new concepts of organization may be welded to produce a single creative synthesis.

Now, what does all this have to do with the problem of organization in administrative science? Organization concepts seem to have gone through the same order of development in this field as in the three just mentioned. It is evident that the classical theory of organization, particularly as in the work of Mooney and Reiley, is concerned with principles common to all organizations. It is a macro-organization view. The classical approach to organization, however, dealt with the gross anatomical parts and processes of the formal organization. Like classical physics, the classical theory of organization is a special case. Neither are especially well equipped to account for variation from their established framework.

Many variations in the classical administrative model result from human behavior. The only way these variations could be understood was by a microscopic examination of particularized, situational aspects of human behavior. The mission of the neoclassical school thus is "micro-analysis."

It was observed earlier, that somewhere along the line the concept of the social system, which is the key to understanding the Hawthorne studies, faded into the background. Maybe the idea is so obvious that it was lost to the view of researchers and writers in human relations. In any event, the press of research in the microcosmic universes of the informal organization, morale and productivity, leadership, participation, and the like forced the notion of the social system into limbo. Now, with the advent of modern organization theory, the social system has been resurrected.

Modern organization theory appears to be concerned with Eddington's "and." This school claims that its operational hypothesis is based on a macro point of view; that is, the study of organization as a whole. This nobility of purpose should not obscure, however, certain difficulties faced by this field as it is presently constituted. Modern organization theory raises two questions which should be explored further. First, would it not be more accurate to speak of modern organization theor*ies*? Second, just how much of modern organization theory is modern?

The first question can be answered with a quick affirmative. Aside from the notion of the system, there are few, if any, other ideas of a unifying nature. Except for several important exceptions,[56] modern organization theorists tend to pursue their pet points of view,[57] suggesting they are part of system theory, but not troubling to show by what mystical means they arrive at this conclusion.

The irony of it all is that a field dealing with systems has, indeed, little system. Modern organization theory needs a framework, and it needs an integration of issues into a common conception of organization. Admittedly, this is a large order. But it is curious not to find serious analytical treatment of subjects like cybernetics or general system theory in Haire's, *Modern Organizational Theory* which claims to be a representative example of work in this field. Beer has ample evidence in his book *Cybernetics and Management* that

---

[56] For example: E. Wight Bakke, *op. cit.*, pp. 18-75.
[57] There is a large selection including decision theory, individual-organization interaction, motivation, vitality, stability, growth, and graph theory, to mention a few.

cybernetics, if imaginatively approached, provides a valuable conceptual base for the study of systems.

The second question suggests an ambiguous answer. Modern organization theory is in part a product of the past; system analysis is not a new idea. Further, modern organization theory relies for supporting data on microcosmic research studies, generally drawn from the journals of the last ten years. The newness of modern organization theory, perhaps, is its effort to synthesize recent research contributions of many fields into a system theory characterized by a reoriented conception of organization.

One might ask, but what is the modern theorist reorienting? A clue is found in the almost snobbish disdain assumed by some authors of the neo-classical human relations school, and particularly, the classical school. Re-evaluation of the classical school of organization is overdue. However, this does not mean that its contributions to organization theory are irrelevant and should be overlooked in the rush to get on the "behavioral science bandwagon."

Haire announces that the papers appearing in *Modern Organization Theory* constitute, "the ragged leading edge of a wave of theoretical development." [58] Ragged, yes; but leading no! The papers appearing in this book do not represent a theoretical breakthrough in the concept of organization. Haire's collection is an interesting potpourri with several contributions of considerable significance. But readers should beware that they will not find vastly new insights into organizational behavior in this book, if they have kept up with the literature of the social sciences, and have dabbled to some extent in the esoteria of biological theories of growth, information theory, and mathematical model building. For those who have not maintained the pace, *Modern Organization Theory* serves the admirable purpose of bringing them up-to-date on a rather diversified number of subjects.

Some work in modern organization theory is pioneering, making its appraisal difficult and future uncertain. While the direction of this endeavor is unclear, one thing is patently true. Human behavior in organizations, and indeed, organization itself, cannot be adequately understood within the ground rules of classical and neo-classical doctrines. Appreciation of human organization requires a *creative* synthesis of massive amounts of empirical data, a high order of deductive

[58] Mason Haire, "General Issues," in Mason Haire (editor), *Modern Organization Theory* (New York: John Wiley and Sons, 1959), p. 2.

reasoning, imaginative research studies, and a taste for individual and social values. Accomplishment of all these objectives, and the inclusion of them into a framework of the concept of the system, appears to be the goal of modern organization theory. The vitality of administrative science rests on the advances modern theorists make along this line.

Modern organization theory, 1960 style, is an amorphous aggregation of synthesizers and restaters, with a few extending leadership on the frontier. For the sake of these few, it is well to admonish that pouring old wine into new bottles may make the spirits cloudy. Unfortunately, modern organization theory has almost succeeded in achieving the status of a fad. Popularization and exploitation contributed to the disrepute into which human relations has fallen. It would be a great waste if modern organization theory yields to the same fate, particularly since both modern organization theory and human relations draw from the same promising source of inspiration—system analysis.

Modern organization theory needs tools of analysis and a conceptual framework uniquely its own, but it must also allow for the incorporation of relevant contributions of many fields. It may be that the framework will come from general system theory. New areas of research such as decision theory, information theory, and cybernetics also offer reasonable expectations of analytical and conceptual tools. Modern organization theory represents a frontier of research which has great significance for management. The potential is great, because it offers the opportunity for uniting what is valuable in classical theory with the social and natural sciences into a systematic and integrated conception of human organization.

57. PRINCIPLES OF
GOOD ORGANIZATION [1]

S. Avery Raube [2]

The word "organization" probably has as many different interpretations as any other single term in the vocabulary of management. In this report, the word is used in its planning sense. It is used in this sense in the following definitions:

> *"Organization is the machine of management in its achievement of the ends determined by administration."* [3]
> *"Organization is the analysis and grouping of all the activities necessary to the objectives of any undertaking so as to provide a structure of duties and responsibilities."* [4]

Neither of these definitions, it will be noted, mentions people. Staffing is a subject apart from organization planning. As discussed here, organization is independent of persons. It is the design, the blueprint for action.

Both definitions refer to the goals of the business—what the company is trying to achieve. The first uses the word "ends"; the second, "objectives." The organization planner begins by knowing where his company wants to go; organization is a plan for getting there. *The objectives determine the structure needed.*

COMPANY OBJECTIVES

Does the company plan to manufacture a single product, or does it intend to add products as financing permits? Does it propose to adhere to a line of allied products, or does it wish to diversify? The decision of a company which makes glass jars to become a manufacturer of containers generally takes the company into the tin can and fiberboard carton businesses and has a marked effect on its organization planning. When a company that has manufactured only agricultural machinery decides to add refrigerators and air condi-

---

[1] From *Company Organization Charts*, National Industrial Conference Board, pp. 5-13. Reprinted by permission of National Industrial Conference Board.
[2] S. Avery Raube, Director, Division of Personnel Administration, National Industrial Conference Board, Inc., 1954.
[3] Oliver Sheldon.
[4] Samuel L. H. Burk.

tioners to its line, that necessarily affects its organization structure. A firm decision, on the other hand, to hew to one line of allied products, may mean the lopping off of unrelated activities that have crept into an organization.

Does the company plan to make and sell a quality article? That decision affects organization for research, development, and quality control. Does the company plan to be in business for a long time? Is it to its interest, for instance, to build customer good will and good public relations? If there is no thought of repeat sales, it may not need a sales servicing department or special public relations activities.

Does the company plan to obtain its own raw materials or to purchase them? Some steel companies mine their own ore; some paper manufacturers run their own tree farms; some newspapers manufacture their own newsprint. Such activities affect their organization structure.

Does the company intend to expand into other regions of the country, or will it confine its operations to a single territory? When a bank which has operated only locally decides to establish a branch in another city or state, it has made a decision that affects organization. How about foreign operations? Does the company wish to sell its products abroad? If so, will the company handle the sales itself, or will it depend on other companies for foreign distribution? Will it do any manufacturing in foreign lands, or will it assemble parts there that are made in domestic factories?

To whom does the company plan to sell its products? Does it plan to reach the ultimate consumer, or sell to manufacturers of end-products, or sell the larger part of its production to the government?

Does the company plan to increase the number of its employees indefinitely as business grows? Management of some companies has concluded that there are advantages in keeping the total employment within a certain figure. When business comes in that cannot be handled by that number, orders are refused, or contracts sublet.

With objectives such as the foregoing in mind, the organization planner designs an ideal structure for meeting them. Necessary duties are grouped into packets and divided into manageable parts.

Initial Steps in Planning

There are few instances where managements have planned the organization at the start of their enterprises. Most companies have grown without design. When management has become aware of the advantages of planning, it is a matter of reorganization, rather than organization.

The initial step, however, is the same. That is, the company objectives are determined and stated, and a chart is drawn which it is believed would best meet them. In the case of reorganization, at the same time that the ideal chart is being prepared, an inventory of present organization structure is made. A written description is prepared of each supervisory position in the company, perhaps to the level of department head. Each person who holds a supervisory position is asked to write out what he thinks are his responsibilities and to whom he reports. A comparison of their statements usually reveals considerable overlapping, as well as areas that are left uncovered.

The most obvious defects are eliminated, through decisions by top management, and then the planner prepares an organization manual. This is made up of primary and subsidiary charts which show the organization as it exists and descriptions of the duties of the various positions as they exist at the time the manual is written.

The planner also prepares what are known as phase charts and plans. An estimate is made of the time it will probably take for the company to reach the ideal organization structure. Phase charts show stages through which the company can proceed to get there. One, for instance, may show the organization structure at the end of a year, another at the end of three or five years.

It may be possible to make some changes easily. These can be put into effect at once. Others may have to wait until an individual holding a given position retires, or resigns, or dies. Some companies have believed it advisable to make an immediate drastic change in structure. For instance, they have shifted from completely functional division of its operations to division by product.

The organization planner helps management reach the goals set in both the phase and the ultimate designs. This is organization control, and it is a continuous process. A change in company objectives usually necessitates a revision of both ultimate and phase charts.

Since the structure is designed to meet the individual company's objectives, it follows that a management cannot expect satisfactory results merely through copying another's plan of organization. Alvin Brown, vice president for finance of the Johns-Manville Corporation, emphasizes this with an apt comparison.[5] Many, he says, point to existing structures of organization and say, "See! That is how you go about organizing." One could as sensibly point to a bridge, Mr. Brown comments, and say, "See! There is how you build a bridge." He continues: "I doubt that bridges could ever be built by imitation. Conditions differ. The bridge that may serve one need will not serve another. I think the engineer must return to his principles every time he builds a new bridge, however much the new product may resemble the old. . . . In the same way, I cannot believe that the author of an enterprise could afford to imitate some other enterprise when his circumstances and his need may be different."

ORGANIZATION PRINCIPLES

Like the engineer who designs his bridge to meet special needs, the organization planner, in designing a company structure, applies principles. For through years of experience it has been learned that if certain principles are followed, regardless of the size of the enterprise, the result will be good organization. Some of these basic laws follow:

1. *There must be clear lines of authority running from the top to the bottom of the organization.*

Lt. Col. Lyndall Urwick [6] defines authority as "the formal right to require action of others." Mr. R. E. Gillmore [7] says it is "the right to direct, coordinate and decide."

Clarity is achieved through delegation by steps or levels from the leader to the working level, from the highest executive to the employee who has least responsibility in the organization and no authority over others. From the president, a line of authority may proceed to a vice president, to a general manager, to a foreman, to a leadman, and finally to a worker on an assembly line. It should be possible to trace such a line from the president, or whoever is top coordinating executive, to every employee in the company.

Following military parlance, this line is sometimes referred to as "the chain of command." The principle is known as the "scalar principle." It is the vertical division of authority.

[5] In an address, "Organization: A Neglected Science," delivered at the Massachusetts Institute of Technology, November 26, 1946.
[6] Eminent British specialist in the field of organization.
[7] Vice-President, the Sperry Corporation, and author of many articles on organization subjects.

2. *No one in the organization should report to more than one line supervisor. Everyone in the organization should know to whom he reports, and who reports to him.*

This is known as the "unity of command" principle. Stated simply, everyone should have only one boss.

This principle is one of those most frequently violated and the cause of many internal difficulties. It may be a matter of several stenographers working for a group of executives, any one of whom can require directly the services of any of the individual girls. The best of the stenographers is overloaded with work; the least efficient has nothing to do.[8] It may be a matter of partners running a business, with each giving orders independently to the executive vice president.

The harassed individual who receives orders from several bosses is faced with problems such as whose orders to follow first, how to allocate his time so as to displease none and satisfy all, what to do if he receives conflicting orders from different sources. The lazy employee is afforded an excellent opportunity to avoid work by explaining to one boss that he cannot accept more tasks because he is busy carrying out (imaginary) assignments given by another.

3. *The responsibility and authority of each supervisor should be clearly defined in writing.*

Putting his responsibilities into writing enables the supervisor, himself, to know what is expected of him and the limits of his authority. It prevents overlapping of authority, with resultant confusion. It avoids gaps between responsibilities. And it enables quick determination of the proper point for decision.

Many executives say complacently, "We all know what we are supposed to do. There is no need to put our duties in writing." But in many companies, management has been startled when top executives have been asked, independently, to list their duties. It is an eye-opener to discover that three and four individuals believe themselves responsible for an identical function, and that time and money are being wasted in duplicated effort. Therein, too, lie the seeds of jurisdictional dispute.

When an executive is lost suddenly, through death or lure of a competitor, it is not uncommon to find that no one knows exactly what the executive did, and therefore what to require of his successor.

---

[8] In secretarial "pools," this situation is avoided and the principle adhered to by having all of the stenographers report to a single supervisor who receives all requests for stenographic assistance and assigns work to the individuals.

Even when a vacancy is expected, it is difficult to train a replacement without an accurate knowledge of the content of the position.

4. *Responsibility should always be coupled with corresponding authority.*

This principle suggests that if a plant manager in multi-unit organization is held responsible for all activities in his plant, he should not be subject to *orders* from company headquarters specifying the quantity of raw materials he should buy or from whom he should purchase them.[9] If a supervisor is responsible for the quality of work put out in his department, he should not have to accept as a member of his working force an employee who has been hired without consulting him.

There are many executives who delegate authority and then undermine it by making decisions that belong to the individual who is being held responsible. Over a luncheon table a company president makes a promise of delivery to a favored customer, which upsets the carefully planned schedules of the sales manager. A plant superintendent makes a casual statement to the press which strews rocks in the path of the director of public relations.

This principle can be stated conversely: "Authority should always be coupled with corresponding responsibility." Those given authority, unless they are held accountable, may easily become dictators.

5. *The responsibility of higher authority for the acts of its subordinates is absolute.*

Lt. Col. Urwick has expressed the principle in these words. Another way of saying it is that although a supervisor delegates authority, he still remains responsible for what is done by those to whom he has delegated it.

The head of maintenance is responsible for keeping the plant lighting system in order. He does not screw a new electric light bulb in place when an old one burns out. That responsibility has been delegated to the plant electrician. But if the electrician fails to replace a bulb when one is needed, the head of maintenance is as accountable as the electrician. He is responsible for the electrician's inefficiency.

---

[9] He may, however, welcome advice or suggestions from a purchasing specialist on the company's central staff.

In accord with this principle, an executive cannot disassociate himself from the acts of his subordinates. He is as responsible as they, for what they do and neglect to do.

6. *Authority should be delegated as far down the line as possible.*

Permitting decisions to be made on as low a level as possible releases the energies of those on higher levels for matters which only they can attend to. The head of a pottery factory does not concern himself with whether the rose on the breakfast plate is to be red or yellow. The head of a large company does not personally sign every paycheck or personally approve the salary increase of every typist. For those are duties that may easily and efficiently be delegated farther down the line.

Application of this principle can be observed in the current trend toward decentralization of large companies. Decision-making power is being placed nearer the scene of action. The plant or division manager is allowed to make all decisions in his unit, within the confines of company-wide policy. This enables members of top corporate management to devote more time to over-all thinking and planning.

7. *The number of levels of authority should be kept at a minimum.*

The greater the number of levels, the longer is the chain of command, and the longer it takes for instructions to travel down and for information to travel up and down within the organization.

Too many levels encourage "run-arounds." To obtain a quicker decision, a worker fails to consult his immediate supervisor, but appeals to an executive higher up the line.

Mr. Gillmor has figured out mathematically that most organizations would never need more than six levels of supervision, including that of the top executive. With six such levels, he says, with a span of control of five at the top levels, and twenty workers reporting to each supervisor at the lowest level of supervision, there is room in an organization for 62,500 workers and 3,905 executives.[10]

8. *The work of every person in the organization should be confined as far as possible to the performance of a single leading function.*

---

[10] "A Practical Manual of Organization," by R. E. Gillmor, Funk & Wagnals Company, New York, 1948.

This is the principle of specialization. It applies to departments and divisions as well as to individuals. It concerns delegation of authority *horizontally*, rather than vertically, as in the case of the scalar principle.

The total duties in the organization are divided according to functions, and a department or division is made responsible for each.[11]

There may be functional division according to the *kind* of work to be done—manufacturing, sales, finance, or engineering. Or, within a department, for example the financial department, a company may have subdivisions for billing, receiving, payroll, etc.

There may also be functional division according to the *way* in which the work is done. For example, divisions may be set up for typists, comptometer operators, etc.

This principle requires that if a person is held responsible for more than one duty, and this is often the case in small companies, the duties should be similar. Public relations is grouped with industrial relations, rather than with engineering. The specialist specializes. In the interests of efficiency, he concentrates on the things he can do best.

In organizations which have been allowed to grow without design, individuals are frequently found who are performing two or more unrelated duties. Sometimes this comes about because a certain individual happens to have a little free time when an activity is added. Sometimes it is because a man happens to have some experience in his background which qualifies him to handle the new assignment, even though it has nothing to do with his major duties. Sometimes it is because he has a particular interest in the activity. Sometimes an individual seizes a floating activity simply because he is a power-grabber.

A combination of ill-related assignments often seems to work satisfactorily, so long as a particular person holds a post. But it is not considered good organization. Should he leave, the prospects of finding another person who has the identical abilities to handle the widely different duties are usually slim. The organization structure which has to be changed to fit persons cannot adhere to a design which it is believed will best achieve the company's objectives.

---

[11] There is no uniformity in the use of the terms "department" and "division." They mean whatever a company wants them to mean. Some companies have departments within divisions; some have divisions within departments. Some use "department" for their staff units, and "division" for the operating units.

9. *Whenever possible, line functions should be separated from staff functions, and adequate emphasis should be placed on important staff activities.*

Line functions are those which accomplish the main objectives of the company. In many manufacturing companies, the manufacturing and distribution functions are considered line. The manufacturing and sales departments are considered the departments that are accomplishing the main objectives of the business.

In companies that are not attempting to reach the ultimate consumer with their products, for example those that sell their products to outside distributors or to the government, the sales function may not be considered a line function.

In some companies in which engineering is practically a part of production, it is considered a line function. In certain chemical companies, research is so closely integrated with production that it is thought of as a line activity. Procurement of raw materials may be considered line by a metal manufacturing company that does its own mining and quarrying.

Line departments are often called "operating" departments.

Staff functions are those which aid in, or are auxiliary to, the line functions. Some companies call their staff departments "auxiliary departments."

Members of staff departments provide service, advice, coordination and control for the line or operating departments. (They may perform one or more of these functions.) Purchasing and advertising departments, for instance, provide service. Legal and public relations departments provide advice. Production planning serves as an example of a coordinating agency. Industrial engineering and accounting departments are examples of departments that provide control. Many of these departments serve more than one of the purposes. The department which provides service may also provide advice; the department that coordinates may also help with control.

Committees are usually considered staff agencies. Their members advise, coordinate, and control.

There are also individuals, who are not members of a department or committee, who perform staff functions. These are called staff assistants. The specialist retained from an outside firm, such as a legal consultant or public relations consultant, is an example. Or, within an organization, there may be an assistant to the president who has no supervisory duties but who investigates problems that are referred to him by the president, putting before the president data upon the basis of which the chief executive can make decisions. The staff assistant's duties are chiefly the detailed work of command, so that the energies of the line executive can be released for larger activities.

10. *There is a limit to the number of positions that can be coordinated by a single executive.*

This is known as the "span of control" principle.

The number of positions (groups of activities) which an executive is able to coordinate, depends on:

a. The similarity or dissimilarity of the subordinate positions and how interdependent they are. The more positions interlock, the greater is the work of coordination.
b. How far the people and activities are apart geographically. The manager who is coordinating activities within a single plant can coordinate more than if these activities are carried on at widely scattered locations.
c. The complexity of the duties of each of the positions to be coordinated.
d. The stability of the business.
e. The frequency with which new types of problems arise. If a company has been in business for many years, the problems which come up from day to day have probably been encountered before, and the work of coordination is therefore less than if the problems were brand new.

The span of control is seldom uniform throughout an organization. At the upper levels, where positions are interdependent and dissimilar, many organization specialists urge that the span of control embrace not more than five or six subordinates. In some decentralized companies, however, in which the operating units are practically autonomous, the top executive is successfully coordinating as many as twelve or fifteen positions.

At the lowest supervisory level—the level of the last executives who have any supervisory responsibilities—organization specialists say that a supervisor may supervise as many as twenty workers. This might be a foreman or leadman supervising men on an assembly line.

As attention has been given to the human relations aspects of the supervisor's responsibilities, there has been a tendency to shorten the span of control even at the lowest level. While a foreman might be able to supervise the work of twenty men, all of whom are performing an identical, simple operation, he might not have time to give them individual attention as persons. He might not have time to communicate information on company policies, listen to their suggestions or grievances, learn the causes of poor performance. For these reasons a large paper company announced that it had decided to limit the number of workers supervised by each of its foremen to ten. A manufacturer of metal products, because of such reasons, has adopted a maximum ratio of twelve workers to the lowest supervisor.

In separating packets of duties into manageable parts, so that no individual's span of control need be too great, three types of division are commonly employed: (1) functional, (2) product or service, and (3) regional or geographical. The functional type of division has been discussed in connection with the principle of specialization. A company that has a radio manufacturing department and a television manufacturing department is using product division. Examples of service divisions are provided by a public utility company which has a lighting department and a heating department, or a bank that has an insurance department and a mortgage department.

When operations are widely scattered, the most effective plan is sometimes to set up a unit in each geographical area. In public ultilities such as railroads, this is a natural way of assigning duties. Life insurance companies, too, often have regional divisions.

Many companies use a combination of these methods. Within a sales department (a functional division) there may be a western and an eastern sales office (regional divisions). Or the refrigerator division of an electrical products company (product division) may use the functional basis for separating its activities into manageable parts—engineering, manufacturing, sales, etc.

Some point out that there is danger in oversupervision as well as in undersupervision, that is, in having the span of control too short. At the top levels, the executive coordinates dissimilar positions. He should not coordinate too many positions simply because they are dissimilar. Account must be taken of the frequency with which new problems arise and other factors which influence the span of control. If, however, the executive is not given enough positions to coordinate, he may have time on his hands. Such a person may have a tendency to inject himself into operational decisions, undermining authority which has been delegated.

11. *The organization should be flexible, so that it can be adjusted to changing conditions.*

The organization plan should stand up, in boom and in depression, in war and in peace, when new markets appear and when old ones disappear. The plan should permit expansion and contraction without disrupting the basic design. Good organization is not a straitjacket.

12. *The organization should be kept as simple as possible.*

Too many levels of authority, as has been noted, make communication difficult. Too many committees impede rather than achieve coordination.

All of these principles (there are more than the dozen listed, but these are ones that are frequently referred to in discussions of organization) are based on the idea of leadership and delegation of authority. Complete authority is delegated by the board of directors to an individual, who is able to carry out his responsibilities by delegating authority to others.

BENEFITS OF GOOD ORGANIZATION

A few of the benefits of the application of these principles have been touched upon in describing the precepts. The following reiterate some of them, but include additional benefits that companies attribute to organization planning. Application of the principles

Disposes of conflicts between individuals over jurisdiction.

Prevents duplication of work.

Decreases likelihood of "run-arounds."

Makes communication easier through keeping the channels clear.

Shows promotional possibilities, which is useful in executive development. Organization charts and position descriptions show where a man can expect to go, what qualifications are needed to fill a superior job, what additional training is needed to prepare a man in one position for a superior post.

Provides a sound basis for appraisal and rating of individual performance and capabilities. If one knows what an individual is supposed to be doing, it is then possible to measure how well he is living up to the requirements of the job.

Aids in wage and salary administration. The analysis of duties for the higher executives performs the same service as job descriptions for those in the lower echelons.

Permits expansion with adequate control, and without killing off top executives. Activities are administered in manageable units, so that no one person has too heavy a load.

Permits changes to be made in the right direction as opportunities present themselves. In the absence of a plan, changes are likely to be made on the basis of expediency, with the likelihood of perpetuating original mistakes.

Increases cooperation and a feeling of freedom. Each person works best with others when he knows for what he is responsible, to whom he is responsible and the value of cooperative relationships with others. A feeling of freedom comes when responsibilities are definite and known and when delegation is actually practiced.

*   *   *

58. ORGANIZATIONAL REALITIES [1]

Rocco Carzo, Jr. [2]

Organizing is easy—at least, that is what one is led to believe from traditional writings on the subject. Traditional theory prescribes that organization be built around the work to be done. For maximum efficiency, this theory specifies that the work be divided into simple, routine, and repetitive tasks. These tasks or jobs should then be grouped according to similar work characteristics and arranged in an organization structure in which an executive has a limited number of subordinates reporting directly to him. Also, every member of the organization should be accountable to only one boss. Personnel assignments are to be made on the basis of the requirements of the job and each individual's ability to do the work.

These are not doctrinaire beliefs reserved for academic minds. In many quarters, they have gained enough stature to be called "principles" of management and/or organization, and they are also widely accepted in practice. Administrators and academicians will recognize the traditional organization pyramids that are based on these seemingly reasonable propositions. As an example, one administrator recommends the following for a "sound, flexible, and dynamic" organizational structure: [3]

1. Determine the objectives and the policies, programs, plans, and schedules that will best achieve those objectives for the company as a whole and, in turn, for each component of the business.
2. Determine the work to be done to achieve those objectives under such guiding policies.
3. Divide and classify or group related work into a simple, logical, understandable, and comprehensive organizational structure.
4. Assign essential work clearly and definitely to the various components and positions.

[1] From *Business Horizons* (Spring, 1961), pp. 95-104. Reprinted by permission of *Business Horizons*.
[2] Rocco Carzo, Jr., Associate Professor of Management, College of Business Administration, The Pennsylvania State University.
[3] Ralph J. Cordiner, *New Frontiers for Professional Managers* (New York: McGraw-Hill Book Company, Inc., 1956), pp. 52-53.

5. Determine the requirements and qualifications of personnel to occupy such positions.
6. Staff the organization with persons who meet these qualifications.
7. Establish methods and procedures that will help to achieve the objectives of the organization.

Now, however, there is enough research evidence to raise some significant doubts about the validity of prevailing organizational theories. Traditional theory is based on logical division of work. More recent social research is concerned with organizational arrangements that will facilitate the joining of human efforts. Realistic organizational theory must be based on the real behavior of real people in real organizations, that is, the ways in which people join their efforts in any kind of cooperative system. The real test of organizational theory is not abstract logic based on work but on arrangements that facilitate effective cooperative relationships. These relationships are the key to productivity. It is the purpose of this article to explain and illustrate the lack of concern for these realities in the traditional approach. In addition, some suggestions will be made for realistic organization.

TRADITION VS. RESEARCH

Specialization

The advantages of specialization are primarily economic. Both economists and formal organization theorists emphasize that greater efficiency and productivity are achieved through division of work. Adam Smith, in his *Wealth of Nations,* illustrated his thinking with his description of a pin factory. By dividing the work into specialized tasks, the factory could produce thousands of pins per man per day. But if the complete manufacturing process were left to individual workmen, each might produce only a few dozen per day. F. W. Taylor went a step further by proposing that management jobs be specialized so that "each man from the assistant superintendent down shall have as few functions as possible to perform. If practicable, the work of each man in the management should be confined to the performance of a single leading function." [4]

The approach that divides the work into simple, routine, and repetitive tasks utilizes *minimum* skills and abilities. James Worthy has attacked this approach as follows:

[4] Frederick W. Taylor, *Scientific Management* (New York: Harper & Brothers, 1941), p. 99.

The gravest weakness [of specialization] was the failure to recognize and utilize properly management's most valuable resource: the complex and multiple capacities of people. On the contrary, the scientific managers deliberately sought to utilize as narrow a band of personality and as narrow a range of ability as ingenuity could devise. The process has been fantastically wasteful for industry and society.[5]

Recently, the effect of specialization on employee attitudes have received more study. For example, Chris Argyris feels that congruency is lacking between the needs of healthy individuals and the demands of the formal organization. In his research of a seemingly healthy manufacturing operation that had very low indexes of employee turnover, absenteeism, and grievances, Argyris found the employees to be apathetic and indifferent toward management and the organization. He has said that the formal organization, with its emphasis on task specialization, utilizes a narrow range of skills and minimum abilities, and tends to create needs that are not characteristic of healthy, mature individuals.

The administrator and the social scientist might argue that these criticisms involve value judgments and are not really their concern. They may ask: Does it matter if human resources are not fully utilized; and does it matter that employees are apathetic and indifferent, as long as organization objectives are accomplished efficiently or as long as profits are maximized in the case of a business enterprise? The administrator may argue further that he is forced to adopt specialization because it promises the greater efficiency and productivity. The social scientist may point out that, as a scientist, he cannot consider values; his concern must be limited to means and not ends.

Both administrators and social scientists would accept the position, however, that greater utilization of the physical and mental capabilities of the human resource may increase the scope of organizational accomplishment. They would also accept the argument that apathy and indifference may have long-run implications for the efficient attainment of goals. For example, Argyris predicts that the dissatisfaction of employees manifested by apathy and indifference will result in demands for increased wages; these increases will be viewed "not as rewards for production but as management's moral obligation for placing the employees in the kind of working world

[5] James C. Worthy, *Big Business and Free Man* (New York: Harper & Brothers, 1959), pp. 69-70.

where frustration, failure, and conflict are continuously being experienced." According to this thesis, wage costs will tend to rise
regardless of productivity changes. The employee in this situation
views the increase as compensation for continued frustration.

Perhaps these realities imply even broader organizational objectives than those of maximum efficiency, productivity, and profits.
The narrower view of organizations in terms of material achievements, such as profits as the prime goal (and some say the only
goal) of business institutions, has permeated the classical as well as
the popular and current versions of organized activity. The materialistic goals attributed to organizations are abstractions and serve
only to facilitate simplified descriptions of organization and group
behavior. These descriptions are usually devoid of human and moral
values. Such values are important not only as ends in themselves
but also for understanding human behavior. Over-simplification
with regard to the multiple objectives of organizations and the complex motivations of individuals will not lead to realistic organizational structure. Worthy has decried the prevailing theories of
business organization and has called for a new theory that more
adequately reflects and explains reality:

> Such a theory will recognize that business is a social organ with
> functions far beyond the mere promotion of material prosperity, and
> with motivations far broader than simple self-interest. It will give
> consideration to the pervasive influence of religious forces in American
> life, the profound consequences of the rise of the large, publicly owned
> corporation, and certain unique features of American historical develop
> ment. It will, in other words, shake off outmoded economic doctrine and
> take a fresh look at the truth about today's business.[6]

This broader view of organizational goals implies that the administrator has responsibilities far beyond those dictated by material
achievements. The fragmentation and routinization of work to the
point where it loses significance has dire implications, not only for
organizations that live by this action, but also for society in general.
The organization may suffer because the rewards for submissive
compliance produce apathy, indifference, noninvolvement, and alienation on the part of group members. They become highly dependent
and incapable of solving problems and making decisions. The organization may become rigid and its members unwilling to accept and
adapt to changes necessary for growth and changing socio-economic

[6] *Big Business and Free Man*, pp. 31-32.

conditions. Furthermore, a democracy built on a foundation of free choice will suffer because the dependency rewarded and fostered in organizations may carry over into everyday life.

Grouping

After the work has been divided into specialized tasks, the advocates of formal organization prescribe the grouping of these tasks according to similar work characteristics. This is called the principle of "functional homogenity." According to one definition, the principle ". . . says that organizational effectiveness is increased and the cost of executive and operative labor is reduced when duties are grouped in accordance with functional similarities. The members of a group are able to *coordinate* and *cooperate* with one another directly when they are dealing with similar problems." [7]

The grouping of persons according to similarities in their work may be contrary to the natural development of human organization. Early researchers found that people tend naturally to organize on a basis other than the technical requirements of work. They organize in terms of sentiments, social customs, codes of behavior, status, friendships, and cliques. The significance of these findings lies in the researchers' conclusions that cooperation depends upon the natural relationships of informal organization and not necessarily on groupings based on work arrangements and/or economic incentives.

The simplicity and rationale of formal structuring is open to further criticism when one examines another prescription for organizing. The principle of "span of control" stipulates that the number of subordinates supervised directly by any one executive be limited. Some eminent students of administration have gone so far as to specify how many subordinates a superior can effectively manage. Urwick, for example, has said, "No superior can supervise directly the work of more than five or, at the most, six subordinates *whose work interlocks*." [8] Two of the most outstanding criticisms (many have been made) of the span of control are those of Herbert A. Simon and Waino W. Suojanen. Simon points out that there is a basic contradiction between this principle and the principle that there should be as few levels as possible in an organization. By

---

[7] Ralph C. Davis, *Industrial Organization and Management* (New York: Harper & Brothers, 1957), p. 70. The emphasis is mine.
[8] Lydall F. Urwick, "The Manager's Span of Control" *Harvard Business Review*, XXXIV (May-June, 1956), p. 41.

restricting or limiting the span of control, an organization—especially one that is growing—must increase the number of scalar levels and the administrative distance between individuals. This development inevitably produces excessive red tape and waste of time and effort. Obviously, adherence to the principle of span of control conflicts with the principle that requires a minimum number of organizational levels. Suojanen states:

> If both principles are actually applicable to the large organization, then it must follow that many large government agencies and business corporations are less efficient than their smaller counterparts. However, large corporations not only continue to grow in size but also comparisons of various sizes of corporations are not convincing as to the superiority of smaller, as opposed to larger corporations.[9]

While Urwick's argument for the span-of-control concept is based on those situations where the work of subordinates interlocks, Suojanen offers this very reason as an explanation for the success of large organizations. Common purpose, willingness to cooperate, and coordinated action are characteristics of the executive unit. According to Suojanen, the ease of communication, the informality of relationships, and the personal satisfactions gained in association actually reduce rather than increase the number of relationships and the demands made on the superior.

If this is not enough to raise doubts about the span-of-control doctrine, one can consider the research done at the Institute for Social Research, University of Michigan. One of the researchers there has concluded that an organization will function best and will achieve the highest motivation when the people in the organization hold overlapping group memberships.[10] The very characteristic (interlocking relationships) that seems to make the span of control operative is in reality a necessity for cooperative and coordinated effort.

Effects of interaction. Evidence indicates that an organization initially framed according to work groupings will eventually function in a manner that parallels the natural social tendencies and personality characteristics of the persons in it.

---

[9] Waino W. Suojanen, "The Span of Control—Fact or Fable," *Advanced Management*, XX (November, 1955), p. 5.
[10] Rensis Likert, "A Motivational Approach to a Modified Theory of Organization and Management," in Mason Haire (Ed.), *Modern Organization Theory* (New York: John Wiley & Sons, Inc., 1959), pp. 184-217.

In laboratory research undertaken by the author (the results have not yet been published), an attempt is being made to predict organizational success on the basis of the composition and interaction of group members. We have seen organizations, initially departmentalized according to similarities in work, actually operate under different systems. The new systems were based on the personalities and interaction of group members. In another study, where departments were established on the basis of work similarities and authority was delegated on the basis of work performance, researchers found that a system of relations had developed that was quite distinct from the formal organization. Furthermore, they suggest that difficulties of industrial cooperation could be avoided if organization would adapt the formal organization to the real relationships that develop over a period of time.[11]

Separation of line and staff

Another area where reality differs from theoretical prescriptions is the traditional separation of line (command) and staff (advisory) authority. According to traditional theory, staff departments are recommended for assisting line executives in work that requires technical knowledge and detailed attention. While the staff is supposed to remain advisory, it usually develops into a line capacity with both the higher and lower elements of the organizational hierarchy. Staff specialists become "experts" in their specialty and top management officials rely on them for "authoritative" advice. As lower management officials realize that staff recommendations are backed by top management, a line of command is established that covers a particular aspect of the work—in addition to general supervision of the line.

The development of this arrangement serves to obviate the neat separation of line and staff. Also, there is reason to question whether the unity-of-command doctrine (one boss) really operates in practice. The acceptance of staff recommendations and suggestions by lower management officials as authoritative and representative of the views of higher management creates a much more complicated

[11] Conrad M. Arensburg and Douglas McGregor, "Determination of Morale in an Industrial Company," *Applied Anthropology*, I (January-March, 1942), pp. 12-34. In a more recent study, Melville Dalton, *Men Who Manage* (New York: John Wiley & Sons, Inc., 1959), Chapter 3, the author found that "real" or "actual" organization and authority differed from prescribed or formal organization and authority.

organization than that portrayed by the simple line-and-staff (unity-of-command) type of structure.

The line-and-staff type of structure seems to suffer from some false assumptions: (1) staff specialists are able and willing to operate without formal authority, and (2) their advice, suggestions, and recommendations will readily be accepted and applied by lower line officials. Under the true line-and-staff arrangement as it works out in practice, the staff officer finds he has little power. His advice may go unheeded and unheralded because he has no authority to implement his decisions in the organization. The lower line officers may resent and reject staff advice because it threatens the sacred position of the line. Melville Dalton, after a study of three industrial plants, concluded that line officers fear staff innovations for a number of reasons.

> In view of their longer experience, presumably intimate knowledge of the work, and their greater remuneration, they fear being "shown up" before their line superiors for not having thought of the processual refinements themselves. They fear that changes in methods may bring personnel changes . . . and quite possibly reduce their area of authority. Finally, changes in techniques may expose forbidden practices and departmental inefficiency.[12]

These frustrations lead to a power struggle. The staff officer seeks more authority by reporting his frustrations and criticisms of line operations to higher line officials. Evidence indicates that staff officers, by virtue of their specialized knowledge, their continual contact with top management, and better education, are able to gain from top management the necessary functional authority over line operations. Some would bemoan this development because it violates the principle of unity of command and causes the lower line officials no end of confusion. However, as explained earlier, the overlapping and the various relationships are the basic ingredients for cooperation and coordination. Thus they should be encouraged, not circumscribed by the contrivances of those who draw organization charts.

Motivation

The doctrine of self-interest has long prevailed in traditional theory as well as in practice. The self-interest doctrine is illustrated

---

[12] Melville Dalton, "Conflicts Between Staff and Line Management Officers," *American Sociological Review*, XV (June, 1950), p. 349. Also see *Men Who Manage*, Chapter 4.

in one of Adam Smith's basic assumptions: Every individual is continually exerting himself to discover the most advantageous employment for whatever capital he can command. It does not take much study to realize that this same doctrine still prevails. As an example, note the view of the president of one of the world's largest corporations: "Of all the motivations to which the human mechanism responds, none has proved so powerful as that of financial gain . . . self enrichment is a dream which must rank with the most compelling forces in shaping the destinies of the human race." [13]

While the concept of self-interest based on financial reward is important in explaining human behavior, it presents an incomplete and inadequate picture of human needs. It says nothing of the desire to feel important, to be respected, and to have prestige. Of even greater significance for the study of organizations is the basic human desire to associate, to belong, or to be accepted as a member of a group. This need far exceeds monetary enrichment as a factor in motivating human behavior. Elton Mayo has said, "The desire to stand well with one's fellows, the so-called human instinct of association, easily outweighs the merely individual interest and the logical reasoning upon which so many spurious principles of management are based." [14] He concluded that "If one observes either industrial workers or university students with sufficient care and continuity, one finds that the proportionate number actuated by motives of *self-interest logically elaborated* is exceedingly small. They have relapsed upon self-interest when social association has failed them."

The self-interest thesis falls down in another important respect. It was stated earlier that people organize naturally on a basis other than the technical requirements of work. This organization has been called the social structure or the informal organization. By satisfying men's basic needs for association, friendship, and belonging, it provides the setting that makes them willing to cooperate. Furthermore, individual behavior is influenced by the customs, traditions, and pressures of the group. Thus, individual interests and desires become subordinated to those of the social organization.

In this respect, one is reminded of the Coch and French experiments, which dealt with the problem of employee resistance to change

[13] Crawford H. Greenewalt, *The Uncommon Man* (New York: McGraw-Hill Book Company, Inc., 1959), pp. 37-38.
[14] Elton Mayo, *The Social Problems of an Industrial Civilization* (Boston: Division of Research, Graduate School of Business Administration, Harvard University, 1945). This and the following quotation are from p. 43.

at the Harwood Manufacturing Corporation.[15] The company had tried to solve this problem with monetary allowances for transfers. It would seem from the self-interest doctrine that economic incentives such as a transfer bonus should create acceptance toward job changes and attitudes favorable to relearning after transfer. On the contrary, the researchers found the general attitudes toward job changes markedly negative. Analysis of the relearning curves of several hundred experienced operators, rating standard or better prior to change, showed that 38 per cent of the operators recovered to the standard unit rating; the other 62 per cent either became chronically substandard operators or quit during the relearning period.

Four different groups were studied. One group was merely told of planned changes; a second group was allowed to participate through representation in designing changes; and the two remaining groups participated fully. The researchers found that the total participation groups not only returned to the previous production rate faster than the other groups, but showed sustained progress toward a higher rate. Coch and French concluded that resistance to change in methods of work can be overcome by stimulating group participation in planning the changes.

This study dramatizes the significance of factors other than financial gain in motivating human behavior. First of all, the researchers observed that work standards, informally set by the groups, were important in determining output levels before and after the change. The nonparticipation group seemed to be governed by a standard set before the change, while the two total-participation groups were governed by a standard set when competition developed between them. However, it is important to note the authors' observation that a major determinant of the strength of these standards was probably the cohesiveness of the group. The power of the group over the members to increase or decrease productivity seemed to depend upon the amount of participation.

Secondly, changes in the social system that would be produced by technical or work changes may cause resistance to change. For example, the researchers indicated that employees would resist change because of the possibility of failure on the new job and a loss of status in the eyes of fellow employees. Furthermore, employees may

[15] Lester Coch and John R. P. French, Jr., "Overcoming Resistance to Change," *Human Relations*, I August, 1948), pp. 512-32.

resist because they are reluctant to leave friends or break social ties and are uncertain about being accepted in a new and different social system.

Thirdly, and most important for overcoming resistance and motivating human behavior, is the very nature of participation. Participation requires interaction, association, and involvement; as noted earlier, these are essential for cooperative effort.

Comparison and evaluation. The self-interest doctrine has prompted another organizational practice that is believed to stimulate greater productivity. This is the arrangement of individuals in a manner that permits their performance to be compared and evaluated. Rating and reward are based on how one individual compares to another doing similar work. Control is supposed to be easier because the organization has built-in standards for comparison and evaluation. Furthermore, it is believed that individuals will compete when they learn that they are being compared, and greater productivity will result.

Does competition increase production? Perhaps a more important first question is: Does competition stimulate cooperation? Competition is characterized by rivalry; one organization member strives against another for an objective of which he will be the principal beneficiary. Cooperation, on the other hand, is characterized by collaborative behavior; group members strive together for the attainment of a goal that is to be shared equally by each participating individual or unit. Cooperation, therefore, suppresses individual drives and goals so that common group objectives may be attained. An organization that promotes competition among its members will not have cooperation; it will have conflict. Group members have little reason to act jointly or collaborate with those against whom they are being measured or compared, or with whom they are competing.

Moreover, evidence indicates that a group will be more productive when its members are cooperative rather than competitive. Morton Deutsch, in an experiment designed to study the behavior of different groups (some cooperative, others competitive), found greater productivity among the cooperative groups.[16] Also, he found that the

---

[16] Morton Deutsch, "A Theory of Co-operation and Competition," *Human Relations*, II (April, 1949), pp. 129-52. and "An Experimental Study of the Effects of Cooperation and Competition Upon Group Process," *Human Relations*, II (July, 1949), pp. 199-231.

productivity was of a higher quality; these groups produced more fruitful ideas and showed more insight and understanding of problems. Measurement and reward of individual performance in the cooperative groups were made on the basis of group achievement. In this situation, each member received the same reward. Each member in the competitive groups was rated and rewarded on the basis of comparison with the efforts of the members in his group. In this situation, the reward each member received was different and was determined by his relative contribution to the solution of the problem with which the group was confronted. In contrast, the emphasis on group behavior in the cooperative groups produced the motivation, cooperation, and coordination that is necessary for the successful achievement of organization objectives.

Decentralization. Decentralization and "management by objectives" have often been offered by administrators and theorists as the best organizational arrangement for overcoming the suppressive aspects of a large organization while providing for the greatest motivation. Decentralization, as defined by its advocates, gives maximum authority and responsibility to the manager of each decentralized unit. Control by top management is exercised primarily by measuring end results and comparing performance with predetermined standards and the performance of other units. Once these measurements have been defined and applied, they are supposed to provide motivation. They are also used by top management as a basis for giving rewards such as promotions and bonuses. This practice may not only emphasize the wrong things in cooperative behavior, as explained earlier, but there is the possibility that measurements based on end results, such as earnings, production, costs, and sales, will encourage managers of decentralized units to adopt a pressure-oriented management. In other words, they may exercise pressure on the organization to meet the end results expected, while ignoring the quality of the human organization.

From a number of research studies, Rensis Likert has found that pressure-oriented supervision can achieve impressive short-run results. He reports that:

> . . . Putting pressure on a well-established organization to produce can yield substantial and immediate increases in productivity. *This increase is obtained, however, at a cost to the human assets of the organization.* In the company we studied, for example, the cost was clear: hostilities increased, there was greater reliance upon authority,

loyalties declined, and motivations to produce decreased while motivations to restrict production increased. In other words, the quality of the human organization deteriorated as a functioning social system.[17]

On the other hand, he has found that managers who are employee-centered and who support their subordinates will foster team spirit, greater productivity, and better employee satisfaction than pressure-oriented or production-centered managers.

Decentralization can, of course, provide the means for maximum utilization and development of the human resource as well as the basis for cooperative behavior. In contrast to organizations where there are many levels of supervision and elaborate systems of control, Worthy found that the flat type of structure with maximum decentralization develops self-reliance and initiative, and more fully utilizes individual capacities. At Sears, Roebuck and Co., for example, the typical store manager has forty-odd department managers reporting directly to him (thus violating the traditional limitations of the span-of-control doctrine), and has no alternative but to delegate decision-making authority to subordinates. When managers of departments were asked to manage, they learned to manage. Having to rely heavily on department managers, store managers at Sears took greater care in the selection, placement, and development of subordinates. Furthermore, Worthy says:

> This pattern of administration not only gets today's job done better, but permits the individual to grow and develop in a way that is impossible in more centralized systems. Furthermore, it contributes strongly to morale because employes work in an atmosphere of relative freedom from oppressive supervision and have a sense of individual importance and personal responsibility which other types of arrangements often deny them.[18]

It is important to note also that Worthy attributes much of the success of the Sears organization to its ability to meet the personal and social demands of its employees and not to any "logical technology, division of labor, or hierarchy of control." The study showed that both low output and low morale prevailed where jobs were broken down minutely. The most sustained efforts were exerted by employees who performed the more complete sets of tasks; these like-

---

[17] Rensis Likert, "Measuring Organizational Performance," *Harvard Business Review*, XXXVI (March-April, 1958), p. 48.

[18] James C. Worthy, "Organizational Structure and Employe Morale," *American Sociological Review*, XV (April, 1950), p. 178. Worthy also observes that not all individuals can function effectively in this type of arrangement and that the system will tend to weed them out.

wise exhibited the highest levels of morale and *esprit de corps*. Further, the research revealed that size of the organization unit was unquestionably a most important factor in determining the quality of employee relationships: the smaller the unit the higher the morale, and vice versa. It was clear that closer contact between executives and the rank and file in smaller organizations tends to result in friendlier, easier relationships.

In Perspective

The research results that have been described are not conclusive, of course, but they do suggest that many of the so-called principles of management and organization are preconceived and have little value as descriptions of behavior or as prescriptions for success. Though specialization has its advantages, it may create employee attitudes and demands that are injurious to the organization. Similarly, efforts to departmentalize according to the requirements of work—while necessary for some degree of order, planning and control—may create arrangements that are contrary to the requirements for cooperative behavior. Also, while the importance of economic and material incentives cannot be denied, reliance on them as the prime or only means of motivation may produce behavior that is contrary to organization needs such as loyalty, honesty, and initiative.

The administrator's task is a difficult one. According to what has been suggested here, the administrator must provide a structure that is loose enough to gain the motivational benefits from the natural social inclinations of organization members, yet he must impose the technical or formal organization and controls so necessary for efficient goal achievement.

As an example of organizing on the basis of natural tendencies, consider the way people associate in small informal groups. They are not only influenced by customs, traditions, and structure, but also receive many satisfactions from and are motivated by membership in these simple social systems.

It seems appropriate, therefore, that the formal organization be structured to take advantage of the benefits provided by smallness. Small, loosely structured organizational units, coupled with maximum employee involvement in organization affairs, can provide the cooperation necessary for successful performance. Seemingly, as the number of organizational units increases, the task of coordination and control will become more difficult. However, the converse may be true, depending on the number of levels, the directness of communication, the amount of interaction and involvement that takes place in an organization. The flat or horizontal type of arrangement (wide spans of supervision and few levels), where the lines of communication are simple and direct, can more readily be coordinated than the organization with many levels where communication is relatively slow and subject to many interpretations. The coordination problem becomes simpler when components of the organization operate autonomously. Left to operate on their own, decentralized units need only to be coordinated on end results.

It is important to re-emphasize that overspecialization and overfunctionalization in decentralized units can create not only the same problems as those experienced in the larger, more centralized organization but also more complex ones. The more a functional unit is defined as a separate entity, the greater the possibility that it will neglect its integrative purpose and be at odds with the over-all objectives of the decentralized unit as well as the whole organization. Furthermore, overfunctionalization may tend to make relationships at both the management and employee levels too formal. Cooperation may then be limited to that required by organization policy or the management hierarchy. Thus, the task of coordination becomes even more burdensome, increasing the necessity for elaborate systems and formal controls. This type of system, characterized by pressure-oriented management with undue regard for end results, can also be detrimental to the human organization. A loosely structured organization, where the emphasis is on teamwork and where there is a high degree of compatibility between goals of group members and the overall objectives of the organization, produces a human organization that is much more cooperative and productive.

Those who argue against organizing on the basis of human characteristics and tendencies emphasize the difficulties inherent in trying to diagnose human problems and in predicting human behavior. Diagnosis, of course, requires a much more learned and analytical administrator. He must be aware of and understand the research **on organization** behavior. He must be able to conduct and supervise research in his own organization concerning problems peculiar to his situation. With understanding and analysis, he should be better equipped to predict the outcome of anticipated courses of action and choose those that promise continued organizational success. Granted, this requires administration of a high order. It is, however, a necessity if organization in accord with reality is desired.

59. COMMENTS ON THE THEORY OF ORGANIZATIONS [1]

Herbert A. Simon [2]

This is an attempt to sketch in very rough form what seem to me some of the central concepts and problems of organization theory. In the first section I have tried to define the field of organization theory and to indicate with some care what justification there is for regarding it as a distinct area of theory, related to, but by no means identical with, the theory of small groups and the theory of social institutions. The comments in the second section on subject-matter areas simply spell out the implications, many of them perhaps obvious, of the central argument of the first section.

This paper is concerned with all kinds of organizations, and not simply with those that fall within the area of public administration. This definition of the scope of organization theory reflects my own conviction that there are a great many things that can be said about organizations in general, without specification of the particular kind of organization under consideration. Moreover, even if we were interested solely in governmental organization, I believe that a great deal can be learned from the comparison of their characteristics with those of other kinds of organizations, and from attempts to explain the similarities and differences that are found. Neither of these statements denies the existence of numerous and important phenomena that are peculiar to governmental organizations or the need for theory in public administration to deal with these phenomena.

The subject of organization theory

Human organizations are systems of interdependent activity, encompassing at least several primary groups and usually characterized, at the level of consciousness of participants, by a high degree of rational direction of behavior toward ends that are objects of

[1] From *The American Political Science Review* (December, 1952), pp. 1130-1139. Reprinted by permission of *The American Political Science Association*.
[2] Herbert A. Simon, Associate Dean and Professor of Administration, Graduate School of Industrial Administration, Carnegie Institute of Technology.

common acknowledgment and expectation. **Typical examples of organizations** are business firms, governmental administrative agencies, and voluntary associations like political clubs.

In complex enterprises the definition of the unit is not unambiguous—a whole agency, a bureau, or even a section in a large department may be regarded as an organization. In such a nest of Chinese blocks the smallest multi-person units are the primary groups; the largest are institutions (e.g., "the economic system," "the state") and whole societies. We will restrict the term "organization" to systems that are larger than primary groups, smaller than institutions. Clearly, the lower boundary is sharper than the upper.

Complexity in any body of phenomena has generally led to the construction of specialized theories, each dealing with the phenomena at a particular "level." Levels are defined by specifying certain units as the objects of study and by stating the propositions of theory in terms of intra-unit behavior and inter-unit behavior. (Cf. the sequence of elementary particle-atom-molecule in physics and the sequence: gene-chromosome-nucleus-cell-tissue-organ-organism in biology.)

Not every arbitrarily selected unit defines a suitable level for scientific study. The most important "unities" that make a level an appropriate one for theory construction and testing appear to be the following:

1. The units at the level in question should exhibit a high degree of internal cohesion relative to their dependence on each other. Under these circumstances we can discover generalizations about the internal properties of the individual units as quasi-isolated systems (e.g., propositions about communications patterns among component primary groups of an organization). We can also discover approximate generalizations about the relations between units as wholes (e.g., propositions about competition between two organizations).
2. The units should exhibit internal properties that are different (or depend on different mechanisms) from those that predominate in the internal properties of sub-units at the next level below (e.g., the determinants of the volume of communication between members of a single primary group).

These two tests are not intended as metaphysical assertions about "wholesome" or "emergent" properties, but simply as criteria determining whether, in fact, verifiable propositions can be constructed employing the units in question as approximations to the full complexity of nature. Even if at some stage in inquiry we should be able to reduce the propositions of theory at one level to those at the next lower level—as the theory of gases has been reduced to statistical mechanics—the former propositions would still retain their usefulness for purposes of application and economy of statement. Indeed, the value of both sets of propositions is enhanced by their translatability from the one to the other.

Human organizations would seem to qualify to a high degree as suitable units defining a level of analysis of systems of human behavior. With respect to the first criterion stated above, the most superficial observation shows that the boundaries between organizations have real behavioral significance, and that it is meaningful, in first approximation, to state propositions about the relations between organizations regarded as wholes. (I trust that I have made clear that no notion of "group mind" is implied in this last statement.)

With respect to the second criterion, I believe that enough is known about the psychological mechanisms that are primarily responsible for cohesion and interdependence in the primary group to show that these mechanisms cannot easily account for the corresponding phenomena in the larger organized aggregates; and that there are important organizational phenomena that do not have exact counterparts at the primary group level. A number of examples of these mechanisms and phenomena, which are central to organizations but absent from or of lesser importance to primary groups, will be given in the next section.

But why speak of a level of organization theory? Do we not need as many levels as there are structural layers between primary groups and institutions? I think not, because I do not believe that these various levels are distinguishable to an important extent in terms of the second criterion suggested above—i.e., there are no important new mechanisms to be discovered at these successive levels. The propositions of organization theory can probably be stated with systematic ambiguity so as to refer indifferently to the relations of divisions within a bureau or the relations of bureaus within a department. As small differences in degree begin to approach qualitative significance at the upper end of the scale, we have probably already reached the level of institutional theory. In the future, of course, the results of research may force us to revise this assumption.

Major problem areas

The study of organizations has hardly progressed to the point where a definitive list can be constructed of the major areas for research. The following list was arrived at primarily by considering which characteristics of organization—particularly those distinctive ones that identify the level of organization theory—require dissection and explanation. I have not tried to construct watertight categories, and it will become evident that several of the items represent different ways of looking at the same problem. Until we know what frames of reference are going to be the most useful for organization theory, it will surely be desirable to retain alternative frameworks, and to take considerable pains to develop means for translating from one framework to another.

1. *The process of decision-making in organization.* A language for the description of decision-making processes appears to offer considerable promise as a framework for the study of organizations. The central notion is that a decision can be regarded as a conclusion drawn (though not in any strict logical sense) from premises; and that influence is exercised by transmitting decisions, which are then taken as premises for subsequent decisions.

When the problem of influence is stated in these terms, our attention is called to some features that are not prominent in other formulations. We see, for example, that the process may depend not only upon interpersonal relations between influencer and influencee, but also upon the structure and accepted rules of transformation of the language employed by them. One can begin investigation here by posing such questions as how influence is transmitted in an organization between professional groups that employ different problem-solving technologies, e.g., accountants and engineers. Work on organization theory utilizing this framework could probably soon be related, in a mutually beneficial way, to research on the sociology of knowledge and on the psychology of the problem-solving process.[3]

2. *The phenomena of power in organizations.* A characteristic feature of the mutual influence of organization members upon one another is that this influence exhibits striking asymmetries—as, for

---

[3] The relation between organizational behavior and individual decision-making and problem-solving processes is discussed in the author's *Administrative Behavior* (New York: 1947), Chapter V. My researches in the decade since this connection occurred to me have steadily deepened my conviction that a very deep relation—not by any means analogical or metaphorical—exists between decision processes in organizations and the processes described by Gestalt psychologists in their study of the problem-solving process. Since the purpose of this paper is to state problems, not to solve them, I will have to be content here with this statement of my belief.

example, in the superior-subordinate relationship. These asymmetries appear to be what we have chiefly in mind in using such terms as "power" and "authority." The following are a number of important tasks in this area:

   a. A fully operational definition of power and methods for observing and measuring power relationships is not yet at hand, but would seem fundamental to the description of organizational behavior.

   b. More needs to be learned about the motivational basis of power in organizations, including the roles of sanctions, identifications, and attitudes of legitimacy in the acceptance of authority. Progress has been made in the study of the analogous phenomena in primary groups (e.g., work on leadership and on group morale),[4] but it is not obvious that the mechanisms of influence within the primary group tell all, or even most, of the story of influence processes in larger organized aggregates.

   c. In elaboration of the last point, the distinction between the "formal" and the "informal" in organizations appears to lie, in part, in differences between the psychological bases of cohesion that are involved. When we refer to power as formal, what we appear to mean is that internalized attitudes toward legitimate authority provide the motivation for acceptance of the relationship. While feelings about legitimacy undoubtedly play a role in primary group relationships, I would conjecture that they take on additional importance when they serve as a substitute for the immediate experience of approval and disapproval in face-to-face relationships.[5]

   d. Another mechanism that is important in the transmission of influence in organizations is the interlocking of primary groups through the dual membership of supervisory employees. In general, each supervisory employee is a member both of a group in which he is formal leader and of another in which his immediate superior is formal leader. The principal research problems here are to determine the behavior patterns that are adopted by executives in these "cross-pressure" situations; and, if there are several such patterns, to find what determines which one will be adopted. The same questions need to be answered with respect to the "staff" man who, because he is attached to a "line" unit, also has potential or actual membership

---

   [4] For an introduction to the literature, see Harold Guetzkow (Ed.), *Groups, Leadership, and Men* (Pittsburgh: 1951), and "Human Relations Research in Large Organizations," *Journal of Social Issues*, Vol. VII, No. 3 (whole number), 1951.

   [5] An overreaction from the excessive emphasis on formal organization in the earlier work on organization theory has led, in the last two decades, to an almost equally serious neglect of the importance of attitudes toward legitimacy. The same overreaction—from legalistic analyses of the state in terms of "sovereignty" to a pure power-politics approach to political behavior—has occurred in the other areas of political science as well. (Lasswell and Kaplan, for example, in *Power and Society* [New Haven: 1951] come very close to treating legitimate authority as an epiphenomenon that has no independent influence on the development of a system of political behavior.) With the reconstruction of "legitimacy" as a psychological, rather than a legal concept, the way is now open to reconciliation of the formal and the informal (legitimate authority and power) within a behavioral framework.

in two primary groups. It remains to be seen whether cross-pressures produce the same behavior in these organizational situations as in the other situations where they have been studied.

3. *Rational and non-rational aspects of behavior in organization.* Organizations are the least "natural," most rationally contrived units of human association. But paradoxically, the theory of an organization whose members are "perfectly rational" human beings (capable of unlimited adaptation) is very nearly a perfectly vacuous theory. It is only because individual human beings are limited in knowledge, foresight, skill, and time that organizations are useful instruments for the achievement of human purpose; and only because organized groups of beings are limited in ability to agree on goals, to communicate, and to cooperate that organizing becomes for them a "problem." [6]

Organization theory is centrally concerned with identifying and studying those limits to the achievement of goals that are, in fact, limits on the flexibility and adaptability of the goal-striving individuals and groups of individuals themselves. The entrepreneur of economic theory is limited only by constraints that are external to himself and his organization—the technology—and by the goal-striving of individuals whose interests are not identical with his. Administrative man is limited also by constraints that are part of his own psychological makeup—limited by the number of persons with whom he can communicate, the amount of information he can acquire and retain, and so forth. The fact that these limits are not physiological and fixed, but are instead largely determined by social and even organizational forces, creates problems of theory construction of great subtlety; and the fact that the possibilities of modifying and relaxing these limits may themselves become objects of rational calculation compounds the difficulties.

In this general area of research, promising suggestions as to the direction in which we might move are contained in oligopoly theory and game theory (formulation of the "outwitting" problem),[7] and in sociological speculations about the self-confirming prophecy. I would single out the following areas for special attention:

   a. Identification of the limits of rationality. We need a more complete and systematic taxonomy of the constraints, internal to the system

---

[6] This point is also elaborated upon in *Administrative Behavior*. See particularly pp. 39-41, 80-84, 96-102, 240-244.

[7] See John von Neumann and Oskar Morgenstern, *Theory of Games and Economic Behavior* (Princeton: 1944); especially Chapter ii.

of social action, that serve as limits to the attainment of goals. This would lead to empirical research on the questions: (i) under what circumstances particular contraints do and do not operate, including inter-cultural uniformities and differences, and (ii) under what circumstances the modification or removal of particular constraints becomes an object of rational calculation.

b. Theory of organizational innovation and change. Plans are regarded as "utopian" when their implementation would require changes in internal constraints that are thought to be unchangeable. Essentially, utopian plans are rejected because "you can't change human nature" in those respects that would be essential to achievement of the plan. Research is needed as to the criteria that are applied by human beings in planning situations to determine which of the behavior variates they will regard as variable (i.e., subject to rational determination), and which as fixed (i.e., constraints on goal attainment).

c. Reification of groups. The limit of human understanding in the presence of complex social structures leads human beings to construct simplified maps (i.e., theories or models) of the social system in which they are acting, and to behave as though the maps were the reality. To the extent that such maps are held in common, they must be counted among the internal constraints on rational adaptation. What we have just said applies, of course, to all systems of classification which, by determining when situations are "similar" and when "different," provide the individual with the social definition of the situation.

My earlier comments about the relation of "formal" organization to attitudes of legitimacy can be generalized in terms of this notion of social classification. The process of organizing involves, among other things, securing acceptance by the organization members of a common model that defines the situation for them, and provides them with roles and expectations of the roles of others, and with commonly accepted classificatory schemes. Attitudes of legitimacy probably provide a principal motivational base for the organizing process.

What is needed here is study of the factors that determine how an organization will be perceived by the persons in it, how the mode of perception affects behavior, and what the effects are of a greater or lesser degree of sharing of such perceptions.

4. *The organizational environment and the social environment.* Members of an organization generally come to it already equipped with the mores of the society in which it operates. To what extent can and do organizations develop and inculcate mores that are distinct from the mores of society? To what extent are there in a society generalized mores about behavior in organizations that pro-

vide the basis for the operation of the individual organizations in the society (e.g., generalized mores about superior-subordinate roles)?

Organization theory has been largely culture-bound through failure to attack this problem.[8] The theory of bureaucracy as developed by Max Weber and his followers represents the furthest progress in dealing with it. The historical data appealed to by the Weberians need supplementation by analysis of contemporary societies, advanced and primitive. A comparison of intra-cultural uniformity and variation in organization patterns with inter-cultural uniformity and variation would provide the evidence we need to determine to what extent the cooperative patterns in organizations are independent of the mores of cooperation of the society.

5. *Stability and change in organizations.* Any theory of the movement of a system of organizational behavior through time must take account of the apparent stability exhibited by organizations. From every evidence, this stability must be an extremely complex phenomenon. It may rest in part on the kinds of bonds, which we might refer to as non-rational, that have been observed in the primary group; it may depend in part on the rational calculations of members that their interests are served by the organization. It is because the role of these, and possibly other, bases of stability needs to be explored that I offer the following suggestions:

a. It is possible that systems in which the "non-rational" type of stabilizing mechanism predominates will behave in a qualitatively different fashion from those in which the "rational" type of stabilizing mechanism prevails. If, by construction of models embodying the two types of mechanisms, a qualitative difference could be deduced, the way would be open to empirical assessment of the importance of the two mechanisms.[9]

b. The work that has been done to date on the theory of the "rational" mechanism would suggest that stability in this case depends on certain relations between the aspiraton levels of members and their achievement levels. If so, we can draw on the psychological research that has already been done on these latter phenomena to design experiments and field studies that would test whether this is, indeed, one of the mechanisms involved in stability.

c. We may borrow the economists' term "entrepreneur" to refer to an individual who specializes as a broker in finding mutually accept-

[8] Cf. Robert A. Dahl, "The Science of Public Administration: Three Problems," *Public Administration Review*, Vol. VII (Winter, 1947), pp. 1-11.

[9] For further discussion of these mechanisms in the context of mathematical models, see Herbert A. Simon, "A Formal Theory of Interaction in Social Groups," *American Sociological Review*, Vol. XVII (April, 1952), pp. 202-211 and "A Comparison of Organization Theories," *Review of Economic Studies*, forthcoming.

able terms on which a group of persons can be induced to associate, or to continue association, in an organization.[10] We need research to determine what the role is of entrepreneurship, so defined, in the process of organizational activity. I conjecture that there are some close relationships both with the "middleman" notion, introduced in topic 2d, and with the kind of stability mechanisms discussed in 6b. Study is also needed of whether the uniqueness or nonuniqueness of the acceptable terms of association is an important determinant of the amount of authority that can be exercised over organization members. This relationship has been exhibited in some formal models, but it needs empirical verification.

d. The two topics just discussed get very close to the heart of the processes of bargaining and the formation of coalitions, insofar as these processes involve rational calculation of advantage.[11] The formal apparatus of game theory appears to provide an appropriate language of theory formulation; and, on the empirical side, some of the problems could probably be examined by means of relatively small-scale laboratory experiments.

e. Another aspect of survival and stability is the question of how organizations adapt themselves to uncertainty and incomplete information. In the past two decades this has been a favorite topic of economists,[12] but only in the last five years has there been much attention to the two aspects of greatest importance to organization theory: (i) reduction in the impact of uncertain events by retention of "flexibility" and (ii) the role of a stable social environment as a means of providing predictability to the individuals who are a part of it.

Under the first heading, research is needed as to the implications of particular ways of organizing behavior for the adaptability of the organization under changing, unpredictable circumstances. Under the second heading research is needed as to the existence and nature of mechanisms in social organizations that are analogous (in the sense of performing the same function) to the homeostatic mechanisms of organisms. Whether organizations are adaptive and possessed of homeostatic mechanisms is an empirical question, but one

[10] I believe that this usage does not do too much violence to the term, at least as it is used by economic historians and those concerned with the dynamic theory of the firm, e.g., Schumpeter. In terms of this definition, entrepreneurship is not peculiar to business concerns but is present (and, I believe, to the same important extent) in governmental and voluntary organizations as well. Examples of important entrepreneurs in governmental, nonprofit, and voluntary organizations would be William Alanson White, Gifford Pinchot, William Rainey Harper, Clarence Streit—the list is inexhaustible. Anyone attempting to describe the roles of men like Charles Merriam and Louis Brownlow within the fields of political science and public administration can hardly avoid using the concepts of entrepreneurial theory.

[11] The process that Philip Selznick refers to as "coöptation" fits in here also. See his *TVA and the Grass Roots* (Berkeley: 1949).

[12] See the excellent survey of the economic literature in Kenneth J. Arrow, "Alternative Approaches to the Theory of Choice in Risk-Taking Situations," *Econometrica*, Vol. XIX (October, 1951) pp. 404-37.

which, in all probability, can be answered in the affirmative. But the important theoretical issue is the nature of the mechanisms—a question that is not solved by reference to the organismic analogy. Moreover, while primary groups and social institutions may also exhibit homeostasis and adaptivity, there is no reason to believe that the mechanisms involved are the same ones that produce these phenomena in organizations. Functional equivalence does not imply structural equivalence.[13]

6. *Specialization and the division of work.* The division of work and the design of the organizational communications system have in the past been the central concerns of persons interested in organization theory for purposes of application. The question usually asked is: "How do we divide the work, and what channels of communication do we establish in order to operate efficiently?"

For purposes of research, the question is more properly stated: "What are the consequences for organizational activity of dividing the work one way rather than another, or employing one set of communications channels rather than another?"

The last half of the question (communications) is best answered in terms of the frames of reference of topics 1 and 2. The subject of the division of work requires further comment. We are considering, of course, not only the question of specialization of the individual organization member, but also the allocation of tasks to whole organization units—in fact, it is the question of specialization among the larger aggregates rather than specialization within the primary group that is the proper concern of organization theory. We are equally concerned with "vertical" specialization, i.e., allocation of decision-making functions to various status and authority levels in an organization—and with "horizontal" specialization—i.e., fixing the jurisdictional boundaries of coordinate organizational units.

    a. Current theories of specialization in organization (excluding the "human relations" approach to the primary group) are largely derived, via the scientific management movement, from Adam Smithian notions that specialization is a means to efficiency, and hence to effective competition. There has been little examination of the alternative Durkheimian idea that specialization is a means of

[13] This last proposition is an important part of our justification, in the first part of this memorandum, for the study of "levels." The issues involved are discussed with great sophistication by T. C. Schneirla, "The 'Levels' Concept in the Study of Social Organization in Animals," in John J. Rohrer and Muzafer Sherif (Eds.), *Social Psychology at the Crossroads* (New York: 1951).

protection from competition.[14] The research problem suggested by the contrast is to examine in what respects specialization (and what kinds of specialization) increases organizational stability; in what respects it jeopardizes stability; and to what extent these considerations enter into decisions about specialization. The problem is also related to 5e in that certain forms of specialization may make an organization less dependent on what other organizations do, and hence may provide a means for dealing with uncertainty.

b. The consequences of specialization depend on the constraints discussed in topic 3. It is an important question as to how far specialization is determined by constraints external to the organization—the technology of its activities—and how far it is determined by internal constraints—the psychological and sociological limitations upon rational adaptation. (The situation is even a bit more complicated because the technology in the sense of the physical, chemical, biological, etc., processes involved in the organization's activity—is not independent of the state of technological knowledge, and the latter may, in turn, be interdependently related to the forms of social specialization that prevail.) In almost every city, the fire department is a recognized organization unit, and in almost every steel mill, the blast furnace department. Here are examples of specialization that appear to be dictated by the technology; the units are "natural" in this sense. On the other side we find units that are "natural" in the sense of being specialized to handle socially-defined purposes, which, in turn, depend on the processes of reification discussed in 3c (e.g., the Children's Bureau). Research into the theory of specialization making use of the framework suggested in topic 3 is needed to clarify these issues, and to formulate and test propositions about the consequences of specialization.

c. The relationship between specialization and the internal constraints on rational adaptation is two-way: the division of work may be determined, partly or wholly, by such constraints; it will in turn create constraints. That is, the form of specialization will be a major determinant of the frames of reference, skills and knowledge, identifications and foci of attention of organization members. Probably this is the most promising viewpoint from which to tackle the nonrational aspects of formation of group identifications (or "interests" in the political sense) and the effects of such identifications upon intergroup processes (cf. 5d on the "rational" aspects).

d. Problems of vertical specialization are closely related to topics 1 and 2. In applied organization theory, the questions are usually stated in terms of "centralization" and "decentralization."

This list of research areas illustrates, I think, that the phenomena of organization constitute an important level of theory—a level that is encompassed neither by the usual conceptualizations of small-group processes nor by those of the more macroscopic analyses of cultures and institutions.

[14] My former colleague, Victor A. Thompson, first pointed out to me the significance of this distinction.

The characteristics of this level that give it its particular "flavor" are the following: (*a*) its focus is on relations among interlocking or non-interlocking primary groups rather than on relations within primary groups; (*b*) it is largely concerned with situations where *zweckrationalität* plays a large role relative to *wertrationalität* (as compared with the study either of small groups or of cultures); (*c*) in these situations the scheme of social interaction becomes itself partly a resultant of the rational contriving of means and the conscious construction and acting out of "artificial" roles; and (*d*) explanation of phenomena at this level requires the closest attention to the fluid boundaries of rational adaptation, including the important boundaries imposed by group frames of reference, perceptual frameworks, and symbolic techniques. In contrast to these characteristics, the level of primary group theory must pay much more attention to the personal values that are emergent from the process of group interaction itself, the acculturalization of individuals to the group, and the particular forms of cohesion that arise out of face-to-face interaction and individual sensitivity to group approval.

It would be wrong, of course, to insist that none of the primary group phenomena are relevant to intergroup relations, or vice-versa. Nevertheless, the important work that has been done on small groups in the past generation—much of it involving the observation of groups that were part of larger organizational structures—has contributed very modestly to the solution of the problems of organization theory.

BIBLIOGRAPHY, CHAPTER XVI

ADAMS, RICHARD N., and JACK T. PREISS. *Human Organization Research.* Homewood, Illinois: The Dorsey Press, 1960.

ARGYRIS, CHRIS. *Understanding Organizational Behavior.* Homewood, Illinois: The Dorsey Press, 1960.

BLAKE, ROBERT R., and JAMES MOUTON. "Managerial Grid," *Advanced Management* (September, 1962), 12-15.

FISCH, GERALD G. "Line-Staff Is Obsolete," *Harvard Business Review* (September-October, 1961), 67-79.

GUEST, ROBERT H. *Organizational Change: The Effect of Successful Leadership.* Homewood, Illinois: The Dorsey Press, 1962.

HAIRE, M. *Modern Organization Theory.* New York: John Wiley & Sons, Inc., 1959.

LEIBENSTEIN, HARVEY. *Economic Theory and Organization Analysis.* New York: Harper and Brothers, 1960.

MARCH, JAMES G., and H. A. SIMON. *Organization.* New York: John Wiley & Sons, 1959.

RUBENSTEIN, ALBERT H., and C. J. HABERSTROH. *Some Theories of Organization.* Homewood, Illinois: The Dorsey Press, 1960.

SHULL, FREMONT, JR. "The Nature and Contribution of Administrative Models and Organizational Research," *Journal of the Academy of Management* (August, 1962), 124-138.

STIEGLITZ, HAROLD. "Optimizing Span of Control," *Management Record* (September, 1962), 25-29.

SUOJANEN, WAINO W. "The Span of Control—Fact or Fable?" *Advanced Management* (November, 1955), 5-13.

THOMSON, JAMES D., et al., *Comparative Studies in Administration.* Pittsburgh: University of Pittsburgh Press, 1959.

URWICK, LYNDALL F. "The Manager's Span of Control," *Harvard Business Review* (May-June, 1956), 39-47.

WICKESBERG, A. K., and T. C. CRONIN. "Management by Task Force," *Harvard Business Review* (November-December, 1962), 111-118.

Chapter XVII
Authority and Staff

In larger organizations which have developed specialized sub-organizations to aid management in its decision making, it is essential that answers be provided to questions concerning the division and placement of formal authority.

The nature of authority in organizations is examined first in this chapter in the article by Robert Tannenbaum. Tannenbaum's article provides a background for the more specialized attention given to the line-staff authority problems in the article by Louis A. Allen and to the nature of staff activity in the article by J. Lewis Powell.

The articles in this chapter examine the horizontal division of formal authority in organizations. Chapter XVIII discusses the division of authority vertically, or at different levels, within an organization.

60. THE NATURE
OF AUTHORITY [1]

Robert Tannenbaum [2]

*   *   *

A superior is able directly to affect the behavior of a subordinate if he possesses authority with respect to that subordinate.[3] [Authority] is commonly viewed as originating at the top of an organizational hierarchy and flowing downward therein through the process of delegation. When viewed in this way, it was called "formal authority." In reality, effective authority does not originate in this manner.

The real source of the authority possessed by an individual lies in the acceptance of its exercise by those who are subject to it. It is the subordinates of an individual who determine the authority which he may yield. Formal authority is, in effect, nominal authority. It becomes real only when it is accepted. An individual may possess formal authority, but such possession is meaningless unless that authority can be effectively used. And it can be so used only if it is accepted by that individual's subordinates.[4] Thus, to be effective, formal authority must coincide with authority determined by its acceptance. The latter defines the useful limits of the former.

The concept "authority," then, describes an interpersonal relationship in which one individual, the subordinate, accepts a decision made by another individual, the superior, permitting that decision directly

[1] From "Managerial Decision-Making," *Journal of Business*, Vol. XXIII, pp. 22-39. Copyright 1950, University of Chicago. Reprinted by permission of the University of Chicago.

[2] Robert Tannenbaum, Associate Professor of Personnel Management and Industrial Relations, Associate Research Economist and Head of the Human Research Group, Institute of Industrial Relations, U. C. L. A.

[3] For purposes of this discussion a "superior" will be defined as one who has effective authority over another, and a "subordinate" will be defined as one who is subject to the effective authority of another.

[4] The term "accept" is used here, in its various forms, to include acquiescence as well as active assent or approval. The import of this will become clear in the discussion which follows.

to affect his behavior.[5] An individual always has an opportunity, with respect to a decision made by another directly to affect his behavior, to accept or reject that decision. If he accepts it, he thereby grants authority to its formulator and, for this matter, places himself in the position of a subordinate. As a subordinate, the individual permits his behavior directly to be affected by the decisions of his superior. If the individual rejects the decision, he does not grant authority to its formulator. Thus the sphere of authority possessed by a superior is defined for him by the sphere of acceptance of his subordinates.

If this line of analysis is to be followed it must be recognized that an individual may possess authority in a given situation without having formal authority. In other words, the channels through which effective authority is exercised do not have to follow the lines of formal organization within a given complex. And these channels may extend outside the given complex.

Determinants of the acceptance of authority

Since the sphere of authority possessed by a superior is defined for him by the sphere of acceptance of his subordinates, it is important to inquire into the factors which determine this latter sphere. Why do subordinates accept, rather than reject, the authority of their superiors?[6] In answering this question, it must be remembered that the choice between acceptance or rejection involves a decision between two alternatives. This choice is made only after the individual has appraised, to the extent possible, the consequences attendant upon each of these alternatives.

[5] Many writers have similarly defined the concept of authority. Some examples of these definitions follow: "Authority can thus be defined as a behavioristic concept describing a relationship between subject and object in which the subject takes an acquiescent attitude to behavior prescribed by the object on the basis of power either possessed by or delegated to the object" (Abram Kardiner, *The Individual and His Society* [New York: Columbia University Press, 1939], p. 40); ". . . the power which operates in and through an authority relation is always in some measure the joint creation of the bearer and subjects of authority. . . . The power of the bearer of authority grows out of the acceptance of his direction and guidance as bearer of authority by the subjects of his authority, not the other way round" (Kenneth D. Benne, *A Conception of Authority* [New York: Bureau of Publications, Teachers College, Columbia University, 1943], pp. 149f.); "Authority is the character of a communication (order) in a formal organization by virtue of which it is accepted by a contributor to or 'member' of the organization as governing the action he contributes; that is, as governing or determining what he does or is not to do so far as the organization is concerned" (Barnard, *op. cit.*, p. 163); " 'Authority' may be defined as the power to make decisions which guide the actions of another. It is a relationship between two individuals, one 'superior,' the other 'subordinate.' The superior frames and transmits decisions with the expectation that they will be accepted by the subordinate. The subordinate expects such decisions, and his conduct is determined by them" (Simon, *op. cit.*, p. 125).

[6] This question has been specifically, though inadequately, dealt with by Barnard, *op. cit.*, pp. 164-71, and by Simon, *op. cit.*, pp. 130-34.

An individual will accept an exercise of authority if the advantages accruing to him from *accepting* plus the disadvantages accruing to him from *not accepting* exceed the advantages accruing to him from *not accepting* plus the disadvantages accruing to him from *accepting*; and, conversely, he will not accept an exercise of authority if the latter factors exceed the former. Thus a decision to accept or reject a given exercise of authority results from a relative evaluation of the consequences—both positive and negative—attendant upon the choice of each of the competing behavior alternatives.[7] To understand better the factors underlying a decision to accept or reject, it will be helpful to consider in more detail the nature of the positive and negative consequences—the advantages and disadvantages—related to each behavior alternative.

The possible advantages accruing to an individual from accepting a given exercise of authority are many. While the following listing of types of advantages is by no means complete, it will serve the end of indicating the variety of such advantages: (1) By accepting an exercise of authority, an individual is able thereby to contribute to the attainment of an enterprise purpose which he recognizes as being good.[8] In the preceding article it was pointed out that group activity involves the specialized service-contributions of individuals which must be co-ordinated in the attainment of an enterprise purpose. Such co-ordination can be achieved only through the exercise of authority on the part of the individual who heads the group.[9] An awareness of this necessity leads individuals who recognize the enterprise purpose as being good to accept authority. (2) By accepting an exercise of authority, an individual may thereby attain the approbation of his fellow-workers. For most individuals, social acceptance is a strong motivating factor. (3) By accepting an exercise of authority, an individual may thereby obtain rewards from his superior. These rewards might be increased pay, promotion, prestige, opportunity for

[7] With respect to a decision to accept an exercise of authority, Roberto Michels has this to say: ". . . submission to authority may result either from a deliberate recognition of it as good or from an acquiescence in it as inevitable, to be endured permanently or temporarily with skepticism, indifference or scorn, with fists clenched but in the pockets" ("Authority," *Encyclopaedia of the Social Sciences,* ed. E. R. A. Seligman, Vol. II [1930]).

[8] See James D. Mooney and Alan C. Reiley, *The Principles of Organization* (New York: Harper & Bros., 1939), pp. 177f.; Henry C. Metcalf and L. Urwick (eds.), *Dynamic Administration: The Collected Papers of Mary Parker Follett* (New York: Harper & Bros., 1940), p. 59; and L. Urwick, *The Elements of Administration* (New York: Harper & Bros., 1943), pp. 94f.

[9] ". . . all men engaged in common enterprises, the most mature, rationally autonomous, self-directing persons among others, need commonly accepted rules, norms, or principles of order to guide and direct the processes of their cooperation" (Benne, *op. cit.,* p. 158).

increased personal power, and the like. (4) By accepting an exercise of authority, an individual may thereby be acting in accordance with his own moral standards. Some individuals believe they ought (that it is right for them) to obey duly constituted authorities. (5) By accepting an exercise of authority, an individual may thereby avoid the necessity of accepting responsibility. Chester I. Barnard has commented on this point as follows:

> . . . if an instruction is disregarded, an executive's risk that the individual cannot and usually will not take unless in fact his position is at least as good as that of another with respect to correct appraisal of the relevant situation. Most persons are disposed to grant authority because they dislike the personal responsibility which they otherwise accept, especially when they are not in a good position to accept it. . . .[10]

(6) Finally, by accepting an exercise of authority, an individual may thereby be responding to the qualities of leadership exhibited by his superior.[11] In part, this point overlaps some of the preceding ones, but it also includes a recognition of the fact that some individuals obey others out of respect for their age, superior ability or experience, character, reputation, personality, and the like.

An individual, after considering the advantages to him, may often decide to accept an exercise of authority. Such a choice would be a free one—one not involving compulsion. But he might also decide to accept an exercise of authority even though the advantages attendant thereto, taken alone, would not be sufficient to induce him to accept. In this case his decision would be compelled by another or others; he would simply acquiesce to authority because of the disadvantages accruing to him from not accepting. When an individual is forced by another to do something against his will—something he otherwise would not have done—coercion is involved. Horace M. Kallen has defined and elaborated upon the concept of coercion in these terms:

> Coercion as a trait of human behavior may be said to obtain wherever action or thought by one individual or group is compelled or restrained by another. To coerce is to exercise some form of physical or moral compulsion . . .
> . . . When it [coercion] is direct we call it physical; when indirect, moral. Both compel or restrain conduct by *force majeure*. . . .

[10] *Op. cit.*, p. 170.

[11] ". . . in general leadership implies a following whose behavior is the result of a conscious consideration of the leader's personality, of its own interests and of the anticipated social consequences" (Richard Schmidt, "Leadership," *Encyclopaedia of the Social Sciences*, Vol. IX [1930]).

> Most social coercion is indirect; it only threatens force. . . . But all coercions involve fear of penalties. Without belief that the coercer can and will impose penalties no indirect coercion can be effective. . . .[12]

There are numerous coercive devices the actual use or fear of which is often effective in obtaining an acquiescence to authority. Some examples of these are social disapprobation, expulsion from a group (ostracism), formal disciplinary action, exertion of economic pressure (monopolistic and monopsonistic power), torture, imprisonment, taking of a life, etc.

In order to understand the full implications of coercion, it will be useful briefly to digress in order to contrast this concept with the concept of sanctions. In every social group there are certain modes of behavior which are generally disapproved. The reactions of approval and of disapproval represent general formal or informal social consensus. Now in every group there are some individuals who have urges toward nonconformity. Sanctions are devices used to induce these individuals to conform to the group will. Sanctions may be positive or negative in character. Positive sanctions are the social reward of conformity, and negative sanctions are the social consequences of nonconformity.[13] All negative sanctions are coercive in their effect—they are used to impel an individual to conform against his will to group norms of behavior. Heads of groups who impose negative sanctions on recalcitrant individuals have the support of the vast majority of the group in so doing. But heads of groups might also induce conformance to behavior patterns which are not generally approved by the group. Here coercion is involved but not negative sanctions. Furthermore, one individual with respect to another individual or a group or one group with respect to another group or an individual outside the group might induce conformance to specified behavior patterns through the use of coercion. But here again negative sanctions are not involved. Thus coercion includes more than negative sanctions. The latter term is applicable only when general group consensus is involved. When the head of a group uses coercion not based upon general group consensus, he is acting in an autocratic or arbitrary manner.

In raising the question as to whether an individual will accept an exercise of authority, only the advantages accruing to him from

---

[12] "Coercion," *Encyclopaedia of the Social Sciences*, Vol. III (1930).

[13] The discussion of sanctions to this point is based upon R. M. MacIver, *Society: Its Structure and Changes* (Toronto: Macmillan Co. of Canada, Ltd., 1931), pp. 248-57; and A. R. Radcliffe-Brown, "Sanctions, Social," *Encyclopaedia of the Social Sciences*, Vol. XIII (1930).

accepting plus the disadvantages to him from not accepting have thus far been considered. But he will accept only if these factors exceed the advantages accruing to him from not accepting plus the disadvantages accruing to him from accepting, as has previously been pointed out. These latter factors, however, are the same in nature as the former ones. An illustration should suffice to make this clear. An employee may be a member of a group most of whose members are restricting output in opposition to a wage-incentive plan. The implied or explicit order of the employee's boss is that each employee should produce the maximum output reasonably possible. Should the employee accept this exercise of authority, or should he restrict his output (i.e., accept the authority of the work group)? If he accepts the authority of his boss, he can earn more, he may get a desired promotion, etc. If he does not accept, he may be demoted or fired. On the other hand, if he does not accept, he may receive the approbation of his fellow-workers, additional status in the group, etc. And if he accepts, he may receive the disapprobation of his fellow-workers or be ostracized from the group. His decision to accept or not accept the boss's exercise of authority will be based upon an evaluation of these and similar relevant consequences.

In order to make complete this discussion of the determinants of the acceptance of authority, one further point calls for attention. Authority is often accepted where conscious processes are not involved. Such acceptance does not entail a conscious choice between acceptance and rejection. Rather, it is reflective of unconscious, habitual processes. Authoritative pronouncements which are unconsciously accepted lie within what Barnard has called the "zone of indifference." [14]

Authority versus influence

The use of authority is one means of affecting the behavior of another. The subordinate who accepts an exercise of authority does not critically evaluate the behavior alternatives underlying the decision of his superior. He accepts the decision and permits it directly to affect his behavior. But there is another means by which one individual can affect the behavior of another. In this case the latter individual is free to make those decisions which directly affect his

---

[14] *Op. cit.*, pp. 167-69. Cf. Simon, *op. cit.*, pp. 12 and 133f. In my judgment, Simon misinterprets Barnard's concept of a zone of indifference when he holds it to be the equivalent of what he calls the "zone of acceptance." In fact, this latter zone is more inclusive and is equivalent to what I have referred to above as the "sphere of acceptance."

own behavior. But, since he never has complete knowledge with respect to all relevant behavior alternatives and to all the consequences related thereto and since the ends toward which he directs his behavior are subject to change, it is possible for another individual or for others to provide him with information which can affect his decisions. This additional information simply adds to or changes the relevant factors (means and ends) which he otherwise would take into account in arriving at his decision. It might or might not result in a decision different from the one that would otherwise be made. In any event, the individual, taking the additional information into account, freely arrives at his own decision. Such provision of relevant information by one person to another (who then takes that information into account in arriving at a decision) will be called "influence." [15] The individual who exercises influence may offer advice, make suggestions, enter into discussions, persuade, use propaganda, and the like; but he does not exercise authority.[16] In so doing, he indirectly affects the behavior of another.

*   *   *

Managers make decisions to affect, both directly (through authority) and indirectly (through influence), the behavior of their subordinates. And, likewise, others make decisions which similarly affect the behavior of managers.

---

[15] No available term is completely satisfactory to connote the meaning here intended. The term used seems most closely to conform to that meaning.

[16] Cf. Gordon, *op. cit.*, pp. 150f., and Simon, *op. cit.*, pp. 126-28. It is recognized that the precise dividing line between authority and influence is sometimes difficult to draw.

61. THE LINE-STAFF
RELATIONSHIP [1]

Louis A. Allen [2]

Inadequate working relationships between line and staff departments are one of the most potent sources of friction and inefficiency in many companies. Frequently staff people are confused and uncertain as to what they are supposed to do and what right they have to do it. Just as often, line managers look upon staff specialists as unnecessary impediments in the otherwise simple and efficient administration of production operations.

Unfavorable effects are usually obvious. Decision-making is often slowed to a feeble walk in the unending hassle between line and staff. There is constant jockeying for position and authority. Important deadlines may be missed. And coordination is often inadequate.

The picture is not all black, however. In many companies, staff and line work together as an integrated team. As a result, line management is supported by a highly effective group of experts who are on call to help with the complicated problems that arise in the highly technical operation of modern industry.

Even where line and staff differences are most troublesome, there is no question about the necessity of staff. Basically, the problem is one of how staff and line can learn to work together in helping the company achieve its goals. But preliminary to the solution of this problem is an understanding of what line and staff mean and what they do.

DEFINING LINE AND STAFF

Every company is organized for a specific purpose. This may be to make, invent, or sell a product or service, or any combination of these. But whether it be production, sales, research, or finance, the line component is the one that has direct responsibility for accomplishing the objectives of the enterprise. Organizationally, the line is the chain of command that extends from the board of directors through

[1] From *Management Record*, Vol. XVII, No. 9 (September, 1955), pp. 346-349, 374-376. Reprinted by permission of the *Management Record*.
[2] Louis A. Allen, Division of Personnel Administration, National Industrial Conference Board, Inc., 1954.

the various delegations and redelegations of authority and responsibility to the point where the primary activities of the company are performed. The line, then, refers to those departments that have the power to initiate and carry through to conclusion the basic activities of the company.

"Line" is identified by the objectives of the company

Since the line is directly responsible for accomplishing the objectives of the company, it follows that line elements can be identified most accurately in terms of these objectives.[3]

To the extent that objectives of companies differ, line activities also differ. For example, a steel company has as its primary objectives the manufacture of quality steel products and their sale at a profit. The line functions in this instance are production and sales.

An oil company is organized to develop sources of crude oil and natural gas, to manufacture petroleum products and by-products, to market these products, and to operate transportation facilities. The line departments are production, manufacturing, transportation, and marketing.

In a department store chain success depends as much upon buying as selling. Both the buying or purchasing and the sales functions are line.

Some functions are line in one company, staff in another

There is little uniformity as to what is line and what is staff from one company to another. For example, one eastern company is organized primarily to manufacture and sell machinery. Engineering the product and providing service to customers are important, but only as a means of selling more effectively. Consequently, in this case, manufacturing and sales are line. Engineering operates in an advisory capacity to the line, and the service function supplies parts, training and assistance to the franchised dealers who service the machines. It is noteworthy that in the organizations of the franchised dealers, sales and service are the line functions.

These same functions receive different emphasis in an aircraft manufacturing company. Here the enterprise can succeed only if it continually invests a good share of its effort in the complex problems

[3] See "Organization Planning," *Management Record*, October, 1954, p. 372.
NOTE: A detailed analysis of staff and line relationships in terms of the philosophy and practice of seventy-two leading companies was published in THE CONFERENCE BOARD'S *Studies in Personnel Policy* series.

of design and engineering of new aircraft, and the testing, servicing and modification of the aircraft it sells. In this organization, the line departments are engineering, manufacturing, sales and service.

The finance function is considered staff in many companies; in others it is line. In a typical manufacturing company, for example, the finance department operates as a specialized staff department, with responsibility for financing, accounting, and reporting or budgeting and control of expenditures. The performance of these duties is a staff service to other units of the company and does not involve the exercise of authority by the finance department over line departments. Necessary uniformity as to accounting, budgeting and reporting procedures is secured through company policy and procedures, which are issued by top line management.

In some companies, however, finance is line. In an eastern manufacturing company, for instance, about half of the company's business comes from products which are leased to customers instead of being sold outright. Because most lessors pay their rental on a usage basis, the accounting group within the finance department is directly concerned with a substantial amount of the company's income. Finance is therefore set up as a line operation, with authority to make final decisions as to leasing arrangements, in the same fashion that manufacturing and sales have the last word in their functions.

Research is line in some companies, staff in others. Again, the reason for the difference can be found in the objectives of the company. In a typical case, research is responsible for providing advice and recommendations aimed at the improvement and maintenance of products and the development of new products. Manufacturing and sales are the line departments in this case.

Another company, however, considers research of equal importance with sales and manufacturing in achieving its objectives. This company believes its future success depends upon a steady flow of new products and processes. Therefore, it has established research as a line department and gives its research director a place comparable to that of the directors of manufacturing and sales.

Some functions are both line and staff in the same company

A function may be both line and staff in the same company. For example, in a decentralized business, the chief executive officer may need specialists in sales and production to advise him on matters of over-all planning, policy making and control. Sales and production thus are specialized staff departments at the corporate level. However, within the operating divisions of this same company, sales is responsible for marketing and distributing the product. At this point it is line. Since production handles the manufacturing in the plants, this function is also line at the operating level.

What Staff Is

Once a line manager's job grows beyond a certain size, he needs help to perform it properly. Staff refers to those elements of the organization which provide advice and service to the line. Actually, staff is best thought of in terms of a relationship. When one *position* exists primarily to provide advice and service to another, it is in a staff relationship. And if the work of a *department* is predominantly that of advice and service to one or more other departments, it is classified as a *staff department*. Staff includes all elements of the organization which are not line.

It is to be noted that a line, or chain of command, runs from the top to the bottom of each staff department, just as it does within each line component. Some positions within the staff department may exist primarily to provide advice and service to other positions within the same department. In this case there is an internal staff and line relationship. For example, in the personnel department in one company the line runs from the manager to the section heads of management development, labor relations and compensation. The personnel department also has a personnel research section which conducts library research and surveys for the management development, labor relations and compensation sections—not for the company as a whole. The personnel research section is staff to the line of the specialized staff department. In the same way, an assistant to the personnel manager is staff to him.

Part of the confusion in identifying staff and in determining its proper relationship to line stems from the failure to recognize that managers need help of two different kinds and that two types of staff provide this help.

Personal staff refers to the positions created primarily to aid the manager in carrying out those parts of his job he cannot, or does not wish to, delegate to others. These reserved responsibilities, which the manager performs personally may include over-all planning for his function, policy making and interpretation, co-ordination, human relations and control.[4]

---

[4] See "The Art of Delegation," *Management Record* (March, 1955), p. 92.

Specialized staff helps the line by performing work that requires special skills or more objectivity than the line can normally be expected to possess. This may include help with accounting, personnel, engineering, purchasing, medical and other problems. Work of this type is so highly specialized that it can be delegated as a separate function to the appropriate specialist.

Personal staff

Personal staff may consist of three kinds of assistants: [5]

> Line assistants
> Staff assistants
> General staff assistants.

Line Assistants. The line assistant assists his chief in the whole range of his duties, except where a more limited delegation is made. He helps the principal to manage the function; that is, he assists with over-all planning, organizing, direction, coordination and control. Although the line assistant is in the direct chain of command, he is staff to his superior because he exists only to advise, counsel and act *for* his principal. The line assistant has no responsibility apart from that of his principal; therefore, he has none to redelegate.

Staff Assistants. The staff assistant is also commonly known as the "assistant to." He usually serves in a much more restricted fashion than does the line assistant. The staff assistant is differentiated from the line assistant in that he has no authority over other employees, except in the case of special assignments. Neither does he take over the department in the absence of his principal.

The work of the staff assistant varies widely from one company to another. He may be anything from a glorified secretary to a vice-president. His duties may range from opening the mail and answering the telephone to sitting in on board of directors meetings of subsidiary companies with power to speak for the president of the company.

Staff assistants may also be called "administrative assistants," "special assistants," and "executive assistants," depending upon the kind of work that they actually do.

General Staff Assistants. Some companies use a general staff, which is an adaptation of army practice. This is, in reality, a group of staff assistants functioning at a high level. These staff assistants

---

[5] For a detailed discussion of assistants and how they can be used most effectively, see "The Uses of Assistants," *Management Record* (May, 1955), p. 174.

usually serve as advisors to top management in specified areas. The general staff is used in addition to the regular corporate specialized staff.

Specialized staff

In contrast to personal staff, the specialized staff advises and serves all line and other staff departments in a functional capacity. For instance, the staff finance department reporting to the president is available not only to advise and serve him, but also to serve other departments that need help in financial matters. The specialized staff thus becomes a reservoir of special knowledge, skills and experience which the entire organization can use. The specialized staff has two identifying characteristics:

1. It has no authority over other parts of the organization. The specialized staff advises and serves; it does not direct.
2. It can be used by all line and staff units of the organization, within the limits of company policy or practice. The activities of each specialized staff department are restricted to one specialized area or function. This differentiates it from the personal staff, which exists primarily to help one executive in carrying out his reserved responsibilities.

The specialized staff assists the line and other staff functions in two ways. First, it performs advisory activities—providing advice, counsel, suggestions, and guidance. Second, it performs service activities—specified work *for* the line, which may include making decisions that the line has asked it to make.

Advisory Activities. Specialized staff managers are, by definition, best qualified to advise the line and other staff managers in matters having to do with their specialties. The advice offered by staff may be of several different kinds.

Staff may offer planning advice to managers by undertaking study, research, analysis and the development of alternative courses of action. These can be of invaluable assistance to the line manager who has to make a final decision. This advice may include planning objectives, policies and procedures which will apply to and govern the operations of the line departments. It may cover the explanation and interpretation of objectives, plans and policies to line and other staff departments.

Staff may offer advice as to how decisions can best be put into practice. It may advise the line on planning performance controls.

This advice may include assistance in establishing standards or yard-sticks, determining the best methods of measuring work in progress, analysis of actual performance compared with the standard, and reporting findings to responsible executives.

Service Activities. Staff may perform service activities by carrying out specified work *for* the line. For example, the personnel department may recruit, select, and employ people for the line and other staff departments. The purchasing department may buy materials and supplies for the line. Finance may install accounting, budgetary and reporting systems for the line organization.

It is to be noted that in each case where staff performs a service for the line, authority for performing that service and final decision as to how it is to be done rests with the line. For example, the accounting department, if it is staff, does not direct the line to conform to standardized accounting procedures necessary for the compilation of a consolidated balance sheet. Such procedures are authorized by the president, who gives either explicit or implied authority to the accounting department to install for *him* the accounting system that will best serve the objectives he has set forth. The personnel manager who recruits college graduates, and who may even hire them, is acting only at the express request of the line departments he serves.

Improving Line-Staff Relationships

Study of company organization brings to light frequent instances of friction and conflict between line and staff. What is at the root of the difficulty? Both line and staff have their viewpoints.

The line viewpoint

Line managers most often have these complaints about the staff organization:

> Staff tends to assume line authority
> Staff does not give sound advice
> Staff steals credit
> Staff fails to see the whole picture

Staff assumes line authority. Line managers are generally keenly aware of their responsibility for results and profits. While they recognize that the staff man is necessary and valuable, they frequently resent what he does, or what they think he is trying to do, because they feel it encroaches upon their duties and prerogatives.

For example, in one company the plant manager had just finished negotiating a contract with a labor union. The central staff labor relations manager had been present all through the proceedings, ostensibly to guide and assist the plant manager in the negotiations.

The plant manager was not complimentary about the staff man's participation. "He knew just what he wanted, and he tried every way he knew to get me to go along. He would have made concessions to the union we didn't have to make at this plant and that we couldn't live with. I know some other plants in the company had to give in on those points, but there is no reason why we should."

Staff does not give sound advice. Many managers complain that the counsel and advice staff offers is not always fully considered, well balanced, and soundly tested. In many companies, staff is considered "academic" or "ivory tower." Responsibility for this attitude can sometimes be laid squarely on staff people. For one thing, since staff is not held accountable for ultimate results, some staff managers show a tendency to propose new ideas without thinking them through or testing them. For another, staff specialists sometimes become enthusiastic advocates of ideas or programs because they work well in other companies. They do not always determine whether these ideas are adapted to the operating conditions of their own organization.

The sad fact is that sometimes the staff man is not well enough acquainted with operating conditions or processes in his own company to be able to identify the limiting factors. For instance, in one company the executive development director attended a seminar in which he heard accounts of the effectiveness of the committee method of executive appraisal. He made an enthusiastic recommendation to two division managers that they install this system in their plants. He did not understand why his idea met with a cold reception until he realized, several months later, that both divisions had many small treating plants with fifteen or twenty people and one or, at the most, two supervisors. As a result, committee appraisal was highly impractical.

Staff steals credit. Another common complaint is the tendency of staff to assume credit for programs that are successful and to lay the blame on line when they are not.

Staff people usually have a strategic advantage because they are closer to the top line manager and have more frequent access to him. In the nature of things, if a division manager accepts his staff industrial engineer's recommendation for installation of a methods improvement program, he will consult with him frequently on how best to go about it. Since the staff man has his chief's ear, he will be able to inject his own opinions and judgments as to why the program does or does not work. As one production superintendent said, "When things go wrong, those staff engineers make sure we're behind the eight ball. But when things click, every staff man in the shop rushes in to take credit."

Staff fails to see the whole picture. Line managers frequently point out that staff people tend to operate in terms of the limited objectives of their own specialty rather than in the interests of the business as a whole. The difficulty here seems to be that the staff man becomes so involved in his own area that he fails to relate it to the task of the line and to the over-all objectives of the company.

The staff viewpoint

Complaints in the staff-line relationship are not entirely one-sided. Many staff men have complaints about the line. These usually center about the following:

> Line does not make proper use of staff
> Line resists new ideas
> Line does not give staff enough authority

Line does not make proper use of staff. In many companies, the advice and help of staff is sought only as a last resort. The line manager possibly prefers to run his own show and does not want to call in a specialist. He may be reluctant to place his actions in public view so they can be criticized. Again, he may distrust the motives of staff, and feel they are trying to usurp his authority. Whatever the cause, staff specialists usually believe that their potential value is minimized if they are only called in when a situation is so far out of hand as to be hopeless.

Most specialized staff managers feel that they should be consulted during the planning stages of a program that involves their own area of specialty. This enables them to anticipate problems and to recommend precautionary measures. As one safety engineer put it: "If I'm called in before machinery or equipment is ordered, I can help specify safety features that the maintenance and purchasing people aren't aware of. It's my business to keep up with our special requirements and new developments in safety engineering. Most times I get in on the show only after accidents have happened."

Line resists new ideas. Many staff men feel that line management tends to be shortsighted and resistant to new ideas. Staff men are usually alert to the newest thinking and innovations in the field of their specialties. The public relations man may be enthusiastic about open-house programs; the personnel man may be convinced that psychological testing is a panacea for many of the ills of the plant; the industrial engineer may be certain that statistical quality control is the cure-all for low quality.

Line management, however, is often cautious and slow to accept new ideas. One industrial engineer who was advocating the use of work sampling and meeting with a great deal of resistance from the plant superintendent summed up this point of view when he said, "They preach 'wait and see' while we're wasting thousands of dollars a day. We'd do better with a little gumption and less caution."

Line does not give staff enough authority. A common theme in the staff manager's complaint is lack of authority. As one industrial engineer said: "We're paid to be experts. Most of us know a lot more in our specialty than line people. But we haven't got the authority to make it stick."

Many staff managers feel that if they have the best answer to a problem, they should be able to enforce the solution on the line man involved. To their way of thinking, knowledge is authority, and there is not much point in throwing organizational barriers between the man who knows and the job that has to be done.

Solutions

The answer to better teamwork between staff and line seems to lie, first, in an understanding of their basic relationship. Company experience indicates that the following important points must be observed if effective teamwork is to exist.

1. The units that are designated as line have ultimate responsibility for the successful operation of the company. Therefore, line departments must be responsible for operating decisions.

2. Staff elements contribute by providing advice and service to the line in accomplishing the objectives of the enterprise.

3. Staff is responsible for providing advice and service to appropriate line elements when requested to do so. However, staff also is responsible for proffering advice and service when it is not requested, but where the staff believes it is needed.

4. The solicitation of advice and acceptance of suggestions and counsel is usually at the option of the line organization. However, in some instances it must be recognized that only the top level of the organization has this option and that top management's decision with respect to the use of staff advice or service is binding throughout lower levels. For instance, if the president decides that all purchasing will be handled by the staff procurement department, an operating department is not at liberty to contract for its own purchases of safety shoes. These decisions may be expressed in company policies or procedures, or they may be conveyed informally.

5. Line is responsible for giving serious consideration to advice and offers of service made by staff units, and should follow the recommendations if it is in the company's best interest to do so. However, except in those cases where the use of staff advice and service is compulsory and subject only to appeal to higher authority, it is not mandatory that the advice of staff be followed. Except as noted above, line managers should have authority to modify, reject or accept such advice.

6. Both line and staff should have the right to appeal to higher authority in case of disagreement on staff recommendations. However, this right to appeal should not be permitted to supersede the line's responsibility for making immediate decisions when required by the operating situation.

How staff can do a better job

How can the staff specialist do a better job in terms of these relationships? Many companies find that the following points help facilitate and improve staff operations.

Operate in terms of policies and objectives of the company as a whole. Written statements of company policy have an important bearing on staff-line relationships. These statements of what the company believes and intends to live by provide guides to both line and staff people over which the staff exercises a watchdog kind of control. In many cases the staff executive is responsible for interpreting these policies with, of course, the final decision resting with the chief executive officer in cases of dispute. Understanding by both line and staff executives of their responsibilities for the development of and adherence to the company policies tend to eliminate much of the friction that can easily develop between line and staff. The objectives of staff departments should be aimed at helping the company accomplish its purposes, and not devoted to the specialized goals of the staff department itself.

For example, the company may not need a program of psychological testing because tests are not capable of identifying the special kinds of talent the company requires. Statistical quality control may not be indicated because the company is trying a new market in which gross tolerances are permissible and in which price is far more important than precise machining. To be able to operate in such terms, the staff man first has to see the over-all picture. He needs to know what the company is trying to accomplish in terms of operations, costs and sales. Then he needs to be able to subordinate his personal and professional interests to the welfare of the company as a whole.

Encourage and educate line to use staff effectively. A line manager cannot use a staff specialist effectively unless he knows what that specialist can do for him. The staff man has the responsibility of letting the line know what he has to offer.

In some companies, this is done through training conferences. Each staff manager appears before conference groups of line and other staff personnel and describes his function to them. He points out how he can be helpful in solving specific problems, and answers questions that may come up.

In other companies, staff managers make a point of talking with line managers individually about their operations. The staff man uses this opportunity to outline his own activities and to introduce any ideas he may have as to how he may be useful to the line operator.

Recognize and overcome resistance to change. One of the important reasons for line opposition to ideas presented by staff is the psychological factor of resistance to change. People tend to resist ideas that threaten to change their way of doing things. The fact that a change is even suggested seems to imply that the old way was not good enough.

It is not so commonly recognized that people are even more set against changes that threaten disturbance or alteration in personal relationships. For example, a maintenance supervisor may be moderately opposed to a suggested change in his job responsibilities. He has always been responsible for the installation of new equipment and he does not want to give it up, even though he is being given responsibility for the lubrication program in its place. However, if the change means that he will also have to move to another part of the plant and work with another group of people, his resistance is likely to be greatly intensified.

Staff specialists can anticipate and overcome this natural resistance to proposed changes. Many companies have found these points helpful:

1. Determine to what extent the proposed change will affect personal relationships. Is the staff man advocating a major, sweeping change which will affect the social patterns established in the group? If so, the traumatic effect and accompanying resistance can be diminished if the change is broken into smaller, more numerous moves which will make gradual adjustment possible.

2. When major changes are involved which will modify the relationships between a manager and the people who work for him, opposition from the manager will be minimized if he participates in the preliminary planning. Then, when announcement of the change is made, the principal directly affected can make it as a working partner with the staff, and not as an unwilling associate. In effect, this gives the line manager an opportunity to make the idea his own.

3. People who will be affected by the change will accept it better if:

> The change is tied in as closely as possible with their personal goals and interests, their jobs, families, and futures, and if they are convinced it will make their own work easier, faster or safer.
> They have an opportunity to offer suggestions, ideas and comments concerning the change as it affects them—provided they are convinced these suggestions are sincerely wanted and will be given serious consideration.
> They are kept informed of the results of the change.
> They are able to check on how well they are doing in terms of the change.

4. Acquire technical proficiency. The primary reason for the existence of staff is that it is highly informed and capable in a specialized field. It follows that the staff specialist, if he is to merit respect and to do his work properly, must be an expert. He needs a detailed and extensive knowledge of his field, and he needs to be able to convey this knowledge and information convincingly to others.

Technical proficiency in a staff man implies more than specialized knowledge. It also requires that the specialist have a knowledge of the company and its operations. The more he knows of line problems and operations, and those of other staff specialties, the better he can develop effective recommendations in his own area.

How line can make better use of staff

The effectiveness of the line manager depends to a large extent upon how he makes use of staff services. The line manager who wants to make most advantageous use of the staff services at his disposal will find the following points of value:

1. *Make maximum use of staff.* The more the line man makes use of staff, the better acquainted the specialists will become with his problems and his way of working. Many line executives find that it is only common sense to make habitual use of staff. In effect, the line manager has on retainer a consultant who can help him perform better.

2. *Make proper use of staff.* Lost motion, duplication and personal irritation often occur because the line manager hasn't made up his mind what advice or service he needs before he calls in the specialist.

In one case, for example, a plant manager asked the purchasing agent to secure data on the comparative costs of a pusher bar conveyor installation as compared to the existing crane and magnet operation. After the purchasing agent had completed his study at considerable time and effort, the plant manager told him: "We haven't got the money for new equipment. I guess what I really wanted to know was how to operate that crane with two men instead of three." He then called in the industrial engineer to make a new study for him.

3. *Keep staff informed.* Line managers frequently take action directly affecting staff activities without notifying the staff people concerned. For example, in one company the executive vice-president and the manager of one of the operating divisions decided to install a fully automatic assembly line in one plant of the division. This necessitated the use of many more maintenance and technical people over a period of years, together with several additional engineers. The personnel manager found out about the new plan only after the work was completed and a request for additional people came through. Instead of having an opportunity to train and upgrade people from within the company over a period of months, he was forced to hire the additional staff from the outside.

Many companies have found that time and effort spent in training and educating managers in proper line-staff relationships is an excellent investment. Evidence seems to show that this is a direct means of improving teamwork, increasing the productive capacity of members of management and reducing friction in personal relationships.

62. COMPLETED STAFF WORK:
KEY TO EFFECTIVE DELEGATION [1] J. Lewis Powell [2]

In any organization, the end product of executive action is decision. Most executives are well aware that their productivity is largely a matter of the quality and quantity of their decisions, and that consequently it is their responsibility to concentrate their time and energy on the actual business of decision-making. Few, however, are wholly satisfied with their own performance in this respect; and a good many suffer from acute frustration over their inability to free themselves from a mass of trivial problems and petty detail.

Basically, of course, the problem is one of delegation, involving the intelligent use of staff assistants—not merely as additional arms and legs for the boss, but as extra brainpower. And probably the best single solution lies in applying the concept of *completed staff work*, a management technique specifically designed to focus executive talent on decision.

The completed staff work concept has been well described by Major General Archer L. Learch:

> Completed staff work is the study of a problem, and presentation of a solution, by a staff officer, in such form that all that remains to be done on the part of the head of the staff division, or the commander, is to indicate his approval or disapproval of the completed action. The words "completed action" are emphasized because the more difficult the problem is, the greater is the tendency to present the problem to the chief in piecemeal fashion. It is your duty as a staff officer to work out the details. You should not consult your chief in the determination of those details, no matter how perplexing they may be. You may and should consult other staff officers. The product, whether it involves the pronouncement of a new policy or affects an established one, should, when presented to the chief for approval or disapproval, be worked out in finished form.

> The impulse which often comes to the inexperienced staff officer to ask the chief what to do, recurs more often when the problem is difficult.

[1] From *The Management Review* (June, 1956). Reprinted by permision of *The Management Review*.

[2] J. Lewis Powell, Associated with the Industrial Planning Branch, Office of the Assistant Secretary of Defense, Supply and Logistics, The Pentagon, 1956.

It is accompanied by a feeling of mental frustration. It is so easy to ask the chief what to do, and it appears so easy for him to answer. Resist that impulse! You will succumb to it only if you do not know your job. It is your job to advise your chief what he ought to do, not to ask him what you ought to do. He needs answers, not questions. Your job is to study, write, restudy, and rewrite until you have evolved a single proposed action—the best one of all you have considered. . . .

The theory of completed staff work does not preclude a "rough draft" but the rough draft must not be a half-baked idea. It must be complete in every respect except that it lacks the requisite number of copies and need not be neat. But a rough draft must not be used as an excuse for shifting to the chief the burden of formulating the action.

The completed staff work theory may result in more work for the staff officer, but it results in more freedom for the chief. This is as it should be. Further, it accomplishes two things:

1. The chief is protected from half-baked ideas, voluminous memoranda, and immature oral presentations.
2. The staff officer who has a real idea to sell is enabled more readily to find a market.

When you have finished your "completed staff work" the final test is this:

If you were the chief, would you be willing to sign the paper you have prepared, and stake your professional reputation on its being right?

If the answer is in the negative, take it back and work it over, because it is not yet completed staff work.

This principle is as valuable to the executive vice president today as it was to the general during World War II—which provided, almost daily, breathtaking demonstrations of how much a single executive could accomplish through the use of this technique.

The pioneer applications of the completed staff work technique in industry in peacetime were often unsuccessful. One reason was that whereas the military executive had been weaned, so to speak, on the completed staff work technique, his civilian counterpart had worked under a different system and had often made the grade through sheer colossal ability to worry about details—i.e., be his own staff—and still make decisions. . . .

Most of us in management are alternately executive and staff. We are seldom exclusively one or the other. Frequently we are staff to those above us and executive to those below us. In consequence, we must understand both viewpoints and apply them simultaneously. This means examining each problem in terms of both our "line" responsibilities and our "staff" responsibilities.

Executive and staff teamwork is a 50-50 proposition. The executive makes the decision and the staff does the work. You can't, obviously, be an executive assistant to a fellow who isn't an executive.

To get completed staff work throughout an organization takes leadership. You can't beat it simply by hanging up a notice. The idea must be sold, and to sell it you must see that its deceptively simple concept is really understood as a profound principle. Once understood, it must be built into your organization as a standard operating procedure. Staff people must always deliver completed staff work, and executives must accept no substitutes. In addition, completed staff work and those who perform it must be awarded management recognition.

The completed staff work principle imposes a number of responsibilities on the executive making an assignment.

1. Before you assign a problem to anyone, be sure you can define the problem. There are no solutions to unknown problems. If you cannot clearly and concisely state or write the problem, you have some more brainwork to do.

2. When you discuss a problem at a staff meeting, make it plain who is carrying the ball. You're the quarterback, but the team needs to know the play.

3. Tell the ball carrier what the problem is and what you expect him to do about it. Communication by administrative osmosis seldom produces much besides confusion and frustration.

4. Contribute your experience. You're the boss because you have superior ability. Share it with your assistants. Tell them what you have learned or what you think you have learned about the problem.

5. When you give an assignment, set a target date. Giving a person an assignment without setting a target is like asking a friend to come to dinner "some evening."

6. Be accessible for legitimate progress reports. If you don't want today's answer to yesterday's problem, or yesterday's answer to today's problem, it will pay you to take an occasional reading on progress.

7. Steadfastly resist the temptation to do your staff's thinking for them. Give guidance and background information, but make them do their own thinking. Remember that it is their job to furnish proposed solutions—not problems—and that your job is to apply management intelligence to their proposed solutions. General Leslie Groves once gave the following example of management intelligence: "You sit down at a conference table with eight scientists, all of whom know infinitely more about the problem than you do. All eight of those fellows disagree with each other. If you can pick which expert is

right, you have 'management intelligence'." Gone are the days when
industry was so simple that the boss could be an expert on everything.
From now on, successful executives will increasingly have to develop
and use management intelligence.

Completed staff work is no panacea. It won't solve all your problems, but it will do this:

> Free you from unimportant detail;
> Multiply your executive effectiveness; and
> Make your organization run better.

It all boils down to this: As an executive, you can either develop
a splendid set of ulcers, or teach your staff to do completed staff
work. It takes about the same amount of energy either way.

BIBLIOGRAPHY, CHAPTER XVII

APPLEY, LAWRENCE A. "Staff and Line," *Management News,* American Management Association, Inc. (May, 1956), 1-2.

CHRISTOPHER, THOMAS W. "Use and Misuse of Authority by Federal Agencies," *Harvard Business Review* (November-December, 1952), 48-58.

DALTON, M. "Conflicts Between Staff and Line Managerial Officers," *American Sociological Review,* Vol. 15 (1950), 342-351.

DUFFY, DANIEL J. "Authority Considered from an Operational Point of View," *Journal of the Academy of Management* (December, 1959), 167-176.

EBY, M. L., and G. C. THOMPSON. "No Magic Formulas for Managing Staff," *Business Record* (October, 1955), 386-392.

FINLAY, W. W., and others. *Human Behavior in Industry.* New York: McGraw-Hill Book Company, Inc., 1955. "The Use and Misuse of Authority," Chapter 10 and "Authority, Responsibility, and People," Chapter 8.

HOLDEN, PAUL E., L. S. FISH, and H. L. SMITH. *Top-Management Organization and Control.* McGraw-Hill Book Company, Inc., 1951. Part B, Section 3.

LEPAWSKY, ALBERT. *Administration—The Art of Organization and Management.* New York: Knoff, 1949. Chapter 10.

MANDEVILLE, MERTEN, J. "The Nature of Authority," *Journal of the Academy of Management* (August, 1960).

MEYERS, CHARLES A. and JOHN G. TURNBULL. "Line and Staff in Industrial Relations," *Harvard Business Review,* Vol. 34, No. 4 (1956), 113-124.

MOONEY, J. D. *The Principles of Organization,* Revised Edition. New York: Harper & Brothers, 1939. Chapters 3, 4, 5, 14, 16, 17, 18.

O'DONNELL, C. "The Source of Managerial Authority," *Political Science Quarterly,* Vol. 67, No. 4 (December, 1952), 573-588.

SAMPSON, ROBERT C. *The Staff Role in Management,* New York: Harper & Brothers, 1955.

SCHLEK, EDWARD C. "Make Your Staff Pay Its Way," *Harvard Business Review,* Vol. 35, No. 2 (1957), 115-122.

THOMPSON, A. S., JR. "Staff Assistant—Wise or Otherwise?" *Personnel,* Vol. 29, No. 2 (September, 1952), 136-140.

URWICK, L. *Profitably Using the General Staff Position in Business.* General Management Series No. 165. New York: American Management Association, Inc., 1953.

Chapter XVIII
Decentralization and Delegation

In this chapter the question of delegation of authority, particularly to divisionalized components of an organization, is compared to a centralization of authority at a headquarters level in a top-management group. As means toward managerial development and the release of the potential capabilities of subordinates, a high degree of decentralization of authority to relatively independent, autonomous operating suborganizations has been suggested. Conversely, the development and growth of decision methods and information systems suggested by others (e.g., Leavitt and Whisler, Article 3, Chapter I) imply that a centralized group of specialists may be able to make better decisions about detailed operations than has been found practicable heretofore.

The articles in this chapter reflect these opposing views. Ralph C. Persons, in Article 63, explains how the problems he faced called for a centralized managerial group to coordinate the diversity of activity in his company. In Article 64 Ernest Dale's discussion of his research experience provides a degree of perspective to the centralization-decentralization issue.

63. HOW TO DIVERSIFY
AND CENTRALIZE [1]

Ralph C. Persons [2]

With the growing trend towards diversification in American industry today, a question in the minds of a great many business executives is why to diversify and how to diversify. We have always followed a program of diversification; but it is only within the last few years that we have realized that in our particular circumstance, diversification must go hand-in-hand with centralization if it is to be successful. This may seem incongruous. We do not take an intransigent stand on the question of centralization versus decentralization. Both have their proper place in various phases of a growing business. However, I think it will be clear by relating the experiences of our corporation that some industries can be centralized and yet remain diversified and achieve results which have never previously been achieved.

The corporation was established in 1929, at which time it operated under the name, General Printing Ink Company. It then consisted of six printing ink companies, each continuing to operate under their individual firm names as divisions of the parent company. By 1945, when the corporate name, Sun Chemical Corporation, was adopted, the corporation had grown to a total of 26 divisions and wholly-owned subsidiaries consisting not only of printing ink companies, but other coating companies as well.

But along with this growth came many problems. At the time I assumed the presidency of the corporation, it was a vast assortment of divisions and subsidiaries which operated practically as separate entities and seemed merged in name only. There were, in addition to the 26 divisions, 29 manufacturing plants, 30 warehouses and 60 sales offices, so widespread and complex that lack of unity was inevitable. This naturally resulted in heavy utilization of facilities for but one product and unavoidable duplication of effort in some fields, particularly sales and research.

---

[1] From *Dun's Review and Modern Industry* (September, 1955), pp. 41-42, 116-117. Reprinted by permission of *Dun's Review and Modern Industry*.
[2] Ralph C. Persons, formerly President, Sun Chemical Corporation.

Because of the diversity and variety of the products manufactured by the corporation, our scope of operations broadened during the post-war period. This, in turn, caused sales to expand greatly. However, earnings growth tended to be more restricted as severe competition began to be experienced in some lines which the corporation had introduced. With the leveling off of sales and the continued rise in costs, profit margins dropped from 12 cents on every sales dollar (from 1951 to 1953) to 7 cents.

In addition to the foregoing, we lacked recognition as a corporate structure. A general lack of information existed on both the part of public and employees as to what actually comprised the corporation. There was the common misunderstanding that Sun was a subsidiary of a larger company and even many persons employed by the corporation did not recognize the divisions which made up the corporation or the companies which made up the divisions.

After studying these problems carefully, I concluded that progress could be accomplished only by incorporating a program of centralization with our established program of diversification. With the aid of the corporate management committee, which is composed of the group chairmen who head each division, such a program was undertaken.

It was readily apparent that the existing organization should first be perfected and the down trend in profit margins halted before any further expansion was considered. With 26 divisions turning out a profusion of products from 29 plants, Sun was a hodgepodge of wasteful operation and the organizational structure was first on the agenda for improvement. The most important step in this direction was consolidation of products and selling organizations into three groups, each covering a more or less specific category—paints, inks, and textile chemicals.

Once this had been accomplished, the way was clear to consolidate sales personnel and management in the company's divisions and subsidiaries. We then integrated our research facilities and attempted to eliminate overlapping of research and development projects. A concerted effort on inefficiencies in production and distribution was initiated as well as a program to consolidate our management and operational functions. Detailed attention was given to the establishment of a unified advertising, marketing, and merchandising program and we incorporated an extensive employee education and training program.

Budget Co-ordination

The inception of a new, unified budgeting procedure was the next step we took in our centralization program. This budgeting system involves forecasts of individual requirements by managers and group chairmen. It enables the purchasing department to buy more effectively and makes it possible for the accounting department to determine what per cent of gross sales is attributable to technical help, advertising, clerical help, and other phases of our business. Generally, in business, managers are cautioned to watch the profit on sales. Our managers are advised to watch their investment and the return they receive on their investment. Any good salesman can raise volume, but only a talented manager can keep costs proportionate.

Finally, we determined to continue an intensive product diversification program incorporating the new centralization program. And we created a new definition for the word, expansion, in the corporation. Whereas in the past it meant only acquisition, at present it also means striving for consistent increases in sales while reducing costs.

When one thinks in terms of the various phases of any industrial operation, the first area which invariably comes to mind is sales. This was our course of thought and we immediately appointed a sales director to co-ordinate and guide the activities of all our sales divisions. In our past experience, it was not uncommon for one customer to be solicited by two or more salesmen, each from a different division. Under our new policy, one salesman sells all products to a single account, thus eliminating duplication of sales effort. Distributorships have been initiated with the aim of converting more target accounts into major customers. New marketing plans have been initiated and studies are being continuously pursued to increase our sales potential and develop additional territories. To stimulate more aggressive selling, several incentive programs for experienced salesmen have been introduced and they have had a considerable and enlivening effect on sales personnel morale.

Industry is rapidly awakening to the increasingly important role research plays to-day in the competitive market. It is only through a never-ending effort to supply the purchaser with the best possible product at the lowest possible price that the leading firms maintain their highly envied standing. A research department must then operate with a maximum of efficiency if it is to reach its peak performance. At the time I became president of the corporation, we had eight chief chemists, each in charge of a divisional laboratory. There was considerable duplication of effort. In fact, it was found that three of our labs were working on the same technical problem while a fourth had already found the answer! A new technical director was appointed to co-ordinate research for all groups. All projects are now channeled through the technical director who sees to it that the men most experienced in a particular field work on the projects in which they have the best chance of achieving the quickest and most satisfactory results and maintaining quality.

We are also continuing to increase our efficiency by an effort to make all divisions more profit-minded through consolidation. As an example, the combined resources of the ten printing ink companies which are a part of Sun Chemical Corporation have been consolidated under the name, General Printing Ink Company—the former corporate name. This division and its twenty branches now afford us nation-wide representation in the East, New England, Midwest, Southwest and Pacific Coast areas, as well as Canada and Mexico. This move has lent itself to an improved operation and a more effective customer service which, in turn, have increased profits.

With this same goal in mind, our Long Island City printing ink manufacturing facilities were relocated in our East Rutherford plant. In a like manner, our Cambridge, Mass., plant was combined with our Norwood, Mass., plant. The combination of these productive energies has already fostered many salutary effects. Production efficiency has been increased because of closer proximity to raw material sources; more up-to-date machinery and equipment are now equally accessible to all plants. Changes like these will help improve the quantity and quality of products. The competitive position will, therefore, be considerably enhanced and there will be more incentive among the employees to maintain and further the position.

CONTINUOUS CHECKING

Other savings in the processing of basic materials used in the manufacture of many lines have also been realized through improved production scheduling by the manufacturing units of the corporation. A constant review of manufacturing operations by our staff of process engineers has improved production methods for uniformity and efficiency.

From a careful analysis of inventory requirements, a new corporate-wide purchasing program has been developed. A policy of central purchasing for all units has resulted in the corporation receiving the best possible price available on purchases made on a quantity basis for all divisions. This has resulted in lower inventories for all departments. In fact, year-end inventory for 1954 was lower than it has been since the pre-Korean war year of 1949.

Faster, lower-cost deliveries of finished products has been achieved by integration of truck movements. In past years, each division had its individual trucks for deliveries. To-day trucks of the same design and color scheme, with the trademark clearly identifying them, deliver the products of all divisions.

Warehousing, too, has been centralized, eliminating wasteful multiple deliveries of small shipments to the same customer.

To meet the sales challenge created by the diversity of products produced by our 26 divisions, a new corporate advertising program has been effected and our advertising, marketing, and public relations activities have been co-ordinated. We formerly had eight advertising agencies handling the various divisions of the corporation and in every case we were too small to get satisfactory results. Within the past few years, all promotional activities have been centralized with the establishment of a single agency-client arrangement. Now, with one budget and working with one agency instead of several, we have found that it is possible, in many instances, to run one ad where we previously ran several.

In a series of moves to increase our corporate identity as the parent firm of its divisions and subsidiaries, we completely overhauled all of the advertising and promotional literature issued by the corporation and initiated a large-scale package redesign program. Letterheads, labels, advertising layouts, and containers, were redesigned, and in an effort to unite all of our divisions and subsidiaries under one symbol, the corporate trademark was revised. A new format was also established for the corporate annual report. With an advertising budget which is the largest in the history of the corporation, we look ahead optimistically to results which are sure to prove profitable.

It is practically impossible for one man to have the final word on details of all operations in the face of the trend toward diversification. With a corporation, such as ours, where there is much diversity, this is completely impossible. Utilizing this theory as the basis of our corporate philosophy, we have initiated a management committee type of business administration. This is one phase of our corporate structure where a policy of decentralization is adhered to rather than centralization. It has always been my belief that if two executives in a company think exactly alike, one is unnecessary.

The management committee consists of fourteen members and administers corporate policy as well as providing a means for exchanging ideas. Managers like this setup as it gives them a direct line to top management. The committee meets regularly; problems are tossed back and forth among the members and solutions arrived at in an efficient manner. We believe in having younger men at the helm of our corporate structure. It is interesting to note that the average age of the members of the management committee is 49, the oldest being 60 and the youngest being 36. These men have an average of sixteen years of service. The average age of the officers in our corporation is 44. Our 26 managers average 50 years of age and have an average length of service totaling eighteen years. This combination of youth and experience is an indisputable advantage to the corporation.

It is our intent to encourage each employee to develop his resources to the maximum so that the groundwork will be laid for promotions from within the ranks when circumstances merit change. The corporation has, therefore, embarked upon an intensive training and development program to help employees become more effective and prepare them for positions of greater responsibility.

Among these programs is the Executive Idea Clinic which is conducted to educate our key people in corporate policy and the uniform application of procedure. This is accomplished by inviting men from the various geographic locations of our divisions to the corporate home office to attend a series of meetings with group chairmen and department heads. At these meetings, the men are given a thorough indoctrination into the operations of the units which comprise the corporate whole. The first meeting they attend is in my office and though they are surprised when I tell them, "Now's your chance to give management hell and we'll be proud of you for it," they are not reticent about doing so. As a result we have received much constructive criticism from them which has brought about productive change in policy and procedure. After approximately a week's intensive training, and when we are sure the men are completely satisfied that they clearly understand every phase of the company's operation and are content with the explanations their complaints have received, they return to their positions better equipped to handle the diurnal flow of their activities.

In addition to our Executive Idea Clinic, we are just about ready to introduce a Junior Executive Club in the corporation. Training of this sort is being carried on for all levels of employment. There is a training program for factory superintendents and a secretarial seminar which meets every week. We feel this phase of our operation reaps dividends in that our employees are more familiar with the operations of the corporation and the products they help manufacture. We have found that the training programs have produced a more interested and efficient personnel and have increased the pride of our people in their work and in their association with a progressive and forward-looking company.

In general, our wages, working conditions and employee benefits have always been as good or better than the prevailing local level, but since the appointment of a director of industrial relations, our employee relations are better than ever before. All union negotiations are conducted by our industrial relations director and while we have 29 different unions to deal with, we negotiated new contracts with 24 of these unions during the past year—a record which gives us a great deal of satisfaction.

Through the appointment of a safety director, we have reduced the number of accidents during the past year by 21 per cent. This has resulted in a reduction of cost of claims for a little more than 24 per cent. Efforts such as these have assisted management to become better acquainted with personnel and more cognizant of employee problems.

The Long-Range View

The closer co-ordination of the various departments and phases of our business has contributed greatly to the corporation's long-term all-around growth and is viewed as a major step in the direction of continued and efficient product diversification.

Our present program calls for an expected 100 per cent increase in sales within the next ten years. The expected increase in sales will result from our obtaining a greater share of the markets available for its products. Definite efforts are being made to increase consumer markets by means of additional areas of supply for the consumer.

However, diversification at this point in our program, does not necessarily mean extension into new markets. It also means the introduction of new products within the markets in which we are already established. All the time that we have been centralizing, we have continued to follow an intensive new products program.

The shift to central control by means of the management committee, together with the dynamic partnership of management, share owner and employee, should be given top honors for the tangible results which have been achieved. The unique arrangement of consolidation and continued diversification affords the corporation unlimited stable market potential on one hand, while permitting unusually close-knit, efficient production on the other. Integration of departments and functions has brought about tremendous results. In 1954, net earnings rose to $1,801,500 as compared with $1,300,300 the previous year, despite the fact that sales volume dipped 3 per cent during the same period. 1954 also saw earnings rise to $1.43 a share, 42 per cent more than the $1.01 in 1953. Share owner's equity at the end of 1954 totaled $15,141,300, or $11.07 per common share, compared with $14,451,300, or $10.49 per common share for the prior year. This established a new all-time high.

First-half figures for 1955 continue to reflect increased earnings as a result of the expanded sales and streamlining program instituted by the corporation. Sales increased 3 per cent and net profit showed an increase of 26.8 per cent for the first six months of 1955 as compared with the same period of 1954. Earnings during the first half of 1955 were 61.8 cents against 48 cents for the first half of 1954. The continued, substantial gain shows the effectiveness of our concentrating on profitable sales while consolidating and realigning our corporate structure.

All of us feel that we have taken the right road in pursuing a policy of centralization combined with diversification. But, to find out which is the best method, which management technique will solve the majority of problems, takes a lot of time, hard work, and thorough investigation. Only in this way can the best results be achieved.

64. CENTRALIZATION VERSUS DECENTRALIZATION [1]

Ernest Dale [2]

"Decentralization" like "politeness" means different things to different people, but in no case should it be taken to imply a value judgment. The term itself means the delegation of business decisions by the owners to their immediate representatives (the board of directors and the chief executive), and then to others further down in the management hierarchy. This is done with the aim of furthering the objectives and values of the enterprise; hence decentralization is only a means to an end.

In addition, "decentralization" is not an absolute term. There are varying degrees of decentralized authority, and the extent to which any company is decentralized must be gauged by tests.

The *locus* or *place* of the decision-making authority in the management hierarchy is one criterion. The lower the rank of the executives who make given decisions, the greater the degree of decentralization. For example, decentralization is greater where larger amounts of money can be spent at lower levels for such things as capital equipment, administrative or operating purposes, or salary changes. The degree of authority for decisions that could result in a loss may also be a test. In a carpet factory, a mistake in the weave would not be serious; hence the function of quality control could be placed far down in the management hierarchy without any great degree of decentralization. In a pharmaceutical company, on the other hand, an error might cause a death, and quality decisions need to be made near the top level.

In addition, the *degree* of decision-making power at the lower levels will be a factor. This can be determined by studying the authority which can be exercised (1) without any check with higher authority at all (routinized decisions such as the billing procedure, safety enforcement, purchase of stock orders); (2) with a check or regular report after the decision is made and carried out (engagement of clerical personnel, purchases of equipment covered by

[1] From *Advanced Management* (June, 1956), pp. 11-16. Reprinted by permission of *Advanced Management*.
[2] Ernest Dale, Associate Professor of Business Administration, Cornell University.

budget); or (3) with a check before the decision is made or put into effect (decisions without precedent, special appropriation requests). Or there may be the simple requirement to check with a superior on all matters of policy changes, of financial appropriations, or potential and actual disagreements.

In determining the degree of decentralization, moreover, it must always be remembered that an enterprise has both *formal and informal decision-making* rules. Official policy statements may decree one type of decision-making, but actual practice may be quite different. Thus there may be a high degree of formal centralization, but if successful business conduct is not possible under such circumstances, decisions may be, in fact, made much lower down.

For instance, in one firm with about a billion dollars of sales, all purchases over $2,500 must be submitted to the president; and all changes in salaries above $4,000, all expense accounts and all public appearances of executives have to be approved by the chief. Obviously, this chief executive is unable to handle all these approvals himself. The large majority of the purchasing decisions are, in fact, made by executives lower down the line, because merchandise has to be bought and sold if the business is to continue.

When objectives clash with the assignment of responsibility and authority, one or the other is likely to be disregarded. Thus, informal, centralized controls may make possible over-riding the effectiveness of formally decentralized responsibility and authority.

Again formal centralization may be offset to some extent by physical decentralization. For example, the production of certain products may be undertaken at a separate physical location; accounting records may be assembled and placed next to the immediate user. Thus in decentralization movements, headquarters are sometimes shifted away from the plant to prevent the close control that can come from propinquity.

Current status in the United States

There is no statistical information on the extent of centralization and its reverse, the decentralization of decision-making, in U. S. industry. Business literature usually carries accounts of corporate decentralization, largely because such moves are considered "progressive" and hence newsworthy (one rarely reads today of a president boasting of centralization.) However, general reasoning will show that centralization is still quite widespread. Probably "one-man control" is found in more companies and affects more employees than "control by the few" or "control by the many."

One-man control stems partly from tradition and partly from human nature. Men in commanding positions like to believe that they are indispensable—secretly hope, perhaps, that they may always be there to carry on. They fear that delegation of authority may foster the creation of "empires within the empire," and make them more dependent on others. In addition, it is hard for the one man in control to jettison all his intellectual investments. He may be committed to a belief in benevolent dictatorship, and the power of vested ideas may be stronger than the power of economic interests.

And this may well be a long-run trend. For there may be a difference (and sometimes an appreciable one) between the maximum profit that a company *could* make and the actual profit it must make to keep the stockholders from complaining too loudly. To this extent the compulsion to maximum profits no longer exists to the same degree that it did 50 years ago when owner-management was much more common. Nor is the maximization of profits as advantageous for the individual executive as it used to be, since income taxes, the decline in the value of money, and the long-run decline in the rate of interest all make large accumulations of wealth difficult and often impossible. Andrew Carnegie made many millions of dollars, but the present heads of the Carnegie-Illinois Steel Corporation have no such prospects, even though the job is probably considerably more difficult and complex than in Carnegie's time. For this reason, it may not be worthwhile to risk public opprobrium by squeezing customers or employees, and the consequent trend to "awareness of social responsibilities" may be affecting even family-owned and operated businesses to some extent.

Hence, one may be justified in studying the shift from profit to power as a major business objective and its effect on decentralization. "Power" may be sought in volume of sales or percentage of market, in professional distinction (i.e., the emphasis on "management as a profession," as an "elite," etc.). The chief executive may demonstrate his power by setting the tone in the local community or the industry, by accepting important positions in government or the foreign service. Or he may simply hold on to all major and many minor decisions in the enterprise. Even in allegedly decentralized companies the delegation of powers may go no further than from the chief executive to his vice presidents, and subordinates cannot complain because the holders of power are their immediate superiors.

Factors making for centralization in an enterprise may be many. Most important, perhaps, is the example of the chief executive. To the extent to which he retains powers, his subordinates are likely to imitate him. To the extent that he welcomes "checking," "consultation" and dependence, his subordinates are likely to do the same. Of course, the chief does not actually have to make each decision himself. He merely needs to "spot-check." For example, if he insists on passing on all increases in salaries above $400 a month and 1,000 such applications reach him every month, he needs to pass on only one or a few of them. If he raises a question (or an eyebrow) everyone will be careful to propose only such increases as can be justified under questioning by the chief.

Measurement of results necessary but complex

Then all the devices used to coordinate an enterprise may be used to foster centralization. Such "tools" as organization and policy manuals, methods and procedures manuals, authority limitation manuals (dealing with authority for capital expenditures, salary and personnel changes, etc.) may actually take away more authority than they confer. Sometimes they enforce systems of communication along the lines of a pyramid. Or the chief executive may set up checks and sources of information that nullify the delegation of powers. Measurement of results is, of course, necessary; the chief must know how the delegated powers are exercised. But the controls may bring about so much checking, transmission of so much information so continuously, and so much correction that the "decentralized" operators may spend a considerable part of their time explaining and defending themselves. In some companies, the saying goes: "It takes two tons of paper to make one ton of product." There is also the possibility that the chief's general staff may deliberately force executives to refer many decisions to headquarters or influence decisions without adequate consultation. Or the special staff may exercise central command powers because of actual or assumed technical knowledge, direct operation of exercises, "concurrent authority," superior articulation, physical proximity to the chief, or simply in default of decision-making elsewhere. There are the possible abuses of group work, the enforcement of compatibility and conformity, the use of manipulative techniques to strengthen centralization.

Finally there are the modern means of communication—telephone, telegraph, teletype, radio, and now television—which make it physically possible for the chief executive to issue direct orders to distant subordinates. And it is even possible that future technical developments may eliminate one of the main reasons for decentralization. If enough information can be brought to a central point quickly enough, there may no longer be a need to have problems settled at a point close to their source. The development of electronic devices, calculators, punch card systems, etc., together with such tools as operations research and Cybernetics, may so greatly and so quickly increase the information available to central management that the basic desire of many chiefs—to continue to make as many decisions as possible or to widen the range of their decision-making—might be gratified.

Forces behind greater decentralization

But even if these powerful factors making for "one-man control" did not exist, extensive delegation might still not be possible. For the personnel who can shoulder the additional responsibilities might not be available. Those who grew up with the chief in the business may not be able (or willing) to take more responsibility. Yet if the chief brings in outside personnel, the newcomers may be thwarted by uncooperative oldtimers.

Thus effective delegation of decision-making may be costly. Difficult personalities may be hard to replace, and both the training of new executives and their initial mistakes may be expensive. Additional functional personnel (accounting, research, industrial relations, etc.) may have to be hired in the now semi-autonomous divisions and branches and the difficult relationships to head-office worked out. Informal work groups and long-established relationships may be upset and destroyed. It is difficult and time-consuming to get executives to assume and exercise additional responsibility.

Finally, hard times and increased competition may foster centralization. When the chief executive feels that the company cannot afford mistakes, he is likely to want more power in his own hands.

So it is clear that the tendencies toward greater centralization or at least preservation of the *status quo* may be strong.

Control by the few

When the founder or sole directing head of the enterprise passes away, or when there is a reorganization, the struggle for succession may be resolved through the assumption of control by a group whose members have more or less equal status. If the major decisions of the enterprise are made by a small number of men, we speak of "control by the few." Usually each of these men handles one or several management functions and makes the major decisions concerning them. Insofar as a decision affects more than one executive—that is, if it requires coordination or cuts across the business as a whole— several executives may have an important voice and the decision-making power of each may be practically equal. Control is often exercised by informal consultation, but there may be formal meetings held at regular intervals—of executive committees, management committees, etc.

Motives for establishing "control by the few" are varied. Sometimes it is believed that the company is too large to be managed successfully by one man. That is how Myron Taylor is said to have felt, after Judge Gary's death, about the management of the U. S. Steel Corporation. So he brought in Fairless to handle production, gave Olds charge of the legal and public relations functions, and Voorhees responsibility for finance. Each had more or less equal power on intra-company problems. In other cases, equality of decision-making is designed to train successors to the chief executive by inducing a number of senior vice presidents to compete for the top position. With the increasing emphasis on the social responsibility of business, new members of the board of directors or new top operating executives may be added to represent the point of view of some of the various "publics" affected by the enterprise. Finally, control by the few may be the end result of one of the plans of "group dynamics" or executive participation.

Genuine equal control by a group of individuals rarely attains long-run equilibrium, and usually only where there is long experience and training, careful selection, an established tradition and long personal acquaintance and respect, such as exists in the Management Committees of the Crown-Zellerbach Company or the Executive Committee of the du Pont Company. If it is to be successful, the group should be homogeneous in outlook, heterogeneous in ability. Objectives and authority must be fairly similar; otherwise disagreements are likely to upset the equilibrium sooner or later. Participants must have a degree of sensitivity toward situations and toward each other, and be broadminded enough to disagree without quarrel, e.g., there must be both informality and careful appreciation of all the usual committee mechanics—definition of functions, agenda, assignment of responsibilities, etc.

The great drawback to control by the few is the potential paralysis of decision-making. It takes time to obtain unanimity, and it may sometimes be achieved only by a compromise that is less effective than the decision of one man; such as agreement on the lowest common denomination. Or the group may split and the majority dominate. The more heterogeneous the composition of the group, the greater the probability of such conflict. For example, the difference in viewpoint between financially minded and production minded executives may make it impossible to arrive at lasting solutions of labor and human problems.

Thus control by the few may be a passing phenomenon. When conditions change to an extent affecting the course of the business perceptibly, one-man control may be restored. Alternately, progress may be made toward "control by the many," that is, participation in important decisions by an increasing number of executives. This tends to develop as members of the "oligarchy" attempt to arrive at genuine joint decisions better than those any one individual or a few of them could reach alone.

Control by the many

The control-by-many type of decision-making may be called "integrative" or "participative." (These are probably better terms than "democratic," because the latter, taken from political science, assumes an equality of men that usually does not exist in this context, certainly not in terms of status and income, and usually not in terms of power to influence business decisions.)

Most frequently this participation takes the form of informal, friendly consultation among leading executives and possibly their subordinates. This is, however, of a haphazard nature and could be quickly changed or destroyed by the whim of any important executive involved. Informal consultation may be useless as a starting point or as a means of continuing and stabilizing far-reaching control by the many. For this reason formal control by the many, often called "decentralization," may be adopted.

History of decentralization in America

The decentralization movement in American business was probably begun by Henry V. Poor in the 1850's through his proposals for the reorganization of American railroads, when he sought to help those first large-scale organizations overcome the drawbacks of diminishing returns from management. This remarkable man coined the phrase "the science of management." Poor's suggestions were first applied by Daniel McCallum, General Superintendent on the Erie Railroad

1854 to 1857 and later one of the chief organizers of the American transport system during the Civil War.

The first successful large-scale plan of decentralization in manufacturing industry was probably that presented in 1920 to W. C. Durant, President of General Motors by Alfred P. Sloan, Jr., then G.M. Vice President. This was a most remarkable and far-sighted document, largely formed the basis of the present General Motors organization and was put into effect by many other companies. This was adopted when General Motors was reorganized in 1921. Independently of this, A. W. Robertson, lately Chairman of the Board of the Westinghouse Electric Corporation; Ralph Kelly, Vice President and F. D. Newbury, Economist (now Assistant Secretary of Defense) developed and carried out such a decentralization program at Westinghouse from 1936 to 1939, and it proved to be extremely successful. Standard Oil of California was a pioneer in systematic organization planning under L. L. Purkey. Outstanding post-war examples of decentralization with a successful record of over seven years include the work of L. F. McCollum at the Continental Oil Co. and the decentralization of the Ford Motor Co. Among successfully decentralized smaller companies the "cooperative capitalism" of the C. J. Bath Company should be mentioned—in this firm all levels of management participate in major policy decisions. Essentially one or more of the following characteristics mark a program of decentralization in a large corporation.

(1) *The administrative unit that usually covers the company as a whole as well as all its plants is broken into smaller administrative units—often on either a geographical or product basis.* Each is headed by a manager who may be compared to the head of a smaller enterprise. Usually he has fairly complete control over basic line functions, such as manufacturing and marketing; if he also has staff services such as accounting, engineering, research and personnel, the unit may be largely self-contained.

(2) *Provision is made for the effective utilization of a centralized staff of specialists to aid the decentralized operations to increased profitability and better relationships in order to combine the advantages of a large unit of management with those of a small one.* Central staff specialists are said to "advise and assist" the chief executive and the line operators, and perhaps handle certain centralized functions for the company as a whole, such as public relations, law and taxation. In other cases, the centralized staff specialists maintain "functional supervision" over divisional operations in their fields of expertise,

such as industrial relations, finance, and possibly manufacturing and sales. Functional supervision may cover formulation of major company objectives, policies, plans and programs for line management's approval and seeing that decisions are carried out, furnishing administrative and technical advice, setting up standards, systems, procedures, controls and measurement of performance, concurring in selection of key personnel and in changes in their assignment.

Delegation of authority to specialists

The essential problem in this area of decentralization is the delineation of the authority of the staff specialists. The theoretical "indirect" authority of the central staff may vary in fact from advice to command. For example, the headquarters staff specialist in personnel administration may be an adviser on personality problems, a coordinator of union negotiations, a policy-maker in job and salary evaluation, a researcher on executive development, a statistical compiler of personnel data, an operator of cafeteria services (and of his own department) or he may "concur" on urgent problems of safety (e.g., prohibiting a worker from continuing on a dangerous machine), a controller of the observance of personnel policies. Clearly there are numerous opportunities for widespread participation by "staff" in the decision-making of the enterprise, through the actual use of authority of various kinds, including the "authority" of knowledge.

(3) *A series of general staffs may be provided for the chief executive* to handle the functions which he cannot delegate and which may become increasingly burdensome as the company increases in size. For example, growth of the enterprise requires more attention to the increasing number of people affected by it. When the chief represents the company personally in these contacts, an increasing proportion of his time is spent away from his subordinates. Or it may be difficult or impossible for the chief executive to handle the growing demands of coordination and communication. Hence he may acquire staff assistance in the person of an "assistant to," who has been called "an extension of the personality of his chief," and as such acts in his name.

Application of military to business organization

The use of a general staff, widely and successfully employed in the armed forces of the world, has been urged by President Eisenhower to the author as "the major application of military to business organization." It is interesting to note that a number of business leaders and pioneers of scientific management started out as "assistants to." For example, Gantt, Barth and S. E. Thompson were assistants to Taylor. Alfred P. Sloan, Jr., and Walter P. Chrysler were assistants to W. C. Durant.

Other staff variants are the "Pentagon Staff" which handles long-range planning for the company as a whole (e.g. the Bell Telephone Laboratories) and the "personal staff" whose job is to make the business life of the chief smoother and more convenient.

(4) *Centralized Controls are designed to find out how well the delegated authority and responsibility are exercised.* Controls may include budgets, standards, reports, audits, visits, regular meetings and exchange of information. Instead of measuring results for the company as a whole, an attempt is made to break down profit or (controllable) cost responsibilities by operating units. This is merely a modernization of the practice of some of the great department store founders who let individual managers alone for a year or two, and then "looked at the record." Perhaps the "decentralization of measurement" partly explains the success of the Standard Oil Company of New Jersey's system of "wholly owned subsidiaries." Furthest in this direction went Orlando F. Webber, for some time the chief executive of Allied Chemical and Dye Company who ran the company on the basis of detailed monthly reports brought to him at the Waldorf Towers, his New York hotel. Not only may costs be effectively controlled by "decentralized measurement," but managerial analysis of results and remedial action are facilitated. A closer tie between effort and reward is made possible.

In a more formal sense there may be a "control office" attached to the chief executive to enable him to "manage on the exception principle." This may be supplemented by manpower controls (varying with the state of business), organization, executive development, planning departments. Essentially the task of the control office is to know the multitude of factors, weigh them and present them in an orderly fashion to someone far removed who makes basic decisions and still has the ultimate cost responsibility, yet can decide only by the rule of "exception."

Deciding the degree of decentralization

Decentralization is not an ideal. It is not a series of principles or prescriptions that a businessman ought necessarily to follow. Decentralization is not necessarily good, nor is centralization necessarily bad.

Centralization or decentralization may be, in part, merely the result of circumstances. Many labor problems are handled centrally because the laws of the country require it or the union insists on it. Many operating or sales decisions are decentralized because it would be physically impossible to operate successfully if they were centralized. Frequently, the centralization or decentralization of a decision is merely an accident. Finally, there is an immense variety of possible human behavior, a vast multiplicity of minute, undiscoverable causes and effects that cannot be encompassed in any principle or standard of evaluation. Thus there is a large area in which necessity, intuition, and luck decide the issue between centralization and decentralization.

Decentralization brings speedier decisions

Where a conscious decision to decentralize is made, ideally it should be based on economic factors. The assignment of a management decision, or any part of it, higher or lower in the management hierarchy, should depend on *the additional revenue to be gained as compared to the additional cost.*

Under decentralization, decisions may be made more speedily because problems of communications are minimized. Often the decisions will be wiser also, because the men who make them will be closer to the problems. Other economies may be achieved through better utilization of lower and middle management, greater incentive, more and improved training opportunities, assurance that some products will not be pushed at the expense of others. In addition, when the administrative unit is smaller—absolutely or as a proportion of the employable population of the community—there are likely to be closer and better employee-management and community relations. And for the business as a whole, the decentralization of activities may mean a more widespread distribution of sales and purchases, which may reduce proportionately the unfavorable impact of sales decline.

Finally, decentralization may result in an increase in the marginal social net product—i.e., benefits to the community as distinct from benefits to the company. These general benefits may include more freedom of action for individuals, more widespread opportunity for constructive individual participation, less social stratification within the business.

The contributions of decentralization to profits must be weighed against the costs, both those that can be measured in dollars and cents and those that are more intangible. Easily measurable are the permanent extra costs that result from the larger staffs necessary, and some temporary expenses of introducing the change in management. More intangible costs are the disturbances caused by the change and their possible effects on morale. In addition, there may be "disguised unemployment" (high-priced men not fully utilized) and losses from watertight thinking or over-specialization. Finally, there are the costs (and gains) of destroying or delaying educational and promotional opportunities from some executives and creating them for others in the process of reorganization.

Basically the economic issue between centralization and decentralization is between lower total administrative costs and more effective performance. This is indicated by a quantitative comparison of centralized and decentralized personnel departments in a recent study by E. C. Weiss of the Department of Psychology, University of Maryland. In a small, but apparently not unrepresentative sample of 38 companies, decentralized organizations had a larger ratio of administrative employees to total employment than centralized firms, but lower rates of labor turnover, absenteeism, accident frequencies and severities.

The stages of decentralization

In reorganization the shift from centralization to decentralization can be compared to a capital investment. There is a heavy initial outlay which may be recovered after some years with a permanent net gain.[3]

In the development of every corporation there comes a point at which the gains of increasing size are such that the still increasing costs of coordination are likely to exceed them. Diminishing returns from the management factor begin to set in when the top executive(s) are no longer intimately acquainted with the major problems of the company and are unable to coordinate them effectively or lose their health in attempting the task. (In this the "managerial optimum" differs from the "technical optimum." The latter merely relates to a minimum scale of operations below which the greatest efficiency cannot be achieved.) But if the managerial optimum is exceeded, costs, through declining managerial efficiency and the need for additional coordination begin to rise. The managerial optimum sets, there-

---

[3] (F. W. Taylor once observed "the building of an efficient organization is necessarily slow and sometimes very expensive," *Shop Management*, p. 62.)

fore, an upper limit to the scale of operations unless there is a reorganization and some decentralization.

Reorganization implies an analysis of basic company objectives to determine how well the existing structure meets them, the elimination of existing deficiencies and the introduction of new organizational techniques to overcome the diminishing returns from the factor management.

Processes of reorganization in three stages

The immediate impact of delegation of decision-making tends to bring about economies. At the top management level the need for coordination of all major decisions is considerably reduced. Top management's time is freed to some extent for more important activities. In the smaller administrative (product) units responsibility for basic operating costs is more clearly fixed. There is likely to be an immediate reduction of "red tape and bureaucracy," and elimination of duplication. Better dissemination of more nearly correct information is obtained and faster action taken. Joint responsibility for costs is reduced. There is a new spirit about, and there are many other immediate savings.

Some immediate increase in cost also occurs, since there must be some increase in the number of executives and specialists. Headquarters requires a larger staff to provide more expert advice and control the results of delegated responsibility and authority; and the heads of the various administrative units each require staff assistance also. Flexible budgets, standard cost systems, and other means of analyzing results may be introduced.

In the second stage, the increase in controllers and staff specialists leads to a net increase in administrative expenses, part of which is permanent, and part of which is due to the necessity of gaining experience in the new system.

Eventually, however, the controls and the expert counsel from headquarters and field staff specialists are likely to make for greater profitability. In the long run, therefore, the corporation should not only recoup its initial outlay, but achieve gains that more than offset the continuing extra costs.

Thus decentralization is clearly a difficult process. This explains the necessity of considering it in balance with centralization. Even if the effort does not result in actual delegation of decision-making, it may still prevent an increase in centralization and afford prestige and opportunity to those receiving it.

BIBLIOGRAPHY, CHAPTER XVIII

CASWELL, W. C. "Taking Stock of Divisionalization," *The Management Review* (October, 1956), 856-858.

DALE, ERNEST. *Planning and Developing the Company Organization Structure.* New York: American Management Association, Inc., 1952. Stage II, VII.

DEARDEN, JOHN. "Mirage of Profit Decentralization," *Harvard Business Review* (November-December, 1962), 140-155.

DRUCKER, P. F. *Concept of the Corporation.* New York: The John Day Company, Inc., 1946. Part II.

GIBSON, EDWIN T. "Polices and Principles of Decentralized Management," *Operating Under Decentralized Management.* General Management Series No. 144. New York: American Management Association, Inc., 1949, 12-20.

KEUFFEL, CARL W. "Breaking Out of a Beehive," *Dun's Review and Modern Industry* (August, 1955), 35, 68-72.

MURPHY, J. A. "Centralized Control in a Decentralized Operation," *Management Methods* (October, 1955), 63-64.

MURPHY, ROBERT W. "Corporate Divisions vs. Subsidiaries," *Harvard Business Review*, Vol. 34, No. 6 (1956), 83-92.

Problems and Policies of Decentralized Management. General Management Series No. 154. New York: American Management Association, Inc., 1952.

SEARES, A. N. "Centralized Control of Decentralized Operations," *Advanced Management* (October, 1957), 10-16, 30.

STAMBAUGH, A. A. "Decentralization: The Key to the Future," *Dun's Review and Modern Industry* (September, 1953), 54-55, 164-174.

SWANK, CLAUDE V. "Some Principles of Decentralized Operation," Production Series No. 176, *Organizing for Efficient Production.* New York: American Management Association, Inc., 1948.

TRUMAN, D. B. *Administrative Decentralization.* Chicago: The University of Chicago Press, 1940.

WORTHY, J. C. "Organization Structure and Employee Morale," *American Sociological Review*, Vol. 15 (1950), 169-179.

Chapter XIX
Organization Methods

In this final chapter devoted to the subject of organization, some techniques and problems of organization not previously discussed are examined. Since most managers deal with already existing organizations rather than with building new groups from the ground up, consideration of reorganizing and of change in organization are of continuing interest. In the light of reorganization needs, the first article by Frank J. Jasinski examines adapting organization to changes in technology. In the second article consideration is given to a review of organization structure to discover whether the classical principles of management have been violated in its design or operation.

The final two articles examine the alternative of using committees or groups to deal with work rather than to assign this same work to an individual managing subordinates. Since committees have so often been misused, Louis A. Allen examines the ways by which management can make better use of committees within organizations. In the last article William H. Mylander explains a successful operation at a relatively high management level in which a committee acted in place of an individual.

65. ADAPTING ORGANIZATION TO
NEW TECHNOLOGY [1]

Frank J. Jasinski [2]

Getting a new machine or production process to live up to advance expectations is often a hard job. Few are the companies that have not had frustrating experiences at one time or another in achieving the improvements that were *supposed* to come from a new line of automatic presses, or a more modern extrusion process, or a promising change in the conveyer system.

Invariably the question comes up: What went wrong? Sometimes, of course, the trouble is simply that the estimates in cost savings or productivity increases were too optimistic. Sometimes the engineering is faulty. Sometimes the loss of a key supervisor, a strike, or a change in some other part of the plant is to blame. And sometimes the new technology is too hard on workers and supervisors, or threatens them in some way so that they resist it.

We are all familiar with such troubles. They are cited again and again. But there is another common type of difficulty—one that is rarely cited. It is a peculiarly *management* problem in that it both begins and ends with management, and no group *but* management can deal with it effectively.

Let me state this problem first in an abstract way; later we can go into detail and illustration. The idea is this: *a change in production or technology affects organizational relationships*. For example, a supervisor may find himself working with other supervisors and groups with whom he has had little contact before, or he may find himself reporting to different people, or different people reporting to him. *When management overlooks these social changes, it generally fails to realize the full potential of a change in technology*, however well thought out the innovation was from an engineering standpoint. The potential may then be achieved only after a difficult and costly period of readjustment. The duration of the readjustment period

[1] From *Harvard Business Review* (January-February, 1959), pp. 79-86. Reprinted by permission of *Harvard Business Review*.
[2] Frank J. Jasinski, Institute of Human Relations, Yale University.

and the degree of technological potential finally attained depend, for the most part, upon management's awareness of the relationship between technology and organization and upon its ability to keep one in harmony with the other through changing times.

Management has established and maintains staffs of engineers who devote considerable time and effort to evaluating new plant sites, designing processes, and making meticulous plant layouts. In contrast, it makes only a nominal, if any, corresponding study of the organizational requirements of a new technological process. Rather, it usually tries to extend the existing organizational structure to the new process. And here is where much of the difficulty lies.

THE OUTMODED VERTICAL

Traditional business organization runs on a vertical line, relying almost solely on superior-subordinate relationships. Orders and instructions go down the line; reports and requests go up the line. But technology, including both integrated data processing and integrated machine production, has developed on what might be called a horizontal plane; that is, the machine cuts across superior-subordinate relationships, affecting the jobs of people in different areas, departments, and work groups. Superimposing a strictly vertical organization structure on a technology which emphasizes horizontal and diagonal relationships can and does cause obvious difficulties.

Typical of the kinds of relationships required by modern technology is the progressive fabricating and assembly line. Here the need to make the right decision or take the necessary action at the right time at the right place is immediate. Managers, in order to solve an immediate problem, have to deal horizontally with their peers and diagonally with people at different levels who are neither superiors nor subordinates. To follow established, formal routes would be too time-consuming, too costly, and too disruptive.

Necessary as these horizontal and diagonal relations may be to smooth functioning of the technology, or work flow, they are seldom defined or charted formally. Nonetheless, wherever or whenever modern technology does operate effectively, these relations exist, if only on a nonformal basis. In other words, certain individuals have developed their own techniques to work satisfactorily outside of (or in place of) the formal framework. They have usually done so after a period of trial and error and emerge as outstanding performers because they can deal effectively with equals, nonsubordinates, and

nonsuperiors—undefined relationships which nevertheless are essential to the technology.

Certainly it is management's job not only to recognize these new
kinds of relationships but also to take steps to enable them to function
definitely and smoothly. A few managers have recognized the discrepancy between organization and technology, and have taken steps
to integrate the two. They have achieved such integration in a
variety of ways, which essentially may be classified as:

1. Changing the technology to conform with the existing organizational
   structure.
2. Changing the organization so as to define and formalize the relationships required by the technology.
3. Maintaining both the existing organization and the existing technology but introducing mechanisms to reduce or minimize the discrepancies between the two.

In appraising these steps we will want to look at the kinds of
problems which arise when technology and organization are not integrated, and at specific examples of what can be and has been done
to recognize and alleviate the basic causes of these problems.

HORIZONTAL RELATIONS

Let us start out by considering a technology which dramatizes
the horizontal nature of the work flow—the automobile assembly
line. I shall present the kinds of problems which can arise and the
nonformal adjustments some members of management have made, as
revealed by the Technology Project at Yale University.[3]

Pressure for short cuts

The automobile assembly line winds its way, almost uninterruptedly, for several miles through the plant. The conveyer carries
each automobile "without a stop" through five departments, past the
areas of 10 general foremen, through the sections of 50 or 60 foremen,
and past the work stations of thousands of workers.

When the "body" starts out, it is a flat sheet of metal comprising
the car floor; at the end of the conveyer the car, now complete, is

---

[3] For previous findings, see Charles R. Walker and Robert H. Guest, *The Man
on the Assembly Line* (Cambridge: Harvard University Press, 1952); Charles R.
Walker, Robert H. Guest, and Arthur N. Turner, *The Foreman on the Assembly
Line* (Cambridge: Harvard University Press, 1956); also Walker and Guest,
"The Man on the Assembly Line," *Harvard Business Review* (May-June, 1952),
p. 71; and Arthur N. Turner, "Management and the Assembly Line," *Harvard
Business Review* (September-October, 1955), p. 40.

driven off into the test area. In between there are innumerable feeder lines or tributaries which bring parts to the main conveyer to be attached to the gradually evolving body. The entire plant and the efforts of all the employees are geared to the task of getting the right part to the right place at the right time.

There is, therefore, considerable interdependence both among production workers and between the production and nonproduction groups. The holes for a particular bit of chromium trim are drilled before the body is prepared for painting; the trim is attached a mile or so down the line. The piece of trim has to be on hand, brought there by a materials handler. And the tools of both driller and "attacher" have to operate at top efficiency—the responsibility of the maintenance man.

In other words, the foreman, to be effective, has to synchronize and coordinate the efforts of many individuals to achieve his production goals. He has to supervise the work of his direct subordinates; he has to make sure that parts are readily and continuously available; he has to ensure peak performance of all equipment in his area; he has to keep "tabs" on quality; and he has to track down and attempt to correct defective work done in previous sections which may be hampering his operators' work.

Yet, despite the importance of all these relations to smooth work flow, the organization does not define them formally. In fact, the formal relations are such that additional difficulties are introduced. For example:

1. Although the workers report to the foreman and he, in turn, to the general foreman, others who are essential to the work flow do not. The materials handler reports up a separate and distinct vertical plane. So do the maintenance man and the inspector.
2. Again, although production defects are within the line production organization, they may be caused by a foreman who reports to a different general foreman and sometimes even to a different superintendent.

Theoretically, the foreman can report any deficiency in services from supporting groups to his general foreman. This procedure is formally and clearly defined. Time on the assembly line, however, is crucial; cars pass a given work station at the rate of one every 1.5 minutes. Unless an error is corrected immediately, the consequences can be far-reaching. The foreman cannot afford to spend time hunting down the general foreman; he has to attend to the matters immediately and directly. To do so he has to deal with other foremen (on the horizontal plane) and also with materials handlers, maintenance men, inspectors, and other foremen's workers (on the diagonal plane).

Readjustments required

In view of the importance of horizontal and diagonal relations to assembly-line technology, the whole concept of superior-subordinate relations is out of place—at least, in much of the plant during much of the time. The formal boxes and directional arrows on the organization chart cannot set the tone for everyday activities. Unless this is recognized, problems can arise.[4] As one perceptive foreman commented: "When you deal with someone from another department, you have to show a smile."

Unfortunately, the Technology Project has revealed that many supervisors, accustomed to behaving according to the usual vertical channels, have not learned to relate effectively on a horizontal plane:

1. In case I get stuff coming into my department that is wrong I usually let my general foreman know . . . and he goes over and gets it straightened out. I couldn't do that myself because, after all, I'm just another foreman.
2. Actually the job I'm doing now is that of a general foreman because I'm checking on these six foremen all the time. I've got the responsibility of letting them know that they're slipping up in one job or another, but I haven't got the authority to *tell* them to button up. Lots of times I have to go to my general foreman.

This lack of patterning and clarity in horizontal relationships frequently creates clashes between foremen. One worker provided this dramatic illustration:

The foremen go around sticking files into one another's heads in front of the men. Just today we thought we were going to see a fist fight between our foreman and another one. They were screaming like washerwomen at one another. Fine example—they hate one another.

Hardly the way to get a job done! Yet these difficulties do not derive from personality clashes. Repeated reports of similar incidents throughout this particular plant strongly indicate a basic shortcoming on the part of the organization to adjust to the incoming technology.

Interestingly enough, there are a number of foremen who have been able to establish and maintain satisfactory nonformal relations

---

[4] Frank J. Jasinski, "Foreman Relationships Outside the Work Group," *Personnel* (September, 1956), pp. 130-136.

with other foremen and with staff and service groups. This means spending much time with persons other than their immediate subordinates. Indeed, contrary to the traditional emphasis on the importance of the vertical foreman-worker relationships, the demands of technology are such that good foremen actually have to interact *most* of the time in horizontal and diagonal relations. As a matter of fact, the foremen judged most effective by their superiors are the very ones who spend the least amount of time with their own workers.

At the time of our study, management was not aware of the relations required by the work flow—or, at least, it had not done much to formalize those relations. In fact, the individual foremen making the necessary adjustments sometimes had to do so in violation of official policy.

Key to success

Horizontal and diagonal relationships, such as those described, exist in virtually all business and industrial organizations.[5] A classic example involves a group of drill line operators in a factory who, even in the face of vigorous management disapproval, resisted the formal logics of an incentive system and continued to devise nonformal methods and relations for getting the work done.

There is no dearth of evidence to indicate that, whether or not the firm operates under the pressing immediacy of an automobile assembly line, the degree of production success depends in good measure upon the mutual adjustment or harmonious integration of the organizational structure and the technology. Where this integration is faulty, those individuals who are able to utilize satisfactorily the nonformal relations required are the successful ones. Where management has recognized the need for integration and has taken steps to achieve it, the efforts of individuals are made that much easier and more effective.

Having considered the kinds of conflict which can arise between the technology and the organization, let us now turn to examples of how some managers have effected a more satisfactory integration. As stated earlier, these methods are: changing the technology, changing the organization and (less radically) introducing mechanisms to reduce discrepancies between organization and technology.

[5] See William F. Whyte, *Money and Motivation* (New York: Harper & Brothers, 1955), pp. 53-66, and "Economic Incentives and Human Relations," *Harvard Business Review* (March-April, 1952), p. 73.

Changing the Technology

Ordinarily, managers consider technology to be inviolate. And frequently it is. After all, in making steel, for example, the metal has certain physical properties which require a certain timing and sequence of operations whether it is made in an American, Russian, or Indian mill. As a result, there are not many dramatic examples available of managers' making changes in the technology to adapt it to the existing organizational structure. The illustrations that are available, however, should serve to make the point. For instance, though it is not generally thought of in these terms, the shift from process to product layout in industry is a fairly widespread technique for effecting just such a change. Most of the integrated machine-processing units would fall into this category.

One-man supervision

Formerly, under the process layout, the manufactured item would go from the rough turning or lathe department to the mill and drill department, to the heat treat department, back to the grinding department, and so on until it finally went to the assembly department —with a different foreman in charge of each department. That is why there are so many meetings in such industrial organizations trying to pin down responsibility for schedule delays and errors in manufacturing.

It is true that, where volume warrants such a change, reorganizing the technology into a product layout brings about considerable savings in materials handling. This is usually the reason given for such a change. The product is no longer shunted between departments but goes uninterruptedly down a single line.

Yet the product layout conforms to the traditional organizational structure, and a number of managers have utilized it for that reason. With the product layout, one man, whether a foreman or superintendent, is responsible for the entire product. He has control over rough turning, mill and drill, heat treat, grinding, and even assembly. The operators who perform these diverse operations all report to him—in an established, clearly defined superior-subordinate relationship. Integration between organization and technology is thus achieved.

This kind of integration is possible only when the product can be made by the number of employees reporting to a specific foreman. When more workers are required, and two, three, or even more foremen are involved, closely knit integration becomes difficult.

As automatic equipment takes over more and more operations and as the actual number of employees is reduced, the number of products which can be manufactured in a product layout supervised by one foreman will increase. However, most industrial products, for one reason or another, still do not lend themselves to "one-foreman product layout" integration. In such instances, managers need to rely on one of the other methods to be discussed here.

CHANGING THE ORGANIZATION

The impact of recent technological innovations has forced many managers to take a second look at their organization, particularly with the advent of modern data-processing equipment. This equipment requires information in a certain form. Where managers have used it as more than simply a change in "hardware," the equipment has triggered sweeping revisions of data-processing departments. To prepare information efficiently for the processing equipment, managers have completely reorganized traditional departments. In this connection there are the telling, though perhaps exaggerated, stories of companies that revised their organizations in anticipation of delivery of data-processing equipment only to realize such great savings through the reorganization process itself that they canceled their orders for the equipment.

Successful solutions

Charles R. Walker in his book, *Toward the Automatic Factory,*[6] describes one instance of conflict between the new technology and the existing formal organization and how that conflict was finally resolved:

> A $40 million installation of a semiautomatic seamless tube mill failed to meet engineers' production estimates for nearly three years. There were a number of variables that were responsible for this delay, and most of them could be termed human factors.
> Among these variables was the fact that the amount of production was pretty much regulated by the automatic machinery. An important variable in the level of production was "downtime"—the length of time it took to make a repair or a mill changeover for a different size of product. As with most industrial organizations, those interruptions of production involved "nonproduction" personnel: crane operators, maintenance men, and repairmen. Most of these nonproduction men did not

[6] New Haven: Yale University Press, 1957, pp. 126-142; see also Walker's "Life in the Automatic Factory," *Harvard Business Review* (January-February, 1958), p. 111.

report to line management directly; they reported vertically along separate lines of authority. Further, while the men on the mill crew were paid for what they produced by an incentive plan, the crane operators and maintenance men were paid on day rates.

In other words, though the technology required the mill crew, the crane operators, and the maintenance men to work as a cohesive unit, management through its formal organization and its incentive plan treated them as separate entities, even to the extent of paying them differently. Productivity suffered as a result.

It was not until the workers convinced management (and the union, as a matter of fact) that the incentive plan should be extended to cover the entire work group—as required by the technology of the semiautomatic steel mill—that productivity increased. Following this and other changes, production not only met the engineers' original estimates of capacity but far exceeded them.

Had management recognized the new organizational structure required and made the necessary adjustments at the outset, then much of the three-year period of costly adjustment might have been avoided.

Undoubtedly, other managers have had similar experiences as one of the consequences of rapid technological innovation. Some may have recognized the nature of the problem and acted to alleviate it. Others may have simply let it ride. It is quite possible for a plant to function for quite some time with a conflict between its organization and the technology—but at less than optimal efficiency. It is also possible for such a plant to benefit from integration even after a lengthy period of such conflict.

A case in point is A. K. Rice's now famous Indian weaving-shed study:

> Organization and technology had been firmly established for a long time. As in the steel mill, the weaving technology required a high degree of coordination between the weavers and a variety of service people—especially during a change of cloth, a break in the yarn, and the loading and unloading of the loom. But the representatives from the servicing units who worked with a particular weaver varied considerably from one group activity to the next. The groups lacked uniformity and continuity over time. There was confusion as to who reported to whom and who had authority over whom. This, and the lack of group continuity, resulted in inefficiencies as well as high damage in production.
>
> Then changes in the organization were introduced so that it would conform more closely with the technological requirements. For example, small work groups were created, with internal leadership, which existed as a unit over time and so were better able to cope with technological requirements satisfactorily. As a result, efficiency jumped 10% and damage dropped 7%.[7]

[7] "Productivity and Social Organization in an Indian Weaving Shed," *Human Relations* (November, 1953), p. 297; see also a subsequent report, "The Experimental Reorganization of Non-Automatic Weaving in an Indian Mill," *Human Relations* (August, 1955), p. 199.

Temporary measures

Obviously, the dramatic and thorough revisions described above are not always feasible or practical in modern business and industry. But managers frequently have made smaller organizational changes that border on being mechanisms. They can be of a temporary or quasi-official nature, or permanently incorporated.

Such temporary measures include coordinators or project heads who provide an organizational short circuit for the duration of a crash program. Best known, perhaps, are the temporary realignments during World War II in invasion task forces. Just prior to and during the invasion one man headed all participating service units. Following the successful completion of the invasion, the task force regrouped into separate and independent units reporting along individual service lines.

In industry, similar groups or teams are temporarily formed to carry out a specified purpose. Many engineering research departments function on a project team basis permanently. Another kind of quasi-official organizational change is the use of an expediter, who, unlike the coordinator or project head, has no direct authority over the individuals with whom he relates.

Still another kind of organizational measure, widely used to cope with horizontal relations, is the meeting. This form enables representatives from the several departments to raise, discuss, and resolve problems requiring the joint efforts of two or more department heads attending the meeting. Here again, the traditional and time-consuming formal channel is bypassed. Usually interdepartmental or interdivisional meetings are held at a top-management level; their usefulness or necessity at lower levels has yet to be fully explored by many organizations.

Other managers have found it expedient to include functions which have been traditionally staff responsibilities under production personnel control. For instance, in an aircraft engine company on the East coast, management transferred its "tool trouble" groups from the master mechanic's department to production and created a new job classification (with quality control functions) under each production foreman.

In fact, considerable attention is currently being given by several large corporations to the question of how many of the service functions can be handed over to the foreman. This is an attempt, it would seem, to fall back on the well-establshed vertical, superior-subordinate relationships and thus avoid the nebulous and consequently difficult line-staff relationships. The limitations described previously in discussing the product-layout plan, however, would apply equally in this instance. The product must be one that requires no more individuals—machine operators and the transferred service personnel—than a foreman can adequately supervise or manage.

INTRODUCING MECHANISMS

Still other managers faced with a discrepancy between technology and organizational structure have attempted to solve the dilemma by changing neither technology nor organization but by introducing new mechanisms. In this case, we are not concerned with minor organizational moves such as have been described in the preceding section, but with procedures or routines.

A dramatic example taken from the restaurant industry of the introduction of a mechanism is provided by William F. Whyte.[8] The problem confronting him was a simple but vexing one:

> Viewing the situation *in formal organizational terms*, the waitresses reported vertically to the hostess; the counterman reported along another vertical line of "command" to the kitchen supervisor. Although not explicit, there was some indication that the countermen considered themselves at a higher organizational level than the waitresses. But *technologically* the work flow was from the customer to the waitress to the counterman. This ran against the formal organization. Not only was the relationship between waitress and counterman formally undefined; it also went diagonally, from a lower to a higher level.

In the cases cited by Whyte, a few individuals were able to adjust to this nonformal relationship, but they emerged as exceptions to the usual conflict pattern. Unfortunately, management did not recognize and take advantage of this adjustment and formalize these effective nonformal relationships in order to extend them to others in the organization.

Recognizing the conflict, Whyte introduced a mechanism to reduce it:

> As an experiment, one waitress wrote out her orders and placed them on a spindle. Her orders were always ready before those of other waitresses who had called theirs in at the same time. If she was not ready for a hot food order, the counterman would voluntarily place it in the warmer for her. Furthermore, he took a liking to her and

---

[8] *Human Relations in the Restaurant Industry* (New York: McGraw-Hill Book Company, Inc., 1948), Chapter 6.

made a bet with the bartender that she, like himself, was of Polish extraction—which she was not.[9]

Thus, an uncomplicated mechanism reduced the conflict between the technological work flow and the organizational setup without changing either.

Other illustrations

The use of paper work as a mechanism to reduce possible conflict in formally undefined relationships is a commonplace in industry. Requests from production foremen, for example, go regularly to personnel, engineering, accounting, and other staff and service groups. Such requests cut across the formal organization both horizontally and diagonally. Conversely, reports may also cut across the organization through the "copy to . . ." technique while going up the line vertically.

Very often, the amount and type of paper work (copies of requests and reports) do not correspond to actual need. Many are destined to end up in the "circular file" simply because the paper work routes do not follow the lines required by the technology. (Machine accountants, aware of this discrepancy and pressed for tabulating time, occasionally run a check on the use made of various reports; they purposely delay circulation of a report for a few days or a week to see how many people will actually call for it. Thus they have been able, unofficially, to eliminate a number of outdated reports.)

The automobile assembly line provides additional illustrations of mechanisms employed by management to meet technologically required horizontal and diagonal relations:

> An operator who hangs doors is in direct contact with the operator who puts them in proper sequence on the overhead conveyer. In the event of a misscheduled door, the line operator has a "squawk" box through which he can call for a substitute door. Here we have a horizontal relationship between two hourly operators, one in production and one in material control.
>
> The worker who loads the overhead conveyor is guided in turn in his door scheduling by the "telautograph," which transmits information from an earlier point on the line from another hourly operator in the material control department. This operator notes the sequence of models and body types of cars passing his station on the line. The information is transmitted simultaneously to various schedulers in the plant who have to synchronize their operations with this sequence.

[9] *Ibid.*, p. 69.

In the event of a mechanical or tool breakdown, time is especially important. When a line worker cannot perform his operation because of such a breakdown, he immediately signals for help through a whistle system: he uses one signal for a mechanical breakdown, another for an electrical one. The appropriate repairman (who is stationed nearby) comes over to repair the defect with a minimum of delay. For a worker to stop the line until he finds his foreman to report the breakdown in the traditional vertical plane would be absurd.

Several managements have adopted programs to facilitate non-formal relations. These range from company-wide social affairs, such as picnics, banquets, or sports teams, to a systematic rotation program whereby individuals at supervisory and middle-management levels transfer periodically from one department to another. Ostensibly, the purpose of such a program is to "broaden" the experience of the individual; actually the more important by-product is that it establishes friendships horizontally and diagonally, and thus encourages and facilitates nonformal relations required by the work flow.

Although many of these and other mechanisms can be effective and may, indeed, be the only means to reduce a discrepancy between technology and organization, it still is worthwhile to make broader and more basic changes in either the technology or the organization.

CONCLUSION

Frequently, the traditional, formally defined vertical relations in business and industrial organization prove inadequate to cope with modern technology. New technologies require new organizational setups, and it is being found increasingly that industrial processes require horizontal and diagonal relations which are not patterned or clearly defined.

Such lack of clarity can impair the production process. The work flow can create difficulty where the vertical lines are strongly emphasized and where the flow violates those lines—as was the case in the restaurant example cited. But when the formal organization is permissive, nonformal relations in the horizontal and diagonal planes arise to cope with the technological process. We saw that the more successful assembly-line foremen learned to relate with other foremen and their workers. But these relationships were not usually recognized formally; they existed on an individual and nonformal basis.

Management can work toward an integration between technology and organization in several ways: (1) by changing the technology,

(2) by changing the organization, and (3) by introducing mechanisms. All these methods have been used effectively to some degree, but the difficulty occurs in that management's attempts toward integration generally lack a systematic and purposeful approach. They may just happen over time, arise as temporary expedients, or emerge as a solution to a crisis situation. Many managers have yet to explore the deeper relation between technology and the organization.

The advent of electronic data processing and integrating machine processing has forced some managers to reorganize departments to meet technological needs. Many such revisions, however, are limited to a small portion of the organization, to the areas of greatest immediate pressure. Cannot more be done? The case studies cited, as well as the successful partial steps taken by businessmen and industrialists thus far, indicate a need for a systematic analysis of technology and organization. This analysis might include the following steps:

1. Examine the work flow of the technology to determine what relations are required.
2. Identify the points where the formal organization meets these requirements and where it does not.
3. Discover what nonformal relationships exist at present to meet the technologically required relations which are not encompassed by the formal organization.
4. Determine what formalization does exist to cope with relations falling beyond the traditional vertical planes.
5. Decide which of the nonformal relations might be profitably formalized.
6. Provide measures to facilitate the nonformal relations which are still required but which may best remain nonformal.

It will not be possible to formalize through new mechanisms or through technology and organization changes all of the nonformal relations required by the work flow. It should be possible, however, to remove or reduce the *major* points of variance between the technology and the organization. It makes sense for a company that has been farsighted enough to bring in a new technology to be equally farsighted in recognizing that established organizational patterns will not usually serve with the same effectiveness as they once did. If the new technology is to live up to production expectations, then management must see to it that organization relationships are carefully restudied and wisely redirected.

66. TWELVE HAZARDS IN
ORGANIZING [1]

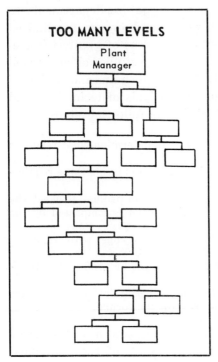

TOO MANY LEVELS

Plant Manager

Hazard No. 1. This set-up has five strikes against it: Besides being poor for communications, decision making, and for wage and salary administration, it's costly to staff. And it cuts authorities and responsibilities so fine, it needs a Philadelphia lawyer to spell them out.

Like the old telephone game, this long chain of command can garble information that's passed down the line: *Some stuff just never trickles all the way to the bottom.* And for information that must move upward, the organizational barriers slow down matters that need quick top-level decisions. Top-level decisions are also hard to make because the plant manager is so far removed from the point of execution.

For front-line action, the numerous levels block the foreman who wants to get something done without checking too far for approval. *Take this case:* A sales representative calls the plant to change an order already on the production line. If the change requires overtime to meet delivery dates, how far up the chain of command must the line foreman go for approval? If the sales representative were to call the change in at the top of the organization, imagine how long it would take to effect the change at six or seven levels. How much production time would be lost.

[1] From *Factory Management and Maintenance* (June, 1957) pp. 102-105. Reprinted by permission of *Factory Management and Maintenance.*

With this elongated structure, there's also the added danger of wage and salary differentials becoming too narrow. This creates another administrative headache.

Better to cut the number of levels down as far as possible. Best rule is never to add another level until all alternative solutions to the problem have been explored.

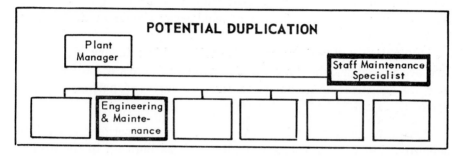

Hazard No. 2. This "gray" set-up is loaded with trouble. Several things can happen. Overlap and duplication of effort, for instance. Or the reverse, a "you first, Gaston," kind of inaction. For others in the organization, the overlap tends to create confusion. Conflicts arising from this type of setup may also drain the plant manager's time and attention in efforts to resolve them.

On this chart, just what is the maintenance specialist supposed to do? Plan? Does his planning aid the maintenance superintendent? Or is it just duplication? What sort of authority relationship is there between the two maintenance areas? Can responsibility for maintenance performance be pinned down? Just who *does* the plant manager turn to with a maintenance problem?

Better to consolidate functional responsibilities by assigning the maintenance specialist to the department superintendent—as a staff assistant, for instance.

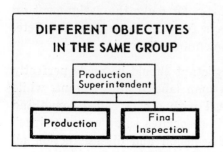

Hazard No. 3. Here one function is to get out production, the other to see that what is produced measures up to product specifications. When final inspection is combined with the output function, inspection is weakened, may lead to dilution of one interest or to harmful collusion.

Certainly the production department must also bear responsibility for quality as well as quantity. But there must be separate checks and balances. Ideally, they should be placed as high up the line as possible—typically in a quality control department reporting at the same level as the manager in charge of production. The production manager should not set the criteria by which he will be judged (standards or specifications). Nor should he be the final judge of his own success any more than a bookkeeper should audit his own books.

Production and maintenance also fall in this category. When the two are placed within the same department, there's a natural tendency to sacrifice maintenance to the pressures of getting out the product.

Better to keep activities with conflicting or divergent objectives separate. Move the responsibility for each as high up in the organization as possible—even though they may take place side by side on the production floor.

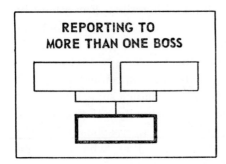

**REPORTING TO
MORE THAN ONE BOSS**

Hazard No. 4. An oldy—but it happens every day. Consequences: conflicting orders, confusion over priority of assignments, no one source of appeal or responsibility for the individual's training, development, promotion.

Anyone who's been caught in this nutcracker knows the dilemma: Which boss's work comes first? When I get conflicting orders, whose do I follow? To whom do I owe my loyalty? Which one will pitch for me for a raise or a promotion?

Better to avoid this one at all costs. Or make the assignment on a time allocation basis—i.e., two days for Joe, three days for Pete. And be sure Joe's and Pete's assignments don't overlap.

Hazard No. 5. The role of an assistant should be made perfectly clear to all concerned. Otherwise a man labeled an assistant, while still on the same organizational level with others called something less important, may be tagged by his associates as a "crown prince" or "favorite son." This leads to dissension and dissatisfaction all through the staff.

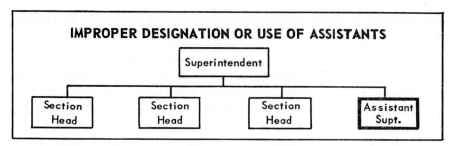

It's a fact that many such improper designations fail to show up until you put your idea of your organization down on paper. But this problem is more than a matter of charting technique.

Take this assistant. Others may not only think he is the heir apparent. They may also want to know specifically: Is he in charge when the superintendent is away? Or is he really just an "assistant to"?

Better to spell out an assistant's real function—right in his job title. Then slot him into the right organizational level.

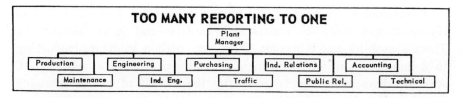

Hazard No. 6. There's no universally "right" number of subordinates. The number that is manageable depends upon many factors. But in general this kind of structure is dangerous because it dilutes the superior's attention, often forcing him to snap decisions and to spend much of his time putting out fires rather than planning his work. It also creates problems in determining what to attend to first, and in coordinating and measuring the performance of so many who report to a single boss.

Further, there is potential duplication of effort in the ranks—with the danger of strong persons assuming responsibilities not really theirs.

Though "span of control" is a hotly debated subject there is no doubt that somewhere for each manager there is a limit to the number of people he can effectively supervise. But in thinking of reducing the number reporting, you must also consider the disadvantages and expenses of extra vertical levels that might result—as in Hazard No. 1.

Better to look at each problem of span of management control individually. In a production department involving several similar and closely related tasks, a manager may be able to provide adequate supervision for a larger number of foremen. But in the case of more difficult and complex work requiring judgment, planning, and coordination, the number of persons who can be properly supervised is more limited.

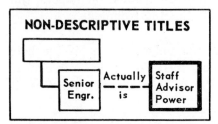

Hazard No. 7. Except that it indicates an organizational level, titles like junior or senior engineer don't tell what the engineer's function actually is. The typical manager's argument, however, is that by pinning down a man's main responsibility (power adviser here) he may lose flexibility of assignment. But descriptive titles do have this advantage—*they fix responsibility.*

Goelz and Efferson feel it's unwise to get too preoccupied with trying to get complete consistency in title and level designation. There's nothing much wrong, they say, with a manager reporting to a manager—or with having a department within a department. Any disadvantages may be offset by the benefit of people knowing exactly what they and others are supposed to do.

Better to select titles that make duties clear to everyone than to lean on more general titles to preserve freedom of assignment.

Hazard No. 8. Not altogether bad, but it has its risks. The assistant may become more of a barrier than an aide, function merely as a messenger boy. If so, he may consciously or otherwise slant communications, slow down decisions, isolate the manager from personal contact with other members of his department.

But this arrangement *can*, and *does*, work in some situations. A superior and his assistant may sit "back-to-back," one handling external matters, the other internal matters. It may be used as a training device, or as a temporary expedient when the superior is nearing retirement age. In unusual circumstances, as when the superior must do much of his work outside the plant—say, 75% or more—it may be the only solution to having an "inside" man on the job at all times.

Better to approach this structure with caution. If the assistant is in fact a staff aide, make him an "assistant to." Or, if he does have responsibility for certain functions in the department, they should be plainly spelled out—and the chart changed to show the exact role the assistant plays.

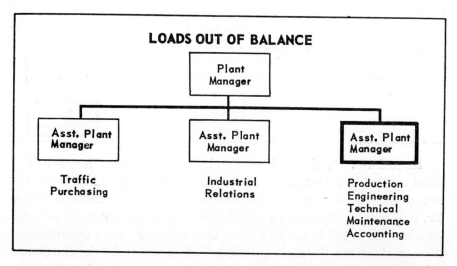

LOADS OUT OF BALANCE

Hazard No. 9. The idea of having three assistant managers is all right—if each has about the same work load. In this case, the assistant who must carry a major plant function—production— must also carry those functions that serve him. Chances are they'll get short shrift from him. Then, too, putting traffic, purchasing, and industrial relations under the other two assistants tends to over-emphasize them in respect to other service functions.

Another serious drawback. This structure makes it difficult to develop three active candidates for the plant manager's job. Keen competition is one of the best advantages of organizational balance.

Another kind of imbalance has to do with inequities in the *importance* of work assigned at the same level. Say the plant manager were to have an assistant in charge of production reporting at the same level as an assistant in charge of janitorial services or stores. This means that the basically important responsibility is downgraded in the eyes of the production man and his associates. And such an arrangement places on the plant manager's time unnecessary demands for details that are best supervised by someone further down the line.

Better to see that people reporting at the same level have nearly equal workloads and that the work itself is equally important.

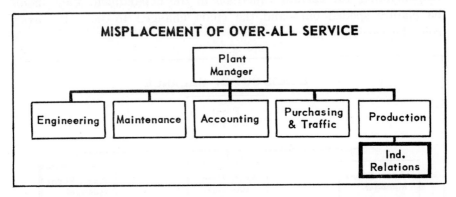

Hazard No. 10. Assigning to a single component a function that must serve the entire plant creates three problems. It restricts the subordinate department's ability to serve all components. It forces the manager (production, in this case) to divide his time between problems close to his eye and those that belong to other departments. Such a structure develops a "production orientation" in the industrial relations group, which can short-change services issued to the plant as a whole.

Better, much better, to raise to equal and separate status any function that must serve several separate components. This is especially true of the traditional service function—such as industrial relations.

Hazard No. 11. As in No. 7, functions, like individuals, need careful labeling. Otherwise a twilight zone of overlap is created. Conflicts between department heads and between employees are unavoidable.

An organization chart best serves its purpose when it clearly tags each function, shows how it is staffed. When this is done properly, the chart then becomes an important guide to indicate where strengths and weaknesses may be in every area of operation.

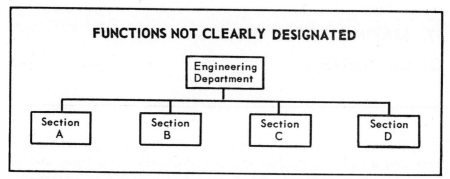

FUNCTIONS NOT CLEARLY DESIGNATED

Better to be explicit in your titles. Clearly define what a section does—e.g., (in this case) "power section," "product design section," "sales service section," "drafting," and so on.

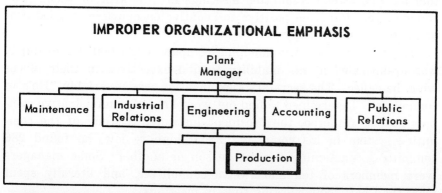

IMPROPER ORGANIZATIONAL EMPHASIS

Hazard No. 12. Here's an example of a single major function that's too far removed from the influence of the plant manager. This structure also hampers communication between production and other major functions.

This situation may look like a remote possibility, but here's the way it can come about. Assume there is a production department in constant trouble. So the plant manager decides to put it under the chief engineer, who has shown he's a good trouble-shooter. A much better solution would have been to develop the production manager, strengthen him with a competent staff. Or, if neither of these two approaches worked, to transfer him to a job better fitting his capabilities.

Better to decide what your major functions are. Then establish them on the same level. Idea is to keep the line of communications as short as possible. Solutions of expediency often cause serious trouble in the long run.

67. MAKING BETTER USE
OF COMMITTEES [1]

Louis A. Allen [2]

If the man-hours spent in committee meetings every working day were added end to end they would undoubtedly total time, and to spare, to run a company the size of General Motors. Attending committee meetings is probably one of the most popular avocational pursuits in American business today. This does not mean, however, that all who attend committee meetings are in favor of them. The range of reaction from positive to negative encompasses a good deal of honest bewilderment.

The president of a Philadelphia company of 10,000, for example, was exasperated at his inability to find executives in their offices when he called. The secretary's explanation was invariably "He's in committee." Determined to find out what kind of administrative complex he had fathered, the president instituted a study of the committee system in his company. From high to low, he found 286 committees functioning for one reason or another. Some managers were members of ten and twelve committees, and literally spent more than half their working time in meetings.

This may be an extreme example. However, to many managers, committees are an unending source of frustration. "If I need a policy decision and the problem gets into a committee, I give up," said one Chicago executive, sales manager for a food company. "Committees are an organized means of passing the buck. The only reason we have them is that some of our top people can't make up their minds and they want a committee to do it for them."

While this viewpoint is prevalent, it is by no means universal. And even where individual executives complain bitterly about the inefficiency of the system, committees still seem to roll along as implacably as a juggernaut.

A great many companies swear by committees as an indispensable tool of management. "We have eight decentralized divisions, and

[1] From the *Management Record* (December, 1955), pp. 466-469, 493. Reprinted by permission of the *Management Record.*
[2] Louis A. Allen, Division of Personnel Administration, National Industrial Conference Board, Inc., 1954.

forty plants, and we are located in five foreign countries as well as the United States," said the president of an equipment company with headquarters in New York City. "I can't be personally acquainted with every issue that comes up, so I rely on committees to give me advice and to help me decide. Without our committee system this company would come apart at the seams."

In spite of the firmly established position of committees and the hot debate as to their merit, THE CONFERENCE BOARD has found in its current study on organization planning that few companies have made a serious analysis of their use of committees. The role of the committee remains only partially evaluated; so, whether or not maligned, it is usually misunderstood.

DEFINITION OF COMMITTEE

Committees are usually relatively formal bodies, with a definite structure. They have their own organization. To them are delegated definite responsibility and authority. A committee is usually given a specific job to do. For example, it may review budgets, formulate plans for new products, or make policy decisions. Or the committee may only have power to make recommendations and suggestions to a designated official. But whatever its task, it is generally given the authority or power it needs to carry it out.[3]

The character and composition of committees is often spelled out in the bylaws or the administrative procedures of the company. Committees usually have a fixed membership. In most cases members are appointed, although, sometimes, as with the board of directors, they may be elected. Membership in a committee is never a casual matter; for example, people don't become members because they happen to join a department, as is true of membership in staff meetings.

In their deliberation, committees usually follow definite rules and procedures, which are often written. But if unwritten, the rules are no less binding. Most committees specify that only the regular members or their designated representatives may vote. Some committees can function if a quorum is in attendance; others must wait until the full membership is present.

Some companies state that their committees are "informal." This is a relative term. Even the most "informal" of committees usually conform to the above criteria. The fact that members may gather

[3] See "Organization Planning," *Management Record*, October, 1954, p. 402.

in a company plane en route from one city to another or around the luncheon table does not detract from the prescribed membership or method of conduct or area of responsibility of the group.

Definition of a committee is difficult because there are many different kinds of committees and the concept of a committee varies widely from one company to another. However, in terms of the criteria outlined above, an acceptable definition might be: *A committee is a body of persons appointed or elected to meet on an organized basis for the consideration of matters brought before it.*

When Should Committees Be Used?

A committee almost invariably is created to carry out responsibilities that would otherwise be delegated to a single individual. Most companies agree that committees are used properly only when individuals in regular, established positions cannot adequately carry out a specific responsibility. It follows that, under certain circumstances, the committee must have inherent capabilities that enable it to operate more effectively than one person.

What unusual properties are found in a committee? Committees have inherent advantages in some situations because people in groups react differently from people as individuals. Group dynamics give the committee certain potential advantages over an individual acting alone.

Pooled knowledge and judgment

A committee is an effective method of bringing the collective knowledge and judgment of a number of people to bear on a problem. One company, in analyzing committee participation, found that the average committee of seven people has over 150 years of composite experience. Representing, as it does, varied viewpoints and backgrounds, this pooled knowledge and judgment may be an invaluable asset when focused on complex problems. In addition, the committee has another closely related characteristic.

Group pressure

The individual members of the group exert pressure or censorship on the ideas, suggestions, comments and judgments of other members. The more loyalty one member feels toward other members of the committee, the more he wants to be liked and respected by them, and, consequently, the more he will tend to conform to this group pressure. The net result may be favorable or unfavorable.

Many executives point out that the very act of pooling and integrating ideas and viewpoints within the group often results in a product that is greater than the sum of the individual contributions. A few executives with outstanding analytical ability or a sense of timing or keen judgment may raise the level of participation of the whole group. A natural question here is: why not throw the problem to such an outstanding individual and let him handle it by himself? The response is that even the outstanding person doesn't have all the answers. If he gets off the beam, or if he is too much influenced by personal prejudices, group pressure will tend to bring him back into line.

This brings up the danger inherent in group pressure. Some specialists claim that this censorship may bring an exceptionally able individual down to the level of a mediocre group. If such an individual's thinking goes beyond the group, or if he shows more imagination than the group can assimilate, or, in fact, if he is very much beyond the capabilities of the group in any way, group pressure may tend to make him conform. Many experienced committee chairmen who have dealt with this situation point out, however, that under proper leadership the group can be encouraged to reconsider ideas it cannot at first assimilate so that eventually the same ideas are reproposed by other members and finally prevail because of their intrinsic merit.

Enforces participation

A third characteristic of group action is that it tends to enforce participation. A major source of resistance to new policies and projects by those who are delegated responsibility for carrying them out is lack of participation on their part at the planning stage. The person who is called upon to suggest, criticize, and make recommendations concerning a policy or project is likely to be motivated to carry it out wholeheartedly. This participation is especially important in decisions which will be binding on all parts of the organization. Many companies find that when department heads who will be affected have an opportunity to participate before the final decision is made, there is better understanding and greater acceptance than will prevail if the decision is by edict.

Obviously, the committee is not the only means of securing this participation. There may be other and more effective opportunities in the normal process of supervision. The chief merit of the committee in this respect seems to be that it makes participation mandatory on the part of members of the committee who are also key people who will be affected by a given decision.

How Are Committees Used?

Committees are most commonly used for the following purposes:

Coordination

When it is necessary to integrate and unify varying points of view, which cannot conveniently or effectively be coordinated by individuals, the committee may be of value in bringing all those concerned together. For example, an eastern chemical company depends largely upon research to provide new products in a competitive market. To determine the feasibility of proposed new products, it is necessary to integrate and unify the ideas and suggestions of the managers of such functions as research, engineering, production, sales, finance and purchasing. At one time the manager of research attempted to coordinate his work by personal visits and discussion with other functional heads. However, he found there were always loose ends, no matter how many personal contacts he made. From this experience, the company concluded that the most effective and economical way to coordinate new product development is through committee meetings which offer opportunity for presentation and resolution of differing points of view.

Advice

Committees may exercise a staff role [4] by providing advice to a specific individual or to the organization at large.

The committee acts in a personal staff role when it restricts its advisory activities to one executive, who may or may not be a member of the committee. It may act in the role of specialized staff when it offers expert counsel and service in one specialized area to the entire organization, as well as to the line principal involved.

Many companies find that committees tend to overlap and duplicate the services available from normal staff agencies when they are used in this fashion. And committees usually have potential handicaps when they act in an advisory capacity. From a procedural viewpoint, a committee is a poor means of gathering and analyzing

[4] See "The Line-Staff Relationship," *Management Record*, Sept. 1955, p. 346.

facts. This usually requires mobility, independent study and investigation. In some companies, the advisory committee has its own staff, or fact-gathering apparatus, in which case the committee acts to review and evaluate the data placed before it.

A committee may be used to advise and counsel a top executive in policy formulation. This has the obvious advantage of pooled knowledge, experience and judgment. It also is a means of bringing out and resolving varying viewpoints so as to ensure a workable policy that will be accepted by those who must put it into effect.

Committees also may provide advice on controls, or the measurement and evaluation of results. Control requires the establishment of standards, recording of current progress, analysis and reporting of variances and exceptions, and appropriate managerial action and follow-up. The committee functions most effectively when it receives reports of progress and variances from fact-gathering and reporting agencies. The committee members study these reports *before* the committee meeting. They devote their meeting time to review and discussion of the data and formulation of recommendations, which are forwarded to the accountable line executive. Committees rarely take control action. This responsibility is usually pinpointed in the line.

Decision-making

Committees sometimes serve as decision-making bodies. This is usually confined, however, to high-level committees. There are those who assert that decision-making should rarely if ever be the responsibility of committees below the level of the board of directors. In other words, committee decision-making seems to be accepted as a sound procedure only when it is not desirable to make a single individual responsible or accountable for the decision. For example, the members of the board of directors share responsibility for making over-all policy decisions and are accountable to the stockholders. In a large manufacturing company, a financial policy committee, comprised of members of the board of directors, decides financial policies. In another company, an executive compensation committee, made up of department vice-presidents, makes final decisions on salary matters for all personnel in specific salary grades.

DANGERS IN THE USE OF COMMITTEES

Some companies have eliminated committees entirely. Others have instituted studies of committee action which have resulted in radical surgery on the committee system. One company, for example, cut down the number of management committees from eighty to twelve; another cut back from two hundred to twenty-four. When this type of curtailment is possible in a well-run, profitable and rapidly expanding company, it is obvious that serious abuses of the committee system are taking place. Company experience shows the following danger points as most prevalent.

1. *Committees encourage managers to shirk or evade decision-making responsibilities.* If a manager has an opportunity to carry a problem to a committee, he may seize upon this as a means of avoiding the necessity for making up his own mind, or to escape the consequences of an unpopular decision. If the chairman of the committee is the accountable person, he can fall back upon the committee as an alibi or scapegoat. If the committee as a whole is held accountable (a nice administrative feat), accountability is so diffuse as to be impossible of assignment.[5] Some managers utilize the committee as a means of avoiding the laborious and difficult process of logical thinking that leads to a sound decision. "I'll bring it before the committee," often serves as an excuse rather than as an acceptable means of administrative action.

2. *Slows decision-making.* Company experience demonstrates that committee action is almost invariably slow and unwieldy, compared to individual decision-making. In some cases this seriously handicaps management of the enterprise. In one company, for example, practically every matter that came to top management had to have the blessing of a committee before the president would make a decision. It was only after a newly styled product was so delayed by committee action that it came out a month behind a similar product of a competitor that the company swept out the overlapping and cumbersome committee system and established straight-line channels for prompt decisions.

The very mechanics of calling people together and providing for discussion is time consuming. And when the managers who are members of the committee are forced to ignore important day-to-day matters to attend a meeting, this compounds the difficulty. There are other mechanical difficulties. Absenteeism, lack of preparation before meetings, and substitutions in membership all slow down decision-making.

3. *May serve to mask ineffective management.* Many companies find that committees are most popular with managers who are inade-

---

[5] See "The Art of Delegation," *Management Record*, March, 1955, p. 90.

quate in their own right. The committee thus serves as a crutch. Since there are likely to be at least a few capable people on the committee, it is able to come to a better decision than an ineffective individual. At the same time, decisions made on the basis of committee participation are likely to be successful to the extent that they have the full support of those members of the committee who participated in the decision. In some cases, committee support is knowingly given an individual by management because there is no capable individual available to do the job. In many instances, however, committees are set up by managers who want to conceal their own weaknesses.

Making Better Use of Committees

Many companies have demonstrated that proper procedures can help cut down the time required for committee meetings, improve the resultant action, and make committees a useful agency of management, rather than a doubtful and much bedeviled administrative gimmick. Such companies usually point to the importance of the following factors.

1. *The committee should have a clearly stated purpose.* A great many committees meet without any clear idea as to what they are supposed to consider. A wage and salary committee, in one company, for example, discusses anything from approval of salary ranges and salaries (its rightful province) to suggestions on how the job evaluation system could be improved—which is a responsibility of the personnel department. The overlap is both wasteful and confusing. Companies that have a systematic approach to the use of committees usually find that this danger can be avoided by setting out a charter in writing for each committee. This specification usually outlines some or all of the following:

> Function and scope of the committee
> Responsibilities
> Authority
> Organizational relationships

2. *Members of the committee should be carefully selected.* Generally, it is wise to have the members of the group of equal status. One of the most common failings of committee action is that one man, who is superior in position to the other members, is able to sway the thinking of the group because of his position. If the members of the group are expected to discuss and contribute on an equal

basis, they should be of similar organizational rank. The manager will think twice before he opposes his vice-president; the vice-president may be uncomfortable if he has to disagree with the chairman of the board. Many companies find, however, that differences in rank are not so critical if the committee members chosen represent different departments.

Some individuals are constitutionally incapable of effective committee action. With subordinates, they are domineering; with superiors, they are obsequious; and with peers, they are quarrelsome. Proper selection of committee members requires a nice judgment as to personality differences, ability in expression, as well as status.

3. *The committee chairman should understand his proper role.* Primarily, the chairman's job is that of expediting and facilitating the progress of the meeting. An executive sometimes wants to use a committee to advise and counsel him, and at the same time to participate as its chairman. When this is the case, he needs to be a highly skilled discussion leader if he is to get the best the group has to offer, rather than an expression of what the group thinks he wants to hear.

The committee chairman's job is to encourage others to express themselves, to settle differences, and to add a touch of humor when the going is rough. He is an arbiter, a peacemaker and an expediter. He should not be a special pleader, an advocate of one point of view or a judge of the opinions being expressed. In practice, the chairman usually finds that he is more the servant of the group than its leader. He does what needs to be done to get maximum cooperation and participation. His job is to get members of the group to think, not to think for them.

4. *The committee should be of proper size.* If the group is too large, many of the members will not have adequate opportunity to express their viewpoints. A large committee with many vocal members may become chaotic. The more people he has to contend with, the more difficult it is for the chairman to keep the discussion moving in productive channels. When the group is too small, it becomes difficult to secure a well-rounded viewpoint. And there is more of a tendency for the members to take sides on every point that comes up. Specialists usually recommend from five to nine as best for the average committee meeting.

5. *There should be adequate preparation for the committee meeting.* If committee meetings are to be productive, little time should be wasted on "make ready" and clerical details during the meeting itself.

The chairman should be provided with adequate clerical and staff assistance, so that he can furnish all available factual data for each member before the meeting starts. Or the chairman or secretary of the group can review the data at the beginning of the meeting. Most companies find it is a waste of time to ask the group to volunteer basic facts and background information during the meeting.

Many committee chairmen recommend that the following steps be taken before every committee meeting:

> Notice of the meeting should be sent out as far in advance as possible. Many feel that at least a month's notice will enable people to schedule trips and appointments before or after the committee meeting and thus help to conserve their time. A week is considered an absolute minimum except in cases of emergency.
>
> Give as much information as possible about the meeting as far in advance as possible. A properly prepared agenda will give the members of the committee an opportunity to think about the subject matter, make inquiries, read and study pertinent data and reports.
>
> Set an exact beginning and ending time for the meeting. This will help the members to arrange schedules, and make it convenient for secretaries to hold telephone calls until the meeting is over.

6. *Follow a logical procedure in conducting the meeting.* Many chairmen limit their leadership to statements such as "Well, what do you think about it?" and "Let's go on to something else." If the time of the committee members is to be invested most wisely, many experienced committee chairmen recommend that some sequence of logical thinking be followed to carry the discussion in an orderly fashion to a logical conclusion. A sequence which has repeatedly yielded good results is the following:

> Review of the pertinent facts by the chairman
> Analysis of the problem in terms of what caused it, if this has not already been brought out, and determining how committee members feel about it
> Suggested solutions
> Group decision or recommendation

The important requirement is that the entire group think together on each step of the sequence. This builds up the necessary background and makes a logical decision possible.

In some companies, the consensus of the meeting is secured by majority vote. Others require concurrence by all members. Still others accept the recommendation of the majority, but record the viewpoints of the dissenters.

7. *Adequate follow-up is necessary.* If the committee presents a recommendation or comes to a decision, appropriate means are necessary to ensure that the intent of the committee is carried out. Usually this is accomplished by making the chairman, secretary or a committee member responsible for whatever follow-up action is required. In all cases, minutes of the committee should be prepared and distributed to each member and to designated members of company management. Some companies require that minutes be prepared and distributed no later than the third working day after the meeting is held.

8. *The work of the committee should be constantly evaluated.* Many companies have periodic reviews of the work of each committee. They determine if it is operating effectively in terms of the purpose for which it was established and whether that purpose is still valid. If this type of control is not instituted, committees often become self-perpetuating. They may waste time, clog administrative channels and take managers from more important work.

68. MANAGEMENT
BY EXECUTIVE COMMITTEE [1]

William H. Mylander [2]

What are the advantages, and the disadvantages, of committee management for the modern American business corporation?

At what point in a company's growth, or product diversification, should consideration be given to committee management?

How does committee management work, and what kind of people are required to make it work successfully?

Questions of this kind were put to 12 of the top executives of E. I. du Pont de Nemours & Company, which has pioneered in using the executive committee form of organization, and this article represents a composite of their replies—their expressions of judgment based on the test of experience.

FORM OF ORGANIZATION

Du Pont, now in its 153rd year, began as a manufacturer of powder on the banks of the Brandywine Creek near Wilmington, Delaware. Its 72 plants in 26 states produce some 1,200 chemical product lines with a sales volume of close to $1.7 billion in 1954.

Until 1921, du Pont was operated with the customary line organization headed by a president assisted by vice presidents in charge of specialized functions such as finance, production, and sales. Then, under the farsighted presidency of Irenee du Pont, now honorary chairman of the board, the company adopted a committee-line system regarded as unique in American industry.

At the top is an executive committee of the board of directors consisting of President Crawford H. Greenewalt and nine vice presidents. These men devote full time to the company's affairs, although relieved of day-by-day functional responsibilities. As a committee, they meet each Wednesday, and oftener if necessary. The bylaws provide that between the monthly meetings of the board the executive committee:

[1] From the *Harvard Business Review*, Vol. 33, No. 3, pp. 51-58. Reprinted by permission of the *Harvard Business Review*.

[2] William H. Mylander, Administrative Assistant, E. I. du Pont de Nemours & Company, 1955.

". . . shall possess and may exercise all the powers of the Board of
Directors in the management and direction of all the business and affairs
of the company . . . in such a manner as the Executive Committee shall
deem best for the interest of the company in all cases in which specific
directions shall not have been given by the Board of Directors."

The only other limitation on the executive committee's powers
involves certain financial decisions which are reserved for the board's
committees on finance, audit, and bonus and salary. The executive
committee constitutes about one-third of the board's membership,
and is, in effect, a daily "working board."

Strangers in Wilmington sometimes are told that "the executive
committee runs the company and the general managers run the business." This is because du Pont operations are decentralized below
the committee level into ten manufacturing departments headed by
general managers with full authority to run their businesses as they
please—so long as they observe over-all company policies and earn a
satisfactory return on the investment of plant and working capital
entrusted to them. At present these departments are electrochemicals,
explosives, fabrics and finishes, film, Grasselli chemicals, organic
chemicals, photo products, pigments, polychemicals, and textile fibers.

Du Pont also has fourteen staff or auxiliary departments. Twelve
of these—advertising, chemical, development, employee relations,
engineering, foreign relations, general services, legal, public relations,
purchasing, traffic, and economist—are headed by directors who are
appointed by and report to the executive committee. The other two
are the departments of the secretary and the treasurer, who are
elected by the board and report to the president and the finance
committee.

The company principle that "authority must be commensurate
with responsibility" extends to the staff groups. The directors organize and run their own departments. In serving the manufacturing
departments, their relations by and large are similar to those of
outside agencies selling specialized services. There is no rule that
requires a manufacturing department to utilize du Pont's staff facilities, but it is rare when a general manager prefers outside counsel.
The staff departments also provide institutional services for the
company as a whole.

The general managers and directors hire their own personnel.
Each selects an assistant who must be approved by the executive
committee since he should be capable of taking over in event of
illness or disability of the general manager or director. "It makes
you a little more careful in your choice," said one general manager.

While careful to preserve the independence of the departments in personnel matters, the committee keeps a watchful eye on the training of managerial talent. Potential executives are noted usually when they are in the early thirties and have been with du Pont from five to ten years. Those who show ability are given the opportunity to round out their experience by taking a hand in all aspects of the business. They are moved across functional fields, such as from research to production or sales, and are even transferred from one manufacturing department to another, in order that their development may be furthered.

The general managers have their own technical, production, and sales divisions, and such others as they deem advisable. They, along with the directors of staff departments, report regularly to the executive committee on their operations. "Our general managers," said one vice president, "have substantially as much power as the average company president."

Origin of the System

When Irénée du Pont and his associates conceived the executive committee-line system of management under which the company has grown and prospered for 34 years, they were seeking a better way to deal with the problems presented by product diversification. The old line organization had been adequate when the company was just making and selling explosives, but by 1921 a deliberate program of expansion into the broad field of chemical products was well under way.

Product diversification

As early as the turn of the century came the modest beginning of du Pont's now famed program of research. Pending the time when its own laboratories would create the present steady flow of new and improved products, the company had bought chemical concerns with know-how and experience in various lines here in this country and had purchased patents and scientific knowledge abroad. Consequently du Pont, with a sales volume in 1921 of $55 million, was suffering growing pains with the new products.

It was one thing to make and sell explosives and quite another to make and sell paint, as du Pont's centralized sales and production divisions soon discovered. The salesmen who knew explosives and how to sell them knew little about paint. Unfamiliar sales and production problems also stemmed from other new products, such as plastic-coated fabrics, dyes, pigments, and the "fibersilk" now known as rayon.

Most chemicals are sold to other industries rather than directly to the consumer (consumer purchases today account for less than 9% of du Pont's production). The successful chemical salesman, therefore, not only must know his own wares, but must be familiar with the needs and problems of the industries to which he sells. He must be able to demonstrate how a chemical can be used to improve the end product manufactured by his customer. Obviously it was demanding too much to expect the sales expert in explosives to be equally expert in dyestuffs.

The centralized manufacturing department encountered the same troubles as the centralized sales department. But unfamiliarity with new products was not the only headache. A veteran of those days recalls an instance when the manager of a paint plant insisted on turning out all the white paint he could make because he knew how to make it at a good profit. The salesmen, however, discovered that the public wanted colored paint. They reported the demand for colors to their manager, who passed the word up the line to the vice president in charge of sales. This vice president in turn took the matter up with the vice president in charge of manufacturing, who sent the word back down the line to the plant manager. But by the time it reached the plant manager and production had been geared to sales, the inventory tanks contained an appalling amount of white paint.

"Our principal difficulty," recalls Walter S. Carpenter, Jr., now chairman of the board, "was that when trouble occurred anywhere in the organization, it had to filter all the way up to the top and all the way back down again before it was corrected."

Company growth

All the executives interviewed felt that the need for the new organization stemmed primarily from diversification and complexity of products, although company growth in itself was a factor.

"There would be far less need for an executive committee," said one, "if a company had only one product line regardless of its size. But even then, the committee might be valuable in considering broad trends and developments without having to be tied down with live issues."

"It would be impossible," said another, "for any one person to administer such diversified operations as we are engaged in. It is necessary always to think in terms of what is best for the company as a whole, rather than for any one of the various components."

"When a company is big enough," said a third, "complex enough or diverse enough to need more than one man to see the sum of the whole, the committee system should be given consideration."

A fourth simply observed, "Ten heads are better than one."

How the Committee Operates

The vice presidents sometimes tell the general managers: "You are the bosses, and we are the philosophers." No one in du Pont, however, and least of all a general manager, would make the mistake of attributing top company authority anywhere but to the executive committee.

Responsibilities

Fundamentally, the committee exercises three important responsibilities:

1. It determines the broad, basic policies for the operations of the company.
2. It selects the men to carry out these operations.
3. It maintains a continuous review, and seeks to make an honest and objective appraisal of the conduct of the business to make sure that the men selected are doing a good job.

The opinions of the committee members command the respect of general managers and other executives down the line. Each member is recognized as an expert in specific fields, which gives to the committee as a whole a prestige seldom possible for a single individual to attain. If a weakness appears in a department, the committee is quick to assist the general manager in determining whether the trouble is in sales, research, or production. When the weak spot is located, committee experts in that field help the general manager to find a solution.

The Wednesday Meetings. Each manufacturing department presents a monthly operating report, which the committee usually considers on the first and last Wednesdays of each month. In addition, the committee averages one meeting a month in a chart room, where the performance and forecasts of sales and earnings for each department are reviewed with the general manager. (A series of departments is considered each time, with every department averaging about four reviews a year.) If there is a slump in either performance or forecast, the general manager is expected to provide a satisfactory explanation and to discuss with the committee the steps which should be taken to bring operations up to standard.

Capital expenditures or long-range commitments of the departments which are above certain amounts must go to the committee for approval, and those above higher limits must be approved by the finance committee as well. This insures committee scrutiny of projects such as new plant construction, plant expansion, or new commercial ventures. The projects, however, are initiated by the general managers.

The committee passes on agreements and contracts proposed by the departments. The staff departments present annual budgets for approval. The operating departments and the chemical and engineering departments present their own research budgets. Construction forecasts are presented four times a year by the engineering department.

Decisions on operating schedules, prices, individual salary raises, and other day-by-day operating problems are left to the general managers, but are subject to the policy framework established over the years by the executive committee. However, if a department gets out of line in these respects with the rest of the company, the committee quickly calls in the general manager for a talk. It should be noted that such talks are rarely necessary.

"The heart of our operation is the Wednesday meeting," said President Greenewalt. "We spend the rest of the week directly or indirectly preparing for it."

Each Friday afternoon, committee members find on their desks a stack of reports two inches high which they are expected to read and digest prior to the next Wednesday. "We are supposed to have time to think," said one vice president indicating the stack. The members, however, do find it helpful to study a proposal in writing before taking it up in oral discussion with the officials concerned.

In the Wednesday meetings, each member of the committee has one vote, including the president, who usually votes only to make or break a tie. Split decisions are uncommon. Five members constitute a quorum, and four affirmative votes are required for the adoption of any resolution. Occasionally the members of the minority ask to have their opposition recorded. Otherwise the action is simply noted as taken, or as taken unanimously.

The practice in some companies of requiring unanimity for committee action finds no support at du Pont. Each member pays careful attention to the views of the others when a question is debated, and minds have been changed by debate. The members feel, however, that it would be stultifying to have to go along with a decision if they sincerely believe it to be wrong, and they pride themselves on being "rugged individualists." A showdown on important questions usually is postponed until all members are present, although, as stated above, five constitute a quorum for ordinary business.

As chairman of the meetings, President Greenewalt has the usual presiding officer's responsibility to see that there is opportunity for full debate, to narrow the issues to their essence, and to call for a decision after adequate discussion. Other members praise his objectivity as chairman, although they know he does not hesitate to speak his mind and express his own views when they differ from others. When fuller explanation of a decision than the customary "advice of action" is warranted, he calls the general managers together and does the explaining.

EXHIBIT I. AGENDA FOR A WEDNESDAY MEETING

CHART ROOM

1. Fabrics and Finishes Department regular report for January.
2. Grasselli Chemicals Department regular report for January.
3. Photo Products Department regular report for January.
4. Pigments Department regular report for January.
5. Foreign Relations Department—annual report and operating budget.

COMMITTEE ROOM

Unfinished business

6. Engineering Department—operating budget.
7. Motion picture program based on the Company's programs re "How Our Business System Operates." Joint report from Advertising, Employee Relations, and Public Relations Departments.

New business

8. Organic Chemicals Department regular report for January.
9. Appropriation project covering partial design, procurement of long delivery equipment, and preparation of construction cost estimate New River Pump House, ash and waste retention facilities, Old Hickory Rayon and Cellophane Plants.
10. Appropriation project—replacement of worn-out pirns, Waynesboro Plant.
11. Credit appropriation—additional power facilities, Spruance Rayon Plant.
12. Appropriation—project for synthesis gas via coal partial combustion—Step #1, Belle Works.
13. Adjustment of permanent investment—QY catalyst facilities, Arlington Works.
14. Supplemental report on accomplishment—second year's operation —continuous polyvinyl alcohol and monomer process, Niagara Falls Plant.

15. History, present status, and future prospects of the "Elvanol"
    polyvinyl alcohol business. Report from Electrochemicals De-
    partment.
16. Miscellaneous items.

The agenda for an executive committee meeting averages at least
12 items. The regular required reports from the manufacturing
departments provide the framework, and either the departments or
members of the committee can initiate additions. "In a live organization, the agenda will take care of itself," was one comment. (See
EXHIBIT I for a sample agenda—typical in breadth and variety
though not necessarily in specific subject matter.)

"Court of Appeals." Since the manufacturing departments compete with each other as well as with outside rivals, and the staff
departments have their own differences of opinion, the executive
committee is available as a court of last resort to settle intracompany
disputes. The committee does not like to be placed in this role,
however, and this fact is emphatically made known to the disputants.
When all consultation and mediation fails, the committee if called
upon will step in and resolve the issue—and the disputants will
resolve never again to let it go as far as the committee.

Review of Department Projects. Members of the committee
believe that the system functions at its best when they are able to
stimulate and encourage the initiation of ideas and projects from
down the line. They do not hesitate, however, to inject their own
proposals when they believe them to be for the best interests of the
company:

> "It is rare when a general manager is turned down on a project,"
> said a vice president. He knows his proposal will be reviewed by experts;
> and since our general managers are able men, they don't bring anything
> to us unless they are pretty sure.
> "Sometimes we don't agree with a general manager," said another,
> "but it is better to let a mistake be made than to order a general manager
> to act against his judgment—unless too many people would be hurt."
> "We err on the side of letting the general managers run their busi-
> nesses according to their own lights," said a third. "When I was a
> general manager, they let me spend half a million dollars playing around
> with superpressures without getting any results."

There is a readiness among the vice presidents to concede that
du Pont has made mistakes—"some of them beauts"—but they do
point out that the initiation of projects by the departments, followed
by executive committee review, provides a built-in weeding-out proc-

ess which disposes of most ill-considered proposals before they ever reach the action stage.

Long-Range Considerations. The committee feels strongly its obligation to look into the future for national trends, and in 1939, for example, it anticipated a country-wide pattern of wage increases. The general managers were called in and encouraged to grant increases promptly in the interest of sound employee relations. It took some convincing in certain departments where general managers were reluctant to curtail department earnings, but the result was regarded as worthwhile.

Operating officials in their planning, too, are encouraged by the committee to take into account long-range considerations of the public interest. For example, du Pont is the sole supplier of neoprene rubber for the free world. When expanded production of this product seemed advisable, the general manager proposed and the committee approved the construction of a second plant rather than enlargement of existing facilities. Among other reasons given in support of this proposal was that a second plant would guarantee an alternate source of neoprene for defense and commercial use in case one plant should be shut down by fire or disaster. As far as the company itself was concerned, the enlargement of the single plant, obviously, would have meant a greater return on investment over the near term.

One of the ways in which the committee seeks answers to its own questions, and stimulates thinking in the departments, is by requesting "whither" reports. These are so named because they ask "whither nylon?" or "whither titanium?" The studies involved in preparation of these documents dealing with the future of specified products are enlightening to the general managers as well as to the committee.

Study and consultation constitute a continuous process at du Pont. In fact, most decisions of the committee are reached only after careful examination of all available facts and opinions and consultation with everyone in a position to make some contribution.

Advisory duties

In a secondary role, members of the committee serve as individual advisers in areas where they are best qualified by skill, training, and experience. But in contrast to formal committee decisions in which they have a vote, as advisers their influence is indirect, and they are quick to say that they can't give orders as individuals "to anybody but my secretary."

Although committee members advise, rather than dictate, it takes a strong-willed general manager or staff department director, who is sure of his ground, to take counteraction after soliciting counsel. This is not because the committee members seek to impose their will upon management down the line, but because everyone in the company looks up to them as experts in specialized areas. Thus:

> Vice President Walter J. Beadle, a former treasurer, advises on foreign relations and legal matters. Another former treasurer, Vice President T. C. Davis, is adviser to the treasurer's department. Vice President Charles A. Cary, up from assistant general manager of the old rayon department, advises on traffic, purchasing, and general services. Vice President J. Warren Kinsman, up from general manager of fabrics and finishes, the company's largest direct sales area, is adviser on advertising and sales. Vice President Henry B. du Pont, who came up from engineering research, advises on engineering. Vice President William H. Ward, a former general manager of explosives, advises on personnel, salaries, and employee relations.
>
> Vice President Walter Dannenbaum, up from general manager of the old ammonia department, advises on manufacturing. Vice President Roger Williams, who was chemical director of the ammonia department and later was in charge of the Hanford atomic energy project as assistant manager of explosives, advises on chemical research and development. President Greenewalt is the adviser on public relations, and is also consulted along with Mr. Williams on technical and scientific problems. Vice President Robert L. Richards, promoted last fall from general manager of textile fibers, awaits his advisership assignment.

Executive committee members also serve on other committees. Messrs. Beadle, Ward, and Williams are members of the company's subcommittee on "B" bonus, while Mr. Dannenbaum is chairman of the "A" bonus committee. Messrs. du Pont, Kinsman, and Dannenbaum are members of a subcommittee on purchases and sales, while Messrs. Beadle, Cary, and du Pont are members of a subcommittee on construction forecasts. In addition, some members of the executive committee are directors of certain subsidiary corporations.

> "We give advice, solicited or volunteered," explained one. "There is no compulsion to follow it, although we sometimes resort to tactful persuasion."
>
> "It is cooperation, contact, the development of a common understanding, and talking out problems," said another. "The key to the company's success is how the general managers run the business. Our task is to create an environment which will help them do a better job."
>
> "We should never attempt to exercise too much power for that would destroy the autonomy of the departments," said a third.
>
> "It is always desirable to avoid sending down pronouncements from on high," observed a fourth. "We try to get the viewpoints of others involved and work out a mutually satisfactory answer."

While individual members of the committee are frequently consulted in advance for their views on special aspects of a project—for example, Mr. Williams on the technical end, Mr. Kinsman on sales, or Mr. Dannenbaum on manufacturing—they are not expected to commit themselves on the project as a whole. The project, as a *project*, is considered on its merits when the general manager formally presents it to the committee, even though the financial, legal, technical, sales, and manufacturing problems connected with it may have already been discussed individually with the special advisers in these fields.

Qualifications for Membership

In selecting the executive committee, the board of directors, in the words of one director, "tries to create a superman by combining the great breadth of experience represented by the various members, so each can contribute his own viewpoint for the benefit of the others and the group as a whole." Specifically, the following qualifications are looked for:

Basic experience and expertness in one or more fields, especially research, production, sales, finance, or engineering, constitute a primary qualification.

A well-rounded background is desirable because, as another put it, "when a man goes on the committee, he is not supposed to look at an issue from the standpoint of his old department or activity, but in the interest of the company as a whole."

Sound judgment, objectivity, breadth of vision, and a willingness to cooperate are essential qualities.

The prospective committee member should be well read, versed in industrial problems, and aware of what's going on in the nation and the world.

He should enjoy good health, and be of an age which will permit him to serve at least 10 years before compulsory retirement at 65.

Other specifications as they were expressed by the board members interviewed include:

"His head should be screwed on right."

"He should be an individualist—we don't want go-alongers."

"He should balance independence of opinion with the grace to submit to the will of the majority."

"He should have ideas but be willing to see them turned down without waiting for an opportunity later to say 'I told you so.'"

"He should have a specialty and as much else as he can bring with him."

"He should be a self-starter willing to be an adviser—with all that the term implies and all that it doesn't imply."

"We want men who won't be earth-bound by logic but have the instinct or intuition to do the right thing whether logical or not."

"He should have forbearance, and recognize that the other fellow has strong convictions, too."

"He should have profound tolerance, and avoid getting provoked."

"He needs personality, a fine mind, and a quick wit."

Two members of the committee separately mentioned "dedication" as a qualification. One defined this quality as "a will to devote all your time and interest to the company's affairs," while the other remarked, "I told a general manager the other day that coming on the committee is like joining a monastery—you work 16 hours a day and get your fun out of the job. You must be dedicated."

It is acknowledged that fate has a hand in the selections. A man with all of the qualifications may miss promotion to the committee because there are no suitable vacancies while he is in the proper age bracket. One of the vice presidents also suggested that "an individual might be an excellent general manager and a poor vice president, or vice versa."

The size of the committee has varied from time to time. Asked why it numbers ten, instead of five or fifteen, a member explained that it was essential to have technical, financial, manufacturing, sales, and engineering experience represented. Then, he continued, it is better to have two from each field, both to insure a quorum for the weekly meetings, despite illnesses, vacations, or business trips, and to make available the judgment of two experts, rather than one, on specialized issues. Also, he felt that ten could function as a committee without the loss of individualism, but twice that number might lead to "herd thinking" or the development of cliques.

"We need a good, wide spectrum," said another, "but not so many as to become unmanageable."

All present members of the committee have come up through the ranks of du Pont, which practices a policy of promotion from within. They absorbed the spirit and became familiar with the theory and practice of the company before assuming their present posts. Committee members believe that outsiders could be brought in if necessary and would soon become accustomed to the system, but they concede it might take time and result in some dissatisfaction.

ADVANTAGES OF THE SYSTEM

When questioned concerning the advantages of the committee-line system, the executives interviewed stressed the following:

1. *The strength and security of group decisions—*

"We are less likely to go to extremes, since the committee assures a balanced viewpoint on every issue."

"If one individual could always come up with the right answer, we would not need a committee."

"When seven men out of ten—all intellectually honest—can reach agreement, the chances are that it is sound."

"It may take longer to get action, but this pays off handsomely in better decisions and ability to follow through on long-range policies."

"We reap the benefit of diversified experience. One of the ten will think of some important angle that may be a blank to everyone else."

2. *Objectivity in decision making—*

"The system permits discussion and consideration of policy by men relieved of day-to-day decisions. This means more than 'time to think.' It means that nobody on the committee will be influenced consciously or unconsciously by the effect of the decision on an operation for which he is responsible, because we aren't responsible for operations."

"We all have more to do than we can get done, but we do have time to concern ourselves with things we couldn't do if we had line responsibilities."

"The discipline of having to work out an agreement with nine others promotes objectivity and thorough analysis of the problems."

"There is some duplication of effort, but we get a combined judgment based on all considerations and weighed without bias."

3. *Continuity of administration—*

"The committee changes so gradually that our management is always on an even keel, whereas, when a dictator dies, there is no successor."

"The committee assures the company of an averaging-out of temperament and ability in top management."

4. *Development of personnel—*

"The system accommodates a greater diversity of executive talent. There is a place for the man who sings solo, and also for the man who sings best in the chorus."

"General guidance by suggestion through the adviserships encourages initiative throughout the organization."

"Our advice always is so worded that a general manager is free to disregard it if he wishes."

"When there is decentralization at the top, there is initiative down the line."

Other advantages briefly mentioned included: increasing the stature of departmental manager, relieving part of the burden which usually falls upon the president or chief executive officer, encouraging the resolution of problems at lower management levels, and flexibility.

Disadvantages of the System

The executives were at a loss for a ready answer when asked to list the disadvantages of the system. After some thought the following were brought out:

1. A few who had come up through departmental management mentioned a certain sense of frustration.

   "On the committee you feel inhibited. You move up to it from an active to an ethereal field, and have to get things done by advice and suggestion."

   "Men who have been on the firing line, making day-to-day decisions, suddenly find when they move up to the committee that they can't give orders as individuals to anybody but their secretaries."

   "There is difficulty in making the transition from line management to the committee, with the danger that departmental allegiances will stay in the picture."

   "Compromise isn't always easy, and expediency must be paid for."

2. Some of the others cited as a minor disadvantage the fact that outsiders frequently are unaware of the division of responsibilities at du Pont, and expect the president and the vice presidents to make decisions on sales or other matters which lie within the province of the general managers.

3. One of the more individualistic members pointed out that ten people had to read every report, but added that there is compensation in the fact that one of the ten occasionally spots something the other nine miss.

4. It was also suggested that in a small company an executive committee might not have enough to do, that autonomy of the departments would be weakened if the committee set up too many rules, and that there might be room even at du Pont for "something to fall between the slats of responsibility."

On the whole, however, the members of the committee were unable to cite serious disadvantages, and two of them suggested that the question be put to one of the general managers.

After some thought the general manager consulted answered that with his title he did find it a little difficult to compete for customers' attention against the head of a competing company, who had the title of president, even though his own department's total output is five times larger than that of the competitor.

"But I just can't think of any other disadvantages of our system," he said. "I would much rather go to ten men with a project than take my chances on one."

In conclusion, the 12 top executives stressed that (1) they are not urging other companies to adopt their committee-line system, (2) they believe unanimously it has been successful for du Pont, and (3) they feel it should work for any other large producer of diversified lines.

BIBLIOGRAPHY, CHAPTER XIX

GIERMAK, EDWIN A. "Individualism vs. the Committee Process," *Advanced Management* (December, 1960), 16-19.

GREEN, ESTILL I. "The Nature and Use of Committees," *Advanced Management* (July, 1959), 24-28.

HENSKY, ROBERT L. "Organizational Planning," *Business Topics* (Winter, 1962), 29-40.

HIGGINS, CARTER C. "The Organization Chart," *Management Review* (October, 1956), 889-893.

LIGHTNER, MILTON C. " 'Patchwork Organization': Causes and Cures," *Management Review*, 80-92.

MAYER, JEROME. "Conference—Profit or Loss?" *Modern Industry* (January, 1956), 47-53.

RICHARDS, MAX D. "Effective Staff Meetings," *Advanced Management* (April, 1959), 18-21.

SAYLES, LEONARD. "The Change Process in Organizations," *Human Organization* (Summer, 1962), 62-67.

SIMON, HERBERT A. *Administrative Behavior*, Second Edition. New York: The MacMillan Company, 1960. 125.

——————————. "The Analysis of Promotional Opportunities," *Personnel* (January, 1931).

STIGLITZ, HAROLD. "Staff-Staff Relationships," *Management Record* (February, 1962), 2-13.

"Stop Misusing Your Management Meetings," *Factory Management and Maintenance* (April, 1960), 210-224.

"Top Management Committees," *Management News* (August, 1960), 6.

SECTION F. STAFFING

Staffing decisions are as important as organization structural decisions since successful performance is determined as much by the capabilities of individual managers as by the structure. In the first chapter of this section, therefore, qualifications important to successful management are examined. The selection and recruitment of managerial personnel are considered in Chapter XXI. Since good managers often are in extremely short supply, staffing decisions are dependent upon internal management development, the subject of the final chapter.

Chapter XX
Managerial Qualifications

The first problem in staffing the positions outlined in an organization structure is to determine the type of man who can successfully carry out the functions of the management job. Consequently, widespread searches have been made to discover those qualities which lead to executive or managerial success.

In Article 69 Robert L. Katz presents his views of the skills (as opposed to knowledge) that his work shows are desirable or necessary for managerial success. Cecil E. Goode in Article 70 summarizes those qualities that a long series of leadership studies show to be important. The difficulty in using these qualities as guides in selecting managers is that they appear to be attributes of good people, not just good managers.

In the final article Saul W. Gellerman examines a common problem in growth companies; the job responsibilities grow, but the man does not.

69. SKILLS OF AN

EFFECTIVE ADMINISTRATOR [1]   Robert L. Katz [2]

Although the selection and training of good administrators is widely recognized as one of American industry's most pressing problems, there is surprisingly little agreement among executives or educators on what makes a good administrator. The executive development programs of some of the nation's leading corporations and colleges reflect a tremendous variation in objectives.

At the root of this difference is industry's search for the traits or attributes which will objectively identify the "ideal executive" who is equipped to cope effectively with any problem in any organization. As one observer of American industry recently noted:

> "The assumption that there is an executive type is widely accepted, either openly or implicitly. Yet any executive presumably knows that a company needs all kinds of managers for different levels of jobs. The qualities most needed by a shop superintendent are likely to be quite opposed to those needed by a coordinating vice president of manufacturing. The literature of executive development is loaded with efforts to define the qualities needed by executives, and by themselves these sound quite rational. Few, for instance, would dispute the fact that a top manager needs good judgment, the ability to make decisions, the ability to win respect of others, and all the other well-worn phrases any management man could mention. But one has only to look at the successful managers in any company to see how enormously their particular qualities vary from any ideal list of executive virtues." [3]

Yet this quest for the executive stereotype has become so intense that many companies, in concentrating on certain specific traits or qualities, stand in danger of losing sight of their real concern: *what a man can accomplish.*

It is the purpose of this article to suggest what may be a more useful approach to the selection and development of administrators. This approach is based not on what good executives *are* (their innate

[1] From the *Harvard Business Review* (January-February, 1955), pp. 33-42. Reprinted by permission of the *Harvard Business Review*.
[2] Robert L. Katz, The Amos Tuck School of Business Administration, Dartmouth College, 1955.
[3] Perrin Stryker, "The Growing Pains of Executive Development," *Advanced Management* (August, 1954), p. 15.

traits and characteristics), but rather on what they *do* (the kinds of skills which they exhibit in carrying out their jobs effectively). As used here, a *skill* implies an ability which can be developed, not necessarily inborn, and which is manifested in performance, not merely in potential. So the principal criterion of skillfulness must be effective action under varying conditions.

This approach suggests that effective administration rests on *three basic developable skills* which obviate the need for identifying specific traits and which may provide a useful way of looking at and understanding the administrative process. This approach is the outgrowth of firsthand observation of executives at work coupled with study of current field research in administration.

In the sections which follow, an attempt will be made to define and demonstrate what these three skills are; to suggest that the relative importance of the three skills varies with the level of administrative responsibility; to present some of the implications of this variation for selection, training, and promotion of executives; and to propose ways of developing these skills.

Three-Skill Approach

It is assumed here that an administrator is one who (a) directs the activities of other persons and (b) undertakes the responsibility for achieving certain objectives through these efforts. Within this definition, successful administration appears to rest on three basic skills, which we will call *technical, human, and conceptual.* It would be unrealistic to assert that these skills are not interrelated, yet there may be real merit in examining each one separately, and in developing them independently.

Technical skill

As used here, technical skill implies an understanding of, and proficiency in, a specific kind of activity, particularly one involving methods, processes, procedures, or techniques. It is relatively easy for us to visualize the technical skill of the surgeon, the musician, the accountant, or the engineer when each is performing his own special function. Technical skill involves specialized knowledge, analytical ability within that specialty, and facility in the use of the tools and techniques of the specific discipline.

Of the three skills described in this article, technical skill is perhaps the most familiar because it is the most concrete, and because, in our age of specialization, it is the skill required of the greatest number of people. Most of our vocational and on-the-job training programs are largely concerned with developing this specialized technical skill.

Human skill

As used here, human skill is the executive's ability to work effectively as a group member and to build cooperative effort within the team he leads. As *technical* skill is primarily concerned with working with "things" (processes or physical objects), so *human* skill is primarily concerned with working with people. This skill is demonstrated in the way the individual perceives (and recognizes the perceptions of) his superiors, equals, and subordinates, and in the way he behaves subsequently.

The person with highly developed human skill is aware of his own attitudes, assumptions, and beliefs about other individuals and groups; he is able to see the usefulness and limitations of these feelings. By accepting the existence of viewpoints, perceptions, and beliefs which are different from his own, he is skillful in understanding what others really mean by their words and behavior. He is equally skillful in communicating to others, in their own contexts, what he means by *his* behavior.

Such a person works to create an atmosphere of approval and security in which subordinates feel free to express themselves without fear of censure or ridicule, by encouraging them to participate in the planning and carrying out of those things which directly affect them. He is sufficiently sensitive to the needs and motivations of others in his organization so that he can judge the possible reactions to, and outcomes of, various courses of action he may undertake. Having this sensitivity, he is able and willing to *act* in a way which takes these perceptions by others into account.

Real skill in working with others must become a natural, continuous activity, since it involves sensitivity not only at times of decision making but also in the day-by-day behavior of the individual. Human skill cannot be a "sometime thing." Techniques cannot be randomly applied, nor can personality traits be put on or removed like an overcoat. Because everything which an executive says and does (or leaves unsaid or undone) has an effect on his associates, his true self will, in time, show through. Thus, to be effective, this skill must be naturally developed and unconsciously, as well as consistently, demonstrated in the individual's every action. It must become an integral part of his whole being.

Because human skill is so vital a part of everything the administrator does, examples of inadequate human skill are easier to describe than are highly skillful performances. Perhaps consideration of an actual situation would serve to clarify what is involved:

When a new conveyor unit was installed in a shoe factory where workers had previously been free to determine their own work rate, the production manager asked the industrial engineer who had designed the conveyor to serve as foreman, even though a qualified foreman was available. The engineer, who reported directly to the production manager, objected, but under pressure he agreed to take the job "until a suitable foreman could be found," even though this was a job of lower status than his present one. Then the following conversation took place:

Production Manager: "I've had a lot of experience with conveyors. I want you to keep this conveyor going at all times except for rest periods, and I want it going at top speed. Get these people thinking in terms of 2 pairs of shoes a minute, 70 dozen pairs a day, 350 dozen pairs a week. They are all experienced operators on their individual jobs, and it's just a matter of getting them to do their jobs in a little different way. I want you to make that base rate of 250 dozen pair a week work!" [Base rate was established at slightly under 75% of the maximum capacity. This base rate was 50% higher than under the old system.]

Engineer: "If I'm going to be foreman of the conveyor unit, I want to do things my way. I've worked on conveyors, and I don't agree with you on first getting people used to a conveyor going at top speed. These people have never seen a conveyor. You'll scare them. I'd like to run the conveyor at one-third speed for a couple of weeks and then gradually increase the speed.

"I think we should discuss setting the base rate [production quota before incentive bonus] on a daily basis instead of a weekly basis. [Workers had previously been paid on a daily straight piecework basis.]

"I'd also suggest setting a daily base rate at 45 or even 40 dozen pair. You have to set a base rate low enough for them to make. Once they know they can make the base rate, they will go after the bonus."

Production Manager: "You do it your way on the speed; but remember it's the results that count. On the base rate, I'm not discussing it with you; I'm telling you to make the 250 dozen pair a week work. I don't want a daily base rate." [4]

Here is a situation in which the production manager was so preoccupied with getting the physical output that he did not pay attention to the people through whom that output had to be achieved. Notice, first, that he made the engineer who designed the unit serve as foreman, apparently hoping to force the engineer to justify his design by producing the maximum output. However, the production

---

[4] From a mimeographed case in the files of the Harvard Business School; copyrighted by the President and Fellows of Harvard College.

manager was oblivious to (a) the way the engineer perceived this appointment, as a demotion, and (b) the need for the engineer to be able to control the variables if he was to be held responsible for output. Instead the production manager imposed a production standard and refused any changes in the work situation.

Moreover, although this was a radically new situation for the operators, the production manager expected them to produce immediately at well above their previous output—even though the operators had an unfamiliar production system to cope with, the operators had never worked together as a team before, the operators and their new foreman had never worked together before, and the foreman was not in agreement with the production goals or standards. By ignoring all these human factors, the production manager not only placed the engineer in an extremely difficult operating situation but also, by refusing to allow the engineer to "run his own show," discouraged the very assumption of responsibility he had hoped for in making the appointment.

Under these circumstances, it is easy to understand how the relationship between these two men rapidly deteriorated, and how production, after two months' operation, was at only 125 dozen pairs per week (just 75% of what it had been under the old system.)

Conceptual skill

As used here, conceptual skill involves the ability to see the enterprise as a whole; it includes recognizing how the various functions of the organization depend on one another, and how changes in any one part affect all the others; and it extends to visualizing the relationship of the individual business to the industry, the community, and the political, social, and economic forces of the nation as a whole. Recognizing these relationships and perceiving the significant elements in any situation, the administrator should then be able to act in a way which advances the over-all welfare of the total organization.

Hence, the success of any decision depends on the conceptual skill of the people who make the decision and those who put it into action. When, for example, an important change in marketing policy is made, it is critical that the effects on production, control, finance, research, and the people involved be considered. And it remains critical right down to the last executive who must implement the new policy. If each executive recognizes the over-all relationships and significance of the change, he is almost certain to be more effective in administering it. Consequently the chances for succeeding are greatly increased.

Not only does the effective coordination of the various parts of the business depend on the conceptual skill of the administrators involved, but so also does the whole future direction and tone of the organization. The attitudes of a top executive color the whole character of the organization's response and determine the "corporate personality" which distinguishes one company's ways of doing business from another's. These attitudes are a reflection of the administrator's conceptual skill (referred to by some as his "creative ability")—the way he perceives and responds to the direction in which the business should grow, company objectives and policies, and stockholders' and employees' interests.

Conceptual skill, as defined above, is what Chester I. Bernard, former president of the New Jersey Bell Telephone Company, implies when he says: ". . . the essential aspect of the [executive] process is the sensing of the organization as a whole and the total situation relevant to it." [5] Examples of inadequate conceptual skill are all around us. Here is one instance:

> In a large manufacturing company which had a long tradition of job-shop type operations, primary responsibility for production control had been left to the foremen and other lower-level supervisors. "Village" type operations with small working groups and informal organizations were the rule. A heavy influx of orders following World War II tripled the normal production requirements and severely taxed the whole manufacturing organization. At this point, a new production manager was brought in from outside the company, and he established a wide range of controls and formalized the entire operating structure.
> As long as the boom demand lasted, the employees made every effort to conform with the new procedures and environment. But when demand subsided to prewar levels, serious labor relations problems developed, friction was high among department heads, and the company found itself saddled with a heavy indirect labor cost. Management sought to reinstate its old procedures; it fired the production manager and attempted to give greater authority to the foreman once again. However, during the four years of formalized control, the foremen had grown away from their old practices, many had left the company, and adequate replacements had not been developed. Without strong foreman leadership, the traditional job-shop operations proved costly and inefficient.

In this instance, when the new production controls and formalized organizations were introduced, management did not foresee the con-

---

[5] *Functions of the Executive* (Cambridge: Harvard University Press, 1948), p. 235.

sequences of this action in the event of a future contraction of business. Later, when conditions changed and it was necessary to pare down operations, management was again unable to recognize the implications of its action and reverted to the old procedures, which, under existing circumstances, were no longer appropriate. This compounded *conceptual* inadequacy left the company at a serious competitive disadvantage.

Because a company's over-all success is dependent on its executives' conceptual skill in establishing and carrying out policy decisions, this skill is the unifying, coordinating ingredient of the administrative process, and of undeniable over-all importance.

Relative Importance

We may notice that, in a very real sense, conceptual skill embodies consideration of both the technical and human aspects of the organization. Yet the concept of *skill*, as an ability to translate knowledge into action, should enable one to distinguish between the three skills of performing the technical activities (technical skill), understanding and motivating individuals and groups (human skill), and coordinating and integrating all the activities and interests of the organization toward a common objective (conceptual skill).

This separation of effective administration into three basic skills is useful primarily for purposes of analysis. In practice, these skills are so closely interrelated that it is difficult to determine where one ends and another begins. However, just because the skills are interrelated does not imply that we cannot get some value from looking at them separately, or by varying their emphasis. In playing golf the action of the hands, wrists, hips, shoulders, arms, and head are all interrelated; yet in improving one's swing it is often valuable to work on one of these elements separately. Also, under different playing conditions the relative importance of these elements varies. Similarly, although all three are of importance at every level of administration, the technical, human, and conceptual skills of the administrator vary in relative importance at different levels of responsibility.

At lower levels

Technical skill is responsible for many of the great advances of modern industry. It is indispensable to efficient operation. Yet it has greatest importance at the lower levels of administration. As the administrator moves further and further from the actual physical operation, this need for technical skill becomes less important, provided he has skilled subordinates and can help them solve their own problems. At the top, technical skill may be almost nonexistent, and the executive may still be able to perform effectively if his human and conceptual skills are highly developed.

We are all familiar with those "professional managers" who are becoming the prototypes of our modern executive world. These men shift with great ease, and with no apparent loss in effectiveness, from one industry to another. Their human and conceptual skills seem to make up for their unfamiliarity with the new job's technical aspects.

At every level

Human skill, the ability to work with others, is essential to effective administration at every level. One recent research study has shown that human skill is of paramount importance at the foreman level, pointing out that the chief function of the foreman as an administrator is to attain collaboration of people in the work group.[6] Another study reinforces this finding and extends it to the middle-management group, adding that the administrator should be primarily concerned with facilitating communication in the organization.[7] And still another study, concerned primarily with top management, underscores the need for self-awareness and sensitivity to human relationships by executives at that level.[8] These findings would tend to indicate that human skill is of great importance at every administrative level, but notice the difference in emphasis.

Human skill seems to be most important at lower levels, where the number of direct contacts between administrators and subordinates is greatest. As we go higher and higher in the administrative echelons, the number and frequency of these personal contacts decrease, and the need for human skill becomes proportionately, although probably not absolutely, less. At the same time, conceptual skill becomes increasingly more important with the need for policy decisions and broad-scale action. The human skill of dealing with individuals then becomes subordinate to the conceptual skill of integrating group interests and activities into a coordinated whole.

[6] A. Zaleznik, *Foreman Training in a Growing Enterprise* (Boston: Division of Research, Harvard Business School, 1951).

[7] Harriet O. Ronken and Paul R. Lawrence, *Administering Changes* (Boston: Division of Research, Harvard Business School, 1952).

[8] Edmund P. Learned, David H. Ulrich, and Donald R. Booz, *Executive Action* (Boston: Division of Research, Harvard Business School, 1950).

In fact, a recent research study by Professor Chris Argyris of Yale University has given us the example of an extremely effective plant manager who, although possessing little human skill as defined here, was nonetheless very successful:

> This manager, the head of a largely autonomous division, made his supervisors, through the effects of his strong personality and the "pressure" he applied, highly dependent on him for most of their "rewards, penalties, authority, perpetuation, communication, and identification."
>
> As a result, the supervisors spent much of their time competing with one another for the manager's favor. They told him only the things they thought he wanted to hear, and spent much time trying to find out his desires. They depended on him to set their objectives and to show them how to reach them. Because the manager was inconsistent and unpredictable in his behavior, the supervisors were insecure and continually engaged in interdepartmental squabbles which they tried to keep hidden from the manager.
>
> Clearly, human skill as defined here, was lacking. Yet, by the evaluation of his superiors and by his results in increasing efficiency and raising profits and morale, this manager was exceedingly effective. Professor Argyris suggests that employees in modern industrial organizations tend to have a "built-in" sense of dependence on superiors which capable and alert men can turn to advantage. [9]

In the context of the three-skill approach, it seems that this manager was able to capitalize on this dependence because he recognized the interrelationships of all the activities under his control, identified himself with the organization, and sublimated the individual interests of his subordinates to *his* (the organization's) interest, set his goals realistically, and showed his subordinates how to reach these goals. This would seem to be an excellent example of a situation in which strong conceptual skill more than compensated for a lack of human skill.

At the top level

Conceptual skill, as indicated in the preceding sections, becomes increasingly critical in more responsible executive positions where its effects are maximized and most easily observed. In fact, recent research findings lead to the conclusion that at the top level of administration this conceptual skill becomes the most important ability of all. As Herman W. Steinkraus, president of Bridgeport Brass Company, said:

---

[9] *Executive Leadership* (New York: Harper & Brothers, 1953); see also "Leadership Pattern in the Plant," HBR (January-February, 1953), p. 63.

"One of the most important lessons which I learned on this job [the presidency] is the importance of coordinating the various departments into an effective team, and, secondly, to recognize the shifting emphasis from time to time of the relative importance of various departments to the business." [10]

It would appear, then, that at lower levels of administrative responsibility, the principal need is for technical and human skills. At higher levels, technical skill becomes relatively less important while the need for conceptual skill increases rapidly. At the top level of an organization, conceptual skill becomes the most important skill of all for successful administration. A chief executive may lack technical or human skills and still be effective if he has subordinates who have strong abilities in these directions. But if his conceptual skill is weak, the success of the whole organization may be jeopardized.

IMPLICATIONS FOR ACTION

This three-skill approach implies that significant benefits may result from redefining the objectives of executive development programs, from reconsidering the placement of executives in organizations, and from revising procedures for testing and selecting prospective executives.

Executive development

Many executive development programs may be failing to achieve satisfactory results because of their inability to foster the growth of these administrative skills. Programs which concentrate on the mere imparting of information or the cultivation of a specific trait would seem to be largely unproductive in enhancing the administrative skills of candidates.

A strictly informative program was described to me recently by an officer and director of a large corporation who had been responsible for the executive development activities of his company, as follows:

"What we try to do is to get our promising young men together with some of our senior executives in regular meetings each month. Then we give the young fellows a chance to ask questions to let them find out about the company's history and how and why we've done things in the past."

[10] "What Should a President Do?" *Dun's Review* (August, 1951), p. 21.

It was not surprising that neither the senior executives nor the young men felt this program was improving their administrative abilities.

The futility of pursuing specific traits becomes apparent when we consider the responses of an administrator in a number of different situations. In coping with these varied conditions, he may appear to demonstrate one trait in one instance—e.g., dominance when dealing with subordinates—and the directly opposite trait under another set of circumstances—e.g., submissiveness when dealing with superiors. Yet in each instance he may be acting appropriately to achieve the best results. Which, then, can we identify as a desirable characteristic? Here is a further example of this dilemma:

> A Pacific Coast sales manager had a reputation for decisiveness and positive action. Yet when he was required to name an assistant to understudy his job from among several well-qualified subordinates, he deliberately avoided making a decision. His associates were quick to observe what appeared to be obvious indecisiveness.
>
> But after several months had passed, it became clear that the sales manager had very unobtrusively been giving the various salesmen opportunities to demonstrate their attitudes and feelings. As a result, he was able to identify strong sentiments for one man whose subsequent promotion was enthusiastically accepted by the entire group.

In this instance, the sales manager's skillful performance was improperly interpreted as "indecisiveness." Their concern with irrelevant traits led his associates to overlook the adequacy of his performance. Would it not have been more appropriate to conclude that his human skill in working with others enabled him to adapt effectively to the requirements of a new situation?

Cases such as these would indicate that it is more useful to judge an administrator on the results of his performance than on his apparent traits. Skills are easier to identify than are traits and are less likely to be misinterpreted. Furthermore, skills offer a more directly applicable frame of reference for executive development, since any improvement in an administrator's skills must necessarily result in more effective performance.

Still another danger in many existing executive development programs lies in the unqualified enthusiasm with which some companies and colleges have embraced courses in "human relations." There would seem to be two inherent pitfalls here: (1) Human relations courses might only be imparting information or specific techniques, rather than developing the individual's human skill. (2) Even if individual development does take place, some companies, by placing all of their emphasis on human skill, may be completely overlooking the training requirements for top positions. They may run the risk of producing men with highly developed human skill who lack the conceptual ability to be effective top-level administrators.

It would appear important, then, that the training of a candidate for an administrative position be directed at the development of those skills which are most needed at the level of responsibility for which he is being considered.

Executive placement

This three-skill concept suggests immediate possibilities for the creating of management teams of individuals with complementary skills. For example, one medium-size midwestern distributing organization has as president a man of unusual conceptual ability but extremely limited human skill. However, he has two vice presidents with exceptional human skill. These three men make up an executive committee which has been outstandingly successful, the skills of each member making up for deficiencies of the others. Perhaps the plan of two-man complementary conference leadership proposed by Robert F. Bales, in which the one leader maintains "task leadership" while the other provides "social leadership," might also be an example in point.[11]

Executive selection

In trying to predetermine a prospective candidate's abilities on a job, much use is being made these days of various kinds of testing devices. Executives are being tested for everything from "decisiveness" to "conformity." These tests, as a recent article in *Fortune* points out, have achieved some highly questionable results when applied to performance on the job.[12] Would it not be much more productive to be concerned with skills of doing rather than with a number of traits which do not guarantee performance?

This three-skill approach makes trait testing unnecessary and substitutes for it procedures which examine a man's ability to cope with the actual problems and situations he will find on his job. These procedures, which indicate what a man can *do* in specific situations, are the same for selection and for measuring development. They will

---

[11] "In Conference," HBR (March-April, 1954), p. 44.
[12] William H. Whyte, Jr., "The Fallacies of 'Personality' Testing," *Fortune* (September, 1954), p. 117.

be described in the section on developing executive skills which follows.

This approach suggests that executives should *not* be chosen on the basis of their apparent possession of a number of behavior characteristics or traits, but on the basis of their possession of the requisite skills for the specific level of responsibility involved.

Developing the Skills

For years many people have contended that leadership ability is inherent in certain chosen individuals. We talk of "born leaders," "born executives," "born salesmen." It is undoubtedly true that certain people, naturally or innately, possess greater aptitude or ability in certain skills. But research in psychology and physiology would also indicate, first, that those having strong aptitudes and abilities can improve their skill through practice and training, and, secondly, that even those lacking the natural ability can improve their performance and effectiveness.

The *skill* conception of administration suggests that we may hope to improve our administrative effectiveness and to develop better administrators for the future. This skill conception implies *learning by doing*. Different people learn in different ways, but skills are developed through practice and through relating learning to one's own personal experience and background. If well done, training in these basic administrative skills should develop executive abilities more surely and more rapidly than through unorganized experience. What, then, are some of the ways in which this training can be conducted?

Technical skill

Development of technical skill has received great attention for many years by industry and educational institutions alike, and much progress has been made. Sound grounding in the principles, structures, and processes of the individual specialty, coupled with actual practice and experience during which the individual is watched and helped by a superior, appear to be most effective. In view of the vast amount of work which has been done in training people in the technical skills, it would seem unnecessary in this article to suggest more.

Human skill

Human skill, however, has been much less understood, and only recently has systematic progress been made in developing it. Many different approaches to the development of human skill are being pursued by various universities and professional men today. These are rooted in such disciplines as psychology, sociology, and anthropology.

Some of these approaches find their application in "applied psychology," "human engineering," and a host of other manifestations requiring technical specialists to help the businessman with his human problems. As a practical matter, however, the executive must develop his own human skill, rather than lean on the advice of others. To be effective, he must develop his own personal point of view toward human activity, so that he will (a) recognize the feelings and sentiments which he brings to a situation; (b) have an attitude about his own experiences which will enable him to re-evaluate and learn from them; (c) develop ability in understanding what others by their actions and words (explicit or implicit) are trying to communicate to him; and (d) develop ability in successfully communicating his ideas and attitudes to others.[13]

This human skill can be developed by some individuals without formalized training. Others can be individually aided by their immediate superiors as an integral part of the "coaching" process to be described later. This aid depends for effectiveness, obviously, on the extent to which the superior possesses the human skill.

For larger groups, the use of case problems coupled with impromptu role playing can be very effective. This training can be established on a formal or informal basis, but it requires a skilled instructor and organized sequence of activities.[14] It affords as good an approximation to reality as can be provided on a continuing classroom basis and offers an opportunity for critical reflection not often found in actual practice. An important part of the procedure is the self-examination of the trainee's own concepts and values, which may enable him to develop more useful attitudes about himself and about others. With the change in attitude, hopefully, there may also come some active skill in dealing with human problems.

[13] For a further discussion of this point, see F. J. Roethlisberger, "Training Supervisors in Human Relations," HBR (September, 1951), p. 47.

[14] See, for example, A. Winn, "Training in Administration and Human Relations," *Personnel* (September, 1953), p. 139; see also, Kenneth R. Andrews, "Executive Training by the Case Method," HBR (September, 1951), p. 58.

Human skill has also been tested in the classroom, within reasonable limits, by a series of analyses of detailed accounts of actual situations involving administrative action, together with a number of role-playing opportunities in which the individual is required to carry out the details of the action he has proposed. In this way an individual's understanding of the total situation and his own personal ability to do something about it can be evaluated.

On the job, there should be frequent opportunities for a superior to observe an individual's ability to work effectively with others. These may appear to be highly subjective evaluations and to depend for validity on the human skill of the rater. But does not every promotion, in the last analysis, depend on someone's subjective judgment? And should this subjectivity be berated, or should we make a greater effort to develop people within our organizations with the human skill to make such judgments effectively?

Conceptual skill

Conceptual skill, like human skill, has not been very widely understood. A number of methods have been tried to aid in developing this ability, with varying success. Some of the best results have always been achieved through the "coaching" of subordinates by superiors.[15] This is no new idea. It implies that one of the key responsibilities of the executive is to help his subordinates to develop their administrative potentials. One way a superior can help "coach" his subordinate is by assigning a particular responsibility, and then responding with searching questions or opinions, rather than giving answers, whenever the subordinate seeks help. When Benjamin F. Fairless, now chairman of the board of the United States Steel Corporation, was president of the corporation, he described his coaching activities as follows:

> "When one of my vice presidents or the head of one of our operating companies comes to me for instructions, I generally counter by asking him questions. First thing I know, he has told me how to solve the problem himself." [16]

Obviously, this is an ideal and wholly natural procedure for administrative training, and applies to the development of technical and human skill, as well as to that of conceptual skill. However, its

[15] For a more complete development of the concept of "coaching," see Myles L. Mace, *The Growth and Development of Executives* (Boston: Division of Research, Harvard Business School, 1950).
[16] "What Should a President Do?" *Dun's Review* (July, 1951), p. 14.

success must necessarily rest on the abilities and willingness of the superior to help the subordinate.

Another excellent way to develop conceptual skill is through trading jobs, that is, by moving promising young men through different functions of the business but at the same level of responsibility. This gives the man the chance literally to "be in the other fellow's shoes."

Other possibilities include: special assignments, particularly the kind which involve inter-departmental problems; and management boards, such as the McCormick Multiple Management plan, in which junior executives serve as advisers to top management on policy matters.

For larger groups, the kind of case-problems course described above, only using cases involving broad management policy and inter-departmental coordination, may be useful. Courses of this kind, often called "General Management" or "Business Policy," are becoming increasingly prevalent.

In the classroom, conceptual skill has also been evaluated with reasonable effectiveness by presenting a series of detailed descriptions of specific complex situations. In these the individual being tested is asked to set forth a course of action which responds to the underlying forces operating in each situation and which considers the implications of this action on the various functions and parts of the organization and its total environment.

On the job, the alert supervisor should find frequent opportunities to observe the extent to which the individual is able to relate himself and his job to the other functions and operations of the company.

Like human skill, conceptual skill, too, must become a natural part of the executive's makeup. Different methods may be indicated for developing different people, by virtue of their backgrounds, attitudes, and experience. But in every case that method should be chosen which will enable the executive to develop his own personal skill in visualizing the enterprise as a whole and in coordinating and integrating its various parts.

Conclusion

The purpose of this article has been to show that effective administration depends on three basic personal skills, which have been called *technical, human,* and *conceptual.* The administrator needs: (a) sufficient technical skill to accomplish the mechanics of the particular job for which he is responsible; (b) sufficient human skill in working with others to be an effective group member and to be able to build cooperative effort within the team he leads; (c) sufficient conceptual skill to recognize the interrelationships of the various factors involved in his situation, which will lead him to take that action which achieves the maximum good for the total organization.

The relative importance of these three skills seems to vary with the level of administrative responsibility. At lower levels, the major need is for technical and human skills. At higher levels, the administrator's effectiveness depends largely on human and conceptual skills. At the top, conceptual skill becomes the most important of all for successful administration.

This three-skill approach emphasizes that good administrators are not necessarily born; they may be developed. It transcends the need to identify specific traits in an effort to provide a more useful way of looking at the administrative process. By helping to identify the skills most needed at various levels of responsibility, it may prove useful in the selection, training, and promotion of executives.

70. LEADERSHIP QUALITIES [1]

Cecil E. Goode [2]

* * *

It is concluded from this study of leadership research that the following represent the qualities which make for successful leadership in working organizations:

1. The leader is somewhat more intelligent than the average of his followers. However, he is not so superior that he cannot be readily understood by those who work with him.
2. The leader is a well-rounded individual from the standpoint of interests and aptitudes. He tends toward interests, aptitudes, and knowledge with respect to a wide variety of fields.
3. The leader has an unusual facility with language. He speaks and writes simply, persuasively and understandably.
4. The leader is mentally and emotionally mature. He has come of age mentally and emotionally as well as physically.
5. The leader has a powerful inner drive or motivation which impels him to strive for accomplishment.
6. The leader is fully aware of the importance of cooperative effort in getting things done, and therefore understands and practices very effectively the so-called social skills.
7. The leader relies on his administrative skills to a much greater extent than he does on any of the technical skills which may be associated directly with his work.

[1] From "Significant Research on Leadership," *Personnel*, Vol. XXVII, No. 5 (March, 1951), pp. 342-349. Reprinted by permission of The American Management Association.
[2] Cecil Goode, Deputy Director of Personnel, Economic Stabilization Administration, 1951.

71. WHEN THE JOB OUTGROWS
THE MAN [1]

Saul W. Gellerman [2]

Sometimes management's thorniest problems are not so hard to solve as they are hard to face. A classic example of this is the problem of the veteran manager who, for one reason or another, is no longer equal to his job. This situation is often at the root of far-reaching problems, especially in a company that is trying to put the accent on progress.

Usually, such men are not hard to identify. In fact, their unsuitability is sometimes painfully obvious, and it is all too clear, that the most appropriate solution to the problems they present would be replacement by better men. But management's reaction frequently consists of doing nothing at all. The problem is shelved, not solved.

Why are these situations allowed to continue? Many "practical" and "humane" reasons are advanced, but when they are examined closely most of them turn out to be rationalizations. It may be argued, for example, that to replace a well-liked manager would disrupt a happy, smooth-running shop—when the shop is actually complacent, and needs a good jolt to wake it up. Or management may balk at hurting the feelings of a loyal old campaigner—which may simply make a more crushing blow to his feelings inevitable later on.

Of course, not every decision to retain an executive who has been antiquated by his job can be dismissed as a rationalization. Sometimes the probability of an early retirement or the prospect of shifts in functional responsibilities makes it far wiser to let nature take its course than to resort to radical action. But management's own underlying psychology when it is confronted with this problem can play hob with its objectivity and give a bogus veneer of realism to what is actually shortsighted decision. The question, then, is how to clear away the underlying barriers to realism. Once this is done,

[1] From *The Management Review* (June, 1960), pp. 4-8, 68-70. Reprinted by permission of American Management Association, Inc.

[2] Saul W. Gellerman, Research in Employee Motivation, International Business Machine.

the alternative courses of action are not nearly so stark, nor the consequences of action so horrendous, as they may have appeared at first.

"There, But for the Grace of God . . ."

Management would do well to examine its own feelings before concluding that it is practical to preserve the status quo for an outgrown executive. Two attitudes, in particular, can debilitate the will to take corrective action: identifying with the "victim," and trying to avoid unpopularity.

When an executive's job is in jeopardy it is quite natural for other managers to feel with a twinge that "There, but for the grace of God, go I." In an era of rapid technological change, it does not take a wild stretch of the imagination to picture oneself in exactly the same predicament some day.

Quite often, however, this type of feeling goes further than mere sympathy and fosters a small but gnawing fear in the back of an executive's mind. It seldom shows itself clearly enough to be put into words, but if it did, it would sound something like this: "Taking action against this man could set a precedent that would eventually trap *me*." This feeling, based more on fear than on logic, lies behind many a softheaded decision by many an otherwise hardheaded executive.

Irrational ideas can sway anybody's thinking, as long as they are too dimly conceived to be recognized for what they are. Consequently, the real danger of this kind of fear does not lie in feeling it, since that is quite natural, but in not facing it. It takes a bold executive to face up to the possibility that he may have allowed a fear to affect his decision, but the only real defense against self-deception is an awareness that it is not at all impossible—or even unusual.

Avoiding Popularity

Many executives dread the thought of being widely disliked within their own organizations. Up to a point, this is quite realistic: grudges and suspicions impose severe handicaps on a man who must get his work done through other people.

But sometimes a manager seems to feel that unpopularity would have a catastrophic effect on his career and must therefore be avoided at all costs. Such a person naturally shrinks from the risk of looking like a hatchet man. He can cheerfully endure another executive's indecision and outmoded ideas when the alternative seems to be a reputation for meanness.

The fact remains, however, that a certain degree of unpopularity is inevitable for anyone who has the power to hurt other people's careers, regardless of whether or not that power is used. The mere possession of power is enough to make an executive unpopular with some of his subordinates, especially those who, fearing that their own work has been inadequate, may have good reason to be wary.

Naturally, when management moves to replace a veteran executive, resentment flares—not only in the man himself, but also in those who may feel, rightly or wrongly, that he was dealt with unfairly. But this resentment is not created by the act of removal; it is simply a stronger and more obvious expression of feelings that are already present in any relationship between managers and the managed.

The real problem, then, is not to avoid unpopularity, but to manage it. Nothing makes this harder than a secret conviction, somewhere in the executive's mind, that his decision may be wrong and that he may deserve to be disliked. This kind of insecurity may not be very becoming in an executive, but it is not uncommon. Excessive fear of unpopularity is often a mask for a lack of confidence in one's ideas. The good will of subordinates is a form of reassurance to the uncertain executive. When this reassurance is lost and people seem to turn against him, he is likely to take it as a sign that he has finally made that colossal blunder he always feared he'd make.

Given such an underlying psychology, it is easy to see why so many "good" reasons are found for avoiding a showdown with an old-timer who has the respect and friendship of many people in the company. Obviously, until such underlying emotional roadblocks as these are cleared away, any proposals for managing executive obsolescence realistically will be purely academic.

THE OBJECTIVE APPROACH

Whether the removal of an obsolete executive precipitates a crisis or is taken in stride by the others in an organization depends to a large extent on the emotional preparation of the executives who do the removing. Because the men who must take action frequently become a major part of the problem themselves, the first step in managing the problem of high-level deadwood is for management to do enough soul-searching to insure that it is being as objective as possible.

Winston Churchill was criticized after the Japanese attack on Malaya for sending a very dignified note to the Japanese ambassador, advising him that Great Britain considered a state of war to exist between their two countries. His reply was, "After all, when you have to kill a man it costs nothing to be polite." It costs even less when one merely has to remove a man from an office he is no longer qualified to hold, and it can save a lot of misunderstanding and dissension for all concerned.

Being in too much of a hurry to get an unpleasant task over with leads to brusqueness, tactlessness, and inadequate explanations to the affected executive and his associates.

Very few men in management need to brush up on Emily Post, but no one is on his best behavior when he is unsure of himself and on the defensive. The men who are faced with this kind of decision must be inwardly convinced of its rightness and of their own qualifications to make it in order to bring it off with the delicacy, timing, and thoroughness that it requires.

INGRATES AND EXECUTIONERS

Realistic planning must take account of the likelihood that, regardless of how well justified removal may be, it will probably be viewed otherwise by those concerned.

The affected executive may see the decision as a potentially destructive blow to his self-esteem. To prevent such a catastrophe in his own psyche, he is likely to take the attitude that the decision is a serious mistake, that the people who made it are incompetent or unworthy, and that in any event this is damned shabby treatment of a man who deserves as much gratitude as he does.

His friends, protegés, and sympathizers in the company will often be indignant at what they consider harsh and unjust treatment. Moreover, they may see the decision as a threat to their own security, partly because it removes a protector and benefactor from the scene, and partly because it reminds them that they are, if anything, even more vulnerable than he was. Their outrage may be at least partially a form of mobilization against what looks like a potential attack on them.

In short, the men responsible for removing an obsolete executive are likely to be perceived as incompetent ingrates on the one hand, and as scheming executioners on the other. There is probably no way to prevent this kind of hysteria altogether. Whether it dies down or persists as a chronic morale-poisoner depends to a large extent on how management handles itself during the initial furor.

If management goes on the defensive by implying that the same fate is in store for those who object too strenuously to the removal, it simply perpetuates animosities that could eventually get out of hand. The same is true when management tries to avoid criticism by refusing to discuss the situation at all. On the other hand, if management takes pains to present its side of the story clearly, to spike rumors and misinterpretations immediately, and above all to accent the importance of getting on with the job, the passions aroused by the removal will tend to run their natural course and fade away.

COURSES OF ACTION

There are several ways of dealing with an executive who must be removed from his position. All of them have their own advantages and disadvantages, so management must choose the one that seems wisest in each case.

A new assignment

Retaining the executive in the organization is often desirable, in order to continue to benefit from his experience and the company's investment in that experience. However, his effectiveness in any new position will be undermined if people suspect that he has become a figurehead. Therefore, the value of retention depends on whether the executive can be assigned to a function that fills a real need rather than a contrived one, and whether he can be entrusted with the full authority that such a job requires.

The functional bypass

When the executive is allowed to keep his title, salary, and status symbols, but is in effect "replaced" by assistants or other executives who take over his duties, appearances are preserved and the turmoil that could be caused by an open break is avoided. But in practice, it often turns out that the by-passing occurs only on paper. The men who are supposed to take over the actual responsibilities of the obsolete executive may approach their new jobs timidly, because they feel awkward and even a little guilty about assuming powers to which another man is supposed to be entitled. In addition, there may be confusion as to where the responsibility and authority really lie, due to equivocal instructions that were originally designed to take the sting out of the change-over. Further, behind-the-scenes politicking by the executive's sympathizers can effectively paralyze his "replacements" by involving them in battles of innuendo regarding their own qualifications.

For these reasons, the functional by-pass is not likely to be effective unless it is feasible to spell out the specific functions of everyone involved (even though the changes may not be made "public") ; to guarantee management support to men assuming responsibilities for which they have no corresponding "official" authority; and to forestall intrigues by clarifying management's position in advance of the change and backing this up with a firm, no-nonsense attitude during the transition.

Each of these conditions presupposes a healthy managerial climate in which an obsolete executive probably would not have been kept in office for very long in the first place—which is another way of saying that the functional by-pass probably has a rather limited range of usefulness.

Assistance in locating a new job

Even though an executive may have been in a sense "outgrown" by one company, he may still have plenty of mileage left in him for another one. This is particularly true of men who are better geared to the dynamics of a smaller, more intimately operated company than to those of an organizational giant. Sometimes, too, company emphasis on a specific technology will "antiquate" executives with no special training or penchant in that area, although their abilities in their own accustomed bailiwicks remain unquestioned. Finally, even a very capable executive may have a personal outlook or trait that does not harmonize with the dominant strains in the company's "personality," in which case he would probably be happier and more effective elsewhere.

Circumstances such as these may make it desirable to help the executive to find a suitable position with another firm. Doing so could preserve the friendship of a man who might otherwise turn into a bitter and perhaps potent foe. It would also tend to bolster the morale of others in the organization who may be apprehensive about their own jobs; and this in turn would alleviate much of the grumbling and insecurity that often occurs after such a change.

However, it is hard to determine just how far this help ought to go, or indeed whether it might not be misinterpreted and therefore boomerang. "Help" can run the gamut from allowing a decent period for winding up one's affairs and for job-hunting all the way to locating a suitable new employer and bringing the parties together. No matter how much notice a man is given, he will tend to consider it inadequate if he has not made an acceptable new arrangement by the time the period is over; and any extensions may simply lead to the same result. On the other hand, directing him to another firm may appear to be a slick way of seducing him into leaving quietly. He may also resent the control over his future that is attempted by a company that has rejected him. Partly for this reason, management sometimes arranges matters so that the executive "happens" to be approached by a recruiter at about the same time that his position becomes precarious.

Early retirement

Early retirement will usually eliminate much if not all of the financial stress imposed by separation, and it tends to be interpreted as a magnanimous gesture by persons who might otherwise feel that the executive was getting a raw deal. However, retirement—even with honors—may carry a stigma in the eyes of the executive who needs to feel that he is important, even indispensable, to his company. To such men, retirement is only a subtle way of being told that they have outlived their usefulness; and this can lead to bitterness or despair.

Early retirement is not an effective solution unless the individual is, or can be, psychologically prepared for it. Unfortunately, a man who has held a position for a long time despite his inability to perform its duties well usually has not been given any reason to doubt that he would keep it indefinitely. Also, being "retired" early is a dubious recommendation for a man who may decide to attempt to resume his career elsewhere later on.

Dismissal

There is merit to the argument that the unequivocal "clean break" avoids drawn-out departures with their attendant strain on everybody concerned and compels the individual to start thinking realistically about his career prospects, rather than dwelling on a lost cause.

Sometimes, in fact, this can provide the very shock a man needs to bring about a long-overdue reappraisal and spur him toward a more suitable and rewarding placement. However, management must recognize that the shock can also be numbing if the executive had become emotionally dependant on his old firm, in which case it could take him a long while to recover his aplomb. Further, if he does not withstand the blow, his demoralization will reflect very poorly on the judgment, not to say the humanity, of management. Instead of forestalling dissension, such a move may only worsen it. Before a "clean break" is attempted therefore, management should consider all other possibilities and should be reasonably sure that the executive will roll with the blow rather than crumple under it.

MAKING THE BEST OF IT

Whatever course of action management considers, it should not temporize with personnel problems that have reached a point of no return. Once the issue of executive obsolescence is postponed, management begins boxing itself into a position from which there are few if any good ways out—and the situation almost always deteriorates from that point on. Any "solution" will probably have its share of uncomfortable or inconvenient aspects. But the longer the issue is postponed, the less palatable the alternatives are likely to become.

Certainly no decision to replace an executive should ever be made rashly. It is axiomatic that every other means of alleviating the situation should be carefully considered first. But once replacement is clearly indicated, the likelihood of bruised egos and tender consciences should not deter management from correcting a bad situation before it gets worse.

BIBLIOGRAPHY, CHAPTER XX

BENNETT, C. L. "Defining the Manager's Job," *Management Review* (November, 1958), 26-30.

BOWER, M. (Ed.). *The Development of Executive Leadership.* Cambridge: Harvard University Press, 1951. Part I.

CANTOR, NATHANIEL. "The Executive as Leader," *Personnel* (November, 1956), 227-235.

ERICSON, RICHARD F. "The Growing Demand for Synoptic Minds in Industry," *Journal of the Academy of Management* (April, 1960), 25-40.

FINE, BENJAMIN. "Most Valuable College Studies Are Listed by Some Graduates in Industry," *The New York Times* (December 2, 1956), E-11.

FLANAGAN, JOHN C. "Defining the Requirements of the Executive's Job," *Personnel*, Vol. 28, No. 1 (July, 1951), 28-35.

GAUDET, F. J. "What Causes Executive Success or Failure," *Iron Age* (September 8, 15, and 22, 1960), 62-63, 69-72, 120-122.

HAY, EDWARD N., and DALE PURVES. "The Analysis and Description of High-Level Jobs," *Personnel*, Vol. 29, No. 4 (January, 1953), 344-354.

HEMPHILL, JOHN K. "Job Descriptions for Executives," *Harvard Business Review* (September-October, 1959), 55-67.

JENNINGS, EUGENE E. "The Anatomy of Leadership," *Management of Personnel Quarterly* (Autumn, 1961).

KRIEGU, JOSEPH L. "Critical Elements of Executive Leadership and Development," *Advanced Management* (June, 1958), 8-9, 13.

"Management Man, Soviet Style," *Management News* (February, 1960), 5.

"Performance Standards for Executives," *Management News* (January, 1960), 6.

ROWLAND, VIRGIL K. *Managerial Performance Standards.* New York: American Management Association, Inc., 1960.

"The Nine Hundred," *Fortune* (November, 1952), 132-135, 232-236.

YNTEMA, THEODORE O. "The Transferable Skills of a Manager," *Journal of the Academy of Management* (August, 1960), 79-86.

Chapter XXI

Recruiting and Selecting Managers

The articles in this chapter present a few of the many techniques of selecting men for the managerial job.

If management is to maintain an upward flow of personnel from the ranks as one means of staffing managerial positions, it must provide ways for identifying individual workers who are promotable. To facilitate the identification of promotable workers, many companies have turned to what has been called the appraisal process. This process consists of periodic evaluations of the man's progress (so that he will not be forgotten) and of counseling him with respect to the improvements he might make. In the first article Douglas McGregor discusses the weaknesses of some of the appraisal programs and presents an alternative approach that overcomes some of these weaknesses.

In spite of the most vigorous attempts by management to provide management replacements from within the organization, the loss of a key man sometimes necessitates the recruitment of a high-level executive from outside the firm. In other instances, management makes it a practice periodically to bring managers in from the outside at all levels to provide new blood. Stephen Habbe discusses the technique of executive recruitment.

As an example of the process of validating a selection device for screening managerial job applicants, Hubert Clay discusses the preliminary steps in that process for testing foremen. The manager is in a position to determine whether such tests are any good only if they have predicted success over a period of time.

The final selection by William H. Whyte, Jr., is a biting criticism of a highly popular type of test for managers: the personality test.

72. AN UNEASY LOOK
AT PERFORMANCE APPRAISAL [1]   Douglas McGregor [2]

Performance appraisal within management ranks has become standard practice in many companies during the past twenty years, and is currently being adopted by many others, often as an important feature of management development programs. The more the method is used, the more uneasy I grow over the unstated assumptions which lie behind it. Moreover, with some searching, I find that a number of people both in education and in industry share my misgivings. This article, therefore, has two purposes:

> To examine the conventional performance appraisal plan which requires the manager to pass judgment on the personal worth of subordinates.
> To describe an alternative which places on the subordinate the primary responsibility for establishing performance goals and appraising progress toward them.

CURRENT PROGRAMS

Formal performance appraisal plans are designed to meet three needs, one for the organization and two for the individual:

1. They provide systematic judgments to back up salary increases, promotions, transfers, and sometimes demotions or terminations.
2. They are a means of telling a subordinate how he is doing, and suggesting needed changes in his behavior attitudes, skills, or job knowledge; they let him know "where he stands" with the boss.
3. They also are being increasingly used as a basis for the coaching and counseling of the individual by the superior.

Problem of resistance

Personnel administrators are aware that appraisal programs tend to run into resistance from the managers who are expected to administer them. Even managers who admit the necessity of such pro-

[1] From the *Harvard Business Review* (May-June, 1957). Reprinted by permission of the *Harvard Business Review*.
[2] Douglas McGregor is Professor of Management, School of Industrial Management, Massachusetts Institute of Technology.

grams frequently balk at the process—especially the interview part. As a result, some companies do not communicate appraisal results to the individual, despite the general conviction that the subordinate has a right to know his superior's opinion so he can correct his weaknesses.

The boss' resistance is usually attributed to the following causes:

A normal dislike of criticizing a subordinate (and perhaps having to argue about it).
Lack of skill needed to handle the interviews.
Dislike of a new procedure with its accompanying changes in ways of operating.
Mistrust of the validity of the appraisal instrument.

To meet this problem, formal controls—scheduling, reminders, and so on—are often instituted. It is common experience that without them fewer than half the appraisal interviews are actually held. But even controls do not necessarily work. Thus:

In one company with a well-planned and carefully administered appraisal program, an opinion poll included two questions regarding appraisals. More than 90% of those answering the questionnaire approved the idea of appraisals. They wanted to know how they stood. Some 40% went on to say that they had never had the experience of being told—yet the files showed that over four-fifths of them had signed a form testifying that they had been through an appraisal interview, some of them several times!

The respondents had no reason to lie, nor was there the slightest supposition that their superiors had committed forgery. The probable explanation is that the superiors, being basically resistant to the plan, had conducted the interviews in such a perfunctory manner that many subordinates did not recognize what was going on.

Training programs designed to teach the skills of appraising and interviewing do help, but they seldom eliminate managerial resistance entirely. The difficulties connected with "negative appraisals" remain a source of genuine concern. There is always some discomfort involved in telling a subordinate he is not doing well. The individual who is "coasting" during the few years prior to retirement after serving his company competently for many years presents a special dilemma to the boss who is preparing to interview him.

Nor does a shift to a form of group appraisal solve the problem. Though the group method tends to have greater validity and, properly administered, can equalize varying standards of judgment, it does not ease the difficulty inherent in the interview. In fact, the superior's discomfort is often intensified when he must base his interview on the results of a *group* discussion of the subordinate's worth. Even if the final judgments have been his, he is not free to discuss the things said by others which may have influenced him.

The underlying cause

What should we think about a method—however valuable for meeting organizational needs—which produces such results in a wide range of companies with a variety of appraisal plans? The problem is one that cannot be dismissed lightly.

Perhaps this intuitive managerial reaction to conventional performance appraisal plans shows a deep but unrecognized wisdom. In my view, it does not reflect anything so simple as resistance to change, or dislike for personnel technique, or lack of skill, or mistrust for rating scales. Rather, managers seem to be expressing very real misgivings, which they find difficult to put into words. This could be the underlying cause:

> The conventional approach, unless handled with consummate skill and delicacy, constitutes something dangerously close to a violation of the integrity of the personality. Managers are uncomfortable when they are put in the position of "playing God." The respect we hold for the inherent value of the individual leaves us distressed when we must take responsibility for judging the personal worth of a fellow man. Yet the conventional approach to performance appraisal forces us, not only to make such judgments and to see them acted upon, but also to communicate them to those we have judged. Small wonder we resist!

The modern emphasis upon the manager as a leader who strives to *help* his subordinates achieve both their own and the company's objectives is hardly consistent with the judicial role demanded by most appraisal plans. If the manager must put on his judicial hat occasionally, he does it reluctantly and with understandable qualms. Under such conditions it is unlikely that the subordinate will be any happier with the results than will be the boss. It will not be surprising, either, if he fails to recognize that he has been told where he stands.

Of course, managers cannot escape making judgments about subordinates. Without such evaluations, salary and promotion policies cannot be administered sensibly. But are subordinates like products on an assembly line, to be accepted or rejected as a result of an inspection process? The inspection process may be made more objective or more accurate through research on the appraisal instrument, through training of the "inspectors," or through introducing group appraisal; the subordinate may be "reworked" by coaching or counseling before the final decision to accept or reject him; but as far as the assumptions of the conventional appraisal process are concerned, we still have what is practically identical with a program for product inspection.

On this interpretation, then, resistance to conventional appraisal programs is eminently sound. It reflects an unwillingness to treat human beings like physical objects. The needs of the organization are obviously important, but when they come into conflict with our convictions about the worth and the dignity of the human personality, one or the other must give.

Indeed, by the fact of their resistance managers are saying that the organization must yield in the face of this fundamental human value. And they are thus being more sensitive than are personnel administrators and social scientists whose business it is to be concerned with the human problems of industry!

A New Approach

If this analysis is correct, the task before us is clear. We must find a new plan—not a compromise to hide the dilemma, but a bold move to resolve the issue.

A number of writers are beginning to approach the whole subject of management from the point of view of basic social values. Peter Drucker's concept of "management by objectives" [3] offers an unusually promising framework within which we can seek a solution. Several companies, notably General Mills, Incorporated, and General Electric Company, have been exploring different methods of appraisal which rest upon assumptions consistent with Drucker's philosophy.

Responsibility on subordinate

This approach calls on the subordinate to establish short-term performance goals *for himself*. The superior enters the process actively only *after* the subordinate has (a) done a good deal of thinking about his job, (b) made a careful assessment of his own strengths and weaknesses, and (c) formulated some specific plans to accomplish his goals. The superior's role is to help the man relate his self-appraisal, his "targets," and his plans for the ensuing period to the realities of the organization.

[3] See Peter Drucker, *The Practice of Management* (New York, Harper & Brothers, 1954).

The first step in this process is to arrive at a clear statement of the major features of the job. Rather than a formal job description, this is a document drawn up *by the subordinate* after studying the company-approved statement. It defines the broad areas of his responsibility as they actually work out in practice. The boss and employee discuss the draft jointly and modify it as may be necessary until both of them agree that it is adequate.

Working from this statement of responsibilities, the subordinate then establishes his goals or "targets" for a period of, say, six months. These targets are *specific* actions which the man proposes to take, i.e., setting up regular staff meetings to improve communication, reorganizing the office, completing or undertaking a certain study. Thus, they are explicitly stated and accompanied by a detailed account of the actions he proposes to take to reach them. This document is, in turn, discussed with the superior and modified until both are satisfied with it.

At the conclusion of the six-month period, the subordinate makes *his own* appraisal of what he has accomplished relative to the targets he had set earlier. He substantiates it with factual data wherever possible. The "interview" is an examination by superior and subordinate together of the subordinate's self-appraisal, and it culminates in a resetting of targets for the next six months.

Of course, the superior has veto power at each step of this process; in an organizational hierarchy anything else would be unacceptable. However, in practice he rarely needs to exercise it. Most subordinates tend to underestimate both their potentialities and their achievements. Moreover, subordinates normally have an understandable wish to satisfy their boss, and are quite willing to adjust their targets or appraisals if the superior feels they are unrealistic. Actually, a much more common problem is to resist the subordinates' tendency to want the boss to tell them what to write down.

Analysis vs. appraisal

This approach to performance appraisal differs profoundly from the conventional one, for it shifts the emphasis from *appraisal* to *analysis*. This implies a more positive approach. No longer is the subordinate being examined by the superior so that his weaknesses may be determined; rather, he is examining himself, in order to define not only his weaknesses but also his strengths and potentials. The importance of this shift of emphasis should not be underestimated.

It is basic to each of the specific differences which distinguish this approach from the conventional one.

The first of these differences arises from the subordinate's new role in the process. He becomes an active agent, not a passive "object." He is no longer a pawn in a chess game called management development.

Effective development of managers does not include coercing them (no matter how benevolently) into acceptance of the goals of the enterprise, nor does it mean manipulating their behavior to suit organizational needs. Rather, it calls for creating a relationship within which a man can take responsibility for developing his own potentialities, plan for himself, and learn from putting his plans into action. In the process he can gain a genuine sense of satisfaction, for he is utilizing his own capabilities to achieve simultaneously both his objectives and those of the organization. Unless this is the nature of the relationship, "development" becomes an euphemism.

Who knows best?

One of the main differences of this approach is that it rests on the assumption that the individual knows—or can learn—more than anyone else about his own capabilities, needs, strengths and weaknesses, and goals. In the end, only he can determine what is best for his development. The conventional approach, on the other hand, makes the assumption that the superior can know enough about the subordinate to decide what is best for him.

No available methods can provide the superior with the knowledge he needs to make such decisions. Ratings, aptitude and personality tests, and the superior's necessarily limited knowledge of the man's performance yield at best an imperfect picture. Even the most extensive psychological counseling (assuming the superior possesses the competence for it) would not solve the problem because the product of counseling is self-insight on the part of the *counselee.*

(Psychological tests are not being condemned by this statement. On the contrary, they have genuine value in competent hands. Their use by professionals as part of the process of screening applicants for employment does not raise the same questions as their use to "diagnose" the personal worth of accepted members of a management team. Even in the latter instance the problem we are discussing would not arise if test results and interpretations were given *to the individual himself,* to be shared with superiors at his discretion.)

The proper role for the superior, then, is the one that falls naturally to him under the suggested plan: helping the subordinate relate his career planning to the needs and realities of the organization. In the discussions the boss can use his knowledge of the organization to help the subordinate establish targets and methods for achieving them which will (a) lead to increased knowledge and skill, (b) contribute to organizational objectives, and (c) test the subordinate's appraisal of himself.

This is help which the subordinate wants. He knows well that the rewards and satisfactions he seeks from his career as a manager depend on his contribution to organizational objectives. He is also aware that the superior knows more completely than he what is required for success in this organization and *under this boss*. The superior, then, is the person who can help him test the soundness of his goals and his plans for achieving them. Quite clearly the knowledge and active participation of *both* superior and subordinate are necessary components of this approach.

If the superior accepts this role, he need not become a judge of the subordinate's personal worth. He is not telling, deciding, criticizing, or praising—not "playing God." He finds himself listening, using his own knowledge of the organization as a basis for advising, guiding, encouraging his subordinates to develop their own potentialities. Incidentally, this often leads the superior to important insights about himself and his impact on others.

Looking to the future

Another significant difference is that the emphasis is on the future rather than the past. The purpose of the plan is to establish realistic targets and to seek the most effective ways of reaching them. Appraisal thus becomes a means to a *constructive* end. The 60-year-old "coaster" can be encouraged to set performance goals for himself and to make a fair appraisal of his progress toward them. Even the subordinate who has failed can be helped to consider what moves will be best for himself. The superior rarely finds himself facing the uncomfortable prospect of denying a subordinate's personal worth. A transfer or even a demotion can be worked out without the connotation of a "sentence by the judge."

Performance vs. personality

Finally, the accent is on *performance*, on actions relative to goals. There is less tendency for the personality of the subordinate to become an issue. The superior, instead of finding himself in the position of a psychologist or a therapist, can become a coach helping the subordinate to reach his own decisions on the specific steps that will enable him to reach his targets. Such counseling as may be required demands no deep analysis of the personal motivations or basic adjustment of the subordinate. To illustrate:

> Consider a subordinate who is hostile, short-tempered, uncooperative, insecure. The superior need not make any psychological diagnosis. The "target setting" approach naturally directs the subordinate's attention to ways and means of obtaining better interdepartmental collaboration, reducing complaints, winning the confidence of the men under him. Rather than facing the troublesome prospect of forcing his own psychological diagnosis on the subordinate, the superior can, for example, help the individual plan ways of getting "feedback" concerning his impact on his associates and subordinates as a basis for self-appraisal and self-improvement.

There is little chance that a man who is involved in a process like this will be in the dark about where he stands, or that he will forget he is the principal participant in his own development and responsible for it.

A NEW ATTITUDE

As a consequence of these differences we may expect the growth of a different attitude toward appraisal on the part of superior and subordinate alike.

The superior will gain real satisfaction as he learns to help his subordinates integrate their personal goals with the needs of the organization so that both are served. Once the subordinate has worked out a mutually satisfactory plan of action, the superior can delegate to him the responsibility for putting it into effect. He will see himself in a consistent managerial role rather than being forced to adopt the basically incompatible role of either the judge or the psychologist.

Unless there is a basic personal antagonism between the two men (in which case the relationship should be terminated), the superior can conduct these interviews so that both are actively involved in seeking the right basis for constructive action. The organization, the boss, and the subordinate all stand to gain. Under such circumstances the opportunities for learning and for genuine development of both parties are maximal.

The particular mechanics are of secondary importance. The needs of the organization in the administration of salary and promotion policies can easily be met within the framework of the analysis process. The machinery of the program can be adjusted to the situation. No universal list of rating categories is required. The complications of subjectives or prejudiced judgment, of varying standards, of attempts to quantify qualitative data, all can be minimized. In fact, *no* formal machinery is required.

Problems of judgment

I have deliberately slighted the many problems of judgment involved in administering promotions and salaries. These are by no means minor, and this approach will not automatically solve them. However, I believe that if we are prepared to recognize the fundamental problem inherent in the conventional approach, ways can be found to temper our present administrative methods.

And if this approach is accepted, the traditional ingenuity of management will lead to the invention of a variety of methods for its implementation. The mechanics of some conventional plans can be adjusted to be consistent with this point of view. Obviously, a program utilizing ratings of the personal characteristics of subordinates would not be suitable, but one which emphasizes *behavior* might be.

Of course, managerial skill is required. No method will eliminate that. This method can fail as readily as any other in the clumsy hands of insensitive or indifferent or power-seeking managers. But even the limited experience of a few companies with this approach indicates that managerial *resistance* is substantially reduced. As a consequence, it is easier to gain the collaboration of managers in developing the necessary skills.

Cost in time

There is one unavoidable cost: the manager must spend considerably more time in implementing a program of this kind. It is not unusual to take a couple of days to work through the initial establishment of responsibilities and goals with each individual. And a periodic appraisal may require several hours rather than the typical 20 minutes.

Reaction to this cost will undoubtedly vary. The management that considers the development of its human resources to be the primary means of achieving the economic objectives of the organization will not be disturbed. It will regard the necessary guidance and coaching as among the most important functions of every superior.

Conclusion

I have sought to show that the conventional approach to performance appraisal stands condemned as a personnel method. It places the manager in the untenable position of judging the personal worth of his subordinates, and of acting on these judgments. No manager possesses, nor could he acquire, the skill necessary to carry out this responsibility effectively. Few would even be willing to accept it if they were fully aware of the implications involved.

It is this unrecognized aspect of conventional appraisal programs which produces the widespread uneasiness and even open resistance of management to appraisals and especially to the appraisal interview.

A sounder approach, which places the major responsibility on the subordinate for establishing performance goals and appraising progress toward them, avoids the major weaknesses of the old plan and benefits the organization by stimulating the development of the subordinate. It is true that more managerial skill and the investment of a considerable amount of time are required, but the greater motivation and the more effective development of subordinates can justify these added costs.

73. WHAT ABOUT
EXECUTIVE RECRUITERS? [1]

Stephen Habbe [2]

Who are these executive recruiters? Can they help us fill top positions? What are their backgrounds? What do they charge? Are they worth it?

Companies are beginning to ask questions like these with increasing frequency. For a new specialty is emerging—executive recruitment. A number of firms now are devoting full time to the business of finding executives for companies.

Good executives and administrators, as everyone knows are in short supply. This situation is not peculiar to business firms. Washington is constantly on the lookout for top men to take important assignments in the government. There are current vacancies for several dozen college presidents. Qualified leaders are needed by the church, by labor unions, by the military services, and by almost every other organization in society that might be mentioned. The shortage of leaders, according to some, is more acute today than ever before in the history of our country.

Persons of high competence always have been attracted to business, and doubtlessly this will continue to be the case. Today, men of outstanding ability are directing American business, but the line of succession appears thin. With business operating at record levels and with further expansion predicted, the need for a full complement of young executives is clear.

But where are these young executives to be found? And can enough of them be found? The depression in the Thirties cut the birth rate. The war in the Forties took young men out of industry for three or four years. And these are only two of many factors which, in combination, have brought about the present shortage of trained executives.

Many companies already have moved to safeguard their future by bringing capable young men from the colleges and elsewhere into

[1] From the *Management Record*, Vol. XVIII, No. 2 (February, 1956), pp. 42-44. Reprinted by permission of the *Management Record*.

[2] Stephen Habbe, Division of Personnel Administration, National Industrial Conference Board, Inc.

their organizations, and then offering them a broad program of managerial development. These companies will need to go outside only rarely when the time comes to replace their present officers. They will have "home-grown" executives ready to move up as vacancies occur.

Of course even with the best of planning there always will be occasions when companies, particularly those that are expanding rapidly and those getting into new-product fields, will go outside their own organizations to get the right man. But the companies that have not looked ahead in anticipating their future needs will be going outside regularly. And these companies, it must be said, are not in the minority.

Two Statements by Executive Recruiters

A Raid or a Service?

We feel that we have a professional obligation to disturb industry as little as possible, and we never raid a company in recruiting a candidate for a client. We try to get a man who is in a situation where he either has a couple of strong assistants who are only a year or two younger than he is, or we try to get the No. 2 man. In such a situation, the candidate's change in position really relieves congestion.

How the Recruiter May Help

In conducting its search the executive recruiting firm becomes in effect a part of the company's management group. In addition to providing counsel on such subjects as the type of experience needed, the compensation to be paid, and the allocation of specific responsibilities, the executive recruiter relieves the president and his key officers of the time-consuming duties of searching, interviewing, appraising and negotiating with potential candidates.

Going outside is not as simple a matter as it may appear to be. Just who is to do it? And just how is it to be done?

Let us suppose that the mythical Whiteside Manufacturing Company needs a sales vice-president and that there seems to be no one in the organization qualified for the job. What does Whiteside do? Is it up to the retiring vice-president to suggest his successor? Or should the president make some discreet inquiries at his luncheon club or among his golf companions? Should an employment agency be asked to recommend two or three candidates?

A Whiteside officer recalls attending a management conference at which he heard a sales manager make a rousing speech. The man impressed him most favorably. Maybe he is just the person for the job. His name is tossed into the hat.

But it turns out this gentleman is employed by a competing firm. And apparently he is happy where he is. Nevertheless, should someone sound him out? And if so, should he be contacted at the office or at his home? How can it be determined if he has the qualifications desired by Whiteside as well as the personality to "fit in" with the Whiteside management family? Finally, aren't there perhaps a dozen other men around the country who should be considered along with this sales manager?

It is at this point that Whiteside, or almost any company, is apt to throw up its hands and cry for help. And help is now available—at a price, of course.

While management and psychological consulting firms have been doing executive recruitment work for client companies for many years, the emergence of specialists devoting full time to executive recruiting is a fairly recent development.[3] Some of the most active firms are less than five years old. A few have been in the business ten or more years. Most of them are located in the large cities, notably New York.

No one is able to say just how many individuals and firms are doing executive recruiting today, but it is known that the activity is mushrooming. It is fast becoming "big business."

In an effort to learn what is going on, THE CONFERENCE BOARD called on a number of companies that have been making use of executive recruiters and also on several of the recruiting firms. All supplied the desired information in detail and without hesitation. Their composite answers to the Board's questions follow.

Q. By what other names are executive recruiters known?

A. They are called talent scouts, "flesh peddlers," pirates, as well as some unprintable names by companies that have been raided.

Q. What are the backgrounds of most executive recruiters?

A. General business; management consulting firms; personnel work; industrial psychological work.

Q. Is executive recruitment a racket?

A. It has been so characterized by some. And there are aspects of the business that lend themselves to fun-poking, and worse. The few articles about executive recruiters that have been published have

---

[3] Consulting firms conduct investigations and advise companies on many different matters. Their recommendations often involve changes in top-level personnel. A company may ask its consulting firm to follow through and find the executives that are needed to carry out the recommendations. The consultants cannot very well refuse this request. Yet they may not feel qualified to do executive recruitment work. And they may do it reluctantly, fearing to lose more friends than they would make during the course of the search.

been on the flip side. But recruiters who have been trying to do a good job resent implications that their work has any of the characteristics of a racket.

Also, these recruiters would like it known that their job is no bed of roses. They work hard, they say, and they have their share of headaches. A few they are quick to mention are: getting companies to understand their services; getting companies to define their needs; interesting good prospects in other opportunities (more money, for example, is no longer sufficient); convincing good prospects that administrative skills are transferable from company to company and even from industry to industry; the handling of a multitude of personality matters, such as problems concerning the wives of some executives and insistence on certain geographical locations.

Q. Are the executive recruiting firms really employment agencies?

A. No. The executive recruiter is engaged by the company; and the company pays a fee whether or not it hires one of the recruiter's candidates. The recruiter can conduct his search anywhere, whereas the employment agency usually is prohibited by law from contacting employed persons and those not registered with the agency. Also, very few employment agencies have had experience in filling top-level positions.

Q. What size and what type of company can executive recruiters serve best?

A. No differences are reported. But recruiters do say they have difficulty in interesting high-caliber executives in small, family-owned businesses.

Q. Under what circumstances are companies likely to engage the services of executive recruiters?

A. There are various circumstances, such as the following:

1. Companies that are expanding rapidly.
2. Companies that are decentralizing, and thus need new executive teams.
3. Companies that are getting into new-product areas.
4. Companies that have failed in their own search to find the "right" man for an important vacancy.
5. Companies that have come to the conclusion that executive recruitment can best be done by specialists.

Q. Does the executive recruiter perform a real service?

A. There are, as might be expected, differences of opinion on this question. Some companies that have used the recruiters regularly for several years in filling important vacancies feel that they are performing a much needed service to business. Other companies point out that since the recruiters do not *create* additional executives, they do nothing more than reshuffle the existing supply. This, they reason, is no service to business in general, although it may be of benefit to individual companies. The recruiters answer this argument by pointing out that almost every placement that is made as a result of their efforts represents a *promotion*, and one or more persons down the line is apt to benefit. Some may be moved into management echelons for the first time. Thus, new executives *are* created.

Q. How does the executive recruiter work?

A. A full answer to this question would require several pages, but the nature and scope of the recruiter's approach may be indicated in outline form.

> He receives a request for help from a company.
> He visits the company, studies its organization, and talks with the top officers.
> The job to be filled is carefully defined, and the type of individual desired by the company is described in detail.
> The recruiter then makes a wide, systematic search for suitable candidates.
> A number of names are obtained and screened. References are checked. Tests may be given. Those who seem best qualified are interviewed—and so are their wives.
> Three or four of the top candidates are "recommended" to the company.
> The company makes the final selection and job offer.

Q. How much does the recruiter charge?

A. One formula is 20% of the first year's base salary plus expenses, or $2,500, whichever is greater. If the recruiter's search is unsuccessful or if the company appoints some one of its own selection, a *per diem* charge of approximately $150 is made. It may be argued that executive recruiters should always be compensated on a straight *per diem* basis, just as other management consultants.

Q. How long does it take a recruiter to find the right man for the job?

A. An average period is about ten to twelve weeks. But the duration of any particular search may vary a great deal depending upon the factors involved.

Q. What degree of success is claimed by executive recruiters?

A. One recruiter answered this query as follows: "We are 85% successful if we have enough time. But a company may become impatient, or it may find its own candidate. About half of our assignments are carried to completion. . . . It should be remembered that we get only the tough cases. Usually the companies come to us after they have failed to find someone through their own efforts."

74. EXPERIENCES IN
TESTING FOREMEN [1]

Hubert Clay [2]

Considerable attention is being given these days to improving the quality of first-level supervision. It is recognized that such supervisors represent a crucial link in the organizational chain. Selection at this level is extremely difficult because there is relatively little on which to base a decision regarding a man's probable competence. At higher levels the candidate has already been observed in supervisory action. His strengths and weaknesses in handling subordinates and in other aspects of supervision can be evaluated with greater accuracy. In elevating a worker from the ranks, none of these advantages is present.

Such problems have given rise to attempts to identify as accurately as possible those persons who will be most likely to succeed as supervisors. The most scientific prediction usually involves a test selection program. In our organization we have instituted such a program, and some of our experiences may be of interest. The present article is concerned primarily with our methods of testing our foremen. It may be well, however, to outline briefly the various steps customarily involved in a test selection program for supervisors. In this way it can be better understood how the testing fits into the picture.

Assuming that no prior testing of a systematic nature has been done, the first step is to evaluate as accurately as possible the present group of supervisors. Accurate evaluation implies some formal method of merit rating. This is a problem which continues to plague investigators. The pages of this and other journals devoted to personnel activities have been filled with the tales of such attempts. The trials of our company in this respect have been as difficult and frustrating as most. Ratings are particularly crucial when they are to be used as criteria for test results. In such a situation the ratings are the foundation on which is built a tremendous amount of statistical

[1] From *Personnel*, Vol. XXVIII, No. 6 (May, 1952), pp. 466-470. Reprinted by permission of the *American Management Association*.
[2] Hubert Clay, Psychologist, Employee Relations Division, The B. F. Goodrich Company (1952).

computation. The conclusions reached, the predictions made, can be no better than the ratings against which they are measured.

The second step in the over-all program is to test the present group of supervisors, using tests which one thinks will sample those abilities and characteristics of supervisors in one's organization. The group should be large enough so that the results can be dealt with statistically to give meaningful answers. Specifically, we try to discover whether high-rated supervisors show different patterns of test scores than do low-rated supervisors.

The third step is to test candidates for supervision and then select those whose scores most nearly match those of presently high-rated supervisors. The idea, of course, is that we can generalize from this sampling (test responses) of the individual's functioning and predict that he will be apt to make good in the way that the high-rated supervisors have made good.

The fourth step in the process, ideally, is to check the accuracy of one's predictions after a year or two.

Having reviewed the over-all program, let us now look at some of the details involved in testing our foremen.

Introducing the tests

Acceptance of the entire project by top management is obviously necessary and important. Acceptance by the men to be tested is also vital. This is especially true where factory foremen are concerned. Many of them have been out of school a good many years and they fear tests. They particularly dislike to be put under the pressure of timing. Moreover, they think of such projects as having a direct bearing on their jobs. Their security feelings are threatened and this easily arouses hostility if not properly handled.

With these factors in mind, we introduced the tests to the foremen as a scientific attempt to help them with their supervisory problems. We also tried to increase their motivation for taking the tests by promising to discuss their test results with each of them individually. The explanatory talk by the personnel manager in one plant, for example, was along these lines:

> Foremen have a lot of headaches, as you all know. Undoubtedly all of you at one time or another have wished that some of the men working with you were easier to get along with, more willing to cooperate, more efficient, etc. You'd like to eliminate all the headaches you can. One way of eliminating them is to select the best possible men for foremen in the future. We all have hunches about men we think would make good

foremen. Frequently we're right. But too often we're wrong and then we wish we could improve our selection batting average.

The desire to make better selections has led to a plan for research into the qualities which make good foremen. It's a study in which we need your help and cooperation. We need to know what makes you "tick." What characteristics do you have? What attitudes? What interests? What ways of handling people?

These qualities are most scientifically measured by means of psychological tests. Probably some of you have taken such tests at one time or another. If you're like most people you found these tests quite interesting. Just taking the tests made you more curious about yourself. But in most instances, unfortunately, you weren't told the results of your tests.

We don't believe it's fair to ask for your help unless you get the benefit of knowing your results. So we'll go over your results with each of you individually after the tests are scored and interpreted by our psychological staff.

We feel certain that you'll enjoy the experience of taking the tests and we are confident that they will be of value to you not only as individuals but to all of you as a group.

It would be a pleasure to report that, with careful introduction, the tests were uniformly welcomed by the foremen in all plants with a great deal of enthusiasm. Such was not the case, however. Within a given plant there was the expected variation in individual reaction. A few foremen thought the tests were unfair. Others enjoyed them immensely. Less expected was the difference in general reaction from plant to plant. Acceptance at a given plant seemed to be related not only to the skillfulness of the introduction but to such factors as average age and mobility of the foremen. The plant at which the tests were least favorably received had the highest average age and, apparently more important, the foremen as a whole were known to be generally unwilling to move from the geographical area in which the plant was located. Naturally this attitude limited their chances for promotion as far as the entire organization was concerned. It also made them less interested in company-wide projects. Still another factor in acceptance was the example set by the plant manager and the production superintendent. At one plant these two men volunteered to take the tests before the plan was announced to the foremen. They were thus able to say to the men, in effect, "We've been through it and it's really an interesting experience." After such statements by their bosses the men were more willing to follow the example.

Administering the tests

It is well known that a test administrator should have a complete understanding of all the tests he plans to administer. Preferably he should have taken the tests himself. Another factor in administration, and one that is related to acceptance of tests by the testees, is the administrator's manner and behavior. People generally come to a testing session in a state of anxiety. A grimly efficient administrator tends to increase this anxiety. A sense of humor is invaluable in putting people at ease and enabling them to do their best.

Some indication of the attitude of a foreman group during testing is seen in the amount of joking comments and complaints which the men make. As in the army, morale is better when people gripe a little about the difficulties in the situation. When foremen are completely silent and impassive, look out!

Our project was so planned that the personnel managers in each plant administered the tests. Although they had some familiarity with test administration prior to the present project, we prepared a test administration manual with detailed explanation of each test in the battery. This insured uniformity in procedure between the various plants. The manual also stressed the advantages of encouraging relaxation as noted above.

Reactions of foremen after testing

An immediate aftermath of the testing was a widespread and spontaneous self-appraisal by a great many of the men. They were chagrined at various items which they realized they had missed and for many days they could be heard exchanging notes on the tests. Frequent comments were:

> "I've been looking up some of those words I didn't know the meaning of."
> "Gosh, I didn't know my arithmetic was so bad."
> "How did you answer that question about the . . .?"
> "These tests make me realize how poor my vocabulary is."

They joked a great deal with each other about the way they had answered various questions on the personality questionnaire, but underneath their banter was a remarkable seriousness. At one plant one of the foremen said to the personnel manager, "These tests are the greatest thing that's happened around here in a long time. They make us realize how little we've kept on our toes."

Reporting the results

There was an unavoidable delay in scoring and interpretation of the tests, and in some of the plants the results were not ready for several months. This was extremely unfortunate. But the delay had one advantage. It revealed the great interest of most of the men in their results. A number of foremen made periodic inquiries of their personnel manager as to when the counseling interviews would take place. The most impatient men were, incidentally, handled first when the test results were finally ready.

We had used a long experimental battery of standard tests intended to measure each foreman's interests, his level of general ability and certain aptitudes, and his personality characteristics. (These tests were: Strong Vocational Interest Blank for Men, Kuder Preference Record, Wonderlic Personnel Test, Classification Test for Industrial and Office Personnel, How Supervise?, General Clerical Test, Test of Mechanical Comprehension, and Guilford-Zimmerman Temperament Survey.) It is hoped that validity studies will "boil down" this long battery to a fraction of its present size. Only those tests which prove most effective *in our situation* will be retained and administered as standard procedure.

The scores were not directly reported to the men but were converted to letter grades (based on decile position) and placed on a profile which each personnel manager could use during the counseling interview. Because we did not know the validity of the tests in our situation the results were based on the general standardization norms for each test. In this way the foremen were not compared directly with each other.

A test interpretation manual was prepared for each personnel manager. The purpose and general tone of this may be understood most readily by quoting some of the most pertinent paragraphs. (These are not rigid test interpretation rules, of course, but merely represent this writer's opinions based on his experiences in numerous interviews of this kind.)

Introduction

Most persons who have been tested are intensely curious about their results. At the same time they are frequently apprehensive. They may come to the interview somewhat tense and nervous, and everything possible should be done to put them at ease.

The test profiles are arranged so that the interest patterns are discussed first, ability and aptitude second, and personality characteristics last. This sequence is followed because it is believed to be most conducive to free discussion.

The interview should be held where interruptions will not occur. Plenty of time should be allowed so that the interview need not be terminated if the interviewee wishes to talk. He may get into a mood for discussion which will never occur again, and an unusual opportunity is lost if he is hurried away. If interruption or too-early termination is positively unavoidable, another appointment should be suggested.

Nothing at this time, not even skilled test interpretation, is so important as a genuine human interest in the individual. This implies an understanding, noncritical attitude which encourages talk. Avoid cross-examinations in regard to test findings and do not use test results as a basis for criticism of job performance. If *he* wants to discuss any problems which the tests bring out, let *him* take the initiative.

Interest Patterns

The discussion of interests provides an easy opening to the interview because nothing threatening to the individual is involved. His scores in an interest area can be either high or low and he is not upset. By the time he has gone through his interest scores and agreed or disagreed with them he is usually relaxed and far better able to accept anything unfavorable which may come up later in the interview. The interviewer, too, has a chance to "size up" the individual and his reactions during this warm-up period and thereby handle the balance of the interview more smoothly.

Ability and Aptitude

The discussion of ability and aptitude has to be carefully handled, especially in the case of an individual whose scores are below the average. This is particularly true of low general ability scores. Avoid using the terms "intelligence" and "I.Q." It can be pointed out to the individual that one reason for reporting the results in letter grades is that some persons get too concerned over differences in numerical scores, even when the differences are too small to be significant.

It may be advisable to stress to the interviewee the research nature of the project and to say quite frankly that we do not know yet how much a given score means as far as supervisory success in our company is concerned. It should be emphasized particularly that the best men do not necessarily get the highest scores.

An important aspect of ability testing is the fact that while we can measure a man's ability we cannot measure his willingness to use that ability. Many men of high ability fail to succeed at a high level because of a lack of persistence, initiative, and other hard-to-measure qualities.

Personality

The discussion of personality is left until last because it often results in the individual "opening up" or unburdening himself of some problem or problems. It is a great advantage to be able to continue such talk, as mentioned earlier.

It should be remembered that scores on a personality questionnaire depend upon the individual's willingness and ability to rate himself frankly and honestly. Some persons merely answer the questions the way they think they should be answered rather than the way they actually feel. It is always well to inquire whether the scores agree with the individual's estimate of himself. For example: "Do you believe that you have more energy than the average man, as this score indicates?" or "This score suggests that you tend to be oversensitive and rather easily hurt. Is that an accurate picture of you?"

Certain personality traits cannot always be accepted literally. The individual's behavior actually may be a cover-up for the opposite tendencies. Aggressiveness, for example, may be an artificial role which a man assumes to cover up feelings of inadequacy and insecurity. This kind of aggressiveness is quite different from a wholesome aggressiveness expressed by a really confident person. Personality scores should always be compared, if possible, with observations of the individual in his everyday living. Scores should never be presented as final and conclusive evidence. Rather, they should be thought of as guideposts which may help a person to gain insight into himself and his relations with others.

In most of the plants the reporting of results was begun by having the psychologist handle the first few interviews in the presence of the personnel manager. In this way the latter became aware of some of the pitfalls in test interpretation. For example, despite all precautions it is a natural tendency to become overly directive in such a situation. Most of us dearly love to give advice, and when we have before us someone whose defenses are down and whose weaknesses stand revealed we are prone to advise him "for his own good." Time and time again psychotherapeutic studies have shown the fallacy of this method. Almost invariably the person being "advised" clams up and leaves the interview openly or secretly hostile. It takes a great deal of practice to be nondirective, to let the individual develop his own insights. But it is highly worthwhile, for then the conclusions he reaches, the decisions he makes, are solely his and more apt to be followed and lived with.

The personnel managers seemed to feel after the interviews that, with a few exceptions, the men were appreciative of the opportunity to discuss their strengths and weaknesses as seen on the tests. At one plant which is located in a college town four of the men, as a direct result of the counseling interviews, enrolled in evening courses at the university. Two others began correspondence courses. Several of the foremen came to the personnel manager for a second talk in order to discuss ways of improving themselves.

It is not easy to fit a great number of such interviews into a busy schedule. In some plants it took many weeks to see all the foremen. It is felt that the time has been well spent, however. There is little doubt that the men have gained a greater understanding of themselves—and understanding which should pay dividends in improved human relations.

75. THE FALLACIES OF
"PERSONALITY" TESTING [1]

William H. Whyte, Jr.[2]

Business is being tantalized by a fascinating possibility. After a long experimentation period with school children, college students, and inmates of institutions, applied psychologists are becoming more and more confident that with "personality" tests they can come close to answering the hitherto elusive question of who will succeed and who won't. As a matter of routine, of course, most managements have been screening job applicants with tests of aptitude and intelligence, but while these have been useful in eliminating the obviously unfit, they have not been able to predict performance, for they tell nothing of a man's motivation and all those intangibles that can make the difference between success and mediocrity. Now, however, psychologists have tests by which they attempt to measure a man for almost any personality trait, and plot with precision his standing compared to the rest of the population.

At first there were only rough measures—such as how introverted and neurotic a man is—but there are now in regular business use tests that tell a man's superiors his decree of radicalism versus conservatism, his practical judgment, social judgment, degree of perseverance, stability, contentment, hostility to society, and latent homosexuality. Some psychologists are tinkering with a test of sense of humor. To probe even deeper, testers are also applying the "projective" techniques like the Rorschach Ink Blot Test, which lead the subject into x-raying himself for latent feelings and psychoses.

Probing adults is not the same thing as probing school children, of course, and the fact that some of the former balk at exposing themselves might appear an important obstacle. But this has not been the case. Testers have learned to attach great significance to the way people respond to the idea of the tests: if a man refuses to answer certain questions psychologists believe they can deduce suppressed anxieties almost as well as if he answered the questions.

[1] Reprinted by Special Permission from the September, 1954, issue of *Fortune Magazine*; Copyright 1954 by *Time Inc.*, pp. 117-120, 204-208.
[2] William H. Whyte, Jr., Assistant Managing Editor, *Fortune*.

America's secondary-school educators were the first to seize upon these tests, but business is catching up very quickly indeed. Two years ago only about a third of U.S. corporations used personality testing; since then the proportion has been climbing—of the sixty-three corporations checked by FORTUNE 60 per cent are using personality tests, and these include such bellwether firms as Sears, General Electric, and Westinghouse. While there are still some executives vigorously opposed to personality testing, all the signs point to a further increase.

The most widespread use of tests has been for the fairly mundane job of screening applicants. Even in companies not notably enthusiastic about personality tests, it is now part of standard operating procedure to add several personality tests to the battery of checks on the job applicant. If business declines, tests may also be applied to cut down the work force. "For trimming inefficiency in the company operation," Industrial Psychology Inc. (Tucson, Arizona) advises clients, "there is no better place to direct the ax than in the worker category." And there is no better way to do this, it adds, than to run the force through tests.

But the really significant development in personality testing lies in another direction. In perhaps 25 per cent of the country's corporations the tests are used not merely to help screen out those who shouldn't get into the organization but to check up on people who are already in it. And the people being checked on, furthermore, are not workers so much as management itself. Some of these companies don't bother to give personality tests to workers at all; aside from the fact that testing can be very expensive, they feel that the limited number of psychologists available should concentrate on the more crucial questions.

How neurotic are executives?

Should Jones be promoted or put on the shelf? Just about the time an executive reaches forty-five or fifty and begins to get butterflies in his stomach wondering what it has all added up to and whether the long-sought prize is to be his after all, the company is probably wondering too. Where once the man's superiors would have threshed this out among themselves, in some companies they now check first with the psychologists to find out what the tests say. At Sears, for example, for the last ten years no one has been promoted in the upper brackets until the board chairman has consulted the tests. At Sears, as elsewhere, the formal decision is of course based on other factors also, but the weight now being given test reports makes it clear that for many a potential executive the most critical day he spends in his life will be the one he spends taking tests.

One result has been the rise of a considerable industry. In the last five years the number of test blanks sold has risen 300 per cent. The growth of psychological consulting firms has paralleled the rise; in addition to such established firms as the Psychological Corp., literally hundreds of consultants are setting up shop. Science Research Associates of Chicago, a leading test supplier, reports that within the last twelve months *seven hundred* new consultants have asked to be put on its approved list of customers. Colleges are also getting into the business; through research centers like Rensselaer Polytechnic's Personnel Testing Laboratory, they have become directly competitive with leading commercial firms.

The types of service offered vary greatly. Some firms will do the entire operation by mail; for example, the Klein Institute for Aptitude Testing, Inc., of New York, within forty-eight hours of getting the completed test back will have an anlysis on its way to the company. Usually, however, the job is done on the premises. Sometimes the consultant group, like the Activity Vector Analysts, will process the entire management group at one crack. More usually the analysts, very often a group of professors in mufti, will come in and study the organization in order to find the personality "profiles" best suited for particular jobs. They will then tailor a battery of tests and master profiles. Though the analysts may help out with the machinery of testing, the company's personnel department generally handles the rest of the job.

A dynamic would appear to be at work. The more people that are tested, the more test results there are to correlate, and the more correlations, the surer are many testers of predicting success or failure, and thus the more reason there is for more organizations to test more and more people. At Westinghouse Electric, for example, 10,000 management men have already been coded onto I.B.M. cards that contain, in addition to vital statistics and work records, the men's personality-test ratings. What with the schools already doing much the same thing, with electronics making mass testing increasingly easy, there seems no barrier to the building of such inventories for every organization.

Except common sense. For a large question remains: leaving aside for the moment the matter of invasion of privacy, have the tests themselves been really tested?

Who flunked

In an effort to find out, FORTUNE did some extensive testing of its own. What was under investigation, let it be made plain, was not the use of tests as guides in clinical work, or their use in counseling when the individual himself seeks the counseling. Neither was it the problem of ethics raised by the work of some practitioners in the field, interesting as this bypath is. What we have addressed ourselves to is the validity of "personality" tests as a standardized way of rating and slotting people. Question: do the tests really discriminate the men of promise from the run of the mill—or do they discriminate *against* him?

What would happen if the presidents of our largest corporations took the same tests that future executives are being judged by? What would happen if the tests were applied to a group of scientists, not just average scientists, but a group of the most productive ones in the world? Would they be rated a good risks? Would their scores jibe with their achievements? By actually giving tests to sixty exceptional persons, we found out. Conclusion: if the tests were rigorously applied across the board today, half of the most dynamic men in business would be out walking the streets for a job.

The effects of the day-to-day use of tests are less spectacular, but they are nonetheless far reaching. For the tests, FORTUNE submits, do not do what they are supposed to do. They do not do what they are supposed to do because, for one thing, they are not scientific. Neither in the questions nor in the evaluation are they neutral; they are, instead, loaded with debatable assumptions and questions of values. The result, deliberate or not, is a set of yardsticks that reward the conformist, the pedestrian, the unimaginative—at the expense of the exceptional individual whom management most needs to attract.

What is "personality"?

To a large degree the growing acceptance of personality tests rests on prestige by association, for these tests at first glance seem no more than an extension of the established methods of aptitude testing. The difference, however, is crucial. What is being measured in aptitude and intelligence testing are responses that can be rated objectively—such as the correctness of the answer to $2 + 2$ or the number of triangles in a bisected rectangle. The conclusions drawn from these aptitude and intelligence scores are, furthermore, limited to the relatively modest prediction of a man's minimum ability to do *the same sort of thing he is asked to do on the tests*. If the tests indicate that a man has only 5,000 words in his vocabulary, it is a reasonable assumption that he won't do particularly well in a job requiring 50,000 words. If he is all thumbs when he puts wiggly blocks together, he won't be very good at a job requiring enough manual dexterity to put things like wiggly blocks together.

To jump from aptitude testing to personality testing, however, is to jump from the measurable to the immeasurable. What the personality testers are trying to do is convert abstract traits into a concrete measure that can be placed on a linear scale, and it is on the assumption that this is a true application of the scientific method that the whole mathematical edifice rests. But merely defining a trait is immensely difficult, let alone determining whether it can be measured as the opposite of another. Can you be 59 per cent "emotional," for example, and if so, is "emotionalism" the precise statistical opposite of "steadiness"? People are daily being fitted onto linear scales for such qualities, and if their dimensions don't fit they are punished, like those on Procrustes' bed, for their deviance.

But what is "personality"? The surface facets of a man—the way he smiles, the way he talks? Obviously not; we must go much deeper, the psychologists tell us. But how much deeper? Few testers would dream of claiming that one can isolate personality from the whole man, yet logic tells us that to be able statistically to predict behavior we would have to do just this.

The mathematics is impeccable—and thus entrapping. Because "percentiles" and "coefficients" and "standard deviations" are of themselves neutral (and impressive sounding), the sheer methodology of using them can convince people that they are translating uncertainty into certainty, the subjective into the objective, and eliminating utterly the bugbear of value judgments. But the mathematics does *not* eliminate values, it only obscures them. No matter how objective testers try to be, even in the phrasing of their questions they are inevitably influenced by the customs and values of their particular world.

Questions designed to find your degree of sociability are an example. In some groups the reading of a book is an unsocial act, and the person who confesses he has at times preferred books to companions might have to be quite introverted to do such a thing. But the question is relative; applied to someone in a climate where reading is normal—indeed, the source of much social talk—the hidden "value judgment" built into the test can give a totally unobjective result. People are not always social in the same terms; a person who would earn himself an unsocial score by saying he would prefer bridge to bowling with the gang is not necessarily unsocial and he might even be a strong extrovert. It could be that he just doesn't like bowling.

If the layman gags at the phrasing of a question, testers reply, sometimes with a chuckle, this is merely a matter of "face validity." They concede that it is better if the questions seem to make sense, but they claim that the question itself is not so important as the way large numbers of people have answered it over a period of time. To put it in another way, if a hundred contented supervisors overwhelmingly answer a particular question in a certain way, this means something, and thus no matter whether the question is nonsensical or not, it has produced a meaningful correlation coefficient.

Logrolling with statistics

Meaning what? This is not the place to go into a lengthy dissertation on statistics, but two points should be made about the impressive test charts and tables that so often paralyze executives' common sense. A large proportion of the mathematics is purely internal; that is, different parts of the tests are compared with each other rather than with external evidence. Second, the external evidence used in many "validation" studies will be found on closer examination to consist of the scores persons made on similar personality tests rather than such untidy matters as how they actually performed on the job. That there should be a correlation between the test scores is hardly surprising; test authors are forever borrowing questions from each other (some questions have been reincarnated in as many as ten or twelve different tests) and what the correlations largely prove is how incestuous tests can be.

But how much have scores been related to individual behavior? Among themselves psychologists raise the same question, and for muted savagery there is nothing to match the critiques they make of each other's tests. The Bernreuter Personality Inventory is a particular case in point. This is by far the most widely used test in business (1953 sales by Stanford University Press, one of several distributors: one million copies). Yet a reading of the professional journals shows a long succession of negative results; when psychologists independently checked Bernreuter scores against other, more objective evidence of what the people tested were like, they found no significant relationships, and sometimes reverse correlations.

As top psychologists point out, a really rigorous validation would demand that a firm hire all comers for a period of time, test them, seal away the tests so the scores would not prejudice superiors, and then, several years later, unseal the scores and match them against the actual performance of the individuals involved. This has rarely been even attempted. To be sure, a good bit of work on the performance of *groups* has been done; for example, a group considered more productive has an average score on a test higher than another group. The average of a group, however, tells us very little about the *individuals* involved, for some of the "best" people will have lower test scores than some of the "poor" ones.

Testers evade this abyss by relying on a whole battery of tests rather than on just one or two. But no matter how many variables you add you cannot make a constant of them. If a man has a high "contentment index" and at the same time a very high "irritability index," does the one good cancel the other bad? Frequently the tester finds himself right back where he started from. If he is a perceptive man he may make a very accurate prognosis, but when, several years later, the prognosis turns out to be true, this is adduced as evidence of the amazing accuracy of test scores.

Sad case of J. J. Jones

As an example of how values get entwined in testing, let's watch as a Worthington Personal History is constructed. This technique is a "projective" one; it is so projective, indeed, that the tester doesn't even have to bother seeing the man at all. The client company has the applicant fill out what seems to be an innocuous vital-statistics blank and then mails it to Worthington Associates. There an analyst studies it for such clues as whether the man used check marks or underlinings, how he designated his relatives, what part of his name he gives by initials, what by the full word.

Let the reader match his diagnostic skill against the testers. In a hypothetical example given in the *Personnel Psychology* journal, we are told that the applicant, one Jonathan Jasper Jones, Jr., writes down that he is twenty-six, that the date of his marriage was November, 1951, that he has only one dependent, his wife, that her given name is Bernardine Butterfield, her age twenty-eight, and that she works as a nurse receptionist in a doctor's office.

Enigma? Carefully, the analyst writes that these clues alone indicate that Jones "may not take his general obligations very seriously, may have a tendency to self-importance, wishful thinking, may be reluctant to assume general adult responsibilities; may be inclined to be passive-dependent, i.e., reliant on others for direction and guidance, in his general work relationships; may be inclined to take pleasure in unearned status or reflected glory."

What's in a name?

How in the world did he deduce all this? Let us peek into the laboratory. The name was the first clue. It told the analyst that Jones was narcissistic. Whenever a man writes his name out in full, the tester notes in his chart that he is "narcissistic." Two initials, last name—"hypomanic." First initial, middle and last name: "narcissistic, histrionic." Any erasure or retracing: "anxious, tense." Characteristically, the applicant gets the short end of every assumption; even if he adopts the customary alternative—first name, middle initial, last name—he is put down as "mildly compulsive."

Deeper and deeper the analyst goes:

Spouse's age: twenty-eight.
    Fact: married a girl two years older than himself.
    Empirical observation—the majority of men marry women younger than themselves.
    Primary deduction—may have been influenced in marrying her by unconsciously considering her as a mother-surrogate.
    Tentative inference—may like to have an older woman, or people, take care of him.
    Provisional extension—may be inclined to be passive-dependent, i.e., reliant on others for direction and guidance, in his general work relationships.

And so on.

Analysts, of course, have just as much right to read between the lines as the next man; what makes their posture interesting is the claim that this is the scientific method. There are all the inevitable tables (the biserial correlation for tenure on Worthington cutoff is 0.34) in which the accuracy of the internal mathematics is confused with the accuracy of the premises. There is the usual spurious humility: the authors caution that no single deduction is necessarily correct; it is only when all the deductions are fitted into a "formal quantitative scoring procedure based on an organized system of psychodynamic factors" that they become correct. Add up enough wrongs, in short, and you get a right.

The analysis of J. J. Jones is a rather extreme example but it leads us to a defect characteristic of all tests. Against what specifications is the man being measured? Assuming for the moment that we are able to diagram Jonathan Jones exactly, how are we to know the kind of work the diagram indicates he is suited for? There is not much point in testing people to find out if they will make good salesmen or executives unless we know what it is that makes the good ones good.

And thus we come to the "profile." Testers collate in chart form personality scores for groups of people in different occupations to show how they compare with other adults on several personality traits. This is generally expressed as a "percentile" rating; if thirty salesclerks' sociability scores average somewhere around the 80 percentile, for example, this indicates that the average salesclerk is more sociable than 79 out of 100 adults. Thus a man being considered for a particular kind of job can be matched against the master profile of the group. If the shoe fits, he is Cinderella.

Profiles are also worked up for jobs in individual companies. At Sears, Roebuck there are charts that diagram the optimum balance of qualities required.

A man does not have to match this profile exactly, but it won't help him at all if his line zigs where the chart zags. Take a man who scores considerably higher than the 10th percentile on aesthetic values, for example; such people, Sears notes, "accept artistic beauty and taste as a fundamental standard of life. This is *not* a factor which makes for executive success. . . . Generally cultural considerations are not important to Sears executives, and there is evidence that such interests are detrimental to success."

The echo

Sears has every right to de-emphasize certain qualities and emphasize others; and in hewing to this type, it should be noted, Sears has built up one of the most alert management groups in the country. But the profile is not to be confused with science. When they are used as selection devices, tests are not a neutral tool; *they become a large factor in the very equation they purport to solve.* For one thing, the tests tend to screen out—or repel—those who would upset the correlation. If a man can't get into the company in the first place because he isn't the company type, he can't very well get to be an executive in it and be tested in a study to find out what kind of profile subsequent executives should match. Long before personality tests were invented, of course, plenty of companies had proved that if you hire only people of a certain type then all your successful men will be people of that type. But no one confused this with the immutable laws of science.

Bias, in short, is no longer personalized; now it's institutionalized. For the profile is self-confirming. When it doesn't screen out those who fail to match it, it will mask the amount of deviance in the people who do pass. Few test takers can believe the flagrantly silly statement in the preamble to many tests that there are "no right or wrong answers." There wouldn't be much point in the company's giving the test if some answers weren't regarded as better than others. "Do you daydream frequently?" In many companies a man either so honest or so stupid as to answer "yes" would be well advised to look elsewhere for employment.

The company "type"

Even when the man who should have looked elsewhere slips through, the profile will be self-confirming. For the profile molds as well as chooses; it is, as Sears puts it, a statement of "the kind of behavior we have found to be desirable." Several years of give and take, and the organization will smooth the man out. Thus when the psychologists do their "validating," or rechecking, later he will score near enough to the median to show them how right they were all along.

Up to a point the company "type" has some virtue; any first-rate organization must have an *esprit de corps* and this implies a certain degree of homogeneity. But the pitfalls are many, for while a self-confirming profile makes for a comfortable organization, it eventually can make for a static one. Even the largest corporations must respond to changes in the environment; a settled company may have its very existence threatened by technological advances unless it makes a bold shift to a new type of market. What, then, of the pruning and molding that adapted it so beautifully to its original environment? The dinosaur was a formidable animal.

The mask of adjustment

The profile can be self-confirming for the individual too. For tests intensify a mutual deception we practice on one another. Who is "normal"? All of us to some degree have a built-in urge to adjust to what we conceive as the norm, and in our search we can come to feel that in the vast ocean of normality that surrounds us only we are different. We are the victims of each other's façades.

And now, with the norm formally enshrined in figures, we are more vulnerable than ever to this tyrant. "Science" seems its ally, and thus, faulty or not, the diagnosis can provoke a sense of guilt or inadequacy; for we can forget that the norm is often the result of the instinctive striving of previous test takers to answer as they think everyone else would answer.

If the organization man escapes the danger of self-tyranny he faces another. At first superiors may scoff at the diagnosis, but if they have been putting reliance on testing they have a stake themselves in its correctness. Suspicion, unfortunately, demands proof, and sometimes it so counterbalances judgment that unconsciously a management will punish the man so that faith in the tests may be confirmed. One large midwestern company was about to promote a man when it decided to have him take a test. The report that the consultant firm mailed back to the company was freighted by the analyst with warnings about the man's stability. The company was puzzled. The man had consistently done a fine job. Still . . . The more the company mused, the more worried it became; at last it decided to tell the man the promotion he had expected so long was going to someone else. Six months later, the company reports, the man had a nervous breakdown. As in all such stories, the company says this proves how accurate the test was.

The fight against talent

Are the people who don't score well necessarily the misfits? Almost by definition the dynamic person is an exception—and where aptitude tests reward, personality tests often punish him. Look at profiles and test scoring keys, and you will find that you will come closer to a high score if you observe two rules:

(1) When asked for word associations or comments about the world, give a conventional, run-of-the-mill, pedestrian answer.

(2) When in doubt about the most beneficial answer to any question, repeat to yourself:

> I loved my father and my mother, but my father a little bit more.
> I was a happy, normal American boy and everybody liked me.
> I like things pretty much the way they are.
> I never worry about anything.
> I love my wife and children.
> I don't let them get in the way of company work.
> I don't care for books or music much.

Choose (a), (b), (c), (d)

The sheer mechanics of the tests also punish the exceptional man. A test with prefabricated answers is precisely the kind of test that people with superior intelligence find hardest to answer. How *big* was that fire in the basement of the theatre? This is not a quibble; it is the kind of question that occurs to the intelligent mind, and the ability to see shadings, to posit alternatives, is virtually indispensable to judgment, practical or otherwise.

Which brings us to FORTUNE'S experiment. With the stipulation by FORTUNE that their individual scores should not be identified, fourteen corporation presidents and board chairmen agreed to take a battery of tests including Personal Audit, Thurstone Temperament, and the Test of Practical Judgment. Next, twelve of the country's most brilliant scientists (previously studied in connection with "The Young Scientists," FORTUNE, June, 1954) agreed to do the same. As a further check, twenty-nine rising middle-management men who had been picked to attend an advanced-management school took the Thurstone and Practical Judgment tests.

Here are the highlights of the test results.

(1) Not one corporation president had a profile that fell completely within the usual "acceptable" range, and two failed to meet the minimum profile for foremen. On the "How Supervise" questions, presidents on the average got only *half* the answers right, thus putting them well down in the lower percentiles. They did particularly badly on the questions concerning company employee-relations policies. Only three presidents answered more than half of these questions correctly.

(2) The scientists' Personal Audit profiles were more even than the presidents'—if anything, they scored as *too* contented, firm, and consistent. They did, however, show up as extremely misanthropic, over half falling under the 20th percentile for sociability.

(3) The middle-management executives scored well on stability and sociability, but on practical judgment only three were at or over the mean indicated for executive work.

(4) The range of scores was so great as to make a median figure relatively meaningless. On the Thurstone "S" score for sociability, for example, only eight of the forty-three management men fell between the 40th and the 60th percentiles, the remainder being grouped at either extreme.

(5) Internally, the scores were highly contradictory. Many of the same people who got high "steadiness" scores on the Personal

Audit scored very badly for "stability" on the Thurstone test. Similarly, many who scored high on "contentment" had very low "tranquility" scores.

The abnormal norms

One explanation for this great variance between results and the standard norms would be that the men in the sample were answering frankly and thus their scores could not be properly compared with the standard norms given. But if this is true, then we must conclude that *the norms themselves embody slanted answers.* Another explanation of their showing would be that they scored low because they were in fact neurotic or maladjusted, as the tests said. But this leaves us with a further anomaly. If people with an outstanding record of achievement show up as less well "adjusted" than the run of the mill, then how important a yardstick is adjustment? FORTUNE'S sample, of course, is small. So is the supply of outstandingly talented people.

The study of a man's past performance, the gauging of him in the personal interview, are uncertain guides; executives are right to use them with humility. But they are still the key, and the need is not to displace them but to become more skilled with them. The question of who will be best in a critical situation cannot be determined scientifically before the event. No matter how much information we may amass, we must rely on judgment, on intuition, on the particulars of the situation—and the more crucial the situation the less certain can we be of prediction. It is an immensely difficult task, perhaps the most difficult one that any management faces. But the question cannot be fed into a computer nor can it be turned over by proxy for someone else to decide, and any management that so evades its most vital function needs some analysis of its own.

The right to privacy

And doesn't the individual have some rights in this matter too? Our society has taught him to submit to many things; thousands of civilians who went into the military meekly stood naked in long lines waiting for their numbered turn in the mass physical examinations. Many civilians who have been asked to work on government projects have submitted to being fingerprinted and to the certainty that government agents would soon be puzzling their friends and neighbors with questions about their backgrounds. In these cases a man can console himself that there is a reason; that if he is to enjoy the benefits of collective efforts he must also pay some price.

But there is a line. How much must a man testify against himself? The bill of rights should not stop at the corporation's edge. In return for the salary the organization gives the individual, it can ask for superlative work from him, but it should not ask for his psyche as well. Here and there, we are happy to report, some declarations of independence have been made. Last year the executives of a large and well-known New England corporation were subjected by the management to psychological examination by an outside consultant. Whether it was because of the consultant's manner or because of the New England character, the executives at length revolted. Let them be judged, they said, for their work. As for their inner feelings—that, as one man said who was almost fired for saying so, that was no one's damn business but their own.

BIBLIOGRAPHY, CHAPTER XXI

BENGE, EUGENE J. "Promotional Practices for Technical Men," *Advanced Management* (March, 1956), 10.

BERTOTTI, J. M. "Selection and Training of Supervisors," *Management Development in Action,* Personnel Series No. 148. New York: American Management Association, Inc., 1952, 3-12.

BUNIN, SANFORD. "The Campus Recruiter," *Advanced Management* (January, 1960), 23-25.

CATTELL, RAYMOND B., and GLEN F. STICE. "Four Formulae for Selecting Leaders on the Basis of Personality," *Human Relations,* Vol. VII, No. 4 (1954), 493-507.

FRASER, JOHN M. "The Group Method of Selecting Executives," *Personnel,* Vol. 26, No. 1 (July, 1949), 50-52.

GELLERMAN, SAUL W. "Seven Deadly Sins of Executive Placement," *Management Review* (July, 1958), 4-9.

GINZBERG, ELI. "The Recruitment and Use of University Graduates by Industry, *Personnel* (May, 1953), 461-466.

HALDANE, BERNARD. "A Pattern for Executive Placement," *Harvard Business Review,* 25 (Autumn, 1947), 652-663.

"Managerial Position Descriptions," *Management News* (July, 1958), 7-8.

MEYER, H. H., and J. M. BERTOTTI. "Uses and Misuses of Tests in Selecting Key Personnel," *Personnel* (November, 1956), 277-285.

O'DONOVAN, THOMAS R. "Can Executive Success Be Predicted?" *Advanced Management* (October, 1961), 23.

RANDLE, C. WILSON. "How to Identify Promotable Executives," *Harvard Business Review,* Vol. 34, No. 3 (1956), 122-134.

"Recruiting Executives from Outside Your Firm," *Management Methods,* Vol. 9, No. 4 (February, 1956), 28-31.

Recruiting the College Graduate. New York: American Management Association, Inc., 1953.

SAXENIAN, HRAND. "Criteria for Emotional Maturity," *Harvard Business Review* (January-February, 1958), 56-68.

STEELE, JOHN E. "Tests Used in Recruiting and Selecting College Graduates," *Personnel,* Vol. 26, No. 3 (November, 1949), 200-204.

TAYLOR, ERWIN K., and C. C. NEVIS. "The Use of Projective Techniques in Management Selection," *Personnel* (March, 1957), 462-474.

"The Older Manager: His Limitations and Assets," *Personnel* (July-August, 1960), 39-48.

TRICKETT, JOSEPH M. "Management Appraisals: A Key to Management Self Development," *Personnel,* Vol. 32, No. 3 (November, 1955), 234-245.

Chapter XXII

Management Development

Even though considerable attention is devoted to hiring excellent people for management positions, the movement of a sufficient number of managers into the higher management levels often occurs too slowly to obtain the benefit of their services for sufficient periods of time. To aid in correcting this situation, many companies engage in management development activities.

In addition to activities designed to advance the knowledge and skill of managers, management development programs often attempt to develop desirable attitudes. In the first article Edgar H. Schein shows how these changes in attitudes may be effected and how different development methods are useful for this purpose.

A different approach to early career development is afforded by Frederic E. Pamp's article which examines the liberal arts as background for managerial positions. In contrast, Robert C. Sampson takes the position that most development will occur on the job.

The final article by Herbert Harris presents one company's approach to their peculiar problems of management development.

76. MANAGEMENT DEVELOPMENT AS
A PROCESS OF INFLUENCE [1]

Edgar H. Schein [2]

The continuing rash of articles on the subject of developing better managers suggests, on the one hand, a continuing concern that existing methods are not providing the talent which is needed at the higher levels of industry and, on the other hand, that we continue to lack clear-cut formulations about the process by which such development occurs. We need more and better managers and we need more and better theories of how to get them.

In the present paper I would like to cast management development as the problem of how an organization can influence the beliefs, attitudes, and values (hereafter simply called attitudes) of an individual for the purpose of "developing" him, i.e. changing him in a direction which the organization regards to be in his own and the organization's best interests. Most of the existing conceptions of the development of human resources are built upon assumptions of how people learn and grow, and some of the more strikingly contrasting theories of management development derive from disagreements about such assumptions.[3] I will attempt to build on a different base: instead of starting with assumptions about learning and growth, I will start with some assumptions from the social psychology of influence and attitude change.

Building on this base can be justified quite readily if we can consider that adequate managerial performance at the higher levels is at least as much a matter of attitudes as it is a matter of knowledge and specific skills, and that the acquisition of such knowledge and skills is itself in part a function of attitudes. Yet we have given far more attention to the psychology which underlies change in the area of knowledge and abilities than we have to the psychology which underlies change in attitudes. We have surprisingly few studies of

[1] From *Industrial Management Review* (May, 1961), pp. 59-76. Reprinted by permission of *Industrial Management Review*.
[2] Edgar H. Schein, Associate Professor of Industrial Management, Massachusetts Institute of Technology.
[3] An excellent discussion of two contrasting approaches—the engineering vs. the agricultural—deriving from contrasting assumptions about human behavior can be found in McGregor, 1960, Chapter 14.

how a person develops loyalty to a company, commitment to a job, or a professional attitude toward the managerial role; how he comes to have the motives and attitudes which make possible the rendering of decisions concerning large quantities of money, materials, and human resources; how he develops attitudes toward himself, his co-workers, his employees, his customers, and society in general which give us confidence that he has a sense of responsibility and a set of ethics consistent with his responsible position, or at least which permit us to understand his behavior.

It is clear that management is becoming increasingly professionalized, as evidenced by increasing emphasis on undergraduate and graduate education in the field of management. But professionalization is not only a matter of teaching candidates increasing amounts about a set of relevant subjects and disciplines; it is equally a problem of preparing the candidate for a role which requires a certain set of attitudes. Studies of the medical profession (Merton, Reader, and Kendall, 1957), for example, have turned their attention increasingly to the unravelling of the difficult problem of how the medical student acquires those attitudes and values which enable him to make responsible decisions involving the lives of other people. Similar studies in other professions are sorely needed. When these are undertaken, it is likely to be discovered that much of the training of such attitudes is carried out implicitly and without a clearly formulated rationale. Law schools and medical schools provide various kinds of experiences which insure that the graduate is prepared to fulfill his professional role. Similarly, existing approaches to the development of managers probably provide ample opportunities for the manager to learn the attitudes he will need to fulfill high level jobs. But in this field, particularly, one gets the impression that such opportunities are more the result of intuition or chance than of clearly formulated policies. This is partly because the essential or pivotal aspects of the managerial role have not as yet been clearly delineated, leaving ambiguous both the area of knowledge to be mastered and the attitude to be acquired.

Existing practice in the field of management development involves activities such as: indoctrination and training programs conducted at various points in the manager's career; systematic job rotation involving changes both in the nature of the functions performed (e.g. moving from production into sales), in physical location, and in the individual's superiors; performance appraisal programs including various amounts of testing, general personality assessment, and counseling both within the organization and through the use of outside consultants; apprenticeships, systematic coaching, junior management boards, and special projects to facilitate practice by the young manager in functions he will have to perform later in his career; sponsorship and other comparable activities in which a select group of young managers is groomed systematically for high level jobs (i.e. made into "crown princes") ; participation in special conferences and training programs, including professional association meetings, human relations workshops, advanced management programs conducted in business schools or by professional associations like the American Management Association, regular academic courses like the Sloan programs offered at Stanford and MIT, or liberal arts courses like those offered at the University of Pennsylvania, Dartmouth, Northwestern, etc. These and many other specific educational devices, along with elaborate schemes of selection, appraisal, and placement, form the basic paraphernalia of management development.

Most of the methods mentioned above stem from the basic conception that it is the responsibility of the business enterprise, as an institution, to define what kind of behavior and attitude change is to take place and to construct mechanisms by which such change is to occur. Decisions about the kind of activity which might be appropriate for a given manager are usually made by others above him or by specialists hired to make such decisions. Where he is to be rotated, how long he is to remain on a given assignment, or what kind of new training he should undertake, is masterminded by others whose concern is "career development." In a sense, the individual stands alone against the institution where his own career is concerned, because the basic assumption is that the institution knows better than the individual what kind of man it needs or wants in its higher levels of management. The kind of influence model which is relevant, then, is one which considers the whole range of resources available to an organization.

In the remainder of this paper I will attempt to spell out these general themes by first presenting a conceptual model for analyzing influence, then providing some illustrations from a variety of organizational influence situations, and then testing its applicability to the management development situation.

A Model of Influence and Change

Most theories of influence or change accept the premise that change does not occur unless the individual is *motivated* and *ready* to change. This statement implies that the individual must perceive some need for change in himself, must be able to change, and must perceive the influencing agent as one who can facilitate such change in a direction acceptable to the individual. A model of the influence process, then, must account for the development of the motivation to change as well as the actual mechanisms by which the change occurs.

It is usually assumed that pointing out to a person some of his areas of deficiency, or some failure on his part in these areas, is sufficient to induce in him a readiness to change and to accept the influencing agent's guidance or recommendations. This assumption may be tenable if one is dealing with deficiencies in intellectual skills or technical knowledge. The young manager can see, with some help from his superiors, that he needs a greater knowledge of economics, or marketing, or production methods, and can accept the suggestion that spending a year in another department or six weeks at an advanced management course will give him the missing knowledge and/or skills.

However, when we are dealing with attitudes, the suggestion of deficiency or the need for change is much more likely to be perceived as a basic threat to the individual's sense of identity and to his status position vis-a-vis others in the organization. Attitudes are generally organized and integrated around the person's image of himself, and they result in stabilized, characteristic ways of dealing with others. The suggestion of the need for change not only implies some criticism of the person's image of himself, but also threatens the stability of his working relationships because change at this level implies that the expectations which others have about him will be upset, thus requiring the development of new relationships. It is not at all uncommon for training programs in human relations to arouse resistance or to produce, at best, temporary change because the expectations of co-workers operate to keep the individual in his "normal" mold. Management development programs which ignore these psychological resistances to change are likely to be self-defeating, no matter how much attention is given to the actual presentation of the new desired attitudes.

Given these general assumptions about the integration of attitudes in the person, it is appropriate to consider influence as a process which occurs over time and which includes three phases:

1. *Unfreezing:* [4] an alteration of the forces acting on the individual, such that his stable equilibrium is disturbed sufficiently to motivate

---

[4] These phases of influence are a derivation of the change model developed by Lewin, 1947.

him and to make him ready to change; this can be accomplished either by increasing the pressure to change or by reducing some of the threats or resistances to change.

2. *Changing:* the presentation of a director of change and the actual process of learning new attitudes. This process occurs basically by one of two mechanisms: (a) *identification* [5]—the person learns new attitudes by identifying with and emulating some other person who holds those attitudes; or (b) *internalization*—the person learns new attitudes by being placed in a situation where new attitudes are demanded of him as a way of solving problems which confront him and which he cannot avoid; he discovers the new attitudes essentially for himself, though the situation may guide him or make it probable that he will discover only those attitudes which the influencing agent wishes him to discover.

3. *Refreezing:* the integration of the changed attitudes into the rest of the personality and/or into ongoing significant emotional relationships.

In proposing this kind of model of influence we are leaving out two important cases—the individual who changes because he is *forced* to change by the agent's direct manipulation of rewards and punishments (what Kelman calls "compliance") and the individual whose strong motivation to rise in the organizational hierarchy makes him eager to accept the attitudes and acquire the skills which he perceives to be necessary for advancement. I will ignore both of these cases for the same reason—they usually do not involve genuine, stable change, but merely involve the adoption of overt behaviors which imply to others that attitudes have changed, even if they have not. In the case of compliance, the individual drops the overt behavior as soon as surveillance by the influence agent is removed. Among the upwardly mobile individuals, there are those who are willing to be unfrozen and to undergo genuine attitude change (whose case fits the model to be presented below) and those whose overt behavior change is dictated by their changing perception of what the environment will reward, but whose underlying attitudes are never really changed or refrozen.

I do not wish to imply that a general reward-punishment model is incorrect or inappropriate for the analysis of attitude change. My purpose, rather, is to provide a more refined model in terms of which it becomes possible to specify the differential effects of various kinds of rewards and punishments, some of which have far more significance and impact than others. For example, as I will try to show, the rewarding effect of approval from an admired person is

[5] These mechanisms of attitude change are taken from Kelman, 1958.

very different in its ultimate consequences from the rewarding effect of developing a personal solution to a difficult situation.

The processes of unfreezing, changing, and refreezing can be identified in a variety of different institutions in which they are manifested in varying degree of intensity. The content of what may be taught in the influence process may vary widely from the values of Communism to the religious doctrines of a nun, and the process of influence may vary drastically in its intensity. Nevertheless there is value in taking as our frame of reference a model like that proposed and testing its utility in a variety of different organizational contexts, ranging from Communist "thought reform" centers to business enterprises' management development programs. Because the value system of the business enterprise and its role conception of the manager are not as clear-cut as the values and role prescriptions in various other institutions, one may expect the processes of unfreezing, changing, and refreezing to occur with less intensity and to be less consciously rationalized in the business enterprise. But they are structurally the same as in other organizations. One of the main purposes of this paper, then, will be to try to make salient some features of the influence of the organization on the attitudes of the individual manager by attempting to compare institutions in which the influence process is more drastic and explicit with the more implicit and less drastic methods of the business enterprise.

ILLUSTRATIONS OF ORGANIZATIONAL INFLUENCE

Unfreezing

The concept of unfreezing and the variety of methods by which influence targets can be unfrozen can best be illustrated by considering examples drawn from a broad range of situations. The Chinese Communists in their attempt to inculcate Communist attitudes into their youth or into their prisoners serve as a good prototype of one extreme. First and most important was the removal of the target person from those situations and social relationships which tended to confirm and reinforce the validity of the old attitudes. Thus the targets, be they political prisoners, prisoners of war, university professors, or young students, were isolated from their friends, families, and accustomed work groups and cut off from all media of communication to which they were accustomed. In addition, they were subjected to continuous exhortations (backed by threats of severe punishment) to confess their crimes and adopt new attitudes, and were constantly humiliated in order to discredit their old sense of identity.

The isolation of the target from his normal social and ideological supports reached its height in the case of Western civilians who were placed into group cells with a number of Chinese prisoners who had already confessed and were committed to reforming themselves and their lone Western cell mate. In the prisoner of war camps such extreme social isolation could not be produced, but its counterpart was created by the fomenting of mutual mistrust among the prisoners, by cutting off any supportive mail from home, and by systematically disorganizing the formal and informal social structure of the POW camp (by segregation of officers and noncommissioned officers from the remainder of the group, by the systematic removal of informal leaders or key personalities, and by the prohibition of any group activity not in line with the indoctrination program) (Schein, 1960, 1961).

The Chinese did not hesitate to use physical brutality and threats of death and/or permanent non-repatriation to enforce the view that only by collaboration and attitude change could the prisoner hope to survive physically and psychologically. In the case of the civilians in group cells, an additional and greater stress was represented by the social pressure of the cell mates who would harangue, insult, revile, humiliate, and plead with the resistant Westerner twenty-four hours a day for weeks or months on end, exhorting him to admit his guilt, confess his crimes, reform, and adopt Communist values. This combination of physical and social pressures is perhaps a prototype of the use of coercion in the service of unfreezing a target individual in attitude areas to which he is strongly committed.

A somewhat milder, though structurally similar, process can be observed in the training of a nun (Hulme, 1956). The novice enters the convent voluntarily and is presumably ready to change, but the kind of change which must be accomplished encounters strong psychological resistances because, again, it involves deeply held attitudes and habits. Thus the novice must learn to be completely unselfish and, in fact, selfless; she must adapt to a completely communal life; she must give up any source of authority except the absolute authority of God and of those senior to her in the convent; and she must learn to curb her sexual and aggressive impulses. How does the routine of the convent facilitate unfreezing? Again a key element is the removal of the novice from her accustomed routines, sources of confirmation, social supports, and old relationships. She is physically isolated from the outside world, surrounded by others who are undergoing the same training as she, subjected to a highly demanding and fatiguing physical regimen, constantly exhorted toward her new role and punished for any evidence of old behaviors and attitudes, and subjected to a whole range of social pressures ranging from mild disapproval to total humiliation for any failure.

Not only is the novice cut off from her old social identity, but her entry into the convent separates her from many aspects of her physical identity. She is deprived of all means of being beautiful or even feminine; her hair is cut off and she is given institutional garb which emphasizes formlessness and sameness; she loses her old name and chronological age in favor of a new name and age corresponding to length of time in the convent; her living quarters and daily routine emphasize an absolute minimum of physical comfort and signify a total devaluation of anything related to the body. At the same time the threat associated with change is minimized by the tremendous support which the convent offers for change and by the fact that everyone else either already exhibits the appropriate attitudes or is in the process of learning them.

If we look at the process by which a pledge comes to be a full-fledged member of a fraternity, we find in this situation also a set of pressures to give up old associations and habits, a devaluation of the old self by humiliations ranging from menial, senseless jobs to paddling and hazing, a removal of threat through sharing of training, and support for good performance in the pledge role. The evangelist seeking to convert those who come to hear him attempts to unfreeze his audience by stimulating guilt and by devaluating their former selves as sinful and unworthy. The teacher wishing to induce motivation to learn sometimes points out the deficiencies in the student's knowledge and hopes at the same time to induce some guilt for having those deficiencies.

Some of the elements which all unfreezing situations have in common are the following: (1) the physical removal of the influence target from his accustomed routines, sources of information, and social relationships; (2) the undermining and destruction of all social supports; (3) demeaning and humiliating experience to help the target see his old self as unworthy and thus to become motivated to change; (4) the consistent linking of reward with willingness to change and of punishment with unwillingness to change.

Changing

Once the target has become motivated to change, the actual influence is most likely to occur by one of two processes. The target finds one or more models in his social environment and learns new attitudes by identifying with them and trying to become like them; or the target confronts new situations with an experimental attitude and develops for himself attitudes which are appropriate to the situation and which remove whatever problem he faces. These two processes —*identification* and *internalization*—probably tend to occur together in most concrete situations, but it is worthwhile, for analytical purposes, to keep them separate.[6]

The student or prisoner of the Chinese Communists took his basic step toward acquiring Communist attitudes when he began to identify with his more advanced fellow student or prisoner. In the group cell it was the discovery by the Western prisoner that his Chinese cell mates were humans like himself, were rational, and yet completely believed in their own and his guilt, which forced him to re-examine his own premises and bases of judgment and led him the first step down the path of acquiring the Communist point of view. In other words, he began to identify with his cell mates and to acquire their point of view as the only solution to getting out of prison and reducing the pressure on him. The environment was, of course, saturated with the Communist point of view, but it is significant that such saturation by itself was not sufficient to induce genuine attitude change. The prisoner kept in isolation and bombarded with propaganda was less likely to acquire Communist attitudes than the one placed into a group cell with more reformed prisoners. Having a personal model was apparently crucial.

In the convent the situation is essentially comparable except that the novice is initially much more disposed toward identifying with older nuns and has a model of appropriate behavior around her all the time in the actions of the others. It is interesting to note also that some nuns are singled out as particularly qualified models and given the appropriate name of "the living rule." It is also a common institution in initiation or indoctrination procedures to attach to the target individual someone who is labelled a "buddy" or "big brother," whose responsibility it is to teach the novice "the ropes" and to communicate the kinds of attitudes expected of him.

In most kinds of training and teaching situations, and even in the sales relationship, it is an acknowledged fact that the process is facilitated greatly if the target can identify with the influence agent. Such identification is facilitated if the social distance and

---

[6] Both are facilitated greatly if the influence agent saturates the environment with the new message or attitude to be learned.

rank difference between agent and target are not too great. The influence agent has to be close enough to the target to be seen as similar to the target, yet must be himself committed to the attitudes he is trying to inculcate. Thus, in the case of the Chinese Communist group cell, the cell mates could be perceived as sharing a common situation with the Western prisoner and this perception facilitated his identification with them. In most buddy systems, the buddy is someone who has himself gone through the training program in the recent past. If the target is likely to mistrust the influence attempts of the organization, as might be the case in a management-sponsored training program for labor or in a therapy program for delinquents in a reformatory, it is even more important that the influence agent be perceived as similar to the target. Otherwise he is dismissed as a "company man" or one who has already sold out, and hence is seen as someone whose message or example is not to be taken seriously.

Internalization, the discovery of attitudes which are the target's own solutions to his perceived dilemmas, can occur at the same time as identification. The individual can use the example of others to guide him in solving his own problems without necessarily identifying with them to the point of complete imitation. His choice of attitude remains ultimately his own in terms of what works for him, given the situation in which he finds himself. Internalization is only possible in an organizational context in which, from the organization's point of view, a number of different kinds of attitudes will be tolerated. If there is a "party line," a company philosophy, or a given way in which people have to feel about things in order to get along, it is hardly an efficient procedure to let trainees discover their own solutions. Manipulating the situation in such a way as to make the official solution the only one which is acceptable can, of course, be attempted, but the hazards of creating real resentment and alienation on the part of the individual when he discovers he really had no choice may outweigh the presumed advantages of letting him think he had a choice.

In the case of the Chinese Communists, the convent, the revival meeting, the fraternity, or the institutional training program, we are dealing with situations where the attitudes to be learned are clearly specified. In this kind of situation, internalization will not occur unless the attitudes to be learned happen to fit uniquely the kind of personal problem the individual has in the situation. For example, a few prisoners of the Communists reacted to the tremendous unfreezing pressures with genuine guilt when they discovered they held certain prejudices and attitudes (e.g. when they realized that they had looked down on lower class Chinese in spite of their manifest acceptance of them). These prisoners were then able to internalize certain portions of the total complex of Communist attitudes, particularly those dealing with unselfishness and working for the greater good of others. The attitudes which the institution demanded of them also solved a personal problem of long standing for them. In the case of the nun, one might hypothesize that internalization of the convent's attitudes will occur to the extent that asceticism offers a genuine solution to the incumbent's personal conflicts.

Internalization is a more common outcome in those influence settings where the direction of change is left more to the individual. The influence which occurs in programs like Alcoholics Anonymous, in psychotherapy or counseling for hospitalized or incarcerated populations, in religious retreats, in human relations training of the kind pursued by the National Training Laboratories (1953), and in certain kinds of progressive education programs is more likely to occur through internalization or, at least, to lead ultimately to more internalization.

Refreezing

Refreezing refers to the process by which the newly acquired attitude comes to be integrated into the target's personality and ongoing relationships. If the new attitude has been internalized while being learned, this has automatically facilitated refreezing because it has been fitted naturally into the individual's personality. If it has been learned through identification, it will persist only so long as the target's relationship with the original influence model persists unless new surrogate models are found or social support and reinforcement is obtained for expressions of the new attitude.[7]

In the case of the convent such support comes from a whole set of expectations which others have of how the nun should behave, from clearly specified role perscriptions, and from rituals. In the case of individuals influenced by the Chinese Communists, if they remained in Communist China they received constant support for their new attitudes from superiors and peers; if they returned to the West, the permanence of their attitude change depended on the

---

[7] In either case the change may be essentially permanent, in that a relationship to a model or surrogate can last indefinitely. It is important to distinguish the two processes, however, because if one were to try to change the attitude, different strategies would be used depending upon how the attitude had been learned.

degree of support they actually received from friends and relations back home, or from groups which they sought out in an attempt to get support. If their friends and relatives did not support Communist attitudes, the repatriates were influenced once again toward their original attitudes or toward some new integration of both sets.

The importance of social support for new attitudes was demonstrated dramatically in the recent Billy Graham crusade in New York City. An informal survey of individuals who came forward when Graham called for converts indicated that only those individuals who were subsequently integrated into local churches maintained their faith. Similar kinds of findings have been repeatedly noted with respect to human relations training in industry. Changes which may occur during the training program do not last unless there is some social support for the new attitudes in the "back home" situation.

The kind of model which has been discussed above might best be described by the term "coercive persuasion." The influence of an organization on an individual is coercive in the sense that he is usually forced into situations which are likely to unfreeze him, in which there are many overt and covert pressures to recognize in himself a need for change, and in which the supports for his old attitudes are in varying degrees coercively removed. It is coercive also to the degree that the new attitudes to be learned are relatively rigidly prescribed. The individual either learns them or leaves the organization (if he can). At the same time, the actual process by which new attitudes are learned can best be described as persuasion. In effect, the individual is forced into a situation in which he is likely to be influenced. The organization can be highly coercive in unfreezing its potential influence targets, yet be quite open about the direction of attitude changes it will tolerate. In those cases where the direction of change is itself coerced (as contrasted with letting it occur through identification or internalization), it is highly unlikely that anything is accomplshed other than surface behavioral change in the target. And such surface change will be abandoned the moment the coercive force of the change agent is lessened. If behavioral changes are coerced at the same time as other unfreezing operations are undertaken, actual influence can be facilitated if the individual finds himself having to learn attitudes to justify the kinds of behavior he has been forced to exhibit. The salesman may not have an attitude of cynicism toward his customers initially. If, however, he is forced by his boss to behave as if he felt cynical, he might develop real cynicism as a way of justifying his actual behavior.

MANAGEMENT DEVELOPMENT: IS IT COERCIVE PERSUASION?

Do the notions of coercive persuasion developed above fit the management development situation? Does the extent to which they do or do not fit such a model illuminate for us some of the implications of specific management development practices?

Unfreezing

It is reasonable to assume that the majority of managers who are being "developed" are not ready or able to change in the manner in which their organization might desire and therefore must be unfrozen before they can be influenced. They may be eager to change at a conscious motivation level, yet still be psychologically unprepared to give up certain attitudes and values in favor of untried, threatening new ones. I cannot support this assumption empirically, but the likelihood of its being valid is high because of a related fact which is empirically supportable. Most managers do not participate heavily in decisions which affect their careers, nor do they have a large voice in the kind of self-development in which they wish to participate. Rather, it is the man's superior or a staff specialist in career development who makes the key decisions concerning his career (Alfred, 1960). If the individual manager is not trained from the outset to take responsibility for his own career and given a heavy voice in diagnosing his own needs for a change, it is unlikely that he will readily be able to appreciate someone else's diagnosis. It may be unclear to him what basically is wanted of him or, worse, the ambiguity of the demands put upon him combined with his own inability to control his career development is likely to arouse anxiety and insecurity which would cause even greater resistance to genuine self-assessment and attitude change.[8] He becomes preoccupied with promotion in the abstract and attempts to acquire at a surface level the traits which he thinks are necessary for advancement.

If the decisions made by the organization do not seem valid to the manager, or if the unfreezing process turns out to be quite painful to him, to what extent can he leave the situation? His future career, his financial security, and his social status within the business com-

---

[8] An even greater hazard, of course, is that the organization communicates to the manager that he is not expected to take responsibility for his own career at the same time that it is trying to teach him how to be able to take responsibility for important decisions!

munity all stand to suffer if he resists the decisions made for him. Perhaps the most coercive feature is simply the psychological pressure that what he is being asked to do is "for his own ultimate welfare." Elementary loyalty to his organization and to his managerial role demands that he accept with good grace whatever happens to him in the name of his own career development. In this sense, then, I believe that the business organization has coercive forces at its disposal which are used by it in a manner comparable to the uses made by other organizations.

Given the assumption that the manager who is to be developed needs to be unfrozen, and given that the organization has available coercive power to accomplish such unfreezing, what mechanisms does it actually use to unfreeze potential influence targets?

The essential elements to unfreezing are the removal of supports for the old attitudes, the saturation of the environment with the new attitudes to be acquired, a minimizing of threat, and a maximizing of support for any change in the right direction. In terms of this model it becomes immediately apparent that training programs or other activities which are conducted in the organization at the place of work for a certain number of hours per day or week are far less likely to unfreeze and subsequently influence the participant than those programs which remove him for varying lengths of time from his regular work situation and normal social relationships.

Are appraisal interviews, used periodically to communicate to the manager his strengths, weaknesses and areas for improvement, likely to unfreeze him? Probably not, because as long as the individual is caught up in his regular routine and is responding, probably quite unconsciously, to a whole set of expectations which others have about his behavior and attitudes, it is virtually impossible for him to hear, at a psychological level, what his deficiencies or areas needing change are. Even if he can appreciate what is being communicated to him at an intellectual level, it is unlikely that he can emotionally accept the need for change, and even if he can accept it emotionally, it is unlikely that he can produce change in himself in an environment which supports all of his old ways of functioning. This statement does not mean that the man's co-workers necessarily approve of the way he is operating or like the attitudes which he is exhibiting. They may want to see him change, but their very expectations concerning how he normally behaves operate as a constraint on him which makes attitude change difficult in that setting.

On the other hand, there are a variety of training activities which are used in management development which approximate more closely the conditions necessary for effective unfreezing. These would include programs offered at special training centers such as those maintained by IBM on Long Island and General Electric at Crotonville, N. Y.; university-sponsored courses in management, liberal arts, and/or the social sciences; and especially, workshops or laboratories in human relations such as those conducted at Arden House, N. Y., by the National Training Laboratories. Programs such as these remove the participant for some length of time from his normal routine, his regular job, and his social relationships (including his family in most cases), thus providing a kind of moratorium during which he can take stock of himself and determine where he is going and where he wants to go.

The almost total isolation from the pressures of daily life in the business world which a mountain chateau such as Arden House provides for a two-week period is supplemented by other unfreezing forces. The de-emphasis on the kind of job or title the participant holds in his company and the informal dress remove some of the symbolic or status supports upon which we all rely. Sharing a room and bath facilities with a roommate requires more than the accustomed exposure of private spheres of life to others. The total involvement of the participant in the laboratory program leaves little room for reflection about the back home situation. The climate of the laboratory communicates tremendous support for any efforts at self-examination and attempts as much as possible to reduce the threats inherent in change by emphasizing the value of experimentation, the low cost and risk of trying a new response in the protected environment of the lab, and the high gains to be derived from finding new behavior patterns and attitudes which might improve back home performance. The content of the material presented in lectures and the kind of learning model which is used in the workshop facilitates self-examination, self-diagnosis based on usable feedback from other participants, and rational planning for change.[9]

The practice of rotating a manager from one kind of assignment to another over a period of years can have some of the same unfreezing effects and thus facilitate attitude change. Certainly his physical move from one setting to another removes many of the supports to his old attitudes, and in his new job the manager will have an oppor-

---

[9] Although, as I will point out later, such effective unfreezing may lead to change which is not supported or considered desirable by the "back home" organization.

tunity to try new behaviors and become exposed to new attitudes. The practice of providing a moratorium in the form of a training program prior to assuming a new job would appear to maximize the gains from each approach, in that unfreezing would be maximally facilitated and change would most probably be lasting if the person did not go back to a situation in which his co-workers, superiors, and subordinates had stable expectations of how he should behave.

Another example of how unfreezing can be facilitated in the organizational context is the practice of temporarily reducing the formal rank and responsibilities of the manager by making him a trainee in a special program, or an apprentice on a special project, or an assistant to a high ranking member of the company. Such temporary lowering of formal rank can reduce the anxiety associated with changing and at the same time serves officially to destroy the old status and identity of the individual because he could not ordinarily return to his old position once he had accepted the path offered by the training program. He would have to move either up or out of the organization to maintain his sense of self-esteem. Of course, if such a training program is perceived by the trainee as an indication of his failing rather than a step toward a higher position, his anxiety about himself would be too high to facilitate effective change on his part. In all of the illustrations of organizational influence we have presented above, change was defined as being a means of gaining status—acceptance into Communist society, status as a nun or a fraternity brother, salvation, etc. If participants come to training programs believing they are being punished, they typically do not learn much.

The above discussion is intended to highlight the fact that some management development practices do facilitate the unfreezing of the influence target, but that such unfreezing is by no means automatic. Where programs fail, therefore, one of the first questions we must ask is whether they failed because they did not provide adequate conditions for unfreezing.

Changing

Turning now to the problem of the mechanisms by which changes actually occur, we must confront the question of whether the organization has relatively rigid prescribed goals concerning the direction of attitude change it expects of the young manager, or whether it is concerned with growth in the sense of providing increasing opportunities for the young manager to learn the attitudes appropriate to ever more challenging situations. It is undoubtedly true that most programs would claim growth as their goal, but the degree to which they accomplish it can only be assessed from an examination of their actual practice.

Basically the question is whether the organization influences attitudes primarily through the mechanism of identification or the mechanism of internalization. If the development programs stimulate psychological relationships between the influence target and a member of the organization who has the desired attitudes, they are thereby facilitating influence by identification but, at the same time, are limiting the alternatives available to the target and possibly the permanence of the change achieved. If they emphasize that the target must develop his own solutions to ever more demanding problems, they are risking that the attitudes learned will be incompatible with other parts of the organization's value system but are producing more permanent change because the solutions found are internalized. From the organization's point of view, therefore, it is crucial to know what kind of influence it is exerting and to assess the results of such influence in terms of the basic goals which the organization may have. If new approaches and new attitudes toward management problems are desired, for example, it is crucial that the conditions for internalization be created. If rapid learning of a given set of attitudes is desired, it is equally crucial that the conditions for identification with the right kind of models be created.

One obvious implication of this distinction is that programs conducted within the organization's orbit by its own influence agents are much more likely to facilitate identification and thereby the transmission of the "party line" or organization philosophy. On the other hand, programs like those conducted at universities or by the National Training Laboratories place much more emphasis on the finding of solutions by participants which fit their own particular needs and problems. The emphasis in the human relations courses is on "learning how to learn" from the participant's own interpersonal experiences and how to harness his emotional life and intellectual capacities to the accomplishment of his goals, rather than on specific principles of human relations. The nearest thing to an attitude which the laboratory staff, acting as influence agents, does care to communicate is an attitude of inquiry and experimentation, and to this end the learning of skills of observation, analysis, and diagnosis of interpersonal situations is given strong emphasis. The training group, which is the acknowledged core of the laboratory approach, provides its own unfreezing forces by being unstructured as to the content of discussion. But it is strongly committed to a method of learning by analysis of the member's own experiences in the group, which facilitates the discovery of the value of an attitude of inquiry and experimentation.

Mutual identification of the members of the group with each other and member identifications with the staff play some role in the acquisition of this attitude, but the basic power of the method is that the attitude of inquiry and experimentation *works* in the sense of providing for people valuable new insights about themselves, groups, and organizations. To the extent that it works and solves key problems for the participants, it is internalized and carried back into the home situation. To the extent that it is learned because participants wish to emulate a respected fellow member or staff member, it lasts only so long as the relationship with the model itself, or a surrogate of it, lasts (which may, of course, be a very long time).

The university program in management or liberal arts is more difficult to categorize in terms of an influence model, because within the program there are usually opportunities both for identification (e.g. with inspiring teachers) and internalization. It is a safe guess in either case, however, that the attitudes learned are likely to be in varying degrees out of phase with any given company's philosophy unless the company has learned from previous experience with a given course that the students are taught a point of view consistent with its own philosophy. Of course, universities, as much as laboratories, emphasize the value of a spirit of inquiry and, to the extent that they are successful in teaching this attitude, will be creating potential dissidents or innovators, depending on how the home company views the result.

Apprenticeships, special jobs in the role of "assistant to" somebody, job rotation, junior management boards, and so on stand in sharp contrast to the above methods in the degree to which they facilitate, indeed almost demand, that the young manager learn by watching those who are senior or more competent. It is probably not prescribed that in the process of acquiring knowledge and skills through the example of others he should also acquire their attitudes, but the probability that this will happen is very high if the trainee develops any degree of respect and liking for his teacher and/or supervisor. It makes little difference whether the teacher, coach, or supervisor intends to influence the attitudes of his trainee or not. If a good emotional relationship develops between them, it will facilitate the learning of knowledge and skills, and will, at the same time, result in some degree of attitude change. Consequently, such methods do not maximize the probability of new approaches being invented to management problems, nor do they really by themselves facilitate the growth of the manager in the sense of providing opportunities for him to develop solutions which fit his own needs best.

Job rotation, on the other hand, can facilitate growth and innovation provided it is managed in such a way as to insure the exposure of the trainee to a broad range of points of view as he moves from assignment to assignment. The practice of shifting the developing manager geographically as well as functionally both facilitates unfreezing and increases the likelihood of his being exposed to new attitudes. This same practice can, of course, be merely a convenient way of indoctrinating the individual by sending him on an assignment, for example, "in order to acquire the sales point of view from Jim down in New York," where higher management knows perfectly well what sort of a view Jim will communicate to his subordinates.

Refreezing

Finally, a few words are in order about the problem of refreezing. Under what conditions will changed attitudes remain stable, and how do existing practices aid or hinder such stabilization? Our illustrations from the non-industrial setting highlighted the importance of social support for any attitudes which were learned through identification. Even the kind of training emphasized in the National Training Laboratories programs, which tends to be more internalized, does not produce stable attitude change unless others in the organization, especially superiors, peers, and subordinates, have undergone similar changes and give each other stimulation and support, because lack of support acts as a new unfreezing force producing new influence (possibly in the direction of the original attitudes).

If the young manager has been influenced primarily in the direction of what is already the company philosophy, he will, of course, obtain strong support and will have little difficulty maintaining his new attitudes. If, on the other hand, management development is supposed to lead to personal growth and organizational innovation, the organization must recognize the reality that new attitudes cannot be carried by isolated individuals. The lament that we no longer have strong individualists who are willing to try something new is a fallacy based on an incorrect diagnosis. Strong individuals have always gained a certain amount of their strength from the support of others, hence the organizational problem is how to create conditions which make possible the nurturing of new ideas, attitudes, and approaches. If organizations seem to lack innovators, it may be that the climate of the organization and its methods of management development do not foster innovation, not that its human resources are inadequate.

An organizational climate in which new attitudes which differ from company philosophy can nevertheless be maintained cannot be achieved merely by an intellectual or even emotional commitment on the part of higher-ranking managers to tolerance of new ideas and attitudes. Genuine support can come only from others who have themselves been influenced, which argues strongly that at least several members of a given department must be given the same training before such training can be expected to have effect. If the superior of the people involved can participate in it as well, this strengthens the group that much more, but it would not follow from my line of reasoning that this is a necessary condition. Only some support is needed, and this support can come as well from peers and subordinates.

From this point of view, the practice of sending more than one manager to any given program at a university or human relations workshop is very sound. The National Training Laboratories have emphasized from the beginning the desirability of having organizations send teams. Some organizations like Esso Standard have created their own laboratories for the training of the entire management complement of a given refinery, and all indications are that such a practice maximizes the possibility not only of the personal growth of the managers, but of the creative growth of the organization as a whole.

Conclusion

In the above discussion I have deliberately focused on a model of influence which emphasizes procedure rather than content, interpersonal relations rather than mass media, and attitudes and values rather than knowledge and skills. By placing management development into a context of institutional influence procedures which also include Chinese Communist thought reform, the training of a nun, and other more drastic forms of coercive persuasion, I have tried to highlight aspects of management development which have remained implicit yet which need to be understood. I believe that some aspects of management development are a mild form of coercive persuasion, but I do not believe that coercive persuasion is either morally bad in any *a priori* sense nor inefficient. If we are to develop a sound theory of career development which is capable of including not only many of the formal procedures discussed in this paper, but the multitudes of informal practices, some of which are more and some of which are less coercive than those discussed, we need to suspend moral judgments for the time being and evaluate influence models solely in terms of their capacity to make sense of the data and to make meaningful predictions.

77. LIBERAL ARTS AS TRAINING
FOR BUSINESS [1]

Frederic E. Pamp, Jr. [2]

It is not hard to predict that the practice of management will be profoundly affected by the rapidly approaching forces of automation and statistical decision making.

Any company with a decent regard for its survival must be trying to forecast the terms of those forces, for it must recruit and promote today the executives who will be running the company tomorrow. Can we write the job description for a vice president of X Manufacturing Company for 1965, or 1975? What will he have to know? What new skills, what new sensitivities will he have to possess to deal successfully with the new elements in management and (what is perhaps more important) the new combinations of old elements?

There have been enough changes just since the end of World War II to make the job grow alarmingly. These changes have in fact been largely responsible for the feverish attention that has been paid to management development in recent years. As Frederick Lewis Allen describes the complicated nature of present executive requirements:

> "The corporation executive today must be the captain of a smooth-working team of people who can decide whether the time has come to build a new polymerization plant, what the answer is to the unsatisfactory employee relations in a given unit of the business, how to cope with a new government regulation, how to achieve a mutually respectful understanding with union representatives and what position to take on price increases in order to maintain the good will of the public. In short, he is confronted with so many questions which require knowledge, intellectual subtlety, political insight and human flexibility that he desperately needs a mental equipment of the sort that the old-time tycoon could do without." [3]

New Demands

Up to now most of the increased demands on management have been quantitative. An executive has had to know more about engi-

[1] From the *Harvard Business Review*, Vol. 33, No. 3, pp. 42-50. Reprinted by permission of the *Harvard Business Review*.
[2] Frederic E. Pamp, Jr., Division Manager of the American Management Association.
[3] "What Have We Got Here?" *Life* (January 5, 1953), p. 50.

neering, about accounting, about his industry, about the position of his company in the industry, about society and the world around him —all to the end of better control of masses of data and information, and better decision making on the basis of such material.

Now we are faced with the fact that many of the quantitative aspects of the executive's job are going to recede into the innards of a computer. Thus, in one company, dozens of clerks used to work laborious days on their slide rules to provide data for what were no more than calculated guesses, on top of which management built a whole pyramid of deliberate decisions. A computer can now take readings of the whole spectrum of data at any time desired, give the relevant figures their proper weights, and come up with production schedules, orders for materials, and financial budgets to ensure maximum efficiency of operation.[4]

Nevertheless, the executive is not likely to join the ranks of the technologically unemployed, just because he will have shucked off many of the problems on which he formerly exercised his executive judgment and "feel." It is inevitable that new problems will crowd in to take the place of the old ones. And, in other than quantitative judgments, a new standard of accuracy and precision will be called for to match the level of accuracy displayed by the computer. A small fable for executives was played out before millions on television at the last election, when the computer performed faultlessly on faulty data and came out blandly with answers that could have ruined a company if they had concerned a gamble on marketing or capital investment.

In any event, the competitive edge acquired by one company by acquisition of a computer will not last long in any industry. Sooner or later all companies will be returned to the equilibrium defined recently by Albert L. Nickerson, Vice President and Director of Foreign Trade, Socony-Vacuum Oil Company:

> If one competitor has a material advantage today it—or a workable counterpart—is likely soon to become common property. An enterprise must rely for survival and progress on the personal qualifications of those who make up its ranks and direct its destinies.[5]

Qualities Needed

Management development has already shaken down from an early concentration on executive manning charts and development of logical

---

[4] See Roddy F. Osborn, "GE and UNIVAC: Harnessing the High-Speed Computer," *Harvard Business Review* (July-August, 1954), p. 99.

[5] "Climbing the Managerial Ladder," *Saturday Review of Literature* (November 21, 1953), p. 38.

succession to key jobs, through a period of sorties into specialized training groups, to a generally accepted set of principles for assessment and development of the candidate on the job under realistic standards of performance. All this prepares for the job as it has shaped up in the past decade and as it exists today (as military staffs are always alleged to prepare for the last war). It is time for the focus to shift again—to the building of the kind of executive quality which will be at a premium tomorrow.

Straight-line extension of the norm that has led the company this far will not necessarily suffice to lead it in the future. Top management cannot expect to pick its succession exactly in its own image and get away with it. Neither is it enough to take the pattern of executive personality that has succeeded in one company (or a thousand) under present conditions. The first question a company must now begin to ask of its candidates for executive responsibility is: "What can you do that a computer can't?"

In more and more companies, the decisive factor is going to be the breadth and depth of executive judgment. As vast areas of what used to be decision making become subject to mechanical computations which are all equally correct in all companies, the edge will be won by the company whose executives do a better job of handling the qualitative factors which remain after the measurable factors have been taken out, and then of putting all the pieces together into a single, dynamic whole—what Peter Drucker calls "seeing a business as a whole in conceptual synthesis." [6]

Breadth of judgment

On one point all authorities have agreed. Narrow specialization is not enough; this is already responsible for most of the inability of middle management executives to be considered for promotion. John L. McCaffrey, President of International Harvester Company, puts it this way:

> . . . the world of the specialist is a narrow one and it tends to produce narrow human beings. The specialist usually does not see over-all effects on the business and so he tends to judge good and evil, right and wrong, by the sole standard of his own specialty.
> "This narrowness of view, this judgment of all events by the peculiar standards of his own specialty, is the curse of the specialist from the standpoint of top management consideration for advancement.

[6] Peter F. Drucker, *The Practice of Management* (New York: Harper & Brothers, 1954), p. 105.

Except in unusual cases, it tends to put a road-block ahead of him after he reaches a certain level. [7]

Thus, there has been a growing call for "breadth" in educational preparation for management, and a surprising degree of agreement on the need for more *liberal arts* in colleges.

Educators, especially those in state-supported colleges, may be forgiven a certain bewilderment if, after bending every effort—and many curricula—to answer insistent demands from business for more and more specialty and vocational courses on all levels, they are now abused for turning out graduates unprepared for the full scope of executive action in management for today, much less for tomorrow. They have responded by pointing out that the company recruiters still come to the colleges with many more demands for technicians than for liberal arts graduates.

Action has been taken to bring educators in the liberal arts and business executives together to discuss the desirable objectives of education for management. A new respect is developing on the part of businessmen for the standards which the privately endowed, liberal arts colleges have been defending for many years. Agreement on ends and, to some extent, on curricular means to these ends has been worked out in conferences such as those held by the College English Association at the University of Massachusetts in 1952, at the Corning Glass Center in 1953, at Michigan State College and the Kellogg Center in East Lansing in 1954, and the most recent one sponsored by General Electric at Schenectady this spring.

Viewed in these terms many subjects and disciplines can lay claim to a role in education for management. It is obvious that wider subject matter, more courses about more things in the contemporary world, will give the student more breadth.

Depth of judgment

But it is also apparent that in a day when the executive will be able to dial the electronic reference library and get all the facts about all the subjects he wants, mere accretion of facts will not warrant his putting in the time to prepare merely to know more facts. The call is for more than "breadth" alone; it is for the ability to move surely and with confidence on unfamiliar ground, to perceive central elements in situations and see how their consequences fall into line in many dimensions. Tomorrow's executive must be able to move

[7] *Fortune* (September, 1953), p. 129.

surely from policy to action in situations that will be different from anything any generation has experienced before.

There have been developments in traditional educational disciplines within the liberal arts which, much to the surprise of those closest to them, will very likely turn out to be far more important to educational preparation for management than many of the flashy subjects that have seemingly been set up to serve business' needs exclusively. The study of the *humanities*—of literature, art, and philosophy, and of the critical terms that these disciplines use to assess the world—is startlingly more pertinent and practical than the "practical" vocational preparation.

Executives should know that recent graduates in the humanities have had a much different experience from those who went through our better colleges ten years ago. They have experienced a much more closely disciplined course in the examination of literature and creative works—of the objectives and the tissue of meanings and symbols which make up the over-all theme of the writing or the painting or the composition, or other form of creative work.

These disciplines have of course other axes to grind than preparing executives to fill job descriptions. They are elements in our civilization which give it life beyond any technologies or economic systems. The arts, education, and management all serve a higher purpose, and business will do society no good if it demands, as do some business leaders, that education serve business directly and solely. That would be the same as insisting that a corporation be restricted only to working capital and forbidden to raise long-term funds.

But the very fact that the humanities serve a larger need than management training is one of the main reasons why they are so valuable for that purpose.

THE EXECUTIVE'S JOB

At first glance, the importance of training in these fields hitherto considered peripheral, if not downright irrelevant, to management may be difficult to see. The contribution of the physical sciences is obvious. Also, at long last, we have come to appreciate the significance of the social sciences, which appear to relate directly to business both because of their content and because of their disciplines. It is obvious that an executive must be able to interpret the social and political environment in which his company operates. Further, he must be familiar with as much of the growing body of knowledge of human behavior as possible. But the liberal arts have always been considered remote from the practical hurly-burly of daily decision making.

To demonstrate that precisely the reverse is true, let us examine the disciplines within which the executive moves. In so doing, we may alter our ideas of his job as it has traditionally been regarded, and bring into focus the parallels between the disciplines of the liberal arts and the disciplines of management.

If we analyze the central activity of the executive, his *process of decision*, we can see three kinds of disciplines which prepare directly for the skills and qualities needed:

1. The executive must distinguish and define the possible lines of action among which a choice can be made. This requires imagination, the ability to catch at ideas, shape them into concrete form, and present them in terms appropriate to the problem.
2. He must analyze the consequences of taking each line of action. Here the computer and operations research techniques can do much, but the executive must set the framework for the problems from his experience and imagination, and work with his own sensitivity and knowledge in the area of human beings where statistics and scientific prediction are highly fallible guides.
3. Then in the decision he must have the grasp to know its implications in all areas of an organism which is itself far from being absolutely predictable: the company, the market, the economy, and the society.

Beyond science

Most executives act on the basis of a definite hypothesis about the nature of business, much as a scientist acts on a hypothesis about the universe. However, many of the elements subconsciously admitted to such a hypothesis are likely to be wrongheaded prejudices based on insufficient data. Indeed, one of the biggest contributions of operations research has been in identifying all the various factors that are involved and in establishing their net weighted relationships. The fact remains that a good proportion of business decisions have been proved pragmatically valid, to judge by the success of American management to date; and this casts real doubt on whether business is quite as "scientific" as many businessmen would like to think.

There has been a good deal of questioning for some time among more thoughtful management authorities whether management is or can be (or even ought to be) considered a science. James Worthy pointed out recently:

> One of the serious stumbling blocks to effective human organization is a deep-seated attitude of mind characteristic of our times. The

physical scientist and the engineer have exercised a profound influence, not only on the outward aspects of modern life, but on our inward thought processes as well. . . . The transference of their mode of thought to a field for which it was never designed has badly distorted our apprehension of our problems and seriously misdirected our efforts to deal with them. . . . All our thinking about organization displays a strongly mechanical turn of mind. . . . The nature of human organization cannot be properly apprehended in terms of mechanistic concepts.[8]

This question is important because of the possibility that much of top management's dissatisfaction with the executives available for promotion today has resulted from the educational and training assumption that management is a science or, worse, a collection of techniques, and can be prepared for in those terms alone.

There is the correlative danger that attempts to make management a science and only a science will destroy its essential nature and vigor in the American system. Peter F. Drucker makes this point:

> . . . management can never be an exact science. True, the work of a manager can be systematically analyzed and classified; there are, in other words, distinct professional features and a scientific aspect to management. Nor is managing a business just a matter of hunch or native ability; its elements and requirements can be analyzed, can be organized systematically, can be learned by anyone with normal human endowment.
> . . . And yet the ultimate test of management is business performance. Achievement rather than knowledge remains, of necessity, both proof and aim. Management, in other words, is a practice, rather than a science or profession, though containing elements of both. No greater damage could be done to our economy or to our society than to attempt to "professionalize" management by "licensing" managers, for instance, or by limiting access to management to people with a special academic degree.
> And any serious attempt to make management "scientific" or a "profession" is bound to lead to the attempt to eliminate those "disturbing nuisances," the unpredictabilities of business life—its risks, its ups and downs, its "wasteful competition," the "irrational choices" of the consumer—and, in the process, the economy's freedom and its ability to grow. [9]

There is an implication here that even if management were not faced with the great changes that are upon us, it would be essential to educate executives for the future who know how to ask impolite questions of the categories of science, just so as to avoid the danger that management as a body of knowledge will freeze into dangerously rigid controls on the whole enterprise system.

[8] "Freedom Within American Enterprise," *Advanced Management* (June, 1954), p. 5.
[9] *Op. cit.*, pp. 9-10.

It is perhaps the most striking fact about the new techniques of management that when they have developed fully, we shall know much better how far the writ of science runs in management; we shall know how far beyond science a man must go to practice management.

Added dimensions

I do not mean to deny that management needs a strong measure of scientific ability. But in organizing and systematizing education for the practice of management it has perhaps been forgotten that more dimensions of hypothesis and experience are involved than are available to science. The practice of management can repeat Hamlet's words to science today: "There are more things in heaven and earth, Horatio, than are dreamed of in your philosophy." The exclusively technical or scientific man is on a tennis court as compared to the generalist who has the added dimensions more like those of a squash court available to him. The latter can get the ball of decision bouncing off more walls. Clarence Randall, President of Inland Steel, puts it thus:

> The weakness of technical education as a preparation for a business career . . . when it is not balanced by participation in liberal disciplines, is that it leaves in the mind of the student the impression that all problems are quantitative and that a solution will appear as soon as all the facts have been collected and the correct mathematical formula evolved. Would life were that simple! Unhappily, the mysteries of human behavior from which come our most complex modern problems do not lend themselves to quantitative analysis, and there is no mental slide-rule which can be distributed as a substitute for straight thinking. [10]

APPROPRIATE DISCIPLINES

In view of all this, what can the humanities offer that is pertinent to the executive's job? For one thing, there is plenty of testimony that a common factor in executive success is the ability to express oneself in language. To illustrate:

> There have been many examinations of the background of executives to discover the secrets of success, which have pointed to other than technical accomplishment. In the most recent of these, by Wald and Doty in this magazine, which is more an examination in depth than any that have gone before, it is clear that the literary aptitude of the 33 executives examined was high compared to the scientific. These execu-

[10] *Freedom's Faith* (Boston: Little, Brown and Company, 1953), p. 90.

tives also felt that English was one of the most useful subjects they could take in college to help them toward success. [11]

It is certainly true that the student in the humanities goes deeper into language, and must get more from it and do more with it. But to assume from this that language is only a tool is to stop far short of the possibilities.

Language is not only a tool; it is the person himself. He makes his language, but his language also makes him. "Speak that I may know thee" is the old saw. Any study of language that stops with "techniques of communication," that sees the relationship as one-directional, is stunting the student's growth as an individual. Thus the study of literature as communication only, and not also as experience, is short-changing the student. Study of literature for its own sake is an activity which widens and deepens the personality.

Arthur A. Houghton, Chairman of the Board of Corning Glass, poses the problem bluntly with his statement opening the College English Association Conference at Corning last year:

> The executive does not deal with physical matter. He deals ex-clusively with ideas and with men. . . . He is a skilled and practical humanist.

Human situations are controlling in a large proportion of business decisions. The executive, it is agreed, must be able to deal with these situations before all else. The instincts for plucking out the fullest implications and keys to human situations are not developed in tech-nical courses of study, nor even in courses in human relations where the techniques pragmatically set the key for action.

There are numerical keys to situations, from accounting; there are quantitative keys, provided by operations research and other techniques drawn from the physical sciences; there are theoretical keys, such as those of Freudian analysis; and there are the keys of the social sciences, which claim to have no preconceptions or assump-tions but which are guided by doctrines nonetheless. But none of these keys provides the executive with the ability to see situations as a whole after and above all the data that are available, to seize on the central elements and know where the entry of action can be made.

[11] Robert M. Wald and Roy A. Doty, "The Top Executive—A Firsthand Profile," *Harvard Business Review* (July-August, 1954), p. 45.

Role of creativity

The fullest kind of training for this ability can actually be given by the practice of reading and analyzing literature and art. In his function the executive must do pretty much what a critic of literature must do, i.e., seize upon the key, the theme of the situation and the symbolic structure that gives it life. The executive must, moreover, create his object for analysis by himself, combining the ingredients of people and data. He must develop insight of an analytic, subjective kind—something he will never get in terms of pure science, for people and things in management situations just will not behave themselves with the admirable regularity and predictability of gases in a test tube!

The fact is, of course, that science itself has had to reconsider its assumptions about the nature of creative activity in its own field. In place of the mechanical concept of the mind as a computer patiently turning over the whole range of possible solutions one by one until it lights on the right one, explanations of scientific discovery now sound more and more like artistic or literary creation—much like John Livingston Lowe's description of how Coleridge inspiredly fused his whole range of experience and impression into "The Ancient Mariner." [12]

The creative element in management, as in the humanities, is developed by the disciplined imagination of a mind working in the widest range of dimensions possible. Some of those dimensions can be more precisely stated. As Clarence Randall has put it:

> My job today is in the realm of ideas. If I must delegate, I must delegate the things that are physical; the things that are material. . . . [13]

Many others have agreed that the most valuable commodity in management is ideas. Yet those disciplines which explore ideas for their own sake, which treat ideas as having life and interaction of their own, have been set off by many as "impractical." Now that the range is widening for management problems, we shall do well to demand that the traditional disciplines, which have dealt in ideas as they interact, in situations as wide as the artist's view of life, become a major part of education for managers. The greater this range of resource for the minds of management, the more and better will be the ideas that emerge.

[12] John Livingston Lowes. *The Road to Xanadu* (Boston and New York: Houghton Mifflin Company, 1927).
[13] Waller Carson, Jr., "Looking Around: Management Training," *Harvard Business Review* (March-April, 1953), p. 144.

Because literature is the disciplined control and development of ideas, it deserves a prominent place in this educational plan. Furthermore, to deal with literature and the arts is to deal with ideas not in the stripped and bloodless way of science, but in the inclusive, pell-mell way that experience comes to us in real life—ideas and practice all muddled up.

The need for order

Lyndall F. Urwick, in a lecture given a few years ago at the University of California, said:

> What the student needs is a universe of discourse, a frame of reference, so that when he encounters the raw material of practical life his mind is a machine which can work fruitfully upon that material, refer his own practical experience, which must be extremely limited, to general principles, and so develop an attitude, a guiding philosophy, which will enable him to cope with the immense responsibilities of business leadership in the twentieth century.

The executive's job, like life, is just one thing after another. The executive must be continually and instinctively making order and relation out of unrelated ideas—sorting, categorizing—to the end of action. The order he is able to impose on this mass of experience and the actions he initiates determine his success as an executive. He must find meanings for his company and his function, not only in control reports, balance sheets, market data, and forecasts, but also in human personalities, unpredictable human actions and reactions; and he must refer all to a scale of values. He must be prepared to answer the demand of the people who work for him: that their work contribute to the meaning of their lives. Without some awareness of the possibilities for meaning in human life he is not equipped for this central job of managing people. That awareness is a direct function of the humanities.

The key to the executive's situation and problem, then, is the fact and type of the network of meanings he must use and deal with. They are his stock in trade. He must remain aware of significance and meaning in the obvious: production rates, standards, absenteeism, and the rest. But today he must be acquiring more awarenesses to keep up. These can no longer be limited to the political and international. They are wider. Here the experience and criticism of the arts—especially literature—are direct preparation; for reading of this kind is above all a search for meanings. The mind that leads this search in literature and art—the author, the artist, the composer—is the most sensitive and aware. The mind that follows—the reader, the listener, the viewer—is itself stretched in the process; it too is going to grow more alert and aware.

Meanings on the widest possible level feed perception on a narrower one. The executive whose experience of meanings is thus widened has a suppleness of perception on narrower problems which can key them to effectiveness and coordination with policies and objectives on up the scale of management.

It is only prudent, then, that the executive's preparation include a participation (actual or vicarious) in the highest development of this process. Every novel and play and poem is an imposition of order in terms of human beings and of meaning in terms of a scale of values on the elements of experience that are found formless and pointless in any human experience. The terms by which this order is achieved over the whole scale of management action uses technology and science as tools, but it must have a sense of the whole and of values to be fully effective.

One of the most perceptive comments on the nature of the executive's job was made by Crawford H. Greenewalt, President of du Pont:

> . . . The basic requirement of executive capacity is the ability to create a harmonious whole out of what the academic world calls dissimilar disciplines. [14]

This ability to see the whole of things is again a central function of the humanities. The sciences have flourished by acute concentration upon those elements of the universe that can be measured, but science itself will today admit that it is not a means to the knowledge of the whole of man or of the universe.

The whole of a play or a poem or a novel is the object of the studies of literature because the meaning and structure of each part of it make sense only in terms of the whole. Thus one can say that this feeling for completeness which must govern management even more in the future than it has in the past is directly served by the humanities.

The search for values

Another, and perhaps the most important, aspect of the executive's job is the fact that he must operate in terms of values. Peter F. Drucker puts this at the center of the management job:

[14] "We Are Going to Need More Executives," *Chemical and Engineering News* (May 25, 1953), p. 2173.

Defining the situation always requires a decision on objectives, that is, on values and their relationship. It always requires a decision on the risk the manager is willing to run. It always, in other words, requires judgment and a deliberate choice between values. [15]

Only in the humanities are values inextricable from the materials that are studied. The significance of this is pointed up by a comment in the Yale Report on General Education:

> The arts are distinguished by the fact that their order already exists in the material studied. . . . The student who works with them learns to deal with intuitive symbolic ways of interpreting experience, ways which combine into one order the rational, the descriptive, and the evaluative.[16]

If there is a better description of the basic elements of management decision than that last sentence, I have not seen it. Men who must deal with situations above all in terms of values must be prepared by being exposed to those disciplines which admit that they are the stuff of all human life. It is here too that the most obvious reason usually advanced for the advantage of the humanities to an executive gains a new significance. With this equipment he is more likely to have interests outside the business. Not only is he thus likely to be less feverishly possessive about his status in the company, but he has available a far more extensive range of values against which to set his relations with others in the company and the policies of the company itself as well (when he is in a position to set those policies).

The tendency on the part of some social scientists—and some professors of literature—to assert the relativity of values is now going out of academic style. Even the most coldly objective of them now agree that some assumption of at least a hierarchy of values is necessary for worthy social action. This concession is of course not enough. The humanities can themselves be explained as the attempt to work out values in the arts, in all the possible terms of human action. Just as every poem, novel, or play is a representation of a scale of values, and thus has a life independent of the society that produced it, so the most objective study of value systems must admit that there are values by which the value systems themselves can be judged. The difference can be simply stated: for the humanities the values are inextricably linked to the materials; the sciences and social sciences attempt to divorce the materials from the value patterns.

[15] "On Making Decisions," *Dun's Review and Modern Industry* (August, 1954), p. 27.
[16] *Report of the President's Committee on General Education*, mimeographed (New Haven, 1953), p. 15.

The attempt to make science and scientific disciplines paramount in education has been responsible for a good deal of the attempt to get along without values. "Detachment from value judgments" was for a time adopted by some of the teachers of the humanities in our colleges and universities. They are turning back today to admission and use of the peculiar element that distinguishes their disciplines—and the social sciences are showing signs of following them, insofar as they can.

Even under teachers who looked at them objectively and skeptically the humanities have been able to convey values. For one thing values and their kind of order are inextricably mixed up in their objects of study. Ralph Barton Perry puts it this way:

> The humanities being defined relatively to the curriculum as those studies which inhuman teachers cannot completely dehumanize, literature and the arts possess an uncommonly stubborn humanity. Courses on literature, for example, are bound to present the literature. . . . The literature will speak for itself in a voice that is never wholly drowned by the hum of academic machinery. Studies accessory to literature, such as phonetics, grammar, linguistics, comparative philology, semantics, are easily dehumanized—more easily, perhaps than the physical or social sciences . . . but in courses on Sophocles, Dante, or Shakespeare, it is difficult wholly to counteract the effect of Sophocles, Dante, and Shakespeare. A course on the documentary technique of attribution, or the chemical technique of restoration, or the historical sources of style, or the administration of museums, though given by a department of fine arts, is easily dehumanized; but he who offers instruction on Titian, Velasquez, or Rembrandt must risk the chance that his students will see and enjoy Titian, Velasquez, or Rembrandt. [17]

Those disciplines in education which provide human and traditional perspective on the sciences and social sciences have always been of the highest importance in developing this ultimate management skill; they will become more important as time goes on, for, as President Nathan Pusey of Harvard has remarked, the humanities draw things back together.

Conclusion

The essence of the humanities, then, is meanings and value judgments on all levels. When they are well taught, they force the student to deal with things as a whole, with the gradations and expressions of meaning, worked out in terms of experience coordinated by values and communicated by the disciplined imagination of the artist or

[17] *The Meaning of the Humanities* (Princeton: Princeton University Press, 1938), p. 38.

writer. These meanings, in a framework of fact, intellect, emotion, and social values, are pulled together in an essentially spiritual complex.

The key to management, and to the executives who make it up, is found in its very nature as an activity. It is easy to define management as a combination of resources, but the fact that the human resources in that combination are in a very special way unique is something that links the humanistic disciplines and management far more firmly than engineering links production to science. Peter F. Drucker puts it this way:

> The enterprise cannot therefore be a mechanical assemblage of resources. To make an enterprise out of economic resources it is not enough to put them together in logical order and then throw the switch of capital. . . . What is needed is a transmutation of the resources. And this cannot come from an inanimate resource, such as capital. It requires management.
>
> But it is also clear that the "resources" capable of enlargement can only be human resources. All other resources stand under the laws of mechanics; they can be better utilized or worse utilized, but they can never have an output greater than the sum of the inputs. On the contrary, the problem in putting nonhuman resources together is always to keep to a minimum the inevitable output-shrinkage through friction, etc. Man, alone of all the resources available to man, can grow and develop. Only . . . the directed, focused, united effort of free human beings can produce a real whole . . . that is greater than the sum of its part (which) has since Plato's day been the definition of the "Good Society." [18]

Participation as a student in the poetic process of turning vision into rhetoric is parallel basically to the central problem of the executive, when he works to get policy and company goals into action, integrating plans and objectifying them. And executive action in its own way is no less an art.

A new synthesis

There are levels of organization in intellectual disciplines as well as in people. On the level of composition, rhetoric, and communication the humanities offer useful tools for the technician in business. But there also are higher levels of organization and integration in work of literary art, which correspond to the integrated personality for which management is looking. Only by exposure to these can we hope to get the character which is essentially the organization of the personality on the highest level of values.

[18] *The Practice of Management,* p. 12.

To neglect the humanities in education is to accept the doctrine of the educationalists as set by John Dewey: "The educational process has no end beyond itself." Management has already discovered that the corporation cannot long exist if it has no end beyond itself. It has now seen its error in giving education the impression that the end of education should be the service of the technical needs of business. There is a new synthesis now in the making through which the true ends of both can best be served. It remains only for management to put it into effect.

Businessmen can of course do the obvious, such as recruiting liberal arts graduates on an equal footing with engineers and technicians. But they can do more. They can ask impolite questions of those who teach the humanities. Do they as teachers produce clarifications of value judgments in their students? Are the students compelled to wrestle with values, as real things or *as if* they were real? Are they driven to see situations as a whole and to analyze them with all the elements in their experience, including their moral values? Businessmen can make it known that their standards for education are not merely technical or specialized. They can thus deeply affect educational policy to the benefit of management and American society.

A realization of these facts can also affect the atmosphere in which potential executives are trained on the job. The procedures which now devote the potential executive's most imaginative years to apprenticeship to figures and techniques can perhaps be changed to take advantage of the stimulated imagination, the taste for general ideas with which the graduate emerges from college, without losing the advantages of buckling down to work and getting a responsible job done. Multiple management no doubt owes a good deal of its success in the many companies using it to its ability thus to harness the most creative elements in the thinking of younger men. There are other ways of working out plans that will tap the liberating qualities of study of the humanities which will not interfere with the necessity for technical training. They should be investigated.

The humanities in the colleges are now struggling to put the pieces of the specialities back together again in order to make the integrated men that management can best use. If they get the sort of direct support already given by Corning Glass Works, General Motors, and General Electric as expressed in their sponsorship of the College English Association's conferences, and in the research projected by that organization, these disciplines can prove the most valuable single resource available for the management of the future.

78. TRAIN EXECUTIVES
WHILE THEY WORK [1]

Robert C. Sampson [2]

In recent years there has been a spectacular increase in plans and programs for executive development. Take in-plant training, for example. A decade ago one large national association found that there were too few programs even to make a survey worth while; today a nationwide canvas would probably reveal that up to 40% or more of major companies have one sort of program or another. Or take the number of formal training courses offered for experienced executives at universities; judging by reliable estimates, there are at least 15 times as many today as there were 10 years ago.

These programs are very helpful. Management has not been expending great sums of money on them foolishly. And yet, it seems to me—and I think that possibly many businessmen would concur—we still have not answered the question: How can we develop the potentials of a *particular* executive for specific higher responsibilities in a *particular* company? For, as I shall point out later, none of the popular solutions advanced thus far meet directly both (1) the individual needs of the executive and (2) the practical needs of the company. Typically, they meet only one or the other of these needs.

In the pages that follow I shall outline an approach which in my opinion does answer both needs at once. It offers a way to stimulate the thinking of executives about the immediate problems before them, to sharpen their administrative skills, and, perhaps most valuable of all, to develop faster and surer executive teamwork; and it does this without taking them out of their offices. In contrast to staff programs which emphasize doing things *to* or *for* management, the new approach is based on the idea that executives can profit most from help *with* the immediate problems of their own work situations.

I feel deeply indebted to line executives of the Chesapeake & Ohio Railway Company—particularly those of the Traffic Division—who have actively participated in working out this approach. They have

[1] From the *Harvard Business Review*, Vol. 31, No. 6, pp. 42-54. Reprinted by permission of the *Harvard Business Review*.
[2] Robert C. Sampson, heads the Staff Services of the Personnel Department of the Chesapeake & Ohio Railway Company.

made important contributions. Their patience, insight, understanding, helpful suggestions, and criticisms as we have worked together have provided a most unusual learning experience; and the case illustrations used in the following discussion are based on some of our cooperative experiences. None of these executives would describe the ideas in this article exactly as I shall describe them. Yet many of them, during the time we have worked together, have developed a keen understanding of what is involved. It is especially gratifying, therefore, that although the new approach is no open sesame, they have accepted it, found it helpful, and welcomed the opportunities it presents for self-development.

The Dilemma

Top-line executives seeking to develop the abilities of the men under them are in a real dilemma:

> For a number of reasons it is virtually impossible for them to do the job adequately themselves. The coaching that they *can* do is invaluable and absolutely essential, but the process of helping an executive to develop new skills and attitudes is an extremely time-consuming one —far too much so to be handled in detail by men who are already overburdened with responsibility. Nor do they have the necessary relationship with the executives in question; they cannot escape from the implications of their status as superiors in the line of command.
>
> On the other hand, if they leave it up to the individual to develop himself, they leave things pretty much to chance. We know from long experience that the individual needs the help of someone else, if for no other reason, so that he can "see himself as others see him."

As a result, top management has turned to special programs of executive development. But here there are major difficulties, too. In these programs we find two major phases of work—executive appraisal and executive training. Typically, the appraisal procedure is worked out by staff experts with top-management approval. The executive is appraised by a committee of his superiors with a personnel man acting as recorder. In subsequent discussions, the immediate superior works out a plan for his training. Little mention is made as to how the superior works *with* the executive on a continuing basis for his development.

The actual training may be handled in a variety of ways. The executive may be given rotation training experiences in various departments and sent on visits to other companies; he may be enrolled in special courses offered by various schools or in intensive training programs conducted by the company or its trade association. All of these methods pull the executive off his immediate job in order to train him presumably to do better on that job. This very circumstance raises some questions about their effectiveness—questions stemming directly from what is now common knowledge about human relations and human reactions to change:

1. *What about the threat of change to the executive?* Many of our current executive development programs are in a real sense a threat to the ego and security of the executive. One might say that he is now faced with what to him may be one of the greatest threats of all: the verdict that he himself must be changed. The implication, no matter how disguised, is that he has been appraised and found wanting in some degree; otherwise there would be no need for his being trained. Generally speaking, however, he has found that his own way of doing things and trying to improve himself has been successful; at least, he has started up the executive ladder. He has made his adjustments, good or bad, in his work situation; and his subordinates have adjusted to him and to each other.

   In view of this, can he be expected to behave much differently after he is trained and sent back to his old situation with its same pattern of traditions, problems, practices, and relationships? Have we given enough attention to the emotional impact of such off-the-job training which, in some measure at least, acts as a check on his being able to change?

2. *What about the executive's desire to change?* This question applies even to those executives who feel no great threat to their ego. Few successful executives view themselves as serious students of management. We find many an executive attending a special training program without real motivation. How is it possible for him to learn if he does not have a strong desire to learn?

3. *What about the executive's capacity for change?* Although he may have been eager for the experience, the training program may be beyond him. It may start at too high a level for him or attempt to carry him too far. He may not be able to find his way in the new experience, the strange terminology, and the unfamiliar concepts.

4. *Can the executive practice what he learns?* In his training programs he may find himself involved in an intellectual exercise without the necessary skills to put his new knowledge into practice. Skills which sounded good in the classroom may not work when he first tries them. The old situation is still there and may well be more powerful than he is; if so, his initial failures will soon cause him to return to his old ways.

There is no denying the contribution of many of the formal training programs, especially those which point to developing men for future positions of greater scope and responsibility; and it is encouraging to note how carefully some of the programs are being devised to meet as fully as possible some of the present limitations of off-the-job training.[3] The fact remains, however, that the kinds of programs

---

[3] See F. J. Roethlisberger, "Training Supervisors in Human Relations," and Kenneth R. Andrews, "Executive Training by the Case Method," *Harvard Business Review* (September, 1951), pp. 47 and 70.

which are mushrooming at such an astounding rate all over the nation usually leave much to be desired. As supplementary training they may be fine, but the primary task must be done on the job— that is, on the man's own regular job. Only in this way is it possible to cope effectively with the problems and obstacles described above.

The Way Out

The way out of the dilemma, it seems to me, is to put qualified staff men in a new role—that of catalytic agents, so to speak, for executive development on the job. In this new role they would be responsible for doing what neither line executives on the job nor staff specialists or instructors off the job can do by themselves: providing the necessary help for administrators who want to increase their capacities for specific positions of higher responsibility in the company.

I have referred to the men who will fill this new role as "staff" men. This classification is necessary, I believe, since they should not have operating responsibilities. At the same time, I want to emphasize that the new role will necessarily involve a departure from many commonly accepted ideas about the nature and function of staff activities. For many of these ideas are incompatible with the requirements of the job I have in mind. Because of them, moreover, the staff assistant for executive development will often have to operate— at the outset, at least—in the face of suspicion and hostility. Let us face up to that fact realistically.

Pitfalls of staff work

Anyone who spends any time with executives cannot help but sense a prejudice against staff people. Many executives are questioning—and for good reason—the intrinsic quality and the ultimate effectiveness of the wide variety of activities which now constitute staff work. Some staff people, too, are showing increasing concern about the end results of their various specialized activities. They are concerned whether their work penetrates deeply enough into management behavior and into the fiber of day-to-day functioning of an organization to be fully effective. If we were to catalogue the various questions which are being raised publicly and privately about the staff people, we would find them subject to these main criticisms:

1. *"Power seeking"*—Executives more and more are concerned about the power-seeking moves of staff people. These moves seldom take

the form of a direct or even a conscious bid for authority; they are usually more indirect and subtle. Ordinarily they are pointed at middle and lower management, with the staff people feeling that they must take over this or that in their particular areas of specialization so that they can do such and such "for top management."

The current emphasis by staff people on the need for top-management support is a symptom of this power seeking. Significantly, it is almost impossible to find any reference by staff people anywhere to their need to earn middle-management or first-line supervisory support. At the risk of overstating the case, one might say that staff people, once they get top-management support, turn their thinking to how they can make middle management "appreciate" their programs.

2. *"Experting"*—There is a feeling on the part of many executives that staff people, in their efforts to do things *to* and *for* management, are failing more and more to recognize that line executives themselves at every level, although not "experts" like the staff people, have much to contribute to staff suggestions or recommendations. Staff people are falling into the habit of approaching their work with statements such as these: "We decide that this program is needed," "We make the investigation," or "We make our recommendations to top management." Perhaps the best single indication of this experting is the emphasis on *programs* and other formal approaches to problems.

3. *"Overspecialized"*—The typical executive reacts negatively to the great variety of specialties in staff work by saying: "For every problem I have, I must use a different staff man; and unfortunately I can get from each staff man only his specialized slant on the problem. What I need is a staff man who can help me on the wide variety of problems I have in my department." Obviously, with the increasing complexity of business, we do need specialists; but if specialization is carried too far, it defeats its own purpose.

4. *"Narrow-minded"*—Stemming in part from their specialization and perhaps in part from the mechanical way in which they approach their jobs is the criticism that many staff people are narrow-minded, that they "don't consider all the angles." As an illustration take the two major trends in human relations. On the one hand, we find many experts emphasizing the overwhelming importance of the *individual*; on the other, we have different experts who feel it is the work *group* in any work situation which is all-important. But are not the individual and the group both important?

New role

How can the staff man avoid these pitfalls and act as an effective catalytic agent for executive development? In approaching this problem we will need to think not in terms of a program but of a way for the executive and the staff man, in light of the needs of the executive's organization, to work together for necessary improvements.

For executives this will mean going at the job the hard way. They will have assistance in starting on those problems which they think are important, but they cannot sit back while someone works out a recommended solution. For the staff man it will mean a more humble, subordinate, comprehensive approach calling for a greater variety of skills with less singleness of theme and effect. The line executive's authority is accepted carte blanche, and the onus on the staff man is to have the capacity and willingness to consult with executives on *their* problems, both in individual and in group counseling, and to help *them* arrive at *their* solutions.

In a very literal sense the staff man's function is that of adjunct to a top-management executive and his subordinates in their efforts to carry out their operating responsibilities. He expands, but does not supplant, the efforts of the head executive to assist his managers in self-development. Not being under the day-to-day operating pressures for immediate results, he can think in larger terms and for more distant results than the executives. He can spend the necessary time for a snails-pace approach. To him the *way* in which he works is of paramount importance. He has no authority, and wants none. As an agent for change, his only power comes from his skill in making full use of the participative process.

PRACTICAL APPROACH

As a practical matter, how can the staff man for executive development go at his job? Specifically, where does he start, how does he prepare himself, and what resistances must be overcome?

Planned opportunism

In keeping the decision-making function with the executives, our staff specialist works for only those improvements which the executives want to make. Let us call his approach "planned opportunism." It is planned because it is positive and purposeful; it is not a capricious catch-as-catch-can activity. It is opportunism because the end is indeterminate; our staff man does not follow the usual program approach of staff work, though programs do evolve out of the joint effort.

In a very real sense, the staff specialist starts with the executives' own perception of their work—the problems they think they have and the kinds of improvement they feel they can make. An executive's work problems are solved, not by adopting or adapting some standard format, but by self-evaluation. The specialist believes that if the problems and facts are critically analyzed, out of the thinking-through process will come sound, realistic solutions.

Problem areas

The staff man concerns himself with executive development primarily in six functional areas: (a) human relations, (b) organization structure, (c) work methods, (d) management practices, (e) personnel practices, and (f) union relations. Because each of these areas is so interwoven with the others and with other facets of a work situation, they should be regarded only as illustrative aspects of our specialist's interest in the *total situation*.

In order to develop his own understanding of the problems and of the particular work situation as a basis for individual or group counseling, our staff man makes his own survey. He gets lost in the organization to get the feel of it. From his questioning and listening come a myriad of facts, opinions, and conflicts, as well as personal perceptions which provide the basis for his insight and understanding about the organization and how it functions.

The survey is in no sense a cataloging of what every executive has to say, but rather what comes through as a group concensus after hours and hours of listening. What are the key problems? What is the situation in each of the six functional areas? The range of specific questions which might develop is shown in EXHIBIT I.

As the result of his survey, our staff man makes no report to anyone. Remember that his primary objective is to aid executives on the basis of their own evaluation of their work situation. Therefore, he does not become overly concerned with the particular things he happens to see as a way for improvement. With his training he can probably see *some* things more clearly and quickly, but—and this is important—he knows full well that he cannot possibly have such unusual insight as to grasp all the ramifications of the problems and the complexities of the personal interrelationships. He is convinced that it makes no difference how he sees things; what counts is how the executives see them.

Gaining acceptance

As we view it here, working out the situational approach in an organization usually means starting at the grass roots—working with a small group of executives in one of the organization units or subdepartments on the problems of that unit. Experience indicates that, at least in the early years, the staff man will usually go where crises have developed (although, significantly, once he gets his function established, the requests for his assistance will probably be in more

EXHIBIT I

Typical Questions in the Six Functional Areas

How sound are the human relations?

What are the people doing *to* each other?
What are the people doing *for* each other?
Do members of the group believe in the purpose of the organization?
Do they believe in the leadership?
Do they believe in each other?
Do they communicate and participate effectively?
Do they believe in the company?

How sound is the organization structure?

Does it work effectively?
How does the informal organization (the informal personal relationships and their use as the means for the functioning of the department) conform to the formal organization?
What kinds of informal subgroups or cliques have been formed?
What marked splits are there between various levels of management or between management and employees?
What is the social hierarchy and what are the status symbols?
Do people understand and accept the organization structure, lines of command, and delegation of authority and responsibility?
Do individuals have an opportunity to use their initiative to demonstrate their ability and to grow?

How effective is the management?

Is there any evidence of planning?
How effectively do the executives direct, delegate and coordinate?
Do they initiate effective action and work with others on a basis of mutuality?
Are they concerned about developing people?
Do people know where they stand as far as their superiors are concerned?

How efficient are the work methods?

Are the executives methods-conscious and economy-minded?
Are the procedures organized or disorganized?
Are there any written instructions ?

What is the quality of personnel practices?

How are individuals selected and promoted?
How are they evaluated and trained?
Do their pay rates correspond to the levels of work?
Are they kept informed about company matters?

Are the union-management relations sound?

What is the attitude toward the contract?
What are the attitudes toward the union representatives?
Are the union rules being followed in spirit as well as in word?
Are the rules understood?

general terms with less crisis implications). Actually, however, the nature of the original assignment is comparatively unimportant. It can be some specific problem of low productivity, low morale, union difficulties, a conflict of personalities, bad organization structure, or poor work procedures, or almost anything else.

These assignments are the staff man's opportunities to begin to practice his counseling role. *But he will be effective only to the extent that he can establish rapport*, winning his way with the executives on a very personal basis to the point where they will look upon him as a source of help. Reliance on lip service or a formal, distant kind of relationship with the line managers will result only in failure; he must get past a shadow-boxing relationship with them to frank and confidential discussions of their views and feelings. And top-management blessings for this kind of staff work is too weak a reed on which to lean.

The obstacles to his establishing rapport are of three kinds:

1. *Resistance to the staff man*—The resistances to our staff specialist as a person run the whole gamut of attitudes and reactions. Almost all of them stem in one way or another from the fact that he is an outsider and not part of the group with which the line executives usually associate in their day-to-day work. Nor is he all wrapped up in their operating problems.

   To make him more of an enigma, he probably does not "know" the operations. How can he know the work well enough to be of any help? Moreover, he is not well versed in the organizational chit-chat, the gossip, and the personal politics which form such a large part of the talk of the executives. Even his experiences are different from those which the executives so well like to recount.

   Finally, he appears to be more interested in listening and asking questions than in trying to get into the conversation with talk about himself. Executives wonder: What kind of a guy *is* this?

2. *Resistance to what the staff man stands for*—He may be likable as an individual and respected as a competent person, but does his appearance in the organizational unit signify that the executives' work and personal competence are being questioned by the management? Rather than view the specialist as a source of help, they may and probably will view him as a threat. What can he do to us? What is he after? Is he an efficiency expert? What ideas can he have for changing our setup or our jobs? Will he put us through a training program? What sort of tales will he carry back to headquarters? Little imagination is needed to see that fears and worries of this sort will magnify each other, especially in the case of executives who feel very insecure personally.

   Even for those executives who have a good measure of self-confidence the arrival of our man may not be a precisely happy experience. It is likely to mean thinking in new terms and along different channels. For the most part, these executives' work experience has been in terms of force, orders, action, and results. Patently, they have not indulged extensively in research (fact getting) and ideas (a long-view analysis of problems). Their organization decisions have usually been one-man decisions, made in terms of an immediate need rather than a complete analysis of the organization structure. Because of their action-oriented approach, over the years they have probably developed the habit of coming pretty quickly to solutions.

3. *Resistance to change*—Executives naturally resist leaving comfortable and familiar ways of doing things and stepping into the unknown. Because of the overwhelming evidence on how difficult and slow behavior changes are for most executives (and, for that matter, most people), the resistance to change itself becomes the significant focal point for our staff man's efforts.

Executive Counseling

We are now ready for the $64 question: How does the staff man overcome resistance to change and help executives to stretch their thinking about themselves, their jobs, and their company?

In a word, it is my belief that the answer lies in the techniques of "counseling." In spite of some of the popular prejudices against the word counseling, there is no satisfactory substitute for it. No other term or phrase so aptly designates the particular task of our staff specialist. But a word of warning is needed: counseling in the sense I shall use it should be in no wise confused with clinical psychology or psychotherapy.

Listening and question-asking skills are especially important in counseling for executive development. Advice, opinions, and preconceived solutions are poor tools for the job if the staff man intends to help the manager help himself. The staff man must submerge his own interests and listen. He *should* participate by asking questions— candid, intensive, and precise questions, because vague inquiries will only get vague answers. At the same time, he must avoid leading or suggestive questions, which are only another means of giving advice or manipulating.

The staff man must try to understand how the executive feels about his situation and his relationships, about his difficulties and possibilities; he must try to sense, without prying questions, what lies behind the words. And he must constantly evaluate as he listens, not in order to discover inaccuracies or to test the ideas, but in order to determine what questions to ask next to keep the process going and stimulate critical and constructive thinking.

Now let us examine some specific types of counseling: preparatory counseling, problem-solving counseling, sympathetic-ear counseling, and value counseling, in particular. These are not mutually exclusive, and all may be used during one interview.

Preparatory

Preparatory counseling comes first in time if not in importance. This is because our staff man must establish rapport and overcome the resistance to himself as a person, as well as to what he stands for and the idea of change itself.

Aside from the usual amenities and a few references to his way of working, our staff man can best start by asking questions about problems. (Later, when he has gained greater personal acceptance, he is very likely to find that the executive's first answers were ones which he thought the staff man wanted to hear or which seemed suitable at the stage of getting acquainted.) This will convey that he is not going to try to "train" the executive, run the show, or make decisions. He will not be too free with advice. He offers his knowledge and skills in terms clearly understandable to the executive as possible suggestions. In other words, the staff man's case for further counseling must be built up gradually in action terms of how he can be a source of help to the executive.

As to the next step, the staff man should move to create an interest in change. Here will come a real test of his skills. In the first place, there probably is little motivation among most executives for improving the functioning of the organization in spite of the numerous platitudes which they frequently use. They may feel that problems, like the poor, are "always with us," always part of their job (as in truth many problems are). They may believe that they have already worked out the best possible solutions to those problems which could be solved; and they have found ways for the most part to be reasonably comfortable with any remaining problems. Then, too, it must always be remembered that it is not unnatural for executives to feel—they virtually *have* to feel—that they are doing a good job, that they have done about all that can be done with their problems.

How can our staff man, in light of these feelings, work for change and at the same time not cast any reflections on the quality of the work which the executives are now doing?

First of all, he must be sure of his own attitudes toward the executives. If he does not have a healthy respect for them as individuals and for the job they are doing, as well as a modest view of his own powers, he becomes his own enemy. Even in those instances where he has been sent out from the front office because of dissatisfaction with the way things are going, he should not give too much recognition to the fact that the executives are under pressure to make improvements. The staff man must also have a high regard for the values and feelings of the executives; he must work to help them maintain their self-respect—yes, in some instances, to rebuild it.

Therefore, his whole approach to them should be couched not in terms of executive self-development or of management failures, but of problems to be solved. If the executives are not so emotionally blocked that they cannot admit even to themselves that there are problems, they will be willing to talk about the problems which stand in the way of their doing the kind of job they believe they should be doing. It is my experience that almost all executives want to do better; the trouble is that they have come to look upon certain problems as practical barriers to progress.

A discussion of problems which are important to the executives is the staff man's "foot-in-the-door." Like most people, executives are inclined to start with those problems which are obvious and for which they have no real feeling of personal responsibility. Oftentimes they have a pat solution for someone else to carry out. In any event, they will have to "give out" before they can "take in"; before they can really be expected to absorb new ideas or think differently, they must have a chance to give vent to their confusions, gripes, and feelings of frustration. The staff man will encourage this. He will try to get the air cleared before proceeding to the next step.

Problem solving

Once the executive has got to talking freely, the staff man can, with further questioning, help him to move from the superficial, easily discussed problems to the underlying ones.[4] It becomes a process of self-diagnosis, since, as he goes deeper, the executive often finds that the source of the difficulties lies at least indirectly in his own behavior or in his own failure to take action at an earlier date.

Problem analyzing is slow and unsystematic, covering much of the same ground over and over again, rehashing many of the same subjects, with new angles gradually coming to the fore. In one session great progress may seem apparent. Then, in the next, it is lost. The exercise of care in not pushing the executive too fast or too far is vital. Sometimes the executive wants to make a quick decision

[4] Douglas McGregor has set forth a comprehensive theory on the problem-solving counseling approach in "The Staff Function in Human Relations," *The Journal of Social Issues* (Summer, 1948), p. 5.

on something fairly superficial and to forget the rest of the problems; the staff man will have to stay with him and go on to discuss such matters as "conflict about technical aspects of projects," "confused relationships among subdepartments," and "too much red tape."

After the analysis is completed, the staff man can help the executive think through the means for getting the facts upon which to determine a solution. He can move from a questioning to a suggesting function, drawing upon his knowledge of the analytical tools of staff work in outlining possible ways for fact gathering. For example, such staff techniques as job descriptions, organization charting, process charting, and work distribution analysis have often proved helpful. The executive is encouraged to participate actively in the fact-gathering process; he decides whether or not the suggested tool is to be used and how much information to gather, and he judges the significance of the facts. He may assign a subordinate to work closely with the staff man in getting the facts or to be trained to do the job under his technical supervision.

Of course, the executive may refuse to use any tool of analysis. He may prefer to settle the matter in his office even though there may well appear to be a real need for facts. In one instance, for example, an executive decided against making a scientific job evaluation study as a basis for revising wage rates and "played it by ear" instead; he and the local union representative sat down together and worked out the rates by mutual judgment. But it was the executive's decision to make, and the staff man properly did not interfere.

Sympathetic ear

Let us turn now to a kind of counseling which has little or nothing to do with problem-solving per se, but is frequently helpful to our staff man. I shall call it "sympathetic ear" counseling; it means that the staff man acts primarily as a listening post. In the normal rough and tumble of competitive relationships executives often need someone to talk *to*. (There is a neat distinction between this and someone to talk *with*.) They expect nothing and want nothing except a chance to talk. Sometimes it enables them to get a better focus on things, to see that things are not as bad as they seem to be; they reduce their anxieties by talking out fears and frustrations. From these confidential sessions they come to realize that they are getting along satisfactorily, that they stand in well with their superiors, and that their jobs are not being threatened. They are ready to think critically and constructively about increasing their skills as administrators.

A sympathetic ear may serve other purposes, too. Frequently, an executive wants to tell someone of a decision he is about to make or an action he is about to take, but he is reluctant to discuss it with his fellow executives. He may want constructive criticism or just moral support. The staff man is in a position to meet his need. Here is a case in point:

> Soon after an executive was informed of his promotion to head a department, the staff man happened to drop into his office and found him weighing the pros and cons of continuing to carry some of his present important technical work along with his new job. He asked the staff man to explore the matter with him.
>
> During the course of the conversation the staff man raised questions such as these: "Do you think you can successfully carry on both jobs when your predecessor didn't feel that one man could handle both functions?" "With all the new things you say you must get acquainted with, do you think you can find time to do both jobs?" "If you continue the technical work which you say takes so much of your time now, do you think you will have time to supervise and develop your people and to keep in touch with your superiors?"
>
> As the result of thinking through the answers to these and other similar questions, the executive came to the conclusion that he could not do justice to both tasks and so assigned the technical work to one of his subordinates. To be sure, he might have reached the same conclusion without help from the staff man; the latter's reactions, however, gave him the benefit of a "backboard" for his ideas and enabled him to reach the decision more surely.

Value counseling

Although value counseling is inextricably interwoven in problem-solving counseling, it is of sufficient complexity and importance to warrant separate treatment.

At almost every turn our staff man will run into the question of executive values or attitudes, expressed or implied. Because it is these values which determine an executive's behavior (the way he views his job, his functions, his way of doing his work, the organization, his superiors, his subordinates, his relationships with them, their relationships with him, and so on), a staff man cannot ignore or pass over attitudes. This is especially true when he views his role as that of providing a means for self-development, for it is axiomatic that to secure a change in behavior, one must first secure a change in attitudes or values.

We have all heard about so many of the typical attitudes of executives that they seem by now to be clichés. It is easy to be facetious about them, but when one is faced with them in a counseling situation—and a staff man often is—they become important and difficult obstacles to executive development. This is especially true when they form such a major part of a manager's outlook that somehow one must try to influence these values if one hopes for self-development. The task is certainly no easier because so many of these values appear to center in the field of human relationships. Can there be more fixed notions in a more intangible area with less ground for factual or logical analysis? On the other hand, attitudes about human problems give excellent insight into a person; they indicate his own view of himself more clearly than anything else.

Let us take some of the expressed values as one finds them in counseling and see what they appear to imply:

> The most obvious and common is the typical set of attitudes toward workers, blaming them for not having the right attitude, for not working hard, and for not being willing to change. As part of this set of attitudes we find that workers are not as ambitious as people used to be, that they expect more with less effort, that they are not as smart, that they want to play and fool around and let the work take care of itself. There is nothing new in these misunderstandings and the resulting tensions. They appear to be an offshoot of the age-old feeling on the part of many adults that the rising generation of people is no good— at least, not so good as the adults.
>
> One often hears an executive say something to the effect that his subordinates cannot be trusted to make sound decisions or do not want to take responsibility. In many instances both of these statements may be partially true, but it is also likely to be true that, by holding to such rationalizations, the executive does not have to face up to his own inability to delegate decision making to others.
>
> An allied statement is that the manager has to know everything that is happening because a superior might ask about some matter. Is it because of the superior? Yes, in some cases it is; but there are more instances in which it turns out that the superior attempted time after time to get the man to put his talents to better use than trying to be a walking encyclopedia. Has the executive blocked the effective functioning of his department because he cannot feel personally secure unless he has everything at his fingertips?

Whatever may be the attitudes of the executive, experience would indicate that they stem not only from the individual's emotional structure but also from attitudes of other executives in the organization. The values have become almost company policy or company thinking, a way of looking at things arrived at over the years which every executive learns as he comes up the organization ladder. One cannot be too hopeful about achieving great change, if change is needed, but a small shift in attitude or a slightly different focus on values often makes an important difference in administration. So our staff man continues to attempt value counseling even though it is nebulous and the direct results intangible. The fact remains that at times he does experience some success, as witness this case:

In one operation there had been for years an inspection type of supervision for the various units of the department. These units were geographically separated, and over each unit there was a first-line supervisor. The supervision from the head office consisted of a small group of inspectors who visited the units unannounced and made their inspections. The work of these units had degenerated to an unsatisfactory state, and there was a great deal of friction between the head office and the units. The inspectors had earned for themselves a particularly unpleasant reputation, both in the units and at the home office.

The executive in charge of the head office was concerned about the poor quality of the work in these units and was blaming the people in the units for their attitudes and also the inspectors for not getting results—a traditional attitude toward a traditional organization plan. Starting with these expressed attitudes, the staff man was able to get the executive to begin thinking about other reasons why the units might be in such poor shape. Gradually, as other problems and other reasons were discussed, the executive came to see that he did not have a good organization plan. He decided to make his inspectors full-fledged supervisors and assigned to each of them a small group of work units. The supervisors were to be totally and completely responsible for the successful functioning of these units and were to *supervise*, not inspect.

After some group sessions in which the staff man helped them to think through their new responsibilities, the supervisors decided how they would do their new job. Although it is safe to assume that they were not able to face about completely after years of traditional inspecting, subsequent checks into the situation indicated that relationships improved and that the units were doing a better job. Moreover, the head executive appeared to have undergone a considerable change in his own supervisory attitudes, viewing himself more as a developer of his supervisors than as a super-inspector.

Perhaps this case points up two morals. The first one is that a crisis can generate enough concern to bring about change. From this moral we might take the second: the more an executive becomes concerned about the quality of his work and wants to do a better job, and the more he becomes aware of himself, looks at himself critically, becomes concerned about his relationships with others, and wants to be accepted by others, the greater are his chances of self-development.

These types of counseling I have been discussing are all, of course, varieties of individual counseling, and there are others in the same category that could be considered. For example, the staff man is in a position to counsel executives personally if opportunities to do so arise—at luncheon or dinner, for instance, when talk turns to hobbies, social life, vacations, and other matters that have no *immediate* bearing on the work situation. What influence such discussions have would depend on a variety of factors, and the decision whether or not to encourage them should be made in the light of individual circumstances. By contrast, the types of counseling so far discussed have all been tested and proved, and I would recommend them without hesitation to any management employing a staff man for executive development.

GROUP CONFERENCES

There is much controversy about the value of conferences in business organizations. But, no matter how one may feel about conferences generally, it must be admitted that they are a necessary part of executive life. While the actions of one man are as a rule comparatively unimportant, the actions of a group are quite significant. This is especially true of industry today, where the various aspects of a business have become so specialized and complex that integration of effort is of the greatest importance.

In any event, I want to go on to consider a very special kind of conference—a problem-solving conference of departmental managers with the staff man acting as group counselor. Such a conference is the final phase of the work of the staff man for executive development; it is the end toward which he has been working. In one sense, individual counseling might be viewed as the means of getting successful management conferences started.

Discussion leader pro tem

As group counselor, the staff man's first function is to act for a time as the discussion leader. Is this prospect inimical to the whole counseling idea as we have looked at it here? From my own experience in this staff role, I should like to make three points in defense of the staff man's acting as the discussion leader:

1. I view the discussion leader's function as a strictly temporary function. Ideally, and for the long practical pull, the department head should be the discussion leader. But in comparatively few instances within my experience have we been able to *start* the conference process successfully with the department head acting as the discussion leader; in those few instances, the executive had a rare combination of attributes which enabled him to act as a good discussion leader at the outset as well as later.
2. Because of the importance in these conferences of providing the opportunity for management self-development, a great deal of em-

phasis must necessarily be placed on the group process per se. Hence, the dominating kind of discussion leadership so typical of many business conferences is not sought after in these conferences. (Of course, the senior executive may not *try* to dominate, but because of his status the other executives may act so as virtually to force him to dominate.) Rather, every possible attempt is made to have the group of managers become aware of the conference leadership functions as a joint responsibility of everyone sitting in the room.

3. The staff man has, by virtues of his position, unique advantages which line executives do not have. I am thinking particularly of the need for the discussion leader to help the members become aware of themselves as individuals and as a group. What the staff man—and only a staff man—can do is to stimulate a free, accepting attitude in the conference by willingly becoming a passive target for hostile and aggressive feelings. In this kind of conference where everyone's work and working relationships are involved and where the usual major personality conflicts of the department and the vested interests exist among the members of the group, he should in fact expect to receive the aggressions which must be released against somebody before there can be much hope of achieving any effective group consciousness.

With hostile feelings reduced, an individual can open his mind to accept new concepts—in short, to learn. In such an atmosphere, our staff man can work toward, but never expect to reach, the point where the members mutually give and accept honest and sincere support and express opinions without fear of ridicule.

Group process

Although the objectives and approach of our specialist in the conferences are similar to the individual counseling situation, there are differences of both degree and kind. The opportunity for achieving improvements is greater. There seems to be more impetus to change in the group process itself; even the laggards are stirred because of an unconscious appreciation that it is not an individual but everyone in the group who is going through a process of self-development.

Typically, the small conference groups, consisting of five to fifteen executives, constitute the three or four levels of management for a particular department. Because the actions of an executive are so much the result of the actions of people above and below him, as well as those of his associates, the fact that all the levels of the unit's management simultaneously are involved provides greater stimulation to reciprocal changes in the people representing the various levels.

The conferences provide for group learning-in-action—not the learning and remembering of principles, a list of rules, or a set of theories, but the sensing and thinking through of relationships and problems in order to come to an action decision. Nowhere is this more true than in human relations. In the individual counseling situation there can be no observation and little practice of human relations skills; in the group conference experience, by contrast, executives learn and can practice how to work together and achieve a greater integration of effort. Thus they become, in fact, conscious of the group process.

In working with a group of managers, our specialist views his approach as similar to that of counseling with an individual executive. He works in three directions:

1. *As a discussion leader* he seeks to stimulate a true learning experience. In no sense does he view himself as a clever manipulator of the group to get it to achieve his ends or his solutions. Nor is it a matter of his trying to get the group to accept any of his ideas as the result of his conducting a stimulating discussion. Yet, at the other extreme, he does not view the conference process as one of a rambling, disorganized discourse, with the group tackling any problem more or less by itself.

    Between the extremes of manipulation and of disorder, our staff man tries to have every suggestion fully considered, thus assuring more mature analysis of the problem and more opportunity for learning. He sets the pace for the time when, with the conference well under way, the department head takes over as permanent discussion leader. (After that the specialist may continue to sit in on the conferences, or he may come into the conferences infrequently, when some special problem comes up.)

2. *As a group developer* our staff man consciously tries to encourage the kind of group experience which will enable the members individually to gain insight into effective group functioning and into their behavior as group members. Right from the start, then, he attempts to arouse this feeling of group consciousness. At the first few meetings he may have to suggest points and raise questions about them to get the discussion going, but later the group will be able to discuss freely its own evaluation of its functioning and eventually develop accurate skills of evaluation.

    The implications for the individual members are quite obvious. They naturally start to question themselves privately about their own behavior. The staff man can expect that, on more than one occasion during a series of conferences with the same group, his views about individual functioning will be privately sought. Then he will have the opportunity for individual counseling again.

3. *As a group consultant* our conference leader directly introduces his knowledge about such things as sound human relations, good organization structure, efficient work methods, good management practices, effective personnel practices, and harmonious union-managment relations. He resists any desire to lecture at great length on the theoretical aspects or to outline a solution. As a means of holding himself in check, he can do one of several things: (a) He can report on what other companies or management groups have done

when faced with a similar problem. (b) He can outline the pertinent observations or research of others, and he can suggest a hypothetical solution which the group may reject or adapt as it chooses. (c) He can supply the steps through which the group may go in problem solving in order to arrive at a solution in an orderly, objective, and analytical manner.

Conference procedure

Group counseling leads to a kind of conference which is unlike the conferences or committee meetings that many members of the group will have experienced before. A discussion of the specific procedures the staff man might use ought, therefore, to be especially appropriate.

Getting Acquainted. The working-rules aspect of the conference is not passed over lightly (as in some types of conference). At the very beginning of the first meeting our staff man, as pro-tem conference leader, starts the participative process. As quickly as possible he gets the members' ideas (to the extent that there is any choice) about the time of the conferences, the length of the conference periods, and the place of the meetings.

The department head then usually makes a few introductory remarks to inform the group that the procedure has his blessing and that decisions reached by the group will be either advisory to him or sent to his supervisors as his recommendations. These remarks tell the group that its work is not entirely for fun. The enthusiastic reaction of a group when it hears the boss say in essence that he wants and will take seriously the ideas that emerge is a major factor in stimulating change.

Throughout the getting-acquainted process, our pro-tem conference leader is assisting the management group in developing further working rules: purposes, limitations, how to operate, how to work together, how to get group action, and procedures for checking regularly on group effectiveness.

As in individual counseling, our staff man must work constantly with opinions, prejudices, and biases which constitute barriers to sound objective thinking and decision making. In his listening and questioning, he constantly tries to get the individual or the group into a self-analysis of the soundness of these attitudes. In this process he will encounter some of the greatest frustrations of his work. For example:

In one organizational unit, the executives felt they were under too much pressure. In thinking through their routine and detailed activities in terms of an ideal executive position, they decided to delegate their clerical duties and thereby improve their working arrangements. By turning over much of their routine work to clerks, they would then be able to spend much of their time in developing their subordinates and handling major technical problems. But although the executives said, "Yes, we want to delegate detail," it became very apparent, as the staff man tried to assist them in reworking their duties, that one of the most comfortable aspects of their job was the routine detail. The net result was that they changed somewhat but could not achieve a true executive role.

Setting Up Problems. In the problem-solving work of these conferences, listing all problems on the blackboard is perhaps the best way of getting started. This census may include anywhere from 40 to 100 items and usually takes at least 6 hours of conference time. Although there is no effort to get group agreement on each problem, there is an attempt to get the sense of the group regarding how the problem should be stated and to obtain specific illustrations of the problem. Listing problems has several advantages. It offers another means for members of the group to get things off their chests, releasing their frustrations and opening their minds, and it gets them thinking and participating along constructive lines.

Bringing together in one listing all the problems, big and little, which the managers can think of oftentimes results in a wide array of detailed and peripheral items which constitute the superficial problems of the organization. Usually no one says right out, "Yes, we have an organizational problem." In all likelihood it will be implied by such statements as: "Stenographers shouldn't be in a pool." "We have to spend too much time getting approvals." "There are too many bosses." "I really don't know what my job is." "I don't know how much authority I have over my employees."

So, in order to get at the underlying problems and combine related problems, the list is next classified into major areas. This may be done by the staff man for the group's final approval, or by the group itself. EXHIBIT II indicates how one group listed and classified some of the problems it wanted to discuss.

After the problems have been classified, the group selects the first category on which it wishes to work. From now on there is little question about its interest in change, for the group is generally completely involved and wants to get at the problems. Often the staff man finds that he has to try to slow things down so that there is careful consideration and thinking through. It is surprising how

EXHIBIT 11

EXAMPLE OF CONFERENCE AGENDA

(PARTIAL LIST)

Organization

No clear-cut assignments and responsibility
Confusion as to clerical assignments
Too many bosses
Stenographic pool
Overload of work

Management

Managers not participating in discussions involving their work
Instructions not always clear

Work Methods

Can't get files quickly
Files too frequently lost
Too many duplicate records

Human Relations

"Square pegs in round holes"
Lack of incentive and initative
Afraid or too lazy to accept promotions
Dissatisfaction of employees

Personnel Practices

Insufficient screening in hiring and promoting
Conglomeration of pay rates
No orderly promotions
No planned training
Supervising clerks not capable of training

Union Relations

Friction with union representatives
Seniority rules hampering promotion

often reviewing problems under one classification brings the group to realize what the major problem is. The members seem to sense that they have listed only the superficial aspects.

In working for critical objectivity in problem solving, the staff man can try several things. One procedure which has been used with success is that of getting a group to think about the problems "theoretically"—to try to forget for the moment the people involved, union rules, company rules, and the traditional ways of doing things. Another way of helping the group to think more objectively is to provide the steps through which the group will go in the analysis of a problem.

Fact Gathering and Analyzing. The fact-gathering and analyzing process is, in the main, quite similar to the approach discussed earlier in connection with individual counseling. At times special studies have to be made and a working committee of the group appointed to get the facts. My own experience indicates that most of the time the group is in possession of the facts or can get them without too much trouble. But, because of guesses and opinions, facts must be evaluated if there is to be clear and logical thinking, and the group usually spends a good deal of time on the analysis of facts in order to develop a basis for working out a solution.

In working out a solution to a problem that has been defined and analyzed, the effect on others outside the group is likely to be reviewed in some detail; also, as part of the plan of execution, the approach to other people is usually worked out. Practice sessions and role playing are used, when appropriate, as a means of thinking through the problem of how to carry out the solution decided on.

Because change in attitude and behavior is a slow process, one can never be sure how much the individuals themselves will change in spite of the drastic alterations they support in such things as organization structure, work methods, or union relations. One can be reasonably sure, however, that the total situation will improve and that, generally speaking, both worker and executive morale will rise. One may expect, too, that the executives will become more conscious of their relationships with their subordinates, associates, and superiors and, as a result, make at least some changes for the better.

What about the quality of group decisions? In coming to its best judgment, the group will undoubtedly fall short of the ideas of its most brilliant thinker. But is this not inevitable if the *group* is to act? Can it carry out anything that it is incapable of thinking through as a group? Unless the executives of a company are better able to act as a *team*, the group counseling has failed in its purpose.

Conclusion

The situational approach described in this article is based on the thesis that most executives have a sincere desire to develop themselves and to improve the functioning of their organizations. But executives, like most people, resent being pushed, being "experted," or being manipulated, because they feel responsible for their own self-development and, more importantly, for the success of their organizations. They and they alone must make the decisions about their organizations. If they cannot make these decisions within the broad framework of company policy and directives, they cannot feel responsible for the results of their organizations. They must have freedom in which to operate, and this applies equally to the first-line supervisor and to the top executive.

The challenge to staff people, therefore, is not one of how many rules they can write or programs they can establish, but of how they can sincerely and humbly unite their efforts with those of the executives. To the extent they can succeed, I believe that there will be less concern about the dollar justification for staff work. It seems to me that just as the counseling approach, as outlined here, is judged by executives on a highly intangible basis, so too are the staff programs, in spite of the claims of dollar savings on the part of staff people. In the final analysis, staff work is being evaluated on the basis of how executives personally react.

One must conclude that, for all the rationale, it is how the executives feel about the staff people as individuals, about the ways in which the staff people work with them, and about the intrinsic purposes of the staff work that really counts. Staff people have tried to get away from feelings, and it just cannot be done. So let us face up to the reality of feelings—let us work with them.

Our greatest obstacle to working creatively with others on a give-and-take basis, whether we are line executives or staff experts, is ourselves. Once we can personally feel secure in participating freely and fully with others within the work situation itself—with line people if we are staff men, or with staff people and subordinates if we are line men—many tasks of management will become far easier. The staff counseling role as outlined in this article is designed to meet that need.

79. HOW MANAGERS
ARE MADE [1]

Herbert Harris [2]

Management development is self-development.

That's the primary finding in the General Electric Company's three-year research study into the factors that make for executive proficiency.

The study also demonstrated that you can't count on a man to get ahead just because he has talent, that experience alone doesn't insure capability on the job, that management is a distinct skill, and that the practice of management is far ahead of its translation into rules and procedures.

General Electric, to meet its own special requirements, used the study to work out perhaps the most elaborate management development project of any in U. S. industry. The company's concern over management development reflects today's upsurge of interest in programs designed:

> To assist the executive to function more effectively in his present position.
> To insure competent replacements for posts vacated by promotion, resignation, discharge, retirement, disability or death and thus strengthen the continuity of an enterprise.
> To correct the narrowness of outlook that derives from over-specialization by cultivating a broader background.

The study and the project provide many pointers for other businesses in the estimate of Harold D. Smiddy, GE vice president for management consultation services, and a distinguished authority on the nature and nurture of the modern executive.

"No company, no industry," says Mr. Smiddy, "can afford to let managers just happen."

General Electric view of management development is about midway between those who see in it a panacea for all problems and those

[1] From the *Nation's Business* (March, 1956), pp. 90-95. Reprinted by permission of the *Nation's Business*.
[2] Herbert Harris, Director, Plans and Research; Gaynor, Colman, Prentis & Varley, Inc., 1957.

who prefer to drift along on the assumption that, somehow, good men will appear in the right slots, when and if needed, ready to take over at an instant's notice.

GE expects no miracles, but is going about the task of executive development in a realistic, purposeful fashion. The company's attitude is in many respects similar to that behind the excellent programs in this field conducted by enterprises as diverse as Standard Oil (N.J.), United Parcel Service, Detroit Edison, Sears Roebuck, Johnson & Johnson, Metropolitan Life, Monsanto, General Motors and other members of the vanguard in the management development movement. The GE pattern differs from most mainly in scope.

For the purposes of the study, GE's own veterans in organization, employee relations and related areas were backed up by a small corps of outside management consultants, psychologists, professors of business administration. They sifted a vast library of books, monographs, records, pamphlets in English, German, French and the Scandinavian. They also interviewed executive personnel in 50 major firms, together with specialists in the American Management Association, the National Industrial Conference Board, the Society for the Advancement of Management and in universities.

Some 300 GE managers, cooperating with the study task force, discussed and argued such points as whether or not it is possible to inculcate management proficiency in the way that the senior surgeon trains an interne.

Detailed experience records of 2,000 GE executives were combed for clues on the elements which comprise that sixth sense, the intuitive grasp which enables the top-flight manager to weigh the known factors and come up with the correct decisions.

The distillation of these findings ("the yield was relatively low at times for the tonnage of data handled," says Mr. Smiddy) served as the working hypothesis out of which GE has shaped its philosophy and approach for management development, increasingly referred to as "MD."

"First of all," says Mr. Smiddy, "We can't engraft talent and ambition on to the personality of someone who hasn't got them. But we can create a favorable climate and give guidance to the man of ability who is his own self-starter.

"In the second place the process of natural selection—the idea that the good man invariably realizes his potentialities and rises to the top or toward it—just doesn't pan out. In our case, it has produced too few managers too late.

"Moreover, we think that the practice of management is ahead of its codification. We are continuing research into method and motivation for a ten or even 20 year pull. Meantime, the responsibility for developing men using the knowledge already at hand, is written into the job assignment of every GE manager.

"Perhaps the most provocative—and important—idea on which we're proceeding is that managing should be regarded as a distinct type of work, with its own disciplines, its own criteria for achievement; something which is both learnable and teachable."

Mr. Smiddy is convinced that experience alone can no longer be counted on to provide appropriate management skills, in sufficient time; that while managing is no longer an art, it is not likely to become an exact science, either; that it is, however, acquiring the characteristics of a profession, that is, a systematic body of knowledge and ethics; that management laws and principles can be, to an increasing extent, discovered, verified, imparted and applied.

It was no accident that GE's high priority stress on management development coincided with the company's vast venture in decentralization during the past five years. It was originated and put into effect by President Ralph J. Cordiner in the belief the future success of GE depended largely upon diffusing its sources of decision making as widely as possible and thus attaining for each GE component the flexibility and humanness of the smaller operation, the kind that "a man can get his arms around."

The aim is to transform every department head, for example, into a highly independent manager. Within the framework of corporate policy, he has a latitude of judgment that would have been regarded as heresy even a decade ago. The same principle applies to his immediate subordinates and so on down the line to supervisor and foreman. It applies also to the people whom the company calls individual contributors—scientists, engineers, accountants and many others.

At every level the well-rounded GE manager is supposed to have the self-confidence and courage to stick his neck out—as did Dr. W. R. G. Baker, chief of electronics, about a year ago. He was sure that 14-inch TV receivers to retail as portable sets at $99.95 could have a huge sale. But market research surveys said this was impossible. He disregarded them, played his own hunch, made his portables and sold 200,000 of them in the first six months, at a decent profit.

GE is determined to supply itself with enough managers of this kind to meet its goal of $5,000,000,000 to $6,000,000,000 a year sales volume in 1963 (as against $3,200,000,000 in 1955) and otherwise to continue its advance for generations thereafter. During the 65 years of its history, it has tried out every form of training for its administrators, from job rotation to having them attend graduate schools of business. But the GE study showed that these and other prevailing methods would not produce the quantity and quality of competence required by the decentralization process, notably in the light of GE's expansion plans. Not customers, not products, not plants, not money, but managers may be the limit of GE's growth," Mr. Cordiner has declared.

Hence GE added two extras to its management development. It fashioned professional business management seminars to be held inside every GE department. And it established a Management Research and Development Institute as the first staff college ever created by a company for the higher education of its own executives.

Everything in the curriculum centers around GE's four basic criteria for the manager who develops himself in the process of developing others:

1. He should be a balanced "generalist" rather than only a functional "specialist." He should be able to plan, organize, integrate, and to measure as his way of getting results mainly through the work of others, and to do all this in terms of department and company objectives as against any excursions for the sake of his own ego enhancement.
2. He should serve the concept of the best balance of interest among customers, employees, shareowners, vendors, dealers, government and community.
3. He should lead by persuasion rather than command, by example of integrity and largeness of view, earning the respect of associates by encouraging participation in contrast to the order-flinging martinet who invokes table pounding to mask immaturity, both administrative and emotional.
4. He should recognize human limitations as well as potentialities for growth; that while everyone has an improvement stretch, it remains impossible to turn a mediocrity into a first-rate executive.

Late last year, the pilot sessions in professional business management were begun at the headquarters of GE's Industrial Power Components Division at Plainville, Conn.

Sixteen members of top and middle management attended three-hour sessions one evening a week for five months. Under the guidance of group leaders, they turned their attention to such problems as:

"In the process of redesigning a new switch, a supplier has been especially helpful and cooperative in working out a part we need. We have been buying that part from him for a year. Everything is satisfactory. But then another supplier offers us the same part at two thirds the price. Does our obligation to the first supplier go beyond placing the facts before him and urging him to lower his costs to meet competition? Or do we have an implied moral commitment to him that should take precedence over the price differential?"

Such questions are threshed out against the background of GE's philosophy of management development pivotal to GE's test-run seminars at Plainville which elicited reactions typified by the comments of four key participants.

"At first," says Allan A. Watson, manager for Assemblies and Component Sales, "some of us thought the course was going to be stratosphere stuff. Others were afraid of too much inbreeding, a rehash at night of what we'd been dealing with all day. The sessions avoided both excesses pretty well. On some points we're not in agreement with the philosophy, the instructors, or each other. I'm not convinced of just how neatly you can separate policy from operations. Sure, you can do it on a chart. You can have lots of pretty boxes— in color—showing who does what and when. But even a quarterback has to back up his line on defense and make a tackle once in a while, or he isn't running his team right.

"I don't believe," he continues, "in the kind of sales managing that means grabbing your hat and hurrying off to wet-nurse the boys in the field every time one of them falls on his face. But we took up the case of a salesman who calls in and says that he has almost got the order. But he can't clinch it. He has tried everything he knows. Some in the class argued that the way to develop him is to let him fight it out alone—and if he misses, okay. But he's asking for help. And while you don't make the pitch for him, you're supposed to manage from authority of knowledge. That means you should pass along to him everything you can. There has to be a happy medium between acting as teacher for your men and the tendency to leave too much distance, too big a gap, between strategy and tactics in marketing."

William C. Wichman, GE vice president and General Manager of the Industrial Components Division, had this to say:

> "Certainly some of us went into these courses with misgivings. There was a show-me attitude. We were as a group, you might say, receptive, but not enthusiastic.
>
> "You must remember," he declares, "that the whole thing was exploratory. Adult education in and for management is still in its infancy. The discussions highlighted the need to give as much thought, every day, to planning management development as to planning production, or purchasing."

To Herschner Cross, General Manager, Distribution Assemblies Department, a special merit of the seminars was that "we had a relaxed atmosphere for rubbing minds together, and for jogging each other's set views. We got to see more sharply the need for even more integrated effort to achieve team goals—to define each operation more precisely in terms of the way it fits in with others.

"Especially useful," he remarks, "is the emphasis upon human assets—the organization of free human beings, with the skills in their hands and the ideas in their heads, the social capital they represent, as being quite as important as plant, or patents, or other property assets.

"Today's whole trend toward management development shows that the day of the autocratic boss is over. Modern business has no place for him.

"Managers are going to be judged more and more by their ability to develop their people, by relating the individual's capacity to his function while keeping in mind the margin for improvement that everyone has. The same foreman, for example, who can easily supervise 50 women in a winding assembly may be overtaxed when it comes to supervising 12 tool setters. But as often as not he could be trained to handle the more difficult chore."

For Lawrence E. Walkely, General Manager, Trumbull Components Department, the best thing about the seminars was "what came out of the spontaneous give and take in restressing the connection between management development and your charter of business, its distinguishing characteristics, as well as what you have as your objective and the steps for reaching them. We intend, for example, to double our sales in the next ten years. We therefore need to do more to standardize parts. We have to intensify research. We have to get a clearer picture of our end-use customers. We need more projections of building construction—perhaps more warehousing— and a thousand other things to enable us to get a fix on the target and have every section make a detailed breakdown of its contribution.

"Utopia," he declares, "would be when you could just set your sights and have the kind of organization that could pick up from there. Since it can never quite happen, our basic problem is developing people at every level to match a developing business. Our manning tables, our replacement charts are put together as carefully and revised as often as our re-tooling estimates.

"One good way of readying your human resources is direct personal coaching. We don't select any crown princes here. But, when a man has proven that he can assume a larger responsibility, we put him to a series of step-up tests, where he has to rely more and more on his own judgment.

"He might handle some minor promotion problems, say, or purchase some materials, or contact a wholesaler, or even check back over a recommendation for a new plant site. We don't look over his shoulder. And if he does well, after a time, he has to take some real risks. So do we.

"You can keep getting your feet wet around the edges of real managing just so long. Then you have to take the plunge."

Central to GE management development is a rigorous performance appraisal system. Every subordinate is regularly assessed by his superior in relation to the current work assignment, the requirements for which are spelled out in a position guide, more specific and detailed than the usual job description. This position guide shows precisely the factors for which the employee is accountable, and to whom, and when. He is then rated on a sliding scale (outstanding, superior, satisfactory, not yet satisfactory, unsatisfactory) for everything from technical proficiency to emotional stability under pressure.

The performance appraisal technique, originally designed to determine salary brackets and compensation, has been extended to detect unsuspected talent and particularly to lay the foundations for a self-development plan worked out jointly between the subordinate and his manager.

The appraisal report of a salesman, for example, may show that he has natural gifts for customer contact and for speaking before small groups, but that he is inadequate in pricing equipment for the more complicated construction project. He and his manager frankly discuss ways to remedy this. It may be a matter of boning up on some manuals, or brushing up on his mathematics by taking a correspondence course.

At the same time, since the purpose of any development plan is to build the individual's strengths while strengthening points of weakness, he may be invited to demonstrate at a sales training class various customer approaches he has found valuable. The psychological dividend here would be that he is simultaneously engaged in a plus activity where he has command of the situation, and a minus activity where he still has to acquire that quality. Yet both activities can lead to improvement.

"All appraisal work, when taken seriously, is difficult," observes Stanley Fell, Training and Education specialist at Plainville, "the human ego being what it is. We try to be on our guard against distortions in evaluating what a man does and can do. He may have struck out on something on the very day his boss is spending two hours in rating him. The temptation is to grade him down. But we have to keep reminding ourselves that we must look at his performance, as a whole, month by month. He may have been batting .300 for the season."

As site for its Management Research and Development Institute GE purchased the 55 acre Crotonville (N. Y.) estate of the late Harry Arthur Hopf, pioneer management consultant, along with his famous collection of management literature. On the campus hill which commands a magnificent view of the surrounding countryside and the Hudson River valley, GE put up two modern functional brick buildings, the one residential, complete with air-conditioned dormitories, lounges, dining hall, and the other educational, with lecture rooms modeled after the surgical theater, class and conference rooms, and offices for the administrative and teaching staff. (The old Hopf home is used as recreation center.)

The Institute's Advanced Management Course is attended by a total of 80 executives for 13 consecutive weeks.

They are recruited from the three levels immediately below that of the President's office; vice presidents, general managers, functional heads of departments, sections and services. (It will take five years to present the course to all GE managers in these classifications.)

The management developings here are guided by Marc A. deSerranti, chief of GE's company-wide manager development consulting service. Also reporting to him are such field consultants as Frank Oglee, who worked as adviser with Messrs. Wichman, Walkely, Cross and their associates in setting up the pioneering seminars at Plainville.

Five classes of 16 men each devote six mornings a week, under the direction of an Institute instructor, to such topics as to whether the Superior Separator Company should have launched its high lift loaders in the corn belt in the way and at the time it did, or whether the merchandise control methods of F. W. Woolworth should be applied to manufacturing stocks, or to other top management problems, either from the casebooks of Harvard's Graduate School of Business Administration, or from GE's experience.

Or they may focus on the pitfalls that will beset a firm that seeks to copy blindly the management development forms and procedures of another despite the fact that management development has to be tailored to a company's individual needs perhaps more meticulously than anything else it does. This has particular relevance for GE managers. Although management development is company-wide, it is no cut and dried doctrine.

It has to be regarded rather as a philosophy, as a source of principles and pointers that can be adapted to the particular requirements of each GE department and plant which differ from each other as widely as a small metal-working establishment differs from a large steel mill.

Afternoons, the members of the separate classes gather in plenary session while one man summarizes for the group the outcome of the morning's parley. Sometimes the meeting is thrown open for general discussion from the floor.

Off to one side of the campus, in the small white house that Dr. Hopf built as his study, is the research operation of the Institute. It is presided over by Mr. Edward D. Kemble, an extremely practical man with theory as preoccupation. His assignment is to look ahead toward 1965 and beyond in shedding light on "the role of the large corporation in a free society" and on similarly momentous issues.

To help him Mr. Kemble has a four-man crew: a sociologist to explore the nature of work and why people do it well or badly; a mathematical scientist to determine the effects on managing of probable rates of changes in technology; an economist to inquire into the large corporation as pacesetter in capital outlays, products, wages; a political scientist to examine it both from the standpoint of its internal administration and its relations with the public, including government, local, state, federal.

The research unit will not have even first tentative results ready for two years or more. But GE believes that research is asking some of the right questions about the proper role of business in fostering an environment where free men can flourish, and not just as managers at GE.

BIBLIOGRAPHY, CHAPTER XXII

ALLEN, LOUIS A. "What Makes for Successful Executive Development?" *Management Record* (June, 1954), 218-220, 246-249.

ANDREWS, KENNETH R. "Executive Training by the Case Method," *Harvard Business Review* (September, 1951), 58-70.

BALTZELL, E. D. "Bell Telephone's Experiment in Education," *Harpers Magazine* (March, 1955), 73-77.

BENNETT, WILLARD E. "Master Plan for Management Development," *Harvard Business Review*, Vol. 34, No. 3 (1956), 71-84.

BROWN, ALVIN. "The Case (or Bootstrap) Method," *Advanced Management* (July, 1956), 11-13.

BUCKLEY, JOHN L. "Seventeen Years of Multiple Management," *Management Review* (April, 1950), 185-186.

HOUSTON, GEORGE C. *Manager Development*. Homewood, Illinois: Richard D. Irwin, Inc., 1961.

JANNEY, J. ELLIOT. "Company Presidents Look at Their Successors," *Harvard Business Review*, Vol. 32, No. 5 (1954), 45-53.

JENNINGS, EUGENE E. "Developing Leadership Status Among Supervisors," *Personnel Journal*, Vol. 33 (1955), 406-409.

MACCULLOUGH, ALLISON V. "Critical Views of Advanced Management Programs," *Advanced Management* (January, 1957), 26-29.

MACHAVER, WILLIAM V., and WILLARD ERICKSON. "A New Approach to Executive Appraisal," *Personnel* (July-August, 1958), 8-14.

MAHLER, WALTER R. "Evaluation of Management Development Programs," *Personnel*, Vol. 30, No. 2 (1953), 116-122.

MARSHALL, DONALD L. "The 'Incident Process' of Supervisory Training," *Personnel* (September, 1954), 134-140.

O'DONNELL, WALTER G. "Role-Playing as a Practical Training Technique," *Personnel* (November, 1952), 275-289.

ROWLAND, VIRGIL K. "Evaluating an Executive Development Method," *Organization Planning and Management Development*, Personnel Series No. 141. New York: American Management Association, Inc., 1951, 23-25.

SURFACE, JAMES R. "Resistance to Training," *Harvard Business Review*, Vol. 32, No. 2 (1954), 73-78.

"Training Understudies," Cleveland Electric Illuminating Company. *Personnel* (March, 1952), 407-415.

WORTHY, JAMES C. "Training Understudies," *Personnel*, Vol. 28, No. 5 (1951), 407-415.

AUTHOR INDEX

A

Alexis, Marcus, 213
Allen, Louis A., 715, 780
Anthony, Edward L., 521
Argyris, Chris, 451, 459, 540

B

Bauer, Raymond A., 91
Berwitz, Clement J., 576
Blum, Fred H., 622
Boulanger, David G., 311
Bowen, Howard R., 65, 67
Branch, M. C., 245

C

Carzo, Rocco, Jr., 679
Chin, Robert, 110
Clay, Hubert, 850
Curley, John Richard, 528
Curran, J. J., Jr., 383

D

Dale, Ernest, 743
Daniel, D. Ronald, 157
Davis, Keith, 183
Drucker, Peter F., 21, 232, 299, 331, 339

G

Geisler, Murray A., 142
Gellerman, Saul W., 825
Goode, Cecil E., 824

H

Habbe, Stephen, 845
Harris, Herbert, 934
Herrmann, Cyril C., 280
Hoslett, Schuyler Dean, 175

J

Jasinski, Frank J., 758
Johnson, Robert H., 345

K

Katz, Robert L., 807
Kircher, Paul, 588
Koontz, Harold, 2

L

Leavitt, Harold J., 34, 495
Levitt, Theodore, 70
Lewis, Robert W., 597
Likert, Rensis, 421

M

Magee, John F., 280
McDermid, Charles D., 408
McGregor, Douglas Murray, 98, 835
Mee, John F., 335
Miller, Ernest C., 351
Moore, David G., 88
Moser, George V., 447
Mylander, William H., 791

N

Nichols, Ralph G., 191

O

Ohmann, O. A., 50

P

Pamp, Frederic E., Jr., 894
Peirce, James L., 393
Persons, Ralph C., 735
Porter, Elias H., 129
Powell, J. Lewis, 729